The Genres of Late Antique Christian Poetry

Trends in Classics – Supplementary Volumes

Edited by
Franco Montanari and Antonios Rengakos

Associate Editors
Stavros Frangoulidis · Fausto Montana · Lara Pagani
Serena Perrone · Evina Sistakou · Christos Tsagalis

Scientific Committee
Alberto Bernabé · Margarethe Billerbeck
Claude Calame · Jonas Grethlein · Philip R. Hardie
Stephen J. Harrison · Stephen Hinds · Richard Hunter
Christina Kraus · Giuseppe Mastromarco
Gregory Nagy · Theodore D. Papanghelis
Giusto Picone · Tim Whitmarsh
Bernhard Zimmermann

Volume 86

The Genres of Late Antique Christian Poetry

Between Modulations and Transpositions

Edited by
Fotini Hadjittofi and Anna Lefteratou

DE GRUYTER

ISBN 978-3-11-099583-1
e-ISBN (PDF) 978-3-11-069621-9
e-ISBN (EPUB) 978-3-11-069623-3
ISSN 1868-4785

Library of Congress Control Number: 2020944903

Bibliographic information published by the Deutsche Nationalbibliothek
The Deutsche Nationalbibliothek lists this publication in the Deutsche Nationalbibliografie;
detailed bibliographic data are available on the Internet at http://dnb.dnb.de.

© 2022 Walter de Gruyter GmbH, Berlin/Boston
This volume is text- and page-identical with the hardback published in 2020.
Editorial Office: Alessia Ferreccio and Katerina Zianna
Logo: Christopher Schneider, Laufen
Printing and binding: CPI books GmbH, Leck

www.degruyter.com

Contents

Acknowledgements —— VII
Abbreviations —— IX

Prelude

Anna Lefteratou and Fotini Hadjittofi
Generic Debates and Late Antique Christian Poetry —— 3

Part I: Fugue in Minor: Epigram, Elegy, *Epyllion*

Gianfranco Agosti
Metrical Inscriptions in Late Antiquity: What Difference Did Christianity Make? —— 39

Arianna Gullo
Writing Classicizing Epigrams in Sixth-Century Constantinople: The Funerary Poems of Julian the Egyptian —— 59

Marco Onorato
The Poet and the Light: Modulation and Transposition of a Prudentian *Ekphrasis* in Two Poems by Sidonius Apollinaris —— 75

Thomas Kuhn-Treichel
Poetological Name-Dropping: Explicit References to Poets and Genres in Gregory Nazianzen's Poems —— 93

James McDonald
The Significance of Meter in the Biblical Poems of Gregory Nazianzen (*carmina* I.1.12–27) —— 109

Maria Jennifer Falcone
Some Observations on the Genre of Dracontius' *Satisfactio* —— 125

Étienne Wolff
Do Dracontius' *Epyllia* Have a Christian Apologetic Agenda? —— 139

Susanna Fischer
Dracontius' *Medea* and the Classical Tradition: Divine Influence and Human Action —— 151

Anna Maria Wasyl
The Late Roman *Alcestis* and the Applicability of Generic Labels to Two Short Narrative Poems —— 169

Part II: Fugue in Major: Epic

Michael Paschalis
The 'Profanity' of Jesus' Storm-calming Miracle (Juvencus 2.25–42) and the Flaws of *Kontrastimitation* —— 191

Maria Sole Rigo
Writing a Homeric-Christian Poem: The Case of Eudocia Augusta's *Saint Cyprian* —— 209

Domenico Accorinti
Did Nonnus Really Want to Write a 'Gospel Epic'? The Ambiguous Genre of the *Paraphrase of the Gospel According to John* —— 225

Fotini Hadjittofi
Nonnus' *Paraphrase of the Gospel According to John* as Didactic Epic —— 249

Andrew Faulkner
Davidic Didactic Hexameters: The Generic Stance of the *Metaphrasis Psalmorum* —— 265

Anna Lefteratou
The Lament of the Virgin in the *I Homeric Centos*: An Early *Threnos* —— 275

Hartmut Leppin
George Pisides' *Expeditio Persica* and Discourses on Warfare in Late Antiquity —— 293

List of Contributors —— 311
Index Auctorum Locorumque —— 313
Thematic Index —— 329

Acknowledgements

This volume is about the reception, reworking, subversion, and reinvention of classicizing genres in the Christian poetry of Late Antiquity, a period that, in this volume, is loosely defined as dating from Constantine to Heraclius. Some of the papers in this volume were presented in two International Workshops held in Lisbon (1–2 June 2017) and Heidelberg (15–16 December 2017), while some others are new additions. We hope that this work will increase our understanding of the changes that Christianity brought about in the classical world, with genre as our main focus but also touching upon the cultural and intellectual developments. The selection of papers and topics, far from being exhaustive, is intended to further discussions about the transformation of the classical heritage in the *moyenne* and *longue durée* of Classical Antiquity.

At this point we want to express our gratitude to the Institutions and funding bodies that have supported this joint endeavor. The Lisbon workshop was hosted by the Centro de Estudos Clássicos, Faculdade de Letras, Universidade de Lisboa, and received funding from FCT (Fundação para a Ciência e a Tecnologia). FCT – through project PTDC/LLT- LES/30930/2017 (national funds) – also covered the expenses associated with the linguistic revision of this volume. The Heidelberg Workshop received support from DFG (Deutsche Forschungsgemeinschaft) and was hosted by Heidelberg University. We are also thankful to the student assistants who helped with the organization of the two workshops (Tomás Ferreira in Lisbon and Eleni Ioakeimdi and Polyxeni Tarpinidou in Heidelberg), and, for precious assistance in the editing stage, Henrike Arnold and Carson Bay. We also want to thank the editor Antonios Regakos for his advice and encouragement throughout the process of publication.

Special acknowledgements are due to Gianfranco Agosti and Hartmut Leppin for their support and, above all, for their decades-long inspiring contributions to the study of Late Antiquity. This volume follows in their footsteps. Finally, we are extremely proud of the thoroughly international team of scholars from various career levels who participated in this endeavor, and we warmly thank them for their thought-provoking papers, inspiring discussions, smooth collaboration, and endless patience with our revisions – without them this publication would not have been possible.

Abbreviations

Abbreviations for Classical authors follow the *Oxford Classical Dictionary*. Abbreviations for Christian authors follow the Society of Biblical Literature Handbook or Lampe's *Patristic Greek Lexicon*; in case of difference in the abbreviation systems or for works that are not listed in either of these sources, we have adopted an abbreviation that appeals to common sense and practice. Journal abbreviations follow the *Année Philologique*; where no *APh* abbreviation is available we cite the full title. Abbreviations used frequently throughout the volume are the following:

Ancient Works:

AAA	*Apocrypha Acta Apostolorum* (e.g. AAPetr.; AAAndr.)
AL	*Anthologia Latina*
Aleth.	*Claudii Marii Victorii Alethia*
AP	*Anthologia Palatina*
Cath.	*Prudentii Cathemerinon*
Chr. Pat.	*Christus Patiens*
CP	*Sedulii Carmen Paschale*
C. Pr.	*Cento Probae; Faltoniae Betitiae Probae Cento Vergilianus de laudibus Christi*
Cypr.	*Eudociae Augustae de Sancto Cypriano*
ELQ	*Iuvenci Evangeliorum Libri Quator*
HC	*Homerocentones* (I HC first edition; II HC second edition; HC^a; HC^b; HC^c (Schembra)
LD	*Dracontii De Laudibus Dei*
Met. Pss.	*Ps. Apollinarii Metaphrasis Psalmorum*
Nonn., Dion.	*Nonni Panopolitani Dionysiaca*
Nonn., Par.	*Nonni Panopolitani Metaphrasis Evangelii secundum Ioannem;* Μεταβολὴ τοῦ κατὰ Ἰωάννην ἁγίου εὐαγγελίου
Orest. trag.	*Dracontii Orestis tragoedia*
Psych.	*Prudentii Psychomachia*
Romul.	*Dracontii Romulea*
Satisf.	*Dracontii Satisfactio*
SHG	*Alcimi Ecdicii Aviti De spiritalis historiae gestis*
Or. Sib.	*Oracula Sibyllina*
Vis. D.	*Visio Dorothei* (PBodmer 29)

Reference Works:

ACO	E. Schwartz (ed.), *Acta Conciliorum Oecumenicorum*, 4 vols., Berlin, 1914–1982.
CA	J.U. Powell (ed.), *Collectanea Alexandrina*, Oxford, 1925.
CCSG	*Corpus Christianorum Series Graeca*
CCSL	*Corpus Christianorum Series Latina*
CH	A.D. Nock/A.-J. Festugière (eds.), *Corpus Hermeticum*, 2 vols., Paris, 1945.
DGE	F.R. Adrados (ed.), *Diccionario Griego-Español*, Madrid, 1980–

DNP	H. Cancik/H. Schneider/M. Landfester (eds.), *Der Neue Pauly*, Stuttgart, 1996–2003.
FGE	D.L. Page (revised and prepared for publication by R.D. Dawe and J. Diggle) (ed.), *Further Greek Epigrams*, Cambridge, 1981.
GDRK	E. Heitsch (ed.), *Die griechischen Dichterfragmente der römischen Kaiserzeit*, 2 vols., Göttingen, 1963²–1964.
HE	A.S.F. Gow/D.L. Page (eds.), *The Greek Anthology: Hellenistic Epigrams*, 2 vols., Cambridge, 1965.
IG	*Inscriptiones Graecae*, Berlin, 1873–.
IGLS	*Inscriptiones greques et latines de la Syrie*, Beirut, 1929–.
Lampe	G.W. Lampe, *A Patristic Greek Lexicon*, Oxford, 1961–1968.
LHS	M. Leumann/J.B. Hofmann/A. Szantyr, *Lateinische Grammatik*, 2 vols., München, 1965–1977.
LfgrE	*Das Lexikon des frühgriechischen Epos*, Göttingen, 1955–2010.
LSA	*Last Statues of Antiquity Database*, https://wiki.digitalclassicist.org/Last_Statues_of_Antiquity
LSJ	H.G. Liddell/R. Scott/H.S. Jones/R. McKenzie (eds.), *Greek-English Lexicon, 9th edition with a revised Supplement*, Oxford, 1996.
Nestle – Aland[28]	E. Nestle/K. Aland (eds.), *Novum Testamentum Graece, 28th revised edition*, Stuttgart, 2012.
NRSV	*The Holy Bible: New Revised Standard Version*, Nashville, 1989.
OCD	S. Hornblower/A. Spawforth/E. Eidinow (eds.), *Oxford Classical Dictionary*, 4th edition, Oxford, 2012.
PG	J.-P. Migne (ed.). *Patrologia Graeca*, Paris, 1857–1866.
PL	J.-P. Migne (ed.), *Patrologia Latina*, Paris, 1841–1855.
PLRE	A.H.M. Jones/J.R. Martindale/J. Morris (eds.), *Prosopography of the Later Roman Empire*, 2 vols., Cambridge, 1971–1992.
RSV	*The Holy Bible: Revised Standard Version*, Nashville, 1952.
SEG	*Supplementum Epigraphicum Graecum*, Leiden, 1923–.
SGO	R. Merkelbach/J. Stauber (eds.) *Steinepigramme aus dem griechischen Osten 1–5*, Stuttgart, 1998–2004.
SH	H. Lloyd-Jones/P. Parsons (eds.), *Supplementum Hellenisticum*, Berlin, 1983.
TLL	*Thesaurus Linguae Latinae*

Prelude

Anna Lefteratou and Fotini Hadjittofi
Generic Debates and Late Antique Christian Poetry

Christian poets on Christian poetry

Ever since Plato criticized the poets and rhapsodes of his time for failing to provide a rational, discursive account of their work, the philosophical standing of poetry was never entirely secure. With the rise of Christianity and the appearance of Christian poetry in classical meter and language, a new set of existential challenges emerges: If the Logos can (and should) reach directly into the hearts of believers through the canonical book *par excellence*, the Gospel, why is poetic elaboration necessary or welcome? To what degree, and in which contexts, is Christian *mimesis* legitimate? How could poetry, which even before Plato was associated with lies, serve the true Christian cause?[1] More importantly for the interests of this volume, why, and to what extent, should Christian poetry follow the blueprint of the classical genres, which were rooted in a pagan past?

The case for Christian poetry will have to be made, time and again, on exclusively Christian, ideological grounds: this poetry proclaims the truth, fights heresy, is divinely inspired, and can bring about the salvation of both poet and audience.[2] What is left implicit in such vocal assertions of superiority is the admission that, when writing poetry, the grip of the classical past is hard to escape. In contrast to the prose genres of, e.g., hagiography, homily, and theological treatise, whose level of literariness may vary and whose debt to classical genres can easily go unnoticed, poetry is composed and read with an eye to generic features such as meter, length, narrativity, structure, and linguistic register,[3] all of which were defined in classical models and codified by generations of grammarians. The continued relevance of such criteria for the composition of Christian poetry is remarkable: in a world that was changing in fundamental ways, the traditional system of poetic genres was not revolutionized, but rather was manipulated to fit the needs and tastes of late antique, and increasingly Christian, audiences.

---

[1] E.g. Pollmann 1999, 69.
[2] Such debates are admittedly more frequent in Latin poetry. See Mastrangelo 2016, 43 for references to specific poems and emphasis on Christian doctrine.
[3] For a list of such generic criteria see Harrison 2007, 22–33.

In the fourth century, the ascetic bishop Gregory Nazianzen is responsible for an extensive (and understudied) poetic production, which includes such culturally enshrined forms as invectives in iambics, epigrams in elegiac distichs, and didactic in hexameters.[4] Gregory is perhaps the only voice in Greek Christian poetry to defend his choice of composing poetry and explicitly to reflect on the usefulness of such an endeavor.[5] In a poem written in iambic trimeter and titled Εἰς τὰ ἔμμετρα (*On His Own Verses*), Gregory presents the rationale behind his classicizing poetic project.[6] Some of his reasons are personal: he hopes that the restraints of meter will slow him down, and prevent him from writing a great deal (vv. 34–36); he also finds in poetry comfort and respite from his illness (vv. 54–57). Another reason he gives is eminently classical – indeed, it seems to be a *topos* of didactic poetry: Gregory hopes that young people, and especially those who enjoy literature, will see in his poems a "pleasant medicine", which sweetens the bitterness of the Commandments,[7] and leads them towards more useful things.[8] For those who are sensible, this new, Christian poetry is, according to Gregory, "a substitute for songs and lyre-playing" (44: ἀντ' ἀσμάτων σοι ταῦτα καὶ λυρισμάτων). But idle fiddling is not all Gregory's poetry aims to replace. His most ambitious reason (and the one presented in the most circumspect manner as, perhaps, petty; 48: μικροπρεπές) is that he feels Christians should have their own poetry that can rival and outstrip the classical canon: "I cannot allow that the

---

[4] See Al. Cameron 2004, 333. For the genres of (and generic debates in) Gregory's poetry see Kuhn-Treichel and McDonald in this volume.
[5] In Latin Christian poetry such protestations are near-obligatory: see the opening verses of Juvencus; Sedulius' preface to *CP*; *C. Pr.* at vv. 13–17; Paulin., *carm.* 10.19–46; and Avitus' prose epistle which introduces his *De spiritalis historiae gestis*.
[6] On this poem see Milovanovic-Barham 1997 and McGuckin 2006.
[7] Lucr. (1.935–50 = 4.10–25) famously compared his poetry to a honeyed cup for bitter medicine (i.e., philosophy). A similar idea is expressed much earlier in Pl., *Leg.* 659e–660a, while in the late 2nd century CE Maximus of Tyre (4.6) compares poets with doctors who administer bitter medicine (i.e., virtue), but only after mixing it with "myths, meter, and the form of song" (μύθους καὶ μέτρα καὶ σχῆμα ᾠδῆς) so as to mitigate the unpleasantness of what they teach (κεράσασα τὴν ἀηδίαν τῶν διδαγμάτων).
[8] II.1.39 = *PG* 37.1329–38, vv. 37–41: δεύτερον δὲ τοῖς νέοις, | καὶ τῶν ὅσοι μάλιστα χαίρουσι λόγοις, | ὥσπερ τι τερπνὸν τοῦτο δοῦναι φάρμακον, | πειθοῦς ἀγωγὸν εἰς τὰ χρησιμώτερα, | τέχνῃ γλυκάζων τὸ πικρὸν τῶν ἐντολῶν ("secondly for the youth; | and especially for those of them who take delight in artful speeches/literature; | so as to give this [= my work] as a kind of pleasant medicine, | an inducement of Persuasion towards more useful things, | which through art sweetens the bitterness of the commandments").

outsiders [= pagans] be superior to us in literature."[9] What is at stake in composing Christian poetry is a twofold challenge: how, on the one hand, to distract from sin, educate and, ultimately, 'save' the audience, while, on the other hand, using and adapting a rulebook established by those "outsiders" whose literary skill was to be emulated but whose religious beliefs should be condemned.

At the turn of the fifth century, another ascetically minded bishop, Paulinus of Nola, grapples with the same issues, albeit in a different language and with more pronounced self-consciousness. In his famous correspondence with his old friend Ausonius, Paulinus denounces poetry on classicizing themes as meaningless and even harmful.[10] Yet he does not seem able (or willing?) to disengage from the form and language of classical poetry. In response to Ausonius, Paulinus mounts a three-pronged offensive, each in its own classical meter (elegiacs, iambics, hexameters). Depending on one's viewpoint, the combination of different meters in one poem might seem either barbarous or a confident rewriting of the classical rulebook.[11] In fact, this relatively brief verse-letter of little more than 300 lines denounces the composition of classicizing poetry by Christian poets while at the same time upholding the 'classical' distinction between meters: the iamb is naturally "lighter", while the hexameter has more *gravitas* and is more appropriate for stern rebukes.[12]

Paulinus' *carmen* 27 presents a second interesting case study of how a 'minor' poem deals with 'major' generic features as well as meta-poetic topics, as it concerns itself with the problem of Christian representational art (and, implicitly, poetry). *Carmen* 27, a poem of roughly 600 hexameters, includes an *ekphrasis* of paintings on biblical subjects that adorned the walls of St. Felix's church. Paulinus clearly feels the need to explain not only the content but also, and more fundamentally, the very existence of the paintings. It is, he confesses, "an unusual custom" (544: *raro more*),[13] but one dictated by societal needs: the cult of St. Felix

---

9 II.1.39 = *PG* 37.1329–38, vv. 48–49: οὐδ' ἐν λόγοις | πλέον δίδωμι τοὺς ξένους ἡμῶν ἔχειν.
10 See *carm*. 10, with commentary in Filosini 2008, and Shorrock 2011, 15–20.
11 On Paulinus' polymentry see, most recently, Consolino 2017, 108–112; also, with stress on continuity and the intertextual indebtedness of Paulinus to classical Latin poetry, Hardie 2019, 12–27. On the polymetry of some poems by Gregory Nazianzen see McDonald in this volume.
12 *carm*. 10.13–15: *et graviore | vindicis heroi sunt agitanda sono. | interea levior paucis praecurrit iambus* ("these [accusations] must be dealt with in the weightier tone of the avenging, heroic meter. But in the meantime, the lighter, iambic meter will briefly run ahead").
13 Translation, here and below, slightly adapted from Walsh 1975. For detailed study of this poem see Herbert de la Portbarré-Viard 2006, 241–255. For Paulinus among other early Christian defenders of images see, recently, Schildgen 2016, 65–66. For the pictorial program of the

draws in a large crowd of country folk, whose unsophisticated minds can be beguiled into fasting and devotion by the paintings that are so pleasing to the eye.[14] Like Gregory's young men, who can be tricked by sweet verses into taking the bitter medicine of the Commandments, the newfangled artistic program of Paulinus' church is not an end in itself, but a conduit to virtue.

Apparently, artistic *mimesis* and its classical forms and traditions cannot be avoided. Just as it deals with broad issues regarding mimetic representation, *carmen* 27 also confronts the grand legacy of hexameter verse. This (relatively) short hexameter poem insistently revisits and reformulates Virgilian epic. At times, the tension between the 'humble', small-scale poem and the perilous heights to which epic hexameter is uniquely suited becomes palpable. As the poem, apparently of its own accord, soars into a Christological hymn, Paulinus wonders how he has come to "fly above the stars" (311: *super astra volans*), when in fact he had wanted to "sing a lighter theme" (310: *materia leviore canens*).[15] The poet's apprehension at his own sublime flight (and likely imminent fall) is expressed with an allusion to Virgil's Icarus: "I dare to trust myself aloft on frail wings" (308: *ausus in excelsum fragili me credere pinna*).[16] A *captatio benevolentiae* as much as a learned allusion, this verse opens up numerous possibilities for dialogue with classical poetry: Is Paulinus appropriating for Christian poetry an elegant, classical turn of phrase and, in doing so, projecting a 'Christian' Icarus back onto the Virgilian text (what modern criticism might call *Usurpation* or *chrêsis*)?[17] Is he implying that, unlike the foolish Icarus, he will not, in fact, fall, because his Christian modesty renders him immune to *hubris* (a form of *Kontrastimitation*)?[18] Or is

---

church, as reconstructed from Paulinus' writings, as an early but sophisticated example of "visual theology" see Elsner 1998, 254–257, and cf. Elsner 1995, esp. 88–124 and 249–287.

14 *carm.* 27.580–592: "This was why we thought it useful to enliven all the houses of Felix with paintings on sacred themes, in the hope that they would excite the interest of the rustics by their attractive appearance, for the sketches are painted in various colors. Over them are explanatory inscriptions, the written word revealing the theme outlined by the painter's hand. So when all the country folk point out and read over to each other the subjects painted, they turn more slowly to thoughts of food, since the feast of fasting is so pleasing to the eye. In this way, as the paintings beguile their hunger, their astonishment may allow better behavior to develop in them. Those reading the holy account of chastity in action are infiltrated by virtue and inspired by saintly example. As they gape, their drink is sobriety, and they forget the longing for excessive wine."

15 For generic experimentation in the poetry of Paulinus (with an emphasis on how this is driven by the poet's asceticism) see, briefly, Basson 1996.

16 See *Aen.* 6.15 (of Icarus): *pennis ausus se credere caelo* ("daring to entrust himself to the sky on wings").

17 For *chrêsis* and its application to the poetry of Paulinus see Gnilka 1984.

18 For the concepts of *Usurpation* and *Kontrastimitation* see Thraede 1962, and Agosti 2011.

it, rather, the self-consciously restricted scale and "lighter theme" of his song that prevents him from rising (even) higher and subsequently falling?

A further possibility is to take the allusion as a formal element with no impact on the content of the poem.[19] A cluster of Virgilian allusions in the same poem has recently been read as 'nonreferential'.[20] The whole passage is interesting, and provides a frame for the examination of Christian poetry in terms of musical metaphors that is central to this volume. It begins with a description of the miracle of the Pentecost:

After this solemn feast (we calculate seven weeks before this holiday comes round for men) comes the day on which the Holy Spirit was of old sent down from the heights of heaven (*caelo demissus ab alto*) in parted tongues of fiery light. Then He, the one God, sped over each mouth (*per ora cucurrit*) and with one voice spoke aloud in tongues of every kind (*ore loquellas*). He gave men the power of speaking to all in languages unknown (*expromere voces*), so that each individual acknowledged his own tongue being spoken by a foreigner, though out of his own mouth he could not converse in a strange language. The barbarian uttered tidings fully comprehended in a language he did not know, for he spoke words foreign to his own. Yet the one Spirit was praising the one God in different languages before all men. Think of a man playing a harp, plucking strings producing different sounds by striking them with the one quill. Or again the man who rubs his lips by blowing on woven reeds; he plays one tune from his one mouth, but there is more than one note, and he marshals the different sounds with controlling skill. (*carm.* 27.60–76)

caelo demissus = *Aen.* 4.575 ~ *Ecl.* 4.7

per ora cucurrit = *Aen.* 11.296;
ore loquellas = *Aen.* 5.842
expromere voces = *Aen.* 2.280

Although the passage does not explicitly present a theory of (Christian) literature,[21] the metaphor of the Holy Spirit as a musician producing one tune out of different strings or notes clearly speaks to the late antique aesthetics of *poikilia/*

---

19 For a *continuum* of late Latin modes of intertextuality that runs from allusions as essential parts of the content to optional parts to merely formal elements see Kaufmann 2017.
20 See Pelttari 2014, 137 for the allusions not referring back to their sources, but pointing towards the "formal emptiness of the signifying word."
21 On the musician as poet and the symbolism of music in Paulinus see Fontaine 1973. For a veritable catalogue of musical instruments, symbolizing various poetic genres, all of which now proclaim Christ in unison see Prud., *Apoth.* 386–392, with the comments of O'Daly 2016, 234–236.

variatio, which is a chief characteristic of the poem.²² Indeed, Paulinus here makes it clear that the variety of voices (71: *voce ... varia*), which throughout remain distinct and un-mixed, might be confusing (in fact, these voices are incomprehensible to those who speak them), but this very variety creates a unity that can be grasped at the level of the listener.²³

Paulinus' conception of the musical work (and, by extension, the literary work) as a set of distinct "strings producing different sounds" (73: *dissona fila*), which are moved with one intent by a single quill (72: *unius verbere plectri*) is particularly relevant for our project in this volume, whose title employs two metaphors from music theory. 'Modulation' is used to describe the process of changing between the major and the minor keys, and 'transposition' is the rewriting of a whole piece onto another key. We have envisioned that both these terms can work as metaphors for how Christian poetry 'transposes', for example, Christian prose into poetry or drama onto epic and 'modulates' between the minor and major genres of the classical grammatical scheme.

Of course, the distinction between poetry on a major or a minor key (and a poet's freedom to 'modulate' between the two) is ancient and has an illustrious pedigree which cannot be fully addressed here. Suffice it to say that Horace, apparently refusing to climb on perilous Pindaric heights for fear of becoming another Icarus, invites, instead, his friend Antonius to take up a song for Caesar, striking with a "grander quill" (*Od.* 4.2.33: *concines maiore poeta plectro*). The presence of Icarus *qua* poetic metaphor in both Horace and Paulinus suggests that this figure was embedded in discussions of genre and scale that resonate throughout antiquity. What is, however, rather different in the case of Paulinus is the degree to which the reader or listener comes to the fore and becomes responsible for disentangling the various keys (or is simply given the option of which strain to listen to). In the passage cited above, the marked echoes of Virgil do not so much direct our attention back to their source text as become they themselves a 'strain' of high epic within a smaller-scale poem. On one interpretation, Paulinus might imply that the words of Virgil speak the truth but have to be rearranged (cento-like) by a Christian poet so that they make (Christian) sense. On another, the significance of authorial intentions retreats and what really matters

---

22 For this late antique aesthetics see the classic study by Roberts 1989, with recent revision in Hardie 2019, ch. 4 on *concordia discors* and *varietas*, and esp. 128–134 on these concepts in Paulinus of Nola. For a recent genealogy of the concept of variety see Fitzgerald 2016. Later in the poem *variatio* will also be an important element in the *ekphrasis* of the paintings, which impress their viewers precisely due to their various colors (583: *fucata coloribus umbra*).
23 Cf. Carruthers 2009, 45–46 on Augustine's views regarding the diverse languages spoken by Christians and whose very variety is an ornament for the Church/bride.

is whether the listener will be able and/or willing to hear the Virgilian tongue (and its higher strain) in Paulinus' mouth. But it is significant that whoever speaks (and quotes Virgil?) during the Pentecost miracle is himself unaware of what he is saying. It is always other listeners who recognize their tongue in another's mouth and hold the key to deciphering it, while acknowledging that, whatever the language, the message is truthful and thus worth spreading/ preaching.

The quest for Christian poetry

Paulinus comes near the end of a long journey that led to the production of Christian poetry in classical form. The classicization of Christian poetry clearly reflects the gradual Christianization of the elites, a process which advanced neither steadily nor uniformly around the Roman Empire.[24] Julian's decree which forbade Christian teachers to use/teach the classics and which was effective from 362 to 364 was one, but by no means the only incentive that drove some fourth-century poets, such as Gregory and the Apollinarii, to reconsider their relationship with classical *paideia*. It would, nonetheless, be unfair to argue that Christian poetry developed as a reaction to such a short-lived decree, especially since poems such as Juvencus' epic or Proba's *Cento* were written before it.[25] It would be equally unfair to see Christian poetry as a by-product of school exercises: despite their didactic tone and their use of rhetorical *topoi*, the stylistic complexity of these poems makes them fit for appreciation beyond the classroom.[26]

If one examines the diachronic production of Christian poetry, it is noteworthy that the earliest prayers and hymns were not composed in classicizing language.[27] The first poems that could be considered Christian are those found in the

---

24 Cf. Leppin 2015, who argues that the mode of appropriation was different for particular genres and texts and that classical texts outside the churches remained, if not pagan, at least 'neutral'. Cf. Leppin 2012. On classicism in late antique literature see, e.g., Johnson 2006.
25 Following here Agosti 2001, 68–74. On the misunderstanding of Julian's School Edict as a kind of Christian persecution see Teitler 2017, chapter 8, esp. 64–67.
26 For school poetry see Hose 2004, who does not recognize the innovative aspect of this poetry; *contra* see Agosti 2009, 320. Cf. Agosti 2001, 68–74, showing that the level of style and exegetical approaches to Old or New Testament texts surpassed the level of school education.
27 Although a model for Christian classicizing poetry may be found in the *Or. Sib.*, it is mainly the Jewish Hellenistic classicizing epics that dealt with material similar to that of Christian poetry, esp. the Old Testament. Tragedies, such as Ezekiel's *Exagoge*, Theodotus' epic on Samaria, or Philon's on Jerusalem, continued to be read, as Eusebius attests (*Praep. ev.* 9.21.1). For further

Old Testament and which became accessible to a Graeco-Roman audience through the Septuagint and then the Vulgate. Accordingly, the earliest samples were the Psalms and verse poems such as the Song of Songs. Traces of poetic language can also be found in the New Testament, for example in the Gospel of John, which begins with a brilliant poetic prologue, akin to a hymn, to the Logos/God.[28] The New Testament Epistles mention prayers and psalms,[29] while in the third-century *Apocryphal Acts of Thomas* we find the *Hymn of the Pearl*, which has an unmistaken Gnostic flavor. *POxy* 1786, a papyrus containing an early Christian hymn with musical annotation in a quantitative meter, is also dated to around this period. Prayers still performed at mass, such as *Phôs hilaron* or *Gloria*, were written between the second and the third centuries in the Hellenistic *koinê* and in the Latin vulgate respectively.[30]

The crucial role of the liturgy in the development of Christian poetry is also amply illustrated in the case of Melito of Sardis, a second-century bishop whose *Homily on the Passion* can be considered a very early precursor of Byzantine hymnography, and especially the poetic homily that came to be known as the *kontakion*. Melito's *Homily*, although not written as a poem or hymn, is marked by its extensive use of anaphora, *homoioteleuton*, antithesis and other rhetorical figures.[31] Even more importantly, several clauses are grammatically parallel and have approximately the same number of syllables, so that they can be conceived of, and written down, as verses, as in this example (731–733):

ὁ κρεμάσας τὴν γῆν κρέμαται.
ὁ πήξας τοὺς οὐρανοὺς πέπεκται.
ὁ στηρίξας τὰ πάντα ἐπὶ ξύλου ἐστήρικται.

He who hung the earth is hanging.
He who fixed the heavens has been fixed.
He who lifted up the world has been lifted up on a piece of wood.[32]

---

reading see Lanfranchi 2006, Kuhn 2012, and Whitmarsh 2013, 211–227. For the patristic reception of the *Or. Sib.* see Toca 2017, and for their influence on Nonnus see Gigli Piccardi 2012 and Lightfoot 2015.
28 For this prologue as hymn see, for instance, Gordley 2009.
29 Cf. Col 1:15–20, 15:3–4, 19:1–8; Phil 2:5–11; 1 Tim 3:16.
30 Cf. the overview in Gordley 2011.
31 See McDonald 1975. For the *Sitz im Leben* of this text (principally, its anti-Judaism and the possibility this is a reaction to the powerful Jewish community of Sardis) see Sykes 1997 and Cohick 1998.
32 Text from Perler 1966. Trans. F. Hadjittofi.

At the same time as Melito experimented with a form that explodes the dichotomy between poetry and prose, other Greek Christian authors were inserting poetic hymns into their prose works. Clement's *Paedagogus* ends with a *Hymn to the Savior* composed in anapaestic meter. This poem draws from the long tradition of classical hymns, as it invokes Christ using a long series of epithets.[33] One century later, Methodius of Olympus similarly ends his *Banquet of the ten Virgins* with an iambic abecedarian *Hymn to the Nymphios*. It has recently been argued that this hymn, which in the 'fiction' of the text is sung by a chorus of virgins dressed in white and bearing lamps, reflects consecration rituals (based upon the rite of marriage), which would already have been familiar in the third century.[34] Once again, then, the liturgical setting and the rites of the Church in general provided an impetus and a context for the development of Christian poetry.

The earliest extensive Christian poetry in classical meter to have survived also dates from the third century, and is written by a shadowy figure named Commodian, author of the *Instructiones* and the *Carmen apologeticum*.[35] This poet describes himself as a former pagan who had seen the light of Christianity late in life and decided to teach others through his poems.[36] The *Instructiones* are particularly interesting as they are a collection of poems each of which contains an acrostic, with the last one, when read from bottom to top, yielding the *sphragis Commodianus mendicus Christi*. In Commodian's verses the hexameter is no longer primarily constructed on the basis of quantity, as accent begins to play a more important role, making these some of the earliest specimens of *versus politici*. For similar early samples of self-standing Christian poems written in classical verse, but from the Greek-speaking East, we have to turn to the fourth century and the poems of the *Codex of Visions* (*PBodmer* 29 and 30–37), all of them fragmentary, but which nonetheless give us a glimpse of semi-popular (as opposed to elite and high-flown) Greek hexametric production. Apart from the *Vision of Dorotheus* – a remarkable poem that perhaps belongs in a category of its own – this Codex includes poems whose topics are drawn from both the Old and the New Testament.[37] In the same century, innovations in the composition of Christian poetry began to move towards the same direction in both the Latin West

---

33 See Gordley 2011, 373–374, with further bibliography.
34 For this argument as well as the general *Sitz im Leben* of this text see Candido 2017.
35 For the date see Pollman 2013, 315, with further bibliography.
36 See the preface of his *carm. apol.*
37 *PBodmer* 29, *Vis. D.*, edited by Hurst/Reverdin/Rudhardt 1984; *PBodmer* 30–37, Hurst/Rudhardt 1999. On the dating and milieu see Agosti 2002.

and the Greek East. Thus, while Pope Damasus wrote metrical epigrams and Ambrose composed iambic hymns, around the end of the fourth century Synesius of Cyrene wrote *Hymns* in complex, ionic meters. This is precisely the juncture at which Gregory Nazianzen, Juvencus, Paulinus, and a host of other poets drew Christian, classicizing poetry into the mainstream.

This (admittedly limited)[38] overview of three centuries of Greek and Latin Christian poetry shows two things: on the one hand, it confirms the almost simultaneous experimentation with classicizing poetry both in the Latin- and in the Greek-speaking milieus and, on the other, highlights the existing, non-classicizing, alternatives. Writing in classical meter was not an one-way option but a conscious choice, and one that was particularly cherished between the fourth and sixth centuries. Indeed, and as many chapters in this volume will argue, classical meter brought with it a range of echoes and overtones which would not have been available in other formats and which contributed to generic adjustments and recalibrations: for example, Agosti's analysis of the hexametric, and probably non-mainstream,[39] *Vision of Dorotheus* has suggested that the poem, besides propagating a Christian agenda of repentance, includes a 'modulation' of didactic epic by adapting Hesiod.[40] Classicizing style, therefore, came attached to a set of a relevant generic expectations shared by both author and audience.

Ancient readers of Christian poetry

Throughout this volume the role of the readers, their preconceptions, and expectations will be central in our investigation of genre and generic development. Our insistence on the continued usefulness of taking the 'classical' scheme of genres into consideration also has to do with how fundamental this was precisely in shaping readerly expectations.[41] Late Antiquity displays a heightened self-awareness when it comes to genre, as we saw in the examples of Gregory and Paulinus above. This does not mean that genres were not important before, but, from the Archaic through to Hellenistic times, the performative context was an important ingredient of genre: the Homeric epics, Archaic lyric poetry, and Attic tragedy are

---

38 For a more detailed overview of Christian production see Miguélez-Cavero/McGill 2018, with further literature.
39 For the *Codex Visionum* as an "oddity" see Miguélez-Cavero 2013, 92.
40 Agosti 2016.
41 For calls to go beyond genre when examining Christian literature see Formisano 2007, 282. Also Kaufmann, forthcoming, on "the implosion" of the generic system.

apt examples.⁴² From the Hellenistic period onwards, and regardless of performative context, a rigorous canonization took place and literary works were categorized by genre, focusing mainly on formal elements such as meter, theme, and *ethos*.⁴³

Furthermore, the formal system of rhetorical education, flourishing from the Hellenistic times onwards,⁴⁴ canonized the works of the past and was simultaneously shaped by the works of the canon, while adapting them to the modern needs of, mainly, epideictic and encomiastic rhetoric. The work of theorists such as Menander Rhetor is particularly important, as it absorbed imperial technography and transmitted it to Late Antiquity and Byzantium, where it enjoyed a long afterlife.⁴⁵ The four surviving Greek treatises on *progymnasmata*, by (or transmitted under the names of) Theon, Hermogenes, Aphthonius, and Nicolaus, display a range of methods and techniques (from *chreia* and encomium to *ekphrasis* and *prosopopoeia*) that were applied to both prose and verse compositions,⁴⁶ and provided a common 'language' shared between all educated individuals. Moreover, precisely because the rules were fixed, at least at the technical level, experimentation was facilitated, as surprise and innovation work better against a canon and an established set of techniques.⁴⁷

---

42 Cf. Fowler 1997, 28–29 on the different nature of intertextuality in classical Greek and in Latin literature.
43 For formal categorization and the ancient understanding of genre from Pl., *Resp.* 3.394b and Arist., *Poet.* onwards, see Farell 2003 and Harrison 2011, 2–6.
44 See Cairns 2007 on how Menander shaped the ancient reception of genre, but cf. the critique by Depew/Obbink 2000, 4 of the application of a rigid Menandrean notion of genre especially onto performance-oriented, and therefore less fixed, works. On how the change of setting influenced the reception of classical genres see also Fantuzzi/Hunter 2002, 24–25. On Menander and his Hellenistic/imperial predecessors see Heath 2004.
45 For the use of poetry in the *progymnasmata* towards rhetorical ends see Webb 2009 and 2010, and the overview in Miguélez-Cavero 2008, 264–370. For rhetoric in Late Antiquity and Byzantium see Kennedy 1983, and the overview in Whitby 2010.
46 It is noteworthy that, while the treatises (as well as Libanius' extensive collection) contain examples only in prose, on the papyri, which preserve real school exercises by Egyptian teachers and students, we mostly find verse *progymnasmata* (primarily *ethopoeiae* and encomia in either hexameters or iambics); see Cribiore 2009, 333. Moreover, poetry, and Homeric poetry in particular, is an important source of rhetorical inspiration; see Webb 2010 for Libanius' case.
47 Cf. Fantuzzi/Hunter 2002, 26: "[in Hellenistic times] ... many of the performance occasions had disappeared, together with archaic culture itself. What remained was a heritage of linguistic and metrical conventions, which had often lost their functional contact with particular subjects and occasions: thus did the possibility of new combinations appear."

This canonization naturally encouraged meta-generic inquiries, leading eventually to further generic experimentation.[48] When a late Greek poet was confronted with the question of how to compose a poem in hexameters – to take the most popular and prestigious meter – there already was a very long tradition of more or less canonized hexametric poetry starting from Homer and Hesiod, continuing with the revisions of Callimachus and Apollonius of Rhodes, and reaching beyond Quintus of Smyrna to Nonnus. On the Latin side this itinerary would have been all the more complex, as Latin literature developed in tandem and in dialogue with Greek literature throughout. Virgil did not emulate Homer only but also wrote the *Aeneid* with the tragedians, the lyric poets, and the Hellenistic revisions in mind. Accordingly, his Dido, for example, is self-consciously as much an epic as a tragic heroine, and it is this particular mélange that is further exploited in Hosidius Geta's *Medea*, a Virgilian cento of the early third century,[49] or in Proba's association of Eve with Dido.[50]

Any discussion of genre in the post-Hellenistic world should also take into consideration the rise of paratext: there was a long tradition of commentaries and exegetical essays on (by then) classical poetry as well as on the Bible, which are particularly important for understanding the Christian poetry of this period.[51] The diffusion of the codex made commentaries all the more accessible. As mentioned above, the Hellenistic critics established the canon that would be taught, commented on, and imitated throughout the rest of antiquity and well into Byzantium. Hexameter poetry, in particular, not only maintained its primacy and was continually taught at school, but also, especially in Late Antiquity, became a means of social advancement through public performance, as skill in composing hexameter poetry paved the way for a successful professional career.[52] Ultimately, the reception and revision of classical genres was given added impetus by the rise of Christianity, which in due time sparked further ideological and eventually generic developments. The Christianization of the classical genres did not proceed uniformly nor was it completed overnight, and, as we shall see in this volume, the adoption of classical genres in late antique poetry differs from century to century and from representative to representative, and even between the

---

[48] Depew/Obbink 2000, 12 note that Plato, who developed one of the first theories of genre, was able to do so once the oral tradition became literary. For the development of the canon of 'classics' see Citroni 2003; cf. Most 2000 on the canonization of tragedy.
[49] See, e.g., McGill 2005, 31–48.
[50] Schottenius Cullhed 2016, 143.
[51] For these paratexts see, e.g., Pollman 2009 and Fuhrer 2013.
[52] Al. Cameron 1965.

works of the same representative, as in the cases of Dracontius and Sidonius, which will be examined in this book.

For these generic experimentations to take place, however, a solid ground of generic expectations was required. Late antique grammarians may be illuminating in this respect as they offered the theoretical framework into which late antique poetry would be received. In the second half of the fourth century the Latin grammarian Diomedes still postulates three kinds of poetry, based on the Platonic and Aristotelian criterion of *mimesis* (whether the poet or the characters speak in the poem): imitative (*dramatikon*), narrative (*enarrativum/enuntiativum/ exegetikon*), and mixed (*mixtum/mikton*). More than a century later, Isidore of Seville classifies poetry along the exact same lines (*Etymologies* 8.7.11), followed by the Venerable Bede, who, in the early eighth century, decides to introduce biblical examples alongside classical ones. Thus, for Bede, the *dramatikon* can easily accommodate the Song of Songs, where no narrator intervenes between the two interlocutors.[53]

Generic classification, then, and indeed on remarkably classical terms, is still an exercise late antique readers undertake and which conveys significance not only when practiced on the classical or classicizing texts composed within that system, but also, and more impressively, when it is superimposed onto texts which hail from a non-classical tradition.[54] When, in response to the decree by Julian the Emperor which forbade the use of classical literary texts by Christian teachers, the two Apollinarii took it upon themselves to set the Bible into classical literary form, each biblical work first had to be mapped onto a corresponding classical genre. According to Socrates of Constantinople (*Hist. Eccl.* 3.15–16), Apollinaris the Elder, a grammarian, 'transposed' the Pentateuch into heroic hexameters and other parts of the Old Testament into drama, while Apollinaris the Younger, who was a sophist, turned the Gospels and the letters of Paul into Platonic dialogues. The division of labor between father and son corresponds to the different competences of each, but certain criteria must also have applied to ensure that each 'transposition' would be plausible and appropriate.

Sozomen (*Hist. Eccl.* 5.18.3–4), another Church historian who reports on the same project but only mentions one Apollinaris, claims that the hexameter paraphrase of the *Pentateuch* was divided into twenty-four books, each identified by

---

[53] *De arte metrica* 7.259 (Keil). For the evolution of the idea of tragedy in Late Antiquity and the Middle Ages see Kelly 1993.
[54] For a mid-4th-century adaptation of a biblical topic along the lines of the classical/rhetorical register see the hexameter *ethopoeia* in *PBodmer* 38: "What Cain would say when killing Abel", with Hurst 199, 125.

a letter of the Greek alphabet (just like the *Iliad* and *Odyssey*). He adds that other works of the Scriptures were transformed into Menandrean comedies, Euripidean tragedies or Pindaric lyric poems. The resulting paraphrases were, according to the historian, "similar in ethos, diction, idiom, and arrangement" to the classical works on which they were modeled.[55] Here, then, is a list of characteristics by which these new, classicizing works could be identified as full members of the canonical genres – and it should be obvious that an entrenched notion of genre is what drove the selection and transformation of the material.

Modern readers of Christian poetry

Although ancient critics are strikingly conservative in their ventures into generic classification, modern scholars highlight radical departures from this system or even argue that it has become irrelevant or that it "imploded".[56] In fact, modern theoretical concerns are always evolving and often, as Hinds observed, each "in reaction to its predecessor."[57] While the nineteenth century was dominated by the quest for genre, the twentieth century increasingly deconstructed the very idea that genres may even exist, focusing on the power of texts and their intertexts. In the late twentieth and early twenty-first century, however, there is a tendency to reach back to genre as a useful category to think with, especially from the reader's perspective.[58] But this was not always the case: in the early twentieth century Wilhelm Kroll invented the extremely influential term *Kreuzung der Gattungen*[59] and argued for a Darwinian, or better Mendelian,[60] understanding of genres as evolving through 'endogamic' cross-fertilization, while his contemporary Russian Formalists suggested that genres develop and adapt to new contexts through 'exogamy'.[61] In the sixties and seventies, however, the critique of authorial inten-

---

[55] Sozom., *Hist. Eccl.* 5.18.4–5: ἤθει τε καὶ φράσει καὶ χαρακτῆρι καὶ οἰκονομίᾳ ὁμοίας τοῖς παρ' Ἕλλησιν. On the importance of genre for the Apollinarian project cf. Sluiter 2000, 198.
[56] Cf. Kaufmann, forthcoming.
[57] See Hinds 2000, 221–223 on Augustan literature and the genre of Ov., *Met.*
[58] For an overview see Silk 2012.
[59] Kroll 1964 (1924).
[60] See the excellent critique of this book as mirroring the ideology of the 1920's in Barchiesi 2001, esp. 146.
[61] See Harrison 2007, 13. For a critique of Bakhtin see Branham 2005.

tion and the deconstruction of the author removed the emphasis from genre altogether, focusing instead on the flexible term intertextuality,[62] as genre was infused with conservative connotations of the 'canon'. In recent years the prominence of reader-response theory, an aftermath of thorough narratological investigations, has shifted attention from author to reader, and thus rendered the question of genre relevant once again, albeit from a different viewpoint.

The idea is not new: Robert Jauss postulated, in the early eighties, the famous concept of a merge of the *Erwartungshorizonte* between reader and text, and thus contributed to the thorough revision of the question of genre from a readerly perspective.[63] This approach has been particularly influential in the field of Augustan poetry,[64] which invites such approaches because of its sheer self-reflexivity. As a result, critics have become extremely sensitive to the mixing of genres, but the jargon to describe such phenomena includes a *poikilia* of terms such as 'hybridization', 'intergenericity', and 'generic enrichment'. These are not in fact synonymous, but more often than not each contributes to the amplification of previous intertextual approaches, again taking genre into consideration, since intertextuality becomes all the more elusive. Terms such as 'hybridization' still bear, we believe, the mark of Kroll's *Kreuzung*, as the term 'hybrid' is strictly applicable to biology and suggests an evolutionary approach that is to be found in the genre itself (and not, e.g., the reader); the tag 'intergenericity' expands the realm of intertextuality by giving it a generic twist, though this too needs to be cautiously defined so as to distinguish (if possible) between genre and intertext; finally, the more recent label 'generic enrichment' adopted by Stephen Harrison – owing much to Gian Biagio Conte and Alistair Fowler – is a chiefly reader-oriented term, but still needs refinement as the threads between intertext and genre are often entangled.[65]

Despite the abundance of theoretical terminology, it is still difficult to trace genre in late antique literature because of the extreme variety of configurations

---

[62] For a critique see Hinds 1998 and now the overview in Pelttari 2014, chapters 1 and 2; for a theoretical overview of intertextuality and genre see Duff 2005.
[63] Cf. the prologue to Jauss/Köhler 1972, VIII: "dass das Gattungshafte eines Textes nicht in zeitlosen Wesensmerkmalen liegt, sondern einem '*modus dicendi*' entspringt, der Werk und Publikum verbindet und über den Erwartungshorizont und 'Sitz im Leben' zu ermitteln ist"; cf. esp. pp. 121–133.
[64] See the pivotal work of Conte 1994.
[65] For other analyses of genre see, esp. in the field of Latin literature, Papanghelis/Harrison/Frangoulidis 2013 and Bessone/Fucecchi 2017; for Greek, esp. Hellenistic, see Fantuzzi/Hunter 2002. The interest in genre is also vivid in other areas where there was no literary canon in the way we find it after the Hellenistic times, e.g., Bakola/Prauscello/Telò 2013.

between form, subject matter and technique. Equally uneven is the reuse of specific genres in particular contexts: the grand, 'major' form of epic is usually reserved for the powerful and for God, such as in the many paraphrases to be examined in this volume, but Paulinus' *carmen* 27 shows that this was not necessarily a straightforward approach. Similarly but in a 'minor' genre, whereas Claudian wrote an *epithalamium* in classicizing form and imagery for the wedding of the emperor Honorius and Maria, Paulinus of Nola composed a subverted, content-wise, Christianized *epithalamium* for the wedding of Julianus, a priest, and Titia. But even in the case of 'new' genres or sub-genres emerging out of rhetorical techniques such as cento-poetry or *paraphrasis*, it is difficult to discern where the rhetorical technique stops and where the 'new' genre begins.[66] Accordingly, it may come as a surprise to scholars of earlier phases of Greek and Latin literature that late antique poets did not strive for innovation in the way poets of the Hellenistic or Augustan times did, since a large portion of the Christian poetic production consists of *paraphrasis* or *cento* compositions, namely poems that – at first sight – might not seem as original as Callimachus' *Hecale*. This kind of poetry, however, was produced in a literary environment where poetry was not only intensively taught at school and was key to administrative success[67] but was also highly appreciated and cherished in its own right, if we judge it from Nonnus' 48 books of *Dionysiaca*.

The complex issue of the genres of Christian poetry has been addressed at different levels at different periods. At the intertextual and source level Fontaine 1975 already talked about the 'mélange des genres' in Prudentius as a characteristic of this late antique poetry. At the formal level recent scholarship tries to adapt the Krollian *Kreuzung* by maintaining the term 'hybrid' but purging it from its Darwinian flavor: Fuhrer 2013, for example, talks about 'hybrids' and 'hypertexts', and argues that the "in-between status (of such works) between heteronomy and autonomy, is in fact programmatic and as a result these works must break the boundaries with the old genre system."[68] Pollmann 2017 is probably more to the point when she describes Late Antiquity as a period of extreme experimentation and of literary hybridity that "chimes with the modern definition of literary genres as open systems with fluid boundaries, consisting of a set of

---

66 Cf. Roberts 1985 on the rhetorical pedigree of biblical paraphrases; he actually argues that cento is a technique that later took up some generic characteristics.
67 For the use of poetry at school see Cribiore 2001; for poetry as allowing entrance to the *cursus honorum* see Al. Cameron 1965.
68 Fuhrer 2013, 87.

characteristics which can overlap; thus one work can potentially be classified under more than just one literary genre."[69]

Another approach is the one that focuses on the readership of such poems. Herzog 1975, xxxvii–xxxvii in his masterful discussion of biblical epic argues precisely for a merge of the *Erwartungshorizonten* shared between a work and its readership.[70] In a more recent work Pelttari 2014 focuses on the late antique reader and argues that whereas in earlier phases of Latin poetry the wit of the text stood out, Late Antiquity shines the spotlight on the reader, who is presented with the challenge of interpreting open and multilayered works.[71] Agosti 2009, on the other hand, claims that the Christianization of poetry in Late Antiquity was more thematically than stylistically oriented and that both secular and Christian poetry were composed to satisfy the needs of a particular audience that delighted in classicizing compositions. The shared *paideia* of such an audience thus encouraged the dialogue between secular and Christian literary production,[72] a point repeated throughout this volume.

This rigorous engagement with, and re-evaluation of, Christian poetry,[73] has removed many of the earlier constraints. For example, the role of school exercises and of patronage has been downplayed in favor of the innovative and learned spirit that permeates Christian poetry.[74] Moreover, the distinction between supposedly highbrow and lowbrow poetry has been challenged, since genres such as the epigram,[75] or the poems of a monastic community, for example those found in the *Papyrus Bodmer* 29–37, show that there was not only one, uniform audience for Christian poetry.[76] What such poetry shows, however, is that without the background of shared *paideia* these generic and thematic experimentations would have been less audacious: because *paideia* permeated most levels of society, the appropriation, deconstruction and subversion of classical genres through

---

[69] E.g., Pollmann 2017, 7, 36; at 22 she argues these literary hybrids may eventually develop into new genres.
[70] Herzog 1977. See also Pollmann 2017, 21 on the importance of genre for shaping readerly expectations.
[71] See also the emphasis on genre and audience in the volume edited by Greatrex/Elton 2015, which deals with a variety of media, both literary and artistic.
[72] A recurring idea in Agosti's important contributions, e.g. Agosti 2002, 2008b, and 2011b.
[73] See the overview in Rebenisch 2009.
[74] See also the revision of late antique aesthetics as something modern in, e.g., Elsner/Hernández Lobato 2017.
[75] See the important contributions of Agosti in this volume and elsewhere, e.g. Agosti 1998 and 2011a.
[76] On more nuanced religious milieus see Gemeinhardt/Van Hoof/Van Nuffelen 2016.

Usurpation and *Kontrastimitation* was made possible.[77] If we aim, therefore, to explore the *Erwartungshorizonte* and the *Sitz im Leben* of this kind of poetry, genre embodies the readerly and textual expectations creating a bridge between text and audience. Genre bears on its delineation the mark of a specific kind of composition and buttresses a certain kind of shared cultural ideology.[78]

This volume: scope, aims, innovation

While it is impossible for this brief introduction to provide a detailed discussion of genre for such a breadth of texts and authors in Greek and in Latin, we hope to have pointed towards the reasons why it is crucial to study the *Sitz im Leben* for each of the poems discussed. This is not a volume on the genres or aesthetics of late antique poetry in general nor is it a diachronic study of specific genres. We have chosen, instead, to focus on the interplay between 'major' and 'minor' genres, which is mirrored in the bipartite organization of the volume according to genres and not chronology: Part 1, 'Fugue in minor', deals with what we understand here as literally small-scale, hence 'minor', genres, such as epigrams, hymns, or *epyllia*; Part 2, 'Fugue in major', discusses larger-scale, literally 'major', poetic works, such as grand-scale heroic or didactic epic. And while 'minor' and 'major' do not reflect the association between major/minor tonality and positive/negative emotional valence as in music, we believe they are useful categories to think with. The contributions in this volume are written by experts in their respective fields, who were given the task of exploring illustrative case studies of how a text manipulates and alternates between major and minor registers, how it negotiates readerly expectations, and how much it deviates, like a fugue, from a given theme, or in our case, genre.[79]

Throughout the volume we ask how Christian poets engage with (and are conscious of) the double reliance of their poetry on two separate systems: on the one hand, the classical poetic models and, on the other, the various genres and sub-genres of Christian prose (Gospel, homilies, hagiographies, passion narratives). At the same time, we did not want to lose sight of the fundamental role of stylistic techniques learned in the schools of rhetoric (e.g. *prosopopoeia*, *ekphrasis*, encomium). When can these be considered as genres in their own right? How

---

77 On *paideia* see, e.g., Brown 1992, chapter 2.
78 See, e.g., Beebee 1994.
79 The musical metaphor echoing Bakhtin's famous polyphony and fugue-like approach to the poetics of Dostoyevsky; cf. Bakhtin 1984, 21.

are they 'modulated' when incorporated into Christian poetry? Does it make a difference for their 'absorption' or 'inclusion' if they are employed within larger- or smaller-scale forms?[80] Still, it was equally important not to overlook the ideological changes reflected in the manipulation and adaptation of classicizing genres in Christian poetry. For this reason the first and the last chapter of the volume specifically address issues of ideology in terms of generic (dis-)continuity. In detail:

The **First Part**, **'Fugue in Minor'**, deals with the small-scale genres of epigram, elegy, and *epyllion*. It opens with Gianfranco Agosti, who looks at ideological shifts in relation to Greek verse inscriptions from the fourth and fifth centuries. Agosti suggests that, although there is no radical break between the classical and the Christian epigraphic production, Christian poetry's conscious adaptation of classical language (in cases of *Kontrastimitation*, but not exclusively so) gradually entered the production of inscriptions, which also started increasingly to reflect and follow these new, Christian literary models. The fact that the same processes are at work in the high-flown epics supposedly read by the elites and the verse inscriptions which were part of the everyday life of ordinary people leads us to think that there were deep-rooted, social interests and needs to which both 'major' and 'minor' poetry (or, both high-flown and more 'everyday' poetry) responded. Following on from Agosti's analysis, but presenting a different take on epigram, Arianna Gullo argues that in the funerary epigrams of the sixth-century poet Julian the Egyptian nothing evinces discontinuity with the past, not least at the level of form. Even though she is able to detect some Christian 'interferences' in Julian's production of funerary epigrams, Gullo maintains that these depend on *a priori* knowledge of the poet's faith and do not have an impact on the way Julian inserts himself in this classical genre. Tackling both epigram and *epithalamium*, Marco Onorato next explores the reception of a Prudentian *ekphrasis* (that is, a Christian, allegorical *ekphrasis*) first in a hexameter *epithalamium* which obliterates the Christian, religious component, and then in an epigram inserted within a letter and celebrating a Christian building: this epigram, written in phalaecean hendecasyllable, a meter usually associated with nugatory frivolity, 'renovates' the Prudentian hexameters and (surprisingly, perhaps) re-instates Prudentius' allegorical intent.

Another cluster of articles in this section showcase different approaches to small-scale forms, chiefly among them the elegiac couplet and the broadly defined 'elegy', an elusive category sometimes (though not necessarily) associated

---

[80] For 'absorption' (one generic example disappears into another or is reduced to a group of *topoi*) vs. 'inclusion' (a separate generic identity is retained) see Cairns 2007, 89–90.

with a mourning mode in classical poetry. Thomas Kuhn-Treichel's contribution begins with an analysis of an elegiac poem by Gregory Nazianzen, in which the poet explicitly refers to a series of classical (dactylic) genres that he aims to surpass. The same competitive attitude is manifest in a hexametric verse epistle, while an iambic poem contains explicit references to tragedy, but also Homer and Theognis. For a markedly different use of elegiacs (side by side with dactylic hexameter and iambic trimeter) we turn to the chapter of James McDonald on the polymetric catalogue poems of Gregory Nazianzen. McDonald argues that these poems were not written for the late antique classroom, as some modern scholars have maintained. Rather, they would have been read as auxiliary material for the study of the Bible and may have been composed in the spirit of confident innovation (albeit one that did not catch on) upon the long-standing didactic tradition. To Gregory's bold experiments we can contrast the quest for innovation in an important Christian poet of the Latin West, Dracontius and especially his *Satisfactio*. Maria Jennifer Falcone studies this complex poem that combines in elegiac couplets modulations of various genres, from *suasoria* to hymn and *precatio*, and most importantly *deprecatio*. Being the first example of prison poetry, Dracontius' elegiac *Satisfactio* creates a new poetic form out of both the classical genre of exile poetry and the extensive adaptation of rhetorical techniques (*exempla, topoi, excursus*).

Dracontius is the focus of a further cluster of articles, dealing with *epyllion*. Here we turn to modulations between the major genres of epic and tragedy, contained within the short epic form. Étienne Wolff argues that the three major mythological poems by Dracontius (*De raptu Helenae, Medea* and *Orestis tragoedia*) do not embark on an allegorical or moralizing interpretation of classical myths. Focusing as they do on the characters' passions, these small-scale poems remain tied to the private sphere, as opposed to the more ambitious and metaphysical large-scale epic. Next, taking the *epyllion Medea* as a case study, Susanna Fischer examines the representation of the gods and their influence (or lack thereof) on human actions. Reaching the same conclusions as Wolff, Fischer argues that, despite some phrases which could be perceived by a Christian audience as parodic criticism of the gods, Dracontius does not set out to denounce paganism, but to combine tragic, epic, and elegiac motifs in a new generic 'transposition' of the story. This first part of the volume ends with Anna Maria Wasyl's comparison and reevaluation of two short *epyllia* concerning Alcestis: the *Alcestis Barcinonensis* and the cento *Alcesta*. For the *Barcinonensis*, Wasyl argues that the pervasive influence of pantomime, which she views as a means of concretization and not a genre in its own right, would have made a difference in how a contemporary audience would receive (especially, visualize) the work, while for the cento, whose narrator has a stronger presence, the label '*epyllion*' would be more appropriate. While the poems cannot be interpreted as Christian, Alcestis' appeal to both Christian and pagan audiences, as a figure who transcends death, must surely be significant.

The **Second Part**, **'Fugue in Major'**, deals with large-scale epic. The first group of contributors examines the impact of heroic epic on the Christian matrix and vice versa. The discussion opens with Michael Paschalis' examination of the miracle of the Calming of the Storm in what is probably the earliest large-scale Christian epic, that of Juvencus. Paschalis argues that the classical intertexts should not be read solely within the framework of ideological *Kontrastimitation*: the self-reflexive passages in Juvencus' *Evangeliorum Libri Quattor* show that the text places itself in the tradition of grand mythological/historical epic illustrated by the *Aeneid*. By assimilating Jesus to Aeneas, Juvencus would have prompted his readers to make further associations between Virgil and himself, but also between Augustus and Constantine. Another take on the encomiastic potential of the grand epic tradition is illustrated by Eudocia's transposition of a hagiographical prose work into a 'Homeric hagiography': Maria Sole Rigo shows that large-scale epic was well suited to the encomiastic project, and Homeric language was used to elevate the converted magician Cyprian into a new, holy epic hero, who, like his Homeric counterparts, battles against the divine, be it God or Satan. The grand epic mode, however, does not always transform the Christian text into a thoroughly heroic poem: Domenico Accorinti challenges the Homeric pedigree of Nonnus' *Paraphrase of the Gospel According to John* and questions the very intention of Nonnus to write a 'Gospel epic'. Unlike Juvencus, who transforms Jesus into an epic hero, Nonnus modulates between 'major' and 'minor' (whether hexametric or not) genres, such as fables or didactic epic. Accorinti emphasises, thus, the amalgamated nature of the *Paraphrase* and illustrates Nonnus' intent to build a new poem on the foundations of both Homer and John by composing an epic poem appreciated for its exegetical and aesthetic appeal.

The next two chapters explore the didactic character of Christian epic. Fotini Hadjittofi examines the didactic flavor of Nonnus' *Paraphrase of the Gospel According to John*. Not only does the *Paraphrase* expand John's *Ur*-didactic setting – Jesus teaching his disciples – but it also abounds in didactic terminology and allusions to the Archaic and Hellenistic didactic tradition. Nonnus transposes the Gospel into a didactic poem following the Hellenistic trend of rewriting prose treatises into hexameters, while stressing the limitations faced by the human mind as it tries to grasp the transcendental truth of Christian revelation. Andrew Faulkner too examines Apollinaris' *Metaphrasis Psalmorum* in terms of didactic epic, and highlights the poem's debt to the Hesiodic tradition. Faukner also underlines the poetic aspirations of the author that go beyond simple didacticism, suggesting that the poet portrays himself as a new kind of biblical epic bard, a "Davidic Hesiod."

The last two papers show the (dis-)continuity of some themes introduced in Late Antiquity (and taken up into the Middle Ages) at both the literary and the ideological level. Anna Lefteratou examines an early Marian lament, to be found in the *I Homeric Centos*, as a 'modulation' between grand epic and tragic lamentations: in order to compose one of the earliest Marian laments the poet of the *I Homeric Centos* uses not only the Homeric *gooi* but also a long tradition of tragic and dramatic laments/monologues filtered through imperial epideictic rhetoric. The last contribution of the volume deals with yet another transformation of grand epic in Late Antiquity. Hartmut Leppin examines the discourses of warfare in George Pisides' *Persian Expedition* from both a historical and an ideological point of view. George Pisides sets out to praise Heraclius' victory against the Persians, following in the steps of historiographers and other imperial panegyrists, and composes an epic poem written in iambs, thus inaugurating a long Byzantine tradition of such iambic poetry.[81] This is a case of discontinuity in relation to the classical canon, as not only meter but also the poem's ideological agenda changes: this poem stands out for its remarkably 'totalizing' Christian discourse, as opposed to the earlier (fourth and fifth century) dialogical relationship between classicizing and Christian culture: Pisides' poem is about a holy war and about the Emperor's role in it as the representative of God on earth.

Afterthoughts and new horizons

This volume aspires, above all, to draw more attention to early Christian poetry, its diverse audiences, and its appropriation of classical genres. Specifically:

Sitz im Leben

All the chapters in this volume show the importance of the historical context of the poems, their *Sitz im Leben*, as a parameter entangled with genre. Agosti's examination of epigrams dating from the fourth to the sixth century illustrates

---

[81] For Pisides' debt to Homeric heroic themes and verse see Demoen/Verhelst 2019, 186–187 with literature.

the discontinuity of the pagan thematic repertoire despite the perseverance of the form. His findings stand in stark contrast to Gullo's treatment of literary epigrams that were circulated among the literati. Another important issue that emerges from this volume is the downplaying of the idea that the 'birth' of Christian poetry was a reaction to Julian's edict. All contributions on fourth-century poets such as Gregory Nazianzen, Juvencus, and the author of the *Metaphrasis Psalmorum* suggest that these poems, apart from championing a Christian cause, had clear aesthetic aspirations that go well beyond mere didacticism. Furthermore, we may see how other historical contexts might have influenced particular artistic expressions: Lefteratou's reading of Mary's lament in the *I Homeric Centos* associates it to the post-Ephesus debates about the motherly features of the Theotokos; even more importantly, Leppin's article shows how the historical changes and critique of *urbanes Kaisertum* in Heraclius' times contributed to the emergence of a new discourse of holy war.

Another important historical parameter is the understanding of the **pagan/Christian dichotomy** and its usefulness, if at all, for deciphering Christian poetry. This volume shows that the response of Christian poetry to previous literature differs significantly from century to century and author to author. Kuhn-Treichel's and McDonald's contributions suggest that an earlier poet such as Gregory felt the need to create a theoretical framework to support the case of Christian classicizing poetry. Yet the fact that Gregory was a clergyman might have underpinned his motivation. The same goes for the other priest of our collection, Juvencus (in Paschalis' contribution), and possibly also for the writer of the *Metaphrasis Psalmorum*, as both poets preface their works with programmatic proems. As far as we know, this is not the case for the fifth- or sixth-century non-ordained poets such as Nonnus and Dracontius, who felt freer to experiment with both pagan and Christian themes, as shown in the chapters by Hadjittofi, Gullo, Falcone, Wasyl, and Wolff. In fact, different social milieus are crucial for shaping the reception of classicizing genres, such as the Cycle of Agathias for Julian the Egyptian (Gullo), whose poetry is disengaged from his own religious beliefs. Yet even within a poet's lifetime, the understanding and reception of classicizing poetry and genres may shift, as is the case in Onorato's analysis of Sidonius Apollinaris, who moves from a rhetorical to a more symbolic reception of Prudentius' epic allegory.

In order to understand the impact of historical setting on genre, it is important to keep in mind the different settings of the **Greek-speaking East** and the **Latin-speaking West**. Whereas in the West an uninterrupted tradition leads from Damasus and Juvencus to Fortunatus, which might as well explain why

Latin Christian poetry is more rigorously studied,[82] the Greek poetry of the same period appears more polyphonic, if not heteroclite, and includes important works whose date is still contested. In the East, besides classicizing Christian poetry another thread continued to develop, especially in Syria, in non-classicizing form and in a different language and meter. Ephraim the Syrian in the late fourth century wrote hymns that later inspired not only a great tradition of Syriac and Armenian poetry, but also the sixth-century poet of *kontakia*, Romanos the Melodist, and subsequent Byzantine hymnography.[83] More intriguing are cases such as the so-called *Akathist Hymn*, traditionally considered later but now dated to the fifth century, which, if accepted, might make it a poem contemporary with Nonnus.[84] This volume attempts to redress the scholarly balance between Latin and Greek Christian poetry by focusing on the latter, while addressing key Latin poems too.

Readership

Another important issue is the question of **readership**. All the contributors of the volume stress the importance of readerly reactions. The reconfiguration of readerly expectations emerges not only because of the shared *paideia* in which Homer and Virgil (Rigo, Paschalis, Wolff) or drama (Fischer, Wasyl) had the leading role but also because of the rigorous rhetorical training undertaken in Graeco-Roman schools. Yet, the engagement with other genres, such as the Archaic and Hellenistic didactic tradition (Faulkner, Hadjittofi) or the literary epigram (Gullo), shows that the poems in this volume are indebted to forms and texts well beyond the school canon. It should also be kept in mind, however, that even the engagement with the canon takes place in different ways and at different points in the East and the West: Juvencus' transformation of the Gospel into a (more or less classical) epic (Paschalis) and Proba's recomposition of the Bible out of Virgilian Centos occur a generation or so before Eudocia transcribes the hagiography of

---

[82] The most recent contribution on the East/West dialogue is the forthcoming edited volume by Verhelst/Scheijnen. For the Latin see, e.g., Otten/Pollmann 2004, Pelttari 2014, Schottenius Cullhed 2016, Pollmann 2017, Elsner/Hernádez Lobato 2017. By contrast, on the Greek side the interest in late antique poetry, besides den Boeft/Hilhorst 1993 and Johnson 2006, is mainly sustained in the volumes dedicated to the most influential poet, Nonnus; see Spanoudakis 2014, Accorinti 2016, Bannert/Kröll 2017, and Verhelst, forthcoming; see also Agosti/Rotondo, forthcoming, exclusively on the *Paraphrase*, on which Goldhill 2020, 81–86 offers some observations.
[83] Tomadakis 1993.
[84] Peltomaa 2001.

Cyprian or the Gospels in Homeric verse. Does that mean that the status of Virgil for Latin-speaking poets was different from that of Homer? Was the intertextual potential offered by Virgil different from that offered by Homer? These topics remain open for further investigation.

This volume, moreover, stresses another important area in which Graeco-Roman *paideia* impacts readerly expectations: the influence of a **rhetorical education** and the poet's manipulation of rhetorical tropes. Michael Roberts long ago stressed the importance of rhetorical *paraphrasis* for biblical epic, and the contributions in this volume show that rhetorical training was a shared code between poets and their audiences. Falcone, for example, highlights the rhetorical pedigree of the *Satisfactio*, e.g. in its modulation of *suasoria*; Wasyl inquires how *ethopoeia* and *controversia* are implemented in the *Alcestis Barcinonensis*; and Lefteratou shows the importance of imperial *progymnasmata* for the characterization and the composition of Mary's lament in the *I Homeric Centos*. By thus highlighting the experimental and innovative aspect of the Christian compositions this volume places particular stress on the self-reflexive elements of this poetry.

A sub-category of reader-related questions is the issue of the scholarly tools often used to describe the engagement of Christian poetry with its pagan models at both the level of intertextuality and generic engagement. While the Church Fathers used the term *chrêsis*,[85] the modern and popular terms are **Kontrastimitation** and **Usurpation**:[86] for *Kontrastimitation* and *Usurpation* to take place an educated audience is assumed – an audience that could decode them accordingly. But whereas both concepts are useful for understanding the ideological engagement of Christian poetry with the classical models, the current scholarly emphasis on the intercultural and dialogical aspects of Christian poetry might press for a new, more flexible, understanding of these terms: Paschalis, for example, questions the strict definition of *Kontrastimitation*, as this would dismiss other possible, and equally valuable, intertextual readings of a passage. Similarly, according to Lefteratou, the Homeric counter-analogues for Mary as a *mater dolorosa*, e.g. Anticlea and Thetis, do not simply help to craft a superior version of the Mother of God against her pagan models but also to fill out the details in this *ethopoeia* of her suffering.

---

85 Gnilka 1984.
86 See Agosti 2011b, 287 for *Usurpation* as "the attribution to God or Christ of predicates typical of pagan gods;" and *Konrastimitation* defined as "contrasting imitation, with respect to an original context which is reversed: the citation therefore shows the falsity of the pagan model and the superiority of Christianity" (trans. A. Lefteratou).

Modulations and transpositions of classical genres

An important characteristic of this collection of articles is the focus on the significance of meter and how this influences reception and interpretation. If, in Late Antiquity, metrical virtuosity aims more at an *epideixis* of the author's skill (a distinct possibility for Synesius' metrically elaborate *Hymns*), in what cases is it also (and still) valid to read generic affiliation into meter? Should we dismiss the traditional 'baggage' of meter and assume that (most) meters no longer evoke an ethos? Throughout the volume we observe that meters such as the elegiac couplet were important for particular genres such as elegy and epigram. On the other hand, we note that dramatic modulations can take place in hexametric poems and even in cento compositions (Lefteratou, Wasyl, Wolff). The reason for such a shift was not only the gradual disappearance of the performative contexts of some genres (e.g., theater), but also the absorption of certain dramatic features and modes by epideictic rhetoric throughout imperial times, a tendency also reflected in the *progymnasmata*.

The same is valid for form and scale. Just as meter was, in earlier times, frequently coupled with specific performative contexts, the length of the poem was equally determined by external criteria, some of which were also linked with performance or setting. In many ways this system is largely still in place, in spite of modern criticism's tendency to look for discontinuity and rupture. While little can change in the length of inscriptional epigram, for example, it has been argued that such poetry ceases to be read in Late Antiquity, and is only appreciated as visual art. Our view, argued in more detail by Agosti in relation to inscriptional epigram, is that Christian poetry (both large- and small-scale) demands an involved audience. Whether or not a poem was the subject of public performance still appears to be linked with meter as well as scale.[87] Magnelli 2008 has convincingly and lucidly shown that smaller-scale poetry in elegiac distichs increasingly becomes private and bookish, while larger-scale iambic and hexametric compositions seem to indicate a public, performative context. The contributions on Gregory and Sidonius show precisely how small-scale poems were intended for private appreciation – in fact, Sidonius includes his epigram in a letter to the young rhetor Hesperius. Contrarily, the use of formulae and the epideictic nature of Mary's lament in the *I Homeric Centos* display actual performative characteristics, such as references to body language.

---

[87] For performance of epic poetry in Late Antiquity see Agosti 2008a.

This volume is yet another testament to the difficulty of disentangling intertexts and genres. A way to 'solve' this Gordian knot was to place particular emphasis on other generic characteristics besides subject matter: meter and context in this respect have been particularly useful (McDonald, Falcone). Performative indicators or paratexts that would have enhanced the reception of a particular text in terms of a specific genre are equally underscored: from the *didaskalia* of Mary's body language (Lefteratou) and the *deixis* in the Alcestis *epyllia* (Wasyl) to the didactic 'you' function in the *Paraphrase* (Hadjittofi), markers of genre seem to be incorporated in a variety of techniques. There are, however, cases where generic debt is not highlighted, as the model was so popular that a simple intertextual allusion would suffice, as in the reception of Virgil in Juvencus (Paschalis) or cases where allusions to other texts and genres aim to display the poet's erudition and virtuosity, as in the case of the reception of Mesomedes' *ekphrasis* of the sponge in Nonnus' *Paraphrase* (Accorinti).

If we now turn to the kind of works transposed from a Christian genre to a classical one, then we observe a tendency to 'transpose' prose works such as the Gospels and hagiographies into larger-scale epics (Paschalis, Rigo) – a tendency also influenced by the rise of encomiastic and panegyric poetry throughout imperial and Byzantine times. Grand epic and praise have inherent affinities and provide a good vehicle to praise the *vitalia gesta* of God, an emperor, or an exemplary holy man (Paschalis, Leppin, Rigo). On the other hand, dramatic genres, and tragedy in particular (Fischer, Wasyl, Lefteratou), are more apt for pathetic touches and, after centuries of rhetorical manipulation, offer a good tool to develop *pathos*, which is why in hexametric poems they are used to modulate between the grand epic and the intimate, emotional key. That being said, what is perceived as tragic varies significantly between works such as the *Orestis tragoedia*, the Alcestis *epyllia* and the cento Marian lament (Wolff, Wasyl, Lefteratou), as the new Christian faith might have influenced the way of addressing the divine, morality, or the *condition humaine*.

Ultimately, what emerges from this volume is that the reception and appropriation of the classical past and its literary forms by Christianity was above all ideological.[88] While our immediate focus is genre, most of the contributors engage, to some extent, with the ideological ramifications of the transposition of Christian themes into classicizing literature. Some genres were more and some less ideologically inflected: for example, on the long run, epigram did not necessarily have to display a particular ideological agenda and Christian epigrams such as those of Gregory do not replace classicizing ones (Gullo). Tragedy, on the

---

88 Cf. Agosti 2009 and 2011a.

other hand, was ideologically loaded. Plato, Plutarch, and Basil, each according to his time and background, questioned the need to 'read' let alone 'perform' dramas,[89] and the two later authors argued for a moralizing reuse of classical plays. Although Fischer, Wasyl and Wolff do not treat the Alcestis *epyllia* and Dracontius' mythological *epyllia* as Christian or apologetic works, they do discern in them moralizing undertones, highlighted by dramatic and especially tragic influences, and suitable for their respective Christian milieus. Lefteratou sees in Mary's lament the emergence of a new kind of *pathos*, one befitting the human mother of the Son of Man. Paschalis' reappraisal of *Kontrastimitation* in a work that is too early to display the exegetical potential of later Christian classicizing poems also touches upon ideology, and so does Leppin's understanding of George Pisides' innovative reworking of Heraclius' holy war. Far from unravelling such issues the contributions in this volume point towards the need for further, in-depth examination of genre and ideology, intrinsically entangled with the *Sitz im Leben* of this poetry.

These conclusions are preliminary, and the questions set forth here are answered in greater depth in each of the volume's contributions. We are also aware that other important poems, such as those of the *Codex of Visions* or Fortunatus, did not find their way into the volume, but as Eudocia rightly warns her audience in the *apologia* regarding her own editorial practice, "we are all Necessity's laborers."[90] What this brief introduction shows, nonetheless, is the perseverance of classicizing forms well into the sixth and seventh century, a boundary, artificial as it is, that frames the chapters of this volume. From that moment on, Christian poetry took a different turn, away from the classicizing forms and prosody, as is wonderfully illustrated in the work of Romanos the Melodist or the poetry of Cassia. This is not to say that classicizing poetry was not written after the seventh century.[91] Late Antiquity is only the first, and a very experimental, step into a tradition that leads into the Middle Ages and the Renaissance. If we were to seek an end to this productive period of classicizing Christian poetry, which would necessarily be imposed externally and *a posteriori*, we would only find it, approximately, with the rise of Humanism. Erasmus in a letter urges his contemporary Christian poets not to imitate the "römischen Klassiker" but their "spätantike

---

89 Barnes 2008.
90 *Apologia* 18 (*Vat. suppl. gr.* 388): ἴστω τοῦθ', ὅτι πάντες ὑποδρηστῆρες ἀνάγκης.
91 For the highly debated *moyenne* and *long durée* of Antiquity see, e.g., Inglebert 2012, Fowden 2014, and Preiser-Kapeller 2018.

Vorläufer",[92] bearing testimony to the parallel existence of two kinds of aesthetic paradigms inherited by Humanism. For centuries, then, Paulinus' "one Spirit" continued "praising the one God in different languages before all men," displaying the amazing polyphony of Christian poetry.

Bibliography

Accorinti, D. (ed.) 2016. *Brill's Companion to Nonnus of Panopolis*, Leiden.
Agosti, G. 1998. "L'alba notturna", *ZPE*, 121, 53–58.
Agosti, G. 2001. "L'epica biblica nella tarda antichità greca. Autori e lettori nel IV e V secolo", in F. Stella (ed.), *La scrittura infinita. Bibbia e poesia in età medievale e umanistica*, Firenze, 67–104.
Agosti, G. 2002. "I poemetti del *Codice Bodmer* et il loro ruolo nella storia della poesia tardoantica", in A. Hurst/J. Rudhardt (eds.), *Le Codex des Visions*, Genève, 74–113.
Agosti, G. 2008a. "L'epica greca tardoantica tra oralità e scrittura", in R. Uglione (ed.), *Arma virumque cano. L' epica dei greci e dei romani. Atti del convegno nazionale di studi, Torino, 23–24 aprile 2007*, Alessandria, 231–259.
Agosti, G. 2008b. "Literariness and levels of style in epigraphical poetry of Late Antqituiy", *Ramus*, 37, 191–213.
Agosti, G. 2009. "Cristianizzazione della poesia greca e dialogo interculturale", *CrST*, 31, 311–335.
Agosti, G. 2011a. "Le brume di Omero. Sofronio dinanzi alla paideia classica", in L. Cristante/S. Ravalico (eds.), *Il calamo della memoria: riuso di testi e mestiere letterario nella tarda antichità, IV*, Trieste, 33–50.
Agosti, G. 2011b. "Usurper, imiter, communiquer: le dialogue interculturel dans la poésie grecque chrétienne de l'antiquité tardive", in N. Belayche/J.D. Dubois (eds.), *L'oiseau et le poisson. Cohabitations religieuses dans les mondes grec et romain*, Paris, 275–299.
Agosti, G. 2016. "Esiodo nella tarda antichità: prime prospezioni" *Seminari Romani di cultura greca*, 5, 179–246.
Agosti, G./Rotondo, A. (eds.) Forthcoming. *Studies on Nonnus' Paraphrasis*, Berlin.
Bakhtin, M. 1984. *Problems of Dostoevksy's poetics*. Minneapolis/London. Trans. C. Emerson.
Bakola, E./Prauscello, L./Telò, M. (eds.) 2013. *Greek comedy and the discourse of genres*, Cambridge.
Bannert, H./Kröll, N. (eds.) 2017. *Nonnus of Panopolis in context II. Religion and society*, Leiden.
Barchiesi, A. 2001. "The crossing", in S.J. Harrison (ed.), *Texts, ideas, and the Classics: scholarship, theory and classical literature*, Oxford, 142–163.

---

92 For the full reference see Herzog 1977, 375. See also the importance, *a posteriori*, of biblical epic in early modern times, in Czapla 2013.

Barnes, T. 2008. "Christians and the theater", in I. Gildenhard/M. Revermann (eds.), *Beyond the fifth century. Interactions with Greek tragedy from the fourth century BCE to the Middle Ages*, Berlin, 315–334.

Basson, A. 1996. "A transformation of genres in late Latin literature. Classical literary tradition and ascetic ideals in Paulinus of Nola", in R.W. Mathisen/H.S. Sivan (eds.), *Shifting frontiers in Late Antiquity*, Aldershot, 267–276.

Bažil, M. 2009. *Centones christiani: métamorphoses d'une forme intertextuelle dans la poésie latine chrétienne de l'antiquité tardive*, Paris.

Beebee, T.O. 1994. *The ideology of genre. A comparative study of generic instability*, Pennsylvania (PA).

Bessone, F./Fucecchi, F. (eds.) 2017. *The literary genres in the Flavian Age*, Berlin.

Branham, R.B. (ed.) 2005. *The Bakhtin Circle and ancient narrative*, Groningen.

Brown, P. 1992. *Power and persuasion in Late Antiquity: towards a Christian Empire*, Wisconsin (WI).

Cairns, F. 2007. *Generic composition in Greek and Roman Poetry. Corrected and with new material*, (first ed. 1972) Ann Arbor (MI).

Cameron, Alan 1965. "Wandering poets: a literary movement in Byzantine Egypt", *Historia*, 14, 470–509.

Cameron, Alan 2004. "Poetry and literary culture in Late Antiquity", in S. Swain/M. Edwards (eds.), *Approaching Late Antiquity. The transformation from Early to Late Empire*, Oxford.

Candido, F. 2017. "The *Symposium* of Methodius: A witness to the existence of circles of Christian women in Asia Minor?", in K. Bracht (ed.), *Methodius of Olympus: State of the art and new perspectives*, Berlin, 103–124.

Carruthers, M. 2009. "*Varietas*: a word of many colours", *Poetica*, 41, 33–54.

Citroni, M. 2003. "I canoni di autori antichi: alle origini del concetto di classico", in L. Casrsa/L. Cristante/M. Fernandelli (eds.), *Culture europee e tradizione latina*, Trieste, 1–22.

Cohick, L.H. 1998. "Melito of Sardis's *Peri Pascha* and its Israel", *HTR*, 91, 351–372.

Consolino, F.E. 2017. "Polymetry in late Latin poems. Some observations on its meaning and functions", in J. Elsner/J. Hernández Lobato (eds.), *The poetics of late Latin literatrue*, Oxford, 100–124.

Conte, G.B. 1994. *Genres and readers*, Baltimore. Trans. G.W. Most.

Cribiore, R. 2001. *Gymnastics of the mind: Greek education in Hellenistic and Roman Egypt*, Princeton (NJ).

Cribiore, R. 2009. "Education in the papyri", in R. Bagnall (ed.), *The Oxford Handbook of papyrology*, Oxford, 320–337.

Czapla, R.G. 2013. *Das Bibelepos in der Frühen Neuzeit: zur deutschen Geschichte einer europäischen Gattung*, Berlin.

den Boeft, J./Hilhorst, A. (eds.) 1993. *Early Christian poetry: a collection of essays*, Leiden.

Depew, M./Obbink, D. (eds.) 2000. *Matrices of genre: authors, canons, and society*, Cambridge (MA).

Demoen, K./Verhelst, B. 2019. "The tradition of epic in Byzantine poetry", in C. Reitz/S. Finkmann (eds.), *Structures of epic poetry: vol. I: Foundations*, Berlin, 175–210.

Duff, D. 2005. "Intertextuality versus Genre Theory: Bakhtin, Kristeva and the questions of genre", *Paragraph*, 25, 54–73.

Elsner, J. 1995. *Art and the Roman viewer. The transformation of art from the pagan world to Christianity*, Cambridge.

Elsner, J. 1998. *The art of the Roman Empire, AD 100–450*, Oxford.

Elsner, J./Hernández Lobato, J. (eds.) 2017. "Notes towards a poetics of late antique literature", in J. Elsner/J. Hernández Lobato (eds.), *The poetics of late Latin literatrue*, Oxford, 1–24.
Fantuzzi, M./Hunter, R.L. 2002. *Tradition and innovation in Hellenistic poetry*, Cambridge.
Farell, J. 2003. "Classical genre in theory and practice", *New Lit. Hist.*, 34, 383–408.
Filosini, S. 2008. *Paolino di Nola. Carmi 10 e 11*, Roma.
Fitzgerald, W. 2016. *Variety: the life of a Roman concept*, Chicago (IL).
Fontaine, J. 1973. "Les symbolismes de la cithare dans la poésie de Paulin de Nole", in W. Den Boer (ed.), *Romanitas et Christianitas*, Amsterdam, 123–143.
Fontaine, J. 1975. "Le mélange des genres dans la poésie de Prudence", in *Forma futuri. Studi in onore di M. Pellegrino*, Torino, 755–777.
Formisano, M. 2007. "Towards an aesthetic paradigm of Late Antiquity", *AntTard.*, 15, 277–284.
Fowden, G. 2014. *Before and after Muhammad: the First Millennium refocused*, Princeton (NJ).
Fowler, D.P. 1997. "On the shoulders of giants: intertextuality and Classical Studies", *MD (Memoria, arte allusiva, intertestualità)*, 39, 13–34.
Fuhrer, T. 2013. "Hypertexts and auxiliary texts: new genres in Late Antiquity?", in T.D. Papanghelis/S. Harrison/S. Frangoulis (eds.), *Generic interfaces in Latin literature*, Berlin, 79–89.
Gemeinhardt, P./Van Hoof, L./Van Nuffelen, P. (eds.) 2016. *Education and religion in late antique Christiantiy: reflections, social contexts, and genres*, London.
Gigli Piccardi, D. 2012. "Ancora su Nonno e la poesia oracolare", *Aitia* 2, §§ 1–43 (url: http://aitia.revues.org/486).
Gnilka, C. 1984. *Chrêsis. Die Methode der Kirchenvater im Umgang mit der antiken Kultur*, Basel.
Goldhill, S. 2020. *Preposterous poetics: the politics and aesthetics of form in Late Antiquity*, Cambridge.
Gordley, M. 2009. "The Johannine prologue and Jewish didactic hymn traditions: a new case for reading the prologue as a hymn", *JBL*, 128, 781–802.
Gordley, M. 2011. *Teaching through song in Antiquity: didactic hymnody among Greeks, Romans, Jews, and Christians*, Tübingen.
Greatrex, G./Elton, H. (eds.) 2015. *Shifting genres in Late Antiquity*, Farnham.
Hardie, P. 2019. *Classicism and Christianity in late antique Latin poetry*, Berkeley (CA).
Harrison, S. 2007. *Generic enrichment in Vergil and Horace*, Oxford.
Heath, M. 2004. *Menander. A rhetor in context*, Oxford.
Herbert de la Portbarré-Viard, G. 2006. *Descriptions monumentales et discours sur l'édification chez Paulin de Nole. Le regard et la lumière (epist. 32 et carm. 27 et 28)*, Leiden.
Herzog, R. 1977. "Probleme der heidnisch-christlichen Gattungskontinuität am Beispiel des Paulinus von Nola", in M. Fuhrmann (ed.), *Christianisme et formes littéraires de l'antiquité tardive en occident*, Genève, 373–423.
Herzog, R. 1975. *Die Bibelepik der lateinischen Spätantike 1. Formgeschichte einer erbaulichen Gattungen*, München.
Hinds, S. 1998. *Allusion and intertext: dynamics of appropriation in Roman poetry*, Cambridge.
Hinds, S. 2000. "Essential epic: genre and gender from Macer to Statius", in M. Depew/D. Obbink (eds.), *Matrices of genre: authors, canons, and society*, Cambridge (MA), 221–244.
Hurst, A./Reverdin, O./Rudhardt, J. (eds.) 1984. *Papyrus Bodmer XXIX. Vision de Dorothéos*. Genève.

Hurst, A./Rudhardt, J. (eds.) 1999. *Papyri Bodmer XXX-XXXVII, 'Codex des Visions': poèmes divers*, München.
Hose, M. 2004. *Poesie aus der Schule. Überlegungen zur spätgriechischen Dichtung*, München.
Inglebert, H. 2012. "Introduction: Late antique conceptions of Late Antiquity", in S.F. Johnson (ed.), *The Oxford Handbook of Late Antiquity*, Oxford, 3–30.
Jauss, H.-R./Köhler, E. (eds.) 1972. *Grundriss der romanischen Literaturen des Mittelalters I. Généralités*, Heidelberg.
Johnson, S.F. (ed.) 2006. *Greek literature in Late Antiquity: dynamism, didacticism, classicism*, Hampshire.
Kaufmann, H. 2017. "Intertextuality in late Latin Poetry", in J. Elsner/J. Hernández Lobato (eds.), *The poetics of late Latin literature*, Oxford, 149–175.
Kaufmann, H. Forthcoming. "The implosion of poetic genre in Late Antiquity", in B. Verhelst/T. Scheijnen (eds.), *Walking the wire: Latin and Greek late antique poetry in dialogue*.
Kelly, H.A. 1993. *Ideas and forms of tragedy from Aristotle to the Middle Ages*, Cambridge.
Kennedy, G.A. 1983. *Greek rhetoric under Christian emperors*, Princeton (NJ).
Kroll, W. 1964. *Die Kreuzung der Gattungen. Studien zum Verständnis der römischen Literatur*, (first printed: 1924) Darmstadt.
Kuhn, T. 2012. *Die jüdisch-hellenistischer Epiker Theodot und Philon. Literarische Untersuchungen, kritische Edition und Übersetzung der Fragmente*, Göttingen.
Lanfranchi, P. (ed.) 2006. *L'Exagoge d'Ezéchiel le tragique: introduction, texte, traduction et commentaire*, Leiden.
Leppin, H. 2012. "Christianisierungen im Römischen Reich: Überlegungen zum Begriff und zur Phasenbildung", *ZAC*, 16, 247–278.
Leppin, H. 2015. "Einleitung", in H. Leppin (ed.), *Antike Mythologie in christlichen Kontexten der Spätantike*, Berlin, 1–18.
Lightfoot, J.L. 2016. "Nonnus and prophecy: between 'pagan' and 'Christian' voices", in D. Accorinti (ed.), *Brill's Companion to Nonnus of Panopolis*, Leiden, 625–643.
Magnelli, E. 2008. "I due proemi di Agazia e le due identità dell' epigramma tardoantico", in A.M. Morelli (ed.), *Epigramma longum: da Marziale alla tarda antichità. Atti del convegno internazionale (Cassino, 29-31 maggio 2006). 2 vols. Collana Scientifica 21*, Cassino, 559–570.
Mastrangelo, M. 2016. "Toward a poetics of late Latin reuse", in S. McGill/J. Pucci (eds.), *Classics renewed: reception and innovation in the Latin poetry of Late Antiquity*, Heidelberg, 25–46.
McDonald, J.I.H. 1975. "Some comments on the form of Melito's *Paschal Homily*", *Studia Patristica*, 12, 104–112.
McGill, S. 2005. *Vergil recomposed: the mythological and secular centos in antiquity*, Oxford.
McGuckin, J. 2006. "Gregory: the rhetorician as poet", in J. Børtnes/T. Hägg (eds.), *Gregory of Nazianzus: images and reflections*, Copenhagen, 181–212.
Miguélez-Cavero, L. 2008. *Poems in context: Greek poetry in the Egyptian Thebaid 200–600 AD*, Berlin.
Miguélez-Cavero, L. 2013. "Rhetoric for a Christian community: The poems of the *Codex Visionum*", in A.J. Quiroga Puertas (ed.), *The purpose of rhetoric in Late Antiquity*, Tübingen, 91–121.
Miguélez-Cavero, L./McGill, S. 2018. "Christian poetry", in S. McGill/E.J. Watts (eds.), *Blackwell's Companion to late antique literature*, Hoboken (NJ), 259–280.
Milovanovic-Barham, C. 1997. "Gregory of Nazianzus: ars poetica (*In suos versus, carm.*

2.1.39)", *JECS*, 5, 497–510.
Most, G. 2000. "Generating genres: the idea of the tragic", in M. Depew/D. Obbink (eds.), *Matrices of genre: authors, canons and society*, Cambridge (MA), 15–35.
O'Daly, G. 2016. "Prudentius: the self-definition of a Christian poet", in S. McGill/J. Pucci (eds.), *Classics renewed. Reception and innovation in the Latin poetry of Late Antiquity*, Heidelberg, 221–239.
Otten, W./Pollmann, K. (eds.) 2004. *Poetry and exegesis in premodern Latin Christianity*, Leiden.
Papanghelis, T.D./Harrison, S./Frangoulidis, S. (eds.) 2013. *Generic interfaces in Latin literature. Encounters, interactions and transformations*, Berlin.
Pelttari, A. 2014. *The space that remains: reading Latin poetry in Late Antiquity*. Ithaca (NY).
Peltomaa, L.M. 2001. *The image of the Virgin Mary in the Akathistos Hymn*, Leiden.
Perler, O. (ed.) 1966. *Méliton de Sardes: sur la Pâque et fragments (SC 123)*, Paris.
Pollmann, K. 1999. "The transformation of epic genre in Christian Late Antiquity", *Studia Patristica*, 36, 61–75.
Pollmann, K. 2009. "Exegesis without end: forms, methods, and functions of biblical commentaries", in P. Rousseau (ed.), *A Companion to Late Antiquity*, Chichester (MA), 285–269.
Pollmann, K. 2013. "Establishing authority in Christian poetry of Latin Late Antiquity", *Hermes*, 141, 309–330.
Pollmann, K. 2017. *The baptized Muse. Early Christian poetry as cultural authority*, Oxford.
Preiser-Kapeller, J. 2018. *Jenseits von Rom und Karl dem Großen: Aspekte der globalen Verflechtung in der langen Spätantike, 300–800 n. Chr.*, Wien.
Rebenisch, S. 2009. "Late Antiquity in modern eyes", in P. Rousseau (ed.), *A Companion to Late Antiquity*, Chichester (MA), 77–90.
Roberts, M.J. 1985. *Biblical epic and rhetorical paraphrase in Late Antiquity*, Liverpool.
Roberts, M.J. 1989. *The jeweled style: poetry and poetics in Late Antiquity*, Ithaca (NY).
Schildgen, B. 2016. *Heritage or heresy: preservation and destruction of religious art and architecture in Europe*, New York.
Schottenius-Cullhed, S. 2016. *Proba the prophet. The Christian Virgilian Cento of Faltonia Betitia Proba*, Leiden.
Shorrock, R. 2011. *The myth of paganism: Nonnus, Dionysus and the world of Late Antiquity*, London.
Silk, M.S. 2012. "Literary Theory and the Classics", *OCD*[4], 845–450.
Sluiter, I. 2000. "The dialectics of genre: some aspects of secondary literature and genre in Antiquity", in M. Depew/D. Obbink (eds.), *Matrices of genre: authors, canons, and society*, Cambridge (MA), 183–201.
Spanoudakis, K. (ed.) 2014. *Nonnus of Panopolis in context I. Poetry and cultural milieu in Late Antiquity with a section on Nonnus and the modern world*, Berlin.
Sykes, A.S. 1997. "Melito's anti-Judaism", *JECS*, 5, 271–283.
Teitler, H.C. 2017. *The last pagan emperor: Julian the Apostate and the war against Christianity*, Oxford.
Thraede, K. 1962. "Epos", *RAC*, 5, coll. 983–1042.
Toca, M. 2017. "The Greek patristic reception of the *Sibylline Oracles*", in D. Batovici/K. De Troyer (eds.), *Authoritative texts and reception history. Aspects and approaches*, Leiden, 260–277.
Tomadakis, B.N. 1993. Ἡ Βυζαντινὴ ὑμνογραφία καὶ ποίησις: ἤτοι εἰσαγωγὴ εἰς τὴν Βυζαντινὴν φιλολογίαν Β΄, (first published: 1965) Athens.

Verhelst, B. (ed.) Forthcoming. *Nonnus of Panopolis in context IV. Poetry at the crossroads*, Leuven.

Verhelst, B./Scheijnen, T. (eds.) Forthcoming. *Walking the wire: Latin and Greek late antique poetry in dialogue*.

Walsh, P.G. 1975. *The poems of St. Paulinus of Nola*, New York.

Webb, R. 2009. *Ekphrasis, imagination and persuasion in ancient rhetorical theory and practice*, Farnham.

Webb, R. 2010. "Between poetry and rhetoric: Libanios' use of Homeric subjects in his *Progymnasmata*", *QUCC*, 95, 131–152.

Whitby, Mary 2010. "Rhetorical questions", in L. James (ed.), *A Companion to Byzantium*, Chichester (MA), 239–250.

Whitmarsh, T. 2013. *Beyond the Second Sophistic. Adventures in Greek Post classicism*, Berkeley (CA).

Part I: **Fugue in Minor: Epigram, Elegy, *Epyllion***

Gianfranco Agosti
Metrical Inscriptions in Late Antiquity: What Difference Did Christianity Make?

"What difference did Christianity make?" is a question put by E.A. Judge to A.H.M. Jones, which later became familiar to historians of Late Antiquity thanks to Ramsay MacMullen. The latter reported it in his 1984 book on the Christianization of the Roman Empire, and attempted to answer "its devastating simplicity" in an article of 1986 of the same title.[1] MacMullen was particularly interested in how Christian doctrine changed broad patterns of the secular life and morality of the Later Empire, not in the "external and self-evident changes" (like churches replacing the temples, for example), which still dominate our discussions of Christianization. Contrary to the straightforwardly negative answer by Jones ("none", he is said to have replied), MacMullen in his 1986 article demonstrated that Christianity had a significant impact in numerous areas of moral and social life.

After the last thirty years of painstaking research on late antique society and culture, we cannot now phrase the question in the same crude terms. One of the most productive approaches in historiography on late antiquity is the study of the *consequences* of Christianization, whose impact on Roman society and morality is generally regarded not only as an established fact, but also as one of the decisive factors that created 'Late Antiquity' as an autonomous period of history, according to the prevailing 'Brownian model'.[2] In a fascinating book, Inglebert extended the enquiry to the literary and scientific culture, exploring more broadly the *mutation des savoirs* in the Christian world.[3] More recently, Johnson's monograph on cartographical thinking dramatically illustrates the development of a new way of thinking and ordering knowledge in Late Antiquity.[4] Moreover, scholars are now prompted to accept that the narrative of Christian triumph in Christian sources was grounded in a rhetorical strategy, meaning that we cannot take literary sources at face value, due to their ideological content and orientation.[5]

---

1 MacMullen 1984, 154 n. 25, and MacMullen 1986, respectively. See also MacMullen 2003.
2 For a recent discussion of this (and other) interpretative models see Humphreys 2017.
3 Inglebert 2001.
4 Johnson 2016.
5 Cf. Av. Cameron 2015, esp. 8–12. On Christian self-definition see Piepenbrink 2015. Needless to say, to take into account the rhetorical discourse is particularly important for the study of literary and inscriptional poetry.

https://doi.org/10.1515/9783110696219-002

A renewed emphasis on the 'ideological mode' of Christian literature has also had important consequences for the "postmodern" vision (as Athanassiadi defined it)⁶ of the conflict between pagans and Christians in the fourth and fifth centuries CE. This emphasis has also influenced critical debate about the use of religious categories to characterize literary trends, including genres. Within this framework, literary analysis of Christian poetry has found new spaces and new critical approaches. Current concerns in the scholarly agenda include the peculiar features of Christian *mimesis*, the nature of the relationship between authors and audience, the gradual transition from an autonomous to a heteronomous aesthetics, the means and consequences of the replacement of the classical tradition with new Christian models and *auctoritates*, and, in the case of poetry written in hexameters, the transformation of epic language into something entirely different. If we compare the current state of research on Christian poetry to that of twenty-five years ago – when studies on crucial texts like the poems of the *Codex of Visions* (*PBodmer* 29–37) and Nonnus' *Paraphrase* were in their infancy – it is evident that the landscape has changed dramatically. Many contentious and thorny issues have now been resolved: for example, the occurrence of both profane and Christian poems in a single author's body of work (as with Nonnus) is no longer considered problematic, nor is it any longer necessary to emphasize the basic point that Greek Christian literature is an integral part of late Greek literature.⁷

Even scholarly perceptions of literary values have gradually and markedly changed. One of the many merits of Livrea's edition of Book 18 of the *Paraphrase of the Gospel According to John* was to illustrate the relevance of Nonnus' 'minor' poem in terms of its literary qualities.⁸ Almost thirty years later, in the *Companion to Nonnus* edited by Accorinti, the *Paraphrase* received the same attention as the

---

6 Athanassiadi 2006.
7 In the words of the late Pierre Chuvin 2018, 17: "To my mind, the main point here is to recognize, in two works at first glance as different as the *Dionysiaca* and the *Paraphrase*, the work of one and the same author, who was undoubtedly familiar with theological problems, and who faced the ancient traditions of his world with a mixture of fascination and contempt, reverence and irony, the latter perceptible here and there in an attitude which emerges, as one might expect, mainly towards the end of the vast work." Significantly, a recent companion on late antique literature has two chapters dealing with Christian poetry (Miguélez-Cavero/McGill 2018 and Whitby/Roberts 2018).
8 Livrea 1989, a groundbreaking volume which reenergized the study of Nonnus' Christian poem (for a complete list of editions of single books of the *Paraphrase*, see my entry *Nonnus* in the *Oxford Bibliographies* [https://www.oxfordbibliographies.com/view/document/obo–9780195389 661/bo–9780195389661–0332.xml]).

Dionysiaca.⁹ Furthermore, current critical approaches to Greek Christian poetry focus on its cultural and social roles, and on how Christian poets, responding to earlier literary traditions, reshaped both intertextual engagement and literary genres more broadly.¹⁰

I share the opinion of scholars who think that one of the main aims of Christian poetry was precisely to explore new communicative functions, both challenging and usurping the classical tradition, and creating a new poetic system. From this perspective, I would like, in this paper, to address a 'grey area' in Greek Christian poetic production, where the question of what difference Christianity made is fundamental, namely the production of metrical inscriptions from the fourth to the sixth centuries CE –of the significant features of late antique epigraphy.¹¹ Previously neglected by literary scholars, Greek metrical inscriptions have recently been receiving growing attention. A major result of the new critical approach (represented by a handful of scholars) was that poems on stone proved to be a significant part of the so-called "resurgence of poetry" in Late Antiquity.¹² Indeed, verse inscriptions and literary poems are two sides of the same coin, and

---

9 Accorinti 2016, where relevant chapters are devoted to the *Paraphrase*. See also the overall statement on Nonnus' project by Spanoudakis 2014, 4: "The *Paraphrasis* and the *Dionysiaca* ... are two parts of a great cultural project which aims at recounting the history of the world. The perspective is essentially Christian."

10 Fuhrmann 1976 was a groundbreaking collection of essays. See more recently Stella 2005 (with further bibliography); Pollmann 2017. It is significant that a classicist such as Hardie prefers to emphasize continuity, e.g. Hardie 2019, 3: "Change there certainly is, transformation even, but not sufficient, in my view, to arrive at something qualitatively quite other. This is particularly the case with allusion and intertextuality, where I am not persuaded by various attempts to diagnose a quantum shift in writers' and readers' response to earlier texts." Contrarily, a specialist of Christian poetry such as Pollmann emphasizes innovation, e.g., Pollmann 2017, 2–3: "Early Christian poetry was one expedient and an effective device by which Christianity managed to establish its agenda in a forceful way. By usurping the established authority of pagan poetry as a cultural identity marker, Christianity opened up a plethora of possibilities for invading this pagan elitist cultural space and for using it to disseminate Christian messages, thereby making them more ubiquitous, reaching educated audiences of a high social status."

11 For surveys on late antique epigraphy, after the ground-breaking collection of papers in Donati 1988, see Salway 2015 and Bolle/Machado/Witschel 2017b, who at p. 20 emphasize the "profound transformation in epigraphic practice" in the period; Van der Vliet 2017 offers an insightful reappraisal of monastic epigraphy and its innovations. Roueché/Sotinel 2017, 512 make a strong case for the "study of late antique inscriptions in their own right." For figures see Antonopoulou 2002 and the chapters in Bolle/Machado/Witschel 2017a. On the shift in the epigraphic habit represented by the 7th century CE see Toth 2016.

12 Cf. Agosti 2012, 361–362 and Al. Cameron 2016, 166–167.

there were meaningful interrelationships between them, as I have tried to demonstrate elsewhere.¹³ Literary analyses of stone epigrams read these inscriptions against the background of high literary poetry, in order to detect influences and echoes. This approach, however, being focused on the literary qualities of the texts, risks perpetuating the traditional interpretative model based on 'the high' *vs* 'the low' (or 'the correct' *vs* 'the awkward', i.e. 'good inscriptions' *vs* 'bad ones'). As legitimate in terms of literary criticism as this model might be, it is surely inadequate for understanding the social functions of inscriptions. Indeed, we cannot measure the literariness of a text in terms of its success or failure in comparison with highbrow poetry. If metrical inscriptions were, according to an apt definition by Roueché, "literary artefacts, whose prime aim was not to convey information but to emphasize the culture of those involved in the transaction",¹⁴ it is fundamental to evaluate this display of culture in the context of its social and cultural background, i.e., the commissioners and the audience.¹⁵ Many lower-level metrical inscriptions, for example, are valuable attestations to the living social prestige of Greek *paideia*,¹⁶ even in small communities and provincial areas. They represent another aspect of the 'democratization of culture' in late antique society.¹⁷

This applies particularly well to the Christian verse inscriptions. It is true that our evaluation of literary poetry has radically changed; for example, Eudocia's *St Cyprian*, traditionally dismissed because of its faulty prosody and awkward language, is now regarded as one of the most intriguing poems of the fifth century. For verse inscriptions, however, inappropriate value-judgments on the 'poetic quality' of the poem, or the degree of the author's proficiency in 'Homeric' language,¹⁸ are still predominant. In this respect, the history of scholarship on Greek Christian poems on stone is radically different from that on Latin Christian ones, where literary analysis has a long-established tradition.¹⁹ Among the various reasons for this is that in the Greek East there was no prominent figure like Damasus and his "special talent for writing tasteful verse" (as Jerome says of him: *De vir. ill.* 103). Damasus' project of celebrating Christian martyrs through poems

---

13 Agosti 2015a.
14 Roueché 1997, 365.
15 Roueché 1997; Agosti 2015a and 2105b (assessment and bibliography: add now Sironen 2017 and Staab 2018).
16 This argument is highlighted in many chapters in this volume; see particularly Gullo, Rigo, and MacDonald.
17 Agosti 2016a.
18 In Agosti 2017 I deal with the limits of the definition of 'Homeric language'.
19 See, e.g., Trout 2015; Liverani 2014; Grig 2017, with further bibliography.

on stone created a new Christian poetic genre and found immediate success in Rome. In Greek, it is quite possible that some of Gregory Nazianzen's epigrams were real inscriptions (like some other epigrams of the fifth and sixth centuries CE transmitted in the *Greek Anthology*), but we do not have any ideological and literary epigraphic programme comparable to the *epigrammata Damasiana*. Only in a few exceptional cases is it possible to identify the patrons, often bishops, who commissioned or authored epigraphic poems. The extant versified inscriptions are isolated cases which must be studied within their context, and against late antique metrical epigraphic conventions, in order to be evaluated. This highlights the urgent need for an updated *corpus*, or at least a largely representative selection of texts with commentary, whose absence is the other main reason for their neglect in current scholarship.

In what follows, I present a few characteristic examples of Christian verse inscriptions, considering them in their broader context. My aim is to give a precise definition of their Christian features, a definition which acknowledges their profound discontinuity with the 'pagan' past, and the dissonance between their Christian content and classical form.

In general, the simple fact that a metrical inscription is Christian belongs to the category of 'external and self-evident changes' and does not necessarily imply a real break from the past.[20] This applies to the text composed for the erection of the cathedral of Antioch around the mid-fourth century and transmitted by John Malalas (111 Preger = *IGLS* 832 = *SGO* 20/03/03).

> Χριστῷ Κωνστάντιος ἐπήρατον οἶκον ἔτευξεν
> οὐρανίαις ἀψῖσι πανείκελα παμφανόωντα
> Κωνσταντίου ἄνακτος ὑποδρήσσοντος ἐφετμαῖς·
> Γοργόνιος δὲ κόμης θαλαμηπόλος ἔργον ὕφανε.
>
> For Christ Constantius made this lovely dwelling, alike in all respects to the vault of heaven, bright-shining, with Constantius obeying the commands of the ruler; the *comes* Gorgonius, cubicularius, carried out the work (trans. Downey, modified).

Leaving aside the textual problems related to the name of the emperors (vv. 1 and 3),[21] it is notable that the poem was written in an elevated style, not different from that of many other dedicatory epigrams of the period, using patterns which later became popular. Despite the mention of Christ at v. 1 and the fact that the text

---

[20] On the issue of continuity in the epigraphic practice of Late Antiquity see, e.g., Kajava 2009–2010.
[21] See Feissel 2016, 1229–1230, with further bibliography.

extols the erection of a church, nothing in the language of this epigram can be labeled as specifically Christian. This is the lofty language typical of the poetry of the period and of inscriptions commissioned by members of the civic elites (for example, the four-word hexameter at v. 2 and the clause ἔργον ὕφανε at v. 4 are frequent in Nonnus' poems). This language in general remains unaffected by religious allegiance. From this point of view, then, this is not a Christian epigram, but *an epigram commissioned by Christians*.[22]

We can draw similar conclusions from a poem of the fifth century CE from Kanatha (Nabatea), describing the dedication of a church on behalf of the unknown bishop Cassius Epiodorus (*SGO* 22/35/02).[23]

εὐχέο νῦν πρώτιστα καὶ εὐξάμενος πάλιν <ἄθρει>
τέρπεο ὀφθαλμοῖσιν ἰδὼν πολυδαίδαλα ἔργα
νηοῦ τειμήεντος ὃν ἀκαμάτοισιν ἐπέργοις
Κάσσιος Ἠπιόδωρος ἐπίσκοπος αἴσιμα εἰδώς
σπουδῇ καὶ ταχύτητι ὑποστὰς ἐξετέλεσσεν   5
Πατρὶ Θεῷ καὶ παιδὶ καὶ ἁγίῳ πνεύματί τε ξύν.
οἷος δ' ἐκ δαπέδου κλυτοεργέος ἤραρε κόσμος
ἐκταδὸν ἀργεννῇσι φαινόμενος πλακέεσσι,
κείοσιν εὐρύθμοις ἀμφισταδόν· ἐνθάδε πάντες   10
εὐχὰς ὁμοῦ τελέουσιν ὅσοι Χριστὸν δοκέουσιν·
νηοῦ δ' αὖ μετόπισθεν ἐπ' αὐχένι πείονι γαίης
πύργους ἀστερόεντας ἐδείματο καλλιθεμείλους·
οἱ μὲν ἴσοις κανόνεσσιν ἀπ' ἀλλήλων βεβαῶτες
διπλόοι ἐξ ὁμόθεν γλυπτοὺς ἀνέχουσι τένοντας,   15
τῶν δὲ μάλ' ἀγλαΐη πολυήρατον εἶδος ἔχουσα{ς}
πνεύματος ἐξ ἁγίου πελιάδας ἀμφὶς ἀνέλκ[ε].

First of all, address your prayer now; and having prayed observe. Delight yourself seeing the skilful works of the precious church, which thanks to unresting labors Bishop Cassius Epiodorus, who has right knowledge, accomplished zealously and quickly with the aid of God the Father, the Son and the Holy Spirit. From the famous well-worked ground the ornament fits outstretched, resplendent with bright slabs of stone, with white columns around from each side: here all people who believe in Christ say their prayers. In the rear of the Church on the neck of fertile earth the Bishop built magnificent towers that reach the

---

22 On the difference between "Christian epigraphy" and "epigraphy of the Christians" see Roueché/Sotinel 2017, 510, referring to fundamental studies by Carlo Carletti (see also Felle 2016). For a thorough regional study (Macedonia) see now Ogereau 2018.
23 Donceel 1987; *SEG* 37, 1587; Agosti 2008, 203–204; Agosti 2017, 235. For the restoration in v. 1 see Magnelli 2007; l. 13: R.A. Tybout in *SEG* 37, 1587 (online: http://dx.doi.org/10.1163/1874-6772_seg_a37_1537).

stars: they, rearing at the same height and distance, both hold together carved tendons, which have lovely and dazzling form, holding up doves from the Holy Spirit.

The author (perhaps the bishop himself) mentions the Trinity in v. 6, Christ in v. 11, and the Holy Spirit in v. 16. But this is not (or not only) a theological poem. The author's main concern was to celebrate the technical skills of the builder and the beauty of the church, like dozens of standard late antique descriptions, displayed on the walls or inside both profane and religious buildings (and sometimes copied and preserved in the *Greek Anthology*). The inscription illustrates very traditional themes, like the *thauma–topos* at vv. 1–2, the miraculous swiftness of the accomplishment (v. 5), the building rising to the heavens (v. 12), and its brightness (v. 16). Any *ekphrasis* of buildings worthy of the name in Late Antiquity showcases this rhetorical imagery. Cassius Epiodorus was one of the many late antique bishops whose *lithomania* was due to social and political reasons, as Peter Brown pointed out in a groundbreaking article forty years ago.[24] Bishops sought to displace governors in their control of public spaces, and they necessarily used the same tools; in this respect also, Christianity did not make any real difference.

Nonetheless, a close reading of the poem nuances one's initial impressions. The language is comprised of the standard 'Homeric' phraseology very common in this type of inscriptions. It seems, however, that the author of the epigram was aware of two of the main literary techniques of Christian poetry – the principles of *Usurpation* and *Kontrastimitation*, whose meaning is rooted in the interaction between an allusion and the context (transposed or reversed) of the hypotext. For example, at v. 1 εὔχεο νῦν is an *incipit* from the *Odyssey* (3.43), where the prayer is addressed to the god Poseidon (*Usurpation*). The definition of the bishop's wisdom at v. 4 adapts a Homeric *formula*, but transposes its meaning: αἴσιμα εἰδώς in Homer is referred to the quality of the king (in the speech by Mentor).[25] Furthermore, at v. 7 there is an (apparently) new pattern, δαπέδου κλυτοεργέος, in which κλυτοεργός is taken from *Odyssey* 8.345, where it is used as an epithet of Hephaestus. Although the adjective had already entered epigraphic language (we have a couple of occurrences in Imperial texts), here it is probably reemployed against its classical source (*Kontrastimitation*), suggesting that the skilfulness of the floor decoration is due to the Christian God, not to Hephaestus.

---

24 Brown 1980.
25 *Il.* 2.231 = 5.9: φρεσὶν αἴσιμα εἰδώς (and *Il.* 14.433: περὶ γὰρ φρεσὶν αἴσιμα ᾔδη; 15.207: αἴσιμα εἰδῇ).

The language of this inscription is a good example of how the conscious manipulation of classical diction by Christian literary poetry gradually entered epigraphic production.[26] It is an *ekphrasis* which already displays some of the literary features which later became widespread in Christian ekphrastic poems, like John of Gaza' description of a cosmic painting, or the description of Haghia Sophia by Paul the Silentiary.

We are not dealing simply with written texts, of course; the physical *media*, and the context in which an epigram on stone was placed, were part of its message. Before reading the text, the audience visually experienced the monument as a whole and its place in the urban or private setting. The viewer then proceeded to decipher and eventually read and understand the text. The choice of the physical support where the text was carved, and the layout and use of paratextual signs, played a significant role in conveying the message. Apart from the crucial question of the competence of the audience (how many people were able to read and understand an epigraphic poem), it is evident that, in this respect, the only significant element of novelty introduced by Christianity was the use of the cross, or the *Chrismon*. But the use of the cross also constitutes an important difference when it assumed a semantic value, as it did, for example, in the inscription carved on the marble lintel of the basilica at Palaiopolis (Corfu), recently re-edited by Kiourtzian (*IG* IX 1, 720–721 = 569 Felle).[27] The first line consists of the quotation of *Psalm* 117:20 (written in bigger letters), followed by the metrical text written in two consecutive lines. Nonetheless, the metrical structure of the epigram is indicated by crosses and blank spaces:

✝ αὕτη ἡ πύλη τοῦ κυρίου. δίκεοι εἰσελεύσοντ‹αι› ἐν αὐτῇ.
πίστιν ἔχων βασίλιαν ἐμῶν μενέων συνέριθον *vacat*
σοί, μά‹κα›ρ ὑψιμέδον, τόνδ' ἱερὸν ἔκτισα νηὸν ✝ |
Ἑλλήνων τεμένη καὶ βωμοὺς ἐξαλαπάξας *vacat* ✝
χειρὸς ἀπ' οὐτιδανῆς Ἰοβιανὸς ἔδνον ἄνακτι. |

This is the gate of the Lord. The just shall enter into it. With the faith of our Emperor, helpmate of my desires, for You, Blessed on High, this holy temple I did found, having destroyed the precincts and altars of the Hellenes. From a humble hand, Jovian [dedicates this], a gift for the Lord.

---

26 For a detailed commentary see Donceel 1987; note also καλλιθεμείλους that is found only in Paul. Sil., *ambo*. 105 De Stefani: τὸ καλλιθέμειλον ἕδος πετραῖον (cf. Mus. 71: καλλιθέμεθλον).
27 See Kiourtzian 2013–2014, 5, who suggests the age of Justinian for the date of the inscription; Agosti 2018, 260–261.

The lintel, as well as the columns, are *spolia* from a profane building (probably an *ôdeion*). It is remarkable that 'humble' Jovian wanted a stylistically elevated epigram at the entrance of the church. Such a choice was, of course, intended to convey an ideological message. This text carefully employs typical late antique language, characterized by elements of the new Christian poetry, like the adjective ὑψιμέδων at v. 2. The humility *topos* at v. 4 (οὐτιδανός) is frequent in this kind of inscription.[28] The only typically Homeric word is ἐξαλαπάξας at v. 3, a verb which always refers to the fall of Troy (*Il.* 1.129 *et al.*), and which can be viewed as another instance of *Usurpation*. V. 3 was obviously the most important of the epigram, marked by paratextual signs (a blank space and a cross)[29] in order to emphasize Jovian's victory over paganism. The material *spolia* reused for the entrance conveyed an immediate sense of defeat of the Hellenic past, and the viewer was invited to read the epigram as a sort of enacted commentary on the *spolia*. Moreover, the language of the text suggested that the pagan literary past had been defeated, a victory described by a Homeric word, taken from the very same tradition which was being overcome and superseded.

In some cases, Christian verse inscriptions explicitly called the viewer's attention to the idea of contrast with the pagan past, in a sort of physical *Konstrastimitation*. In a group of four statue-bases from Stratonikeia in Caria dedicated to a certain Maximus, who is celebrated for paying taxes "on behalf of the poor", the language fluctuates between traditional civic phraseology and specifically Christian language, according to the context. Three statues were erected in secular contexts (the Gymnasium and the main gate of the city), and accompanied by prose and verse texts, all written in the standard language of honorific inscriptions. The paratextual signs, like the crosses and the ΧΜΓ, confirmed that the honorand was a Christian. A fourth statue bearing an inscription, however, was set in a religious context, in front of a church, and its language clearly suggests Christian faith (*LSA* 657 = *SGO* 02/06/15, Stratonikeia, Caria, fifth c.?; stone apparently lost).[30]

Μά|ξι|[μ]ος. | Θεός.
Μάξιμον εἰσοράαις με τὸν ἄστεϊ καὶ ναετῆρσιν
ἡμετέρων καμάτων πολλὰ χαριζόμενον·
τοὔνεκα δ' ἡ βουλή με καὶ ἀκτέανοι πολιῆται
στῆσαν κυδαλίμαις εἰκόσι λαϊνέαις

---

28 See e.g. *SGO* 16/43/06, vv. 5–6; *SGO* 21/22/01.1–4.
29 Further examples of the semantic relevance of paratextual signs in Agosti 2015a. On the cross see also the insightful article by Jacobs 2017.
30 Ward-Perkins 2015.

εὐαγέων Χρειστοῖο δόμων προπάροιθε θεοῖο,
ὡς ἀγαθὸν τελέθει μὴ κτεάνων ἀλέγειν.

Maximos. / God. You see me, Maximos, who, through our toils, have given much to the city and its inhabitants. Therefore, the Council and the citizens without wealth set me up in glorious images of stone in front of the sacred houses of Christ God. How good it is not to care for wealth! (trans. Ward-Perkins)

At v. 5, the church is defined as εὐαγέων Χρειστοῖο δόμων, employing an epithet also used by Eusebius for a church (*Vit. Const.* 2.40); moreover, v. 6 pertains to a Christian motivation, *philanthrôpia* ("how good it is not to care for wealth"). Ward-Perkins recently characterized this inscription as a failed attempt at Christianizing the statuary practice of late antique cities. Among the large collection in the *Last Statues of Antiquity* database, this is actually the only example of a statue erected in a Christian context instead of the usual civic space. The only other possible example of which I am aware, *SGO* 20/06/01 = *LSA* 878 (Epiphaneia, Syria, fifth or sixth century), an honorific epigram to Elias, who was 'merciful towards the poor folk of the city', is more doubtful.

ἄνδρα μοι ἔννεπε, κοῦρε· τίς | ἔπλετο οὗτος ἄριστος; |
ξεῖνε, φιλ', Ἡλίαν μιν ἐπάξια |τεῖσαν ἄνακτες· |
στεινόμενον γὰρ ἔτοιξεν ἑοῖς | κτεάτεσσι λοετρόν |
χειμερινὸν πλατύνας, πτόλιός δ' | ἐλέαιρε πένητας, |
τέχνης οἵ τὰ ἕκαστα δαήμονε[ς] | ἀμφιπένονται, |
ἐκ σφετέρης παρέχων τὰ | τελέσματα οὐσίας αὐτός. |

Name me this man, young man; who is this felicitous man? Friendly stranger, it is Elias. The emperors have rewarded him as he deserved. Because from his own funds he widened the narrow winter-bath, showing mercy towards the poor folk of the city each of whom pursues his own craft, and he paid the salaries himself, from his own funds (trans. U. Gehn).

The original context of the inscription is unknown, and Cyril Mango makes an unverified assumption that it came from the church in Epiphaneia. The language displays Homeric phraseology (with the *detorsio* of the beginning of the *Odyssey*), and is more traditional in comparison to the epigram for Maximus, and it is only from the name that we assume that the honorand was a Christian, but he might equally have been a Jew.

It is indeed well known how difficult it is to glean reliable information about the religious faith of the honorand when the context of the inscription is lost or insufficiently clear, due to the ambiguity of poetic language (sometimes intentional, especially in multicultural environments, like Aphrodisias in Caria). From the approach I have adopted here, however, the context is not enough; it is the conscious and evident manipulation of poetic language which makes the crucial difference. In brief, Christian verse inscriptions marked a discontinuity with the past when they transformed traditional language into something new, following the principles literary poetry experimented with (as we have briefly seen), by inserting expressions and phraseology from the Scriptures, and/or by displaying a clear departure from classical literary models in favor of new Christian ones.

I shall now focus on these two last points, and firstly on the insertion of Scriptural quotations and the adoption of new models. My first case is an epigram from Crete, the funerary epigram for Magnus (*IC* II 24, 13 = 80 Bandy), dated to the fourth or fifth century CE.[31]

ἡμετέρης κάλλιστον ἔχεις, Λόγε Χ(ριστ)έ, | χορίης |
Μάγνον ἐν εὐσεβίεσσιν πανηγυρίεσσι | δικέων |
τῶδε πόνος κλυτόκαρπος ἐπουρανίων | ἀνέωξε |
τιμὴν ἀγγελόεσσαν, ἐπ‹ε›ὶ σέβας ἱερὸν ἔσχε. |
τίμα{ς} δὲ <σ>ὴν μεγάλην βασιληείδα, τὴν θεότε|κνον|
ἀειδίην θεότητα. τὸ σὸν δ' ὑπεδέχνυτο πν(εῦμ)α,
εὔσχολον ἐκτανύων ψυχῆς πολυχανδέα κόλπον,
εἶδος ὅπως θεϊκὸν βροτοείκελον ἀμφιβά|λοιτο
σῆς, μάκαρ, ἀντολίης θεεϊκὴν δόσιν | ἀγλ‹α›οφεγγές. |

5 τίμα{ς} δὲ <σ>ὴν Guarducci: τιμὰς δ' ἐήν Bandy

Thou hast, o Christ the Word, the best of our chorus, Magnus, among the pious assemblies of the just. Toil after celestial things, crowned with fruits of glory, has opened for him angelic honor since he revered everything holy and honored Thy great Kingdom and eternal divinity begotten of God. He received Thy tranquil spirit, extending the capacious bosom of his soul, in order that his mortal form might put on a splendidly divine one, a divine gift of Thy resurrection, Blessed One (trans. Bandy, modified).

Beyond its use of epic patterns, the text shows a certain acquaintance with the phraseology of Christian poetry (at vv. 1 and 7);[32] more importantly, vv. 5–6 are inspired by a Pauline passage (1 Cor 15:35–58), as Bandy rightly pointed out. The merging of Scriptural models and traditional poetic language is one of the essential features of Christian literary poetry across genres. As far as we can observe,

---

31 See Bandy 1963, 241–245; Guarducci 1978, 412–414. Funerary inscriptions are, of course, the largest part of Christian late antique inscriptions. Cf. Toth 2016, 23. For recent literary analysis of Christian funerary poems, see e.g. Franceschini 2016.
32 1 χορείης cf. Greg. Naz., *AP.* 8.82 et al.; **3** κλυτόκαρπος: Pind., *Nem.* 4.76; **7** ἐκτανύων cf. ἐκτανύσας *Il.* 11.844; 24.18 πολυχανδέα κόλπον: Nonn., *Par.* 6.51 = 21.34 πολυχανδέι κόλπῳ; **8** βροτοείκελον *hapax*, cf. Jo 1:12–14, and Nonn., *Par.* 1.40–41 ἐν ἀρρήτῳ τινὶ θεσμῷ | ξυνώσας ζαθέην βροτοειδέι σύζυγα μορφήν; **9** ἀγλαοφεγγής: *Or. Sib.* 13.65 ἀγλαοφεγγέι πλούτῳ, *Theos. Tub.* 13 ἀστέρας ἀγλαοφεγγεῖς, Max., π. κατ. 189 Zito.

Christian literary poetry was experimenting with traditional forms and language from at least as early as the mid-fourth century CE (as in the Bodmer poems, which I have mentioned at the very beginning); this experimentation was later realized in full by Gregory Nazianzen. Interestingly, it also began to appear in Christian verse inscriptions around the mid-fourth century CE. Another, and very simple, example is this funerary epigram from the Hauran (*IGLS* XXI 323 = *SEG* 59.1723, Arabia, Hauran, Umm al-Jimāl, 344 CE):

Ἰουλιανοῦ τόδε μνῆμα, μακ|ρῷ βεβαρημέν(ου) ὕπν(ῳ),
ᾧ Ἄγαθος δείματο πατὴρ κατὰ | δάκρυ(ον) εἴ<βω>ν,
κοιμητηρίου παρὰ τέρμα κοι|νοῦ λαοῦ Χρειστοῦ
ὄφρ' αὐτὸν ἀείδοιεν ἀμείνω|ν εἰς ἀεὶ λαὸς
ἀμφά{ι}δια, Ἀγάθῳ πάροιθεν | πρεσβυτέρῳ
πιστὸν ἐόντ' ἀγαπητόν, ἐτέω|ν ιβ' ὄντα

1 βεβαρημένῳ ὕπνου, lapis

This (is) the memorial of Julianus, weighed down with long sleep, for whom Agathus (his) father built (it), shedding a tear, hard by the bounds of (the) public cemetery of (the) people of Christ, to the end that the better folk might forever sing his praises publicly, as being aforetime a trusty (son) to Agathus, (the) presbyter, (and) well beloved, being twelve years (old). (trans. Butler).

At v. 1, the pattern βεβαρημένον ὕπνῳ, known in a couple of literary epigrams, is more likely to come from the Gospel of Luke (Lk 9:32: ὁ δὲ Πέτρος καὶ οἱ σὺν αὐτῷ ἦσαν βεβαρημένοι ὕπνῳ) than from Statilius Flaccus (*AP* 7.290.3 = *GPh* 3809: βεβαρημένον ὕπνῳ; *AP* 16.98.1: οὗτος ὁ νῦν ὕπνῳ βεβαρημένος ἠδὲ κυπέλλῳ).[33] The novelty of these inscriptions, despite a certain awkwardness, is evident when compared to other Christian epitaphs, like that of Dioscorus the physician (*SEG* 34.1003 = 493 Samama, Milan, end of the fourth century CE). The language and concepts of this elegant epigram are entirely traditional, and its only allusion to Christianity is a brief mention of Paradise.[34] It is especially in funerary poems that this new language, which was to become predominant in the subsequent century, is displayed. Official texts are characterized by a more traditional, classicizing language, related to their public function. This difference in metrical inscriptions corresponds to what Feissel observed regarding the Constantinian age

---

33 On the use of biblical quotations in public inscriptions see Felle 2015.
34 Agosti 2008, 202–204.

between "acts officiels" which "témoignent ... d'une indulgence persistante envers les cultes traditionnels" and private inscriptions which are much closer to a Christian epigraphy.[35]

The change in literary models is the other feature which marks a strong discontinuity with the pagan past. This is evident from the beginning of the fifth century CE, and certain examples illustrate, somewhat unexpectedly, the culmination of this process in the sixth century CE. I shall mention here two instances belonging respectively to the beginning and to the final stage of the process.

The first inscription is a limestone fragment preserving two columns of a long funerary epigram in hexameters on one side, and a cross on the other. The stone comes from the antiquities market, probably originating from Egypt (*SEG* 24.1243).[36] Unfortunately, the epigram went mostly unnoticed, and did not even feature in Bernand's collection of metrical inscriptions from Egypt (probably because he did not have access to the stone or to reproductions of it).[37] It is a funerary *epigramma longum* (a kind of epigram exceeding the usual length – a frequent typology in Late Antiquity) for a pious person, comparable to the martyrs, of demonstrable and orthodox faith (according to the allusion to the Holy Trinity at vv. 19–23), and who was probably engaged in pastoral activities. The metrical features (such as the absence of proparoxytone accents at the end of the lines), as well as some echoes of Nonnian phraseology from the *Dionysiaca* and the *Paraphrase*, and typically Nonnian rhetorical devices such as the *epanalepses*, point to an author who was acquainted with Nonnus' poetry. These affinities with Nonnian style suggest a date around the mid-fifth century CE, and Alexandria or Panopolis as its place of origin. This metrical inscription is probably the earliest surviving example of the spread of the so-called 'modern style' in Nonnus' homeland, and, importantly for us, its author was familiar with the *Paraphrase*. It was clearly an ideological and conscious choice, following a principle shared by other Christian inscriptions, namely the adoption of Christian literary models (mainly Nonnus and Gregory Nazianzen) instead of classical ones. It was a long process, whose final stage is evident in an epigram of the mid-sixth century CE from a small town northeast of Apamea on the Syrian *limes*, celebrating defensive works protecting a *domus* against Saracene attacks (*SGO* 20/05/06, I'gaz, Syria; 546–547 CE):[38]

---

35 Feissel 2016, 1230.
36 Agosti 2008, 195–196.
37 Bernand 1969, 8.
38 See Agosti 2008, 194–195, referring to previous bibliography (and to the fundamental new edition of the text by Feissel); Felle 2015, 366–367.

ἡ Τριάς, ὁ θεός, πόρρω διώκοι τὸν φθόνον.
εἰκὸν ἐπουρανίοιο θεοῦ, Λόγε, μειλίχιον φῶς,
ὃς Χριστὸς τελέθεις, ὃς ἐδείμαο κόσμον ἀλήτην
ὄλβον ἐμοὶ προίαλλε, τεὴν χάριν ἄφθιτον αἰεί.
Χριστὸς ἀειζώων λυσ[ι]πήμονα χεῖρα κομίζει.
τοὔνεκεν οὐ τρομέο[ι]μι κακορρέκτοιο μεγοινάς
δαίμονος, οὐδ' ἀνδρὸς στυγερὸν καὶ ἀθέσμιον ὄμμα.
νεύμασιν ὃς μούνοισι θεμείλια πῆξαο γαίης,
ῥίζας τ' οὐρανίας καὶ ἀτρυ[γ]έτοιο θαλάσσης,
τόνδε δόμον λίτομαί σε, [κ]αὶ ἐσσομένοισιν ὀπάζοις
[εὔ]διον ἀστυφέλικτον, [ἀ]οίδιμον αἰὲν ὁρᾶσθαι.

Might the Trinity, God, chase away Envy!
Image of heavenly God, Word, gracious light, you who are the Christ, you who built the wandering world, send forth to me happiness, your eternal grace. Christ ever-living offers his hand that ends sorrow. So, I could not fear eager desires of the devil, nor the hateful and impious eye of men. You who only with your will established earth's foundations, and the roots of heaven and of unharvested sea, I pray to you to give this home to future generations, gracious, unshaken and always famous to see!

The author(s) was well acquainted not only with Nonnus' *Paraphrase*, but also, more surprisingly, with Eudocia and the *Metaphrasis Psalmorum*.[39] This text eloquently attests to a discontinuity in the composition of poetry, and in education. Comparison with the contemporary Dioscorus of Aphrodito shows that Nonnus and probably the *Metaphrasis Psalmorum* entered the school curriculum by this time.[40]

In addition to the manipulation of epic language and the selection of new models, I would like to mention another major feature of the Christianization of verse inscriptions in Late Antiquity. Many epigrams, especially epideictic, adopt the characteristic and ubiquitous narrative of triumphalism over the pagan past;

---

39 2 ἐπουρανίοιο θεοῦ: *Par.* 1.134, 5.70 **3** κόσμον ἀλήτην: cf. Nonn., *Dion.* 1.399, 32.54, *Par.* 9.29, 15.105, 16.74; **5** Χριστὸς ἀειζώων: = [Apol.], *Met. Pss.* πρ. 110; Nonn., *Par.* 1.34, 201; **5** λυσιπήμων: [Orph.], *Hymn* 2.11 λυσιπήμονα χεῖρα κομίζει, 59.20 [Μοῖραι] λυσιπήμονες; **6** κακορρέκτοιο: cf. Eud., *Cypr.* 2.374; **7** ἀνδρὸς στυγερὸν καὶ ἀθέσμιον ὄμμα: [Apol.], *Met. Pss.* 36.14 ἀνδρὸς ... ἀθέσμου; **8** νεύμασιν ὃς μούνοισι: cf. [Apol.], *Met. Pss.* 36.50 νεύμασι θεσπεσίοις ἰθύνεται ἴχνια φωτός; Nonn., *Par.* 17.11 νεύμασιν ὑμετέροισι τό μοι πόρες; Jo. Gaz. 1.159 νεύμασιν ἀτρέπτοισι; **8** θεμείλια πῆξαο: Callim., *Hymn* 2.58; Nonn., *Par.* 17.14, *Dion.* 5.50, 17.135, 43.3; [Apol.], *Met. Pss.* 96.8 θεμείλια πάντοσε γαίης, 88.22 θεμείλια θήκατο κόσμον, 103.18 θεμείλια πῆξαο χώρων (and *AP* 9.808.2 [Cyrus?] θεμείλια καρτερὰ πήξας); **11** ἀστυφέλικτον very frequent in Nonnus (e.g., *Par.* 18.48).

40 See also the contribution by Gullo in this volume on the Christian clues in Julian's funerary epigrams.

this, in Cameron's effective words, "may be a heroic narrative, or an anxious narrative, or a contested narrative, but it is more often intended to be a victorious one."[41] This firm narrative choice characterizes several metrical inscriptions, especially the poems carved on public buildings and churches, whose social and ideological function was to re-enact Christian identity against polytheism and the pagan past.

One of the most representative categories of these inscriptions is that of texts inscribed on the doorways of churches, as instances of the more general strategy of Christianizing the civic space of late antique cities.[42] A particularly apposite example is that of two epigrams from Jerash (Jordan) celebrating the church of St Theodore dedicated between 494 and 496 CE, after decades of progressive Christianization of the urban space (*SGO* 21/23/03 and 04).[43] The texts were carved respectively on the lintel above the central door to the atrium, and on the inner face of the lintel, therefore being arranged in order for the faithful to view and read them upon entering and leaving the church. The triumphalism of both epigrams (the church extols its own purity, the reputation of the martyr spreads across the world, and he is now the 'bulwark' of the city)[44] corresponds to the 'visual triumphalism' represented by *spolia* of pagan buildings incorporated into the church, and pagan inscriptions cut and reused to pave the floor.[45] Although it is not always possible to pinpoint ideological reasons behind the use of *spolia*, it is evident in this case that it was done intentionally.[46] Moreover, the presence of verse inscriptions on the two faces of the lintel conveyed an ideological and literary message in itself. Displaying Greek *paideia* at the entrance of the church also involved the idea of capturing the prestigious literary pagan tradition and transforming it into something radically different. The reuse of epic language, merged with the new language of Christian poetry, in the two inscriptions on the lintel is parallel to that of the *spolia* in the pavement of the floor. The metrical inscriptions take on the function of strengthening the Christian identity of the community which they were addressing, commemorating its triumph over the pagan past.

---

[41] Av. Cameron 2015, 8. See also the chapter on the rhetoric of war by Leppin in this volume.
[42] I summarize here Agosti 2018. On the 'written display' in late antique city see Roueché 2006. On 'depaganization' see now the fine essay by Hahn 2015.
[43] Moralee 2006; Agosti 2010, 171.
[44] Vv. 5–6: ἕρκος | ἀλεξίκακ[ο]ν τελέθει κἀγήραον ἕρμα | ἄστει καὶ ναέτῃσι καὶ ἐσσομένοισι πολίταις. On these images see Rapp 2014, 158–159.
[45] As Moralee 2006 perceptively demonstrated.
[46] In his book on Christian attitudes towards pagan statues, Kristensen 2013, 244 adduces a similar case from Ephesus, where the atrium pavement in front of the church of Mary is paved with fragmentary inscriptions facing up.

Conclusions

In summary, I think we can give a positive answer to the initial (and somewhat provocative) question. Christianity made a difference in the practice of verse inscriptions, introducing and spreading features like the transformation of epic language and the display of triumphalist rhetoric, emphasizing the ideological function of poetry. It is especially in the presence of these features that we can confidently speak of a 'new' Christian metrical epigraphy. It is not coincidental that the re-semantization of classical language and the assertion of identity through the triumphalist narrative characterize Christian literary poetry of the fourth and fifth century; suffice it to consider the preface to the *Metaphrasis Psalmorum*,[47] where the author sets out a literary manifesto declaring that Homeric language was created by God as the language of poetry. Indeed, it is crucial to take into account metrical inscriptions in our agenda, because they reveal the 'everyday side' of Christian poetry. Verse inscriptions are extremely helpful in assessing the impact of poetry on a wider audience, and the relevance of poetic communication in Christian society. Furthermore, although authors of metrical inscriptions were primarily addressing ideal readers able to understand the complex poetic language (and who cherished their recondite knowledge of classical literature), their pragmatic communicative functions were not limited to the upper class. Any late antique Roman city inscription, carved on public buildings, on the bases of statues, and so forth, was part of the everyday life of ordinary people. By placing inscriptions in religious buildings, Christians often aimed at pointing out the contrast with the pagan and municipal epigraphic habit. Verses added something more; they showed that pagan *paideia* was defeated, both reversing and transforming 'Homeric' language, and adopting the diction of the new Christian poetry. This applies especially to inscriptions placed in symbolic spaces, such as church doorways. Given the symbolism inherent in the act of entering a church, it is evident that inscriptions placed in the liminal zone were intended to be part of this moment, which was laden with meaning for every worshipper. One need not imagine that people entering churches stopped on every occasion to read the inscriptions. Their content was probably well known, either through performance on the occasion of annual feasts, or owing to readers in churches who explained the content of the inscriptions to illiterate people.[48] They

---

[47] On the author of this poem cf. Faulkner in this volume.
[48] See Agosti 2010; Liverani 2014, both with further bibliography. As Kajava 2009–2010, 112 rightly remarks: "We know that the phenomenon existed in the Greek world from early times,

continuously conveyed through their presence a sense of victory over the past, proclaiming the new world of Christian *paideia*.

Furthermore, I suggest that verse inscriptions, together with literary poems, were one of the most prominent arenas in which Christians reflected on and asserted their position vis-à-vis anything 'Hellenic' or 'Greek'.[49] Beyond their immediate practical function, they reveal deeper and broader attitudes behind Christian poetic production, at the core of which was the rethinking of pagan heritage in order to transform it into something new. Nevertheless, the fact that verse inscriptions are written with the same techniques of imitation as those undertaken in highbrow poems reminds us that these latter poems were not isolated, bookish products, but instead vibrant texts which engaged with actual interests and needs.

Bibliography

Agosti, G. 2008. "Literariness and levels of style in epigraphical poetry of Late Antiquity", *Ramus*, 37, 191–213.

Agosti, G. 2010. "*Saxa loquuntur*? Epigrammi epigrafici e diffusione della *paideia* nell'Oriente tardoantico", *Ant. Tard.*, 18, 149–166.

Agosti, G. 2012. "Greek poetry", in S.F. Johnson (ed.), *The Oxford Handbook of Late Antiquity*, Oxford, 361–404.

Agosti, G. 2015a. "Per una fenomenologia del rapporto fra epigrafia e letteratura nella tarda antichità", in L. Cristante/T. Mazzoli (eds.), *Il calamo della memoria. Riuso di testi e mestiere letterario nella tarda antichità. VI*, Trieste, 13–34.

Agosti, G. 2015b. "La *mise en page* come elemento significante nell'epigrafia e nei libri tardoantichi", in P. Orsini/M. Maniaci (eds.), *Scrittura epigrafica e scrittura libraria: tra Oriente e Occidente*, Cassino, 45–86.

Agosti, G. 2016a, "Epigrafia metrica tardoantica e democratizzazione della cultura", in L. Cristante/V. Veronesi (eds.), *Forme di accesso al sapere in età tardoantica e altomedievale. VI*, Trieste, 131–147.

Agosti, G. 2016b. "Les langues de l'épigramme épigraphique grecque: regard sur l'identité culturelle chrétienne dans l'Antiquité tardive", in E. Santin/L. Foschia (eds.), *L'épigramme dans tous ses états: épigraphiques, littéraires, historiques*, Lyon, 276–295.

Agosti, G. 2017. "Présence d'Homère dans les épigrammes épigraphiques tardives", in Y. Durbec/F. Trajber (eds.), *Traditions épiques et poésie épigrammatique. Présence des épopées archaïques dans les épigrammes grecques et latines*, Groningen, 225–244.

---

but I have the impression that the reading aloud of inscriptions in public, and listening to the reading, was perhaps even more important in Byzantium than it had been before."

49 In general, see now Piepenbrink 2015.

Agosti, G. 2018. "*Versus de limine* and *in limine*. Displaying Greek *paideia* at the entrance of early Christian churches", in E. van Opstall (ed.), *Sacred thresholds: the door to the sanctuary in Late Antiquity*, Leiden, 254–281.

Antonopoulou, T. 2002. "A quantitative survey of the Christian-Byzantine inscriptions of Ephesus and Thessalonica", in H. Friesinger/F. Krinzinger (eds.), *100 Jahre Österreichische Forschungen in Ephesos*, Wien, 169–178.

Athanassiadi, P. 2006. "Antiquité tardive: construction et déconstruction d'un modèle historiographique", *Ant. Tard.*, 14, 311–324.

Bandy, A.C. 1963. "Early Christian inscriptions of Crete", *Hesperia*, 32, 222–247.

Bernand, E. 1969. *Inscriptions métriques de l'Égypte gréco-romaine*, Paris.

Bolle, K./Machado, C./Witschel, C. (eds.) 2017a. *The epigraphic cultures of Late Antiquity*, Stuttgart.

Bolle, K./Machado, C./Witschel, C. 2017b. "Defining the field – The epigraphic cultures of Late Antiquity", in K. Bolle/C. Machado/C. Witschel (eds.), *The epigraphic cultures of Late Antiquity*, Stuttgart, 15–30.

Brown, P. 1980. "Art and society in Late Antiquity", in K. Weitzmann (ed.), *Age of spirituality: a symposium*, New York, 17–27.

Cameron, Alan 2016. "Poetry and literary culture in Late Antiquity", in *Wandering poets and other essays on late Greek literature and philosophy*, Oxford, 163–184 (repr. from: S. Swain/M. Edwards (eds.) 2004. *Approaching Late Antiquity: the transformation from Early to Late Empire*, Oxford, 327–354).

Cameron, Averil 2015. "Christian conversion in Late Antiquity: some issues", in A. Papaconstantinou, with N. McLynn, and D.L. Schwartz (eds.), *Conversion in Late Antiquity: Christianity, Islam, and beyond*, London, 3–22.

Chuvin, P. 2018. "Introduction: Nonnus, from our time to his. A retrospective glance at Nonnian studies (notably the *Dionysiaca*) since the 1930s", in H. Bannert/N. Kröll (eds.), *Nonnus of Panopolis in context II. Poetry, religion, and society*, Leiden, 1–18.

Donati, A. 1988. *La terza età dell'epigrafia*, Faenza.

Donceel, R. 1987. "L'évêque Epiodôre et les basiliques de Kanatha d'après une inscription grecque inédite", *Le Muséon*, 100, 67–88.

Feissel, D. 2016. "L'épigraphie d'orient, témoin des mutations de l'empire constantinien", in O. Brandt/V. Fiocchi Nicolai/G. Castiglia (eds.), *Acta XVI congressus internationalis archaeologiae Christianae*, Città del Vaticano, 1221–1231.

Felle, A. 2015. "Esporre la Scrittura. L'uso di testi biblici in epigrafi d'ambito pubblico fra tarda antichità e prima età bizantina (secoli IV–VIII)", *Ant. Tard.*, 23, 335–370.

Felle, A. 2016. "Una lunga svolta costantiniana. Tradizione e mutamenti nella prassi epigrafica dei cristiani di Roma prima e dopo Costantino (260–320)", in O. Brandt/V. Fiocchi Nicolai/G. Castiglia (eds.), *Acta XVI congressus internationalis archaeologiae Christianae*, Città del Vaticano, 1159–1178.

Franceschini, A. 2016. "Il pascolo, la colomba e la stella: virtú dei pastori cristiani e lessico omerico nell'epigramma funerario greco dell'Asia Minore", *Prometheus*, 42, 207–218.

Führmann, M. (ed.) 1976. *Christianisme et formes littéraires de l'antiquité tardive en occident*, Vandœuvres/Genève.

Grig, L. 2017. "Cultural capital and Christianization: the metrical inscriptions of late antique Rome", in K. Bolle/C. Machado/C. Witschel (eds.), *The epigraphic cultures of Late Antiquity*, Stuttgart, 427–448.

Guarducci, M. 1978. *Epigrafia Greca IV*, Roma.

Hahn, J. 2015. "Public rituals of depaganization in Late Antiquity", in A. Busine (ed.), *Religious practices and Christianization of the late antique city (4th–7th cent.)*, Leiden, 115–110.
Hardie, P. 2019. *Classicism and Christianity in late antique Latin poetry*, Berkeley (CA).
Humphreys, M. 2017. "Late Antiquity and World History", *Studies in Late Antiquity*, 1, 8–37.
Inglebert, H. 2001. *Interpretatio christiana. Les mutations des savoirs (cosmographie, géographie, ethnographie, histoire) dans l'antiquité chrétienne (30–630 après J.-C.)*, Paris.
Jacobs, I. 2017, "Cross graffiti as physical means to Christianize the classical city. An exploration of their function, meaning, topographical, and socio-historical contexts", in I. Garipzanov/C. Goodson/H. Maguire (eds.), *Graphic signs of identity, faith, and power in Late Antiquity and the Early Middle Ages*, Tournhout, 175–221.
Johnson, S.F. 2016. *Literary territories: cartographical thinking in Late Antiquity*, Oxford.
Kajava, M. 2009–2010. "Byzantine Greek inscriptions and urban context", *Acta Byzantina Fennica*, 3, 105–115.
Kiourtzian, G. 2013–14. "Les inscriptions de la basilique de Iovianos à Corfou", *Cahiers Archéologiques*, 55, 5–15.
Kristensen, T.M. 2013. *Making and breaking the gods. Christian responses to pagan sculpture in Late Antiquity*, Aarhus.
Liverani, P. 2014. "Chi parla a chi? Epigrafia monumentale e immagine pubblica in età tardoantica", in S. Birk/T.M. Kristensen/B. Poulsen (eds.), *Using images in Late Antiquity: identity, commemoration and response*, London, 3–32.
Livrea, E. (ed.) 1989. *Nonno di Panopoli. Parafrasi del vangelo di S. Giovanni. Canto XVIII*, Napoli.
MacMullen, R. 1984. *Christianizing the Roman Empire (A.D. 100–400)*, New Haven.
MacMullen, R. 1986. "What difference did Christianity make?", *Historia*, 35, 322–343.
MacMullen, R. 2003. "Cultural and political changes in the 4th and 5th centuries", *Historia*, 52, 465–495.
Magnelli, E. 2007. "Notes on four Greek verse inscriptions", *ZPE*, 160, 37–40.
Miguélez-Cavero, L./McGill, S. 2018. "Christian poetry", in S. McGill/E. Watts (eds.), *A Companion to late antique literature*, Malden (MA), 259–280.
Moralee, J. 2006. "The stone of St. Theodore: disfiguring the pagan past in Christian Gerasa", *JECS*, 14, 183–215.
Ogereau, J.M. 2018. "Authority and identity in the Early Christian inscriptions from Macedonia", in C. Breytenbach/J.M. Ogereau (eds.), *Authority and identity in emerging Christianities in Asia Minor and Greece*, Leiden, 217–239.
Piepenbrink, K. 2015. "Der christliche Identitätsdiskurs im spätantiken Römischen Reich: Griechischer Osten und lateinischer Westen in komparatistischer Perspektive", *Millennium*, 12, 75–101.
Pollmann, K. 2017. *The baptized Muse. Early Christian poetry as cultural authority*, Oxford.
Rapp, C. 2014. "City and citizenship as Christian concepts of community in late antiquity", in C. Rapp/H.A. Drake (eds.), *The city in the Classical and post-Classical world: changing contexts of power and identity*, Cambridge, 153–166.
Roueché, C. 1997. "Benefactors in the Late Roman period: the Eastern Empire", in M. Christol/O. Masson (eds.), *Actes du Xe congrès international d'épigraphie grecque et latine*, Paris, 353–368.
Roueché, C. 2006. "Written display in the late antique and Byzantine city", in E. Jeffreys (ed.), *Proceedings of the 21st International Congress of Byzantine Studies I: Plenary Papers*, London, 235–253.

Roueché, C./Sotinel, C. 2017. "Christian and late antique epigraphies", in K. Bolle/C. Machado/C. Witschel (eds.), *The epigraphic cultures of Late Antiquity*, Stuttgart, 503–514.

Salway, B. 2015. "Late Antiquity", in C. Bruun/J. Edmondson (eds.), *The Oxford Handbook of Roman epigraphy*, Oxford, 364–393.

Sironen, E. 2017. "The epigraphic habit in late antique Greece", in K. Bolle/C. Machado/C. Witschel (eds.), *The epigraphic cultures of Late Antiquity*, Stuttgart, 449–472.

Spanoudakis, K. (ed.) 2014. *Nonnus of Panopolis. Paraphrasis of the Gospel of John. Book XI*, Oxford.

Staab, G. 2018. *Gebrochener Glanz. Klassische Tradition und Alltagswelt im Spiegel neuer und alter Grabepigramme des griechischen Ostens*, Berlin.

Stella, F. 2005. "Epic of the biblical God: intercultural imitation and the poetics of alterity", in M. Paschalis (ed.), *Roman and Greek Imperial epic*, Rethymno, 131–148.

Toth, I. 2016. "Reflections on a period of transformation in early Byzantine epigraphic culture", in C. Stavrakos (ed.), *Inscriptions in the Byzantine and post-Byzantine History and History of Art*, Wiesbaden, 17–40.

Trout, D. 2015. *Damasus of Rome. The epigraphic poetry*, Oxford.

Van der Vliet, J. 2017. "The wisdom of the wall: innovation in monastic epigraphy", in M. Choat/M. Giorda (eds.), *Writing and communication in early Egyptian monasticism*, Leiden, 151–164.

Ward-Perkins, B. 2015. "Four bases from Stratonikeia: a (failed) attempt to Christianize the statue habit", in A. Busine (ed.), *Religious practices and Christianization of the late antique city (4th–7th cent.)*, Leiden, 179–187.

Whitby, Mary/Roberts, M. 2018. "Epic poetry", in S. McGill/E. Watts (eds.), *A Companion to late antique literature*, Malden (MA), 211–240.

Arianna Gullo
Writing Classicizing Epigrams in Sixth-Century Constantinople: The Funerary Poems of Julian the Egyptian

*To Alan Cameron, in loving memory,
with the deepest fondness and endless gratitude.*

This chapter deals with the funerary epigrams of the sixth-century CE Greek Christian poet Julian the Egyptian, one of the most prolific contributors to the *Cycle* of Agathias: his *corpus* of epigrams is inferior in number only to Agathias himself or Paul the Silentiary.[1] Julian perfectly assimilated the preceding epigrammatic tradition into his own poems, which can thus be considered 'Hellenistic' in content and style. This chapter aims to show that, despite the Hellenistic mode that sets the tone of his poems, there are some echoes of what I call involuntary 'interferences' of Julian's Christianity. In what follows I will explore in what way Julian's poems may or may not be considered Christian epigrams.

My analysis will focus on those funerary epigrams whose themes and motifs cannot be unambiguously interpreted as either classical, often misleadingly styled 'pagan', or Christian, as they could perfectly inhabit both systems of reference. In this respect, sepulchral epigrams are a privileged *locus* for cultural ideology and genre investigation because, on the one hand, they engage with the religious sphere more than any other epigrammatic sub-category; on the other hand, this particular sub-category – rather than the votive, sympotic, satirical, or erotic – is the one in which the epigrammatists of the *Cycle* most employ classicizing features, as Averil Cameron has highlighted.[2] More generally, the stereotypical character and continuity of epitaphs as an epigrammatic subgenre provide fertile ground for diachronic considerations of genre, *topoi*, and religious and cultural milieus.

---

[1] I am currently preparing a new edition with introduction, translation and commentary of the epigrams of Julian the Egyptian. I present here some preliminary results.
[2] Funerary epigrams often express beliefs and views about the afterlife, thus sometimes providing clues about the religious identity of the deceased, as well as of the poet/author. See Av. Cameron 1970, 19: "It is in the funerary epigrams above all that the *Cycle* poets tended to express themselves in conventional and hence pagan-seeming imagery, though usually only in the weakened formulae acceptable even in contemporary Christian inscriptions." For the more accentuated Christianization of Christian inscriptional epigram, as opposed to Julian's literary variety, see Agosti in this volume.

Greek classicizing epigrams: the case of the *Cycle* of Agathias in the sixth-century CE between Christianity and *paideia*

Around 567/568 CE, under the reign of Justin II, the historian and poet Agathias Scholasticus published the *Cycle* (Κύκλος), a collection of epigrams of various kinds. Here he assembled (some of) his own poems together with those of several roughly contemporary epigrammatists, more or less celebrated.[3] The epigrams of the *Cycle*, many of which survive today in the so-called *Greek Anthology*, provide for the most part a cultural snapshot of Justinian's reign, and chiefly reflect that historical and literary milieu.[4]

Current research has convincingly argued that the *Cycle* poets, who were mostly rhetors and imperial officials with rhetorical education,[5] were Christians who, following a long series of Greek and Roman epigrammatists, composed classicizing epigrams in full awareness of the preceding, unbroken tradition. In doing so they took up and combined, to a greater or lesser degree, Hellenistic and Graeco-Roman epigrammatic motifs with the stylistic features of the 'Nonnian School'[6] and also with the epigraphic tradition, which stands in a relationship of mutual cross-fertilization with literary epigram.[7] As a consequence, and in contrast to the obviously Christian epigrams of Gregory Nazianzen or those preserved

---

[3] So, cogently, Al. Cameron/Av. Cameron 1966, 6 and 21–25; see also Av. Cameron 1970, 15–16; Al. Cameron 1993, 16 and 70–75; 2016, 279; McCail 1969, 87. Baldwin 1977, 298–301, and 1980 argues that the *Cycle* was published around the end of Justinian's reign.
[4] McCail 1969, 94–96.
[5] For a list of the *Cycle* poets see Al. Cameron/Av. Cameron 1966, 8, with Al. Cameron/Av. Cameron 1967 for additions and further remarks; see also Al. Cameron 2016, 278–279.
[6] On the definition of the so-called 'stile moderno' ('modern style'), that is the metrical and language style codified in late antique literary poetry, which finds its supreme manifestation in Nonnus of Panopolis (hence it is called 'Nonnian', though it was not properly elaborated and developed by him), see, e.g., Whitby 1994; Agosti/Gonnelli 1995. The label of 'Nonnian' poets applied to the *Cycle* epigrammatists should now be put into perspective: see Gullo, forthcoming b.
[7] I prefer not to distinguish between literary and epigraphic epigram, but consider them a single tradition, especially in Late Antiquity: see recently Garulli 2012; Agosti 2015a; Christian 2015. It is crucial to stress, however, that in the *Cycle* poems, which were basically literary compositions addressing a learned audience and imitating the work of the Hellenistic predecessors, Christian elements, as we shall see, are little pronounced, especially in comparison with late antique verse inscriptions. On the relevant presence of Christian culture in late antique inscriptional epigrams see Agosti's chapter in this volume.

in Book 1 of the *Greek Anthology*, there is no way to infer clearly the religious beliefs of these poets solely on the basis of their epigrams: indeed, their poems are so soaked in epigrammatic *topoi* that, in most cases, it is almost impossible to discern between Christian beliefs and secular forms.[8]

In the past, the heavy presence of classicizing themes in the epigrams of the *Cycle* often raised doubts about the religious identity of these poets, whose Christianity has been considered only superficial.[9] It should now be obvious, however, that the clear-cut opposition between pagans and Christians in literary culture is an interpretative category created in modern times, and not at all perceived as such in Late Antiquity.[10] Nowadays any doubt concerning the religious beliefs of these poets must be ruled out once and for all: the old-fashioned idea that the Christian faith of these poets was only a facade – or that it even concealed a sort of cryptopaganism – was simply formulated on the basis of a mistaken assumption about the inclusion/use of classical themes as an expression of pagan beliefs.[11] Our understanding of the religious and cultural milieu of the period necessarily leads to the realization that the *Cycle* poets were in every way Christians who composed literature in classicizing form. The inclusion of classicizing elements, particularly in their funerary epigrams,[12] is not, therefore, a sign of pagan self-representation, as is proved by Agathias himself, who clarifies (and justifies) this attitude through a programmatic declaration in the prologue of his collection: upon introducing the votive and funerary poems, he states that the former were written "as though they were dedicated to the gods of the past" (ὡς προτέροις μακάρεσσιν ἀνειμένα),[13] while in respect to the latter the poet wishes that: τάπερ Θεὸς ἐν μὲν ἀοιδῇ | ἐκτελέειν νεύσειεν, ἐν ἀτρεκίῃ δὲ διώκειν ("God may allow us to accomplish them in song but to chase them away in reality").[14] Thus, on the one hand, Agathias firmly reiterates his and his fellow contributors' Christian faith, even calling upon God himself as the guarantor of literariness. On the

---

8 Av. Cameron 1970, 106–107.
9 Baldwin 1984; Kaldellis 1999 and 2003. See also what Giommoni 2017, 15 n. 82 reports.
10 Cf., in this volume, the ambiguous nature of the Alcestis myth as examined by Wasyl.
11 See Madden 1995, 43: "the probability is that the Christianity of Macedonius was more than a mere façade;" see further Av. Cameron 1970, 105–106; Madden 1977; Al. Cameron 2016, 277–281, who discusses and contests Kaldellis' theories (see above n. 9); McCail 1971 is still fundamental for Agathias.
12 See above n. 2. See further Av. Cameron 1970, 106: "There is after all a large area of common ground between Christianity and late paganism which is nowhere so apparent as in the field of funerary epigram."
13 Agath., *AP* 4.3b.115 = 2.69 Viansino.
14 Agath., *AP* 4.3b.122–123 = 2.76–77 Viansino.

other hand, by advertising the purposely elaborate and refined character of these epigrams, he explicitly voices his (and his fellow poets') intention to compose epigrams which cleverly imitate their predecessors, and which primarily find their *raison d'être* in the art of poetry.[15] Therefore, the use and/or the imitation of classicizing models, forms and features has nothing to do with the religious beliefs of the poets of the *Cycle*, who, from time to time and against the undeniably 'pagan' (that is, classical) matrix which dominates their poetry, betray a genuine Christian mindset, as is demonstrated by certain 'interferences' in their poems or, more unambiguously in the case of Agathias, by the clearly Christian subjects of some of his epigrams.[16]

Since we no longer deal with the alleged cryptopaganism of these poets, references to the *topoi* of funerary epigram, as well as the mention of Moira, Hades, or any other classical deity, are rarely sufficient to classify the epitaph (whether it is literary or inscriptional) as pagan. The use of Hellenistic *topoi* and formulas was part of the poetic tradition of (in this case) funerary epigram, employed by pagans, Christians,[17] and Jews alike,[18] and a product of the classical *paideia*, that secular literary, cultural and educational legacy[19] shared between Romans, Greeks, and the Hellenized people of the East,[20] and in which the poets – above all Homer and Virgil – played a dominant role. *Paideia* was, above all, a distinctive mark in Late Antiquity, a *status symbol* for the representatives of the upper classes, and as such a sign communicated between the poet/composer and the

---

15 Yet it would be totally naive to reject outright the possibility that some of the *Cycle* epigrams, especially the funerary ones, were actually inscriptional.
16 I refer namely to the three poems on the Archangel (presumably Michael), transmitted in Book 1 of the *Greek Anthology* (*AP* 1.34–36 = 18, 7 and 17 Viansino). Nonetheless, it is quite sure that these poems were not originally included in the *Cycle*, but eventually reached the *Greek Anthology* through the epigraphic collection assembled by Gregory of Campsa: see McCail 1969, 92–93; Al. Cameron 2016, 281. For the Christian dimension of Agathias' *Histories* see Av. Cameron 1970, 89–111. Another notable *Cycle* epigrammatist, Paul the Silentiary, reveals explicitly his Christian sentiments in the *Soph.*, a work that also contains classical imagery (see, for example, vv. 195; 221; 273).
17 For a detailed, though now a little dated, analysis of the pagan elements in Christian epitaphs see Lattimore 1942 §§ 83–100, 301–340.
18 Van der Horst 1994.
19 Agosti 2006–2007; 2008; 2009; 2010a; 2010b; 2011; 2013; 2015b; 2016a; 2016b; see also Waltz 1931, particularly 10–12 and 14–15; Av. Cameron 2006, 14–15; Al. Cameron 2007.
20 See particularly the works by Gabriel Sanders on Latin pagan and Christian funerary inscriptions collected by Sanders/Donati/Pickhaus/van Uytfanghe 1991 (especially papers nos. 2; 4; 8; 13; 16).

addressee and/or consumer of this kind of literature, independently of their religious beliefs.[21] It is through and because of this elite education that the classical tradition endured by embracing the new, foreign elements introduced by Christianity. Julian, as will be shown below, is a typical poet of his times, as he juggles successfully Christianity and Graeco-Roman *paideia*.

A poet of the *Cycle* of Agathias: Julian the Egyptian

Julian was presumably a native of Egypt, as the ethnic Αἰγύπτιος suggests,[22] although he lived in Constantinople around the first half of the sixth century CE.[23] The two manuscripts of the *Greek Anthology* correctly style Julian ἀπὸ ὑπάρχων ("the ex-prefect") in most cases. The title ἀπὸ ὑπάτων ("the ex-consul"), which appears in some lemmata relating to Julian's epigrams in the Palatine manuscript, but never in the Planudean manuscript, is without doubt a mistake that arose from a misunderstanding of the abbreviation ἀπὸ ὑπ-, contained in the Palatine manuscript in the lemmata of three epigrams surely to be attributed to Julian.[24] According to an intriguing hypothesis,[25] it is likely that the epigrammatist Julian the Egyptian, styled "former prefect" (ἀπὸ ὑπάρχων), should be identified with the *praefectus praetorio Orientis* of 530–531 CE,[26] who was dragged by the crowd to the hippodrome together with the usurper Hypatius and Pompeius during the Nika riot, according to the account of the *Chronicon Paschale*.[27] It is less likely that the title ἀπὸ ὑπάρχων is an honorific title, to which the ethnic

---

21 See, e.g., Brown 1992, 35–70. In Christian epigrams the phenomenon of accepting or maintaining elements of the ancient classical tradition lasts at least until the 6th century CE, when, following the assimilation and Christianization of *paideia*, as well as the consequent development of Christian verse epigraphy, we then pass, as suggested by Agosti 2016a, 143: "all'*epigraphic habit* bizantino, in cui le iscrizioni metriche cambiano forma espressiva a partire dal VII secolo (adozione del dodecasillabo) e il sostrato culturale risulta ormai completamente modificato."
22 *Pace* McCail 1969, 90.
23 All Julian's dateable poems fall before the mid-6th century CE.
24 See Gullo 2009.
25 Al. Cameron/Av. Cameron 1966, 13; see also Al. Cameron 1977, 42–48.
26 *PLRE* IIIA, 729–730 (Iulianus 4). In the sources this Julian always bears the title *praefectus praetorio* or ἔπαρχος πραιτωρίων ("praetorian prefect").
27 Cf. *s.a.* 531, where he is styled: Ἰουλιανὸν τὸν ἀπὸ ἐπάρχων πραιτωρίων ("Julian the ex praetorian prefect").

Αἰγύπτιος might have been added to distinguish the poet from his contemporary prefect.[28]

The funerary poems of Julian the Egyptian

In his work Julian the Egyptian routinely engages with and imitates his predecessors in both subject matter and lexical/stylistic formulas. Since the formal elements he employs continually recall Hellenistic epigrams, his poems, distributed into the thematic Books 5, 6, 7, and 9 of the *Greek Anthology*, with a few additions from the *Planudean Anthology* and the so-called *Sylloge Σπ*, might seem at first glance to consist largely of stereotypical and tiresome imitations in terms of meter and genre. Yet in many cases a careful reading reveals how Julian endows conventional generic elements with new nuances.

In Book 7 of the *Greek Anthology*, Julian's funerary epigrams are mostly gathered in a long sequence largely derived from the Cycle (*AP* 7.551–614).[29] Constantine Cephalas, the compiler of the early-tenth-century CE epigrammatic anthology from which the two major collections forming the *Greek Anthology* – the *Palatine Anthology* and the *Planudean Anthology* – descend, might have copied them in the same order in which they appeared in the third book of the *Cycle* of Agathias, which was dedicated to funerary epigrams (he might have then added a few poems from other sources, including epigraphic). The re-use of popular Hellenistic epigrammatic themes such as death by shipwreck or fictitious epitaphs for ancient Greek poets and philosophers is not the only focus of Julian's funerary epigrams. He also dedicated poems to the memory of several contemporaries, and it may well be that at least some of these poems were originally inscribed.

As a Christian, for whom it is mostly the Afterlife that matters, Julian should not have cared about being remembered in this world – one of the most recurrent motifs in Greek and Latin epitaphs and, chiefly, the fundamental idea which underpins both the presence and the need of the tomb μνῆμα ("memorial") in Classical Antiquity –, nor should he have cared about writing epitaphs to commemorate the dead. Indeed, from a Christian point of view the commemoration of the dead by the living is futile, since their earthly story is only the vehicle of their

---

28 *PLRE* IIIA, 733 (Iulianus 11).
29 A few others are scattered and dislocated in thematic sections of Book 7 but are in mixed chronological order.

salvation. This new Christian concept, however, hardly influences even those epitaphs which are manifestly Christian:[30] the bishop Gregory Nazianzen, for example, composed more than 250 fairly classicizing epitaphs,[31] preserved in Book 8 of the *Greek Anthology*. This should not be surprising at all, firstly because writing funerary epigrams was a social custom, which does not change in spite of the rise of Christianity. Secondly, what the cases of both Julian and Gregory demonstrate above all is that they were *pepaideumenoi* and that they were addressing a similarly cultivated audience.

A characteristic case is *AP* 7.581. The poem is modeled after a group of (mostly) anonymous Hellenistic epigrams[32] from Book 7 of the *Greek Anthology* on the subject of the murderer who buries the corpse of the person he killed in order to hide the crime; Julian contributes to this series by composing two variations on the same theme (the other one is *AP* 7.580), according to a common epigrammatic convention:[33]

ἀντὶ φόνου τάφον ἄμμι χαρίζεαι· ἀλλὰ καὶ αὐτὸς
ἴσων ἀντιτύχοις οὐρανόθεν χαρίτων.

In exchange for your murder you gift me with a tomb, but may you
as well receive from heaven the same present in return. (*AP* 7.581)

In the poem, the deceased speaks in the first person from the tomb, and brutally addresses his murderer, reversing the common *topos* of greeting the passerby, whom the murderer replaces here. At the end of v. 1 the Homeric (and Nonnian)

---

30 See, for example, Greg. Naz., *AP* 8.171.1–4: παῖδες χριστιανῶν, τόδ' ἀκούσατε. οὐδὲν ὁ τύμβος; | πῶς οὖν ὑμετέρους χώννυτ' ἀριπρεπέας; | ἀλλ' ἔστιν καὶ πᾶσι γέρας τόδε, μηδὲ τάφοισιν | βάλλειν ἀλλοτρίοις δυσμενέας παλάμας ("Listen to this, sons of Christians. Is the tomb nothing? How come, then, you bury your own in magnificent mounds? But this reverence is due to all, not to lay hostile hands on the tombs of others"), trans. A. Gullo.
31 See, for example, the mention of Hades (*AP* 8.97.6; 8.104.6; 8.218.1) and Tartarus (*AP* 8.246.1; 8.247.1; 8.248.1), as in the Gospels; the use of the Homeric (and then sepulchral) metaphor of death as an eternal sleep (*AP* 8.12.4; 8.60.1); typical funerary imagery like the shedding of tears on the tomb (*AP* 8.107.6; 8.192.4; 8.226) or formulas like ἐνθάδε κεῖται (*AP* 8.71.1; 8.81.1; 8.126.1). The series on the tomb desecrators (*AP* 8.170–172 and 176–254), on which see Floridi 2013, shows affinities (the anonymity of the dead and the employment of the so-called *arai epitymbioi*) with Hellenistic epitaphs such as those dedicated to the tomb of Timon the misanthrope or the series on the deceased buried by his own murderer (see *infra*).
32 Anon., *AP* 7.310, Anon., *AP* 7.356–360, and [Simon.], *AP* 7.516 = 'Simon.', *FGE* LXXXIV 1026: for this series see Gullo, forthcoming a on Anon., *AP* 7.356 = *FGE* XXIX 1160.
33 All translations are my own. The text of Julian's epigrams is the one I have established for my forthcoming critical edition.

clausula ἀλλὰ καὶ αὐτός[34] stands out in a privileged metrical position, which is also the standard one in both Homer and Nonnus. Attention should be drawn to the expression οὐρανόθεν ("from heaven") at v. 2, which may be considered at first glance one of those interferences which reveal Julian's Christianity. In this case, however, the plain mention of οὐρανός does not necessarily refer to the Christian heavenly kingdom as it does in Gregory Nazianzen's poems, where the word needs no further specifications because of the markedly and unambiguously Christian context.[35] In fact, similar generic expressions are quite common in Hellenistic funerary epigrams,[36] especially in contexts dealing with the *topos* of the separation of body and soul after death, which is already attested in Homer.[37] Such expressions are present in Christian epitaphs too.[38] Yet, although in *AP* 7.581.2 the mere presence of the word οὐρανόθεν cannot be considered with certainty a Christian interference, the idea of a punishment coming from heaven is fully Christian. Therefore, the sentence ἀλλά ... χαρίτων operates on both the classical and Christian levels, and may well have been perceived by some readers as a Christian interference.

The mention of οὐρανός in connection with the verb εἰσαναβαίνω ("go up to") in *AP* 7.587, an epitaph for the philosopher Pamphilus,[39] who died at sea and is otherwise unknown,[40] appears to be another interesting case of Christian interference in a classicizing context:

χθών σε τέκεν, πόντος δὲ διώλεσε, δέκτο δὲ θῶκος
 Πλουτῆος· κεῖθεν δ' οὐρανὸν εἰσανέβης.
οὐχ ὡς ναυηγὸς δὲ βυθῷ θάνες, ἀλλ' ἵνα πάντων
 κλήροις ἀθανάτων, Πάμφιλε, κόσμον ἄγῃς.

The earth gave birth to you, the sea killed you, Pluto's throne
 received you, and from there you went up to heaven.
You did not perish in the depth of the sea like a shipwrecked man, but in order
 to bestow ornament, Pamphilus, to the domains of all the immortals. (*AP* 7.587)

---

34 See Gullo, forthcoming a *ad loc.*, with bibliography.
35 *AP* 8.8.3: ἐς οὐρανόν; 8.33.1: πρὸς οὐρανόν; 8.35.5: οὐρανόθεν; 8.53.2: πρὸς οὐρανόν; 8.59.1; 8.61.1; 8.69.1; 8.82.4.
36 See, e.g., Theodorid., *AP* 7.529.1 = *HE* X 3544: τόλμα καὶ εἰς Ἀίδαν καὶ ἐς οὐρανὸν ἄνδρα κομίζει ("Bravery brings a man to Hades and to heaven").
37 *Od.* 11.64–65; 218–222; see also *Od.* 11.601–604.
38 See, e.g., Greg. Naz., *AP* 8.12; 8.33.1–2; 8.72.1.
39 According to the lemma of the Palatine manuscript: see *PLRE* IIIB, 962 (Pamphilus 1).
40 *Pace* Al. Cameron/Av. Cameron 1966, 14.

The sequence of clauses "χθών … Πλουτῆος" (vv. 1–2) follows the typical tripartite (or bipartite) structure of both literary and epigraphic funerary epigram, whereby the places where the deceased was born, lived, and eventually died are listed sequentially.[41] Despite the mention of the ἀθάνατοι in the last line of Julian's epigram, at v.2 the motif of the deceased entering heaven (οὐρανὸν εἰσανέβης) from the reign of Pluto is not attested in any other funerary epigram, and leaves little doubt as to its Christian flavor:[42] Church Fathers resort to speaking of 'the House of Hades' in order to describe the intermediate place where the souls of all the departed either waited until the death of Christ or still wait for the day of judgment.[43] It is, therefore, likely that Julian is here reproducing this view.[44] Regarding οὐρανὸν εἰσανέβης, the *iunctura* is not formulaic Christian phrasing *per se*, but if considered in the light of the imagery it expresses, then it acquires a Christian flavor. Moreover, the use of the compound εἰσαναβαίνω with οὐρανός here seems to reflect two important *termini technici* in the Christology of the Gospel of John, ἀναβαίνω ("go up") and καταβαίνω ("come down from"), which are employed to express respectively the theme of ascent to and descent from heaven, as well as the journey to and the departure from Jerusalem and the Temple.[45] It is my argument, then, that the combination of all these aspects can be identified as a Christian interference.

The next poem, *AP* 7.590 is an epitaph for the ἄωρος ("untimely deceased") John,[46] structured as a dialogue between two passersby who comment on the dead man's earthly life, contrasting it to his mortality:

"κλεινὸς Ἰωάννης." – "θνητὸς λέγε." – "γαμβρὸς ἀνάσσης."
"θνητὸς ὅμως." – "γενεῆς ἄνθος Ἀναστασίου."

---

41 See Gullo, forthcoming a on Eryc., *AP* 7.368.1–4 = *GPh* VI 2232–2235 for parallels. The most famous representative of this *tournure* is the famous epitaph of Virgil (2 Courtney) transmitted by his biographical sources: *Mantua me genuit, Calabri rapuere, tenet nunc | Parthenope* ("Mantua gave birth to me, the Calabrians snatched me away, Parthenope now holds me"), trans. A. Gullo.
42 It further develops the motif of the separation of soul and body in a Christian perspective.
43 See the numerous parallels collected by Prestige 1922; I would like to thank Fotini Hadjittofi for drawing my attention to this article. See also, more recently, Ainalis 2018.
44 Hartigan 1975, 45, had already observed that the first two lines of the poem attest Julian's Christianity.
45 See Livrea 2000 on Nonn., *Par.* 2.71 ἀνέβαινεν, 252; Agosti 2003, 267–268 on Nonn., *Par.* 5.1 ἀνέβαινεν.
46 This John (d. ca. 549 CE), a descendant of the emperor Anastasius, is the son of Pompeius and the nephew of Hypatius: the brilliant identification was first made by Du Cange 1680, 86, and has been accepted by modern scholars.

"θνητοῦ κἀκείνου." – "βίον ἔνδικος. οὐκέτι τοῦτο
  θνητὸν ἔφης." – "ἀρεταὶ κρείσσονές εἰσι μόρου."

"This is the famous John." – "Say, rather, mortal." – "The son in law
  of a queen." – "Mortal anyway." – "The flower of the family
of Anastasius." – "Mortal was he as well." – "A just man in his life. And about this
  you have not said 'mortal' yet." –"Virtues are stronger than death." (*AP* 7.590)

From the two final sentences βίον ... ἔφης and ἀρεταί ... μόρου (vv. 3–4) one may infer that Julian is here alluding to the Christian idea according to which death is not really the end – because actually the true life of a Christian starts right after death. These expressions, thus, primarily echo the view that being righteous in life is a virtue which is superior to secular and short-lived 'virtues' like noble birth or titles, and which allows Christians to claim immortality in the heavenly kingdom. While this latter interpretation in particular is certainly tempting, it should also be noted that Julian is equally influenced by classicizing ideas about the immortality of earthly virtue,[47] such as the Homeric ἄφθιτον κλέος or, more prominently, the incompatibility between good men and death, an idea which, in funerary epigram, is at least as old as Callimachus.[48] Nonetheless, although it is imperative to acknowledge Julian's heavy literary debt to his predecessors, not only on the formal level but also in terms of the content, the word ἔνδικος at v. 3 seems to be the unequivocal mark of a Christian mindset, and thus works very well as a Christian interference.[49]

Another intriguing case, which also displays a Christian flavor, is *AP* 7.594, an epitaph for the grammarian Theodorus,[50] who will be remembered forever not for his material, sepulchral monument, but for his written work. With his work

---

[47] The final sentence ἀρεταὶ κρείσσονές εἰσι μόρου, in particular, is a paraphrase of the widespread motto αἱ δ' ἀρεταὶ ἀθάνατοι ("virtues are immortal"), attributed to Periander of Corinth, Stob. 3.1.172.
[48] Callim., *AP* 7.451.2 = 9 Pf. = *HE* XLI 1232: θνήσκειν μὴ λέγε τοὺς ἀγαθούς ("Do not say that good men die"), a very popular model in epigraphic poetry, where the expression is often quoted almost *verbatim*: see Gullo, forthcoming a *ad loc*. See also Tull. Laur., *AP* 7.17.1–2 = *GPh* I 3909–3910: μή με θανοῦσαν | τὰν Μιτυληναίαν ἔννεπ' ἀοιδοπόλον ("Say not that I, the poetess of Mitylene, am dead"), which depends on the Callimachean model too, or expressions like *GVI* 1268.8 = *IG* X 2, 1, 876 = 23 Vérilhac (Thessalonike, 1st century CE): ἀρετὴν μὲν οὐκ ἔμαρψεν ἐχθρὸς Ἅιδης ("Hateful Hades did not snatch away virtue").
[49] One may quote Mt 5:6: μακάριοι οἱ πεινῶντες καὶ διψῶντες τὴν δικαιοσύνην, ὅτι αὐτοὶ χορτασθήσονται ("Blessed are those who hunger and thirst for righteousness, for they will be filled").
[50] Kaster 1988, no. 266, 434–435; *PLRE* IIIB, 1261 (Theodorus 53).

Theodorus saved from oblivion hundreds of ancient poets by copying their works (and probably providing them with exegetical remarks):

> μνῆμα σόν, ὦ Θεόδωρε, πανατρεκὲς οὐκ ἐπὶ τύμβῳ,
> ἀλλ' ἐνὶ βιβλιακῶν μυριάσιν σελίδων,
> αἷσιν ἀνεζώγρησας ἀπολλυμένων ἀπὸ λήθης
> ἁρπάξας νοερὸν μόχθον ἀοιδοπόλων.

> Your real monument, Theodorus, is not on the tomb,
> but on the countless columns of writing
> in which you recalled to life and snatched away from oblivion
> the ingenious labor of dead poets. (*AP* 7.594)

The idea that the real tomb is not the material monument, but, rather, the significant or heroic deed(s) for which the deceased will be remembered forever (vv. 1–2) is a common motif in funerary epigrams.[51] Julian wonderfully plays with the material dimension offered by the funerary monument and the written/copied book, as well as the epigrammatic conventions, by shifting the role of 'carrying memory' from the tomb/funerary inscription to Theodorus' work as a scribe (and commentator). In doing so, he uses another popular classical theme: the idea that a poet gains immortality through his works.[52] At v. 3 the compound ἀναζωγρέω ("recall to life") is a Nonnian neologism attested both in the *Dionysiaca* and the *Paraphrase*,[53] where it is used for the healing of the paralytic (*Par.* 5.41 ἀνεζώγρησε). The verb thus seems to belong to specifically Christian phraseology:[54] it stems from Julian's Christian background, although it is here applied to a context not directly implying a religious dimension (the literary *topos* of the immortality of the poet guaranteed by his works translates into Theodorus' being "recalled to life" by his copying activity).

AP 7.603 is dedicated – according to the lemma in the Palatine manuscript – to another John, otherwise unknown, whose untimely death allowed him to avoid the troubles of adult married life, a common comic motif from the Archaic Age onwards:

> "ἄγριός ἐστι Χάρων." – "πλέον ἤπιος." – "ἥρπασεν ἤδη
> τὸν νέον." – "ἀλλὰ νόῳ τοῖς πολιοῖσιν ἴσον." –

---

51 See Gullo, forthcoming a, on Anon., *AP* 7.45.1–2 = 'Th.', or 'Tim.', *FGE* I 1052–1053: μνᾶμα μὲν Ἑλλὰς ἅπασ' Εὐριπίδου, ὀστέα δ' ἴσχει | γῆ Μακεδών ("All Hellas is Euripides' monument; but the Macedonian land holds the bones").
52 See Gullo, forthcoming a, on Anon., *AP* 7.12.5–6 = *FGE* XXXIX 1226–1227.
53 See Agosti 2003 *ad loc.*, 385.
54 See also the use of ζωγρέω e.g. in Nonn., *Par.* 5.80 (with Agosti 2003 *ad loc.*, 443); 82.

> "τερπωλῆς δ' ἀπέπαυσεν." – "ἀπεστυφέλιξε δὲ μόχθων." –
> "οὐκ ἐνόησε γάμους." – "οὐδὲ γάμων ὀδύνας."
>
> "Charon is fierce." – "Kind instead." – "He snatched away
>   a young man." – "Yet for his mind equal to elderly men."
> "He prevented his joy." – "He rather drove him away by force from pains."
>   "He did not know marriage." – "Nor the troubles of marriage." (*AP* 7.603)

Charon, portrayed as Hades, the snatcher *par excellence*,[55] is rather conventional.[56] At v. 2 (ἀλλὰ νόῳ τοῖς πολιοῖσιν ἴσον) the poem employs another funerary *topos*, that of the *puer-senex*:[57] although it appears in two epigrams by Gregory Nazianzen[58] and in Paul the Silentiary (*AP* 7.604.6 = 6 Viansino) as well, it cannot be counted as a Christian interference.

The last poem to be considered here, *AP* 7.605, is probably the only case where some Christian flare is clear and unambiguous. In it, a husband celebrates his newly found freedom as a widower by erecting a magnificent tomb for his wife, thanking her for dying so early:

> σοὶ σορὸν εὐλάιγγα, Ῥοδοῖ, καὶ τύμβον ἐγείρει
>   ῥύσιά τε ψυχῆς δῶρα πένησι νέμει
> ἀντ' εὐεργεσίης γλυκερὸς πόσις, ὅττι θανοῦσα
>   ὠκύμορος κείνῳ δῶκας ἐλευθερίην.
>
> Your sweet husband raises a coffin made of precious stone and a tomb for you, Rhodo,
>   and distributes presents to the poor to save your soul,
> in exchange for the good you did to him: for by dying
>   early you gave him his freedom. (*AP* 7.605)

The word ῥύσια (v. 2: "offerings in thanksgiving for deliverance")[59] here indicates the almsgiving for the dead bride's soul, and is an unequivocal Christian feature.[60]

---

[55] See Gullo, forthcoming a, on Leon., or Mel., *AP* 7.13.2–3 = Leon., *HE* XCVIII 2564–2565: Ἤρινναν Μουσῶν ἄνθεα δρεπτομέναν | Ἅιδας ... ἀνάρπασεν ("As Erinna was gathering the flowers of the Muses | Hades ... snatched her away").

[56] See Anon. or Bianor, *AP* 7.671 = *GPh* V 1667; Floridi 2014 on Lucill. 42.5 = *AP* 11.133 ὁ Χάρων, 245.

[57] See Griessmair 1966, 51–52; Vérilhac 1978–1982, II, § 11, 19–22; Strubbe 1998, 50–51 and 68–69.

[58] Greg. Naz., *AP* 8.85b.3; 8.152.1.

[59] Pers., *AP* 6.274.4 = *HE* III 2870 (to Eilithyia in thanksgiving for childbirth).

[60] Compare Justinian's almsgiving for Theodora's soul in Michael the Syrian, *Chron.* 9.29, II, 243 (Chabot).

This satirical poem may mock Justinian's puritan propaganda and program of reforms advancing moral behavior, which particularly affects Agathias' epigrams, as well as the strict legislation concerning divorce over the years 542–566 CE.[61]

Lastly, I shall point to two final cases which show how Julian's Christian faith influences traditional funerary *topoi*. Both poems suggest a play between the classicizing *topos* and the name of the deceased. *AP* 7.599 is an epitaph for a woman named Καλή ("the beautiful"), which has mistakenly been interpreted as satirical;[62] the eulogistic φρεσὶ δὲ πλέον ἠὲ προσώπῳ ("more beautiful in mind than in face") that appears at v. 1, probably reflects the idea of the (pure) soul's beauty and its superiority in comparison with the body, a distinction that becomes more prominent with Christianity. The second, and final, example is the characterization of Charon in *AP* 7.600.4, as πορθμεὺς δάκρυ χέει νεκύων ("the ferry-man of the dead pours tears") for a girl with the very suggestive name Anastasia. This may be a representation of pity which is not attested elsewhere, for Charon is usually portrayed as a cruel deity. Moreover, the name of the girl, with its allusion to resurrection, seems to stress the contrast between the classical *topos* of untimely death and the Christian belief in the Afterlife.

Conclusions

This analysis manifestly shows how difficult it is to infer the religious identity of Julian the Egyptian from the classical language and form of his epigrammatic production alone. On the one hand, we need to bear in mind that the subgenre 'funerary epigram' did not need to 'convert' in Late Antiquity. It was certainly not the poet's aim nor the audience's priority to show or spot Christian elements in these poems, which belonged to a long-standing literary tradition of intertextuality and genre, exploited by poets composing with a more or less marked Christian agenda, like Gregory Nazianzen and Julian respectively. Julian's Christian faith does not influence his epigrams and the way he inserts himself in the genre. Therefore, in his case we cannot speak of a 'transposition' nor of a 'modulation' of the classical form, as for example it might be the case for Gregory, because in Julian's epigrams there is nothing specifically Christian except for some instances that I here label 'Christian interferences', in *AP* 7.581; 7.587; 7.590; 7.594; 7.605

---

[61] McCail 1968, 78; see also McCail 1969, 95–96; Garland 2011, 153–154.
[62] By Hartigan 1975, 48–49, but see the serious praise of Anon., *AP* 7.695.2–3 (a late epitaph for Cassia, perhaps originally inscribed): ταῖς ἀρεταῖς γνωρίζεται | ψυχῆς τὸ κάλλος μᾶλλον ἢ τοῦ σώματος ("The beauty of her soul is revealed by her virtues rather than her body").

(possibly in *AP* 7.599 and 7.600 too). On the other hand, what I identified as Christian in these poems becomes evident precisely because we are *a priori* aware of Julian's Christianity. Therefore, any firm assertion about these epigrams risks being a *petitio principii* if not supported by a detailed textual analysis of Julian's poems alongside other, clearly labeled Christian epitaphs.

Bibliography

Agosti, G. (ed.) 2003. *Nonno di Panopoli. Parafrasi del Vangelo di S. Giovanni. Canto V*, Firenze.

Agosti, G. 2006–2007. "Cultura greca negli epigrammi epigrafici di età tardoantica", in L. Cristante/I. Filip (eds.), *Incontri triestini di filologia classica, 6: Atti della giornata di studio in onore di Laura Casarsa, Trieste, 19 gennaio 2007*, Trieste, 3–18.

Agosti, G. 2008. "Literariness and levels of style in epigraphical poetry of Late Antiquity", *Ramus*, 37, 191–213.

Agosti, G. 2009. "Niveaux de style, littérarité, poétiques: pour une histoire du système de la poésie classicisante au VIe siècle", in P. Odorico/P.A. Agapitos/M. Hinterberger (eds.), *"Doux remède…." Poésie et poétique à Byzance. Actes du VIe Colloque international philologique, Paris, 23–24–25 février 2006*, Paris, 99–119.

Agosti, G. 2010a. "*Paideia* classica e fede religiosa: annotazioni sul linguaggio dei carmi epigrafici tardoantichi", *CCG*, 21, 329–353.

Agosti, G. 2010b. "*Saxa loquuntur?* Epigrammi epigrafici e diffusione della *paideia* nell'Oriente tardoantico", *AnTard*, 18, 163–180.

Agosti, G. 2011. "Usurper, imiter, communiquer: le dialogue interculturel dans la poésie grecque chrétienne de l'antiquité tardive", in N. Belayche/J.-D. Dubois (eds.), *L'oiseau et le poisson. Cohabitations religieuses dans les mondes grec et romain*, Paris, 275–299.

Agosti, G. 2013. "Classicism, *paideia*, religion", in R. Lizzi Testa (ed.), *The strange death of pagan Rome. Reflections on a historiographical controversy*, Turnhout, 123–140.

Agosti, G. 2015a "Per una fenomenologia del rapporto fra epigrafia e letteratura nella tarda antichità", in L. Cristante/T. Mazzoli (eds.), *Il calamo della memoria: riuso di testi e mestiere letterario nella tarda antichità, 6: Raccolta delle relazioni discusse nel VI incontro internazionale di Trieste, Biblioteca statale, 25–27 settembre 2014*, Trieste, 13–33.

Agosti, G. 2015b. "Paideia greca e religione in iscrizioni dell'età di Giuliano", in A. Marcone (ed.), *L'imperatore Giuliano: realtà storica e rappresentazioni*, Firenze, 223–239.

Agosti, G. 2016a. "Epigrafia metrica tardoantica e democratizzazione della cultura", in L. Cristante/V. Veronesi (eds.), *Forme di accesso al sapere in età tardoantica e altomedievale VI. Raccolta delle relazioni discusse nell'incontro internazionale di Trieste, Biblioteca statale, 24–25 settembre 2015*, Trieste, 131–147.

Agosti, G. 2016b. "Les langues de l'épigramme épigraphique grécque: regard sur l'identité culturelle chrétienne dans l'antiquité tardive", in E. Santin/L. Foschia (eds.), *L'épigramme dans tous ses états: épigraphiques, littéraires, historiques*, Lyon, (online: https://books.openedition.org/enseditions/5621).

Agosti, G./Gonnelli, F. 1995. "Materiali per la storia dell'esametro nei poeti cristiani greci", in M. Fantuzzi/R. Pretagostini (eds.), *Struttura e storia dell'esametro greco*, I, Pisa, 289–434.
Ainalis, Z.D. 2018. "From Hades to hell. Christian visions of the Underworld (2nd–5th centuries CE)", in G. Ekroth/I. Nilsson (eds.), *Round trip to Hades in the Eastern Mediterranean tradition. Visits to the Underworld from Antiquity to Byzantium*, Leiden, 273–286.
Baldwin, B. 1977. "Four problems in Agathias", *ByzZ*, 70, 295–305 (repr. in: B. Baldwin 1984. *Studies on Late Roman and Byzantine history, literature & language*, Amsterdam, 347–358).
Baldwin, B. 1980. "The date of the *Cycle* of Agathias", *ByzZ*, 73, 334–340 (repr. in: B. Baldwin 1984. *Studies on Late Roman and Byzantine history, literature & language*, Amsterdam, 359–363).
Baldwin, B. 1984. "The Christianity of Macedonius Consul", *Mnemosyne*, 37, 451–454 (repr. in: B. Baldwin 1989. *Roman and Byzantine papers*, Amsterdam, 279–282).
Brown, P.R.L. 1992. *Power and persuasion in Late Antiquity*, Madison (WI).
Cameron, Alan 1977. "Some prefects called Julian", *Byzantion*, 47, 42–64 (repr. in: Al. Cameron 1985. *Literature and society in the Early Byzantine world*, London, 42–64).
Cameron, Alan 1993. *The Greek Anthology from Meleager to Planudes*, Oxford.
Cameron, Alan 2007. "Poets and pagans in Byzantine Egypt", in R.S. Bagnall (ed.), *Egypt in the Byzantine world 300–700*, Cambridge, 21–46 (repr. in: Al. Cameron 2016. *Wandering poets and other essays on late Greek literature and philosophy*, Oxford, 147–162).
Cameron, Alan 2016. "Paganism in sixth-century Byzantium", in Al. Cameron, *Wandering poets and other essays on late Greek literature and philosophy*, Oxford, 255–286.
Cameron, Alan/Cameron, Averil 1966. "The *Cycle* of Agathias", *JHS*, 86, 6–25.
Cameron, Alan/Cameron, Averil 1967. "Further thoughts on the *Cycle* of Agathias", *JHS*, 87, 131.
Cameron, Averil 1970. *Agathias*, Oxford.
Cameron, Averil 2006. "New themes and styles in Greek literature, a title revisited", in S.F. Johnson (ed.), *Greek literature in Late Antiquity. Dynamism, didacticism, classicism*, London, 11–28.
Chabot, J.-B. (ed.) 1963. *Chronique de Michel le Syrien: Patriarche Jacobite d'Antioche (1166–1199)*, I–IV, Bruxelles.
Christian, T. 2015. *Gebildete Steine: zur Rezeption literarischer Techniken in den Versinschriften seit dem Hellenismus*, Göttingen.
Courtney, E. (ed.) 1993. *The fragmentary Latin poets*, Oxford.
Du Cange, C. 1680. *Historia Byzantina I. Familiae Byzantinae*, Paris.
Edson, C. (ed.) 1972. *Inscriptiones Graecae Epiri, Macedoniae, Thraciae, Scythiae. Pars 2. Inscriptiones Macedoniae. Fasc. 1. Inscriptiones Thessalonicae et viciniae (IG X)*, Berlin.
Floridi, L. 2013. "The epigrams of Gregory of Nazianzus against tomb desecrators and their epigraphic background", *Mnemosyne*, 66, 55–81.
Floridi, L. (ed.) 2014. *Lucillio. Epigrammi*, Berlin.
Garland, L. 2011. "Public lavatories, mosquito nets and Agathias' cat: the sixth-century epigram in its Justinianic context", in L. Garland/G. Nathan (eds.), *Basileia. Essays on imperium and culture in honour of E.M. and M.J. Jeffreys*, Brisbane, 141–158.
Garulli, V. 2012. *BYBLOS LAINEE. Epigrafia, letteratura, epitafio*, Bologna.
Giommoni, F. (ed.) 2017. *Νέης γενετῆρες ἀοιδῆς. Gli epigrammi dei "minori" del Ciclo di Agazia*, Alessandria.

Gow, A.S.F./Page, D.L. (eds.) 1965. *The Greek Anthology: Hellenistic epigrams (HE)*, I–II, Cambridge.

Gow, A.S.F./Page, D.L. (eds.) 1968. *The Greek Anthology: The Garland of Philip (GPh)*, I–II, Cambridge.

Griessmair, E. 1966. *Das Motiv der mors immatura in den griechischen metrischen Grabinschriften*, Innsbruck.

Gullo, A. 2009. "Un epigrammista del *Ciclo* di Agazia: Giuliano d'Egitto", *Maia*, 61, 345–347.

Gullo, A. (ed.) Forthcoming a. *Antologia Palatina. Epigrammi funerari (Libro VII)*, Pisa.

Gullo, A. Forthcoming b. "Nonnian poets (?): the case of Julian the Egyptian", in B. Verhelst (ed.), *Nonnus of Panopolis in context IV. Poetry at the Crossroads (Gent 19–21 April 2018)*, Leuven.

Hartigan, K.V. 1975. "Julian the Egyptian", *Eranos*, 73, 43–54.

Jones, A.H.M./Martindale, J.R./Morris, J. (eds.) 1971–1992. *The Prosopography of the Latin Roman Empire (PLRE)*, I–III, Cambridge.

Kaldellis, A. 1999. "The historical and religious views of Agathias: a reinterpretation", *Byzantion*, 69, 206–252.

Kaldellis, A. 2003. "Things are not what they are: Agathias *Mythistoricus* and the last laugh of classical culture", *CQ*, 53, 295–300.

Kaster, R.A. 1988. *Guardians of language: the grammarian and society in Late Antiquity*, Berkeley (CA).

Lattimore, R. 1942. *Themes in Greek and Latin epitaphs*, Urbana (IL).

Livrea, E. (ed.) 2000. *Nonno di Panopoli. Parafrasi del Vangelo di S. Giovanni. Canto B*, Bologna.

Madden, J.A. 1977. "Macedonius Consul and Christianity", *Mnemosyne*, 30, 153–159.

Madden, J.A. (ed.) 1995. *Macedonius Consul. The Epigrams*, Hildesheim.

McCail, R. 1968. "Three Byzantine epigrams on marital incompatibility", *Mnemosyne*, 21, 76–78.

McCail, R. 1969. "The *Cycle* of Agathias: new identifications scrutinised", *JHS*, 89, 87–96.

McCail, R. 1971. "The erotic and ascetic poetry of Agathias Scholasticus", *Byzantion*, 41, 205–267.

Page, D.L. (ed.) 1981. *Further Greek Epigrams (FGE)*, rev. R.D. Dawe and J. Diggle, Cambridge.

Peek, W. (ed.) 1955. *Griechische Vers-Inschriften (GVI)*, Berlin.

Prestige, L. 1922. "Hades in the Greek Fathers", *JThS*, 24, 476–485.

Sanders, G./Donati, A./Pickhaus, D./van Uytfanghe, M. (eds.) 1991. *Lapides memores. Païens et chrétiens face à la mort: le témoignage de l' épigraphie funéraire latine*, Faenza.

Strubbe, J.H.M. 1998. "Epigrams and consolation decrees for deceased youths", *AC*, 67, 45–75.

van der Horst, P.W. 1994. "Jewish poetical tomb inscriptions", in J.W. van Henten/P.W. van der Horst (eds.), *Studies in early Jewish epigraphy*, Leiden, 129–147.

Vérilhac, A.-M. (ed.) 1978–1982. *ΠΑΙΔΕΣ ΑΩΡΟΙ. Poésie funéraire*, I–II, Athens.

Viansino, G. (ed.) 1963. *Paolo Silenziario. Epigrammi*, Torino.

Viansino, G. (ed.) 1967. *Agazia Scolastico. Epigrammi*, Milano.

Waltz, P. 1931. "L'inspiration païenne et le sentiment chrétien dans les épigrammes funéraires du VIe siècle", *L'Acropole*, 6, 3–21.

Whitby, Mary 1994. "From Moschus to Nonnus: the evolution of the Nonnian style", in N. Hopkinson (ed.), *Studies in the Dionysiaca of Nonnus*, Cambridge, 99–155.

Marco Onorato
The Poet and the Light: Modulation and Transposition of a Prudentian *Ekphrasis* in Two Poems by Sidonius Apollinaris

In the late Latin literary scene Sidonius Apollinaris, a fifth-century Gallo-Roman writer, bishop, and a leading exponent of the so-called 'jeweled style',[1] stands out for being particularly sensitive to the relationship between major and minor genres. An explicit reference to this issue can be found in the introductory poem of Sidonius' *nugae* (*carmen 9*), which attributes the *novitas* of the texts included in the *sylloge* not only to their discontinuity in terms of form and content,[2] but also to the *recusatio* of themes and *auctores* who had become canonical in Greek and Latin literature.[3] In such a context a disregard for high-flown, large-scale forms such as epic and tragedy is not surprising.[4] It is less obvious, however, why Sidonius, while compulsively repeating his *non dicam*, uses an informal meter such as the Phalaecian hendecasyllable to create his fascinating synthesis of a centuries-old literary tradition, demonstrating his wide-ranging (albeit not always deep nor direct) knowledge of preceding literature.[5] As the poems of the *sylloge* show, even high genres and authors find their place: although they are apparently ignored, in reality they are the target of obvious or – at times – subtle and refined references.

One of the most renowned predecessors subject to Sidonius' *furtiva lectio*[6] is Prudentius,[7] whose re-use attests to the Lyonnais writer's tendency to exploit his

---

[1] Roberts 1989, 11–12, 50–52, and 63–64; Onorato 2016b.
[2] The rest of the collection includes two wedding poems (*carm.* 11 and 15; the latter is an unparalleled example of philosophical *epithalamium*) with their respective prefaces (10 and 14), six epigrams (12 and 17–21), a polymetric *precatio* to the emperor Majorian (13), an *eucharisticon* to the bishop Faustus of Riez (16), an elaborate *ekphrasis* of a sumptuous estate (22), a long and articulated encomium of a friend (23) and, finally, a *propempticon ad libellum* (24).
[3] On this programmatic poem, one of the most debated among critics, see Consolino 1974, Santelia 1998 and 1999, Condorelli 2008, 81–116, Onorato 2016b, 169–233.
[4] See esp. vv. 65–167.
[5] For a detailed discussion of this feature see Onorato, forthcoming.
[6] About this concept see Gualandri 1979.
[7] Besides the *loci similes* listed by Geisler in the appendix to Lütjohann 1887, see Thraede 1965, 47–48, Gualandri 1979, 5–6 and 157–158, Condorelli 2004, 570, Santelia 2007, 316–317, and 2012,

hybrid cultural background to involve both Christian and pagan models in some fascinating intergeneric experimentations. This chapter will investigate the relationship between the two authors by focusing on a passage of the *Psychomachia* which influences two of Sidonius' poems: an *epithalamium* and an epigram. It would be reductive to define such an intertextual dialogue as an adaptation of some elements of the solemn Prudentian allegorical *epos* to humbler literary forms. In fact, the second text analysed here is also the result of a transposition of the original materials in a new metrical context, apparently in contrast with the nobility of the theme.

Prudentius

The Prudentian passage which undergoes a double rewriting by Sidonius is the famous *ekphrasis* of the temple of *Sapientia*, built by the Virtues guided by *Fides* and *Concordia*,[8] in *Psychomachia* 823–887. Its thorough description is justified by the special value of the sanctuary, already expressed in vv. 804–822 by *Fides* when addressing the Virtues: the temple, constructed after the conclusion of the bloody battle against the Vices, is explicitly modeled on the one built in Jerusalem under Solomon's peaceful reign.[9] The section on *virtutum gemmae*, gems that function as *ornamenta animae* and cover the walls of *Sapientia*'s temple, is particularly interesting for the purposes of the present analysis:

> quin etiam totidem gemmarum insignia textis
> parietibus distincta micant, animasque colorum
> viventes liquido lux evomit alta profundo.
> ingens chrysolitus, nativo interlitus auro,
> hinc sibi sapphirum sociaverat, inde beryllum,   855
> distantesque nitor medius variabat honores.
> hic chalcedon hebes perfunditur ex hyacinthi
> lumine vicino; nam forte cyanea propter
> stagna lapis cohibens ostro fulgebat aquoso.
> sardonicem pingunt amethystina, pingit iaspis,   860

---

passim (on *Psych.* see esp. 86–92 and 109), Hecquet-Noti 2013, 225, Onorato 2016b, 137–143. Sidonius, in a letter written in 465 to his friend Donidius (*ep.* 2.9.4), quotes Prudentius' works among the favorite readings of the Gallo-Roman nobles.

8 On the role of these personifications in the *Psych.* see Smith 1976, 194–206 and Cambrionne 2002, 454–457.

9 About the relationship between the two buildings see Gnilka 1963, 125–128, Cambrionne 2002, 458–460 and 464–465.

sardium iuxta adpositum pulcherque topazon.
has inter species smaragdina gramine verno
prata virent volvitque vagos lux herbida fluctus.
te quoque conspicuum structura interserit, ardens
chrysoprase, et sidus saxis stellantibus addit. 865

And more, the same number of gems, set singly in the fabric of the walls, sparkle conspicuously, and out of their clear depths the light from on high pours living, breathing colors. A great chrysolite, speckled with natural gold, had partnered with it on one side a sapphire, on the other a beryl, and the lustre between them gave varying tones to the beauties it parted. Here a dull chalcedony is flooded with color from the light of its neighbour jacinth; for as it chanced that stone with the dark depths imprisoned within it was shining nearby with its pellucid flash of crimson. The amethyst's hue tinges the sardonyx, jasper and fair topaz the sardius set beside them. Amid these beauties are emeralds like grassy meadows in the spring, whose green light rolls out ever-changing waves. Thou too, gleaming chrysoprase, hast a conspicuous place in the structure, thy star is added to the glittering stones.[10] (*Psych.* 851–865)

Prudentius draws inspiration only in part from the bare passage of John's Apocalypse on the foundations of the celestial Jerusalem, where the combination of ordinal adjectives with the names of precious stones puts an emphasis on the number twelve:[11] "*fundamenta muri civitatis omni lapide pretioso ornata: fundamentum primum iaspis; secundus sapphyrus; tertius carcedonius; quartus zmaragdus; quintus sardonix; sextus sardinus; septimus chrysolitus; octavus berillus; nonus topazius; decimus chrysoprassus; undecimus hyacinthus; duodecimus amethistus*" (Apoc 21:19–20, Vulgate).[12] This attribute is also shared by the *lapides* and the gates distributed on the four sides of the city walls. Prudentius is sensitive to such a detail and imagines that *Sapientia*'s temple, reproducing the celestial Jerusalem, has a qadrangular shape[13] traced by *Concordia*'s golden slide rule and, on all sides, three doors with golden inscriptions of the names of the apostles above them (826–850). The gems used to decorate the temple walls are also twelve.

---

10 For the Latin text I follow Cunningham 1966. The translation is by Thomson 1949.
11 On the symbolism of this number see Cambrionne 2002, 461–462.
12 "The foundations of the wall of the city are adorned with every jewel; the first was jasper, the second sapphire, the third agate, the fourth emerald, the fifth onyx, the sixth carnelian, the seventh chrysolite, the eighth beryl, the ninth topaz, the tenth chrysoprase, the eleventh jacinth, the twelfth amethyst;" cf. Apoc 21:12–16, and 21 (on the twelve gates).
13 For the meaning of the detail see Gnilka 1963, 95–97.

Besides this homage to the biblical text, however, the poet, in line with a late antique tendency to play with light and colors,[14] is more prone to evoke the splendor of the building's decorations now endowed with a precise theological value. In the epilogue of the *Psychomachia*, it becomes clear that the allegory of the temple is an interpretive key for the whole poem: the conflict between *lux* and *tenebrae* attested in the description mirrors the conflict between virtues and vices and is presented as a constant element in the human soul until Christ's salvific intervention, which confirms the triumph of light by placing the *virtutum gemmae*[15] in a purified site.[16]

Prudentius eliminates the numerals present in the *Apocalypsis* and, although he does not spare references to the collocation of the *ornamenta* (see the whole v. 855; *vicino* and *propter* in v. 858; *has inter species* in v. 862), he is less interested in the stones' reciprocal position than in the visual effects of their combination. The beginning is cautious: in v. 856 the denotative *variabat* clarifies that the golden gleaming of the chrysolite marks a chromatic distinction in the transition from the sapphire to the beryl. Starting from vv. 857–859, however, the poetic strategies become more elaborate: the lively reflection of the hyacinth on the chalcedony is evoked by *perfundo*, a verb recalling not only the spreading of colors in painting, but even the act of soaking,[17] and thus perfectly suitable to the following metaphors of the *cyanea ... stagna* and the *ostrum aquosum*. The painting connotation of this *Farbenmischung*[18] returns in vv. 860–861: the amethysts paint the sardonyxes in the same way as the jasper and the topaz do with the sard. After the suggestive image of the *smaragdina ... | prata*[19] crossed by green flashing similar to sea waves,[20] the poet ends with the *chrysoprasus*, shining like a star and symmetrical (even linguistically) to the *chrysolithus* quoted at the beginning.

---

14 On this trend see Charlet 1988, 80–81, Roberts 1989, 72–78, and 2011–2012, Gualandri 1994, 330.
15 Some parallels of such an image are collected by Gnilka 1963, 108–109.
16 Paul's allegory on man as the temple of God (1 Cor 3:16) is the obvious starting point; see Gosserez 2001, 249. On other influences: Gnilka 1963, 83–86.
17 *TLL, s.v. perfundo*, 1418.69–1419.8.
18 Gnilka 1963, 107.
19 The metaphor of meadows, which occurs also in Prud., *Perist.* 12.54 and has some parallels in Gregory of Nyssa's description of the *martyrion* of Saint Theodore at Euchaita as well as in Procopius' and Paul the Silentiary's *ekphraseis* of the church of Hagia Sophia in Constantinople (Schibille 2014, 20–21 and 99–109), is central to late antique literary aesthetics (Roberts 1989, 75–76) and enriches the metapoetic resonance of these lines (on which see *infra*).
20 On Prudentius' tendency to use nature as a term of comparison for buildings' beauty see O'Hogan 2016, 127–131.

Prudentius is clearly interested in the interaction between the hues of the *lapides* and the light (852: *micant*; 853 and 863: *lux*; 856: *nitor*; 858: *lumine*; 859: *fulgebat*; 864: *ardens*; 865: *sidus*; *stellantibus*). Brightness is a quality of stones such as chrysolite, hyacinth and chrysoprase; in v. 863, the enallage of *herbidus*, referred to *lux* rather than to *fluctus*, gives the impression that the *lapis*' color saturates even sunrays. The overall meaning is, however, determined by vv. 852– 853, where the poet claims that *lux alta* penetrates the transparent bottom of the *lapides* pouring out (*evomit*)[21] their colors, their souls, like an uncontainable gush. This is how this fascinating "poésie de lumière"[22] constructs its allegorical message: only a divine, salvific intervention can make the virtues residing in the human soul shine, preventing them from being obscured by vices.

There is also a metaliterary discourse, revealed by the first two lines of the passage, in which the poet gathers four terms (851: *gemmarum*; *insignia*; 852: *distincta*; *colorum*) commonly used to designate rhetorical as well as literal *ornatus*[23] and puts an *enallage* in *enjambement* to assure *textis* a prominent position: *gemmarum insignia textis | parietibus distincta micant* = *gemmarum insignia texta | parietibus distinctis micant*.[24] This ambiguous phraseology suggests that the target of Prudentius' admiring *ekphrasis* is not only the luxurious decoration of the walls of *Sapientia*'s temple, but also the verbal artifact that describes it and is characterized by an ostentatious 'jeweled style'.[25] What is still more relevant, however, is that in rhetorical occurrences terms such as *insigne* and *distinguo* are commonly associated with the metaphor of light to indicate the effect of a refined *ornatus* on the speech.[26] The poetology of the *Psychomachia* passage is the obvious result of the Christianization of this rhetorical perspective: Prudentius, while mentioning the *lapides*' naturally radiant chromatism and, thus, the intrinsic

---

21 Cf. *infra*, n. 27.
22 I am of course referring to the title of Gosserez 2001, an essay useful also for the analysis of further Prudentian occurrences of the theme of light.
23 On *gemma* see the analysis of Mart., *epigr.* 5.11.3–4 and Tac., *Dial.* 22.4 by Roberts 1989, 52– 53. For *insigne*, *distinguo* and *color* (often attested together) see *Rhet. Her.* 4.11.16, 4.13.18 and 4.23.32, Cic., *De or.* 1.50, 1.218, 2.36, 3.96 and 3.201, *Orat.* 134, *Part. or.* 72. On *color* (which in the rhetorical tradition acquires further meanings, apparently ignored by Prudentius: Lévy 2006; Spangenberg Yanes 2013 and 2015) see also the *loci* listed by *TLL*, 1720.43–68. Finally, it should not be overlooked that, with a fascinating *Ringkomposition*, the last line of the Prudentian passage (865) has both *sidus* and *stellans*, clearly reminiscent of the use of *stella* for stylistic embellishment (Cic., *De or.* 3.170 and *Orat.* 92).
24 For another possible purpose of this *enallage* see Onorato 2016b, 140.
25 About this feature of Prudentius' poetry: Fontaine 1975, 758–759; Roberts 1989, 28–30, 75– 76, 132–133 and 146.
26 See the appearance of *lumen* in most of the *loci* quoted *supra*, at n. 23.

qualities of his own verses, assigns a decisive role to an external element, the *lux alta* that brings out[27] the colors of precious stones and symbolizes the importance of divine inspiration[28] in the creative process of such a dense literary device.[29]

Sidonius Apollinaris, *carmen 11*

The Prudentian *ekphrasis* of *Sapientia*'s temple is significantly rewritten in Sidonius Apollinaris' *carmen* 11, an *ephitalamium* composed around 460[30] for the wedding of the Gallo-Roman nobles Ruricius and Hiberia.[31] The poem is marked by a strong ekphrastic tendency, already evident in vv. 17–33, which describe the Corinthian temple of Venus, a love token of her husband Vulcan:

> hic lapis est de quinque locis dans quinque colores
> Aethiops, Phrygius, Parius, Poenus, Lacedaemon,
> purpureus, viridis, maculosus, eburnus et albus.
> postes chrysolithi fulvus diffulgurat ardor;   20

---

27 As Fotini Hadjittofi has suggested to me, the attribution of *evomere* to the *lux alta* in v. 853 is perhaps also metapoetic, since Prudentius seems to use this verb as an alternative to *(e)ructare*, widely attested for the pouring forth of speech (the source is the *Psalms* [Vulgate] 18:3: *eructat verbum*; 44:2: 118:171, and 145:7; cf., e.g., August., *Tract. Ev. Jo.* 20.1 and 124.7, Jer., *ep.* 65.5, Iuvenc. 2.828, Prud., *Apoth.* 93, Paul. Nol., *ep.* 15.4, 19.1 and *carm.* 27.103–105; in the Greek context, see, e.g., ἐρεύγομαι in Nonn., *Par.* 5.144); cf. Gualandri 1979, 131 n. 88. The choice might have been further supported by passages such as Jer., *ep.* 69.2: *quasi per mentis crapulam ructans et nausians evomebat: apostolus dixit, Paulus haec docuit* ("At last his mouth opened and he vomited forth the contents of his mind. Certainly, he blurted out, that is the doctrine of the apostle Paul"); the letter dates to 397 and, thus, is chronologically close to the *Psychomachia*, where *ructare* and *evomere* occur as synonyms, even if with a negative connotation; for a later parallel see August., *C. Jul. op. imp.* 4.55: *tu, qui non potes nisi ructare calumnias, et vomere contumelias* ("You, who can do nothing but belch out slanders and throw up insults").
28 Cf. the proemial invocation at vv. 5–11 (*dissere, rex noster...*), on which see Santelia 2012, 82–84.
29 On this point I mostly agree with Gosserez 2001, 262–70; it should be added that the synergy between the *lux alta* and the splendor of the precious stones might suggest also that the display of a jeweled style is legitimized by an edifying hidden meaning. Gnilka 1967, 109 instead argues that *lux alta* indicates "das Licht in der Tiefe (der Edelsteine)", but such a reading seems denied by the explanation of the allegory at the end of the poem, where God's intervention is presented as crucial.
30 On the chronology see Filosini 2014, 13–17.
31 For a biographical sketch of bride and groom: Filosini 2014, 18–21. On Ruricius see also Loyen 1943, 169–173, Hagendahl 1952, 51–89, Mathisen 1999, 19–45, Gasti 2006, 157–159 and Neri 2009, 7–10.

myrrhina, sardonyches, amethystus Hiberus, iaspis
Indus, Chalcidicus, Scythicus, beryllus, achates
attollunt duplices argenti cardine valvas,
per quas inclusi lucem vomit umbra smaragdi;
limina crassus onyx crustat propterque hyacinthi   25
caerula concordem iaciunt in stagna colorem.
exterior non compta silex, sed prominet alte
asper ab adsiduo lympharum verbere pumex.
interiore loco simulavit Mulciber auro
exstantes late scopulos atque arte magistra   30
ingenti cultu naturae inculta fefellit,
huic operi insistens, quod necdum noverat illa
quae post Lemniacis damnavit furta catenis.

Here is stone from five regions, giving forth five hues, Aethiopian, Phrygian, Parian, Punic, Spartan-purple, green, mottled, ivory, white. The yellow glow of topaz flashes through the doorpost; porcelain, sardonyx, Caucasian amethyst, Indian jasper, Chalcidian and Scythian stones, beryl and agate, form the double doors that rise upon silver pivots, and through these doors the shadowy recess beyond pours out the sheen of the emeralds that are within. Onyx thickly encrusts the threshold, and hard by the blue color of amethyst casts upon the lagoon a harmonious hue. Outside is no dressed stone, but towering walls of rock that has been roughened by the constant lashing of the waters. In the inner part Mulciber mimicked in gold the crags that rise up far and wide, and with his skill to guide him counterfeited with mighty art the artless creations of Nature, plying his work diligently-for not yet did he know of that deception which afterwards he punished with his Lemnian chains.[32] (*carm.* 11.17–33)

References to the hypotext are evident in the lines focusing on the materials used for jambs, shutters, the doorstep and the interior of the building (20–26): twelve precious stones, the first of which to be mentioned, like in the *Psychomachia*, is the chrysolite. Two important lexical details also point to Prudentius: firstly, the syntagma of v. 24 *lucem vomit*, which reverses the *lux evomit* occupying the same metrical *sedes* as in *Psychomachia* 853; secondly, the simultaneous mention of the hyacinth and the *stagna* (25–26), with another perspicuous shift from the Prudentian passage (*Psych.* 857–859), since *stagna* is not a metaphor for the hue of the lapis, but rather a reference to the seawater where the hyacinth casts a similar color. These elements are sufficient to suggest that a peculiarity of Sidonius' rewriting of Prudentius' work is an exaggerated mannerism, which isolates, modifies and reconstitutes some elements of the model in a merely formalistic *lusus*.

---

[32] The translation of this and other Sidonian *loci* is by Anderson 1936; for the Latin text of the poem I follow Filosini 2014.

Another prominent feature is the treatment of precious stones that become a pervasive presence: no longer limited to the walls (as in Prudentius), they decorate several parts of the building, almost obscuring its architectonic structure. This effect is also emphasized by the use of personification, which at v. 23 gives the impression that the precious stones mentioned in the two previous hexameters replace the *artifex* in elevating the temple's doors: once again, the *aemulatio* of Prudentius, who attributes the act of *pingere* to the amethyst and the jasper at v. 860, is evident.

The most evocative element, however, is the use of *congeries* at vv. 21–22: Sidonius draws inspiration from the list included in John's Apocalypse, but also selects and orders the words according to a strategy which goes beyond metrical constraints. Simplification of syntax and high proximity between words, thus, make the juxtaposition of lexical items the perfect linguistic equivalent of the combination of precious stones (cf. the list of marbles at vv. 17–19).[33] Sidonius treats words with the same virtuosity that Vulcan displays with setting the *lapides* and, in both cases, the result is a fascinating chromatic *iter*, strategically introduced at v. 21 from the murrha, which, by combining glass brightness with red purple or candid white tinges, functions as a 'bridge' between the chrysolite's glow of the *postes* and the white-red nail of the sardonyx in turn and in harmony with the amethyst cited right after it. A series of stones follows marked by a wide variety of greens or blue-green: the three types of jasper (*iaspis Indus, Chalcidicus, Scythicus*) evoke respectively a color similar to emerald, dark green and a cerulean. Similarly, the transition from the blue-green to the beryl to the emerald's vivid green is mediated by a variety of agate. The epilogue is entrusted to the hyacinth, whose color is harmonized with that of the sea rather than with another stone. The relationship between the temple and the surrounding environment is also addressed in the *synkrisis* of vv. 27–31, between the outside of the building, made with a *non compta silex*, and the interior, where Vulcan reproduces the rocks of the steep sea landscape in gold.

It is worth noting the small number of references to the light, limited to the words referring to the chrysolite (20) and the emerald (24). More space to the light is instead given in the hexameters before this *ekphrasis* (7–16), gradually introducing the scenery of the gulf of Corinth invaded by the brightness of the day, which seems to come from the entire sky and to penetrate the transparent waters, reaching the depths of the sea:

---

33 For a more detailed analysis of such a technique see Onorato 2016b, 124–136.

inter Cyaneas, Ephyraea cacumina, cautes
qua super Idalium levat Orithyion in aethram
exesi sale montis apex, ubi forte vagantem,
dum fugit, et fixit trepidus Symplegada Tiphys,
atque recurrentem ructatum ad rauca Maleae   5
exit in Isthmiacum pelagus claudentibus alis
saxorum de rupe sinus, quo saepe recessu
sic tamquam toto coeat de lumine caeli,
artatur collecta dies tremulasque per undas
insequitur secreta vadi, transmittitur alto   10
perfusus splendore latex, mirumque relatu,
lympha bibit solem tenuique inserta fluento
perforat arenti radio lux sicca liquorem.
profecit studio spatium; nam Lemnius illic
ceu templum lusit Veneri fulmenque relinquens   15
hic ferrugineus fumavit saepe Pyragmon.

Between the Dark-blue Rocks, Ephyra's peaks, where the summit of a sea-worn mountain raises Orithyion above Idalium to the sky, in which place, as it chanced, the wandering Symplegades were fixed fast by the trembling Tiphys even as he fled from them, *and the waves vomited again, which return to the hoarse rocks of Maleas,*[34] there emerges into the sea of the Isthmus a bay enclosed by wings of piled rocks jutting from the cliff; in which retreat, just as if the whole radiance of the sky were concentrated there, the daylight is gathered together into a narrow space, and penetrating the quivering waters it searches out the secluded depths, and so the ripples pass on, bathed in deep-shining brightness, and, wondrous to tell, the water drinks in the sun and the light, pushed into the limpid stream, bores unwetted through the wet with arid ray. This site favoured a labour of love; for there the Lemnian god amused himself by building a mimic temple for Venus, and swarthy Pyragmon, abandoning the thunderbolt, raised his smoke in the place many a time. (*carm.* 11. 1–16)

Despite their debt to Prudentius (see *alto* in v. 10 and *perfusus* in v. 11), these verses are indicative of the transformation of the *Psychomachia*'s elements after being inserted in a nugatory text. The metaphysical connotations of the Prudentian image disappear in an *ekphrasis* which privileges concettism and visual suggestions of Ausonian (as well as Ovidian and Martialian) ancestry.[35] It is a worthy prelude to the temple of Venus, where purely literary strategies prevail and where

---

[34] In italics my addition to Anderson 1936, who did not translate v. 5, an example of the textual and interpretive problems posed by the poem's beginning; cf. Santelia 2010 and Filosini 2014, 97–103.
[35] Cf. Rosati 2017, 126–130.

there is no space for the complex hidden meanings related to the precious stones in the hypotext.[36]

It should be further observed that Sidonius, unlike Prudentius, does not explicitly claim that it is the light that brings out the temple's materials, whose beauty seems to result from their respective colors and careful *compositio*. The metaliterary horizon, thus, changes and the intrinsic value of the text becomes evident together with an aesthetics founded on *varietas*. The role of the poet changes too in that he is no longer subject to the illumination of the Christian god, but rather becomes an *alter ego* of *Mulciber*, embodying a creative art of light and color. Vulcan creates a sumptuous building not only as a love token towards Venus and her sparkling beauty, but also to show his *ars*. While the outside is made of rough stones and exposed to the modeling power of natural forces, the splendor of the rest of the temple, thanks to a combination of marbles, precious stones and gold, competes with the gulf of Corinth, and can even reproduce the *inculta* of the marine landscape through its *cultus*. At the same time, for Sidonius, the representation of the god's wedding gift offers a pretext for a sample of ekphrastic virtuosity, whereby individual words, already loaded with suggestions, become even more evocative thanks to a wise combination. In the same way as Vulcan is at ease with materials of various geographical origins, Sidonius manages to combine echoes of the Prudentian *epos* with those of works belonging to minor genres, such as Statius' *Silvae* (particularly 1.2, but also 1.5 and 2.2) and Claudian's *epithalamium* for Honorius and Maria.[37]

The mirroring between Vulcan and the poet thus neutralizes the epic flavor of the scene where the blacksmith Cyclops Pyragmon interrupts the forging of Jupiter's thunders (15–16), a clear hint at Virgil's verses on the making of Aeneas' shield, abruptly prioritized over that of weapons and other attributes of Jupiter, Mars and Minerva (*Aen.* 8.369–453; see esp. 439–443). This passage – an ekphrastic archetype, as well as a hypotext appropriate to an *epithalamium* due to the

---

[36] Such a radical shift of perspective, all the more conspicuous in light of the modest time lapse (approximately 60 years) between the *Psych.* and this wedding poem, does not necessarily indicate a weak Christian reference system in Sidonius' poetry before his election as a bishop in 470/471 (the question is more complex: see Santelia 2012, 9–17). More likely, a Christian revision – even if only partial – of a genre such as the *epithalamium* (in the manner of *carm.* 25 by Paulinus of Nola: cf. the Introduction to this volume) was considered of little appeal to the recipients (whose religious interests would have intensified several years after, for which see Neri 2009, 9).

[37] On these further influences see Filosini 2014, 94–97 and 114–116, Onorato 2016a. Cf. *infra*, n. 60.

scene where Vulcan is seduced by Venus and to the insistence on the god's devotion to his wife (387–406) – undergoes a substantial *Umkehrung*.[38] Sidonius' Vulcan, rather than creating a typical weapon for the epic hero, builds a monument to *cultus* and refinement, by paying tribute not only to Venus' beauty, but also to the ideal of a disengaged (v. 15: *lusit*) and precious poetry.[39] The nugatory modulation of another epic hypotext such as the *Psychomachia* passage runs parallel to this, and one might suspect that the syntagma *ceu templum* ("a sort of temple") at v. 15 aims subtly to reveal that the building is a frivolous counterfeiting of the Prudentian sanctuary.

The peculiar treatment of Prudentian reminiscences is part of a strategy, evident from the first lines, where the reference to the passing of the Symplegades by Tiphys, the Argo's helmsman,[40] is not only aimed at an isotopy with the allegoric *praefatio* (*carm*. 10), which re-evokes Peleus and Thetis' wedding according to the rhetorical norms of the *epithalamium*,[41] but also recalls the famous incipit of Catullus' *carm*. 64 (vv. 1–15).[42] This text, due to both its combination of *epyllion* and *epithalamium*, and its assimilation of epic and tragic elements in a heterodox poetic form, undoubtedly places itself at the crossroads of major and minor genres. The Gallo-Roman poet seems to have been influenced by the syntagmatic development of Catullus' poem, which, after the Argonauts' backstory, includes in the wedding section a long ekphrastic passage of the *vestis* decorated with images drawn from Ariadne's myth, an authentic compendium of an experimental and Alexandrian rewriting of epic canons.[43] In the Sidonian *epithalamium*, in fact, the first six and a half lines (full of thematic and lexical references to epic)[44] create a horizon of expectations to be immediately denied in vv. 7–12, where mythology is set aside and an interest in the light effects in the gulf of Corinth prevails. Sim-

---

38 Since it must be assumed that, as in *Aen*. 8.418, the Cyclops stops his work at the behest of Vulcan, *alter ego* of Sidonius, it is not hazardous to say that vv. 15–16 of the *epithalamium* disclose a poetic agenda that aims to 'interrupt' the epic model by displacing it to a minor genre. I thank Fotini Hadjittofi for drawing my attention to this.
39 In the Latin context, the metaliterary value of precious stones, attested since the Augustan Age and then re-emerging in Martial and, more frequently, in late authors (Roberts 1989, 52–55), derives perhaps from the influence of Posidippus' *Lithika* or similar poems, which established an analogical correspondence between the gems and the epigram, an exquisite and iridescent genre by definition: cf. Petrain 2005, 344–353 and Elsner 2014.
40 For a possibile allegorical meaning of this hint see Santelia 2010, 236–237.
41 Men. Rhet. 400.15–22 and 409.5; [Dion. Hal.], *Rhet*. 2.5.
42 Also recalled by Sid. Apoll., *carm*. 9.65.
43 On the hybrid generic identity and the poetic technique of Catullus' poem see Fernandelli 2012.
44 Filosini 2014, 104–110.

ilarly, in the verses on Venus' temple (13–33), allusions to the *Psychomachia*, rather than consolidating the epic feel of references to the *Aeneid*,[45] become central to an aestheticized poetry whose privileged tool is *ekphrasis* and whose perfect symbol is the *lapides*' polychromy.[46]

Sidonius, *Epistle* 2.10.4

The *Psychomachia* verses are again recalled by Sidonius approximately nine years later[47] in an epigram in Phalaecian hendecasyllables enclosed in a letter to the young rhetor Hesperius, the *Epistle* 2.10.4. To satisfy his friend's request of *versiculi*, Sidonius sends him a poem meant to be inscribed in the apsis of a church in Lyons,[48] whose construction had been encouraged by the bishop Patient. Echoes of the hypotext are evident in those lines dedicated to the luxurious interior of the building (vv. 8–15), characterized by a golden *lacunar*, by the polychrome marbles of the *camera*, the *solum* and the *fenestrae* and by a *crusta* of emeralds on which compositions of glass tiles imitating sapphires are inserted:

> intus lux micat atque bratteatum
> sol sic sollicitatur ad lacunar,
> fulvo ut concolor erret in metallo.   10
> distinctum vario nitore marmor
> percurrit cameram solum fenestras,
> ac sub versicoloribus figuris
> vernans herbida crusta sapphiratos
> flectit per prasinum vitrum lapillos.[49]   15

Within it the light flashes and the sunshine is so tempted by the gilded ceiling that it travels over the tawny metal, matching its hue. Marble diversified by various shining tints pervades the vaulting, the floor, the windows; forming designs of diverse color, a verdant grass-green encrustation brings winding lines of sapphire-hued stones over the leek-green glass. (*ep.* 2.10.4.8–15).

---

[45] A more than legitimate expectation given Virgil's influence on the Prudentian poem, on which see: Mahoney 1934; Magazzù 1975; Smith 1976, 234–300; Ludwig 1977, 309–310; Bruno 1995; Gosserez 2002, 72–73; Lühken 2002, 33–184; Mastrangelo 2008, 14–40; Pelttari 2014, 154–157.
[46] On this see Onorato 2016a.
[47] Cf. Loyen 1970, 247.
[48] The identification of the building is still uncertain: see Santelia 2007, 320 n. 38.
[49] For the Latin text I follow Loyen 1970.

The prominence of light in the aesthetic experience of the Lyonnais church[50] is expressed in a vocabulary of undoubtedly Prudentian origin: *micat* (8) and *distinctum* (11) recall *distincta micant* of *Psychomachia* 851; *vario nitore* (11) is inspired by *nitor … variabat* of v. 856 of the model; the original image of the *lux herbida* becomes that of the *herbida crusta*.[51] Moreover, unlike *carmen* 11, this epigram, written for religious purposes, does not overlook Prudentius' allegorical praxis: sunrays cast towards the golden *lacunar* evoke the presence of God in a suitable site both from a chromatic and from a spiritual perspective.[52]

The metaliterary implications, however, are once again different from those of the Prudentian verses. The attraction of the sun emphasizes the building's precious craftsmanship (equipped with light and color)[53] and, indirectly, of the poem, whose intrinsic qualities bring about celestial illumination.[54] The basilica, which attracts, in the same way, sunrays and passing-by worshippers,[55] becomes the symbol of a poetry which can draw readers' interest thanks to its formal as well as religious qualities. Sidonius, even though referring to a *tumultuarium carmen*, inferior to those of the *eminentes poetae* Constantius and Secundinus[56] inscribed in the side nave of the basilica, does not hide his pride for the *ars* of an epigram which can even compete with the demanding legacy of the Prudentian *epos*.

---

[50] From this point of view Sidonius' epigram anticipates the aestheticism of light in the Byzantine *ekphraseis* of the church of Hagia Sophia in Constantinople; cf. Schibille 2014.

[51] Parallels with Prud., *Perist.* 12.49–54 are also present; see Santelia 2007, 316–317; Hecquet-Noti 2013, 225; Herbert de la Portbarré-Viard 2014, 383 and 386–387.

[52] The meaning of the allegory is evident; cf. Santelia 2007, 316 and Hernández Lobato 2012, 504. Hecquet-Noti 2013, 222–227 identifies a prefiguration of Paradise.

[53] This is an original development of a *topos* of late antique *ekphraseis* of sacred buildings, which usually focus instead on the irresistible attraction of some architectural details on the viewer's eye: cf. Schibille 2014, 18–19.

[54] The movement is symmetrical to that of *carm.* 11.25–26: there the hyacinths of the temple's thresholds virtually unite themselves with the sea thanks to a *concors color*; here the golden roof of the basilica attracts the *concolor sol*.

[55] Vv. 22–27: *hinc agger sonat, hinc Arar resultat, | hinc sese pedes atque eques reflectit | stridentum et moderator essedorum, | curvorum hinc chorus helciariorum | responsantibus alleluia ripis | ad Christum levat amnicum celeuma* ("On one side is the noisy high-road, on the other the echoing Arar; on the first the traveller on foot or on horse and the drivers of creaking carriages turn round; on the other, the company of the bargemen, their backs bent to their work, raise a boatmen's shout to Christ, and the banks echo their alleluia.

[56] 2.10.3; on Costantius and Secundinus see Santelia 2007, 306 n. 10. The *topos modestiae* continues in 2.10.4: compared to the rival poems, Sidonius' epigram is like a bride less beautiful than the *pronuba* or like a man whose dark skin is emphasized by a white dress or, even, like a flute surrounded by trumpets.

What is remarkable here is the choice of the Phalaecian hendecasyllable (an isosyllabic verse, thus a rigid one) for an incisive representation of the building, whose interior, as well as the roof (5–7) and the porches (16–21), is described by the poet. Resorting to the hexameter of *carmen* 11 – but also of *carmen* 22, a long description of the *Burgus* of the poet's friend Pontius Leontius – would have been easier for Sidonius; moreover, hexameters were used in some famous Statian *ekphraseis* of buildings (*Silv.* 1.3, 1.5 and 3.1)[57] and in Constantius' and Secundinus' epigrams, with which the Sidonian text competes. The Phalaecian, which allows Sidonius' epigram to stand out among other poems inscribed in the basilica while generating expectations of *tenuitas*,[58] is first of all chosen because of the poet's great familiarity with this metrical form: it is the one most commonly used in his non-political poems. Sidonius is clearly interested in widening the horizons of the Phalaecian in the frame of intergeneric experimentations, as shown by *carmen* 23, an encomium of the poet's friend Consentius from Narbonne which, despite its abnormal length (512 lines) and its borrowing of *topoi* from panegyric and epic, can be considered a nugatory transposition of noble genres. The great space devoted to a chariot race in which the poet's friend participated is emblematic: thanks to a virtuosic treatment of the relationship between word and meter, Sidonius succeeds in enclosing in 121 Phalaecians (vv. 307–427) a narration rich in echoes of Virgilian (*Aen.* 5.114–267) and Statian epic (*Theb.* 6.238–549).[59]

Nevertheless, in the epigram on the Lyonnais church there is also an *aemulatio* of Martial's *epigram* 4.64, the *ekphrasis* of the Janiculum villa of Julius Martial, patron of the poet from Bilbilis. The reference to this *epigramma longum* in Phalaecian hendecasyllables is above all clear through the image of carters and boatmen (24–27), which takes its cues from vv. 19–24 of Martial's poem: *illinc Flaminiae Salariaeque | gestator patet essedo tacente, | ne blando rota sit molesta somno, | quem nec rumpere nauticum celeuma | nec clamor valet helciariorum, | cum sit tam prope Mulvius sacrumque | lapsae per Tiberim volent carinae.*[60] The

---

57 The prestige of such ekphrastic models is recognized by Sidonius in the afterword to *carm.* 22; cf. Stoehr-Monjou 2013, 164–165 and Pelttari 2016.
58 Morgan 2010, 49–113. On Sidonius' treatment of Phalaecians see Onorato 2016b, 402–419.
59 Pavan 2005.
60 "On the other side the traveller on the Flaminian and Salarian Way is in view; but his carriage makes no sound, lest the wheel disturb soothing slumbers that neither boatswain's call nor bargee's shout can interrupt, even though Mulvius be so near and keels glide rapidly down sacred Tiber", trans. Shackleton Bailey 1993; cf. Harries 1994, 112, Santelia 2007, 313, *ad loc.* and Hecquet-Noti 2013, 227–229. Martial does not, however, emphasize the light element and simply clarifies that because of the fog the villa's ground has a particular glare (4–8). From such a perspective, it can be argued that Sidonius combines elements of the *Psychomachia* with others from

Flavian poet describes a villa which embodies an Epicurean ideal of serene detachment from the clamor of *negotia* and which in its moderate ascent towards the sky (9–10: *puris leniter admoventur astris | celsae* culmina *delicata villae*)[61] testifies to the owner's morality, inclined to a sensible enjoyment of material pleasures.[62] Sidonius reinterprets this model and its strategy of legitimation of *cultus* in Christian terms: by adopting the idea of the building as a mirror of the *ethos* of the person who has encouraged its construction (*ep.* 2.10.2: *ecclesia nuper exstructa Lugduni est, quae studio papae Patientis summum coepti operis accessit, viri sancti strenui, severi misericordis quique per uberem munificentiam in pauperes humanitatemque non minora bonae conscientiae culmina levet*),[63] he urges his readers to understand that the pomp of the decorations and the architectural structure is not a mere display of wealth, but a way to offer God and his worshippers a *hospitalitas* which is not less generous than that of Julius Martial, a new Alcinous or Molorcus.[64] Furthermore, unlike the Janiculum villa, the basilica of *Lugdunum* is not isolated from the noises of surrounding life, which reach it as a proof of faith; its ascensional force, brightness and orientation eastwards are a sign of a natural harmony with the celestial light: (*ep.* 2.10.4.5–7) *aedis celsa nitet nec in sinistrum | aut dextrum trahitur, sed arce frontis | ortum prospicit aequinoctialem.*[65]

Conclusions

It becomes clear that Sidonius' strategy in this later poem is the opposite to that adopted in *carmen* 11: in the *epithalamium* of Ruricius and Hiberia the deliberate

---

Mart., *epigr.* 6.42.8–10 and 19–21 (cf. Fabbrini 2007, 188–189), Stat., *Silv.* 1.3.53–55 and 1.5.41–46.
61 "Rising gently to the clear stars are the dainty rooftops of a lofty villa."
62 On the epigram's ideological substratum see Fabbrini 2007, 1–57.
63 "A church has recently been built at Lugdunum, and the undertaking has come to the point of completion through the zeal of Bishop Patiens, a man both holy and active, strict and compassionate, and one who is building up by his noble generosity to the poor and by his kindliness the not less lofty edifice of a guileless conscience."
64 Mart., *Epigr.* 4.64.26–30: *tuam putabis, | tam non invida tamque liberalis, | tam comi patet hospitalitate: | credas Alcinoi pios Penates | aut facti modo divitis Molorchi* ("You will think it your own, so open and ungrudging is its welcome, so liberal and courteous; you would think it the hospitable household of Alcinous, or of Molorchus, newly become rich").
65 "The lofty temple sparkles and does not incline to right or left, but with its towering front faces the sunrise of the equinox."

frustration of readerly expectations prompted by various epic reminiscences prepares the nugatory rewriting of Prudentius' solemn passage on *Sapientia*'s temple. In this later case, the Christianizing and thus ennobling revision of Martial's poem attests to the potential compatibility of epigram with a message of religious edification and sets the generic background against which the inclusion of Prudentian hints in a *tumultuarium carmen* in Phalaecians should be interpreted. This shift reflects the new agenda dictated to Sidonius by his growing religious commitment around 470/471[66] and, at the same time, by his ill-concealed desire not to sacrifice to a non-frivolous conception of literature the familiarity with minor poetry and its meter *par excellence*. In such a framework, the re-use of the *Psychomachia* no longer serves to bring out the aesthetic and thematic distance between major and minor genres, but, on the contrary, is crucial in transforming a humble epigram into a temple of literary mannerism open to the sublimity of divine light.

Bibliography

Anderson, W.B. (ed.) 1936. *Sidonius. Poems. Letters I–II*, Cambridge (MA).
Bruno, C. 1995. "L'approccio escatologico nella *Psychomachia* di Prudenzio", *Pan*, 14, 169–177.
Cambrionne, P. 2002. "Métamorphoses de la Terre Promise. Le Temple de l'Âme dans la *Psychomachia* de Prudence", *REA*, 104, 445–474.
Charlet, J.-L. 1988. "Aesthetic trends in late Latin poetry (325–410)", *Philologus*, 132, 74–85.
Condorelli, S. 2004. "L'officina di Sidonio Apolinare: tra *incus metrica* e *asprata lima*", *BStudLat*, 34, 558–598.
Condorelli, S. 2008. *Il poeta doctus nel V secolo d.C.. Aspetti della poetica di Sidonio Apollinare*, Napoli.
Consolino, F.E. 1974. "Codice retorico e manierismo stilistico nella poetica di Sidonio Apollinare", *ASNP*, 4, 423–460.
Cunningham, M.P. (ed.) 1966. *Aurelii Prudentii Clementis carmina*, Turnhout.
Elsner, J. 2014. "Lithic poetics: Posidippus and his stones", *Ramus*, 43, 152–172.
Fabbrini, D. 2007. *Il migliore dei mondi possibili. Gli epigrammi ecfrastici di Marziale per amici e protettori*, Firenze.
Fernandelli, M. 2012. *Catullo e la rinascita dell'epos. Dal carme 64 all'Eneide*.
Filosini, S. (ed.) 2014. *Sidonio Apollinare. Epitalamio per Ruricio e Iberia*, Turnhout.
Fontaine, J. 1975. "Le mélange des genres dans la poésie de Prudence", in M. Bellis (ed.), *Forma futuri. Studi in onore del cardinale Michele Pellegrino*, Torino, 755–777.

---

[66] On Sidonius' life and literary career in the years close to his election as a bishop (cf. *supra*, n. 36) see Loyen 1960, xxi–xxiii and Harries 1994, 169–186.

Gasti, F. 2006. "Ruricio poeta. Analisi e commento di *epist.* II 19", in L. Cristante (ed.), *Incontri triestini di filologia classica V - 2005–2006*, Trieste, 155–170.
Gnilka, C. 1963. *Studien zur Psychomachie des Prudentius*, Wiesbaden.
Gosserez, L. 2001. *Poésie de lumière. Une lecture de Prudence*, Leuven.
Gosserez, L. 2002. "Le combat de *Sobrietas* contre *Luxuria*, miroir de la *Psychomachie* (*Psych.*, 310 à 453)", *VL*, 167, 66–79.
Gualandri, I. 1979. *Furtiva lectio. Studi su Sidonio Apollinare*, Milano.
Gualandri, I. 1994. "Aspetti dell'*ekphrasis* in età tardo-antica", in *Testo e immagine nell'Alto Medioevo. Settimane di studio del Centro Italiano di Studi sull'Alto Medioevo. Spoleto. XLI. 15–21 aprile 1993*, Spoleto, 301–341.
Hagendahl, H. 1952. *La correspondance de Ruricius*, Göteborg.
Harries, J. 1994. *Sidonius Apollinaris and the Fall of Rome. AD 407–485*, Oxford.
Hecquet-Noti, N. 2013. "Le temple de Dieu ou la nature symbolisée: la dédicace de la cathédrale de Lyon par Sidoine Apollinaire (*Epist.* 2,10)", in F. Garambois/D. Vallat (eds.), *Le lierre et la statue. La nature et son espace littéraire dans l'épigramme gréco-latine tardive*, Saint-Étienne, 217–231.
Herbert de la Portbarré-Viard, G. 2014. "Les descriptions et évocations d'édifices religieux chétiens dans l'œuvre de Sidoine Apollinaire", in R. Poignault/A. Stoehr-Monjou (eds.), *Présence de Sidoine Apollinaire*, Clermont-Ferrand, 379–406.
Hernández Lobato, J. 2012. *Vel Apolline muto. Estética y poética de la Antigüedad tardía*, Bern.
Lévy, C. 2006. "La notion de *color* dans la rhétorique latine. Cicéron, Sénèque le Rhéteur, Quintilien", in A. Rouveret/S. Dubel/V. Naas (eds.), *Couleurs et matières dans l'Antiquité: textes, techniques et pratiques*, Paris, 185–199.
Loyen, A. 1943. *Sidoine Apollinaire et l'esprit précieux en Gaule aux derniers jours de l'empire*, Paris.
Loyen, A. (ed.) 1960. *Sidoine Apollinaire. Tome I. Poèmes*, Paris.
Loyen, A. (ed.) 1970. *Sidoine Apollinaire. Tome II. Correspondance. Livres I–V*, Paris.
Ludwig, W. 1977. "Die christliche Dichtung des Prudentius und die Transformation der klassischen Gattungen", in M. Fuhrmann (ed.), *Christianisme et formes littéraires de l'antiquité tardive en Occident*, Genève.
Lühken, M. 2002. *Christianorum Maro et Flaccus. Zur Vergil- und Horazrezeption des Prudentius*, Göttingen.
Lütjohann, C. (ed.) 1887. *Gai Sollii Apollinaris Sidonii epistulae et carmina* (*Monumenta Germaniae Historica. Auctorum antiquissimorum tomus VIII*), Berlin.
Magazzù, C. 1975. "L'utilizzazione allegorica di Virgilio nella *Psychomachia* di Prudenzio", *BStudLat*, 5, 13–23.
Mahoney, A. 1934. *Vergil in the works of Prudentius* (diss.), Washington (DC).
Mastrangelo, M. 2008. *The Roman self in Late Antiquity. Prudentius and the poetics of the soul*, Baltimore (MD).
Mathisen, R. 1999. *Ruricius of Limoges and friends. A collection of letters from Visigothic Gaul. Letters of Ruricius of Limoges, Caesarius of Arles, Euphrasius of Clermont, Faustus of Riez, Graecus of Marseille, Paulinus of Bordeaux, Sedatus of Nîmes, Sidonius Apollinaris, Taurentius and Victorinus of Fréjus*, Liverpool.
Morgan, L. 2010. *Musa pedestris. Metre and meaning in Roman verse*, Oxford.
Neri, M. (ed.) 2009. *Ruricio di Limoges. Lettere*, Pisa.
O'Hogan, C. 2016 *Prudentius and the landscapes of Late Antiquity*, Oxford.

Onorato, M. 2016a. "Amore e Venere nel *c*. 11 di Sidonio Apollinare: tra culto della *varietas* ed *aemulatio* staziana", *BStudLat*, 46, 79–109.

Onorato, M. 2016b. *Il castone e la gemma. Sulla tecnica poetica di Sidonio Apollinare*, Napoli.

Onorato, M. Forthcoming. "*Pinguia alabastra*: metaliterature and intertextuality in Sidonius Apollinaris' *carmen 9*", in J. Hernández Lobato/Ó. Prieto Domínguez (eds.), *Literature squared: Metaliterary reflections in Late Antiquity*, Turnhout.

Pavan, A. 2005. "Consenzio o le virtù dell'*auriga*. Una rielaborazione della gara delle quadrighe di Stat. *Theb*. VI in Sid. Ap. *carm*. 23 *ad Consentium* 304–427", *Aevum (ant)*, 227–250.

Pelttari, A. 2014. *The space that remains. Reading Latin poetry in Late Antiquity*, Ithaca (NY).

Pelttari, A. 2016. "Sidonius Apollinaris and Horace, *Ars poetica* 14–23", *Philologus*, 160, 322–336.

Petrain, D. 2005. "Gems, metapoetics, and value: Greek and Roman responses to a third-century discourse on precious stones", *TAPhA*, 135, 329–357.

Roberts, M. 1989. *The jeweled style. Poetry and poetics in Late Antiquity*, Ithaca (NY).

Rosati, G. 2017. "*Et latet et lucet*: Ovidian intertextuality and the aesthetics of luxury in Martial's poetry", *Arethusa*, 50, 117–142.

Santelia, S. 1998. "Le dichiarazioni del poeta: il carme IX di Sidonio Apollinare", *InvLuc*, 20, 229–224.

Santelia, S. 1999. "Sidonio Apollinare e gli dèi pagani (a proposito di *Carm*. 9, 168–180)", *InvLuc*, 21, 341–355.

Santelia, S. 2007. "Sidonio Apollinare autore di una epigrafe per l'*ecclesia* di Lione: epist. 2, 10, 4 (= Le Blant *ICG* 54)", *VetChr*, 44, 305–321.

Santelia, S. (ed.) 2012. *Sidonio Apollinare. Carme 16. Eucharisticon ad Faustum episcopum*, Bari.

Schibille, N. 2014. *Hagia Sophia and the Byzantine aesthetic experience*, Farnham.

Shackleton Bailey, D.R. (ed.) 1993. *Martial. Epigrams*, Cambridge (MA).

Smith, M. 1976. *Prudentius' Psychomachia. A reexamination*, Princeton (NJ).

Spangenberg Yanes, E. 2013. "Il χρῶμα e la dottrina degli *status* negli scolii tardoantichi a Ermogene", *RPL*, 16, 5–36.

Spangenberg Yanes, E. 2015. "Sulla nozione di *color* e χρῶμα nella retorica della prima età imperiale", *MD*, 75, 79–104.

Stoehr-Monjou, A. 2013. "Sidonius and Horace: the art of memory", in J.A. van Waarden/G. Kelly (eds.), *New approaches to Sidonius Apollinaris*, Leuven, 133–169.

Thomson, H.J. (ed.) 1949. *Prudentius*, Cambridge (MA).

Thomas Kuhn-Treichel
Poetological Name-Dropping: Explicit References to Poets and Genres in Gregory Nazianzen's Poems

Gregory Nazianzen has bequeathed to us not only a voluminous, but also an extremely versatile poetic oeuvre.[1] Following the classification of Kristoffel Demoen, one may divide the poetic corpus into dogmatic poems, biblical poems, hymns and prayers, moralia, gnomologies, laments, autobiographical poems, verse epistles and epigrams.[2] The poems range from a single distich to almost two thousand verses, comprising hexameters, elegiac couplets, iambic trimeters and occasionally even some lyric meters, while there is only partial overlap between a poem's content and its metrical form.[3] This conspicuous variety of both form and content may be explained from different perspectives: It may be a consequence of the fact that Gregory is one of the first Christians to write extended Greek poetry in the classical tradition,[4] but it can be also seen as reflecting the late antique aesthetics of *poikilia*. Julian's edict, though effective only from 362 to 364, may have provided an additional stimulus for experimentation with classical forms.[5] However the puzzling complexity of Gregory's poetry is to be explained, it prompts the question as to what extent Gregory had a sense for distinct poetic genres at all. Scholars have been struggling with this question for many years. By way of example, I cite two contrasting assessments dating from the mid-

---

[1] I would like to thank the participants of the Heidelberg workshop and most of all Fotini Hadjittofi and Anna Lefteratou for their valuable comments. Additional thanks to Christos Simelidis, with whom I discussed an earlier version of this paper, and to Alex Poulos, who improved both the language and content of the final version.
[2] Demoen 1996, 61–63. His division is much more detailed and does more justice to the poems than that of the Maurists in the *PG* (*carmina dogmatica, moralia, de se ipso*, and *quae spectant ad alios*). Cf. also the comparison of classifications in Prudhomme 2006, 59–70.
[3] The most exhaustive contribution on the issue is Prudhomme 2006, 71–83 (with tables on p. 77). In some cases there are clear tendencies (e.g., dogmatic poems are mostly written in hexameters), in others (e.g., hymns and prayers) the metrical form seems to be chosen more or less arbitrarily; cf. also the remarks by Dihle 1994, 605, Kuhn 2014, 112, and McDonald in this volume.
[4] Whether the poems of the *Codex Visionum* were written before or after Gregory is not quite clear, but scholars tend to date them after Gregory (for an extensive discussion, see Kalish 2009; cf. also Agosti 2012, 372). For an overview of earlier poetry see also the Introduction to this volume.
[5] The exact influence of the edict is debated; modern scholars tend to relativize its impact; cf. Whitby/Roberts 2018, 226 and the Introduction to this volume.

https://doi.org/10.1515/9783110696219-005

twentieth century. In a paper published in 1953, Rudolf Keydell (1953, 142) draws the conclusion:

> Ueberhaupt hatte er für den Kunststil der einzelnen Gattungen kein Empfinden ... das hellenische Gefühl für die Schönheit und die Besonderheit der Form hatte er nicht.

A rather different view on Gregory was expressed by Bernhard Wyss in an article published four years earlier; describing Gregory's relation to Homeric epic on the one hand and Attic tragedy on the other hand, Wyss (1949, 187) states:

> Gregor übernimmt auch den besondern Wortschatz, der jeder dieser Gattungen eigentümlich ist, ihren Dialekt, ihre Stilisierung: Elemente also der künstlerischen Ausdrucksweise, die den Leser sofort in die Atmosphäre sei es der homerischen Welt, sei es des klassischen Athens versetzen.

Subsequent scholarship tends to side with Wyss rather than with Keydell, but Gregory's handling of genres remains an elusive issue.[6] Broadly speaking, there are two major ways to approach the problem: One way is to study how far Gregory follows the conventions of a certain genre when choosing a certain metrical form (e.g., the conventions of didactic epic in some of the hexameter poems, or the conventions of elegy in a poem in elegiac couplets). Another possibility is to investigate to what extent Gregory imitates poets belonging to the respective generic tradition (e.g., Hesiod for didactic, or Theognis for elegy). Both approaches are concerned with how Gregory *implicitly* positions himself in relation to traditional genres and both are undeniably important. There are, however, several poems in which Gregory refers to certain classical genres or canonical poets *explicitly*, a fact that makes him stand out in Greek Christian poetry of the fourth and fifth centuries.[7] Here I consider

---

[6] To give just a few examples: Sykes 1970, 39 points out that with his *Poemata Arcana* Gregory quite clearly places himself in the tradition of didactic, concluding that "in drawing vocabulary, forms, and direct reminiscences from his predecessors ... Gregory is doing no more than showing that he understood the conventions of his chosen form" (as to didactic features in the *Arcana*, see also Meinel 2009, esp. 90f.). Dihle 1994, 605 speaks of the "natural ease with which he uses the linguistic and metrical forms of the individual poetic genres." Al. Cameron 2004, 333–337 argues that besides poems that "look familiar ... in form and style: hymns and didactic poems in hexameters, epigrams and occasional poems in elegiacs, and a few invectives in iambics", even in peculiar cases as didactic poems in trimeters Gregory stands in a well-established tradition. Cf. also Kuhn 2014, 111f.

[7] Eudocia comes closest, who mentions Homer in the *Apologia* to the *HC* (*Vat. suppl. gr.* 388). Nonnus mentions Homer, too, but only in *Dion.*, e.g. 25.265; Hopkinson 1994 and Accorinti in this volume. In Latin Christian poetry, explicit references to classical authors and genres are more common: Iuvenc., *praef.* 9f.; *C. Pr. praef.* 3f.; Sedul., *CP* 1.17–22; Alc. Avit., *SHG* 3.336f.

what these explicit references reveal about Gregory's attitude towards genres, discussing first passages from two poems in dactylic meters (elegiacs and hexameters), then passages from an iambic poem.

Dactylic meters: From Homer to pederastic elegiacs

Three poems are most important in this respect because they contain clusters or catalogues of explicit references. The first one I examine is the elegiac poem Εἰς τὴν ἐν ταῖς νηστείαις σιωπήν A (*carm.* II.1.34A). The poem, which deals with the silence Gregory imposed on himself in the Lent of 382, contains a self-reflexive middle part in which the poet sets out his literary program – and refers to several classical texts and genres (vv. 69–76):[8]

> ὄργανόν εἰμι Θεοῖο καὶ εὐκρέκτοις μελέεσσιν
> ὕμνον ἄνακτι φέρω, τῷ πᾶν ὑποτρομέει.   70
> μέλπω δ' οὐ Τροίην, οὐκ εὔπλοον οἷά τις Ἀργώ,
> οὐδὲ συὸς κεφαλῆν, οὐ πολὺν Ἡρακλέα,
> οὐ γῆς εὐρέα κύκλα ὅπως πελάγεσσιν ἄρηρεν,
> οὐκ αὐγὰς λιθάκων, οὐ δρόμον οὐρανίων·
> οὐδὲ πόθων μέλπω μανίην καὶ κάλλος ἐφήβων,   75
> οἷσι λύρη μαλακὸν κρούετ' ἀπὸ προτέρων.

> I am an instrument of God, and with fair-sounding songs I bring a hymn to the Lord before whom everything trembles. But I do not sing of Troy, not, like someone did, of the fair-sailing Argo, nor of the boar's head, nor of mighty Heracles, nor how the earth's wide circles are fit to the seas, nor of the gleams of stones, nor of the course of heavenly bodies; nor do I sing of the madness of passions and the beauty of young men, for whom the lyre was gently plucked by the poets of old. (*carm.* II.1.34A.69–74)

Lines 71–76 constitute a veritable catalogue of genres, arranged, as it seems, in a sort of hierarchy: The first couplet (vv. 71–72) alludes to mythological poetry or, more specifically, mythological epic. The references to Troy and the Argo are obviously intended as allusions to the two most prominent representatives of this

---

8 The poem is quoted from Kuhn 2014, 22–25, where I also provide a German translation and further notes (the text is based on the critical edition of Piottante 1999). All translations given here are my own (as to this poem, cf. White 1996, 169–171).

genre, Homer and Apollonius of Rhodes.[9] Homer might also be alluded to by the "boar's head", which points to the Meleager myth,[10] while the mention of "great Heracles" can be seen as a reference to lost Heracles epics.[11] The next couplet (vv. 73–74) is devoted to didactic epic, exemplified by geography, mineralogy and astronomy.[12] The third couplet (v. 75f.) is slightly more difficult to assign to a specific genre. It covers erotic subjects, and the reference to the lyre at first sight suggests lyric (or melic) poetry; however, one can also think of epigrams and other dactylic poems with pederastic contents, and given that lyric was not a very common genre in Gregory's time and that Gregory himself alluded to pederastic elegiacs and hexameters in other poems (and was very well acquainted with the epigrammatic tradition), this second interpretation seems more plausible.[13]

But what kind of attitude does the text display towards these classical genres? First of all, the list shows that Gregory is highly aware of his poetic predecessors. Moreover, the fact that he repeatedly presents himself as a musical instrument (ὄργανόν εἰμι; cf. v. 91: γλῶσσαν ἔχω κιθάρην)[14] and a singer (ὕμνον ... φέρω, μέλπω) makes it clear that he uses the same medium of communication as the pagan poets.[15] Gregory's poetry does not claim to be a *creatio ex nihilo*, but rather to surpass classical genres using their own means while treating the Christian contents listed in the following lines (vv. 77–91):

---

9 Of course, these subjects were also dealt with by other poets, but they are most prominently linked to these two epicists; cf. Kuhn 2014, 22 n. 62.
10 Gregory uses a similar juncture in *carm.* I.2.15.84 (συὸς κεφαλῇ), and since that verse is preceded by a quotation of *Il.* 9.529, one can assume that in both cases Gregory thinks of the Homeric version of the Meleager myth (*Il.* 9.528–599); cf. Kuhn 2014, 22 n. 62.
11 E.g. those of Peisander and Panyassis, both of whom were adopted into the Alexandrian canon of epic poets and therefore held in esteem throughout antiquity, although their works soon ceased to be widely read.
12 Topics treated for example in Dionysius Periegeta, the anonymous *Lithica* and in Aratus' *Phaenomena*; cf. Hollis 2002, 47 n. 54. By contrast Agosti 1994, 34f. associates v. 73 with cosmogonies and v. 74a with the Orphic *Lithica*; cf. Kuhn 2014, 22 n. 63.
13 Cf. Simelidis 2009, 41. 118f., who notes allusions to pederastic Theognidean elegiacs (1253f., 1335f., and 1375f.) and to Theocritus' pederastic *Id.* 12, both of which can be seen as cases of *Kontrastimitation*. In lyric, a possible reference would be the Anacreontics.
14 With these metaphors of embodied music (cf. the polysemous term μέλος), Gregory follows patristic allegory but at the same time underlines his role as an inspired poet, cf. Kuhn 2014, 52–55; one may also compare Gregory's older contemporary Ephraim the Syrian, who is known as "the harp of the spirit" in the Syriac tradition, (taken up in Greek by Thdrt., *ep. S* 146: ἡ τοῦ Πνεύματος λύρα); cf. Horn 2004, 36.
15 This does not, of course, preclude other associations; especially κιθάρα may recall David, with whom Gregory compares himself explicitly in *ep.* 101.73 (cf. Simelidis 2009, 28). Cf. also Faulkner in this volume p. 271.

μέλπω δ' ὑψιμέδοντα Θεὸν μέγαν, ἠδὲ φαεινῆς
 εἰς ἓν ἀγειρομένης λάμψιν ἐμῆς Τριάδος,
ἀγγελικῶν τε χορῶν μεγάλους ἐριηχέας ὕμνους
 πλησίον ἑσταότων, ἐξ ὁπὸς ἀντιθέτου,   80
κόσμου θ' ἁρμονίην καὶ κρείσσονα τῆς παρεούσης,
 ἥν δοκέω πάντων εἰς ἓν ἐπειγομένων,
καὶ Χριστοῦ παθέων κλέος ἄφθιτον, οἷς μ' ἐθέωσεν,
 ἀνδρομέην μορφὴν οὐρανίῃ κεράσας.
μέλπω μίξιν ἐμήν. οὐ γὰρ φατὸν ἔργον ἐτύχθην,   85
 ἔργον, ὅπως πλέχθην θνητὸς ἐπουρανίοις.
μέλπω δ' ἀνθρώποισι Θεοῦ νόμον, ὅσσα τε κόσμου
 ἐρύματα καὶ βουλὰς καὶ τέλος ἀμφοτέρων·
ὄφρα τὰ μὲν κεύθῃς σῇσι φρεσί, τῶν δ' ἀποτῆλε
 φεύγῃς, καὶ τρομέῃς ἦμαρ ἐπερχόμενον.   90
τόσσων γλῶσσαν ἔχω κιθάρην ...

I sing of the great God ruling on high, and of the light of my shining Trinity united into one, and of the great, clear-voiced hymns of the angelic choirs standing close by with antiphonal voices, and of a cosmic harmony stronger than the present one,[16] which I await when all things come together, and of the imperishable fame of Christ's sufferings, by which he has deified me, blending the human form with the heavenly. I sing of my mixture. For I have been made an ineffable creature, such a creature that I, being mortal, was intertwined with heavenly beings. I sing to the men of God's law, and of all the works and plans of the world and the outcome of both, so that you may keep these things in your mind but flee far away from the other ones and tremble before the coming day. (*carm.* II.1.34A.77–91)

At least to a certain degree, the contents listed here can be interpreted as counterparts to the subjects of the classical genres.[17] The opposition between the old forms and mediums and the new themes is crafted around a series of *antitheseis* presenting Gregory's poetry as a sort of *Kontrastimitation* of classical genres: The "imperishable fame" (v. 83: κλέος ἄφθιτον) that was supposed to be conferred upon heroes in mythological epic[18] is replaced by the fame of Christ that can much more justly be called everlasting. Instead of the physical order treated in didactic, Gregory describes a cosmological harmony far surpassing natural phenomena (v. 81). And finally, instead of the corporeal beauty and sexual desire of erotic poetry, he sings of a heavenly splendor (v. 77–80) and, ultimately, of his

---

16 Or: "and of the world's harmony and a harmony that is stronger than the present one", cf. Kuhn 2014, 23 n. 66.
17 Cf. Simelidis 2009, 34, who also comments on Gregory's "attempt to find 'common' elements between the pagan past and the Christian present." For a different reading of the passage see Demoen 1993, 241f., who notes that "[a]lthough mythology, natural phenomena, and earthly love are not the main subjects in Gregory's poetry, they are not absent in it either."
18 The juncture is attested in *Il.* 9.413; cf. Simelidis 37 with n. 50 (with literature).

own μίξις (v. 85). The *antitheseis* seem to suggest that, although drawing on the classical tradition, Gregory's poetry can claim to be something fundamentally new and different. Taking up Harold Bloom's famous concept of 'anxiety of influence', one might say that Gregory is 'anxious' to downplay the influence of those authors who are in some respect obviously his models.[19] One last remark has to be made about the term μίξις (v. 85), which is also important for understanding the poem as a whole: It can denote sexual intercourse but is here applied to the union with God, while, at the same time, alluding to the mix of genres and poetic traditions dealt with by Gregory.[20]

The parallels between the catalogue of genres and the positive program are not entirely cogent but add up to the impression that Gregory aims to surpass all classical genres at the same time – or at least a certain group of genres: If I am right to associate vv. 75f. with pederastic elegiacs and hexameters, all genres referred to in the catalogue are associated with dactylic meters, one of which, elegiac distichs, Gregory has used for this poem. Here it appears that Gregory's poems are intended to compete in particular with those classical genres with which they are more or less connected by meter. In fact, such a tendency can be observed in another poem, a hexametric verse epistle addressed to the Cappadocian governor Nemesios, to whom Gregory also sent several letters in prose (*carmen* II.2.7).[21] Nemesios was an educated pagan, and the poem can be summarized as an invitation to become a Christian. Already the beginning is interesting regarding the question of genre (vv. 7–22).[22]

> ἄλλοι μὲν μολπῇσιν, ἐριγδούποισί τ' ἀοιδαῖς,
> καὶ ῥήτρην πυρόεσσαν ἀπὸ στομάτων προχέοντες
> τὴν σήν, ᾗ ῥα σὺ πάντας ἀπόπροθε πολλὸν ἔθηκας,
> σὸν κλέος ὑμνείοιεν ... 10
> αὐτὰρ ἐγώ (δὴ γάρ με Θεὸς μέγας ἴδριν ἔθηκεν 18

---

19 Cf. Bloom 1973. Gregory's case is complicated by the religious conflict underlying the process of poetic self-formation, but nevertheless Bloom's terms can help to describe his attitude towards his predecessors.
20 Cf. *LSJ* s.v. μίξις II. Simelidis 2009, 36, notes that πλέχθην (v. 86) evokes sexual associations, too: πλέκω itself is not attested in this sense, but συμπλέκομαι is applied to sexual intercourse several times, cf. *LSJ* s.v. II.2. Interestingly, πλέκω is also used in poetological metaphors (e.g., π. ὕμνον, cf. *LSJ* s.v. πλέκω II.2).
21 Greg. Naz., *ep.* 198–201, cf. McGuckin 2001, 395 n. 143; cf. the summary of the poem in Crimi/Costa 1999, 35. It remains disputed whether this Nemesios can be identified with the Christian philosopher and bishop Nemesios of Emesa; cf. Brisson 2000.
22 The poem is quoted from *PG* 37.1551f., 1569f. An annotated Italian translation can be found in Crimi/Costa 1999, 275f., 285f. Note that v. 22a = *AP* 8.15.3a.

οὐρανίων, χθονίων τε, νόος δ' ἐπὶ πάντα φορεῖται,
βένθε' ἀνιχνεύων μεγάλου σὺν Πνεύματος αἴγλῃ)   20
φθέγξομαι, ἄσσ' ἐπέοικε θυηπόλον ἄνδρ' ἀγορεύειν,
    ἄγγελον ἀτρεκίης ἐριηχέα ...

Let others with songs and loud-sounding chants and pouring forth from their mouths your ardent eloquence, by which you outrank everybody by far, praise your fame ... But I (for the great God made me knowledgeable in heavenly and earthly things, and my mind is taken along everywhere, investigating the depths with the shining of the great spirit), I will say whatever befits a priest to speak, a clear-voiced messenger of truth ... (*carm.* II.2.7.7–22)

In these lines, Gregory explicitly contrasts his poem to the eulogies that others might have composed for Nemesios and which would most probably have been written in hexameters. Even more important, however, is a passage in the second half of the poem where Gregory directly addresses the pagan poets (vv. 239–252):

λήξατ', ἀοιδοπόλοι, ναὶ λήξατε, μαινόμενοί τε
δαίμονες, ἐμπνείοντες ἀθεσμοτάτοισιν ἀοιδαῖς.   240
Ὀρφεὺς θῆρας ἄγοι, Πέρσῃ δ' Ἀσκραῖος ἀείδοι
Ἡσίοδος, Τροίην δὲ καὶ ἄλγεα κλεινὸς Ὅμηρος.
Μουσαῖός τε Λίνος τε θεῶν ἄπο μέτρα φέροιεν,
οἵ ῥα παλαιοτάτῃσιν ἐπικλέες εἰσὶν ἀοιδαῖς.
Ἑρμῆς ὁ τρισάριστος ἐμοῖς ἐπέεσσιν ἀρήγοι,   245
οὐδ' ἐθέλων, σταυρὸν δὲ σέβοι μέτροισι Σίβυλλα,
τῆς μεγάλης θεότητος ἐλαυνόμενοι βελέεσσιν·
οὐδὲν ἐπιστρέφομαι, καὶ εἴ τινες ἆσσον ἴκοιντο,
οὐ Θεόθεν, Βίβλων δὲ παρακλέψαντες ἐμεῖο.
οἱ μὲν γὰρ καὶ πάμπαν ἀλαμπέες, οἱ δ' ὀλίγον τι   250
ἀστεροπὴν πάλλουσαν ἐσέδρακον, ὦκα δ' ἄμερθεν.
τοὔνεκεν εἴξατ' ἔμοιγε, καὶ ὀψέ περ εὖ φρονέοντες.

Stop, you poets, yes stop, and you raging demons breathing most unlawful songs.[23] Let Orpheus lead animals, let Hesiod the Ascraean sing to Perses, and the renowned Homer of Troy and pains. Let Musaeus and Linus, who are famous for the oldest songs, take their

---

23 The verse is oddly constructed: One would expect either the dative of a person or the accusative of an abstract (cf. *DGE* and Lampe s.v. ἐμπνέω). In other comparable contexts, Gregory connects the verb with an accusative (*ep.* 114.4: ἐμπνεῖν ἡδύ τι; *Or.* 27.9: ἐμπνεῖς τὴν παίδευσιν; *Or.* 44.10: ἐμπνέουσι μέλος). But since Gregory is not always fully precise with vocabulary and syntax, one may assume a similar sense here (cf. Costa's translation in Crimi/Costa 1999, 285: "che ispirate canti empissimi"). The lines make it clear that the pagan idea of poetic inspiration (including divine μανία) has become untenable for a Christian poet like Gregory (a development described in detail by Shorrock 2011, 13–48).

verses from the gods.²⁴ Let Hermes the thrice-best²⁵ help my songs, even if he does not want, let the Sibyl venerate the cross with her verses, both stricken by the darts of the great godhead. I do not mind even if some should come near, not by divine inspiration, but stealing from my Bible. For some were utterly unilluminated, others have for a short time seen a quivering lightning but were soon bereft of it. Therefore yield to me, thinking rightly albeit late. (*carm.* II.2.7.239–253)

The list curiously combines existing works and collections such as Homer's *Iliad*, Hesiod's *Works and Days* and the *Sibylline Oracles* with famous mythical singers such as Orpheus, Musaeus and Linus, who, to be sure, were believed to be the authors of existing poems, too.²⁶ The most puzzling case, though, is that of Hermes: One could think of the very few non-hexametric hymns and prayers inlaid in the prose treatises of the *Corpus Hermeticum*, which indeed express monotheistic ideas.²⁷ That being said, there seems to have been also a larger collection of Hermetic hymns, including hexameter poems, so that we might not know with certainty what kind of poems Gregory had in mind here and whether he really thinks of existing Greek hymns or rather of their alleged Egyptian models, or both.²⁸ However that may be, it is conspicuous that all names that can be unambiguously matched with existing poems are connected with hexameters. If one adds the eulogies mentioned in the beginning and a later reference to Empedocles, one can hardly escape the impression that with his hexameter poem Gregory aims to confront not just pagan poetry in general, but at least to a certain degree specifically pagan poetry in hexameters.²⁹

---

24 Gregory probably alludes to mythical traditions according to which both Musaeus and Linus were sons of gods; cf. Crimi/Costa 1999, 285 n. 37.
25 Gregory's τρισάριστος seems to be an attempt to adjust the common form Ἑρμῆς τρισμέγιστος to dactyls.
26 As to Orpheus and Musaeus, the respective Suda entries provide lists of the works attributed to each of them; Linos was credited with of a cosmological poem surviving in fragments; for details see West 1983.
27 Most prominently, *CH* 1.31 and *CH* 13.17–20, cf. van den Broek 2000, 82–84. Other hymns and prayers are known in Coptic from "On the Ogdoad and Ennead" (*Nag Hammadi Codices* VI 6); cf. Holzhausen 1997, esp. 204.
28 One hexametric poem ascribed to Hermes is cited in Stobaeus (= *CH* fr. 29). The tradition of an Egyptian book of hymns ascribed to Hermes (the *interpretatio Graeca* of Thot) is also attested in Clem. Al., *Strom.* 6.4.35.3 on the singer opening the Egyptian procession: τοῦτόν φασι δύο βίβλους ἀνειληφέναι δεῖν ἐκ τῶν Ἑρμοῦ, ὧν θάτερον μὲν ὕμνους περιέχει θεῶν ("They say that he must have learned two of the books of Hermes, one of which contains hymns of the gods").
29 Empedocles is mentioned at v. 281f.: Ἐμπεδόκλεις, σὲ μὲν αὐτίκ' ἐτώσια φυσιόωντα, | καὶ βροτὸν Αἰτναίοιο πυρὸς κρητῆρες ἔδειξαν ("Empedocles, the craters of Etna's fire demonstrated at once that you were puffed up in vain [notice the pun between φυσιόωντα vs. φυσιολογοῦντα]

While this strategy can be compared to the poem discussed above, the attitude towards poets displayed here is partly different. The poets of old mentioned in vv. 240–244 are rejected with similar harshness; they are "utterly unilluminated" (v. 250: πάμπαν ἀλαμπέες).[30] According to Gregory, however, there is also a kind of pagan poetry that partly supports Christian views (vv. 245–251). The idea of pagan writings containing elements of truth which are in fact adopted from the Bible was widespread in early Christianity,[31] and even 'Hermes' and the 'Sibyl' were mentioned in this context before Gregory.[32] Nevertheless, it is remarkable to find this apologetic *topos* combined with a discussion of poets. In this context, it supports not only an argument to believe Christian authors more than pagan ones, but also a justification for writing Christian poetry: As the examples show, poetry in itself is capable of expressing the truth; it is only the poets who had no or limited access to it. What is needed, therefore, is a poet who takes the beginnings of 'enlightened' poetry represented by 'Hermes' and 'the Sibyl' a step further – i.e., someone like Gregory, who stands in the poetic tradition but to whom the full truth has been revealed.

Iambs: Between epic and tragedy

Having examined passages from two dactylic poems, it would be interesting to cross-check the reception of meter and genre in Gregory by looking at another major metric form: iambs, the medium of dramatic poetry. An important case study for this paper is the iambic poem on virtue entitled Περὶ ἀρετῆς Βʹ (*carm.*

---

and a mortal"). It is interesting to note that Gregory calls his own text ἔπη (v. 245), in accordance with the technical sense of the word (*LSJ* s.v. IV). In fact, Gregory uses ἔπος mostly in dactylic poems, but contrast *carm.* I.2.10.277–279 (τραγῳδίας ἔπη); cf. below n. 37 on ἴαμβος, τραγῳδία and κωμῳδία.

30 Probably alluding to Call., *Hymn* 1 (*Iov.*) 60: δηναιοὶ δ' οὐ πάμπαν ἀληθέες ἦσαν ἀοιδοί ("The ancient bards were not entirely truthful") – suggested to me by A. Poulos.
31 For a detailed study see Droge 1989; for similar ideas in Gregory's writings see Demoen 1996, 209 n. 1. Interestingly, by accusing authors such as 'Hermes' and 'the Sibyl' of having stolen elements from the Bible, Gregory comes close to what really happened, for both collections incorporate ideas developed within Judaism and Christianity.
32 E.g., Clem. Al., *Strom.* 6.4.35 (stating that pagans have adopted their best doctrines 'from us', mentioning Hermes) and 6.5.43 (mentioning the Sibyl); cf. Simelidis 2009, 37 n. 41. Christian attitudes towards Hermeticism varied, but the strategy of appropriation was adopted by several authors; cf. Löw 2002 and Herrero de Jáuregui 2010, esp. 243–246. On Gregory's reception of the *Or. Sib.* cf. Sykes 1970, 38f. (similarly Moreschini/Sykes 1997, 58) and Simelidis 2009, 227.

II.1.10), which stands out from the passages discussed so far as it refers to pagan poets in a more affirmative way. The poem is directed to a promising young man (v. 3: νέος),[33] to whom Gregory shows that the Christian way of life and doctrine is superior to pagan models and authorities. Consequently, pagan poets, philosophers, and other notables are mentioned many times.[34] Two passages are most interesting for this article. In the first one, Gregory relates an anecdote about Plato and Aristippus that can be found in similar forms in several prose authors and collections since the second century CE and which is here employed to exemplify Aristippus' mixture of laudable παρρησία and blameworthy τρυφή (v. 319f.).[35] The two philosophers are offered a woman's dress (in other sources, it is described as a purple robe); Plato declines, citing a verse from Euripides' *Bacchae* (*Bacch.* 836), while Aristippus accepts with another quotation from the same play (317f.). Due to the identical meter, Gregory can insert the verses without problems, and he even goes so far as to mention Euripides as their author (v. 327–334):[36]

> ... Πλάτων μὲν οὐ προσήκατο,
> ἴαμβον εἰπὼν καίριον ἐξ Εὐριπίδου·
> "οὐκ ἂν δυναίμην θῆλυν ἐνδῦναι στολήν."
> ὁ δ', ὡς τὸ δώρημ' ἦλθεν εἰς αὐτοῦ χέρας,   330
> φέροντος ἀνδρός, καὶ προθύμως λαμβάνει,
> καὶ τὴν ἰάμβου κομψότητ' ἰαμβίῳ
> βάλλει, τόδ' εἰπών· "καὶ γὰρ ἐν βακχεύμασιν
> οὖσ' ἥ γε σώφρων, οὐ διαφθαρήσεται."

---

[33] Whether the young man is a real person or a literary fiction is an open question cf. Crimi/Kertsch 1995, 30f.

[34] Already in vv. 25–58, there is catalogue of men considered to be best in their area (including Demosthenes, Homer, and Plato), but whose achievements cannot be compared to life with God; cf. Demoen 1993, 248; 1996, 178–181.

[35] Cf. Sext. Emp., *Pyr.* 3.204; Diog. Laert. 2.78; Stob. 5.38; *Gnom. Vat.* 41; *Suda* α 3909. There seems to be a special connection between Gregory and Sextus Empiricus, who share the verb προσήκατο, but Gregory differs from all other versions in that he has Archelaus, not Dionysius, offer the dress; cf. Crimi/Kertsch 1995, 259.

[36] The poem is quoted from Crimi/Kertsch 1995, where an Italian translation and a commentary are also provided. In the *Bacchae*, Plato's line is spoken by Pentheus, Aristippus' response by Tiresias. However, inferring that Gregory favors Pentheus instead of Tiresias because he sides with Plato rather than with Aristippus would probably be to read too much into the passage: Gregory's aim is to discredit Aristippus (Plato was criticized before); the original context of the lines is not relevant for this aim (although the *Bacchae* was discussed at some length by earlier Christian authors like Origen and Clement of Alexandria; cf. Friesen 2015).

... Plato did not accept, quoting a fitting iamb from Euripides: "I could not put on a female dress." But he [sc. Aristippus], when the gift came into his hands, brought by a man, took it readily and attacked the iamb's elegance with an iambic verse, saying the following: "For even in Bacchic revelries she who is prudent will not be corrupted." (*carm.* II.1.10.327–334)

The references to tragedy foreground a genre that is strikingly absent in the dactylic passages studied above. Repeating ἴαμβος no less than three times (v. 328, and twice at 332), Gregory draws attention to the metrical kinship between his poem and tragedy and to the opportunity for quotations and allusions provided by this kinship. In a certain sense, the passage seems to imply, Gregory's iambic poetry can inherit the tragic tradition (though in this case mediated through an anecdote), and indeed there are several other passages in this and further iambic poems where Gregory explicitly cites iambic verses indicating their affinity with τραγῳδία or the like.[37] What is conspicuous, however, is that in nearly all these cases Gregory uses the lines as *gnomae*; to be sure, Gregory is deeply indebted to tragedy in some of his poems (e.g., in his famous poem *On His Own Life*, *carm.* II.1.11: 249–264),[38] but when it comes to explicit references, he receives tragedy in a very reduced form, and one could say that by this reception he transforms tragedy to a collection of more or less moralizing sayings – sayings of an incisiveness that is not even compromized by their pagan origin.

---

[37] *carm.* I.2.10.277–279: ... τραγῳδίας ἔπη, | ὧν ἕν τι καὶ τόδ' εὐστόχως εἰρημένον· | ὦ ξένε, τυράννοις ἐκ ποδῶν μεθίστασο [Eur., *Phoen.* 40] ("... the tragic verses, one of which, aptly put, runs: 'stranger, make way for kings'"); *carm.* I.2.10.585–588: ἤκουσα τοῦτο τῆς σοφῆς τραγῳδίας· | γαστρὸς δὲ πειρῶ πᾶσαν ἡνίαν κρατεῖν· | μόνη γὰρ ὧν πέπονθεν οὐκ ἔχει χάριν. | ἐν πλησμονῇ δὲ Κύπρις, ἐν πεινῶσι δ' οὔ ("I heard the following from wise tragedy: I attempt to hold tight the reins of the belly; for it [belly] alone does not show gratitude for how it is treated; Cypris is found in prosperity, not among the hungry") – only v. 588 can be attributed to a tragedy as Eur., fr. 895 K.; vv. 586f. probably derive from the gnomic author Chares, cited as *Sent.* 2.2f. Jäkel; v. 586 is also transmitted as Men., *Sent.* 137 Jäkel; cf. Crimi/Kertsch 1995, 302); *carm.* II.1.11.1804f.: κάπροι δ' ὅπως θήγοντες ἀγρίαν γένυν [= Eur., *Phoen.* 1380] | (ὡς ἂν μιμήσωμαί τι τῆς τραγῳδίας) ("Just as boars whetting their wild teeth – to imitate a bit of tragedy"). The only case where the quotation is not gnomic is *carm.* II.1.12.134f.: ὦ πόλις, πόλις, [= Soph., *OT* 629] | ἵν' ἐκβοήσω καί τι καὶ τραγῳδικόν ("Oh city, city – to cry out something in tragic manner"). The terms ἴαμβος, τραγῳδία and κωμῳδία and their derivations occur in Gregory's iambic poems only; this may be partly due to the fact that τραγῳδία and κωμῳδία do not scan in dactyls, but since ἴαμβος and derivations like τραγῳδικός or κωμικός would do, one can take this as further evidence for the connection between the iambic poems and the iambic tradition.

[38] An even more impressing example would of course be the *Christus patiens*, which most scholars deemed non-Gregorian: cf. most recently Rimoli 2016; Most 2008; see also Pollmann 2017, 145–149.

Although the poem refers to tragedies and tragedians several times, other poets and genres that are not related by meter are represented as well. Homer is mentioned twice, the second time, which I will focus on here, together with the elegist Theognis (vv. 393–398):[39]

> ληρεῖ δέ μοι Θέογνις ὡς λῆρον πλατύν,
> κρημνοὺς προτιμῶν τῆς ἀπορίας καὶ βυθούς,
> κακῶς τε Κύρνῳ νομοθετῶν εἰς χρήματα.   395
> Ὅμηρε καὶ σύ, πῶς τοσοῦτον ἀστάτῳ
> πράγματι νέμεις, ὥστε φράσαι που τῶν ἐπῶν,
> ὀπηδὸν εἶναι τὴν ἀρετὴν τῶν χρημάτων;

But what a plain nonsense is Theognis talking in my eyes, preferring cliffs and depths to poverty,[40] and poorly laying down for Kyrnos laws on possessions. And you, Homer, how can you allot so much to an unstable thing that you say somewhere in your verses that virtue is a companion of possessions? (*carm.* II.1.10.393–398)

The reference to Homer is remarkable in that the lines are phrased like the introduction to a direct quotation. What follows is the attempt to give an iambic version of a hexameter (which, by the way, derives not from Homer but from Hesiod's *Works and Days* v. 313: πλούτῳ δ' ἀρετὴ καὶ κῦδος ὀπηδεῖ).[41] After several quotations from tragedy, this quasi-citation of a hexameter appears like a jeu d'esprit, a demonstration that an iambic poem may draw not only on iambic literature, but also on any other genre. If he chooses to do so, the lines seem to suggest, Gregory can deal at whim with whatever genre seems relevant, be it in an affirmative or, as here, in a dissenting manner.

One last question deserves to be raised: If in most poems Gregory deals with the poetic tradition only implicitly, why does he sometimes explicitly mention poets and genres at all? This question is all the more salient as Gregory is the only Greek Christian poet who discusses his relation to the poetic tradition in such a prominent way (some Latin Christian poets could be compared).[42] One answer would be that the explicit references reflect Gregory's personal struggle with the

---

[39] The first time he is mentioned at v. 42: κἂν τὴν Ὁμήρου μοῦσαν ἐν στέρνοις ἔχῃς ("even if you carry the Homeric Muse in your heart"); cf. n. 34 above.

[40] The allusion is probably to Thgn. 175f.; cf. Crimi/Kertsch 1995, 268f.

[41] Gregory may be confused by a similar-sounding phrase in *Hymn. Hom.* 30.12 (Gaia): ὄλβος δὲ πολὺς καὶ πλοῦτος ὀπηδεῖ ("and much fortune and wealth attend them").

[42] Cf. above n. 7. One explanation for the more explicit (and more agonistic) references to the classical tradition in Latin Christian poetry is that Latin poets are influenced by the idea of *aemulatio* developed in relation to their Greek predecessors; cf. Hose 2004, 34–37.

tradition that was so omnipresent for him because of his erudition. A second possibility is that Gregory is inspired by literary models that contain explicit reflections on other poets themselves, especially by Callimachus, who is known to have exercised much influence on Gregory. A third aspect is the social and communicative context of the poems.[43] Especially when addressing educated persons, as is the case at least in *carmen* I.2.10 and *carmen* II.2.7, Gregory might have felt it necessary to explain his objectives by relating his poems to genres and authors that were familiar to the addresses.[44] This way he not only builds a bridge for his readers but also underpins his ambitions as a poet – a poet who can face authorities like Homer, Hesiod and Euripides and coopt their tradition for the truth of Christianity.[45]

Conclusions

The results of this study are somewhat disparate. To sum up, two basic attitudes towards classical genres can be identified: On the one hand, Gregory presents his poetry as something opposed and in some sense superior to all classical genres at the same time,[46] and sometimes he almost seems eager to break up generic boundaries, e.g. by quasi-quoting a hexameter in an iambic poem. On the other hand, Gregory is aware that with each poem he inserts himself in a specific generic tradition and that a poem written in a certain meter competes with those genres in particular that are metrically related (although meter is of course not

---

43 This aspect is particularly relevant due to the fact that in modern theory genres are often understood as norms of communication (cf., e.g., Zymner 2010, 3f.), which establishes a link between generic reflections and communication, too.
44 In *carm*. II.1.34A, the addressee is not clearly specified. One line addresses the priests (91: φράζεσθ', ἱερῆες), but probably other friends and relatives were supposed to read the poem, too.
45 This also corrects Hose 2004, 33, who sees Greek Christian poetry under the spell of school poetry: "Die christliche lateinische Poesie erhebt damit für sich den Anspruch, nicht epigonal zu sein, sondern vielmehr, da neu in Bezug auf den Inhalt, qualitativ der vorangehenden paganen Dichtung überlegen gegenüberzustehen. Nirgendwo in der griechischen Poesie vermag ich einen solchen Anspruch zu erkennen." Although Hose's assessment has many merits (cf. the affirmative references in Pollmann 2017, 6 and 74), this study shows that there is (at least) one clear exception: Gregory.
46 This does not necessarily imply that Gregory intended to *replace* all classical poetry. Many of his poems cannot be fully appreciated unless the reader is acquainted with the canonical authors. Gregory's poetry can thus be seen as a supplement to pagan poets, which is superior to its models but nevertheless based on them; cf. Simelidis 2009, 78–80 with literature.

the only relevant aspect). Both attitudes can be found in both dactylic and iambic poems, although it has to be noted that the dactylic tradition is generally given more weight by Gregory as it figures in both dactylic and iambic poems, while explicit references to drama are restricted to the iambic poems. The two attitudes can be seen as a consequence of the same basic situation: Since Gregory is one of the first Christians to write Greek poems in classical forms, he is constantly struggling with this tradition (or, in Bloomian terms, with his anxiety of influence) in order to find his own place, and unsettled as he was throughout his life, he found different solutions at different times, and sometimes even at the same time.[47] Gregory's ambiguity can be seen as reflecting the overall situation of genres in Late Antiquity, when there were new, especially Christian, texts resisting generic classification, while on the other hand the traditional system of genres was still alive.[48]

Bibliography

Agosti, G. 1994. "La 'Cosmogonia' in Strasbourg", *A&R*, 39, 26–46.
Agosti, G. 2012. "Greek poetry", in S.F. Johnson (ed.), *The Oxford Handbook of Late Antiquity*, Oxford, 361–404.
Bloom, H. 1973. *The anxiety of influence. A theory of poetry*, New York.
Brisson, L. 2000. "Nemesios", *DNP*, 8, 817.
Cameron, Alan 2004. "Poetry and literary culture in Late Antiquity", in S. Swain/M. Edwards (eds.), *Approaching Late Antiquity: the transformation from Early to Late Empire*, Oxford, 327–354.
Crimi, C./Costa, I. (eds.) 1999. *Gregorio Nazianzeno. Poesie, 2*, Roma.
Crimi, C./Kertsch, M. (eds.) 1995. *Gregorio Nazianzeno. Sulla virtù*, Pisa.
Demoen, K. 1993. "The attitude towards Greek poetry in the verse of Gregory Nazianzen", in J. den Boeft/A. Hilhorst (eds.), *Early Christian poetry. A collection of essays*, Leiden, 235–252.
Demoen, K. 1996. *Pagan and biblical exempla in Gregory Nazianzen. A study in rhetoric and hermeneutics*, Turnhout.
Dihle, A. 1994. *Greek and Roman literature of the Roman Empire: from Augustus to Justinian*, London. Trans. M. Malzahn.
Droge, A.J. 1989. *Homer or Moses? Early Christian interpretations of the history of culture*, Tübingen.

---

[47] Of course references to the poet's personality are always a risky matter, but the fact that Gregory tended to oscillate between different ideals (e.g., between *vita activa* and *vita contemplativa*) is so obvious from his biography that it seems legitimate to draw a parallel to his literary principles.
[48] Cf. Fuhrer 2013, 79f., with focus on Latin literature.

Friesen, C.J.P. 2015. *Reading Dionysus. Euripides' Bacchae and the cultural contestations of Greeks, Jews, Romans and Christians*, Tübingen.
Fuhrer, T. 2013. "Hypertexts and auxiliary texts. New genres in Late Antiquity?", in T.D. Papanghelis/S.J. Harrison/S. Frangoulidis (eds.), *Generic interfaces in Latin literature. Encounters, interactions and transformations*, Berlin, 79–89.
Herrero de Jáuregui, M. 2010. *Orphism and Christianity in Late Antiquity*, Berlin.
Hollis, A.S. 2002. "Callimachus. Light from Late Antiquity", in F. Montanari/L. Lehnus (eds.), *Callimaque. Sept exposés suivis de discussions. Vandœuvres-Genève, 3–7 septembre 2001*, Genève, 35–54.
Holzhausen, H. 1997. "Corpus Hermeticum", *DNP*, 3, 203–207.
Hopkinson, N. 1994. "Nonnus and Homer", in N. Hopkinson (ed.), *Studies in the Dionysiaca of Nonnus*, Cambridge, 9–42.
Horn, C.B. 2004. "Überlegungen zur Rolle der Pneumatologie Ephräm des Syrers im Umfeld des Ersten Konzils von Konstantinopel", in M. Tamcke (ed.), *Syriaca II. Beiträge zum 3. deutschen Syrologen-Symposium Vierzehnheiligen 2002*, Münster, 29–51.
Hose, M. 2004. *Poesie aus der Schule. Überlegungen zur spätgriechischen Dichtung*, München.
Keydell, R. 1953. "Die literarhistorische Stellung der Gedichte Gregors von Nazianz", in *Atti dello VIII congresso internazionale di studi bizantini (Studi bizantini e neoellenici 7)*, Roma, 134–143.
Kalish, K.J. 2009. *Greek Christian poetry in classical forms. The "Codex of Visions" from the Bodmer Papyri and the melding of literary traditions* (diss.), Princeton (NJ).
Kuhn, T. 2014. *Schweigen in Versen. Text, Übersetzung und Studien zu den Schweigegedichten Gregors von Nazianz (II,1,34A/B)*, Berlin.
Löw, A. 2002. *Hermes Trismegistos als Zeuge der Wahrheit. Die christliche Hermetikrezeption von Athenagoras bis Laktanz*, Berlin.
McGuckin, J.A. 2001. *Saint Gregory of Nazianzus. An intellectual biography*, Crestwood (NY).
Meinel, F. 2009. "Gregory of Nazianzus' *Poemata Arcana*: ἄρρητα and Christian persuasion", *CCJ*, 55, 71–96.
Moreschini, C./Sykes, D.A. (eds.) 1997. *St Gregory of Nazianzus. Poemata Arcana*, Oxford.
Most, G.W. 2008. "On the authorship of the *Christus Patiens*", in A. Jördens (ed.), *Quaerite faciem eius simper. Studien zu den geistesgeschichtlichen Beziehungen zwischen Antike und Christentum. Dankesgabe für Albrecht Dihle zum 85. Geburtstag aus dem Heidelberger Kirchenväterkolloquium*, Hamburg, 229–240.
Piottante, F. 1999. *Gregorio Nazianzeno. Inni per il silenzio [carm. II,1,34A/B II,1,38]*, Pisa.
Pollmann, K. 2017. *The baptized Muse. Early Christian poetry as cultural authority*, Oxford.
Prudhomme, J. 2006. *L'œuvre poétique de Grégoire de Nazianze* (diss.), Lyon.
Rimoli, P. 2016. "La paternità del *Christus patiens* tra Gregorio di Nazianzo e Teodoto di Ancira", *Adamantius*, 22, 215–230.
Shorrock, R. 2011. *The myth of paganism. Nonnus, Dionysus and the world of Late Antiquity*, Bristol.
Simelidis, C. 2009. *Selected poems of Gregory of Nazianzus. I.2.17; II.1.10, 19, 32*, Göttingen.
Sykes, A.D. 1970. "The *Poemata Arcana* of St. Gregory Nazianzen", *JThS*, 21, 31–42.
van den Broek, R. 2000. "Religious practices in the Hermetic 'lodge': new light from Nag Hammadi", in R. van den Broek/C. van Heertum (eds.), *From Poimandres to Jacob Böhme: Gnosis, Hermetism and the Christian tradition*, Amsterdam, 77–95.
West, M.L. 1983. *The Orphic poems*, Oxford.

Whitby, Mary/Roberts, M. 2018. "Epic poetry", in S. McGill/E.J. Watts (eds.), *Blackwell's Companion to late antique literature*, Hoboken (NJ), 221–240.
White, C. 1996. *Gregory of Nazianzus. Autobiographical poems*, Cambridge.
Wyss, B. 1949. "Gregor von Nazianz. Ein griechisch-christlicher Dichter des 4. Jahrhunderts", *MH*, 6, 177–210.
Zymner, R. (ed.) 2010. *Handbuch Gattungstheorie*, Stuttgart.

James McDonald
The Significance of Meter in the Biblical Poems of Gregory Nazianzen (*carmina* I.1.12–27)

The Biblical Poems of Gregory Nazianzen have been the subject of scholars' scorn, dismissiveness, and – often – perplexity throughout the ages. Billius's metrical Latin translation of the poems in the *Patrologia Graeca* does not even bother to finish the poem on the Lucan and Matthean genealogies;[1] and West in his *Greek Metre* (1982, 183) only mentions *carmen* I.1.12 (the most metrically varied of the poems) in a footnote, clearly perplexed by this "curious mixture" of meters.[2] It is also often the case that the lines do not scan very well, which has led to corruptions in the text (as discussed by Palla 1989) and scorn from scholars who dismiss his meter as shoddy.[3] Palla has provided the most in-depth scholarly discussion of this series of poems thus far, upon whom later authors such as Dunkle (who published an edition and translation of these poems in 2012) have very much depended. Palla, however, does not really deal with the scansion of these polymetric poems but concerns himself much more with the correct ordering of the poems and possible corruptions that have seeped into these poems through editors' mistakes over time in the manuscript tradition. This has certainly advanced our understanding of these peculiar, if plain, poems; but Palla (1989, 175) and other scholars who have come after him[4] have unquestionably presumed that the purpose of the polymetry in these poems is to aid the reader in memorizing the scriptural data within them whilst learning their scansion at the same time. Meter was a formal characteristic of classical Greek poetry, and particular meters were traditionally used for particular genres – such as dactylic hexameter for epic or didactic poetry, or iambics for invective (though this is not a hard and fast rule, especially in Late Antiquity, as noted below). Therefore, it would make sense that scholars would ask what function this polymetry had in these poems.[5]

---

[1] *PG* 37.485 fn. 60, as noted by Dunkle 2012, 20–21.
[2] Arist., *Poet.* 1447b20–22 and 1459b37–1460a2 also expresses a certain scorn for polymetric poetry.
[3] See Whitby 2008, 93, who cites various scholars' criticism of Gregory's mastery of verse composition.
[4] Such as Dunkle 2012, 21–22, 30 and McGuckin 2006, 201.
[5] A sound grasp of Greek meter was essential, for Gregory, to the proper writing of poetry – as Milovanovic 1997, 502–503 has pointed out. See also Harder 1998 for the use of generic allusion

But were the Biblical Poems made for a young, specifically schoolroom, reader in order for him/her to learn both scansion and Scripture?

Palla and Dunkle seem to imply this,[6] and McGuckin explicitly states that these poems were for a "schoolroom audience, whom [Gregory] obviously intends to learn the various forms of Greek meter while they are at the task of memorizing the biblical books."[7] Moreover, Martin Hose (2004, 36–37) argues that late antique Greek Christian poetry in general is bound to the school, and that it is no more than versified prose. This paper will argue, however, that Gregory did not intend these poems to be (specifically) for a classroom, but rather a much wider – and more mature – audience; an audience that could deal with the complexity of the meters, as I will demonstrate. The metrics of these poems, far from helping schoolchildren grapple with the meter of canonical literature such as Homer and Hesiod, are a reflection of a conscious, forward-thinking development in the regulation of Greek meters. In arguing this, I will show that the Biblical Poems were not a shoddy mish-mash of meters[8] whose sole purpose was helping schoolchildren learn their scansion and Bible at the same time, but rather an innovative and interesting approach to creating a piece of auxiliary literature that would provide a gateway to the poems' primary text, the Bible, for Gregory's learned and well-read contemporaries.[9] I begin my argument by showing that Gregory nowhere

---

in Hellenistic poetry; Fantuzzi/Hunter 2004; and also, Gutzwiller 2007 for the development and uses of meter amongst Hellenistic poets. For the entanglement of meter and theme in Gregory see Kuhn-Treichel in this volume.

6 Palla 1989, 175: "Il fatto stesso che Gregorio ricorra al metro può essere considerato una novità, ma non deve sorprendere e va visto in questa prospettiva didascalica: anche oggi maestri e genitori ricorrono spesso a filastrocche rimate o ritmate perché i bambini possano memorizzare con facilità maggiore regole grammaticali e nozioni di vario genere (ad esempio di quanti giorni sono formati i vari mesi dell'anno)." Dunkle, 2012, 22: "Although [the Biblical Poems] may not suit every grown-up's taste, his poems are, as he puts it, 'a helpful plaything for children'." Dunkle 2012 here is quoting an acrostic present in the poem I.2.31.31–47: ἐσθλὸν ἄθυρμα νέοις. He also states more explicitly at p. 20 that these poems were perhaps for neophytes and children to introduce them to the "basics of the scriptural narrative."

7 Palla 1989, 201.

8 There are some false quantities and metrical 'mistakes' in the poems, which I will point out, but overall this is not the case, and we must do more than simply dismiss these poems if we are to better understand the writings of Nazianzen.

9 Given the length of this paper, I do not have a chance to discuss this aspect of the poems further, but will do so in my PhD thesis. For more on such texts, see Dubischar 2010, which discusses the necessity of condensing large texts – like the Bible; Fuhrer 2013, who looks at auxiliary texts in late antique Christian literature; and Whitmarsh 2001 on the use of – and high respect for – such literature in the Second Sophistic. For an in-depth discussion of the inter-play between scriptural and classical language in these poems and the poems' didactic functions, see

states that his poetry is intended/designed for the classroom. Then I discuss the polymetry of the poems, as analysed by Palla, and highlight how such polymetry would make these works ill-fitting for a classroom context. Finally, I outline my own metrical analysis of these poems and compare my findings to those of other such studies conducted by scholars on Gregory's poetic corpus and discuss what implications my analysis of the meter has for better understanding the intended audience and contemporary appeal of these compositions.

Gregory in the classroom

Firstly, it should be noted that Gregory nowhere states that his poetry was designed for a classroom audience. Gregory certainly wanted his literature to be read, and to be read by the *pepaideumenoi* of his age, but his Christianization of *paideia* was not carried out through creating textbooks for schools, but literature to be read and enjoyed by those who cared to read such Christian compositions once sweetened by Gregory's *paideia*. His poetry was to be literature that equalled, if not surpassed, that of the classical poets – something Gregory *does* explicitly state.[10] Whether or not Gregory succeeds in that objective (in the Biblical Poems or any other of his poems) is beside the point here. What must be emphasized is that Gregory did not explicitly want his work to be for the classroom. Gregory does say in the poems *On His Own Verse* and in his *On His Own Life* that he wants his work to be a τερπνὸν φάρμακον (*carm.* II.1.39.30: "pleasant medicine") and παίδευμα καὶ γλύκασμα τοῖς νέοις ἅμα (*carm.* II.1.11.7: "both a lesson and a source of sweetness for the young"), but this is hardly a statement of intent to write specifically for the young in the classroom, or of creating an educative program through his poetry. Simelidis (2009, 75–88) has pointed out that the poems of Gregory were, in later years, read in schools, at times used to replace the erotic (classical) poetry of antiquity, but again, this does not at all mean that any of his work was intended for the classroom – in the same way that Homer or Virgil

---

Prudhomme 2006 – though I disagree that we can see these poems as biblical paraphrases (such as that of Nonnus), as they lack the sustained narrative which other biblical paraphrases have. See in this volume Paschalis, Accorinti, and Hadjittofi for the narrativity of Latin and Greek biblical paraphrases, all with further bibliography.
10 See the poem *On His Own Verses* (*carm.* II.1.39.47–49) with some further comments in Faulkner and the Introduction to this volume. In using the word 'pagan' I am following the translation of White 1996, 5 of the Greek τοὺς ξένους, which could perhaps mean not only pagans, but Christians (or perhaps intellectuals in general) with whom he disagreed or considered enemies.

did not write their *opera magna* for the classroom, despite their use in classrooms for millennia.

We also have little evidence of Gregory's formal teaching. It would not be controversial to make the claim that Gregory taught, but we know little about the context or content of his teachings – excepting, of course, his theological teachings, which more likely have an ecclesiastical as opposed to a pedagogical setting. Gregory tells us in the poem *On His Own Life* (*carm.* II.1.11.249–264) that he was begged (if not intimidated) by his colleagues at Athens not to follow Basil in departing from the city, and he even hints at the promise of some sort of κράτος to be voted to him if he were to stay (perhaps a coveted public chair as a teacher of rhetoric in Athens).[11] When he does return home to Cappadocia, we know that he teaches a certain Evagrius, and that Gregory was a good teacher to him.[12] But again we know little of what was actually taught, and it is likely that this did not particularly differ from the education in basic grammar and rhetoric that all young men of upstanding families were expected to undertake. Therefore, from the little evidence we have of Gregory's teaching career, we can only assert that he very likely did teach in Athens and Nazianzus, but not that he attempted some sort of amalgamation of Christian and Hellenic *paideia* through such poems as the Biblical Poems discussed here.[13] Furthermore, in turning to the poems themselves we will see that the peculiarity of these poems goes beyond their mere polymetry.

---

11 I would like to conjecture that Gregory was perhaps a *hetairos* (see Watts 2006, 51–53 for the meaning of the term) to a leading teacher in Athens (perhaps Prohaeresius?), and so would have taken some of the teaching responsibilities within that school. But this is, of course, only my conjecture.

12 See McGuckin 2001, 86–87.

13 There does not seem to be any evidence of Christian (episcopal) schools at Gregory's time – that is, schools that combined Christian doctrine with a Classical education. Marrou 1956, 325 can find only one in the Thebaid around 372 CE. Szabat 2015, 254 notes that the school at Gaza has been called a Christian school, but only because all in attendance were most likely Christian; the curriculum would have been no different from a 'pagan' school.

Gregory's Use of Polymetry

Carmen I.1.12 is the most metrically varied of the poems and runs as follows:

θείοις ἐν λογίοισιν ἀεὶ γλώσσῃ τε νόῳ τε
στρωφᾶσθ'· ἢ γὰρ ἔδωκε Θεὸς καμάτων τόδ' ἄεθλον,
καί τι κρυπτὸν ἰδεῖν ὀλίγον φάος, ἢ τόδ' ἄριστον,
νύττεσθαι καθαροῖο Θεοῦ μεγάλῃσιν ἐφετμαῖς·
ἢ τρίτατον, χθονίων ἀπάγειν φρένα ταῖσδε μερίμναις.   5
ὄφρα δὲ μὴ ξείνῃσι νόον κλέπτοιο βίβλοισι
(πολλαὶ γὰρ τελέθουσι παρέγγραπτοι κακότητες),
δέχνυσο τοῦτον ἐμεῖο τὸν ἔγκριτον, ὦ φίλ', ἀριθμόν.
ἱστορικαὶ μὲν ἔασι βίβλοι δυοκαίδεκα πᾶσαι
   τῆς ἀρχαιοτέρης Ἑβραϊκῆς σοφίης.   10
   πρώτη Γένεσις, εἶτ' Ἔξοδος, Λευϊτικόν[14]
   ἔπειτ' Ἀριθμοί. εἶτα Δεύτερος Νόμος.
   ἔπειτ' Ἰησοῦς, καὶ Κριταί. Ῥοὺθ ὀγδόη.
ἡ δ' ἐνάτη δεκάτη τε βίβλοι, Πράξεις βασιλήων,
   καὶ Παραλειπόμεναι. ἔσχατον Ἔσδραν ἔχεις.   15
αἱ δὲ στιχηραὶ πέντε, ὧν πρῶτός γ' Ἰώβ·
   ἔπειτα Δαυΐδ· εἶτα τρεῖς Σολομωντίαι.
   Ἐκκλησιαστής, Ἆσμα καὶ Παροιμίαι.
   καὶ πένθ' ὁμοίως Πνεύματος προφητικοῦ.
μίαν μέν εἰσιν ἐς γραφὴν οἱ δώδεκα·   20
   Ὡσηὲ κ' Ἀμώς, καὶ Μιχαίας ὁ τρίτος·
   ἔπειτ' Ἰωήλ, εἶτ' Ἰωνᾶς, Ἀβδίας,
   Ναούμ τε, Ἀββακούμ τε, καὶ Σοφονίας,
   Ἀγγαῖος, εἶτα Ζαχαρίας, Μαλαχίας.
μία μὲν οἵδε. δευτέρα δ' Ἡσαΐας.   25
   ἔπειθ' ὁ κληθεὶς Ἱερεμίας ἐκ βρέφους.
   εἶτ' Ἰεζεκιήλ, καὶ Δανιήλου χάρις.
ἀρχαίας μὲν ἔθηκα δύω καὶ εἴκοσι βίβλους,
   τοῖς τῶν Ἑβραίων γράμμασιν ἀντιθέτους.
ἤδη δ' ἀρίθμει καὶ νέου μυστηρίου.   30
Ματθαῖος μὲν ἔγραψεν Ἑβραίοις θαύματα Χριστοῦ·
   Μάρκος δ' Ἰταλίῃ, Λουκᾶς Ἀχαϊάδι·
πᾶσι δ' Ἰωάννης, κῆρυξ μέγας, οὐρανοφοίτης.
   ἔπειτα Πράξεις τῶν σοφῶν ἀποστόλων.
δέκα δὲ Παύλου τέσσαρές τ' ἐπιστολαί.   35
   ἑπτὰ δὲ καθολικαί, ὧν, Ἰακώβου μία,

---

[14] Calliau in the *PG* 37.473 prints this line as a hexameter (πρωτίστη, Γένεσις, εἶτ' Ἔξοδος, Λευϊτικόν τε) but I, following Palla 2008, 176, believe it makes much more sense here structurally to have a trimeter.

δύω δὲ Πέτρου, τρεῖς δ' Ἰωάννου πάλιν·
Ἰούδα δ' ἐστὶν ἑβδόμη. πάσας ἔχεις.
εἴ τι δὲ τούτων ἐκτὸς, οὐκ ἐν γνησίαις.[15]

Abide always in the divine Scriptures in speech and mind. For God has given this prize of labor to make known some glimmer of hidden light; and, most importantly, to pierce through the great commandments of the pure Godhead; and thirdly to lead our mind away from the worries of the world. Therefore, lest you should steal away your mind in strange books (for many spurious and wicked works exist) receive, dear friend, this authoritative account of mine. In total there are twelve historical books of ancient Hebraic wisdom. First is Genesis, then Exodos, and Leviticus. Thereafter we have Numbers, then Deuteronomy. Then Joshua, Judges and eighth is Ruth. Books nine and ten are the books of Kings, then you have Chronicles, and finally Ezra. There are five books of poetry, the first of which is Job. Then David [Psalms], then the three books of Solomon: Ecclesiastes, The Song of Songs, and Proverbs. Similarly there are five books of the prophets of the Holy Spirit. Twelve prophets are placed into one book: Hosea, Amos, and Micah; then Joel, Jonas, Obadiah, Nahum, Habakkuk, Zephaniah, Haggai, Zechariah, and Malachi. They make one book. Second is Isaiah. Then Jeremiah, who was called whilst in the womb. Then Ezekiel, and the fortune of Daniel. I have set out the twenty-two books of the Old Testament, which is equal in number to the letters of the alphabet of the Hebrews. Now recount the new Mystery. Matthew wrote of the miracles of Christ for the Hebrews, Mark for Italy, and Luke for Greece. But John, the great herald, who walks in the heavens, wrote for all men. Then there is the Acts of the wise Apostles; then the fourteen Epistles of St. Paul. Then there are the seven epistles addressed to the whole Church: One by James, two by Peter, three by John and the seventh by Jude. You have all the books. If any book differs from the above, it is not counted among the legitimate books. (*carm.* I.1.12.1–29)

As Palla (1989, 176–177) also notes, verses 1–8 are written in dactylic hexameter. They outline the purpose of Scripture: knowledge of hidden "light", understanding the commandments of God, and freeing the mind of earthly cares. Then it finishes with an invitation to receive Gregory's authoritative numbering of the canonical books of the Bible. Verses 9–10 form an elegiac couplet that introduces the first 12 books of the Old Testament which Gregory calls Ἱστορικαί. There follows three lines of iambic trimeter (11–13) followed by an elegiac couplet which closes the series of Ἱστορικαί (14–15). Verses 16–18 recount the στιχηραί in iambic trimeter, which continue into vv. 19–27 recounting the book of prophets. Verses 28–29 make up an elegiac couplet that closes the catalogue of the Old Testament. 30 is another invitation to receive the correct numbering of the New Testament written in iambic trimeter. Verses 31–33, which recount the four Gospels, form

---

[15] For the absence of the book of Revelation see Thielman 1998. There is a paraphrase of this poem in *PG* 38.841–846.

another elegiac couplet followed by a dactylic hexameter. John's Gospel is given particular prominence by having a whole line to itself in hexameter. The poem closes with the rest of the New Testament being recounted in iambic trimeter with a final comment that, if there be any supposedly biblical book that is different from Gregory's catalogue, then it is not ἐν γνησίαις. Therefore, we can analyse the poem's metrical scheme as follows: (1) The poem is introduced in dactylic hexameters; (2) The books of the Bible are written in straightforward iambic trimeter in accordance with the conventions of comic dialogue, in which anapaests and resolution are admitted more freely than in tragedy, and there are many lines which have no caesura;[16] (3) Elegiac couplets are used to introduce and conclude the list of books of the Old Testament; the Gospels are given special prominence by being recounted in an elegiac couplet and a hexameter, and surrounded by iambic trimeters.[17] Palla then notes that the metrical changes would have helped the reader to learn the poem by heart, but how?[18]

I think this poem, as well as the other Biblical Poems, as Palla notes, uses polymetry better to organize the content, and to highlight important information. Sometimes it is used to note a change in subject matter, such as in the poem on the genealogies of Christ (*carm*. I.1.18.33–35)[19] when Gregory briefly changes from hexameter to iambic trimeter in order to make an authorial aside (or summary) of his argument – that Matthew's genealogy is according to nature, and Luke's according to (Judaic) law.[20] But the metrical changes within the poems would have posed a challenge to the reader, especially if that reader was just learning Greek meter; and even the well-read would never (or perhaps rarely) have come across such polymetry.[21] Furthermore, the verses (even when the meter is identified) often do not scan in a straightforward manner. The iambic trimeters are the best

---

16 See West 1987, 24–28 for a good summary of these conventions.
17 As I note below, iambic trimeter is used here (as in many later writers) for didactic writing, but see Hawkins 2014, 142–180 for Gregory's use of iambic as invective.
18 Palla 1989, 177: "Difficile avere dubbi sui fini catechetici della composizione e sul fatto che i cambiamenti di metro volessero anche fornire un aiuto a chi doveva imparare a memoria."
19 It should be noted that Palla 1989, 179 and Dunkle 2012, 43 n. 5 who follows him, believes this poem to be actually two poems. I disagree with them and prefer the interpretation of Sicherl 2002, 313–314 that the poem is in fact a unity, and that the manuscripts that have a *Zwischentitel* are wrong to divide it.
20 Therefore, I disagree with Hose's 2004, 36 statement that: "die lateinische Dichtung enthält damit ein hermeneutisches Potential, das der griechischen fehlt." There is little space to discuss this further here.
21 Amphilochius' *Iambi ad Seleucum* provides a parallel to this poem, in that it also discusses the canon of Scripture in iambic trimeter, but switches to hexameters for the last three verses. However, the polymetry here is nowhere near as varied as *carm*. I.1.12.

example of this. One could say that they broadly fit into the conventions of comic dialogue in drama, which West (1982, 81) notes became popular for didactic poetry in later writers. However, verse 10 of *carmen* I.1.16 introduces a peculiarity into what is otherwise a straightforward iambic-didactic poem:

x − ⏑ −| x − − − |x − ⏑ −
ἔφλεξεν ἄρδην πεντηκοντάρχας δύω.

He utterly burnt up the two companies of fifty men.[22] (*carm.* I.1.16.10)

The second metron scans as a tetrasyllabic dochmiac, a metrical scheme more likely found in dramatic song.[23] Finally, the following poem has a line that scans as two choriambs and one iambus:

− ⏑ ⏑ −| x ⏑ ⏑ − |x − ⏑ −
τοῦτο δ' ἀφειδῶς μεταδοῦσα τῷ ξένῳ

She gave this [flour and oil to make bread] freely to her guest [Elijah] (*carm.* I.1.17.7):

Again, such a metrical scheme is the kind one would find in dramatic song.[24] It could well be that Gregory and his audience did not have an ear for the quantities of ancient Greek,[25] and that these lines are an examplary antecedent of the later Byzantine dodecasyllable, as argued by West (1982, 185). But given that the trimeter elsewhere is in line with comic convention, and so admits anapaests and resolution within lines (thus allowing more than twelve syllables in a line), to read these lines as a sort of forefather of the dodecasyllable would bring us no closer to understanding Gregory's metrics.

The elegiac couplets often admit *brevis in longo* in the pentameter at the caesura, such as at *carmen* I.1.14.12 on the plagues of Egypt:

---

22 This is a reference to 2 Kgs 1:12.
23 See West 1982, 100 for examples.
24 For the use of choriambs in drama in general see West 1982, *passim*.
25 Simelidis 2009, 54 following Maas 1962, 14 mentions the lack of understanding of quantities among Gregory's contemporaries. Al. Cameron 1971, 120–121 notes the work of Marianus of Eleutheropolis (active only a little after Gregory's time) who converted hexameter poems into iambic trimeter. Agosti 2001, 224 believes that such a 'translation' must have been made so that hexameter poets could be more easily read by a wider audience. Horrocks 2010, 160–187 provides the most thorough analysis of the changes happening in the Greek language at this time (although its evidence is mainly based in Egyptian papyri). See especially p. 169: "The change from a primary pitch accent to a primary stress accent was directly associated with the loss of vowel-length distinctions and was widespread by the middle of the 2nd century BC."

```
– ⏑ ⏑ | – ⏑ ⏑ | ⏑ | – ⏑ ⏑ | – ⏑ ⏑ | ⏑
```
πρωτοτόκων δὲ μόρος ἡ δεκάτη βάσανος.

The tenth torment, the death of the first born. (*carm.* I.1.14.12)

And *carmen* I.1.25.6 on the parables in the Gospel of Mark:[26]

```
– ⏑ ⏑ | – –| ⏑ | – ⏑ ⏑ | – ⏑ ⏑ | ⏑
```
Ἑλλάδι Παύλοιο Λουκᾶς ἔγραψε τάδε·

Luke wrote these [parables] for Paul's Greece. (*carm.* I.1.25.6)

This is a phenomenon which only begins to develop in the third and fourth centuries.[27] It should also be noted that the -ᾶς of Λουκᾶς should be long. However, on this phenomenon Sicherl in Oberhaus' edition of I.2.25 has this to say (1991, 26): "Die Verwendung naturlanger Silben in den brevia ist oft bemerkt worden, aber infolge des Fehlens einer vollständigen Erschließung des Wortschatzes Gregors war es bisher schwer festzustellen, daß er langes α, υ und ι in manchen Wörtern immer kurz wertet, also diese nie im longum, sondern nur im breve oder anceps erscheinen."

More peculiarities are found in the hexameter. At I.1.27.15 the *princeps* position of the second metron is occupied by a short vowel:

```
– – | – ⏑ ⏑ | – ⏑ ⏑ | –   ⏑ ⏑ | – ⏑ ⏑ | – x
```
αἰνῶ τὸν ὀλίγον νάπυος σπόρον, ὡς ὀλίγος μὲν[28] (*carm.* I.1.27.15)

I praise the small mustard seed, because while small…

Simelidis (2009, 55) – following Sicherl's metrical analysis of Gregory's poetry in Oberhaus' (1991, 29–30) edition of *carmen* I.2.25 – notes that "[t]here are several 'long' syllables with a short vowel [in Gregory's prosody], almost always before ν, σ and ῥ." This could help us to explain another metrical puzzle at I.1.20.7:

```
– ⏑ ⏑ | – ⏑ ⏑ | – ⏑ ⏑ | –   – | – ⏑ ⏑ | – x
```
δαίμονας ἧκε σύεσσι τὸ πέμπτον, ἐν Γεργεσηνοῖς.[29] (*carm.* I.1.20.7)

In the fifth (miracle) he drove the demons into the swine, in the country of the Gergesenes.

---

26 Palla 1989, 183 seems to think that only lines 1, 2, and 4 are authentic, in accordance with his reading of the manuscript tradition.
27 See West 1982, 81. Also noted by Sykes 1979, 14–15 and Simelidis 2009, 56–57.
28 See, also, *carm.* I.1.18.28.
29 *PG* 37.489 has Γεργεσσηνοῖς, but Γεργεσηνοῖς is attested elsewhere; see Bauer 2000 *s.v.*

This scansion would give us a bucolic diaeresis, but would still leave us with a 'long' syllable in *brevis* position in the first syllable of Γεργεσηνοῖς. Perhaps the comment of Sicherl quoted above could help us better to understand this phenomenon too. However, the initial epsilon of Γεργεσηνοῖς is not long by nature but by position, and so it is not quite the same phenomenon as Sicherl describes. Nevertheless, we can add to this that the Biblical Poems show a certain flexibility in the quantities of words when it comes to biblical names.[30]

The poem on the genealogies of Christ (I.1.18) provides a few examples, such as the different scansions of the name Ἰακώβ where it is scanned as ⏑ ⏑ – at v. 28 and ⏑ – – at v. 30. Later on, we have Ἀρών scanned – ⏑ at verse 42,[31] but at verse 45 it is ⏑ –. The following poem that lists Christ's apostles (I.1.19) also has two different scannings of the same name in one line (5), where the first word Ἰούδας scans – – –, but the last word of the line with the same name scans ⏑ – x. Maas (1962, 20) notes the difficulty that Semitic, biblical names caused Christian poets, as such names "could be given only an arbitrary quantitative value." Even the more prosodically correct poets such as Synesius and Nonnus find it impossible to fit such names into Greek meter without allowing false quantities. We cannot, therefore, judge the quality of Gregory's verse too much based on these Biblical Poems, and we should add that – given the difficulty of writing biblical poetry in correct meter – it would seem an odd choice of topic to learn one's scansion.

Finally, we can compare the Biblical Poems with studies already conducted on the meter of Gregory. The study of Agosti/Gonnelli (1995, 289–409) has been most influential on later scholars who discuss Gregory's meter.[32] Sykes (1979, 15) notes that the ratio of dactyls to spondees is 5:1 in Gregory, which is an increase from earlier authors such as Homer and Hesiod (2.5:1), but in line with the trend of poets later than Homer and Hesiod and Gregory's contemporaries (as well as the later Nonnus), who have a ratio of dactyls to spondees much similar to Gregory. Both Simelidis (2009, 54–57) and Whitby (2008, 93–94) – who conducts her own study on the poem to Olympias (*carm.* II.2.6) – follow Agosti/Gonnelli in noting what Simelidis (2009, 56) describes as follows: "Gregory's favourite patterns of hexameters are ddddd (31.69%) and sdddd (19.20%); other sequences which Gregory favours to a lesser extent are dsddd (15.22%) and dddsd (8.50%); σπονδειάζοντες: 1.44%." Dunkle (2012, 22), also following these findings, states that "[i]n the poems on Scripture, the ratio [of dactyls to spondees] is even higher

---

30 Such flexibility can also be found in Homer as noted by West 2011, 226–228.
31 The *PG* prints this name as Ἀαρών, but this does not scan, and we have Ἀρών in the same poem regardless. So, it is not an excessive emendation to the text.
32 See also Sykes 1979 who has more or less the same results as Agosti/Gonnelli 1995.

[than 5:1], around six resolved dactyls for every spondee. Gregory's preference for resolved dactyls in these poems appears at least to help students recite or even sing the verses." Dunkle does not state why such a ratio would help them recite (not to mention sing!) these poems, but the ratio of 6:1 is completely unfounded.

My own study of these particular poems has returned a result of approximately 3 dactyls to every one spondee (or 76.83% dactyls to 23.17% spondees). This would mean that these poems are even more spondaic than the poems covered in previous studies. There are similar results, however, when we look at the line patterns for the hexameters. Gregory's favored pattern is still ddddd (21.35%) followed by sdddd (19.09%). The pattern dsddd still comes in third (13.26%), followed by dddsd (8.41%). Fifth foot spondees only make up 0.64% (2 lines), but given that the percentages here are slightly lower for Gregory's favored patterns than in previous studies, this means that there are more examples of lines with two or more spondees (31.02%). The reason for this higher ratio of spondees is best explained by the large presence of Semitic names in these poems, which Gregory prefers to scan with *longa elementa*. If we look at verses with 2 or more spondees, we see that the spondees predominantly fall upon the Semitic names such as in the following poem:

```
 - ⏑   ⏑|- -|-   -|  - -  |-   ⏑ ⏑|  - x
```
Κωσάμ, ἔην Ἀδδί. τοῦ, Μελχί. τοῦ δ' ἄπο, Νηρί.
...
```
 - - |-   -|-    ⏑ ⏑|-  -|   - - |- x
```
Ἰούδας, Ὡσώκ, Σεμεεί τ' αὖ, Ματθίας τε,

```
  -  -|-   - | -  -|  - -|  -   ⏑ ⏑ |- x
```
καὶ Μαάθ, Ναγγαί, καὶ Ἐσλείμ· τοῦ δ' ἄπο Ναούμ,
...
```
 - -  |-  -|- -   |-   -| - ⏑  ⏑|- x
```
Μελχί, καὶ Λευί, καὶ Ματθάν, Ἠλεί, Ἰωσήφ.[33] (*carm.* I.1.18.83, 85–86, 88)

Many other examples of such lines can be found in the Biblical Poems.[34] Therefore, we can say that Gregory's Biblical Poems are in agreement with metrical analyses already carried out upon different parts of his poetic output. However, given the difficulty posed by the Semitic names that make an essential part of his subject matter, Gregory has a higher ratio of spondees in these poems compared to other parts of his corpus. Maas, as noted above, has already discussed the difficulty such names caused Gregory's contemporaries and poets after him, and so

---

33 An example of epic correption, as the final syllable of Ἠλεί is short.
34 See *carm.* I.1.13.2, 3, 5; I.1.18.100; and I.1.19.2, 3.

it was only inevitable that Gregory would have to forgo slightly his favored style of (heavily dactylic) metric in order to accommodate these names.

Conclusions

To conclude, we have shown that these poems were unlikely to be intended for use as a school textbook, through which the pupil could learn both Scripture and scansion. Gregory nowhere states that he embarks upon such a pedagogical program in his extant writings, but rather that he intends to write poetry that would rival that of the classical poets (such as Homer, Callimachus, and so on). The polymetry of the poems that has seemingly led scholars to suspect such a pedagogical purpose to these poems is in fact one of the main reasons why these texts would not be suitable for learning Greek meter, as the reader would have to scan not only their lines correctly but figure out what kind of meter each verse is (as there is no guarantee that one poem has one meter). Furthermore, our metrical analysis has shown that the meter of these poems is not shoddy, as previous scholars have suggested, but a reflection of contemporary developments in poetic composition. Gregory's quirks in the meter, such as a short vowel before certain consonants scanning as long, can be found as far back as Homer (Oberhaus 1991, 29); and they show that he, like Nonnus and other contemporary poets, is looking to further regulate and order his poetry, but with an ear to the changes in the Greek language of his time, which no longer distinguished the long and short quantities of more ancient Greek. It should be noted that, if Gregory had intended for these poems to be used in elementary education, then surely they would seek to reflect the meter of poets such as Homer or Callimachus who were part of the literary canon, and more likely studied by schoolchildren.

Also, it should be noted that these poems are a transposition of sorts, for they transform the books of Scripture both through the use of meter (as discussed here) and also through the use of classical – as opposed to biblical – language. However, it is difficult to say how, or if, they in any way modulate Scripture. Unlike other biblical paraphrases written in meter, these poems lack the extended narrative of Nonnus' *Paraphrase* or its Latin equivalents. In fact, these poems are unlike any other poem this author has seen, and function much more as a paratext (in the sense that Genette intends) to Scripture than a *paraphrasis* (that would elucidate Scripture for the reader) or a *metaphrasis* (that would seek to embellish Scripture). It is difficult, therefore, to say what genre these poems might fit into, if the question of genre is relevant at all, and the register seems to oscillate between major and minor genres – even within a single poem through the change of meter.[35]

When these poems are read with Gregory's poetic manifesto (*On His Own Verses*) in mind, we see that, firstly, given the innovative approach to meter that reflected the practices (and, therefore, tastes) of contemporary poets (and readers), Gregory clearly sees his Biblical Poems as among those that he wished to equal or surpass the poems of the pagans. These poems could be considered as auxiliary texts, a genre of texts that are secondary to a primary source (the Bible) and that aim to both guarantee a readership for the primary text (that is, to engage and increase the readership of the primary text) and provide a gateway to it. Often such texts were not seen as inferior to the texts to which they were subservient – as they are today – but were deemed literature in their own right. As noted above, the change in meter has a clear function within the poems: to highlight authorial asides and to note changes in subject matter (such as a transition from one catalogue of biblical books to another). Therefore, what we have in Gregory's Biblical Poems may be seen as an example of didactic poetry, which reflects the developments in meter and style of the didactic genre in Late Antiquity. Didactic was no longer written in just hexameters, but iambic trimeter as well; Gregory does both and often within the same poem. That we find no such mixture of meters anywhere else is not a reflection of Gregory's mediocrity, but rather provides an example of a late antique poet looking to push the boundaries of what can be done with meter and to innovate further upon a received didactic tradition – such a style just seems not to have caught on.[36]

The Biblical Poems are a fine example of the real struggle that Gregory faced in creating this poetry, as the Semitic names of the Bible often forced him to abandon his preferred metrical patterns – which are very dactylic – in order to accommodate these names (a struggle he refers to in *carmen* II.1.39.34–37). Therefore, we see quite clearly here Gregory's first stated reason for writing poetry in the poem *On His Own Verses*: the need to bring measure (μέτρον) to his own "measurelessness" (ἀμετρία).[37] This struggle also led him to be much more flexible with quantities in these names, as can be seen from the various scansions of the same

---

[35] On paratext see Genette 1997 (again, this aspect will be discussed in more detail in my PhD thesis). See Roberts 1985 on the difference between *paraphrasis* and *metaphrasis*. Rosenmeyer 2006 questions the usefulness of the concept of genre in ancient literature.
[36] For a less adventurous adaptation of the Psalms in a more classicizing meter and form see Faulkner in this volume.
[37] For more on this poem see Milovanovic 1997 and the Introduction to this volume.

name. In going forward with the study of Gregory's poetry, a much more extensive and detailed analysis of his meter is needed in order to find and better understand the rules and regulations that the poet seems to have developed for his own poetry. Such a scientific study – as carried out by Agosti/Gonnelli, and others (including my own analysis of the Biblical Poems) – will, no doubt, further confirm the growing academic consensus that Gregory (although not, perhaps, an excellent poet) was not as careless or as mediocre as previous scholars have concluded.

Bibliography

Agosti, G. 2001. "Late antique iambics and *iambikè idéa*", in A. Cavarzere/A. Aloni/A. Barchiesi (eds.), *Iambic Ideas*, Oxford, 219–255.
Agosti, G./Gonnelli, F. 1995. "Materiali per la storia dell'esametro nei poeti cristiani greci", in M. Fantuzzi/R. Pretagostini (eds.), *Struttura e storia dell'esametro greco*, I, Pisa, 289–434.
Bauer, W. 2000. *A Greek-English lexicon of the New Testament and other early Christian literature*, (third ed.) Chicago (IL).
Cameron, Alan 1971. "*Pap. Ant.* III. 115 and the iambic prologue in late Greek poetry", *CQ*, 20, 119–129.
Dubischar, M. 2010. "Survival of the most condensed? Auxiliary texts, communications theory, and condensation of knowledge", in M. Horster/C. Reitz (eds.), *Condensing texts – condensed texts*, Stuttgart, 39–67.
Dunkle, B. 2012. *Poems on Scripture*, New York.
Fantuzzi, M./Hunter, R. 2004. *Tradition and innovation in Hellenistic poetry*, Cambridge
Fuhrer, T. 2013. "Hypertexts and auxiliary texts: new genres in Late Antiquity?", in T.D. Papanghelis/S.J. Harrison/S. Frangoulidis (eds.), *Generic interfaces in Latin literature : encounters, interactions, transformations*, Berlin, 79–92.
Genette, G. 1997. *Paratexts*, Cambridge. Trans. J.E. Lewin.
Gutzwiller, K. 2007. *A guide to Hellenistic literature*, Oxford.
Harder, M.A. 1998. "Generic games in Callimachus' *Aetia*", in M.A. Harder/R.F. Regtuit/G.C. Wakker (eds.), *Genre in Hellenistic poetry*, Groningen.
Hawkins, T. 2014. *Iambic poetics in the Roman Empire*, Cambridge.
Horrocks, G. 2010. *Greek: a history of its language and its speakers*, (second ed.) Oxford.
Hose, M. 2004. *Poesie aus der Schule. Überlegungen zur spätgriechischen Dichtung*, München.
Maas, P. 1962. *Greek metre*, Oxford. Trans. H. Lloyd-Jones.
Marrou, H. 1982. *A history of education in Antiquity*, Madison (WI).
McGuckin, J. 2001. *Saint Gregory of Nazianzus: an intellectual biography*, Crestwood (NY).
Milovanovic, C. 1997. "Gregory of Nazianzus: ars poetica", *JECS*, 5, 497–510.
Oberhaus, M. 1991. *Gregor von Nazianz: Gegen den Zorn*, Paderborn.
Palla, R. 1989. "Ordinamento e polimetria delle poesie bibliche di Gregorio Nazianzeno", *WS*, 102, 169–185.

Prudhomme, J. 2006. *L'œuvre poétique de Grégoire de Nazianze* (diss.), Lyon.
Roberts, M. 1985. *Biblical epic and rhetorical paraphrase in Late Antiquity*, Liverpool.
Rosenmeyer, T.G. 2006. "Ancient literary genres: a mirage?", in A. Laird (ed.), *Ancient literary criticism*, Oxford, 421–439.
Sicherl, M. 2002. "Verschmolzene Gedichte Gregors von Nazianz", in W. Blümer/R. Henke/ M. Mülke (eds.), *Alvarium Festschrift für Christian Gnilka*, Münster, 313–323.
Simelidis, C. (ed.) 2009. *Selected poems of Gregory Nazianzus*, Göttingen.
Skyes, D.A. 1979. "The *Poemata Arcana* of St. Gregory Nazianzen: some literary questions", *ByzZ*, 72, 6–15.
Szabat, E. 2015. "Late Antiquity and the transmission of educational ideals and methods: the Greek world", in W.M. Bloomer (ed.), *A Companion to ancient education*, Oxford, 252–263.
Thielmann, F. 1998. "The place of the *Apocalypse* in the canon of St. Gregory Nazianzen", *Tyndale Bull.*, 49, 155–157.
Watts, E.J. 2006. *City and school in late antique Athens and Alexandria*, London.
West, M.L. 1982. *Greek metre*, Oxford.
West, M.L. 1987. *Introduction to Greek metre*, Oxford.
West, M.L. 2011. "Homer's meter", in I. Morri/B. Powell (eds.), *A new Companion to Homer*, Leiden, 218–237.
Whitby, Mary 2008. "Sugaring the pill: Gregory of Nazianzus' advice to Olympias (*Carm.* 2.2.6)", *Ramus*, 37, 79–98.
White, C. 1996. *Gregory of Nazianzus: autobiographical poems*, Cambridge.
Whitmarsh, T. 2001. *Greek literature and the Roman Empire: the politics of imitation*, Oxford.

Maria Jennifer Falcone
Some Observations on the Genre of Dracontius' *Satisfactio*

As scholars have abundantly demonstrated, not only is it difficult to offer a clear classification of the literary genres in Late Antiquity, but the very idea of 'genre' is problematic and subject to debate.[1] Indeed, it has been said that, "the sharpest resistance to a classification in the traditional genre, or of any genre system, occurs in Christian literary works."[2] Far from being an exception in this regard, Dracontius' *Satisfactio* is a prime example of a very complex literary work.[3] It offers an interesting, concrete case study for those who aim to analyze the poetry of a Christian author, as this poem's classification in terms of literary genre is a particularly vexing question.[4] In fact, in stressing different aspects, scholars have interpreted the poem in a variety of ways: as an elegy[5] due to both metrical choice and the connection with Dracontius' main model, namely Ovid (and in particular *Tristia* 2); as a Romanized psalm[6] focusing on analogy with the Penitential Psalms; as a poetic *suasoria* emphasizing the poem's rhetorical aspects and its structure of arguments;[7] and finally, as a composite genre.[8] The plurality of these interpretive attempts confirms the complexity of the poem, yet none seems to be completely satisfactory on its own.

Rather than search for what seems to be an ellusively exact definition, this chapter offers a pragmatic approach, and in doing so, identifies the text-type (to

---

1 The bibliography on this topic is sizeable. After Kroll 1924, 202–224, see on different aspects: Rossi 1971; Fontaine 1977; Fowler 1982; Fedeli 1989; Depew/Obbink 2000; Consolino 2003; Farrell 2003; Rosenmeyer 2006; Wasyl 2011, 7–8; Fuhrer 2013 (with further references).
2 Fuhrer 2013, 80.
3 One may observe that the genre of this Christian-themed poem of Dracontius seems to be more convoluted and complex than what we find in his mythological poems, where he reinterprets the usual genres (such as *epithalamium* or *epyllion*) as a late antique author would do. On the mythological poems see in this volume Fischer and Wolff, both with further bibliography. I argue that the heightened complexity of the *Satisf.* is related to the fact that the poet is dealing here more deeply with the problem of his imprisonment. As for the, also complex, genre of his other Christian poem, the *Laudes,* see Stella 1988.
4 For an overview until 1996 see Mariano 1997, 122–123.
5 See Arevalo 1791, 65; de Duhn 1873. On Ovid as a model see Fielding 2017.
6 So Fontaine 1981, 276 : "Psaume romanisé."
7 See Schetter 1990, 90: "poetisches Gnadengesuch"; Galli Milić 2009, 246: "plaidoyer en verses"; Goldlust 2015, 245: "*deprecatio.*"
8 See Moussy 1988, 148: "le genre littéraire de la *Satisfactio* est donc composite."

https://doi.org/10.1515/9783110696219-007

which Dracontius himself primarily hints at) as belonging to the penitential genre. The poet offers a peculiar interpretation of this Christian genre, the '*paenitentia*', (typically addressed to God), which he intermingles with the '*deprecatio*' (the invocation addressed to the king). Moreover, several other elements further increase the poem's complexity. First, the presence of hymnal and precatory sections shows how the boundaries between different Christian genres are often blurred. Second, certain elements are not easily linked to a precise literary genre, namely the presence of *exempla*, the long *excursus* (vv. 53–92 and 215–264) and the strategic use of *topoi*, deriving both from prosaic argumentative texts and from the classical poetic tradition (and primarily from Ovid). Finally, as the first example of 'a prison poem' in the history of Western literature, the *Satisfactio* contains references to the poet's imprisonment[9] and its fictional representation; these demonstrate how, when faced with this new factual situation, Dracontius readapts the classical exile literature, which he highlights, *inter alia*, through his choice of meter.

Confessio, Paenitentia, Satisfactio

The main theme of the work is the confession of Dracontius' fault and his request for forgiveness, one that is characteristic of the penitential genre, common in Africa during the fifth and sixth centuries CE.[10] An important peculiarity of Dracontius' work is a hint at the originally juridical meaning contained in the title *satisfactio*, which is related to the payment of any kind of obligations.[11] This is common in various prosaic penitential works of the Church Fathers, who represented sin as a debt undertaken by man, who must pay for it through acts of penance in order to obtain forgiveness. A paradigmatic example of this is Tertullian's treatise *On Repentance* (*De paenitentia*).[12] In this work, the Church Father describes the path of reconciliation between the human sinner and God as the result

---

9 This is one of the most debated issues regarding Dracontius: probably due to a literary work in which he allegedly celebrated someone as a king (see *infra*, n. 14) he was imprisoned by Gunthamund: for an overview see Moussy 1988, 143–145 and the bibliography mentioned in this paper, at n. 14.
10 On the specificities of this genre see Bianco 1984, 27–29; Quacquarelli 1995, 140–142; Nosarti, forthcoming.
11 See Santini 2006, 182 for further literature. Fielding 2017, 98–99 interprets the word as a hint at the second addressee of the poem, the king, whom Dracontius promises to celebrate in a poem.
12 Rahner 2007, esp. 116–126.

of three phases, which also plays an important role in Dracontius' poem. These are the *confessio*, the *paenitentia*, and the *satisfactio*.[13] In order to single out the elements hinting at this genre, it is useful to compare them with passages of Verecundus of Junca's *Carmen de satisfactione paenitentiae*. This later poem, perhaps written during the poet's exile in Chalcedony (after 551 CE), consists of 212 hexameters (thus confirming the possibility that Dracontius' choice of the elegiac couplets may have been intended to emphasize the Ovidian literary model) and is the only other extant poetic work belonging to the penitential genre.

Similarly to Verecundus, (e.g., at vv. 22–23 and 40–41), Dracontius devotes a number of passages to his admission of guilt, the *confessio*. He represents his fault as a sin of idolatry, and, although he resorts to a meta-literary language, he never clearly explains exactly what he did:

a) The first mention of his sin occurs at vv. 19–26: Here his admission of guilt is related to the complex theory of human responsibility and free will, and in this section the poet's fault itself occupies only the second half of v. 25 and syntactically only an absolute ablative: *tacitis tot regibus almis* ("passing over in silence so many benevolent kings").

b) Next (vv. 41–44: *peccando regi dominoque Deoque*) the poet admits his fault against both God and king and represents himself as worse than a dog – for while the latter can use its tongue to treat its wounds, the poet's tongue (i.e. his poetry) has indeed caused his own wounds.

c) Later (vv. 53–54: *culpa quidem gravis est*) he admits his serious fault but at the same time stresses the fact that it deserves forgiveness.

d) The next passage (vv. 93–94: *culpa mihi fuerat dominos reticere modestos | ignotumque mihi scribere vel dominum*, "it was my fault not to praise the gentle masters and to write of an unknown man as a lord") is one of the most hotly debated in Dracontius' entire oeuvre, as it seems to contain an allusion to the composition of a poem that the Vandal king did not appreciate. Two infinitive clauses follow the admission of guilt, clearly expressed at the beginning of the distich with *culpa mihi fuerat*. They refer to the poet's twofold fault: 1) not having praised the actual kings (*dominos reticere modestos*); 2)

---

13 See in particular Tert., *Paen.* 8.9: *confessio enim satisfactionis consilium est* ("for confession is counseled by a desire [to make] satisfaction"); and 9.2: *satisfactio confessione disponitur, confessione paenitentia nascitur* ("by confession satisfaction is settled, of confession repentance is born").

having celebrated an "unknown" person (*ignotumque mihi scribere vel dominum*) – despite the interpretative issues because of the meaning of *ignotus* here.[14]

e) In the following line, (v. 107: *post te, summe Deus, regi dominoque reus sum*, "after You, Supreme God, I am guilty before my lord and king"), Dracontius again admits his guilt against God and king.

f) Additionally, vv. 105–106 contain a new reference to the poem that caused Dracontius' imprisonment (*carminis ullius*) and also mention the two first steps on the path of reconciliation as described by Tertullian (see above), namely the *confessio* (*fateor*) and the *paenitentia* (*paenitet*). *Hysteron proteron* and *zeugma* (genitive properly occurs only with *paenitet*) amplify the poetic stress on these verbs.

Penitential works naturally contain references to God's mercy and to the theological theme of forgiveness.[15] Just like other authors, Dracontius links these topics to the classical *topoi* related to *clementia* and *ira*, key themes of the poem.[16] These arguments occur explicitly twice in the *Satisfactio*:

a) At vv. 95–100 (*idola vana*), the reference to the sin of idolatry, which both the pagans and the Israelites committed, establishes a parallel between them and the poet. They are all guilty of ingratitude and of celebrating the wrong 'deity'. The (implicit) consequence is that if God forgave them, the poet too can hope to be forgiven, provided he repents. The explicit reference to God's mercy is declared at v. 99: *et tamen indulges veniam poscentibus, auctor* ("and yet, Creator, You are kind to those who ask for forgiveness").

b) In the closure, (vv. 305–308: *qui poscit hac lege deum ut peccata relaxet, | debet et ipse suo parcere ubique reo*, "Whoever on account of this precept beseeches God to forgive his sins, should himself on every occasion be merciful to the one who offends him") the poet hints at theological issues related to the theme of forgiveness. Namely, if a man asks God for forgiveness, he in

---

14 The identification of the *ignotus ... dominus* is problematic. Zenon, Odoacer, Theodoricus are the traditional answers, for which see Camus-Moussy 1985, 18–26 and Comparelli 2003, 114–115. Wolff 1988 and Merrills 2004 identify this person with someone within the Vandal family itself, based on the legal problems around dynastic succession. For an overview see Luceri 2007, 25; Wolff 2015, 212–213; Labarre 2015, 231–232 (with reference also to the *Laudes Dei*, henceforth *LD*); Steinacher 2016, 278–279; Fielding 2017, 91–92.
15 The poetic representation of theological issues is an important argument of late antique Christian poetry, as shown by Gasti/Cutino 2015.
16 Cf. esp. Verecundus, vv. 64–65. There are parallels with Seneca's treatises, but also, e.g., with Lactantius' *De Ira Dei*.

turn must show mercy to others. This is the key theme of the Lord's Prayer (*Vulg.* Mt 6:12). For Dracontius, forgiveness has no limits (vv. 307–309: *non semel ignosci dixit lex sancta reatum, | sed quotiens culpa est, sit totiens venia*, "The Holy Law stipulates that the delinquent be pardoned not merely once; but as often as the fault occurs, let there be endless forgiveness"), following Jesus' admonition to Peter in Matthew 18:21–22 (Vulgate): *non dico tibi usque septies, sed usque septuagies septies* ("not seven times, but, I tell you, seventy-seven times").[17]

When it comes to the explicit requests for forgiveness, another important element of penitential works,[18] Dracontius' peculiar interpretation of this genre comes into play. Instead of addressing his request to God, he asks the king to forgive him, though still invoking God as well. This is a consequence of the hierarchy between God and king, which acts nearly as a thematic refrain throughout the composition, starting from its very first words, as evidenced by the richly meaningful expression *rex immense deus*. In invoking God, the poet chooses to focus on his royalty, and in doing so, he naturally hints at the Vandal king as well, the second addressee of the poem and the one responsible for his punishment.[19] This use of a double addressee indicates a double aim as well: In fact, it is to God that the poet admits his sin, but when it comes to asking for forgiveness, he mentions Gunthamund. This leads to a primary blending of literary genres: The penitential poem is intermingled with a *deprecatio* (in this respect, Claudian may have been an important model for Dracontius).[20] At the same time, Dracontius presents the king as a quasi-'divine' figure: As a result, the interference works in both directions, so that the penitential genre strongly modifies the characteristics of the *deprecatio*.[21] Dracontius' requests for forgiveness occur in the following passages:
a) At vv. 107–108, the request is addressed to the king (v. 108: *cuius ab imperio posco gemens veniam*, "from his sovereignty, groaning, I ask for mercy"), who needs to be guided by God (for vv. 109–114 see *infra*).

---

17 St. Margaret 1936, 99–100 has already compared the biblical passages.
18 See e.g. Verecundus vv. 68 and 117: *expiet erroris pietatis dextera culpas | ... cerne, precor, mitis manibusque attolle iacentem* ("Cleanse the sins of error with your merciful right hand; look upon me gently, I beseech, and lift up with your hands him who is prostrate on the ground").
19 See also Polara 1987, 76; Galli Milić 2009, 253; Labarre 2015, 232–233; Goldlust 2015, 248–249; Luceri 2015, 277; Fielding 2017, 113.
20 Cf. Claud., *carm. min.* 22 and 23. Galli Milić 2009 has thoroughly focused on the interpretation of Dracontius' poem as a *deprecatio*, and its similarities with Claudian's works.
21 On the representation of God with the characteristics of the emperor, common in late antique Christian texts, see Stella 1988, 268 (with further bibliography).

b) The following lines, vv. 117–120, contain a new heartfelt request to the king, not coincidentally addressed as *princeps* (v. 117) by a suppliant (*supplex* emphatically at the end of v. 117), who presents himself as an 'Ovidian' poet, perhaps also thanks to the reference to the *topos* of the poem-ship.[22] The interaction between the two genres is here particularly evident, because of a stronger presence of penitential elements. The representation of the sinner is highlighted: He prays with his whole body and soul (vv. 118: *pectore mente rogans, voce manuque petens*), a sign that these gestures are the external expression of an inner feeling; he seeks God's hand (v. 119: *da dextram misero*) and he invokes his forgiveness (v. 119: *veniam concede precanti*).

c) At the closure, the request is addressed, as before, to the king (vv. 311–312: *da veniam, miserere, precor, succurre roganti | pristina sufficient verbera vincla fames*, "Give forgiveness, take pity, I beg you, help the one who beseeches you, let there be an end to the lashes, chains, hunger of days bygone"). In the pentameter, the poet refers to the fact that thanks to his punishment, now he has paid his debt: In other words, he has accomplished his *satisfactio*, and consequently he can be forgiven with the expressive final tricolon: *pristina sufficiant verbera vincla fames*.

The following passages also evince a close relationship between God and king. Therefore, they confirm the very strong interference of the *deprecatio* in Dracontius' peculiar penitential poem:

a) In the first passage, (vv. 49–52: *ipse meo domino Deus imperat atque iubebit | ut me restituat respiciatque pius, | servet, avi ut laudes dicam patriasque suasque | perque suas proles regia vota canam*, "God Himself, governs my lord and He will order him to care for me, and, just man that he is, restore me and save me so that I may sing the praises of his grandfather, his father, and his own, and among his children chant prayers for the royal house"), the hierarchy between God, king, and poet is very clear: Since the king obeys God, the poet is sure that if God orders his release, the king will acquiesce – and once free, the poet will be able to celebrate the king's family.

b) At vv. 101–114, a parallel implicitly established between God and Gunthamund confirms and strengthens this hierarchy. The poet, in fact, insists on the king's *pietas* as the main characteristic which would connect him most closely with God. He recalls the expression *pietas tua* (v. 109, referring to God) at v. 112, where *pietate sua* (with remarkable polyptoton) refers to the

---

[22] For *mea vela retorqueo* ("I turn my sails away") cf. Ov., *Tr.* 1.1.84.

king. Dracontius stresses this argument even more: he places *pius* emphatically at the end of v. 110 and recalls this adjective using the synonyms *bonus* and *placidus* at v. 112.[23]

c) The next lines, (vv. 149–151: *ignoscendo pius nobis imitare Tonantem, | qui indulget culpas et veniam tribuit. | principis Augusti simile est ad regna polorum*, "In pardoning us you piously imitate the God of thunder Who has mercy on our faults and bestows pardon. The kingdom of a sovereign Augustus is like that of heaven"), strengthen this claim by a reference to the parallels between the reign of heaven and that of the Vandal kingdom. The equivalence between divine and imperial sovereigns was very important for the Augustan poets, and the explicit mention of *Augustus princeps* is not by chance here, but rather hints at the Romanization of Vandal Carthage, a concept which has already been studied by scholars commenting on various literary works of this period.[24] Its interpretation in Late Antiquity was strongly influenced by Augustine's *City of God*, and the God-king hierarchy in the *Satisfactio* confirms this tendency. Ovid's poems of the exile, and above all *Tristia* 2,[25] play an important role as well.

In religious poetry, the exact boundaries of a single genre are even more difficult to define than in other cases. In particular, modulations of hymnal and precatory poems are frequently found in every kind of Christian poetry.[26] The following passages of the *Satisfactio* evince characteristics of these two religious genres, enriching the complexity of the poem in terms of literary genre:[27]

a) vv. 1–18: As is typical of Dracontius,[28] the poem begins with a hymnal section. God's invocation is followed by his attributes (v. 1). The *Relativ-Stil* (vv. 2–4; 11–14) alternates with *Partizipial-Stil* (vv. 5–7); the *Du-Stil* is prevalent

---

23 *Pietas* is a key argument of the poem. It occurs, e.g., also at vv. 192–195 with the expression *rex dominusque pius*, used for the Vandal kings as shown by coinage; see St. Margaret 1936, 61–62; Steinacher 2016, 181–183.
24 Cf. Paolucci 2008 with further literature.
25 For the relevant presence of Ovid in Dracontius' works, with the aim of emphasizing the common situation of suffering, see Bouquet 1982; Galli Milić 2009, 259–260; Goldlust 2015, 251; Luceri 2015, 279–282. Fieldling 2017, 89–129 has analyzed in depth the presence of Ovid (in particular his exile works, and – above all – *Tr.* 2) in Dracontius' *Satisfactio*.
26 Regarding Dracontius see Stella 1988 on the genre of the *LD*. For a 'modulation' of hymn in Nonnus' *Paraphrase* see Hadjittofi in this volume.
27 In this section I use the terminology of Norden 2002.
28 See also the first sections of each book of *LD*, (esp. 2.1: *omnipotens aeterne Deus, fons auctor origo* "omnipotent, eternal God, source, Creator, origin"), but also the hymnal sections of some *Romulea*, listed and commented by La Bua 1999, 407–415.

throughout the section, while the *Er-Stil* appears only at vv. 15–16 in order to stress the keywords of the poem *ira favorque Dei*.

b) vv. 81–86: With a focus on the sun, the tone of this example is higher than that of any other in the same sequence, owing to the use of forms typical of the hymn: namely, the presence of a cletic attribution at v. 81 (*species gratissima mundi*), and the passage from *Partizipial-Stil* (*parans* and *fovens*) to *Relativ-Stil* (*per quem*).[29]

c) vv. 101–116: This prayer is traditionally addressed to God (*te precor, omnipotens*). It contains the formal characteristics of the precatory genre: *Du-Stil* with anaphoric *te* and *tua*, alternating with *Er-Stil* (vv. 114–116); the *Relativ-Stil* (vv. 101–104; v. 108, here in reference to the king; vv. 115–116); the invocations (v. 101: *omnipotens*; v. 107: *summe Deus*); the use of independent conjunctive (vv. 109 and 112); the presence of the keywords of the *precatio*, namely *precor* v. at 101; *posco* at v. 108 (and here it is interesting to note that the addressee is no longer God, but the king); *exorent*, v. 115.

Rhetorical *topoi*

The strong presence of *exempla* and the strategic use of *topoi* on the one hand strengthen the persuasive and argumentative aim of the poem while also showing Dracontius' reliance on previous poetic traditions. Scholars have already sufficiently described the argumentative structure of the *Satisfactio*.[30] Therefore, it will only be necessary to touch on certain rhetorical elements which Dracontius adapted into a poetic language, just as Ovid had done before him.

a) *Exempla*: At vv. 27–48, the poet mentions Nebuchadnezzar and Zacharias as examples of people forgiven by God. The presence of these figures in the works of Church Fathers on the theme of sin and forgiveness is relevant and

---

29 It is important to note that references to the sun occur often in late antique literary texts (see Paolucci 2008, 300–301 and 312). It is sometimes related to the representation of the Vandal kings: so in *AL* 389 R. = 385 Sh.-B. (see Zurli 2008) and in *AL* 376 R. = 371 Sh.-B., vv. 3s.: *toto sic clarior orbe | sol radiante micans cunctis super eminet astris* ("thus brighter than the whole globe, a sun that sparkles radiant stands out above all the stars", about Thrasamund). In other texts, it is connected with the representation of the Christian God or the pagan gods: Macr., *Sat.* 1.17.2–3; Aus., *prec.* 2; Paul. Nol., *carm.* 10.49; Mart. Cap., *nupt.* 2.185ff.
30 See in particular Schetter 1990; Galli Milić 2009; Bisanti 2010, 212–213; Goldlust 2015.

could have played a role in Dracontius' choices.³¹ The tone of the verses, however, is fully poetical and 'Ovidian'.³² At vv. 152–190, there is a (debated) list of Christians (David, Solomon, Stephen Protomartyr) and Romans (Caesar, Augustus, Titus, Commodus) who had shown *pietas* during their lives. Scholars think that Dracontius may have found similar lists in rhetorical handbooks.³³ Finally, at vv. 297–302, Dracontius tells the story of the forgiveness accorded to a man named Vincomalos by an ancestor of the king, to whom the poet refers at v. 299 with the expression *vestrae pietatis origo*. The last term supports the identification of the king with Genseric, though the identity of Vincomalos is not clear.³⁴

b) *Topoi*: The strategic use of *topoi* and the way in which they are inserted in the poem divulge Dracontius' literary models. In fact, at vv. 137–148, the theme of the lion's *clementia* is a *topos* (see Plin., *HN* 8.48; but also Gell., *NA* 5.14, with the story of Androcles and the lion)³⁵ and already in use in poetry by Ovid (*Tr.* 3.5.33–36)³⁶ and Claudian (*carm. min.* 22.28–32).³⁷

c) *Excursus*: The long sequences of vv. 53–92 and vv. 215–264 are two *excursus*. In the first case, the main theme is the coexistence of *mala* and *bona* in every aspect of creation; the second section is about the *temporis ordo*. In both cases, the first verses are devoted to the description of the main theme: See for the first passage vv. 56–58 (and especially v. 58: *et bona mixta malis et mala mixta bonis*, "and good mixed with evil, and evil mixed with good"),³⁸ and for the second vv. 215–216, in particular 216 (c). As is often the case in Ovid's poems,³⁹ strategies of multiplication and repetition both at a phonic and at a syntactic/lexical level characterize the sequences. See, e.g., vv. 65–

---

31 See, Jer., *Expl. Dan.* 1.4.1, *CCSL* 75 A at p. 810f. for Nebuchadnezzar, and August., *Serm.* 293.2 for Zacharias.
32 I focus elsewhere on the meaning and the models of this passage. See recently Fielding 2017, 103–104 (with further insights).
33 Alfonsi 1961, 298–299; for possible sources of Dracontius' *exempla* see Labarre 2015, 234–238 and 241, where the scholar stresses the importance of analyzing this aspect in order to highlight the coherence between the Christian and classicizing works of the author.
34 For further information see Moussy 1988, 223.
35 For the tradition of this story see Spina 2008.
36 See Fielding 2017, 113.
37 Cf. Galli Milić 2009, 255.
38 The verse offers a perfect description of the concept, and had a rich *Nachleben*, starting from Corippus (*Ioh.* 7.25: *hic mala mixta bonis*). As pointed out by scholars starting from Arevalo 1791, *ad* v. 58, the verse is quoted in Goldoni's *Molière*.
39 See Fielding 2017, 106–109, who analyzes in depth the relations between Dracontius' first *excursus* and Ovid's *concordia discors*.

66: *aspis habet mortes, habet et medicamina serpens | vipera saepe iuvat, vipera saepe nocet* ("The asp brings death, and the serpent brings remedies; the viper often aids, the viper often harms"), with antonyms and synonyms, anaphoric repetitions and perfect parallelism in the structure of the pentameter; and vv. 219–220: *omnia tempus agit, cum tempore cuncta trahuntur | tempora eunt vitae, tempora mortis eunt* ("Time drives everything, with time everything is driven along; the time of life passes; the time of death passes"), with synonymic variation, polyptoton, anaphoras and an almost perfect parallel structure (with the exception of the position of the first *eunt* in the pentameter, which creates a variation and avoids metrical problems). Similarly, in the first passage the very end of the *excursus* recalls the general theme. In fact, the poet alludes to the *incipit* at v. 87, in the second-last example of the list, where he explicitly uses for the first (and only) time after v. 58 the keywords *mala* and *bona*: *omnia nec mala sunt nec sunt bona sidera caeli* ("the stars of heaven are neither all good nor all evil"). Thanks to this echo, the reader is prompted to recognize the initial theme and prepare for the very end of the section, where the poet reasserts his argument with the new impetus provided by the long series of examples: vv. 91–92: *quod caelum, quod terra, fretum, quod purior aer | non meruere simul, hoc homo quando habeat?* ("What the heaven, what the earth, the sea, the pure air, what all these together do not have, how can a man possess?"). In the hexameter, it is notable that the *cumulatio* of substantives recalls the very first example of the section, namely the Empedoclean elements, which were already mentioned at vv. 59–60 through the equivalent adjectives: *sic elementa potens contraria miscuit auctor, | umida cum siccis, ignea cum gelidis* ("thus the mighty Creator mixed together the opposite elements, the wet with the dry, the fiery with the icy"). The pentameter confirms the main defensive argument, namely the fact that, just like all creatures, human beings are naturally made of opposites, and consequently there is no possibility for them to be completely free from sin (see v. 54: *quod sine peccati crimine nemo fuit*).

Finally, elements regarding the poet's imprisonment contribute to the increased complexity of this poem in terms of the genre classification. While the final words of the *explicit* in manuscript V (*Vat. Reg. Lat.* 1267) confirm the factual situation (*dum esset in vinculis*), the poet himself refers to his current imprisonment in many passages of the poem, both in direct and indirect ways.[40] As mentioned

---

40 Wolff 2004 and Luceri 2015 particularly focused on Dracontius' representation of his imprisonment, both in the *Satisf.* and in *LD*.

above, this is a characteristic of prison literature,[41] of which the *Satisfactio* happens to be the first poetic example in Western literature. In order to describe his captivity, Dracontius readapts the classical form and content of exile literature. This also explains the choice of the elegiac distich instead of the hexameter (used for his main Christian work, but also by Verecundus in his more conventional penitential poem).

In the following passages, there are major and minor references to Dracontius' imprisonment:

a) The first mention of his captivity and misfortune occurs at v. 26, with the semantically pregnant adjective *miser* placed at the end of the verse: *ut peterem subito certa pericla miser* ("so that suddenly I was exposed to real danger, wretched me").

b) In the important section on Nebuchadnezzar and Zacharias analysed above, the poet introduces the parallel between himself and a dog at v. 42: *peior sum factus deteriorque cane* ("I have become worse than and inferior to a dog"). In this case, he refers only indirectly to his punishment and to the inhumane prison conditions. Dracontius intensifies the proverbial expression *peior cane*[42] resorting to synonymy and hyperbaton.

c) Further indirect hints at prison, prisoners, and the good prison conditions under Vandal rule are found in the poem with a clear persuasive and celebratory objective. In particular, at vv. 121–136 Dracontius focuses on the themes of silence (127: *captivus securus agit*; 128: *praeda quieta sedet*) and good food (122: *captivosque tuos deliciis epulas*; 129–130: *victum super ipse ministras | ne sit vita gravis subripiente fame*).

d) For the clearest description of the ill-treatment he suffered in captivity, Dracontius uses an expressive tricolon. This occurs only at almost the very end of the poem at v. 312: *verbera vincla fames*. A similar expression, with an adjective instead of the second noun, occurs at v. 284: *frigus inopsque fames*. Here too the poet complains that his family too must have suffered (v. 284: *culpa meorum*), even though he himself was the only one guilty.

---

41 For research on prison literature, which particularly flourished since the 1980s in relation to modern texts, see Weigel 1982 and Keßler 2001.
42 See Moussy 1988, 199.

Conclusions

In conclusion, the difficulties in attributing the *Satisfactio* to a precise literary genre are due both to a tendency common in late antique literature[43] and to the peculiarities of Dracontius' work itself. Nevertheless, it is still possible to single out a text-type, one to which the poet consciously refers: the penitential poem. He both establishes a hierarchy between God and the Vandal king throughout the work while also hinting (more or less implicitly) at the presence of a double addressee starting from the very first word of the poem (*rex*). Thus, Dracontius interprets the penitential genre in a very distinctive manner and harmonizes it with the *deprecatio*. The insertion of minor secondary voices enriches this major polyphony. Prayers and hymns, rhetorical devices such as *topoi*, *exempla*, and *excursus* readapted and inserted in the poem à la Ovid, as well as the elegiac meter, guarantee variation and strengthen the complexity in terms of literary genre. Finally, references to the factual experience of his imprisonment act as a constant countermelody, reverberating through the interlaced points of this 'literary knot' of a work.

Bibliography

Alfonsi, L. 1961. "Commodo in Draconzio", *RFIC*, 89, 296–300.
Arevalo, F. (ed.) 1791. *Dracontii Aemilii Carmina (= PL 60, 901–932)*, (editio princeps), Roma.
Bianco, M.G. (ed.) 1984. *Verecundi Iuncensis Carmen de paenitentia*, Napoli.
Bisanti, A. 2010. "Retorica e declamazione nell'Africa vandalica. Draconzio, l'*Aegritudo Perdicae*, l'*Epistula Didonis ad Aeneam*", in G. Petrone/A. Casamento (eds.), *Studia... in umbra educata. Percorsi della reotrica latina in età imperiale*, Palermo, 189–221.
Bouquet, J. 1982. "L'imitation d'Ovide chez Dracontius", in R. Chevallier (ed.), *Colloque Présence d'Ovide (Tours, 26–28 septembre 1980)*, Paris, 177–187.
Camus, C./Moussy, C. (eds.) 1985. *Dracontius, Œuvres, Louanges de Dieu, Livres I–II*, Paris.
Comparelli, F. 2003. "La *Satisfactio* di Draconzio 1", *Schol(i)a*, 5, 111–141.
Consolino, F.E. (ed.) 2003. *Forme letterarie nella produzione latina di IV–V secolo. Con uno sguardo a Bisanzio*, Roma.
de Duhn, F. (ed.) 1873. *Dracontii Carmina Minora*, Leipzig.
Depew, M./Obbink, D. (eds.) 2000. *Matrices of genre: authors, canons, and society*, Cambridge (MA).
Farrell, J. 2003. "Classical genre in theory and practice", *New Literary History*, 34, 383–408.

---

43 See above, n. 1.

Fedeli, P. 1989. "Le intersezioni dei generi e dei modelli", in G. Cavallo/P. Fedeli/A. Giardina (eds.), *Lo spazio letterario di Roma antica, I: la produzione del testo*, Roma, 375–397.
Fielding, I. 2017. *Transformations of Ovid in Late Antiquity*, Cambridge.
Fontaine, J. 1977. "Unité et diversité du mélange des genres et des tons chez quelques écrivains latins de la fin du IVe siècle: Ausone, Ambroise, Ammien", in Alan Cameron/ M. Fuhrmann et al. (eds.), *Christianisme et formes littéraires de l'antiquité tardive en Occident*, Vandœuvres, 425–472.
Fontaine, J. 1981. *Naissance de la poésie dans l'Occident chrétien. Esquisse d'une histoire de la poésie latine chrétienne du IIIe au VIe siècle*, Paris.
Fowler, A. 1982. *Kinds of literature. An introduction to the theory of genres and modes*, Oxford.
Fuhrer, T. 2013. "Hypertexts and auxiliary texts: new genres in Late Antiquity?", in T.D. Papanghelis/S.J. Harrison/S. Frangoulidis (eds.), *Generic interfaces in Latin literature. Encounters, interactions and transformations*, Berlin, 79–89.
Galli Milić, L. 2009. "Stratégies argumentatives dans la *Satisfactio* de Dracontius", in H. Harich-Schwarzbauer/P. Schierl (eds.), *Lateinische Poesie der Spätantike (Internationale Tagung in Castelen bei Augst, 11.–13. Oktober 2007)*, Basel, 245–266.
Gasti, F./Cutino, M. (eds.) 2015. *Poesia e teologia nella produzione latina dei secoli IV–V. Atti della X Giornata Ghisleriana di Filologia classica (Pavia, 16 maggio 2013)*, Pavia.
Goldlust, B. 2015. "La persona de Dracontius dans la *Satisfactio*: quelques réflexions sur la posture discursive du poète", in É. Wolff (ed.), *Littérature, politique et religion en Afrique vandale*, Paris, 243–256.
Keßler, N. 2001. *Schreiben, um zu überleben. Studien zur Gefangenenliteratur*, Mönchengladbach.
Kroll, W. 1924. *Studien zum Verständnis der römischen Literatur*, Stuttgart.
Labarre, S. 2015. "Dracontius et les 'crimes' des héros païens: historiographie, quête du salut et drames humaines", in É. Wolff (ed.), *Littérature, politique et religion en Afrique vandale*, Paris, 229–242.
La Bua, G. 1999. *L'inno nella letteratura poetica latina*, San Severo.
Luceri, A. (ed.) 2007. *Gli epitalami di Blossio Emilio Draconzio (Rom. 6 e 7)*, Roma.
Luceri, A. 2015. "'Notus et ignotus desunt': Draconzio e i suoi (presunti) amici", in É. Wolff (ed.), *Littérature, politique et religion en Afrique vandale*, Paris, 275–286.
Mariano, B.M. 1997. "Satisfactio", in L. Castagna (ed.), *Studi Draconziani (1912–1996)*, Napoli.
Merrills, A.H. 2004. "The perils of panegyric: the lost poem of Dracontius and its consequences", in idem (ed.), *Vandals, Romans and Berbers. New perspectives on late antique North Africa*, Burlington (VT), 145–162.
Moussy, C. (ed.) 1988. *Dracontius, Œuvres, Louanges de Dieu Livre III. Réparation*, Paris.
Munier, C. (ed.) 1984. *Tertullien, La pénitence*, Paris.
Norden, E. 2002. *Agnostos Theos. Dio ignoto. Ricerche sulla storia della forma del discorso religioso*, Brescia. Trans. C.O. Tommasi-Moreschini.
Nosarti, L. Forthcoming. *L'inno alla luce di Draconzio*.
Paolucci, P. 2008. "Interferenze tra il *Carmen saeculare* di Orazio e il carme *In laudem Solis* dell'*Anthologia Latina*", in L. Cristante/F. Ireneo (eds.), *Incontri triestini di filologia classica. 7, 2007–2008: atti del III convegno, Il calamo della memoria: riuso di testi e mestiere letterario nella tarda antichità, Trieste, 17–18 aprile 2008*, Trieste, 293–319.
Polara, G. 1987. *Letteratura latina tardoantica e altomedievale*, Roma.
Quacquarelli, A. 1995. *Retorica patristica e sue istituzioni interdisciplinari*, Roma.

Rahner, K. 2007. *Sämtliche Werke 6/1. De paenitentia I. Dogmatische Vorlesungen zum Bußsakrament*, Roma.
Rosenmeyer, T.G. 2006. "Ancient literary genres. A mirage?", in A. Laird (ed.), *Ancient literary criticism*, Oxford, 421–439.
Rossi, L.E. 1971. "I generi letterari e le loro leggi scritte e non scritte nelle letterature classiche", *BICS*, 18, 69–94.
Santini, C. 2006. *Inter iura poeta. Ricerche sul lessico giuridico di Draconzio*, Roma.
Schetter, W. 1990. "Zur *Satisfactio* des Dracontius", *Hermes*, 118, 90–117.
Spina, L. 2008. "Memento te esse leonem", *I Quaderni del Ramo d'Oro online*, 1, 217–237.
Steinacher, R. 2016. *Die Vandalen: Aufstieg und Fall eines Barbarenreichs*, Stuttgart.
Stella, F. 1988. "Fra retorica e innografia. Sul genere letterario delle *Laudes Dei* di Draconzio", *Philologus*, 132, 258–274.
St. Margaret, M. 1936. *Dracontii Satisfactio* (diss.), Philadelphia (PA).
Wasyl, A.M. 2011. *Genres rediscovered: studies in Latin miniature epic, love elegy, and epigram of the Romano-Barbaric Age*, Kraków.
Weigel, S. 1982. *'Und selbst im Kerker frei...!' Schreiben im Gefängnis. Zur Theorie und Gattungsgeschichte der Gefängnisliteratur 1750–1933*, Marburg.
Wolff, É. 1988. "L'*Aegritudo Perdicae*, un poème de Dracontius?", *RPh*, 62, 79–89.
Wolff, É. 2004. "*Poeta inclusus*: le cas de Dracontius", in C. Bertrand-Dagenbach/A. Chauvot/J.M. Salamito/D. Vaillancourt (eds.), *Carcer II.: prison et privation de liberté dans l'Empire romain et l'Occident médiéval*, Paris, 123–128.
Wolff, É. 2015. "Dracontius: bilan et aperçu sur quelques problèmes de sa vie et de son œuvre", in É. Wolff (ed.), *Littérature, politique et religion en Afrique vandale*, Paris, 211–225.
Zurli, L. 2008. *Anonymi in laudem Solis*, Hildesheim.

Étienne Wolff
Do Dracontius' *Epyllia* Have a Christian Apologetic Agenda?

Specialists of Dracontius generally label poems 2, 8, and 10 of the *Romulea* (*Hylas*, *De raptu Helenae*, and *Medea*) as well as the *Orestis tragoedia* as *epyllia*. These relatively long mythological poems (apart from poem 2, which is quite short and was written when the poet was young, and so does not really concern us here) raise at least two questions: that of their generic affiliation[1] and that of their intended purpose. This contribution will address these two questions, considering, in particular, how to reconcile their pagan themes with the otherwise Christian faith of the author. Do these poems, at least partially, have a Christian apologetic function?

In his *epyllia* Dracontius relates either a complete story (*Medea*, *Orestis tragoedia*), at the risk of restricting the whole tale to a simple overview, or a specific episode (*Hylas*). The *De raptu Helenae* is halfway between the two. Dracontius' intention was to transform the way the stories were told by merging literary genres and traditions. The problem of generic affiliation applies especially to *Medea* and *Orestis tragoedia*. In effect, Dracontius adopted the form of *epyllion* to deal with subjects that had previously been exclusively (*Orestis tragoedia*) or principally (*Medea*) dealt with in tragedy (Medea is also the subject of epics, such as those of Apollonius of Rhodes, Valerius Flaccus, and Ovid's *Metamorphoses*). Dracontius was well aware of this, since in the proem of his *Medea* (vv. 16–30), Calliope is made to transcend Polymnia and Melpomene, while in the proem of *Orestis tragoedia* (vv. 13–15), he appeals to Melpomene, asking her to relinquish the tragic buskin and the iambus to make the dactyl foot reverberate in their place, thus revealing the shift from tragedy to epic.[2] On the other hand, in the *De raptu Helenae* and, to a lesser extent, in the *Hylas*, the link to the epic genre is very clear. Some tension remains, however, between the magnitude of epic and the Alexandrian-style miniaturization. In poem 8 (*Helen*), Dracontius invokes Homer and Virgil in the context of a commonplace declaration of humility (vv. 11–30). Here, his self-proclaimed inferiority is both qualitative and quantitative: He lacks the boldness to rival Homer and Virgil, and, in addition, he writes short

---
1 This problem of generic affiliation also arises in the Christian poems of Dracontius, *De laudibus Dei* (henceforth, *LD*) and *Satisfactio*. On the latter poem see Falcone's contribution in this volume.
2 Cf. Fischer in this volume.

epic poems, *epyllia*, not grand epic. Furthermore, and in line with late antique literary aesthetics, it is obvious that Dracontius mixes genres, which allows for the inclusion of epithalamic and other rhetorical devices in his epic poems (especially in the *Medea* and *De raptu Helenae*).³ Symmetrically, in poem 5 of *Romulea*, a rhetorical piece in verse (titled *Controversia de statua viri fortis*), the worlds of declamation and epic merge, as the first verse, a cento of Virgil and Lucan, suggests.⁴ At the same time, Dracontius delivers a romanesque adaptation of the myths, blending versions and introducing episodes of his own making.⁵ For instance, in the *Orestis tragoedia* (vv. 44–107), he imagines an encounter between Agamemnon and Iphigenia in Tauris, which allows him to write a scene that features all the pathos of a reunion between father and daughter.

The *epyllia* and the tragic

Orestis tragoedia, which has come down to us through a manuscript tradition distinct from that of *Romulea* and without the name of the author, poses a specific challenge: how should we understand the word *tragoedia* in a poem that is not a tragedy at all? There are two possible, non-exclusive explanations: First, the author's intention was to indicate that the poem's subject matter was drawn from ancient tragedies;⁶ or, second, the word *tragoedia* takes the sense of "tragic story" – a meaning it already had in classical Latin, and particularly fitting in this case, since Dracontius recounts the whole of Orestes' story. Annick Stoehr-Monjou, however, rejects the title *Orestis tragoedia* as inauthentic and adopts *Orestis*.⁷

---

3 For the long-standing history of incorporating such rhetorical devices (some of which arguably attain the status of genres in themselves) see Cairns 2007. On Dracontius' *Medea* see Fischer's contribution in this volume.
4 On this verse see Wolff 2017.
5 Bureau 2003, 4 defines as "romanesque" the echoes of what we now consider as novelistic tropes – "dont le caractère à la fois hautement fantaisiste et largement romanesque" – irrespective of the existence or the reception of the ancient novel.
6 It is difficult to determine with certainty which tragedies (Greek and Latin) on the subject Dracontius would know. In his time, performed tragedy was to take exclusively the form of the pantomime, to which the poet alludes through Polymnia in the proem of the *Medea*. The *Latin Anthology* mentions several pantomime shows (111 and 310 Riese) and specifies two subjects (Andromache and Helen, 310). See also Wasyl in this volume.
7 Stoehr-Monjou 2009.

Whichever hypothesis we accept, it is clear that in this work, Dracontius experiments with generic mutation. "Melpomène s'est adaptée à l'écriture épique pour créer un genre hybride et neuf," as A. Stoehr-Monjou justifiably wrote.[8]

More widely, Dracontius' poetic design lies, at least in part, in a play on the reassignment of genres and the inclusion of intergeneric elements. The term '*epyllion*' is aptly applied to poems 2, 8, and 10 of *Romulea* and *Orestis tragoedia*. As in larger-scale epic, these poems involve prodigious actions by gods, heroes and prominent men in texts which deftly combine narrative and dialogue. However, the metaphysical and political dimensions are missing, while the emphasis is on personal adventure and emotions (love and criminal passion). This is an epic drawn back to the private sphere. The secularization and the romanesque tone of the narratives help to pull these legends closer to everyday experience.

Dracontius thus rewrote myths by transforming them and emphasizing certain aspects. This brings us to the question of the nature and purpose of the inflections to which Dracontius subjects the myth. One of the most striking aspects of Dracontius' writing of myths is his taste for horror. In *Medea*, it is black magic, while in *Orestis tragoedia* it is the depiction of gruesome murders.[9] Dracontius lingers over the scene of Aegisthus' body being chopped to pieces (vv. 719–728), an episode that he appears to have invented, and emphasizes Clytemnestra's ordeal at her death, dragged by the hair (v. 732) and pitilessly killed despite her cries for mercy, followed by her suffering in spasms of agony (vv. 792–794). This penchant for the bloodthirsty reaches an incredible level of intensity in the poem, leading us to question his moral incentive. Punishing Aegisthus and Clytemnestra in an awfully cruel way certainly reflects the horror of their own crime, but other episodes share the same gruesome style without any obviously uplifting justification, such as Agamemnon's death, when his head is split in half, causing his brains to spill out (vv. 258–262). Dracontius apparently tries to exaggerate the crime and perversity of the characters: Rather than being driven by the hatred which, in other versions, is legitimately inspired by the supposed murder of her daughter by her husband, this Clytemnestra seeks above all to pursue her illicit love affair with Aegisthus (vv. 153–203). Thus, the myth is clearly eroticized. While this may make her punishment seem all the more warranted, the main impression is that Dracontius wants to create personalities prone to psychological excesses, whose troubled behavior he can subsequently explore. Accordingly, Medea too becomes a flat, evil character, without nuance. The insistence on certain episodes and the skimming of others at the expense of the coherence of the

---

8 Ibid.
9 See Bureau 2003 for very good arguments on the subject, some of which are picked up on here.

whole enable the poet to select elements that allow him to indulge his taste for violence and to create pathos underpinned by strong emotions. By depicting extreme situations, Dracontius delves into the representation of monstrous or criminal behavior, without the occasional moral overtones appearing to be the motivation of the work.

A Christian or moralizing agenda?

The question of the purpose of Dracontius' *epyllia* divides critics, whose interpretations diverge significantly.[10] Some, noting Dracontius' clear intention to rewrite the myths, consider his aim to be mainly literary, with his classicizing works having only a poetic function. Others,[11] drawing from the argument that Dracontius was raised a Catholic and that he clearly asserts in *De laudibus Dei* that the pagan gods are idols and have no existence (2.588–593), consider that his secular pieces need to be understood in the light of his Christian beliefs. How can we otherwise explain a poem in which Diana of Tauris is so prevalent, even though the poet denounces this goddess in his Christian poem (*LD* 3.217–221)?

Unfortunately, few elements support the theory that the *epyllia* are Christianized. There is no reason to give a moral or Christian sense to the *Hylas*, insofar as the poet adds no commentary. A curious expression at v. 3 of the *De raptu Helenae*, where the poet refers to Paris' crime by *aggrediar meliore via* ("Let me approach from a better route"), has sometimes been understood in a moral sense,[12] reflecting Dracontius' moralizing purpose, namely, to denounce adultery. But, even though Paris was ultimately punished by death and the city of Troy was destroyed, it is paradoxical to claim that the poet wanted to write a moral work by narrating such an immoral mythological episode. Second, what should we make of a moral lesson that is virtually only apparent in the prologue and the last verse of the text (v. 655: *crimen adulterii talis vindicta sequitur*, "let such vengeance follow the crime of adultery"), and which appears to be forgotten elsewhere in the narrative? Finally, the question of sin in the poem is complex, and there is a dilution of responsibility. Paris is certainly guilty and Dracontius is extremely harsh towards him. Nevertheless, the text is just as insistent on the role of destiny (vv.

---

10 See Simons 2005, 15–16 and 20–21; Stoehr-Monjou 2015, 140; Wolff 2015, 218–219.
11 Among recent studies that adopt this position see Klein 2001; Kaufmann 2005–2006. On the contrary, the Christian interpretation of *Medea* is refuted by Schetter 1980, picked up on in Schetter 1994, and by Van Zyl Smit 2003, 151–160.
12 See a summary of interpretations of this verse in Simons 2005, 286–287.

57–60, 131, 191, 198). Similarly, in vv. 535–539 Helen repeatedly says that it was Jupiter (her father) and the destinies that ordered her to leave her husband. It is unclear whether this is a purely rhetorical argument designed to exculpate her. Finally, a curse weighs over the royal house of Troy since the double perjury of Laomedon (cf. vv. 80, 185–187). We may note that the poet seems surprised by the violence of the gods' resentment (vv. 55–56), which adds nuance to Paris' condemnation. In short, the moralizing explanation does not hold water.

In the *Medea* and the *Orestis tragoedia*, we have slightly more ground for a moralizing reading. The two poems effectively end with an intervention by the author-narrator. In the last verses of the *Orestis tragoedia* (vv. 763–774), Dracontius speaks out, asking the (pagan) gods to spare Greece from the return of such horrors. The hemistich at v. 973 *vestro iam parcite mundo* ("spare henceforth your world") could indicate that the poet is stepping back to some extent. In the *Medea* (vv. 570–601), his remarks are more complex. He requests a certain number of nefarious personified abstractions (Madness, Crime, Desire, Impiety, etc.) to leave the mortals alone, to pardon the world and to spare Thebes, before entreating Venus, Cupid and Bacchus to do the same, arguing that it would be paradoxical and unjust to punish a city that had given birth to, and hosted the gods.[13] Strictly speaking, however, this is not a curse against the pagan gods but, at the most, a denunciation of their cruelty. It should be noted, though, that classical authors themselves criticized the notion that gods are cruel beings with strong passions (cf. Lucretius 1.62–101; Virgil, *Aeneid* 1.11; Seneca, *Letters to Lucilius* 95.45 and 50), and Dracontius' words reveal nothing that is specifically Christian.

Moreover, the proem of the *Medea* contains a violent denunciation of magic.[14] In the context of an anti-pagan, apologetic argument, magic is the antithesis of miracles. In this respect, Medea, escaping on her poisoned chariot (vv. 556–569), appears to counterbalance the prophet Elijah, who rose to Heaven on a chariot of fire (2 Kgs 2:1). This aspect, however, is not picked up on in the poem's conclusion. Dracontius could have also shown the ineffectiveness of magic by pointing out, for example, that Medea is unable even to keep her husband, but he does not do so.

Bruno Bureau (2003, 168–169) concludes his comparative analysis of Claudian's *De raptu Proserpinae* and Dracontius' *Orestis tragoedia* as follows: "Le

---

[13] Venus is the mother of Harmony, wife of Cadmus, the founder of Thebes; Cupid is Harmony's half-brother; Bacchus is Harmony's son who, after his journey to India, went back to Thebes and founded his cult there.

[14] For the interpretation of the *epyllia* as a denunciation of pagan magic see Stoehr-Monjou 2013.

monde du mythe apparaît ainsi, relu à travers le filtre de l'histoire tragique, comme un monde parfaitement haïssable dont le lecteur doit rendre grâces d'être sorti." He adds that: "Pour Dracontius (...), si le mythe est exemplaire c'est parce qu'il témoigne d'une époque obscure de l'humanité où la vérité chrétienne ne venait pas éclairer les esprits (...), un monde sans la lumière divine où l'homme réduit à ses seules forces montre sa cruauté, sa folie, son dérèglement." This is excessive. It is true that we find in Dracontius elements of criticism against the gods, but these are voiced from within the classical tradition. Critics also tend to agree that the pagan gods in Dracontius' work have little substance (Venus and Cupid for instance are nothing more than a personification of love), possibly with the exception of Apollo in *De raptu Helenae* and Diana in the *Medea*. It has also been pointed out that Dracontius secularizes the myths and transforms them into stories that deal with human passions. If this is true, it indicates a possible contradiction in seeing his work as a criticism of false gods.

At this point, we have to distinguish between an anti-pagan and a moralizing objective. As Stoehr-Monjou argues,[15] the theme of marriage is important throughout Dracontius' work, appearing in *De laudibus Dei* (1.363–370), in poems 6–10 of the *Romulea* and in the *Orestis tragoedia*. The poet indeed associates matrimony with very positive values. This stance is particularly clear in *De raptu Helenae*: legitimate marriage is glorified through Telamon and Hesione (vv. 286–290 and 304–308); Menelas mourns his broken marriage (vv. 571–585); the poem ends with an anti-*epithalamium* that curses the adulterous union between Paris and Helen (vv. 638–651). Dracontius doubtlessly denounces the violation of marriage. At the same time, the four *epyllia* emphasize the power of sexual attraction (the Nymphs and Hylas, Clytemnestra and Aegisthus, Helen and Paris, Medea and Jason, Glauce and Jason), which is irresistible and always destructive,[16] and which is symbolized by Venus and Cupid. There is, thus, a positive and a negative depiction of love (hence the fundamental ambiguity of the god Cupid and the force he embodies), and this could well be the message Dracontius intends to highlight.

We can, therefore, accept that Dracontius' work contains a set of moralizing considerations on evil and passion. As Bureau notes (2003, 169), however, "le moraliste chez Dracontius n'est pas sans failles," since the poet also gives the reader the literary pleasure of the story and the strong emotions it contains: (ibid.) "Le lecteur peut sans frais et sans risque se délecter du plaisir trouble de la transgression, tout en se pinçant le nez devant ce qu'il découvre." In short, it

---

15 Stoehr-Monjou 2014, 144 and 148–149.
16 Herren 2016, 305.

is difficult to accept the idea that Dracontius' somewhat unedifying stories were solely devised to give readers the ardent desire to see such behaviors eradicated.

Stoehr-Monjou, however, rightly warns us not to pin Dracontius to a sole objective or attitude.[17] In reality, nothing prevents us from believing he had several complementary, rather than mutually exclusive, purposes. His work reflects a literary goal that involves rewriting and reinventing the myth. This rewriting is performed in a romanesque key, resulting in a shift of focus to the characters' passions, with a strong preference for the most extreme and the most criminal of human behaviors. Dracontius thus adapts traditional themes to a new situation and to new values in order to make them even more eloquent. He thus introduces a twofold outlook: On the one hand, he deals with universal issues like the dangers of blind passion, punishment of crime, tyranny as the opposite of fair authority, responsibility, and the freedom of man; on the other hand, his chosen theme may also allude to contemporary events.

This last aspect has rarely been considered by scholars. With regard to poem 5 of the *Romulea*, a declamation in verse, Michel d'Annoville and Stoehr-Monjou (2008) have demonstrated that it would be difficult not to perceive in the emphatic condemnation of tyranny echoes of the political situation in Africa. With regard to the *epyllia*, Gualandri (1990, 69) and De Gaetano (2010) make some interesting observations. The situation of Hesione, held hostage and then married to Telamon, and the subsequent abduction of Helen in *Romulea* 8, would (going beyond the differences in situation)[18] remind the audience of the fate of the widow and the two daughters of Valentinian III, abducted in 455 by Genseric during the Sack of Rome.[19] Similarly, in poem 8 and in the *Orestis tragoedia*, Paris and Aegisthus, who, moving from the status of shepherd to that of king, exchanged their animal skin garments for purple cloth, could be reminiscent of the barbarian chieftains, previously *pelliti*, who adopted the purple chlamys and the imperial crown. The multiple murders in the family of the Atrides, mentioned in the *Orestis tragoedia*, could be likened to the assassinations in the royal Vandal family. In his attempt to seize Agamemnon's wealth, the usurper Aegisthus may conjure up the behavior of the Vandals.

All these possible allusions to contemporary events are ostensibly intended especially for an audience of Romans in Africa. Nevertheless, in considering the

---

17 Stoehr-Monjou 2015/2016, 123.
18 See Simons 2005, 371.
19 Certainly the theme of the 'Abduction of Women' appealed to audiences all over the Empire; Morales 2016.

purpose of Dracontius' *epyllia*, we need to think about his wider audience. Unfortunately, we do not have much information on this aspect. The *subscriptio* of poem 5 informs us that Dracontius declaimed the controversy in the thermal baths of Gargilius in Carthage (the same place that hosted the famous conference of 411 between Catholic bishops and Donatists) in front of an audience which included as prominent a figure as the proconsul of Carthage, Pacideius. Whatever his exact powers, Pacideius was a Roman. We do not know if there were any Vandals in the audience, but in any case, they, at least some of them, were not excluded from Graeco-Roman culture. In poem 1 of *Romulea*, Dracontius praises his master Felicianus for bringing back the radiance of Roman culture to Carthage, in other words, a form of culture preceding the Vandals. But Felicianus did more: he brought the Romans and the Vandals together in the lecture hall (v. 14: *barbaris qui Romulidas iungis auditorio*). Vandals could thus have access to Latin literature and, consequently, to the works of Dracontius. Elsewhere, the interest of the Vandals in Roman culture is confirmed by certain poems in the *Latin Anthology*, especially those of Luxorius.[20] It is, then, quite likely that Dracontius also wrote with the Vandals in mind, even if he did not compose a poem celebrating them specifically. Perhaps one of his objectives was to spread Roman culture among these new rulers. This possibility could, in turn, reinforce the argument in favor of the literary intent of his *epyllia*.

Dracontius himself, now, could boast a different kind of dual identity: he had a vast classical education and a well-grounded Christian culture. His writings reflect this dual outlook, and do not exclude a certain osmosis or continuity between the Christian and the classicizing works. For instance, we have seen that the theme of marriage was important in both types of work. The miracle of the phoenix appears in both the *Medea* (vv. 102–109) and the *De laudibus Dei* (1.653–655). Several passages in the *De laudibus Dei* have a strong classical influence:[21] e.g., the listing of omens and miracles (*LD* 1.52–91), the mention of the sun (*LD* 2.15–27) and the description of Paradise before The Fall (*LD* 2.440–463), which evokes Virgil's Golden Age in the fourth *Eclogue* or the one of Ovid in the first Book of the *Metamorphoses*. This work's literary sources are also largely classical.

In general, however, Christian and classicizing works have different functions, different goals, and a different message. Although Dracontius' *epyllia* could have been read by all kinds of audiences, their emphasis on destiny and

---

20 See Wolff 2016 and forthcoming.
21 Herren 2016, 301–302.

the punishment of innocents²² would be unacceptable for Christians. Nevertheless, the Christian and classicizing works may be contemporary, even if the chronology is very hard to establish.²³ One thing is certain: the two *epithalamia*, in which the place of mythology is extremely important, are more or less contemporary with the two Christian poems. But we cannot be certain with regard to poems 8–10 or the *Orestis tragoedia*. Their literary aspect suggests they were written with a certain degree of maturity. This aesthetic criterion, however, needs to be used with caution since some scholars consider them, on the contrary, to be influenced by the author's rhetorical training, and thus date them to his youth. Whatever the truth, we cannot apply a scenario of conversion to Dracontius. He did not first write his classicizing pieces and then his Christian pieces. Prison did not make him reject mythological poetry. Both forms of expression continued to coexist within his work.

Conclusions

With regard to his *epyllia*, we can conclude, it seems highly unlikely that they are intended as an attempt at Christian apologetics or as a polemic against the pagan gods: they are not programmatic pieces.²⁴ Dracontius also did not aim to make the pagan myths acceptable by providing them with an allegorical interpretation, as Fulgentius the Mythographer did, also in Vandal Africa, during the same period or a little later. Doreen Selent's book,²⁵ which attempts to explain Dracontius' work as allegory, is not particularly compelling in this respect. On the other hand, we find in Dracontius' writing an interrogation and a reflection on the passions, values, limits, rights and the place of humans in the world which is not incompatible with Christianity, and confirms a basic unity in Dracontius' view of the world. The elements of Stoicism observed in the *Romulea* by Michael W. Herren²⁶ may to some extent serve as a bridge between his classicizing and his Christian

---

22 See De Gaetano 2009, 149–158.
23 See Wolff 2015, 212–214.
24 Furthermore, certain elements of humor, in the vocabulary (Jason called *callidus heros* when he makes a stupid decision, at 10.41) as well as in situations (Jason on the verge of being sacrificed sees Cupid fluttering above him, at 10.199–200, on which see Fischer in this volume; the sudden change of mind of Medea's father, at 10.328–329) invite us to see these *epyllia* with more distance than modern scholars usually allow for.
25 Selent 2011.
26 Herren 2016, *passim*.

poetry. It is not convincing, however, that this Stoic, moralizing reflection can account for the many differences in comparison to established versions of the myths.

The fact that mythology could still serve as poetic subject matter at a time when Christianity had otherwise prevailed is not in itself surprising. The *Latin Anthology* contains many epigrams with a mythological theme. Indeed, Christians no longer saw such stories as a danger or as competition. The poetic choice of mythology was no longer perceived as a compromise with paganism: it was the exploitation of a common cultural capital. And it was certainly less risky under Arian Vandal rule to write about Orestes, Medea and Paris than about the nature of Christ.

Bibliography

Bureau, B. 2003. "Épique et romanesque: l'exemple de deux épopées tardives, *l'Enlèvement de Proserpine* de Claudien et la *Tragédie d'Oreste* de Dracontius", *Interférences-Ars scribendi online* 1. http://ars-scribendi.ens-lyon.fr/spip.php?article12.

Cairns, F. 2007. *Generic composition in Greek and Roman poetry. Corrected and with new material*, (second ed.) Ann Arbor (MI).

De Gaetano, M. 2009. *Scuola e potere in Draconzio*, Alessandria, 149–158.

De Gaetano, M. 2010. "Simbologia animale e lettura storica del mito in Drac. *Romul*. 8, 453–480", *Auctores nostri: studi e testi di letteratura cristiana antica*, 8, 137–184.

Gualandri, I. 1999. "Gli dei duri a morire: temi mitologici nella poesia latina del quinto secolo", in G. Mazzoli/F. Gasti (eds.), *Prospettive sul Tardoantico*, Como, 49–68.

Herren, M.W. 2016. "Dracontius, the pagan gods, and Stoicism", in S. McGill/J. Pucci (eds.), *Classics renewed: reception and innovation in the Latin poetry of Late Antiquity*, Heidelberg, 297–322.

Kaufmann, H. 2005–2006. "Missing hierarchy. The gods in Dracontius' *Medea* (*Romul*. 10)", *Archivum Bobiense*, 27–28, 79–101.

Klein, R. 2001. "Medea am Ausgang der Antike. Bemerkungen zum Epyllion *Medea* des christlichen Dichters Dracontius", *WJA*, n.s., 25, 229–238.

Michel d'Annoville, C./Stoehr-Monjou, A. 2008 "Fidélité à la tradition et détournements dans la controverse de Dracontius (*Romulea* 5): un poème à double sens", in C. Sotinel/M. Sartre (eds.), *L'usage du passé entre antiquité tardive et haut Moyen Âge*, Rennes, 29–45.

Morales, H. 2016. "Rape, violence, complicity: Colluthus' *Abduction of Helen*", *Arethusa*, 49, 61–92.

Schetter, W. 1980. "Medea in Theben", *WJA*, n.s., 6a, 209–221.

Schetter, W. 1994. *Kaiserzeit und Spätantike. Kleine Schriften, 1957–1992*, Stuttgart, 314–327.

Selent, D. 2011. *Allegorische Mythenerklärung in der Spätantike: Wege zum Werk des Dracontius*, Leidorf.

Simons, R. 2005. *Dracontius und der Mythos: christliche Weltsicht und pagane Kultur in der ausgehenden Spätantike*, München.

Stoehr-Monjou, A. 2009. "Le rejet de la *tragoedia* et les tragiques dans l'*Orestis* de Dracontius à la lumière du manifeste inaugural: *te rogo, Melpomene, tragicis descende cothurnis* (Drac. *Orestis* 13)", *Mosaique* 1, June 2009 (online: 1.10.2018: Https://revuemosaique.files.wordpress.com/2010/03/mosaique-1-12_stoehr-monjou.pdf).

Stoehr-Monjou, A. 2013. "Une *ekphrasis* tardive entre traditions poétique et iconographique: le char de Médée, symbole du Mal (Dracontius, *Romul*. X, 556–569)", *AntAfr*, 49, 161–176.

Stoehr-Monjou, A. 2015. "Dracontius, *Poèmes profanes* VI-X, fragments", in A. Rolet/S. Rolet (eds.), *Silves latines 2015–2016*, Neuilly sur Seine, 87–191.

Van Zyl Smit, B. 2003. "A Christian Medea in Vandal Africa? Some aspects of the *Medea* of Blossius Aemilius Dracontius", in A.F. Basson/W.J. Dominik (eds.), *Literature, art, history. Studies on Classical Antiquity and tradition: in honour of W.J. Henderson*, Frankfurt a.M., 151–160.

Wolff, É. 2015. "Dracontius: bilan et aperçus sur quelques problèmes de sa vie et de son œuvre", in É. Wolff (ed.), *Littérature, politique et religion en Afrique vandale*, Paris, 211–225.

Wolff, É. 2017. "Un vers centon programmatique: le vers initial de la pièce 5 des *Romulea* de Dracontius ", in F. Garambois/D. Vallat (eds.), *Varium et mutabile. Mémoires et métamorphoses du centon dans l'Antiquité*, Saint-Étienne.

Wolff, É. Forthcoming. "La culture des cités africaines à l'époque vandale d'après le témoignage de *l'Anthologie latine* et de Dracontius", in C. Goddard/H. Inglebert/V. Fauvinet-Ranson (eds.), *Actes du Colloque "Cités et religions dans l'Afrique tardoantique (IIIe-VIIe siècles). Hommage à Claude Lepelley" (Université Paris-Ouest, 7–8 September 2016)*.

Susanna Fischer
Dracontius' *Medea* and the Classical Tradition: Divine Influence and Human Action

> Per alta vade spatia sublime aetheris,
> testare nullos esse, qua veheris, deos.
>
> Seneca, *Medea* 1026–1027

Seneca's tragedy *Medea* closes with Jason's declaration that there are no gods where Medea is. The interpretation of these lines has caused much consternation: How can Medea triumph at the end of a drama written by a Stoic? Are the gods being criticized? Five centuries later, and despite its different genre and radically different historical, political, and religious circumstances, the end of Dracontius' *Medea* (*Romul.* 10)[1] poses similar no less pressing questions about the theological world of the poem. Just as some scholars expect that the Stoic Seneca ought to write Stoic tragedies, so for some others the predominant understanding is that the Christian Dracontius, who wrote manifestly Christian poems like the *Satisfactio* discussed in a previous chapter of this volume, ought to write pagan poems only in order to criticize the pagan gods.[2]

But when dealing with late antique Christian authors such as Dracontius, whose poetic production is heterogeneous, we need to question whether the mythological poems need to be interpreted in the light of Christian theology.[3] This paper will contribute to the interpretation of Dracontius' *Medea* and raise the question of Christian criticism of the pagan gods as represented in this poem. I will address the central topic of the volume, 'transposition', in two contexts. The first part will examine the prologue of *Medea* and the transposition and transformation of genre. The second part will focus on the transposition and transformation of myths regarding the gods in *Romulea* 10. This part will also examine

---
1 On the title *Romulea* cf. Zwierlein 2017a, 39; Schmidt 1984. Translations, unless otherwise stated, are my own.
2 For such a Christian interpretation see Klein 2001, 9 n. 54. On the *Satisf.* see Falcone in this volume, with further literature. For the lack of explicit Christian allusion in Christian literary epigram see also Gullo in this volume.
3 Cf. Wolff 1996, 45 in the introduction to the edition. A counter paradigm from the Greek East is Nonnus of Panopolis, author of the mythological *Dionysiaca* and the Christian *Paraphrase of John's Gospel*; on the latter poem see Accorinti and Hadjittofi in this volume.

the poem's structure and central passages, which help us to explore the theological perspective – if there is any – of Dracontius' *Medea*. The close reading of the episodes concerning the gods will stress the difficulties any interpretation has to face. Finally, I will re-evaluate the poem's epilogue. My aim will be to show that Dracontius' focus is on a creative rewriting of the myth in a new genre and not on a Christian recasting of the myth with the ulterior motive of criticizing the pagan gods.

Prologue and genre

Blossius Dracontius Aemilianus, a Carthaginian poet who flourished around 500 CE,[4] wrote a highly original version of the Medea myth. The most illustrative example of his revision is the change of place: Medea's bloody revenge is situated no longer in Corinth but in Thebes.[5] Moreover, Dracontius innovates not only in re-interpreting the myth, but also in revising the structure of the narrative itself, now comprising, in two parts, two different episodes of the myth, the Colchian (*Romul.* 10.32–339) and the Corinthian (situated in Thebes, *Romul.* 10.366–569), which were traditionally dealt with in different genres – epic for the first (Apollonius, Valerius Flaccus) and drama for the latter (Euripides, Seneca). But Dracontius' chief innovation is the self-conscious modulation of the mythical narrative between various minor genres before settling on the major tonality and the writing of an epic poem in a short form.

Medea's story was treated in Euripides' drama and was already part of epic myth from Apollonius Rhodius onwards, but there are no close parallels with Euripides in *Romulea* 10 which would suggest that Dracontius knew Greek.[6] Besides, Medea was a popular theme among Roman poets throughout antiquity. The first extant Latin versions are Seneca's eponymous play, Ovid's *Heroides* 12 and his *Metamorphoses* 7.1–424, where the narration focuses more prominently

---

[4] On Dracontius' life and education see Bright 1987, 14–29; Wolff 2004; Kaufmann 2006a, 19–23. The date and relative chronology of the poems in his mythological work *Romulea* (consisting of *epithalamia*, one *controversia* and one *deliberativa* and three epic poems in short form), written in hexameter, are unclear. See the discussion in Kaufmann 2006a, 20–24.
[5] Cf. the discussion in Schetter 1985.
[6] On Dracontius' knowledge of Greek cf. Kaufmann 2006a, 43–44. There are no traces in his poems that can lead us to assume that he knew Greek. It is highly unlikely that he had access to Apollonius Rhodius', Dionysius Skytobrachion's or Euripides' versions of the myth.

on the figure of Medea.[7] In Ovid and Seneca, Medea's very name becomes synonymous with her power and infamous murders, as shown by the Senecan proclamation "*Medea nunc sum*"[8] right before the murder of her children. Valerius Flaccus' *Argonautica* offers yet another epic version of the myth. Additionally, the myth's popularity in Late Antiquity is attested by the frequency with which it appears on Roman sarcophagi.[9] When Dracontius rewrote the myth, he had at his disposal a multiform material that included treatments of the tale not only in literature but also in art and theater. It is precisely this generically multi-layered appropriation of the myth that is reflected in the prologue of Dracontius' work.

Kaufmann shows in her commentary that linguistic debts to older versions of the Medea myth are difficult to trace in Dracontius alltogether.[10] Her results make those cases all the more remarkable where Dracontius alludes directly to texts (mainly, in the case of Ovidian allusions) which do not treat the Medea myth. The beginning of the text (v. 1: *fert animus vulgare nefas et virginis atrae | captivos monstrare deos*, "my mind moves me to reveal the crime and to show the gods prisoners of an evil virgin")[11] alludes to Ovid's *Metamorphoses* (vv. 1–2: *in nova fert animus mutatas dicere formas | corpora*, "my mind moves me to tell of shapes changed into new bodies") and Lucan's equivalent passage (at v. 67: *fert animus causas tantarum expromere rerum*, "my mind leads me to reveal the causes of such great events").[12] The echo clearly highlights Dracontius' innovation when compared to the epic work of Lucan and, above all, Ovid, whose own originality is programmatic in his opening line: *in nova*.[13] Through intertextual reference,[14] then, Dracontius characterizes his work as an epic poem already in his opening words. In fact, the prologue itself contains reflections on the poem's genre. First, the myth's dramatic pedigree is highlighted. The two episodes of the story clearly

---

7 Several fragments of Medea-themed tragedies are transmitted from Ennius, Accius, Pacuvius, and Ovid. From Lucan we know only of the title. Varro Atacinus wrote the epic *Argonautae* (1st century BCE), which is also only transmitted in fragments. On Medea in Roman literature see Boyle 2012 and Manuwald 2013. Cf. also the overview in Kaufmann 2006a, 48–52.
8 Sen., *Med*. 910. Cf. Hypsipyle in Ov., *Her*. 6.151: *Medeae Medea forem*. For the stereotypical aspect of some mythical characters in Latin literature see also Gualandri 2009.
9 Zanker/Ewald 2004, 82–85.
10 Kaufmann 2006a, 50.
11 Dracontius, *Romul*. 10.1. I use the edition of Zwierlein 2017a.
12 On Dracontius' imitation of Ovid cf. Bouquet 1982. See also Kaufmann 2006ab on intertextuality in *Romul*. 10.
13 Cf. Pollmann 2001, 98 and now Pollmann 2017, 43.
14 On intertextuality in Late Antiquity in general cf. Stenger 2015.

show that Medea, for Dracontius' audience, evoked primarily theatrical associations. Characteristically, for the first part of the text, situated in Colchis, Dracontius refers to Polymnia, whose sphere of activity is wide but who is addressed here as the muse of pantomime:[15]

> nos illa canemus,
> quae solet in lepido Polyhymnia docta theatro
> muta loqui
>
> For our part, we will sing what erudite Polymnia usually voices without words in delightful theater. (*Romul.* 10.16–18)

The second part of the poem is guided by Melpomene, the muse of choruses and tragedy,[16] and develops the popular theme of *Medea furens*.[17] Dracontius mentions not only Melpomene as a guiding deity, but also the characteristic meter of tragedy, iamb:

> vel quod grande boans longis sublata cothurnis
> pallida Melpomene, tragicis cum surgit iambis
>
> or what pale Melpomene bellows grandiloquently when she stands to recite tragic iambs on her high buskins. (*Romul.* 10.20–21)

Yet all the other genres that had previously treated the Medea myth are rejected in favor of epic. A third muse, Calliope, is finally evoked to assist:

> Te modo, Calliope, poscunt optantque sorores:
> dulcior ut venias (...)
> ad sua castra petunt.
>
> It's you now, Calliope, that your sisters ask and desire: they request that you come gracefully to their camp. (*Romul.* 10.26–28)

---

[15] Cf. Wasyl 2011, 85. On Polymnia's sphere of activity see Walde 2001. Polymnia is connected to pantomime in several testimonies; e.g., Nonn., *Dion.* 5.104 or *AL* 664R, 8. On pantomime see Rotolo 1957; Zimmermann 1990; Benz 2000; Hall/Wyles 2008; Zanobi 2014. From Procopius' book on the Vandal war, dated to the end of the 5th century, we know that the theater in Carthage was visited by many people (*Vand.* 2.6.7). Cf. Puk 2014, 310–313. On the possible audience of Dracontius' mythological poems cf. Wolff in this volume.
[16] On Melpomene cf. Walde 1999; Kaufmann 2006a, 122–123; and the similar text in *AL* 88R,4.
[17] Cf. Stoehr-Monjou 2009 on the rejection of Melpomene in *Orest. Trag.*

In the *Medea*, Polymnia and Melpomene, who seem inappropriate for the genre Dracontius is writing in, are only mentioned to request the Muse of grand epic to inspire the poet. The generic allusions to prior versions of Medea's story are dismissed together with the mentions of the two Muses. By addressing Calliope, the poem is assigned to the epic genre, in spite of its shorter form.[18]

After exposing these generic reflections, the prologue ends with an antithetic question – a very short resume of the irrational plot to come. In these final words, we get a glimpse of the two-fold structure adopted in the poem: vv. 30–31: *cur hospes amatur | qui mactandus erat, vel cur mactatur amatus?* "Why did the guest that ought to be sacrificed become a beloved, and why was the beloved sacrificed?"). This question bears the traces of Dracontius' rhetorical training and exemplifies his fondness of "l'écriture du contraste."[19] But Dracontius' modulation of the Medea myth between grand scale epic and theatrical representations shows that beyond his rhetorical education, he composed the Medea not as a school exercise[20] but in self-conscious generic and intertextual dialogue with his predecessors.

The gods in *Medea* and the structure of the poem

The poem begins with the depiction of Medea as a strong character – just as we know her, for example, from Senecan drama. In Dracontius, Medea is portrayed as a bloodthirsty priestess of Diana (*sacerdos*),[21] resembling Iphigenia, who, like Medea, dwells in a barbarian land. Dracontius, like Seneca, also gives the heroine

---

18 Shorter epics, even those of Dracontius, tend to be labeled as either '*epyllia*' (e.g., Wolff) or 'miniature epics' (e.g., Wasyl 2011). The volume by Baumbach/Bär 2012 has opened up the category of *epyllion*, allowing for all types of short(er) epics to be included. Wolff 2015, 222–223 uses the term '*epyllion*' for *Romul.* 2, 8, and 10 and the *Orest. trag.* The same term, however, is rejected for these poems on the grounds of style and theme: e.g., Weber 1995, 228–247; Simons 2005, 9–10; Kaufmann 2006a, 35–36; Pollmann 2017, 41. See also Bright 1987, 3–8 and Bureau 2015. On the forms of late antique short(er) epic, especially the difference between *epyllion* and *Kleinepik*, see Koster 2002, 32, who argues that *epyllia* are more focused on eros than other shorter epics.
19 Stoehr-Monjou 2013, 166. Cf. Pollmann 2017, 44. On the influence of declamation on Dracontius see Bouquet 1996, and also De Gaetano 2009.
20 On school in Late Antiquity see in general Vössing 1997 and Kaufmann 2006a, 16; on school poetry see Hose 2004 and Stotz 1982. On Dracontius' education see Kaufmann 2006a, 13–20.
21 Medea as a priestess is connected to the figure of Iphigenia in Tauris. See Schetter 1985, 317; Simons 2005, 185–189; Wasyl 2011, 60. On Medea as *sacerdos* and *virgo/virago* see Kaufmann 2006a, 55 and 156–157. On human sacrifice see Rives 1995, 80–83.

superhuman power.²² Medea's magic is of a cosmic origin, an aspect stressed in the second part of the poem.²³ With such a strong lead as the protagonist the poem raises issues about the role of the gods: if Medea is such a powerful, almost superhuman, being, then who is responsible for the tragic events of her tale, she or the gods?

This question is also raised by the parallel structure of the two main parts of the poem, Colchis and Thebes,²⁴ whereby events are, at the same time, mirrored and contrasted: in the first part, there is a clear emphasis on the gods, as the narrative focuses mainly on divine actions²⁵ and their impact on the mortal characters, whereas in the second part mortal characters act without being influenced by the divine.²⁶ The structure is reflected in the epilogue, where the gods are only mentioned in the second part (587–601). In questioning the role of the gods, Dracontius follows his predecessors in the treatment of the myth (Seneca) and within the genre in which he writes (Lucan and Statius).²⁷

Tab. 1: Structure of *Romulea* 10²⁸

1–31 Proemium
32–339 Part I: Colchis (Divine action)
32–49 Jason's arrival
49–170 Juno - Venus - Cupid
171–254 Sacrificial scene with Cupid's appearance
255–283 Wedding with Bacchus' appearance
284–311 Diana's curse
312–339 Aletes - Bacchus
340–365 Interlude

---

[22] The powers mentioned at the beginning are repeated in the words of Venus later in the poem (136–140). On magical practices in this context cf. Tupet 1976, 68–70 and 85. Cf. also Korenjak 1996 on Erictho 20f.
[23] Vv. 431–433, 461–463, 568–569. Cf. Simons 2005, 215.
[24] Bright 1987, 82. Cf. Wasyl 2011, 59 and Milić 2015, 324 on the two parts as *Medea amans* and *Medea furens*.
[25] Bright 1987, 82 strangely calls the divine action of the first part "digression."
[26] Cf. Simons 2005, 173.
[27] For a discussion of the role of the gods in Seneca see Fischer 2008; for Lucan and Statius see Ambühl 2015, 232–234.
[28] On the structure of the poem see Bright 1987, 82; Van Zyl Smit 2003, 152; Kaufmann 2006a, 54.

366–569 Part II: Thebes (Medea's action)
    366–390 Preparations for the wedding of Jason and Glauce
    391–435 Medea's prayer to Diana
    436–469 Medea's prayer to the Furies
    470–483 Wedding of Jason and Glauce
    484–509 Medea's preparations for the murders – Medea's prayer to the Sun (497–508)
    510–569 The murders and Medea on the chariot
570–601 Epilogue
    570–573: Invocation of personifications of negative effects
    574–586: The context of the house of Thebes
    587–592: Invocation of Venus, Cupid and Bacchus
    592–601: The narrator's commentary

In the following, I will show how Dracontius reworks the Medea myth by combining motifs from different genres. First, I turn to the antagonism between Diana and Venus/Amor, a major theme in part one. This motif is very common in literature, famously exemplified in Euripides' *Hippolytus*, where Aphrodite seeks revenge because Hippolytus despises her and only worships Artemis.[29] In Dracontius' *Medea*, Juno states in her speech (49–85)[30] that Medea is to stop venerating Diana (64–65) and worship only Venus (67–68). Also, in the scene between Venus and Amor,[31] the rivalry between Amor and Diana is a central motif. Amor picks up the arrows that made Luna/Diana herself fall in love (146–150) and ends his speech in 152–155 by comparing his *tela* with Diana's. Amor's power in the human and divine realm is a poetic motif of which we find many examples, for instance in Ovid's love elegy (*Am.* 1.2.37) as well as in the Senecan *Phaedra* 186–189,[32] or in Ovid's *Metamorphoses*, where Amor competes with Apollo in the art of archery (*Met.* 1.454–465). The mention of Luna's love is interesting, because Bacchus will

---

[29] For a discussion of the role of the gods in the Euripidean tragedy see Matthiesen 2004, 67–69 and Fletcher 2017. Cf. Herren's remark 2016, 319 on Eur., *Hipp.* and Dracontius' *Medea* as "a mirror image of each other."
[30] Cf. Wolff 1996, 192 n. 31; Kaufmann 2006a, 149.
[31] On Amor as a powerful principle (in the words of Venus at vv. 127–134) and as the flying love god with his characteristic attributes cf. Kaufmann 2006a, 196 and Selent 2011, 149–189. The combination of both aspects is not unusual in poetry and especially in *epithalamia*, for example in Ap. Rhod. 3.132–150. Cf. Kaufmann 2006a, 196 and Selent 2011, 149–189, esp. 182–189. Cf. the depiction of Amor in *Hylas* (*Romul.* 2) with Selent 2011, 170–182.
[32] Cf. Kaufmann 2006a, 200.

also refer to it later on (326–327), thus undermining the legitimacy of Diana's curse.[33]

But Dracontius' revision of the myth also employs non-literary sources and modes. When Amor comes into the temple to intervene, the scene displays comic elements[34] that could be traced back to pantomimic representations, thus reminding the reader of the prologue:[35] Jason, who is on the altar about to be sacrificed, notices Cupid flying above him, and the two start to chat at this point. This surprising development undercuts the serious effect of the sacrifice scene. The following scenes, where everything happens quite fast, are also comic in tone. Right after Medea drops the sword, she asks her victim whether he is married and, when he says he is not, at 254 she asks him straightaway to marry her: *vis ergo meus nunc esse maritus?* ("Would you like to be my husband now?").

The effect of Amor's arrows is depicted in a pantomimic scene with the nurse as a commentator (225–236). This type of scene, where a character or the chorus comments on the affective movements of another character, can also be found in Senecan tragedy.[36] In Seneca's *Medea* 382f., the nurse describes the protagonist's *furor*. Contrarily, at 230 the Dracontian Medea's behavior is described as an anti-*furor*: *non furit aut tremuli strident in murmure dentes* ("she does not rage, her teeth do not clatter and gnash with rumbling noise"). Nevertheless, the description of Medea losing control in the heat of the moment and the allusions to her body language are a perfect theme for pantomimic presentation through movement and gestures. The combination, therefore, of motifs from different genres shows how confidently and playfully Dracontius reworks the Medea myth, and demonstrates that this poem is written entirely within the classical tradition.

The treatment of Diana's curse (291–300), for instance, is also developed in intertextual dialogue with the prologue of Seneca's *Medea*. The curse anticipates future events (such as Jason's love for another woman, the death of the children and Jason) but not everything mentioned in the curse will come to pass later in the poem.[37] The final words of the curse are particularly interesting: Medea will be groaning when she recognizes herself as *auctor* of the pain (299–300). In Dracontius' poem, Medea is very aware that she is the initiator of the events, and

---

[33] In the mythological tradition, Luna's love of Endymion is mentioned and compared to Medea's love for Jason; see Ap. Rhod. 4.54–65 and Val. Flacc. 8.27–31. Cf. Kaufmann 2006a, 213.
[34] Cf. van Zyl Smit 2003, 158 and Malamud 2012, 180.
[35] On a comic form of pantomime see Zanobi 2014, 5–6.
[36] See Zimmermann 1990, 164 and Zanobi 2014.
[37] Dracontius' Medea is not grieving, as the words *natos plangat, viduata (...) lugeat* (297) suggest, but is content with the killing: *nihil ipsa dolebo* (545). See the discussion in Simons 2005, 212; Kaufmann 2006a, 294–295; Wasyl 2011, 64; Zwierlein 2017b, 160.

the embedded comment of Diana confirms that the power and passion of Medea lie at the root of what will unfold. Thus, Medea is not "Diana's instrument for punishment," as Wasyl (2011, 91) states, because this contradicts the protagonist's otherwise active portrayal.[38] The curse suggests that the future 'tragedy' is doubly motivated, and its roots can be found in the divine as well as in the human realm.

The motif of the antagonism between Amor/Venus and Diana is again reflected in the last scene of part one, where Bacchus appears successfully to calm down Medea's upset father, Aietes.[39] It is remarkable that Aietes is depicted at v. 321 and 324 as *furens*,[40] and thus his behavior parallels that of his daughter in her later crime. Bacchus begins his speech (322–327) with words which sound very unlikely for a divine speaker to proffer (322–323): *sic tibi, rector, ait, mentem possedit inanis | religio?* ("King, he says, is your mind so much obsessed with inane *religio*?") Here, a god tries to convince a human to disregard religious rules. The words of Bacchus are striking in their dubious sense of morality. This reworking of the myth, then, raises questions in terms of a possible Christian perspective. If one imagines a recitation among Christians, motifs like this could amuse the audience, but need not present a serious criticism of the gods.

Aietes plans to kill his child (323), just as Medea plans to kill hers in the second part of the poem. Kaufmann stresses that both murders are religiously motivated, but a god intervenes only here, in the first part.[41] Bacchus' intervention correlates with the logic of the myth. Dracontius modifies the myth to make it suit his purpose, but he does not change its essence: namely, that Medea kills her children. He thus abides by Horace's rules regarding revisions of mythological themes that are outlined in his *Epistle* 3.119–123: *aut famam sequere aut sibi convenientia finge | scriptor. (…) sit Medea ferox invictaque* ("You, writer, either follow the tradition or invent congruently. (…) Let Medea be wild and undefeated").

In fact, the theme of *Medea ferox invictaque* is described in the traditionally Corinthian part of the myth that now takes place in Thebes.[42] This setting sets the

---

38 On Medea as an instrument see Gualandri 1999 and Glaser 2001, 75. Diaz de Bustamante 2002 also emphasizes the vengefulness of the gods. For a different view see Kaufmann 2006a, 302.
39 Bacchus does not appear in other versions of the myth that we know of; cf. Kaufmann 2006a, 284. In most versions of the myth Aietes does not consent to the wedding: cf. Kaufmann 2006a, 310.
40 Cf. Kaufmann 2006a, 320–324.
41 Kaufmann 2006a, 317. In Eur., *Hipp.* 1328f. Artemis explains in the end that she cannot act against the will of the other gods. This explanation is already missing in the Senecan *Phaedra*. Dracontius also does not explain the actions of the gods.
42 On the transfer of Medea's revenge to Thebes see Schetter 1980.

Medea myth in a new frame – as a continuation of the crimes of the Theban royal house. But the change of place is also a statement on genre. Not by coincidence does the second half of the poem start with a citation from Statius' *Thebaid* 2.65:[43] *ventum erat ad Thebas* (366: "they came to Thebes"), re-locating the poem into the context of epic, the target genre of the prologue. As opposed to the narrative in Statius, however, in Dracontius the action takes place without divine appearances or major divine intervention. No god initiates Glauce's desire to marry Jason. When Creon consents to the marriage, he mentions Jupiter but speaks only in conditional clauses (374–375). Creon is depicted in a morally negative way as a *tyrannus* and as *nocens* and *iniquus* (380f.), a characterization that highlights the altogether questionable actions of the human characters in this second part of the poem. Additionaly, Glauce's wish to marry Jason is characterized as moral corruption, *turpe* (376). Jason's wrongdoing against Medea is also emphasized.[44] It thus becomes clear that humans are themselves responsible for their misfortunes, which are due to their misconceived goals and erroneous beliefs and are manifestly not prompted by the gods.[45]

While in the first part the gods' speeches were an important element of the action, in the second part mortals dominate the stage. It is telling that Medea prays for about 100 verses: first to Diana (396–430), then to the Furies (436–469), and finally to the Sun (497–508). In the first two prayers, we can find close connections to prayers in both tragedy and epic: especially in Seneca's Medea[46] and Lucan's Erictho.[47] The three prayers reveal Medea's magical and cosmic authority through the reactions of both earth and sky. Her power verges on replacing that of the gods, which was manifest in the first half of the poem. For example, as Medea prepares the presents for Glauce, she prays to the Sun (497-508) and asks for his help in order to inflame the crown. Divine intervention is later severely reduced and can only be found in v. 518: *has (sc. flammas) radians nam Phoebus alit* ("Phoebus nourishes the flames"). The power of Medea, programmatically announced in the prologue, becomes concrete reality. Thanks to her magic, she now has the Sun under her command. This is illustrated by the shame a deity like the Sun experiences, and which is narrated later on, as he is said to blush and

---

[43] On Dracontius' imitation of Statius see Moussy 1989 and Galli Milić 2015.
[44] Already in the first part, beside the description of happiness during the wedding, the personifications of *Ingratia* and *Oblivio* appear and foreshadow the events of the second part of the poem, where Medea calls Jason *ingratus* (384, 519, 545f.) and Jason forgets his union with Medea.
[45] Cf. Simons 2005, 220; Malamud 2012, 181.
[46] Cf. Fischer 2008, 169–172.
[47] Cf. Korenjak 1996. Cf. the prayers in the first part of Dracontius' poem: Medea to Diana (188–194); Jason to Amor (201–208).

shine even brighter (568–569). But we cannot speak of the Sun's willful assistance, as Klein states,[48] as he appears to be threatened by Medea, *minax* (510). The depiction of Medea's magical powers culminates in the end with her triumphal ride in the sky on her chariot. Kaufmann states in her commentary that, in a Christian interpretation, it is not Medea's apotheosis that is described, but her likely journey to a remorseful afterlife.[49] But we do not read that in the text. Unlike Seneca's, Dracontius' Medea does not end at this point. The epilogue, which will be discussed next, is central for understanding the role of the gods in the poem.

The epilogue

The last two verses have led scholars to different interpretations of the poem as a whole, and raise the question of whether we find Christian criticism and anti-pagan polemics in the poem or, alternatively, criticism of the pagan gods from within the literary tradition. At 600–601 we read: *sit\<que\> nefas coluisse deos, quia crimen habetur | religionis honos, cum dat pro laude pericla* ("and it may be a sacrilege to have worshipped the gods, since honoring a religion is considered a crime when it causes ruin instead of evoking praise").[50] Modern scholarship has given different solutions to these riddling verses, revealing the complexity of the issue and the multi-layered character of the gods depicted by Dracontius.[51]

Regarding the view that these verses constitute Christian criticism, I follow the view of Wolff that it is paradoxical to suppose that Dracontius wrote poems about pagan myths in order to denounce paganism, especially since the explicit

---

48 Klein 2001, 235. Cf. the discussion of Simons 2005, 215–216.
49 Kaufmann 2006a, 302. Cf. Stoehr-Monjou 2013 on the chariot as a symbol of evil.
50 Translation by Kaufmann 2005/2006, 83.
51 On the question of the interpretation of Dracontius' mythological works see the overview in Wolff 2015, 218–219. Klein 2001, 233 argues that Dracontius intends to show the preeminence of the Christian belief against the pagan deities and the curse of the demons on the humans. Simons 2005, 209–211 convincingly rejects Klein's views. Already Quartiroli 1947, 24–25 sees polemics against the gods in the epilogue (570–601), but he does not directly connect his interpretation of the epilogue to the poem as a whole. Kaufmann 2005/2006 also argues for an anti-pagan interpretation that she mainly bases on the missing hierarchy of the gods, but the question remains whether the missing hierarchy is the main focus in the poem. In contrast, van Zyl Smit 2003, 160 states that: "There are no positive pointers to Christian morality in the poem: this is not a Christian version of the myth."

criticism of the immorality of pagan 'crimes' is limited to a few verses.[52] To write a mythological poem on Medea, for example, as a rhetorical exercise, does not have to lead to a theological problem for a Christian, as already Augustine's words from his *Confessions* 3.6.2 show: *volantem autem Medeam etsi cantabam, non asserebam, etsi cantari audiebam, non credebam* ("Though I sang about Medea flying, I did not assert this; though I heard this sung, I did not believe it").

Similar to *Medea*, Dracontius' *Orestis tragoedia*[53] also ends with a prayer to the gods to save the world at 973: *vestro iam parcite mundo* ("spare henceforth your [own] world"). The words *vestro mundo* may point to a distant perspective, but if we consider the verses in the context of the whole epilogue and not in isolation,[54] the use of *vestro* is not completely surprising, as *vos* is emphasized in the preceding verses: it is the world of the gods – their own world – they have to save.

In the epilogue, we hear the narrator's voice, which provides a generalized view of events. The gods are the focus of interest, and some form of criticism is traceable. The epilogue can be divided into two main parts, mirroring the twofold structure of the poem as a whole. In the first part of the epilogue, the focus is on the humans (570–586), while in the second part it is on the gods (587–601).[55] The epilogue starts with an invocation of physical embodiments of negative emotions that are asked to spare Thebes (570–573). The Medea story is embedded in the history of the house of Thebes from Cadmus to Eteocles and Polyneices (574–586), and Thebes is characterized as the place from which all *nefas* derives (575).

In the next step (587–592), the guardian gods of Thebes, Venus, Cupid and Bacchus – gods appearing in the first part of the poem – are asked to spare the city. In the finale of the epilogue (592–601), Thebes is the starting point for a list of places which may regret the fame of being a god's birthplace. Crucial for the interpretation of the epilogue are these verses with the word *erit*, with Zwierlein's text reading *si* instead of *sic*: 591–593: ... *pro munere Thebae | et pro tot meritis si(c) funera tanta merentur, | crimen erit genuisse deos!* ("If [or: Thus] Thebes has merited such great catastrophes in return for this honor [for having Harmonia as patronesss] and after such merits [becoming the homecity of Dionysus], it shall

---

52 Wolff 2015, 218, also 1996, 45. Cf. already Schetter 1980, 326 opposing the interpretation of Christian polemics against the gods.
53 Cf. Schetter 1985; Simons 2005, 349; Wasyl 2011, 47–49.
54 *Orest. trag.* 963–966: *Di* ... *| vos Pietas miseranda rogat, vos mitis Honestas, | vos bona Simplicitas, Affectus sanguinus orat | vos Genus humanum* ... ("Gods, ... it is you that pitiable Piety is begging, you the gentle Honesty, the good Simplicity, the Familial Affection, you the Humankind begs"). Cf. the different view of Herren 2016, 319; cf. Wasyl 2011, 48.
55 Cf. Simons 2005, 216.

be a crime to have begotten gods!").⁵⁶ Even if we do not read *si* with Zwierlein (2017a, 181), the translation of *erit* makes the difference between a hypothetical or a factual annihilation or deconstruction of the god's birthplaces.⁵⁷ In late Latin, future and subjunctive can be used interchangeably.⁵⁸ Regarding the subsequent subjunctives, it is possible to take *erit* as a substitute for the subjunctive: "it may be a *crimen* to have begotten gods." The following catalogue of birthplaces mentions gods connected to the preceding poem, but not exclusively so, and thus provides a generalized view of the story of Medea. For example, Bacchus is not mentioned, but we hear of Pallas Athene and Vulcan. The emphasis on Venus is notable (Venus, connected to Amores and Dione), but Diana is not mentioned by name like the other gods.⁵⁹ Given her important role in the first part, this may be surprising and confirms her marginalization in the second part.

It is striking that the word *religio* is mentioned in the last line of the poem (v. 601: *religionis honos*). But this is about *religionis honos*, namely worship, and not pagan *religio* itself. The extreme example of Medea therefore demonstrates a mistaken human understanding of religious worship.⁶⁰ Medea *furens* is responsible for the crimes. It is no accident that the epilogue at v. 571 begins with the personification, *saeve Furor*.⁶¹ A main difference between Dracontius' Medea and all the other Medeas is that her *furor* is not caused by her love of Jason, but is rather a religious *furor*. As the second part of the poem shows, the main interest is not polemics against the gods,⁶² but the consequences of human actions. The background story of the house of Thebes puts the Medea myth into a wider context of crime that repeats itself, and points to generic connections with the tragedies and epics dealing with these myths. With the intertextual references to Statius' *Thebaid*, Dracontius reinforces his affiliation with the epic genre, while maintaining the tragic potential of his story despite using it in a short epic.

---

56 *Ad* v. 592: *sic* β Baehrens: *si* Zwierlein 2017a. Cf. Herren's translation 2016 and Zwierlein 2017a *ad loc.*
57 Pollmann 2017, 45 calls this finale an "anti-prayer" and sees the gods annihilated because of the deconstruction of the aetiological function of their myths: "The mythological narration of the supposed *nefas* of Medea (...) is used to reveal pagan piety itself to be *nefas*;" cf. also Pollmann 2001.
58 Cf. Kaufmann 2006a, 163 with LHS 2,309 §17. Cf. differently Herren's 2016, 307 interpretation of the finale as Dracontius' (Christian) voice.
59 Cf. Simons 2005, 213.
60 See the discussion of Simons 2005, 213.
61 On *furor* cf. Kaufmann 2006a, 125 and 425; see also Selent 2011, 165.
62 Cf. Simons 2005, 220.

Conclusions

My aim has been to interpret Dracontius' *Medea* with a focus on the transposition and transformation of genre and myth, as well as on the question of Christian criticism of the gods. To achieve this, I analyzed the structure of the poem in its two parts. In the prologue, the genre of the poem is defined within the epic tradition but is also explicitly indebted to pantomimic (part I) and dramatic (part II) representations of the myth. In the first part of the poem (vv. 32–339), the appearances and interventions of the gods Juno, Venus, Amor, and Bacchus dominate the action. As the example of the rivalry between Venus/Amor and Diana showed, their presentation combines tragic and epic, as well as elegiac motifs. The gods are cruel and egocentric, but their depiction is not different from that found in the classical tradition. In the second part (366–569), the gods do not appear. Medea is the central figure, and the cosmic reactions to her prayers are a clear indication of her magical powers. Only the last two verses show a critical attitude towards the gods.

Regarding the potentially Christian interpretation of the poem, it is important to differentiate between a possible Christian perspective – namely passages that would appeal to a Christian audience – in the selection of the episodes and motifs of the myth and serious criticism of the pagan gods. In my opinion, Dracontius' transposition of the Medea myth does not turn *Romulea* 10 into a Christian poem. In fact, the focus is on the generic transposition, not on a Christian recasting of the story. The generic considerations of the prologue place emphasis on the epic reworking of the myth, strengthened by citations from Lucan and Statius in the central parts of the poem and by the transfer of the second part of the action to Thebes. The compelling figure of Medea dominates the second part and is a reflection of the Senecan Medea combined with the Ovidian Medea from *Metamorphoses* 7, reworked in Dracontius' epic verse. His new recasting of the Medea myth is a self-conscious generic and intertextual presentation in dialogue with the literary and theatrical representation of the myth.

Bibliography

Ambühl, A. 2015. *Krieg und Bürgerkrieg bei Lucan und in der griechischen Literatur. Studien zur Rezeption der attischen Tragödie und der hellenistischen Dichtung im Bellum Civile*, Berlin.

Baumbach, M./Bär, S. (eds.) 2012. *Brill's Companion to Greek and Latin epyllion and its reception*, Leiden.

Benz, L. 2000. "Pantomimos", *DNP*, 9, col. 274–276.
Beltrán-Noguer M.T./Sánchez-Lafuente Andrés, A. 1998. "Es la figura de Medea de Draconzio la Medea de Séneca?", in R.M. Aguilar/L. Gil/M. Martínez Pastor (eds.), *Corolla complutensis. In memoriam J.S. Lasso de la Vega contexta*, Madrid, 295–302.
Bisanti, A. 2017. "Responsabilità e (de)merito negli epilli di Draconzio", *Hormos*, 9, 649–663.
Bouquet, J. 1982. "L'imitation d'Ovide chez Dracontius", in R. Chevallier (ed.), *Colloque Présence d'Ovide*, Paris, 177–187.
Bouquet, J. 1996. "L'influence de la déclamation chez Dracontius", in J. Dangel/C. Moussy (eds.), *Les structures de l'oralité en latin. Colloque du Centre Alfred Ernout, Université de Paris IV, 2–4 juin 1994*, Paris, 245–255.
Boyle, A.J. 2012. "Medea in Greece and Rome", *Ramus*, 41, 1–32.
Bright, D.F. 1987. *The miniature epic in Vandal Africa*, Norman (OK).
Bureau, B. 2015. "L'annonce du sujet dans les épopées profanes de Dracontius, inflexions du genre épique?", in É. Wolff (ed.), *Littérature, politique et religion en Afrique vandale*, Paris, 287–301.
De Gaetano, M. 2009. *Scuola e potere in Draconzio*, Alessandria.
Díaz de Bustamante, J.M. 2002. "El epilio *Medea* de Draconcio", in A. López/A. Pociña (eds.), *Medeas: versiones de un mito desde Grecia hasta hoy*, Granada, 697–708.
Fischer, S. 2008. *Seneca als Theologe*, Berlin.
Fletcher, J. 2017. "Euripides and religion", in L.K. McClure (ed.), *A Companion to Euripides*, Chichester, 483–499.
Friedrich, W.H. 1967. *Vorbild und Neugestaltung. Sechs Kapitel zur Geschichte der Tragödie*, Göttingen.
Galli Milić, L. 2015. "Valérius Flaccus et Stace à Carthage: la matrice flavienne du *Romulea* 10 de Dracontius", in É. Wolff (ed.), *Littérature, politique et religion en Afrique vandale*, Paris, 323–340.
Gasti, F. 2016. *Blossio Emilio Draconzio, Medea*, Milano.
Gosserez, L. 2015. "L'*ekphrasis* de Cupidon dans la *Médée d*e Dracontius", in É. Wolff (ed.), *Littérature, politique et religion en Afrique vandale*, Paris, 303–322.
Gualandri, I. 1999. "Gli dei duri a morire: temi mitologici nella poesia latina del quinto secolo", in G. Mazzoli/F. Gasti (eds.), *Prospettive sul Tardoantico*, Como, 49–68.
Gualandri, I. 2009. "*Sit Medea ferox invictaque, flebilis Ino:* spunti di teorizzazione sul personnagio nella letterature latina", *Acme*, 62, 7–19.
Hall, E./Wyles, R. (eds.) 2008. *New directions in ancient pantomime*, Oxford.
Herren, M.W. 2016. "Dracontius, the pagan gods, and stoicism", in S. McGill/J. Pucci (eds.), *Classics renewed. Reception and innovation in the Latin poetry of Late Antiquity*, Heidelberg, 297–322.
Hose, M. 2004. *Poesie aus der Schule. Überlegungen zur spätgriechischen Dichtung*, München.
D'Ippolito, G. 1962. "Draconzio, Nonno e gli idromimi", *A&R*, 7, 1–14.
Johnson, W.R. 1988. "*Medea nunc sum*: the close of Seneca's version", in P. Pucci (ed.), *Language and the tragic hero: essays on Greek tragedy in honour of G.M. Kirkwood*, Atlanta, 85–102.
Kaufmann, H. 2005/2006. "Missing hierarchy. The gods in Dracontius' *Medea* (*Romulea* 10)", *Archivum Bobiense*, 27/28, 79–101.
Kaufmann, H. (ed.) 2006a. *Dracontius, Romulea 10 (Medea)*, Heidelberg.

Kaufmann, H. 2006b. "Intertextualität in Dracontius' *Medea (Romulea* 10)", *MH*, 63, 104–114, (online: 1.10.2108: http://doi.org/10.5169/seals-48695).

Koster, S. 2002. "Epos – Kleinepos – Epyllion? Zu Formen und Leitbildern spätantiker Epik", in J. Dummer/M. Vielberg (eds.), *Leitbilder aus Kunst und Literatur*, Stuttgart, 31–51.

Klein, R. 2001. "Medea am Ausgang der Antike. Bemerkungen zum Epyllion *Medea* des christlichen Dichters Dracontius", *WJA*, 25, 229–238.

Korenjak, M. (ed.) 1996. *Die Ericthoszene in Lukans Pharsalia. Einleitung, Text, Übersetzung, Kommentar*, Frankfurt a. M.

Malamud, M. 2012. "Double double. Two African Medeas", *Ramus*, 41, 161–189.

Manuwald, G. 2013. "Medea: transformations of a Greek figure in Latin literature", *G&R*, 60, 114–135.

Matthiesen, K. 2004. *Euripides und sein Jahrhundert*, München.

Moussy, C. 1989. "L'imitation de Stace chez Dracontius", *ICS*, 14, 425–433.

Pollmann, K. 2001. "Das lateinische Epos in der Spätantike", in J. Rüpke (ed.), *Von Göttern und Menschen erzählen: Formkonstanzen und Funktionswandel vormoderner Epik*, Stuttgart, 93–129.

Pollmann, K. 2017. *The baptized Muse. Early Christian poetry as cultural authority*, Oxford.

Puk, A. 2014. *Das römische Spielewesen in der Spätantike*, Berlin.

Quartiroli, A.M. 1947. "Gli epilli di Draconzio II", *Athenaeum*, 25, 17–34.

Rives, J.B. 1995. "Human sacrifice among pagans and Christians", *MH*, 51, 54–63.

Rotolo, V. 1957. *Il pantomimo*, Palermo.

Schetter, W. 1980. "Medea in Theben", in O. Zwierlein (ed.), *Willy Schetter, Kaiserzeit und Spätantike, Kleine Schriften 1957–1992*, Stuttgart, 1994, 314–327.

Schetter, W. 1985. "Über die Erfindung und Komposition des '*Orestes*' des Dracontius. Zur spätantiken Neugestaltung des klassischen Mythos", in O. Zwierlein (ed.), *Willy Schetter, Kaiserzeit und Spätantike, Kleine Schriften 1957–1992*, Stuttgart, 1994, 342–369.

Schetter, W. 1987. "Dares und Dracontius: Zur Vorgeschichte des Trojanischen Krieges", *Hermes*, 115, 211–231.

Schmidt, P.L. 1984. "*Habent sua fata libelli*. Archetyp und literarische Struktur der *Romulea* des Dracontius", in *Vestigia. Studi in onore di Giuseppe Billanovich*, Roma, 681–697 (repr. in: P.L. Schmidt (ed.) 2000. *Traditio Latinitatis. Studien zur Rezeption und Überlieferung der lateinischen Literatur*, Stuttgart, 73–83).

Selent, D. 2011. *Allegorische Mythenerklärung in der Spätantike: Wege zum Werk des Dracontius*, Rahden.

Simons, R. 2005. *Dracontius und der Mythos: christliche Weltsicht und pagane Kultur in der ausgehenden Spätantike*, München.

Stenger, J. (ed.). 2015. *Spätantike Konzeptionen von Literatur*, Heidelberg.

Stoehr-Monjou, A. 2009. "Le rejet de la *tragoedia* et les tragiques dans l'*Orestis* de Dracontius à la lumière du manifeste inaugural: *te rogo, Melpomene, tragicis descende cothurnis* (Drac. *Orestis* 13)", *Mosaique* 1, June 2009 (online: 1.10.2018: Https://revuemosaique.files.wordpress.com/2010/03/mosaique-1-12_stoehr-monjou.pdf).

Stoehr-Monjou, A. 2013. "Une *ekphrasis* tardive entre traditions poétique et iconographique: le char de Médée, symbole du Mal (Dracontius, *Romulea* X, 556–569)", *AntAfr*, 49, 161–176.

Stotz, P. 1981. "Dichten als Schulfach – Aspekte mittelalterlicher Schuldichtung", *MLatJB*, 16, 1–16.

Tupet, A.-M. 1976. *La magie dans la poésie Latine, Vol. 1: Des origines à la fin du règne d'Auguste*, Paris.

Van Zyl Smit, B. 2003. "A Christian Medea in Vandal Africa? Some aspects of the *Medea* of Blossius Aemilius Dracontius", in A.F. Basson/W.J. Dominik (eds.), *Literature, art, history. Studies on Classical Antiquity and tradition: in honour of W.J. Henderson*, Frankfurt a. M., 151–160.
Vössing, K. 1997. *Schule und Bildung im Nordafrika der Römischen Kaiserzeit*, Bruxelles.
Walde, C. 1999. "Melpomene", *DNP*, 7, 351.
Walde, C. 2001. "Polyhymnia", *DNP*, 10, 61.
Wasyl, A.M. 2011. *Genres rediscovered: studies in Latin miniature epic, love elegy, and epigram of the Romano-Barbaric Age*, Kraków.
Weber, B. (ed.) 1995. *Der Hylas des Dracontius: Romulea 2*, Stuttgart.
Wolff, É. (ed.) 1996. *Dracontius, Œuvres, t. 4*, Paris.
Wolff, É. 2004. "Poeta inclusus: le cas de Dracontius", in C. Bertrand-Dagenbach (ed.), *Carcer II. Prison et privation de liberté dans l'Empire romain et l'Occident médiéval. Actes du colloque de Strasbourg (décembre 2000)*, Paris, 123–128.
Wolff, É. (ed.) 2015. *Littérature, politique et religion en Afrique vandale*, Paris.
Zanker, P./Ewald, B.C. 2004. *Mit Mythen leben. Die Bilderwelt der römischen Sarkophage*, Müchen.
Zanobi, A. 2015. *Seneca's tragedies and the aesthetics of pantomime*, London.
Zimmermann, B. 1990. "Seneca und der Pantomimus", in G. Vogt-Spira (ed.), *Strukturen der Mündlichkeit in der römischen Literatur*, Tübingen, 161–167.
Zwierlein, O. 2017a. *Die Carmina profana des Dracontius. Prolegomena und kritischer Kommentar zur Editio Teubneriana. Mit einem Anhang: Dracontius und die Aegritudo Perdicae*, Stuttgart.
Zwierlein, O. (ed.) 2017b. *Blossius Aemilius Dracontius, Carmina profana*, Stuttgart.

Anna Maria Wasyl
The Late Roman Alcestis and the Applicability of Generic Labels to Two Short Narrative Poems

It is undeniable that in late antique literature, next to long hexametric compositions, there is a strong tendency toward miniaturization, and indeed within various narrative forms. At the same time, most such poems, despite their minor format, have quite major 'ambitions', so to speak, aiming to explore themes so far reserved for grand genres. The two texts on Alcestis, i.e. the one referred to as *Alcestis Barcinonensis* and the cento *Alcesta*, are representative of this trend. Both are extremely short (122[1] and 162 hexameters, respectively), and yet concern themselves with a (*par excellence*) tragic protagonist, presenting her story *in extenso*, though understandably with major shortcuts. Both are composed in narrative mode,[2] and yet show similarities with dramatic forms, thus provoking intriguing questions concerning their performative contexts. In addition, one of these texts, the *Alcesta*, happens to be a Virgilian cento.[3] This material provides excellent grounds for a discussion on late antique approaches to genres and generic divisions, on the applicability of certain generic labels (those coined in antiquity and those invented by modern scholars), and – last but not least – on the reinter-

---

[1] For the *Alcestis Barcinonensis* (henceforth, *Alc. Barc.*) see recent commented editions by Nosarti 1992 and Nocchi Macedo 2014, *pace* Marcovich 1988 and Lebek 1983.
[2] In other words, in both poems one can detect a diegetic frame, obtained through the presence of the speaking 'I'. This differentiates them, and in particular the cento *Alcesta*, from Hosidius Geta's cento *Medea*, where the diegetic frame is absent (as is the narratorial voice) and the whole poem, however composed of Virgilian units, has the formal appearance of a drama. For Geta's cento as an example of rewriting Virgil's epic as a tragedy see McGill 2002.
[3] The *Alcesta* is one of the twelve Virgilian centos transmitted in the initial part of the *Anthologia Latina* (Riese 1894) and one of the sixteen ancient Virgilian centos that are still extant. Interestingly, all but one of the centos from the *AL* (7–18 R) are secular and most of them deal with mythological topics: 9 R *Narcissus*; 10 R *Iudicium Paridis*; 11 R *Hippodamia*; 12 R *Hercules et Antaeus*; 13 R *Progne et Philomela*; 14 R *Europa*; 15 R *Alcesta*; 17 R *Medea* by Hosidius Geta. As for other Latin centos, Ausonius' *Cento nuptialis* is secular (as is 18 R, Luxorius' *Epithalamium Fridi*), whereas *C. Pr.* by Faltonia Betitia Proba, *Versus ad gratiam Domini* by Pomponius, and the anonymous *De Verbi incarnatione* are Christian. The cento *De ecclesia* (16 R) is also Christian, but was most probably mistakenly included in the *Salmasian Anthology*; see Mondin/Cristante 2010, 318.

pretations of a classical myth in a culture that was already, if not wholly Christianized, at least thoroughly permeated by Christian concepts of familial love, sacrifice, and (im)mortality.

In fact, in the late antique cultural *koinê* Alcestis was the example of the brave wife and, more generally, the mature human being, who was ready to accept his/her fate; she thus appealed with the same intensity to both pagans and Christians. Jerome uses her paradigm in advocating for the sacrosanctity of marital bonds (*Against Jovinianus* 1.45). The mythographer Fulgentius, active in late fifth-century Carthage and thus contemporary with the author of the cento, proposes, in his *Fable of Admetus and Alcestis* (*Myth.* 1.22), an allegorical interpretation of the myth. In this reading, every protagonist personifies a single quality: Admetus fear; the lion spiritual, the boar physical strength; Apollo wisdom; Hercules virtue; and finally, Alcestis bravery. Therefore, his interpretation is not strictly a Christian allegoresis,[4] but rather an insight into a deeper, moral sense of the story, which would be acceptable for the majority of his late antique readers, both Christians and pagans.[5] A glimpse at the funerary visual testimonies can provide additional evidence.[6] The so-called Hypogeum in Via Dino Compagni, in Via Latina, datable to the fourth century and discovered in 1955, may have included tombs of the members of a mixed family, of Christians and pagans,[7] as its cubicula display both Christian (Lazarus and Jonah in Cubiculum O and M) and mythical (Ceres and Proserpina in Cubiculum O) characters. Alcestis is depicted in Cubiculum N: The scene of her death appears in the left arcosolium, while her 'ascent', i.e. Hercules leading her out of the Underworld, which could potentially be interpreted as a 'resurrection', is in the right arcosolium. Apparently, the heroic wife was able, thanks to her virtue and generous sacrifice, not just to cross the borders of life and death, but even to unite two worlds, the Christian and the pagan.

Before addressing more specific questions let us briefly summarize some information concerning dating, authorship, and the cultural milieu of the two late Latin poems on Alcestis. The *Alcestis Barcinonensis* is transmitted in the Papyri Montserratenses Roca, named after Ramon Roca-Puig, the purchaser of the codex

---

[4] In the style of medieval exegetical interpretations of the classical mythography, the key example of which is the anonymously published *Ovide moralisé* (1309–1320), the first French translation and allegorical presentation of the Latin *Metamorphoses*.

[5] See generally Hays 2004; on the 'secular middle ground' see Miles 2005 and Merrills/Miles 2010, 225–227.

[6] For a general discussion on the presence of the Alcestis myth in funerary art, including Roman sarcophagi, see Wood 1978; Zanker/Ewald 2012, 306–310; Wasyl 2018, 31–38.

[7] Denzey Lewis 2016, 269.

and the discoverer of the poem in question. Whereas the entire *codex miscellaneus* is datable to the second half of the fourth century and comes from Upper Egypt,[8] the poem itself was probably composed in the early-third to mid-fourth century, and shows stylistic affinities with texts written in Roman North Africa.[9] Quite possibly it was penned there, too, by some anonymous local *litteratus*. The cento *Alcesta* is part of the *Anthologia Salmasiana*,[10] a varied medley of Latin short poetry compiled at the time of the fall of the Vandal kingdom (533–534) or shortly thereafter and surviving solely in the initial part of the manuscript once owned by Claudius Salmasius. Presumably, the *Alcesta* as well as the majority of the centos from the *Anthologia Latina* are datable to the same period,[11] i.e. the late fifth-early sixth century, and belong to authors from the same literary milieu of Carthaginian grammarians and poets.[12] The hypothesis that the author of our poem might have been female, revealing herself under the penname of Siria in the initial acrostich,[13] is worth taking into consideration as (some) women of Late Antiquity happened to be active litterateurs and, interestingly, the cento appeared to be one of their favorite techniques.[14] Besides, the text does convey a subtle 'feminist' message, as we will see, even though it cannot be taken for granted, of course, that female authorship always entails a feminist viewpoint.[15]

Alcestis Barcinonensis

What strikes the reader of the *Barcinonensis* is its schematic structure: five self-contained units, five protagonists (Apollo, Admetus, his father, mother, and Alcestis), usually presented either alone or only in twos, with the action itself

---

8 For a thorough analysis of the codex and its destination see Nocchi Macedo 2014, 125–142.
9 Paolucci 2015, XXXV.
10 For a specific study on the *Salmasian Anthology* see Spallone 1982; Mondin/Cristante 2010.
11 Except for the *Medea* by Hosidius Geta, for which 203 CE is considered the *terminus ante quem* by most scholars; see, e.g., McGill 2005, 31–32, *pace* Rondholz 2012, 84–89, who would antedate it to the times of Quintilian.
12 See Wasyl 2018, 108–115.
13 Paolucci 2014b, 119–121 and 2015, LXXXIV–XCIII.
14 It is worth adding here that the conceptual amalgamation of writing and weaving, of which Proba's patchwork poem is an *exemplum par excellence*, played also an integral part in the rhetoric of the autonomy of early modern women writers; see Schottenius Cullhed 2015, 101–108.
15 As Proba's attitude to Eve (too) often indicates; on the other hand, Proba's 'antifeminism' should not be overestimated, as Laato 2017 justly argues.

shown through single scene-panels. Unity of place is preserved, and the heterodiegetic narrator's interventions and comments are quite rare. Yet interestingly, none of these features affects the aesthetic appreciation of the poem. The protagonists, portrayed in this way, reveal only some general traits and so can be interpreted as embodiments, or even models, of the most basic human virtues and vices. Admetus is just an everyman: average, anti-heroic, mediocre even in his cowardliness,[16] and believing in some sort of generational justice the foundation of which should be the rule that the old should die before the young.[17] Hence, he is not able to confront the suddenness of death courageously or philosophically. The parents, on their part, do introduce some 'philosophical' flavor into the poem. The father appears extremely materialistic, absolutely unable to believe in any form of life after death (vv. 35–40). The mother is casuistic in evoking examples of other women who lost their offspring, as if she were composing a sort of self-consolation (vv. 57–63). It is interesting to note that the poet, intending to portray them as egocentric, negative characters, does not ridicule their physical defects at all, but instead focuses on their attitudes to life. It is as if his objective was to offer a kind of parody of philosophical argumentation, especially the kind that addresses fundamental questions (such as death) and ends up giving only trite, banal answers. If so, it should be concluded that his humor is of an intellectual sort, requiring much erudition and typically school, i.e. rhetorical education on the part of his audience that would have enabled them to recognize in the poem exercises such as 'a consolation' for a lost child. This is an additional hint concerning the possible audience of the anonymous author.

Alcestis, naturally, embodies female virtue as opposed to the egoism of Admetus' mother. She generously relinquishes her own for her husband's life, but in return requires faithfulness on his part. If and only if he obeys, she promises her spiritual presence (in his bedroom, to be exact) on condition that spirits return (vv. 90–92 and 100–101).[18] The passage is somewhat oneiric, and not entirely free from some grotesque overtones, counterbalancing quite well the pathos, but its general message seems to be utterly serious. The anonymous poem does not convey a strictly allegorical reading of the myth, yet it opens up such an interpre-

---

16 Marcovich 1988, 96.
17 Nosarti 1992, XXVIII.
18 The highlighted conditional clause at 90–91: *si redeunt umbrae, veniam tecumque iacebo* ("If the shades return, I shall come to lie down with you") together with the (quite alarming) expression *qualiscumque tamen, coniux* ("whatever shape I, your wife, may have then") indicate that the phrasing can hardly be taken as an allusion to the Christian idea of resurrection.

tation. Admetus the everyman, with no heroic aspirations, thanks to Alcestis' sacrifice, may – and even should – transcend his very self and gain the courage he so much lacks. But he must not deviate from his road to virtue.

Interestingly, the problem of immortality and life after death is central to the miniature poem, yet the way in which the poet evokes it causes some perplexity. Firstly, the mother in her speech ridicules the myth of the 'barbarous' (as she calls it, v. 54) bird, i.e. the phoenix, with an irony that seems not merely anti-Christian but rather, in general, anti-religious.[19] Secondly, Alcestis herself refers to her own immortality and defines it only through the eternal memory of her admirable deed (vv. 77–78) and the life of her legitimately born heirs (vv. 93–95). One could hardly find a more Roman approach to the topic. In the final scene Admetus' wife is shown preparing her own funeral pyre and adorning it with flowers and spices (vv. 109–114). This should provoke some further associations with the phoenix myth, except that there are no hints whatsoever at the possibility of future resurrection.[20] Instead, the sopor into which Alcestis falls (v. 122) matches perfectly the oneiric atmosphere of the poem. At the same time, the *Barcinonensis* reveals quite a lot of bitter realism, and hence pessimism, which, especially if mixed with pathos, makes it, as mentioned above, utterly Roman. The skill with which its author combines all elements, exploiting various sources (Euripides possibly, but in particular Roman literature, both poetry[21] and prose[22]), evoking – but with freedom – the rhetorical schemes of *ethopoeia* and *controversia*, may induce one to conclude that the poem is a mature work, not one by a mediocre litterateur. Yet its schematic structure and rare narratorial interventions – both applied intentionally, though – suggest that the poem's destination might have been different from the one focused only on quiet reading. This seems intriguing enough to provoke further questions concerning its genre.

---

19 See Schäublin 1984, 180–181, Liebermann 1993, 186–187.
20 For the myth of the phoenix see Van Den Broek 1972; in Latin literature specifically see Strati 2007. Contrast the crypto-Christian elaboration of the myth in Lactantius' *De ave Phoenice*, on which see Fontaine 1981 and Roberts 2018; *pace* Richter 1993. Our poet's approach to the topic may compete with Lactantius', as argued by Schäublin 1984 and (from a slightly different viewpoint) Nosarti 1992, XXVI–XXVII.
21 Especially elegy: Prop. 4.11; Ov., *Tr.* 3.3. See in particular Moreno Soldevila 2011.
22 The consolations by Seneca in the first place, see in particular Sen., *Marc.* 10.5, where the author argues that death is inevitable and common to every living creature on earth (compare *Alc. Barc.* vv. 69–70). Some self-consolatory undertones are also perceptible in Seneca, especially in his *Ad Helviam matrem, pass.* (cf. *Alc. Barc.* vv. 57–63).

The cento *Alcesta*

In the cento *Alcesta* the narrator is more active and definitely more self-conscious. The speaking 'I' starts by invoking Apollo, the god of poetic inspiration, and declares his (or rather her, if we accept that the author's (pen) name was Siria) intention to tell the story in its entirety (*prima repetens ab origine pergam* at v. 2, as opposed to the narration *in medias res*). And, in fact, the opening scene – as in Fulgentius (*Mythologiae* 1.22) – is the trial in which Admetus wins Alcestis' hand in marriage after yoking two opposed wild animals, the boar and the lion, to his chariot. The reader is immediately informed that Admetus wins because he is assisted, indeed replaced, by Apollo. Interestingly, all subsequent episodes take place a year later,[23] when the marriage is already fulfilled and fruitful: The couple has two children, which is a clear sign that, unlike in the *Barcinonensis*, the poet(ess) has no intention whatsoever to maintain the unity of time. On the contrary, the passage of time is emphasized with the (typically epic) proverbial "meanwhile" (v. 45: *interea*). First Apollo predicts the approaching *dies nefanda*, next the father (the cento does not mention the mother) rejects his son's request, and finally Alcestis declares her readiness to die in her husband's stead. The description of the *promissa dies* – again the unity of time is broken – comprises two, according to Paolucci (2014a), rather long farewell speeches by Alcestis and Admetus and a very short, and thus moving, finale: the moment of the female protagonist's death. The whole poem gives the general impression that it is a bit more dynamic than the *Barcinonensis*, also because it offers a more variegated combination of descriptive and dialogue-based parts. It is also certainly more comprehensive, providing a sort of 'backstory' for the core of the action as such.

As a cento the *Alcesta* is given extra dimension in portraying the protagonists, since each character and situation is colored with its Virgilian reference point and these associations turn out to be far from random, if not rarely unexpected.[24] Analyzing the hypotexts of the poem, one may notice that Alcestis is usually described through phrases evoking other female characters, and most often the tragic ones (like Lavinia, Creusa, Eurydice, Polyxena, and in particular Dido).

---

[23] Euripides' innovative version of the myth places it much later, and not on the wedding day or the honeymoon time as in the folklore tradition. His dramatic elaboration, however, does not highlight the diachronic perspective in the way Siria's reinterpretation does.

[24] For the Virgilian borrowings see Rossi Linguanti 2013; Paolucci 2015; Wasyl 2018, 121–132. On the 'memory of a quotation' see Audano 2015 and Bažil 2017. On the centos as 'absolute intertextuality' see Okáčová 2009 and 2011.

More surprisingly, however, she also assumes some masculine traits, as her actions and words call to mind several brave youngsters (Nisus and Euryalus, Lausus, Pallas, Turnus, and indeed Camilla, who is represented by Virgil himself in somewhat cross-gender terms).[25] At times, she is even modeled on Mezentius, the most controversial of Virgilian heroes, whose contempt for death, however, is admirable to the same extent as his opponent's, Aeneas', shallowness is disappointing. Admetus, too, is often painted in dark colors, through associations with protagonists who died prematurely (like, notably, Marcellus) or miserably (Deiphobus, Palinurus). Several times he is marked as Aeneas, as is Alcestis as Dido. Yet interestingly, he is also characterized with references to Ascanius, in particular in passages addressed to him by his wife. This infantilization of the main character tells us much about the general message of the poem: In fact, while its aim is certainly protreptic (with Admetus painted as an 'adolescent', if not a 'child', encouraged to pursue virtue), its undertone is 'feminist' (especially in the implication that the male protagonist is actually inferior to his female lead). What is more, Admetus is a few times connoted through phrases describing the traitor Sinon or the cruel Pyrrhus. This is alarming, as the centonic narration is often built upon the tension between the signified and the signifier. Thus, the reader is given a discreet suggestion, on the part of the narrator, that Admetus may not be really worthy of the unique sacrifice of life he was offered.

The cento *Alcesta* differs from the *Barcinonensis* in its portrayal of some protagonists, and in particular the father. Rather than egoistic and materialistic, Admetus' father is indeed severe, yet also noble and realistic. Skeptical about the god's illusory promise (the flavor of religious skepticism is ubiquitous throughout the poem), he also sounds convincing when advising his son to accept his own fate (vv. 79–83). Thus, he cannot be interpreted as a negative character, but instead embodies dignity and steadiness. Steadiness is certainly a feature Admetus lacks; as mentioned above, he appears intriguingly infantile at times, which provides an extra explanation as to his limited self-awareness. But, equally, he is also presented as deeply emotional, eventually even capable of expressing some sort of penitence. Moreover, the love between him and Alcestis is shown as truly mutual, indeed de-eroticized, based on tenderness and mercy, and in Alcestis' case even assuming the flavor of maternal affection. Alcestis is of course superior to him in virtue and self-awareness (which again opens up the possibility of allegorical interpretation) – hence treating him as a child and requiring faithfulness as if it were Admetus who was supposed to remain *univira* –, yet the emotional

---

[25] Since the basic meaning of the Latin term *virtus* is in fact 'manliness' – see McDonnell 2006; Masterson 2014, 22–28 – similar positioning of Alcestis is hardly surprising, if (still) provocative.

language she employs makes her also more human and moving. What is remarkable is her attitude to death. Alcestis seems almost fascinated with the idea of sacrificing herself (vv. 105–113),[26] even though she is also bitterly realistic about its irrevocability. There is no hint whatsoever at any form of existence after death, if not in the memory of the dear ones, nor any promise of the communion of souls (like in the *Barcinonensis*, however oneiric the image may seem). Consequently, the message of the poem is even more pessimistic than its earlier counterpart, the *Barcinonensis*, yet at the same time the virtue of the heroine is all the more emphasized. It seems that Alcestis believes much more in her female bravery and virtue, which will guarantee her being remembered among future generations, than in the legends of eternal life. This is why the poem cannot be interpreted as Christian, although some of its overtones are not far from Christian. Alcestis combines Stoicism with religious skepticism, but even if her figure reveals the true *Weltanschauung* of the poetess Siria, her work fully belongs to the world of the (gradually Christianizing) late antique cultural *koinê*, where it is already the dominant Christian culture that penetrates the classical, or pagan, one.

Alcestis Barcinonensis and ancient pantomime

None of the poems on which this chapter focuses were composed by a renowned classical poet – or at least not one recognizable by a wider readership. Nevertheless, quite a lot has been published on the *Alcestis Barcinonensis*, in particular in recent decades, and these publications include not only strictly scholarly studies but also newspaper notes and articles. This is because this unique version of Alcestis' tragedy was performed as a pantomime spectacle, first in 1999 in Florence (by Sara Cascione, a classical student and professional dancer) and for the second time ten years later, in Milan (by an actor and performer, Paolo Stoppani, during the *La festa del teatro romano*). These performances aroused some interest among the wider audience and, as far as the experts are concerned, provided additional impetus to pondering the destination of the text found in the Egyptian papyrus codex by the Catalan Hellenist. Certain conclusions, however, still require revision. There are some scholars who, following with full acceptance – and indeed fascination – the idea that the *Alcestis Barcinonensis* might be used as a

---

26 Pollina 2007–2008, 103–104.

pantomime libretto (some even conclude it was one),[27] appear to rely on this modern attestation,[28] as if it explained what ancient pantomime really was. Should it be seen as a literary genre in its own right or rather (only) as a performance medium for a certain text, the proper generic status of which should be defined separately and on the basis of different criteria?

The continuing popularity of the *tragoedia saltata/fabula saltica* throughout Late Antiquity is testified in various sources. Pantomime, one of the most interesting theatrical forms that developed from and eventually replaced the old tragedy, was by far the most important and popular mythological spectacle known to the Roman public. It was pantomime that shaped their taste and general consciousness of performative aesthetics and mythology itself. Quantitatively speaking, pantomime played a more important role than other arts in educating the majority of inhabitants of the Roman Empire in mythology.[29] Thus, it can be epitomized as an example of ancient 'popular culture', indeed, especially peculiar to Postclassical Antiquity.

Pantomime involved a highly skilled multi-media combination of speech, song, dance, music, gesture, and scenic design[30] in which, as the narrator described scenes or stories from mythology, the *pantomimus*, wearing a mask whose mouth was closed (as he did not speak), acted out the events and the characters' feelings. He was sometimes joined by an assistant actor, or a group of dancers of either sex, and could dance to the accompaniment of a large orchestra and choir or a single musical instrument and solo singer. He could dance in venues stretching from vast open-air amphitheaters to private dining rooms.[31] Yet in terms of external equipment pantomime was minimalist. The effect was created almost entirely by the dancer's skill and, crucially, his interaction with the audience's knowledge of the stories and characters he represented. The spectators were thus expected to contribute imaginatively to the creation of the scenario, imagining settings and even other characters.[32] The central garment of the performer was a long robe and the whole costume included also a mantle, some props (like hats and weapons), a mask, and sandals. Such a costume would have

---

[27] See in particular Gianotti 1991.
[28] Again Gianotti 1991, but also Hall 2008.
[29] Hall/Wyles 2008, esp. 6–8, and specifically Hunt 2008.
[30] Griffith 2009, 32.
[31] Hall/Wyles 2008, 4.
[32] Webb 2008, 47.

been extremely versatile. It could be used to depict female as well as male characters.[33] There is no suggestion that the *pantomimus* left the stage in order to transform into a new character; quite the opposite, the actor did not seek to conceal the fact that the same performer was playing different roles, only changing masks (and apparently nothing more). Hence, pantomime required the spectator to be alert so as to recognize what was happening through gesture and, since the representation of character and action was partly symbolic and made use of a set of specialized gestures, all these symbols would have been intelligible to the initiated, though not necessarily to the uninitiated.[34]

Scholars have dedicated much attention to the question of ancient pantomime libretti and, as mentioned above, it is the *Alcestis Barcinonensis* that has been pointed to as the most probable candidate for having been one.[35] But before addressing the very problem of theatricality in the *Barcinonensis*, one aspect should be emphasized. As it appears from various sources, what was most frequently and readily performed as pantomimic shows was motifs or scenes taken from well-known and acknowledged literary works, like, indeed, the *Aeneid* (in particular, Books 4 and 6) and, plausibly, Ovid's *Metamorphoses* (especially selected episodes concerning adulterous liaisons of the gods featuring transformation into animals or trees, the story of Daphne being the most obvious example).[36] This shows that pantomime was seen not so much as a genre in its own right but as a medium that concretized already existing literary works and, at the same time, guaranteed them some contact with (possibly) new audiences, different from those that met at private, or even public, recitations. Being a sort of 'pop art', pantomime could certainly make 'high', epic text more accessible to the wider public. As a popular medium, it certainly shaped the mythological erudition but also the aesthetic consciousness, or simply 'taste', and the visual sensitivity of the spectators. Yet interestingly, it also influenced their reception of any

---

33 On the symbolism of costume see Wyles 2008. On pantomime's femininity and feminizing power see Lada-Richards 2003.

34 Augustine comments upon this aspect of pantomime in his *Doctr. Chr.* 2.97: *si quis theatrum talium nugarum imperitus intraverit, nisi ei dicatur ab altero quid illi motus significant, frustra totus intentus est*; "Now if a person unfamiliar with these frivolities goes to the theater his rapt attention to them is pointless unless someone tells him what the movements mean." Trans. R.P.H. Green; see also Green 1995, 103.

35 Already Tandoi 1984, 236 implied the influence of the aesthetics of pantomime on the presentation of the Alcestis myth in the *Barcinonensis*. See Gianotti 1991, briefly Salanitro 2007, 30–32, and in particular Hall 2008.

36 See Galinsky 1996, 265–266; Ingleheart 2008, 169–184; Garelli 2013, 93–118.

work they were reading. The readers, who on other occasions frequented theaters, were 'naturally' trained to imagine certain scenes as if performed on stage. The same is true of the (prospective) authors: It has been shown in recent scholarship that Seneca, for instance, when composing his tragedies, took inspiration from the 'vividness' (or *enargeia/evidentia*) he and his readers were familiar with from (and appreciated in) pantomimic spectacles – although this does not mean that his tragedies were to be only libretti, planned for a pantomimic performance.[37] Pantomime and its specific 'vividness' penetrated the textual culture to the same extent as already existing texts, usually belonging to narrative genres, provided material for a pantomimic spectacle. Pantomime was, indeed, a means of concretization, not a specific literary genre.[38]

Conclusions: The two poems on Alcestis and ancient and modern categories of genre

In seeking the literary genre of the two poems in question, the ancient perspective should be taken into consideration first. The most systematic among ancient classifications of literary genres was provided by Diomedes Grammaticus in the late fourth century CE. As his classification is late and elaborated by a grammarian, it seems a valuable reference point for the two pieces on Alcestis. As a grammarian with experience in describing parts of the speech, Diomedes managed to categorize literary works hierarchically, obtaining a scheme of three major kinds: 1) *activum vel imitativum*; 2) *enarrativum vel enuntiativum* (which he defined as a poetry that is narrative but non-mimetic; thus, it should not be interpreted as epic); and 3) *commune vel mixtum*, divided subsequently in several sub-genres (*species*). The category of *genus mixtum* comprised, in his system, the *species heroica* (exemplified by the *Iliad* and the *Aeneid*; thus, the *species heroica* should refer to epic poetry) and the *species lyrica*.[39] Reading his definition, it appears that Diomedes himself would not have hesitated to include both our poems in the *genus mixtum – species heroica*. Some compositional differences between them seem less important than similarities, taking into account the criteria he applied. In both, we find (several) speaking characters and a narrating voice – its activity is

---

37 See Zanobi 2008 and 2014; earlier Zimmermann 1990 and 2008.
38 See Ingarden 1988, 409–437, esp. §62.
39 For the whole definition see Keil 1857, 482–483.

different in the *Alcestis* and in the *Alcesta*, but Diomedes himself did not elaborate on this particular aspect. What is most relevant, however, is that their heroine fully represents a character apt for a 'lengthy treatment' (interestingly, the protagonist chosen by the grammarian to define this type of treatment is also female: Camilla). Apparently, the length of the poem itself is not of essential importance. Diomedes cites Homer, Virgil, Ennius *et cetera his similia*. The formula is so open that one could hardly argue that he would have excluded a piece in hexameters, provided with a narrator and speaking protagonists, both divine and heroic, only on the basis of its shortness. Therefore, if one aims to avoid anachronistic or misapprehended terms, applying Diomedes' label of *genus commune vel mixtum* in reference to both poems in question may seem a salutary solution.[40] Its advantage is that it allows us to define them objectively, i.e. on the basis of their actual – and textual – form and not taking as a starting point only a possible (but not necessary) concretization such as a pantomime performance. If, however, what one intends to find is a more precise definition, comprising not only basic and compositional but also, say, aesthetic qualities, the terminology attested in ancient sources may turn out not to be specific enough. In such a case it is necessary to employ more controversial terms, coined only in modern classical philology, or even to propose one's own *hapax legomena*.

The notion of the *epyllion* – although its generic status is disputable for some scholars[41] – might be worth considering. The label seems natural enough, considering the very format of our two poems: both are short, indeed minute. Yet, what is much more important, both invite insight into their structure and narrative mode, which is essential in defining and differentiating between the minor and the major within the epic tradition. It has often been stressed in studies on the 'miniature epic' – even by scholars hesitant to call it a separate genre and more prone to see a *genus mixtum* in it[42] – that its narrative style is different from that of grand epic:[43] it is more episodic and, consequently, causing marginalization or elimination of some parts of a story, in particular in between certain episodes of major importance. This implies a panel-like structure, as if composed of separate scenes, often poorly coordinated.[44] Interestingly, the narration as such is usually linear, starting from the origin of a story (rather than *in medias res*), but

---

40 Thus Schetter 1986, 128 in reference to the *Barcinonensis*.
41 Allen's 1940 and 1958 criticism is proverbial; see, recently, Bär 2015. For a more thorough discussion see Wolff 1988, Tilg 2012, and Cichoń 2016; see also Wasyl 2011, 13–29 and 2018, 159–170.
42 See notably Styka 1994, 160.
43 Styka 1994, 157–167.
44 See Richardson 1944, 85; Perutelli 1979, 28.

hardly exhaustive because of the short form. Another aspect worth pointing out is the obtrusive presence of the speaking 'I'.[45] The epyllic narrator has, indeed, a leading role, not merely in telling but also commenting on a story and confidently defining his literary goals at the outset. It is as if he focused less on the plot as such than on his own view on it. Now, these elements are easily found in the cento *Alcesta*. The speaking 'I', declaring his (or rather her) intention to tell the story in its entirety (*prima ... ab origine* is an interesting and presumably not unintended allusion to the opening of Ovid's *Metamorphoses* v. 3: *primaque ab origine mundi*), refers to Apollo as the god of poetic inspiration and the source of the truth. In other words s/he insists that the tale be read not simply as a literary fiction, but as a 'true', 'reliable' account (with the emphasis placed on *fides* and *vera* in v. 3). While later on the speaking 'I' may appear to be missing, his/her presence is felt throughout every line, in every borrowing from Virgil. Marking protagonists with overtones of their Virgilian archetypes (Alcestis as Dido and Camilla, and even Mezentius; Admetus as Aeneas, yet also as Ascanius and Sinon) reveals his/her attitude toward them. Reading the *Alcesta* comparatively with other miniature narrative poems composed in Vandal Africa (by Reposianus, Dracontius, or the author of the *Hippodamia* (11 R), another mythological cento of the *Salmasian Anthology*)[46] demonstrates compositional, aesthetic, and ideological similarities relevant enough to make one believe that they all represent a genre that was fashionable, indeed peculiar to that milieu of Latin literati and grammarians, gathering together and reading aloud their productions, yet presumably hesitant to include any outsiders in their circles. Most probably, the centonic technique, the key to which was not only following the plot but also decoding the intertext(s), required this and only this mode of presentation, by reading aloud or (even) silently. Otherwise, its (inter)textual richness would have been irrevocably lost.

In the case of the *Alcestis Barcinonensis* we cannot say much about the author's environment. What we see, though, is that the speaking 'I', while not wholly absent, appears definitely less self-oriented. There is no narratorial proem, while in the main part of the text the narrator focuses mostly on the protagonists and their 'scenic movement', letting them speak for themselves whenever possible. The final scene is different, as it is 'mute', fully descriptive, and indeed visual if not synaesthetic, especially when it depicts exotic herbs and spices mixed together by Alcestis. So, do the *Alcestis Barcinonensis* and the cento *Alcesta* represent two different genres? As argued above, in terms of ancient

---

45 Perutelli 1979, 64 and 115; Conte 2007, 52.
46 On the cento *Hippodamia* as an *epyllion* see Paolucci 2006, XXXVIII–LXI.

genology, most probably not. Diomedes' label *genus mixtum* would have comprised both of them. Yet paradoxically, the idea of a generic mixture has also appealed to some modern scholars, including those convinced (like myself) about the separate generic status of *epyllion* as such, and in particular in reference to the *Barcinonensis*. Since in the *Barcinonensis* the self-conscious narrator is marginalized and, instead, protagonists' words, actions, and movements are highlighted, it has been maintained that the poem is a pastiche, a mixture of the epyllic and the mimetic.[47] It has also been argued that the piece is a *fabula* rewritten as an *epyllion* and planned for a recitation.[48] Focusing on the performative context(s) of the *Barcinonensis* seems, indeed, a clue here, as the poem, short as it is, turns out to be problematic in terms of defining its interaction with and impact upon its audience. While the cento *Alcesta* reveals its literary dimension in (inter)textuality, the *Barcinonensis* calls for visualization, highlighting the theatrical dimension. The question is, however, how this particular effect of visualization was achieved among its original, late antique public.

I mentioned earlier the example of Seneca who composed his tragedies with an eye to the performative culture of his time, and pantomime in particular. In Vandal Carthage Dracontius is an example of a poet who really mastered drawing upon the visual consciousness of his contemporaries. This poet not only cites the pantomime muse, Polymnia, expressing his admiration for the art she patronizes (labeling her as *docta*, *Romul.* 10.17), but above all reuses motifs from pantomimic spectacles, adjusting them to his epic poetics. The point is made quite clearly in the prologue to his *Medea* (*Romul.* 10.26–28) where he invokes three Muses, Melpomene, Polymnia, and Calliope. Calliope, the epic Muse, is asked to come and enter the "encampments" of her two sisters.[49] In other words, Dracontius declares that his will be epic 're-narrations' of motifs usually explored in tragedy and pantomime.

Dracontius' approach to pantomime is in fact emulative in the sense that he aims at making his readers believe that through verbal description they can see the image not worse – and possibly better – than in the theater. In other words, he relies upon his audience's theatrical consciousness, shaped through viewing various kinds of performances, still popular in Vandal Carthage, hoping thus to achieve the desired effect of *evidentia*. Deictic forms, enumerations, detailed de-

---

[47] Garzya 1985, 14.
[48] Nosarti 1992, XXI.
[49] On pantomime see Bright 1987, 35–37; 53; 219–220. For detailed discussion of this passage see the chapters by Fischer and Wolff in this volume.

scriptions centered upon a protagonist's garment (or, indeed, costume) and scenic movement – these are all techniques he employs to mark his poems with this unique 'aesthetics of pantomime'.⁵⁰

Many similar techniques are applied throughout the *Barcinonensis*: the perceptual *deixis*⁵¹ in protagonists' speeches (especially Alcestis', vv. 101–102), pointing at various parts of the body when speaking (both by Admetus' father and mother, vv. 32–33 and vv. 48–50), Alcestis' adorning of her future deathbed, and her subsequent *rigor mortis*.⁵² Thus, the *Barcinonensis* embodies much theatricality, which it is not difficult to discover. If its readership was endowed with sufficient theatrical consciousness and imagination, i.e. the ability to visualize scenes or stories described through texts, this effect may well have been achieved while reading, especially during recitations. The *Alcestis Barcinonensis* is also performable, and one can easily notice it upon a closer look. Nonetheless, we have no strong evidence that it really *was* performed in antiquity, and in particular as a pantomime spectacle. What we may say, however, is that this short text invites concretization and, paradoxically, that it does so especially today when so many of us are wholly unaware of the richness, diversity, and visuality of the (late) ancient culture.

Thus, it is most fortunate that over the past twenty years the *Barcinonensis* was twice turned into a pantomime spectacle. Concretization through this unique medium allows it to communicate with a wider audience and to reveal its textual and extratextual potential. Nonetheless, the very word 'pantomime' does not define the poem in terms of genre categorization, but only in terms of its (possible) mode of performance. Similarly, the word 'cento' indicates the specific compositional technique adopted (by the poetess Siria?) in a miniature narrative, or indeed epic, poem. The two pieces, *Alcestis* and *Alcesta*, differ slightly as regards certain structural details. While in the *Barcinonensis* the self-conscious narrator is marginalized, in the *Alcesta* his (or again: her, representing Siria) presence is emphasized from the very beginning. While in the *Barcinonensis* protagonists' words, actions, and movements are highlighted, in the *Alcesta* they are at times omitted and replaced by the narrator's panoramic presentation of what has happened within a certain period. Yet, as argued above, ancient genology, and notably Diomedes, would have safely labeled both as examples of a typical *genus commune vel mixtum*. For today's scholarship, however, whereas the *Alcesta* might easily be pointed to as a model late antique *epyllion* (*pace* the 'deconstructors' of

---

50 See Wasyl 2011, 85–86, and especially 2019.
51 On the notion see Stockwell 2002, 45.
52 See Wasyl 2018, 175–179.

the notion) in the tradition of several other *epyllia* composed by the Latin literati in Vandal Africa, the *Barcinonensis* reveals only a few epyllic traits, or indeed a (generic) 'mixture' of the epyllic and the mimetic. What an intriguing coincidence it is, in fact, that the above usage of the expression *genus mixtum* has nothing to do with Diomedes' classification and yet his term, *mutatis mutandis*, turns out to be quite helpful again.

Bibliography

Allen Jr., W. 1940. "The epyllion: a chapter in the history of literary criticism", *TAPhA*, 71, 1–27.
Allen Jr., W. 1958. "The non-existent classical epyllion", *SPh*, 55, 515–518.
Audano, S. 2015. "Riusi centonari di formule virgiliane: l'esempio di *o dulcis coniunx* (*Aen.* 2, 777)", *Sileno*, 41, 53–71.
Bažil, M. 2017. "La mémoire de la citation. Teneur littérale et évocation implicite dans les centons virgiliens de l'Antiquité", in F. Garambois/D. Vallat (eds.), *Varium et Mutabile. Mémoires et métamorphoses du centon dans l'Antiquité*, Saint-Etienne, 49–60.
Bär, S. 2015. "Inventing and deconstructing epyllion: Some thoughts on a taxonomy of Greek hexameter poetry", in C. Walde (ed.), *Stereotyped thinking in Classics. Literary ages and genres re-considered* (= *Thersites* 2), 23–51, (online: http://www.thersites.uni-mainz.de/index.php/thr/article/view/18/18).
Bright, D.F. 1987. *The miniature epic in Vandal Africa*, Norman (OK).
Cichoń, N. 2016. "Epyllion w badaniach naukowych – antyczne *genus mixtum*?", *Terminus*, 18, 311–331.
Conte, G.B. 2007. *The poetry of pathos: Studies in Virgilian epic*. S.J. Harrison (ed.), Oxford.
Denzey Lewis, N. 2016. "The crafting of memory in late Roman mortuary spaces", in K. Galinsky (ed.), *Memory in ancient Rome and early Christianity*, Oxford, 263–285.
Fontaine, J. 1981. *Lactance et la mue de l'oiseau phénix au siècle de Constantin*, in J. Fontaine (ed.), *Naissance de la poésie dans l'occident chrétien. Esquisse d'une histoire de la poésie latine chrétienne du IIIe au VIe siècle*, Paris, 53–66.
Garelli, M.-H. 2013. "Les *Métamorphoses* d'Ovide: un texte à danser dans l'antiquité?", in R. Poignault (ed.), *Présence de la danse dans l'antiquité. Présence de l'antiquité dans la danse. Actes du colloque tenu à Clermont-Ferrand (11–13 décembre 2008)*, Clermont-Ferrand, 93–118.
Garzya, A. 1985. "Ricognizioni sull'*Alcesti* di Barcellona", *Koinonia*, 9, 7–14.
Gianotti, G.F. 1991. "Sulle tracce della pantomima tragica: Alcesti tra i danzatori?", *Dionisio*, 61, 121–149.
Green, R.P.H. (ed.) 1995. *Augustine, De Doctrina Christiana*, Oxford.
Griffith, M. 2009. "'Telling the tale': a performing tradition from Homer to pantomime", in M. McDonald/J.M. Walton (eds.), *The Cambridge Companion to Greek and Roman theatre*, Cambridge, 13–35.
Hall, E. 2008. "Is the 'Barcelona *Alcestis*' a Latin pantomime libretto?", in E. Hall/R. Wyles (eds.), *New directions in ancient pantomime*, Oxford, 258–282.
Hall, E./Wyles, R. (eds.) 2008. *New directions in ancient pantomime*, Oxford.

Hays, G. 2004. "*Romuleis libicisque litteris*: Fulgentius and the 'Vandal Renaissance'", in A.H. Merrills (ed.), *Vandals, Romans and Berbers. New perspectives on late antique North Africa*, Burlington (VT), 101–132.
Hunt, Y. 2008. "Roman pantomime libretti and their Greek themes: The role of Augustus in the Romanization of the Greek Classics", in E. Hall/R. Wyles (eds.), *New directions in ancient pantomime*, Oxford, 169–184.
Ingarden, R. 1988. *O dziele literackim*, (second ed.) Warszawa.
Ingleheart, J. 2008. "*Et mea sunt populo saltata poemata saepe* (*Tristia* 2.519): Ovid and the pantomime", in E. Hall/R. Wyles (eds.), *New directions in ancient pantomime*, Oxford, 169–184.
Keil, H. (ed.) 1857. *Diomedis Artis Grammaticae libri III*, *Grammatici latini*. Ex recensione Henrici Keilii, I, Leipzig, 299–529.
Laato, A. 2017. "Adam and Eve rewritten in Vergil's words: *Cento* of Proba", A. Laato/L. Valve (eds.), *The Adam and Eve story in Jewish, Christian and Islamic perspectives*, Winona Lake, 85–117.
Lada-Richards, I. 2003. "'A worthless feminine thing'? Lucian and the 'optic intoxication' of pantomime dancing", *Helios*, 30, 21–75.
Lebek, W.D. 1983. "Das neue Alcestis-Gedicht der Papyri Barcinonenses", *ZPE*, 52, 1–30.
Liebermann, W.-L. 1993. "Euripides und die Folgen: zur *Alcestis Barcinonensis*", *WS*, 106, 173–195.
Marcovich, M. (ed.) 1988. *Alcestis Barcinonensis*, Leiden.
Masterson M. 2014. "Studies of ancient masculinity", in T.K. Hubbard (ed.), *A Companion to Greek and Roman sexualities*, Malden (MA), 17–30.
McDonnell, M.A. 2006. *Roman manliness: virtus and the Roman Republic*, Cambridge.
McGill, S. 2002. "Rewriting Vergil as tragedy in the cento *Medea*", *CW*, 95, 143–161.
McGill, S. 2005. *Virgil recomposed. The mythological and secular centos in Antiquity*, Oxford.
Merrills, A.H./Miles, R. 2010. *The Vandals*, Malden (MA).
Miles, R. 2005. "The *Anthologia Latina* and the creation of a secular space in Vandal Africa", *AntTard*, 13, 305–320.
Mondin, L./Cristante, L. 2010. "Per la storia antica dell'*Antologia Salmasiana*", *AL. Rivista di studi di Anthologia Latina*, 1, 303–345.
Moreno Soldevila, R. 2011. "El motivo del lecho conyugal en la *Alcestis Barcinonensis*: dos notas de lectura", *Emerita*, 79, 177–188.
Nosarti, L. 1992. *L'Alcesti di Barcellona*, Bologna.
Nocchi Macedo, G. (ed.) 2014. *L'Alceste de Barcelone (P.Monts. Roca inv. 158–161)*, Liège.
Okáčová, M. 2009. *Centones: recycled art or the embodiment of absolute intertextuality?*, (online: http://www.kakanien.ac.at/beitr/graeca_latina/MOkacova1.pdf).
Okáčová, M. 2011. *Centones Vergiliani: intertextuální analýza pozdně antických centonárních epyllií s mytologickou tematikou* (diss.), Brno.
Paolucci, P. (ed.) 2006. *Il centone virgiliano Hippodamia dell'Anthologia Latina*, Hildesheim.
Paolucci, P. 2014a. "Per la costituzione del testo dell'*Alcesta* centonaria. L'epilogo", in M.T. Galli/G. Moretti (eds.), *Sparsa colligere et integrare lacerata. Centoni, pastiches e la tradizione greco-latina del reimpi' testuale*, Trento, 57–78.
Paolucci, P. 2014b. *Studi sull'Alcesta centonaria*, Perugia.
Paolucci, P. (ed.) 2015. *Il centone virgiliano Alcesta dell'Anthologia Latina*, Hildesheim.
Perutelli, A. 1979. *La narrazione commentata: studi sull'epillio latino*, Pisa.

Pollina, R. 2007–2008. "Il centone *Alcesta*: una fonte poco studiata per la storia della mentalità tardoantica", *Seia*, 12–13, 101–106.
Richardson Jr., L. 1944. *Poetical theory in Republican Rome*, New Haven.
Richter, W. 1993. "Zwei spätantike Gedichte über den Vogel Phoenix", *RhM*, 136, 62–90.
Riese, A. (ed.) 1894. *Anthologia Latina sive poesis Latinae supplementum 1. Carmina in codicibus scripta. Fasc. 1 Libri Salmasiani aliorumque carmina*, Leipzig.
Roberts, M. 2018. "Lactantius's *Phoenix* and late Latin poetics", in J. Elsner/J. Hernández Lobato (eds.), *The poetics of late Latin literature*, Oxford, 373–390.
Rondholz, A. 2012. *The versatile needle. Hosidius Geta's cento Medea and its tradition*, Berlin.
Rossi Linguanti, E. 2013. "L'*Alcesta. Cento Vergilianus* e i suoi modelli", *Maia*, 65.2, 227–56.
Salanitro, G. (ed.) 2007. *Alcesta. Cento Vergilianus*, Roma.
Schäublin, C. 1984. "Zur *Alcestis Barcinonensis*", *MH*, 41, 174–181.
Schetter, W. 1986. "Zu den Sprecherangaben in den Papyri Barcinonenses des Alkestisgedichts", *Hermes*, 114, 127–128.
Schottenius Cullhed, S. 2015. *Proba the prophet. The Christian Virgilian Cento of Faltonia Betitia Proba*, Leiden.
Spallone, M. 1982. "Il Par. Lat. 10318 (Salmasiano): dal manoscritto alto-medievale ad una raccolta enciclopedica tardo-antica", *IMU*, 25, 1–71.
Stockwell, P. 2002. *Cognitive poetics. An introduction*, London/New York.
Strati, R. 2007. "La fenice nella letteratura latina", *Annali Online di Ferrara – Lettere*, 1, 54–79.
Styka, J. 1994. *Studia nad literaturą rzymską epoki republikańskiej. Estetyka satyry republikańskiej, Estetyka neoteryków*, Kraków.
Tandoi, V. 1984. "La nuova *Alcesti* di Barcellona", in V. Tandoi (ed.), *Disiecti membra poetae. Studi di poesia latina in frammenti*. Fasc. 1, Foggia, 233–245.
Tilg, S. 2012. "On the origins of the modern term 'epyllion'. Some revisions to a chapter in the History of Classical Scholarship", in M. Baumbach/S. Bär (eds.), *Brill's Companion to Greek and Latin epyllion and its reception*, Leiden, 29–54.
Van Den Broek, R. 1972. *The myth of the phoenix according to classical and Early Christian traditions*, Leiden.
Wasyl, A.M. 2011. *Genres rediscovered: studies in Latin miniature epic, love elegy, and epigram of the Romano-Barbaric Age*, Kraków.
Wasyl, A.M. 2018. *Alcestis barcelońska oraz centon Alcesta. Późnoantyczne spojrzenie na mit i gatunek*, Kraków.
Wasyl, A.M. 2019. "Dracontius's miniature epic and the aesthetics of pantomime. Visualizing myths, theatricalizing reality", in K. Pohl (ed.), *Dichtung zwischen Römern und Vandalen. Tradition, Transformation und Innovation in den Werken des Dracontius*, Stuttgart, 167–188.
Webb, R. 2008. "Inside the mask: pantomime from the performers' perspective", in E. Hall/R. Wyles (eds.), *New directions in ancient pantomime*, Oxford, 43–60.
Wolff, É. 1988. "Quelques precisions sur le mot 'epyllion'", *RPh*, 62, 299–303.
Wood, S. 1978. "Alcestis on Roman sarcophagi", *AJA*, 82.4, 499–510.
Wyles, R. 2008. "The symbolism of costume in ancient pantomime", in E. Hall/R. Wyles (eds.), *New directions in ancient pantomime*, Oxford, 61–86.
Zanker, P./Ewald, B.C. 2012. *Living with myths. The imagery of Roman sacrophagi*, Oxford. Trans. J. Slater.
Zanobi, A. 2008. "The influence of pantomime on Seneca's tragedies", in E. Hall/R. Wyles (eds.), *New directions in ancient pantomime*, Oxford, 227–257.

Zanobi, A. 2014. *Seneca's tragedies and the aesthetics of pantomime*, London.
Zimmermann, B. 1990. "Seneca und der pantomimus", in G.Vogt-Spira (ed.), *Strukturen der Mündlichkeit in der römischen Literatur*, Tübingen, 161–167.
Zimmermann, B. 2008. "Seneca and pantomime", in E. Hall/R. Wyles (eds.), *New directions in ancient pantomime*, Oxford, 218–222. Trans. E. Hall.

Part II: **Fugue in Major: Epic**

Michael Paschalis
The 'Profanity' of Jesus' Storm-calming Miracle (Juvencus 2.25–42) and the Flaws of *Kontrastimitation*

In the preface to his *Evangeliorum libri quattuor* (henceforth *ELQ*), Juvencus programmatically introduces himself as a Christian epic poet who is renewing the classical epic tradition.[1] *ELQ* is a paraphrase of the Four Gospels composed in hexameters. The most distinct feature of Juvencus' paraphrastic technique is not exegesis but the 'poetic elaboration' of particular points of the biblical narrative.[2] What 'poetic elaboration' actually means is transforming the prose Gospel narrative into an epic, in the sense that the text he most frequently borrows from is Virgil's *Aeneid*. Actually, *ELQ* is the first Christian Latin epic. Juvencus' choice of Virgil is perfectly understandable because, according to Roger Green, in the early fourth century CE, when Juvencus' poem was composed, "perhaps the two most widely studied books in the western Roman Empire were Virgil's *Aeneid* and the set of writings known collectively as the Bible."[3]

In the preface Juvencus dwells on the ability of epic poetry to confer long-lasting fame,[4] and refers specifically to Homer and Virgil as the outstanding representatives of Greek and Roman epic who through their poetry have won "almost eternal glory:"[5]

> sed tamen innumeros homines sublimia facta
> et virtutis honos in tempora longa frequentant,
> adcumulant quorum famam laudesque poetae.
> hos celsi cantus, Smyrnae de fonte fluentes,
> illos Minciadae celebrat dulcedo Maronis.   10
> nec minor ipsorum discurrit gloria vatum,
> quae manet aeternae similis, dum saecla volabunt
> et vertigo poli terras atque aequora circum
> aethera sidereum iusso moderamine volvet.

> Still, lofty deeds and honor paid to virtue
> exalt throughout the ages countless men

---

1 Cf. Pollmann 2001.
2 On this subject see Paschalis, forthcoming, with earlier literature.
3 Green 2006, XI.
4 On 'fame' as the main theme of Juvencus' preface see Green 2006, 17–21.
5 The text is quoted from Huemer 1891, and the English translation is by McGill 2016.

>   whose fame and praise the poets amplify.
>   The high-flown verse that flows from Smyrna's spring
>   lifts some, the charm of Mincian Virgil others. 10
>   The poets' glory ranges just as far,
>   almost eternal, lasting long as time,
>   abiding while the spinning axis turns
>   the starry sky on its determined path. (*ELQ praef.* 6–14, trans. McGill)

Next at v. 19, he announces that he will sing of a new kind of heroic deeds, *Christi vitalia gesta* ("the life-giving deeds of Christ").[6] These represent "a gift to nations, cleared of lies, divine" as opposed to poems which "weave together lies with ancient acts have earned such long repute" (vv. 15–16). He furthermore expresses confidence that his epic will not perish together with everything else in the universal conflagration, which will mark the end of the world, and is hopeful that it may even win him a favorable judgement when Christ descends in all his brightness within a blazing cloud (15–24):

>   quod si tam longam meruerunt carmina famam, 15
>   quae veterum gestis hominum mendacia nectunt,
>   nobis certa fides aeternae in saecula laudis
>   immortale decus tribuet meritumque rependet.
>   nam mihi carmen erit Christi vitalia gesta,
>   divinum populis falsi sine crimine donum. 20
>   nec metus, ut mundi rapiant incendia secum
>   hoc opus; hoc etenim forsan me subtrahet igni
>   tunc, cum flammivoma discendet nube coruscans
>   iudex, altithroni genitoris gloria, Christus.
>
>   And yet if poems that weave together lies 15
>   with ancient acts have earned such long repute,
>   my steadfast faith will grant the deathless glow
>   of endless praise to me, my due reward.
>   For I will sing of Christ's life-giving deeds –
>   A gift to nations, cleared of lies, divine. 20
>   Nor do I fear world-wasting flames will seize
>   my work: this might, in fact, deliver me
>   when Christ the gleaming judge, his high-throned Father's
>   glory, descends within a blazing cloud. (*ELQ praef.* 15–24, trans. McGill)

---

[6] On the various possible meanings of the epithet *vitalia* see Carrubba 1993, 305 n. 7.

Some critics stress that the preface stands in contrast to Latin classical epic,[7] but I would prefer to see in it a remarkable sense of continuity. Juvencus does not adopt a polemical attitude towards earlier pagan epic. As a matter of fact, *ELQ* resumes the interrupted Latin epic tradition, since it is the first Latin *epos* to be written after Silius Italicus' *Punica*.[8] It is true that at v. 15, in censuring classical epic poetry for "weaving lies with ancient acts," Juvencus starts what later becomes a *topos* in Christian poetics, namely contrasting Christian truth with pagan lies.[9] From a Roman viewpoint, however, mixing history with fiction would be an accurate description of historical epic and in this respect of Virgil's *Aeneid*. As for the notion that poetry is the art of fiction, it 'officially' begins with Hesiod's *Theogony* 27, where the Muses tell the poet that "we know how to tell lies that sound truthful." In the Hellenistic age Callimachus argued that the question is not whether you lie as a poet, but whether you lie convincingly.[10]

Juvencus recognizes in classical epic the capacity to immortalize lofty deeds (*sublimia facta*) and glory derived from virtue (*virtutis honos*). Furthermore, the Christian poet employs the conventional term *gesta* to describe the 'deeds' of both pagan epic heroes and of Christ. Whatever the exact sense of *vitalia* may be, the term *gesta* is employed at the obvious expense of Jesus' teaching, which carries equal weight to his actions – not to mention that the notion of *gesta* is here extended to include the passion narrative of Jesus as well.[11]

Finally, as regards the theme of poetic immortality, Juvencus enters into an implicit contest with the most ambitious Latin tradition of its kind in a conspicuous effort to outdo the pronouncements, for instance, of Horace in *Odes* 3.30 and of Ovid in the *sphragis* of his *Metamorphoses*. His way of thinking is basically that of a classical poet; only the viewpoint and the context have changed. It is generally accepted that Juvencus insists on the contrast between transient mortal fame

---

7 E.g., Herzog 1975, 62, who notes that: "Juvencus steht im Bewußtsein der Gebildeten näher an Klopstock als an Nemesian;" see also, among others, Gärtner 2004, 431–436; on this point see Malsbary 1985.
8 Cf. Pollmann 2001, 61.
9 Bultot 1998; Mastrangelo 2016, 43.
10 *Hymn* 1.60–65.
11 Green 2004, 215 notes that the word *gesta* (or the phrase *res gestae*) suggests above all military achievements, whether in history or in epic, adding that Juvencus elsewhere uses *gesta* only of wicked deeds (those of Herod at 3.42 and Judas at 4.628), which is indeed intriguing. He therefore wonders if Juvencus "is shedding an ironic light on the supposed similarity between the deeds of Christ and the deeds of epic, explicitly comparing them but implicitly rejecting the parallel."

and Christian salvation and eternal life,[12] but in reality he places a great amount of emphasis on the fame of poets and their "almost eternal" glory (lasting as long as the duration of the earth) and seems more focused on exalting his own forthcoming immortality than on praising Christ. If the conception of epic in Late Antiquity as a genre "praising the outstanding deeds performed by special persons (*gesta laudata*)"[13] is applied to the preface of *ELQ*, the reader will discover to his/her great surprise that praise goes mostly to pagan heroes, earlier epic poets, and especially to the poet himself, and to a much lesser extent to Christ, the 'hero' of the new era, whose deeds Juvencus has undertaken to tell and whom he envisages as his 'savior'. On the whole, the reader does not get the impression that in the preface Juvencus the committed Christian (according to Jerome he was a priest, a *presbyter*) has the upper hand over Juvencus the epic poet. He even retains the venerable invocation to the Muse, now disguised as Holy Spirit,[14] and substitutes the river Jordan for the familiar source of poetic inspiration (25–28). Especially important for my analysis is the fact that he recognizes nobility of action and virtue in classical heroes, first and foremost Virgil's Aeneas.[15]

Classical Latin epic and most prominently the *Aeneid* constitute Juvencus' major source of inspiration for elaborating the Old Latin version of the Bible in order to appeal to cultivated Christian and pagan audiences.[16] Virgilian imitation consisted especially in substituting or adding words and phrases borrowed from classical epic; but given that form and narrative context were inseparable in the memory of Juvencus' learned readers, the combination of biblical content with classical epic form would undoubtedly have raised questions in their minds concerning the relationship between, on the one hand, Jesus and biblical characters and, on the other, Virgilian gods and heroes.

In 329 CE, when, according to Jerome, Juvencus composed *ELQ*, Christian readers did not yet possess the theological-hermeneutical tools required for handling the impact of the Virgilian intertext, especially since, as noted above, Juvencus' was the first Christian Latin epic and the first substantial Christian Latin poem in classicizing form. The 'allusions' to Virgilian epic scenes and episodes, arising from specific verbal parallels, would therefore have triggered perplexing

---

[12] Witke 1971, 199–203; Campagnuolo 1993, 53.
[13] Pollmann 2001, 63.
[14] On the Christianization of the traditional *fons Musarum* see Herzog 1975, LI and n. 158; Gärtner 2004; Agosti 2015, 205–206.
[15] Šubrt 1990; and further Clark/Hatch 1981 on features associating Aeneas with Jesus.
[16] Roberts 2004; Green 2006, 50–71; McGill 2016, 11–18. On Juvencus and earlier Latin epic poems see Testard 1990.

questions in readers' minds,[17] and scholarly projections of straightforward answers contrasting the biblical epic to its classical literary model should be viewed with great caution. As already stated, at the time when Juvencus flourished, Virgil's *Aeneid* and the Bible were perhaps the two most widely studied books in the Western Roman Empire; and since Juvencus recognized and promoted the authority of Virgil through the appropriation of the Roman poet's works, the learned reader (whether pagan or Christian) of Juvencus' paraphrase, whom the epic was intended to attract or train, would have had to balance the authority of the Bible against the authority of Virgil.

As noted above, casting Christian content in classicizing form was not in principle a neutral paraphrastic technique having only a linguistic dimension, since classicizing form evoked well-known pagan contexts. The question, however, of identifying and interpreting 'meaningful' Virgilian 'allusions' in *ELQ* remains wide open. McGill distinguishes between what he calls "referential" and "nonreferential" allusions.[18] Summarizing and rephrasing earlier discussions on late antique intertextuality, Helen Kaufmann has more recently distinguished three categories of 'allusions': "Allusions as essential part of the content", "Allusions as optional part of the content", and "Allusions as formal features."[19] Critics and readers are each time called upon to distinguish among these categories of 'allusions'. More to the point, however, is an earlier contribution to the subject by Michael Roberts. The conclusion of his short but insightful article entitled "Vergil and the Gospels: The *Evangeliorum Libri IV of Juvencus*" reads as follows:[20]

> But Juvencus' adoption of a Vergilian idiom was not unproblematic for the Christian reader. Use of Vergilian language necessary prompted comparisons between contexts of the source and target texts. From one perspective this process could be viewed positively as a spiritualization of Vergil's poetry by bringing it into line with the message of Christianity. But equally, as in the case of the application of language used of the Evander-Pallas relationship to that between God the Father and the Son, it could be read as secularizing and hu-

---

17 I use 'allusion' throughout in order to indicate a first level relation between a text and its source or its particular use in a scholarly work, while the terms 'intertext' and 'intertextuality' indicate a broader, dynamic relation of a text with its source-text and its context and their reconfiguration; the distinction is not, however, uncomplicated; cf. Hinds 1998.
18 McGill 2016, 14–18.
19 Kaufmann 2017, 153–162.
20 Roberts 2004, 59.

manising the biblical text. Such reservations seem to resonate in Jerome's otherwise positive appreciation of Juvencus: "he did not fear (*nec pertimuit*) to submit the majesty of the Gospels to the laws of metre" (*Ep.* 70.5).

In a refreshing manner Roberts discusses the issue not from an authorial viewpoint but from the viewpoint of Christian readers of Late Antiquity. Furthermore he looks for differences and similarities between Virgil and Juvencus with an open mind, raises the question of interaction between the two texts, and, above all, detects striking similarities between Jesus and characters of Virgil's epic.[21] I would only question the validity of a suggested allegorical reading of one Virgilian passage.[22] My interpretation takes into consideration the fluidity of the religious and intellectual milieu of the period. Hence it presupposes a mixed audience for *ELQ*, of Christians as well as pagans, whom Juvencus would have targeted through the reuse of Virgilian language, and considers the authority and influence of the *Aeneid* to be equal to that of the Bible.

My test case is Jesus' stilling of the storm on the Sea of Galilee, which I will use to argue against the widespread interpretation that is based on the theory of *Kontrastimitation* and aims to subvert the Virgilian intertext by exalting the power of the Christian god vis-à-vis the pagan divinity. This theory was first advanced in 1962 by Klaus Thraede, in his article on 'epos' in *Reallexikon für Antike und Christentum*,[23] and has since won wide acceptance. According to this theory, Juvencus' Christian epic is set in opposition to and, in a sense, 'corrects' its classical antecedent, the Virgilian epic. *Kontrastimitation* amounts to a total reversal in content despite linguistic parallels. It has been equated with Gérard Genette's intertextual 'transvaluation', the strategic replacement of the values of the targeted text with new ones.[24] In what follows I will attempt to show that, if we approach Juvencus' transformation of the storm-calming miracle exclusively from the viewpoint of *Kontrastimitation*, we risk disregarding its complex relation to the storm episode of *Aeneid* 1 and the subsequent interpretative potential of such

---

[21] McGill 2016, 16 is more cautious: "All instances of referential allusion to classical sources in Juvencus have at least some measure of contrast in them, because Juvencus applies his pagan/classical source material to Christian content. But Virgil's content can also resemble Juvencus' in a complementary way, so that the reader can recognize similarities between them as well as differences."
[22] In his view *Aen.* 6.662, if seen in the light of *ELQ* 1.27 and of Lactantius' allegorical reading of Virgil, might be found to contain "disguised presentiments of the Christian truth." It would indeed be curious if Juvencus had resorted to allegorizing only in one instance out of hundreds of Virgilian 'allusions'.
[23] Thraede 1962, 1039.
[24] Sandnes 2011, 58.

a comparison. The questions raised and conclusions drawn in this case should also have an impact on other instances of Virgilian 'allusions' in Juvencus.

Jesus calms the storm

I have chosen to discuss Jesus' stilling of the storm on the Sea of Galilee, because the storm is the only epic convention Juvencus has included in *ELQ*[25] and because it has a venerable tradition behind it, which starts with the storm of *Odyssey* 5.291–453. In Rome it was sanctioned by the storm in the first Book of Virgil's *Aeneid* and recurred in all later epics: Ovid's *Metamorphoses* (11.474–572), Lucan's *Pharsalia* (5.560–677), Valerius Flaccus' *Argonautica* (1.574–699), Statius' *Thebaid* (5.335–421), and Silius Italicus' *Punica* (17.236–291).[26] After a gap of more than two hundred years, Juvencus resumed this Latin epic convention. The impressive amplification of the biblical storm into yet another classical epic storm after the Virgilian model suggests generic awareness. Green has furthermore noted that sustained imitation of passages of classical epic is almost nonexistent in *ELQ* and that the storm scene is unique in this respect.[27]

The primary source of the epicized New Testament episode in question (*ELQ* 2.25–42) is the Old Latin version of Matthew 8:23–27 (similar accounts occur in Mark 4:35–41 and Luke 8:22–25). I quote *ELQ* 2.25–38 and the Old Latin version of the same passage, leaving out the reaction of the disciples to Jesus' miracle:

> conscendunt navem ventoque inflata tumescunt
> vela suo, fluctuque volat stridente carina.
> postquam altum tenuit puppis, consurgere in iras
> pontus et immissis hinc inde tumescere ventis
> instat et ad caelum rabidos sustollere montes;
> et nunc mole ferit puppim, nunc turbine proram,
> inlisosque super laterum tabulata receptant
> fluctus disiectoque aperitur terra profundo.
> interea in puppi somnum carpebat Iesus.
> illum discipuli pariter nautaeque paventes
> evigilare rogant pontique pericula monstrant.
> ille dehinc, "quam nulla subest fiducia vobis!
> infidos animos timor irruit!" inde procellis
> imperat et placidam sternit super aequora pacem.

---

25 McGill 2016, 12–13.
26 See Friedrich 1956; Morford 1967, 20–36; and Burck 1978.
27 Green 2004, 208–209.

They embark onto the ship, and the sails filled with the wind billow, and the boat flies over the hissing waves. After the ship reached open water, the sea began to rise to anger and, with the winds let loose from all sides, to swell and to raise raging mountains to heaven; the storm now strikes the stern with a mass of water, now the prow with a hurricane, and the planking of the sides takes in the waves hurled against it, and the sea-bed is opened up as the depths are torn apart. Meanwhile in the stern Jesus was asleep. In panic the disciples and the sailors together ask him to awake and point out the dangers of the sea. He then says. "How there is no faith in you! Fear rushes into faithless minds!" Then he gives orders to the storm and spreads quiet peace over the waters. (*ELQ* 2.25–38, trans. Green)

23. et ascendente eo in navicula, secuti sunt eum discipuli eius. 24. et ecce motus magnus factus est in mari, ita ut navicula operiretur fluctibus, ipse vero dormiebat. 25. et accesserunt et suscitaverunt eum dicentes: Domine, libera nos, perimus. 26. ait illis Iesus: quid timidi estis, modicae fidei? tunc surgens imperavit ventis et mari, et facta est tranquillitas magna.[28]

And as he got up into the boat, his disciples followed him. And behold, a great storm happened on the sea, so that the boat was overcome by the waves, but he was asleep. And his disciples went up and woke him saying: Lord, save us, we are perishing. Jesus said to them: why are you afraid, men of little faith? Then arising he gave orders to the winds and the sea, and a great calm was created. (Mt 8:23–26)

In Juvencus' account, Jesus is asleep on the stern of his ship when a furious storm breaks out, described in a six-line-long epic amplification of the biblical passage. Awakened by the frightened disciples, Jesus laments their lack of faith and then commands the stormy winds to cease, thus causing the sea to become completely calm. The learned Christian or pagan reader would undoubtedly have detected in Juvencus' narrative the 'allusions' to the storm of *Aeneid* 1, which is raised by Aeolus on Juno's command (50–123) and in the context of which the god Neptune sternly rebukes the winds for their overconfidence and calms the sea as a statesman calms a turbulent mob (124–156). The reader would also have recalled the passage in *Aeneid* 4 where Aeneas has fallen asleep on his ship's stern and is warned by Mercury in a dream of the threat lurking in Dido's troubled soul (553–570). Some parallels with Virgil's narrative are noted already in Huemer's 1891 edition of *ELQ*.[29]

---

28 The text is quoted from the Codex Veronensis in Jülicher/Matzkow/Aland 1963, 119–133.
29 For *ELQ* 2.30: *et nunc mole ferit puppim*, Huemer cites *Aen.* 1.115: *in puppim ferit*; for 2.32: *disiectoque aperitur terra profundo*, he cites *Aen.* 1.107: *terram inter fluctus aperit*; and for 2.33: *interea in puppi somnum carpebat Iesus*, he cites *Aen.* 4.554–555: *Aeneas celsa in puppi iam certus eundi | carpebat somnos*. For further parallels see Ratkowitsch 1986, 45–49; Sandnes 2011, 59–60.

The notion that Juvencus' passage anticipates Proba's Christian Virgilian cento, an interpretation advanced by Herzog,[30] should be dismissed without question. Herzog's argument is based on the repetition of single words from *Aeneid* 1.103–104, such as *vela* (<*velum)*, *stridens* (<*stridente*), *sustollere* (<*tollit*), *ferit*, *proram* (<*prora*). Apart from the fact that most of these words recur in changed form, the argument defies the very definition of a Virgilian *cento*, which, according to Scott McGill, is a composition consisting of unconnected *verse units* (a segment of a hexameter, an entire line, a line and some section of the next one, etc.) *extracted* from the works of Virgil.[31] As the similarities quoted above show, Juvencus *does not copy but reworks* sections of Virgil's storm scene, as Latin (epic) poets of the classical period used to do. Here is another example: out of *Aeneid* 1.103 (*fluctusque ad sidera tollit*, "and lifts the seas to heaven") and 1.105 (*insequitur cumulo praeruptus aquae mons*, "a steep mountain of water follows in a mass") Juvencus creates the amalgamated line 2.29: *ad caelum rabidos sustollere montes* ("to raise raging mountains to heaven", trans. Kline).

More significant for my argument here than the storm itself are the agents that calm it respectively in Juvencus' epicized biblical narrative and in Virgil's *Aeneid*. The pivotal question is the readerly reaction to the obvious parallelism between Jesus and Neptune in terms of words, action, and power, and between Jesus and the statesman whom the Virgilian narrator describes at *Aeneid* 1.151 as *pietate gravem ac meritis* ("a man of authoritative virtue and service"). Jesus' similarity with the statesman provides a good point of departure. The readers may have been reminded of Juvencus' preface, where the poet refers in a positive manner to the "lofty deeds" (*sublimia facta*) and "glory derived from virtue" (*virtutis honos*) of pagan heroes. They may also have associated the Virgilian statesman's action of calming the turbulent mob with the epilogue of Juvencus' poem and specifically the following passage:

> haec mihi pax Christi tribuit, pax haec mihi saecli,
> quam fovet indulgens terrae regnator apertae
> Constantinus, adest cui gratia digna merenti,
> qui solus regum sacri sibi nominis horret
> imponi pondus, quo iustis dignior actis
> aeternam capiat divina in saecula vitam
> per dominum lucis Christum, qui in saecula regnat.

---

30 Herzog 1975, 151.
31 McGill 2005, xv.

> Christ's peace gave this to me, and peace today,
> graciously fostered by the wide world's ruler,
> Constantine, duly touched by worthy grace;
> alone of kings he dreads a holy name,
> so that, more worthy by just acts, he wins
> eternal life throughout immortal ages
> through Christ, the Lord of Light, who ever reigns. (*ELQ* 4.806–812, trans. McGill)

The ideal statesman in Virgil's simile has been connected with various Roman leaders, including Augustus and his adoptive father Julius Caesar,[32] and intratextually with Aeneas: The programmatic characterization of Aeneas as *insignem pietate virum* (*Aen.* 1.10) is echoed by that of the statesman as *pietate gravem virum* (*Aen.* 1.151). Some two hundred years later Cyprianus Gallus will substitute God himself for *pius Aeneas* in speaking of *insignem pietate deum*.[33] The learned reader of Virgil's epic knew perfectly well that the calming of the storm and the saving of Aeneas' ships ensured the foundation of the Roman Empire, whose first emperor, Augustus, took pride in his *pietas*[34] and claimed descent from the Trojan hero through his adoptive father Julius Caesar. Michael Roberts has suggested that the epilogue of *ELQ* was inspired by the opening lines of the *sphragis* of Virgil's *Georgics*[35] and that Octavian's battles in the East in comparison to Juvencus' epilogue invite a contrasting association of the *pax Augusta* with the *pax Constantiniana*, the former based on military victory and the latter promoting the peace of Christ.[36] The contrast is there, of course, but this is only part of the story; because the association between Octavian and Constantine, at a time when both had become sole rulers of the Roman world, points in turn to a triple similarity,

---

32 See especially Galinsky 1996 on the association of both Neptune and the statesman with Augustus; on the names of republican statesmen possibly alluded to see Sandin 2000, 189–192.

33 *Heptateuchos*, Exodus 213, cf. *Aen.* 1.10: *insignem pietate virum*; see Malsbary 1985, 64–66.

34 In 27 BCE the Roman senate conferred the title Augustus to Octavian and voted in his honor the inscribed *clipeus virtutis* celebrating his *virtus, pietas, iustitia,* and *clementia*; see Ryberg 1966. Augustus records the event as follows, *RG* 34.2: *virtutis clementiaeque et iustitiae et pietatis caussa testatum est per eius clupei inscriptionem* ("[was given me] on account of my courage, clemency, justice, and piety, as attested by the inscription on that shield").

35 Verg., *G.* 4.559–562: *haec super arvorum cultu pecorumque canebam | et super arboribus, Caesar dum magnus ad altum | fulminat Euphraten bello victorque volentis | per populos dat iura viamque adfectat Olympo* ("So I sang, above, of the care of fields, and herds, | and trees besides, while mighty Caesar thundered in battle, | by the wide Euphrates, and gave a victor's laws | to willing nations, and took the path towards the heavens").

36 Roberts 2004, 48–49. Huemer (1891) *ad loc.* had already cited the passage of the *Georgics* as a *locus similis*.

arising from Jesus' storm-calming miracle, among Virgil's statesman, Augustus, and Constantine.

Indeed Juvencus' epicized storm-calming miracle, its Virgilian intertext and the epilogue of *ELQ* illuminate one another in ways which invest Virgil's narrative with Christian connotations and Jesus' miracle with pagan ones. In the epilogue Juvencus aligns Jesus with Constantine as princes of peace (*ELQ* 4.806: *haec mihi pax Christi tribuit, pax haec mihi saecli*); in the storm-calming narrative Jesus "spreads quiet peace over the waters" (*ELQ* 2.38: *placidam sternit super aequora pacem*), just as Constantine fosters world-wide peace. Jesus' intervention evokes in turn that of Neptune and the ideal statesman in *Aeneid* 1, the latter potentially reminiscent of Augustus' quelling of the civil wars and verbally recalling Aeneas. The calming of the storm in Virgil is a prerequisite for Aeneas' foundation of the Roman Empire; and in Juvencus' epilogue the first Christian emperor and late successor to the first Roman emperor who claimed descent from Aeneas and imposed the *pax Augusta* is portrayed as having achieved the *pax Constantiniana* as the earthly manifestation of the *pax Christi*.

Regarding the association between Jesus and the *gens Iulia*, most illuminating is the 'assimilation' in *ELQ* of Jesus to Iulus, as suggested by Michael Roberts. Roberts aptly compares the telling similarity between the flaming star announcing the birth of Christ in *ELQ* 1.243–245 and the comet that appeared over Troy in *Aeneid* 2.692–698 to confirm the omen of the tongues of flames seen over the head of Iulus. He concludes his discussion as follows:

> In the present instance the reader will perceive the parallels between Iulus and Jesus, both children of special destiny, parallels that will prompt comparison between Christian salvation history and the future allotted to Rome and the Julian line.[37]

Going a step beyond examining Jesus in relation to the ideal statesman, I ask what contemporary readers would have thought of Jesus and Neptune. In the *Aeneid*, as opposed to the *Iliad*, the god is a divinity friendly to the Trojans. He perceives the conspiracy of forces opposing Aeneas' arrival in Italy — in the narrative the plot is called "Juno's anger and stratagems" (*Aen.* 1.130: *nec latuere doli fratrem Iunonis et irae*) — and intervenes to save the Trojan hero and his men. Thus, he ultimately ensures the foundation, as ordained by the *fata*, of the Roman Empire, which is now ruled in Christian peace by the Emperor Constantine. Is it likely that Christian readers would have seen with a favorable eye a pagan god with Virgilian credentials as outlined above? I think it is, because the statesman

---

37 Roberts 2004, 53.

simile reflects on the god and because in exercizing his power Neptune does not display violence, like Aeolus, but relies on his *auctoritas*.[38] In this respect, Neptune and Constantine are not that far apart. One should also consider the visual association between Neptune and Augustus: On a cameo from 30 BCE Octavian is represented as Neptune, holding a trident and riding on a quadriga drawn by sea horses and surging atop the waves over an opponent (Sextus Pompeius or Mark Antony) who disappears into them, in a manner that 'anticipates' his controlling intervention in the storm of *Aeneid* 1.[39] On an intertextual level, then, Jesus would have been aligned with Neptune in a way that could affect a Christian reader's perception of a pagan god and a pagan reader's perception of Jesus. All of the above do not require an allegorical interpretation but are mainly the fruit of intertextual and intratextual associations resulting from the thematic and ideological continuity between a biblical and a classical epic.

The calming of the storm in Sedulius

It is illuminating to compare and contrast in this respect another epicized version of the storm-calming miracle found in the *Carmen paschale* (henceforth *CP*) of Sedulius, who flourished some two hundred years later. Apparently having in mind both Virgil's and Juvencus' storm descriptions, Sedulius hastens to interpret the meaning of the storm in a way that clearly and unequivocally distinguishes Jesus from Neptune. He specifically argues that the violent activity of the natural elements was in fact a gesture of happy exaltation and an act of obedience towards Jesus:

> exsurgens dominus validis mitescere ventis
> imperat et dicto citius tumida aequora placat.
> non erat illa feri pugnax audacia ponti
> in dominum tumidas quae surgere cogeret undas,
> nec metuenda truces agitabant flamina vires,
> sed laetum exsiliens Christo mare compulit imum
> obsequio fervere fretum, rapidoque volatu
> moverunt avidas ventorum gaudia pinnas.
>
> But [the Lord] stood up and gave orders to the powerful winds to cease and, even before he finished speaking, made the swelling seas subside.

---

38 Sandin 2000, 190–191.
39 Galinsky 1996, 20–24; Sandin 2000, 191–192.

> This belligerent boldness of the wild sea was not such
> as to compel the roiling waves to rise against the Lord.
> The winds were exercising their fierce force but were not to be feared;
> rather, the sea in happy exaltation was compelling
> its depths to boil up in obedience to Christ. In their swift flight
> it was the joy of the winds that moved their eager wings. (*CP* 3.62–69, trans. Springer)

On the whole, Roger Green's view that the storm-calming accounts of Juvencus and Virgil constitute "an excellent case of *Kontrastimitation*", which means a clear-cut contrast carrying an unambiguous Christian message, disregards the complexity of the issues outlined above. I refer to his monograph *Latin Epics of the New Testament*,[40] which adopts the conclusions of a 1986 article by Christine Ratkowitsch entitled "Vergils Seesturm bei Iuvencus und Sedulius." Ratkowitsch had emphasized Juvencus' allusion to Jesus' far greater power as manifested by the use of a mere verb commanding the storm-winds (*procellis imperat*) vis-à-vis Neptune's ten-line-long rebuking speech.[41] Accordingly, Ratkowitsch, Green, as well as Sandnes[42] provide a single-minded interpretation of Juvencus' storm-calming miracle in relation to Virgil's epic that leaves out of the picture its complex aspects discussed above and ignores the statesman simile altogether.

In what constitutes a further example of the flaws of *Kontrastimitation*, Green (2006, 62) contrasts as follows Jesus' and Aeneas' awakening, in *ELQ* 2 and *Aeneid* 4 respectively:

> Moreover, he [Jesus] acts very differently from Aeneas: when woken from his sleep (for this we must compare Aeneas at Carthage in *Aen.* 4.554–5 *in puppi ... carpebat somnos*, again extremely close) he does not shout or panic, as Aeneas did both in the storm (*Aen.* 1.94–101) and after Mercury's second appearance to him in Carthage, but quietly asserts his authority.

Of course, in any given passage of Juvencus' biblical epic there are inherent differences with Virgil's pagan epic. But is it not also important to point out that Aeneas, though at that moment catching some sleep on the ship's stern, *was not entirely mindless of his mission*, since he was already resolved to go and had made all necessary preparations for departure (*Aen.* 4.554–555: *iam certus eundi | carpebat somnos rebus iam rite paratis*, "now that everything was ready, and he

---

40 Green 2006, 61–62.
41 Jesus' command (*ELQ* 2.37–38: *inde procellis | imperat*) remains faithful to the brevity of the biblical text but it is worthy of note that Juvencus has replaced the biblical *ventis et mari* with a Virgilian word occurring twice in the storm description (*Aen.* 1.85–86: *creberque procellis Africus*; 102: *stridens Aquilone procella*).
42 Sandnes 2011, 59–60.

was resolved on going, | Aeneas was snatching some sleep, on the ship's high stern", trans. Kline)? As regards his reaction, it is not accurate to say that he "panicked" but was quite naturally "terrified by the sudden apparition" (571); and furthermore he did not actually "shout" to his companions but "kept on at them with extreme urgency" (572–573: *fatigat praecipitis*), in order to wake them up and give them instructions for immediate departure in the face of imminent danger, as he had been commanded by Mercury. Juvencus' learned audience were after all Roman citizens, and the idea of Aeneas' 'awakening' to his Roman future would not have been incompatible with the mission of Jesus: "Render unto Caesar the things that are Caesar's, and unto God the things that are God's" (Matthew 22:21). We should therefore appreciate each of the two scenes involving, respectively, Jesus and Aeneas, in their appropriate contexts.

Conclusions

In this article, I have attempted to show that, based on intertextual considerations with Virgil's *Aeneid*, some reflection of classical 'profanity' on Jesus' epicized storm-calming miracle may have been unavoidable. In this as well as in other cases, Juvencus' Christian and/or pagan readers would have been able to discern the differences and similarities between the Bible and the *Aeneid* and each time they would have had to balance the authority of the former against that of the latter. As suggested above, Juvencus emphasizes in his preface the continuity of his epicized paraphrase of the Four Gospels with earlier epic, recognizes the established hierarchy of poets in Greco-Roman epic, and *mutatis mutandis* conducts himself as a classical epic poet would have done in emulating his predecessors. Accordingly, the profanity of Jesus in the sea-calming miracle does not merely replace the old (Virgil) with the new (Bible), but compels the readership to take into account both these interpretative poles: on the one hand, the epic theme of the storm in *Aeneid* 1 in combination with the hero sleeping on the stern in *Aeneid* 4, the intervenion of Neptune that calms the waters, and especially the Virgilian simile of the statesman and, on the other, the epiphany and sovereignty of the Christian god above the elements of nature. At the same time, transcendental issues are also linked with the earthly world as a discernible line connects epic characters such as Aeneas and Jesus to their imperial analogues, Augustus and Constantine, respectively. At the level of literary criticism, the theory of *Kontrastimitation*, of merely contrasting Christian with pagan values, needs be used carefully, as it may dwell on obvious and expected differences while ignoring significant similarities arising from broader and deeper considerations. It is important, in my view, always to keep in mind: the realities of an Empire that in Juvencus' times was both Christian and Roman;[43] the impact of classical *paideia* on both pagan and Christian writers;[44] and, regarding biblical *exegesis*, the state of affairs in 329 CE, when it was yet too early for the recent Council at Nicaea and later councils to have borne their theological-hermeneutical fruit.[45]

Bibliography

Agosti, G. 2012. "Postfazione. Il fascino discreto del paganesimo", in P. Chuvin (ed.), *Cronaca degli ultimi pagani*, Brescia, 313–324.
Agosti, G. 2014. "Classicism, paideia, religion", in R. Lizzi-Testa (ed.), *The strange death of pagan Rome. Reflections on a historiographical controversy*, Turnhout, 123–140.
Agosti, G. 2015. "'Chanter les dieux dans la societé chrétienne: les *Hymnes* de Proclus dans le contexte culturel et religieux de leur temps", in N. Belayche/V. Pirenne-Delforge (eds.), *Fabriquer du divin. Constructions et ajustements de la représentation des dieux dans l'Antiquité*, Liège, 183–211.
Bultot, R. 1998. "*Ficta et facta*. La condamnation du 'mensonge des poètes' dans la poésie latine chrétienne", *REAug*, 44, 101–121.
Burck, E. 1978. *Unwetterszenen bei den flavischen Epikern*, Mainz.
Campagnuolo, G. 1993. "Caratteri e tecniche della parafrasi di Giovenco", *VetChr*, 30, 47–84.
Carrubba, R.W. 1993. "The Preface to Juvencus' biblical epic: a structural study", *AJPh*, 114, 303–312.
Chuvin, P. 2009. *Chronique des derniers païens. La disparition du paganisme dans l'Empire romain, du règne de Constantin à celui de Justinien*, (first published 1990) Paris.

---

43 The literature on the subject is vast and the issues involved are complex; see, for instance, Fletcher 1997; MacMullen 1997; Curran 2000; Chuvin 2009; Agosti 2012; Leppin 2012; Jones 2014; Agosti 2014; Leppin 2015.
44 Di Berardino 1983, 14–15: "Schools did not exist in the West for those who wanted to deepen their understanding of the faith. The church itself had not organized anything for the clerics who were preparing to serve it. [...] The formation of the Latin Fathers took place outside of schools and ecclesiastical directives; a fact which, thanks to their classical formation, favored their liberty of thought and expression."
45 There is an ongoing debate as to the extent of the presence of exegetical expansion in Juvencus' paraphrase. I would be inclined to agree with the concluding remarks of Roberto Palla 2008, 227: "Possiamo ritenere l'opera di Giovenco e quella dei suoi epigoni una forma di esegesi? Senza dubbio qualche spunto esegetico qua e là si trova [...]: Giovenco propone occasionalmente qualche brevissima aggiunta, limitata ad una parola o poco più." See further Green 2007. On the emergence of theological literature in the West after the Council of Nicaea cf. Di Berardino 1983, 36: "Between 356 and 360, there developed an authentic flowering of doctrinal literature with the great figures of Hilary and Marius Victorinus."

Clark, E.A./Hatch, D.F. 1981. "Jesus as hero in the Vergilian 'Cento' of Faltonia Betitia Proba", *Vergilius*, 27, 31–39.
Curran, J.R. 2000. *Pagan city and Christian capital: Rome in the fourth century*, Oxford.
Di Berardino, A. 1983. *Patrology, IV. The Golden Age of Latin Patristic literature from the Council of Nicea to the Council of Chalcedon*, Allen (TX).
Fletcher, R. 1997. *The conversion of Europe: from paganism to Christianity 371–1386 AD*, London.
Friedrich, W.-H. 1956. "Episches Unwetter", in H. Erbse (ed.), *Festschrift Bruno Snell*, München, 77–87.
Gärtner, T. 2004. "Die Musen im Dienste Christi: Strategien der Rechtfertigung christlicher Dichtung in der lateinischen Spätantike", *VChr*, 58, 424–446.
Galinsky, K. 1996. *Augustan culture: an interpretative introduction*, Princeton (NJ).
Green, R.P.H. 2004. "Approaching Christian epic: the *Preface* of Juvencus", in M. Gale (ed.), *Latin epic and didactic poetry: genre, tradition and individuality*, Swansea, 203–222.
Green, R.P.H. 2006. *Latin epics of the New Testament. Juvencus, Sedulius, Arator*, Oxford.
Green, R.P.H. 2007. "The *Evangeliorum Libri* of Juvencus. Exegesis by stealth?", in W. Otten/ K. Pollmann (eds.), *Poetry and exegesis in premodern Latin Christianity. The encounter between classical and Christian strategies of interpretation*, Leiden, 65–80.
Herzog, R. 1975. *Die Bibelepik der lateinischen Spätantike*, München.
Hinds, S. 1998. *Allusion and intertext: dynamics of appropriation in Roman poetry*, Cambridge.
Huemer, J. (ed.) 1891. *Gai Vetti Aquilini Iuvenci Evangeliorum Libri Quattuor*, Prague.
Jones, C.P. 2014. *Between pagan and Christian*, Cambridge (MA).
Jülicher, A./Matzkow, W./Aland, K. (eds.) 1963. *Itala. Das Neue Testament in altlateinischer Überlieferung, IV, Johannes-Evangelium*, Berlin.
Kaufmann, H. 2017. "Intertextuality in late Latin poetry", in J. Elsner/J. Hernández Lobato (eds.), *The poetics of late Latin literature*, Oxford, 149–175.
Kline, A.S. 2002. *The Aeneid. Poetry in translation project.*
    Online: http://www.poetryintranslation.com/klineasaeneid.php
Leppin, H. 2012. "Christianisierungen im Römischen Reich", *JAC*, 16, 245–276.
Leppin, H. 2015. "Einleitung", in H. Leppin (ed.), *Antike Mythologie in christlichen Kontexten der Spätantike*, Berlin, 1–18.
MacMullen, R. 1997. *Christianity and paganism in the fourth to eighth centuries*, New Haven (CT).
Malsbary, G. 1985. "Epic exegesis and the use of Vergil in the early biblical poets", *Florilegium*, 7, 55–83.
Mastrangelo, M. 2016. "Towards a poetics of late Latin reuse", in S. McGill/J. Pucci (eds.), *Classics renewed: reception and innovation in the Latin poetry of Late Antiquity*, Heidelberg, 25–46.
McGill, S. 2005. *Virgil recomposed: the mythological and secular Centos in Antiquity*, Oxford.
McGill, S. 2016. *Juvencus' Four Books of the Gospels*, London.
Morford, M.P.O. 1967. *The poet Lucan: studies in rhetorical epic*, Oxford.
Palla, R. 2008. "Esegesi in versi? Agli inizi dell'epica biblica", in R. Uglione (ed.), *Atti del Convegno Nazionale di Studi "Arma virumque cano ..." L'epica dei greci e dei Romani, Torino, 23–24 aprile 2007*, Alessandria, 209–229.
Paschalis, M. Forthcoming. "Amplification in Juvencus' *Evangeliorum Libri IV* and in Nonnus' Μεταβολὴ τοῦ κατὰ Ἰωάννην ἁγίου εὐαγγελίου", in F. Doroszewski/K. Jażdżewska (eds.), *Nonnus of Panopolis in context III. Old questions and new perspectives*, Leiden.

Pollmann, K. 2001. "The transformation of the epic genre in Christian Late Antiquity", *Stud. Patr.*, 36, 61–75.
Ratkowitsch, C. 1986. "Vergils Seesturm bei Iuvencus und Sedulius", *JbAC*, 29, 40–58.
Roberts, M. 2004. "Vergil and the Gospels: the *Evangeliorum Libri IV* of Juvencus", in R. Rees (ed.), *Romane memento: Vergil in the fourth century*, London, 47–61.
Ryberg, I.S. 1966. "Clipeus Virtutis", in L. Wallach (ed.), *The Classical tradition: literary and historical studies in honor of Harry Caplan*, Ithaca (NY), 232–238.
Sandin, P. 2000. "The man of authority: images of power in Virgil's *Aeneid* 1.50–156", in A. Jönsson/A. Pilt (eds.), *Språkets speglingar: festskrift till Birger Bergh*, Lund, 187–194.
Sandnes, K.O. 2011. *The Gospel 'according to Homer and Virgil': cento and canon*, Leiden.
Springer, C.P.E. 2013. *Sedulius: The Paschal Song and Hymns*, Atlanta (GA).
Šubrt, J. 1990. "Jesus and Aeneas: The epic mutation of the Gospel story in the paraphrase of Juvencus", *Listy filologické*, 16, 10–17.
Testard, M. 1990. "Juvencus et le sacré dans un épisode des *Euangeliorum libri IV*", *BAGB*, 1, 3–31.
Thraede, K. 1962. "Epos", *RLAC*, 5, 983–1042.
Witke, C. 1971. *Numen litterarum: the old and the new in Latin poetry from Constantine to Gregory the Great*, Leiden.

Maria Sole Rigo
Writing a Homeric-Christian Poem: The Case of Eudocia Augusta's *Saint Cyprian*

The Life of Saint Cyprian (hencefore *St. Cyprian*) is a hexametric poem in three books written in the fifth century CE by Eudocia Augusta, the cultured wife of emperor Theodosius II.[1] The 900-line poem tells the story of the magician Cyprian, a kind of *ante litteram* Faust, who was commissioned by an Antiochene aristocrat, Aglaidas, to seduce a young Christian virgin named Justa with the help of certain demons. The plan, however, failed, as the girl repelled the demons with the power of the Cross. Because of this overwhelming evidence of the power of Christ, Cyprian converted to Christianity and finally became bishop of Antioch. Eudocia's text is a verse paraphrase of a prose hagiographical dossier of the fourth century, the *Conversion, Confession, and Passion of St. Cyprian* of Antioch: we may, therefore, define it as a 'transposition', since it transforms prose hagiographical texts into heroic hexameters.[2] Moreover, the fact that Eudocia decides to use extant material and change the style of the original, adopting epic language, suggests that she breaks free from the traditional classification of genres, creating a special kind of 'Homeric hagiography'.

Here, due to space limitations, I will focus on Book 1 of the *St. Cyprian* that is a 'transposition' of the text of the *Conversion of St. Cyprian*.[3] The aim of this paper is to analyse the literary strategies used in the poem in order to gain a better understanding of the genre of the *St. Cyprian*. As Alan Cameron observed, although the practice of paraphrase as a rhetorical exercise had been widespread since Classical Antiquity, verse paraphrases of prose works in a more elevated style than the original were a new development of Late Antiquity.[4] At that time, classicizing poetry in

---

[1] For this work see Bevegni 2006a and Salvaneschi 1981 and 1982. Some general studies on the author are Al. Cameron 1982 (now in Al. Cameron 2016); Holum 1982; Burman 1994; Sowers 2008.
[2] The three hagiographical texts are the *Conversio*, which corresponds to the first book of the poem, the *Confessio*, corresponding to the second, and the *Passio*, which corresponded to the third book, now lost. I refer to the critical editions of the *Conversio* and the *Confessio* by Radermacher 1927 and Bailey 2009.
[3] For the edition of this text see Ludwich 1897 and Bevegni 1982. The translations here, unless otherwise indicated, are mine.
[4] Al. Cameron 2004, 332. For a more detailed analysis of the practice of paraphrase in antiquity see Roberts 1985, 37–60, in particular p. 58 for what concerns the paraphrastic technique as a separate work of literature.

traditional meters "expanded its field, colonizing areas previously dominated by prose."[5] For this reason, it is even more pertinent to investigate the genre of so complex a text as *St. Cyprian*.

In this chapter I am going to investigate how Eudocia surpassed the prose model by reusing Homeric epic to introduce new meanings into her poem. I will, therefore, focus primarily on Cyprian, the main character of the narrative, examining his depiction as an epic hero. I will pay particular attention to the characterization of the magician by means of Homeric words in the first part of the work, before his conversion to Christianity: as an enemy of Christianity, he is closer to pagan culture and is consequently portrayed using language from the classical tradition. Furthermore, I will attempt to delineate the audience's response to the re-writing of a hagiographic text in hexameters: why did Eudocia choose to write the work in this particular way and what did the audience expect from this kind of poem? In the last part of the paper, I will address the genre of *St. Cyprian*, trying to elucidate how Eudocia was able to create this kind of 'Homeric hagiography'. Through this case study of Eudocia, I will point towards a new approach to the question of the communicative functions of Christian poetry in classical meters.

The impact of Homeric language

In Book 1, Eudocia composes a *paraphrasis* of a hagiographical *Vorlage* of the fourth century, titled *Conversio*, which tells the story of the conversion of Cyprian. Unfortunately, it is not easy to compare Eudocia's Book 1 with the *Conversion of St. Cyprian*, because we have three different redactions of this prose text and it is not clear which one the poetess used. Indeed, it seems that she was either aware of all three of them or read a fourth redaction which is now lost.[6] Hagiographical works such as the *St. Cyprian* were particularly popular in Late Antiquity as they were prose fictions with narrative flair and a popular appeal. The best-known example is probably the reworking of the *Life and miracles of Thecla*.[7] At the same time, the seduction of a virgin with the help of a magician is a frequent theme in

---

[5] Al. Cameron 2004, 327–332; quote from p. 328.
[6] The problem of Eudocia's possible model has been thoroughly discussed by previous scholars, see, e.g., Danesin 2001 and Bevegni 2006b. The studies of Bevegni 2003 and 2006b concluded that she probably used a fourth redaction. Nevertheless, this is difficult to prove, and we cannot easily solve this problem unless we find a manuscript of the fourth redaction.
[7] See Johnson 2006b.

novelistic fiction but not necessarily in Homer-imbued epic.⁸ By transposing, therefore, the hagiographic text onto the epic mode, Eudocia not only switches from prose to hexameter, but also alters the target audience of the work. Below I will show the impact of Homeric language and allusion in transforming the text.

In the first example we see how the author distances herself from the prose model, with Homer in mind, when she describes the seduction of Justa:

τῆνδε λαβὼν βοτάνην κύκλῳ θαλάμου⁹ κατάδευσον
κούρης Αἰδεσίδος, ἀτὰρ ὕστατος ἵξομαι αὐτὸς
καὶ νόον ἐνθήσω κραδίῃ πατρώιον αὐτῇ.
ἡ δέ σοι ἐλδομένῳ μάλα πείσεται ἔν περ ὀνείρῳ.

Take this herb and sprinkle it in a circle around the house of the daughter of Aidesius; at last I'll come and I'll place in her heart the sense of the Father (i. e. the Devil). And she will obey you, even in a dream (*Cypr.* 1.152–155 Bevegni = 1.53–56 Ludwich).¹⁰

In this passage, Cyprian is teaching the first demon how to seduce Justa. To understand these lines, a comparison with the *Conversion* is needed. In the first redaction of the prose text, we read: δέξαι οὖν τὸ φάρμακον τοῦτο καὶ ῥᾶνον τὸν οἶκον ἔξωθεν τῆς παρθένου, κἀγὼ ἐπελθὼν τὸν πατρικὸν ἐπάγω νοῦν, καὶ εὐθέως ἐπακούσεταί σου ("take this potion and sprinkle it outside the house of the girl, and I will come and induce the sense of the Father, and she will immediately obey you"). The second and the third redactions do not show significant differences, apart from the fact that in the third we read καὶ ῥᾶνον κύκλῳ τοῦ οἴκου αὐτῆς ("and sprinkle it in a circle around her house") and πορνικόν ("of unchastity") instead of πατρικόν ("of the Father"). The prose text clarifies Eudocia's lines: the "herb" (βοτάνην) in Eudocia is actually the potion made with the herb (τὸ φάρμακον).¹¹ Moreover, the noun θάλαμος here means 'house' and not 'bedroom', as

---

8 Asking a magician to help to seduce a beloved is a common theme of universal lore (see e.g. Dickie 2003), but also an ingredient of novelistic fiction: e.g., the Egyptian priest and magician Calasiris in Heliod., *Aeth.* 4.7 is asked, unsuccessfully, to make the beautiful virgin Chariclea fall in love with Alcamenes.
9 I accept here θαλάμου, the *lectio* of the manuscript, instead of θάλαμον, Ludwich's correction; see also Salvaneschi 1982, 69.
10 In this paper lines are numbered in two ways, according to Bevegni and according to Ludwich. This is because the only critical edition we have was published by Ludwich in 1897, before the discovery of the first 99 lines of the poem in the sixties and their edition by Bevegni in 1982. Now we have to consider the whole work, so the verses from 1 to 99 of the first book are numbered according to Bevegni, while the following lines are numbered both according to Ludwich's edition, and Ludwich + 99, taking into account the addition of the 99 lines discovered later.
11 Bevegni 2006a, 130 n. 55.

it revises "τὸν οἶκον ἔξωθεν" of the prose redaction.[12] We can observe how difficult it is to identify the source of Eudocia: at v. 1.152 she seems to conform to the third redaction (because it is the only one that mentions κύκλῳ), but at v. 1.154 she revisits the other two texts, because we read in her poem πατρώϊον that corresponds to πατρικόν.[13]

The words "ἔν περ ὀνείρῳ" at v. 1.155, however, are particularly interesting as they do not appear in the prose model. This is a Homeric expression that occurs thrice in the *Odyssey*; at 19.541: αὐτὰρ ἐγὼ κλαῖον καὶ ἐκώκυον ἔν περ ὀνείρῳ ("now for my part I wept and wailed, in a dream though it was"), and at 19.581 and 21.79: τοῦ ποτε μεμνήσεσθαι ὀΐομαι ἔν περ ὀνείρῳ ("which, methinks I shall ever remember even in my dreams", trans. Murray). After Homer, the only poetic text where these words are used is precisely Eudocia's *St. Cyprian*. As Enrica Salvaneschi observes, the meaning of this expression is controversial: It may be used just to fill the hexameter and strengthen the main idea; alternatively, περ could have the function of limiting the meaning ("at least in a dream") or it may clarify the circumstances ("just in a dream").[14] If we assume that it is not a mere filler and is instead a meaningful re-use of Homer, this expression may give us a more structured idea of what is going to happen: Justa is not expected to fall in love with Aglaidas, the man in love with her, but only to obey him "at least in a dream," bewitched by the demon. In fact, we already know that even this project is going to fail.[15] It is interesting to compare Eudocia's text with *Odyssey* 19.581

---

[12] Bevegni 2006a, 130 n. 56. Nevertheless, the use of the noun θάλαμος may not be accidental, since it evokes eroticism.

[13] See Salvaneschi 1982, 5. In Eudocia's text, however, πατρώϊον could also mean 'pagan'.

[14] Salvaneschi 1982, 8–9.

[15] The dream is often connected to the erotic context: see *e.g.* Theoc., *Id.* 20.5: μὴ τύγε μευ κύσσῃς τὸ καλὸν στόμα μηδ' ἐν ὀνείροις ("kiss not my fair lips even in thy dreams", trans. Gow). Another possibility is that Cyprian is suggesting that Justa will submit to sex even if it is only while she sleeps: being raped while sleeping or dreaming was not uncommon amongst mythological women; see Hadjittofi 2019. However, the demon finds Justa awake and praying, so he cannot use his magic while she is asleep. Two similar passages can be found in Nonn., *Par.* 10.125: οἷς τότε μοῦνον ἵκανε θεοῦ λόγος ἶσος ὀνείρῳ ("only the Word of God came like to a dream") and 12.9: εἷς δ' ἦν δαιτυμόνων ἔτι Λάζαρος, ἶσος ὀνείρῳ | πασιφανής ("Lazarus was one of the guests, like to a dream, shining"); here Nonnus is adding the mention of the dream that does not appear in the Gospel. The interpretative problem of these lines is not solved yet. In the first case it is not clear why the Word is compared to a dream: it might mean that the Word appears "as a dream/in a dream", or that "he appears as a dream may appear." The second example may refer to Lazarus and his feelings for being at a banquet after his resurrection or to the other people staring at him. In both cases the simile of the dream is used to give the idea of something insubstantial and far from reality, just like Justa's potential obedience to the demon. For a more detailed analysis of dreams in Late Antiquity see Cox Miller 1994.

and 21.79: here, Penelope is announcing that she will marry the suitor who can string Odysseus' bow and shoot an arrow through a line of twelve axes, and that she is finally ready to leave the house where she has been so happy and which she will remember "even in her dreams." It is noteworthy that the character of Penelope is usually associated with marital fidelity: the poem, then, may be implying that, just as Penelope never betrayed Odysseus, neither will Justa break her promise to Christ, modeling thus the Christian virgin on the archetypal faithful wife.

With this example, we can see how Eudocia employs Homeric vocabulary to modify the prose texts: using just part of a Homeric hexameter, she lets the audience understand how the magic spell of the demon is supposed to work, something that the prose texts do not do. The author resorts to Homeric language in order to enrich the original meaning of the prose models and enhance the characterization of the protagonist, as the reference to Penelope should immediately convey the idea of fidelity.

The Homeric language, therefore, is re-employed to communicate the Christian message, as the Homeric echoes alter their original meaning and become a Christian instrument. A good example can be found at the very beginning of the poem at v. 16 (Bevegni): σεπτὸς ἄγαν πινυτός τε διάκτορος οὐρανίωνος ("very venerable and wise minister of God"). This line refers to Praulius, the holy man that Justa listens to and thanks to whom she converts to Christianity. What is significant here is the word διάκτορος. This word is famously used by Homer as an epithet of Hermes,[16] so this is a case of *Kontrastimitation* (an expression of the classical, pagan world re-appropriated for a superior, Christian usage). As a matter of fact, just as Hermes is the messenger of Zeus and the other gods, here Praulius, the priest, is a messenger of (the true) God. But while in Homeric exegesis διάκτορος usually has the meaning of 'messenger', afterwards, in the works of Christian authors, it acquires the meaning of 'servant' and 'minister of God'.[17]

---

16 See *LfgrE* s.v. διάκτορος. This word appears frequently in Hom., *Il.* 21.497, 24.339, 24.378, 24.389, 24.410, 24.432, 24.445, (always in the formula διάκτορος Ἀργεϊφόντης), 2.103 (διακτόρῳ Ἀργεϊφόντῃ), *Od.* 8.335 (Ἑρμεία Διὸς υἱέ, διάκτορε), 5.43, 5.75, 5.94, 5.145, 8.338, 24.99 (again διάκτορος Ἀργεϊφόντης), 12.390, 15.319 (Ἑρμείαο διακτόρου), 1.84 (διάκτορον Ἀργεϊφόντην).

17 For the meaning of 'messenger' in the Homeric exegesis see *schol. D in Od.* 2.103 = Ap. S. 58.17: διάγων τὰς ἀγγελίας; *schol. in Il.* 9.338; *schol. Q in Od.* 390, and for the meaning of 'servant' see Aesch., *PV* 941 and *Etym. Gen.* B s.v.: διακτόρῳ ... παρὰ δὲ τοῖς ἄλλοις ποιηταῖς ἁπλῶς ἐπὶ τοῦ διακόνου τίθεται = *Etym. Magn.* 268.22 ("by the other poets it is simply used for 'messenger'"). Eudocia uses the word διάκτορος (in 1.379 Bevegni = 1.280 Ludwich and in 1.382 Bevegni = 1.283 Ludwich) and the word διακτορίη (in 1.397 Bevegni = 1.298 Ludwich and in 1.400 Bevegni = 1.301 Ludwich) with the meaning of 'minister of God' and 'diaconate', but she plays with the double

For this reason, it is difficult to give the right translation of this word, because Praulius is at the same time a minister of God and someone who preaches the Gospel. The educated audience of Eudocia was probably aware that the epic διάκτορος was an epithet of Hermes, but it was also used to perceiving this word as 'minister of God'. So, the line plays with this double meaning, making Praulius both a minister and a messenger of God. In this case as well, then, Eudocia uses Homer to enrich the original text, and her audience would have appreciated the implicit comparison of Praulius with Hermes, who was identified at that time with the Λόγος.[18] The whole description of Praulius is, thus, an amplification of the prose texts, which just state that he is a deacon (διάκονος) of God (Πραϋλίου τινὸς διακόνου, Fassung I, II, III).

Characterization and Homeric language

The main character of this poem, however, is not Praulius, but Cyprian. The wizard is the one who has the characteristics of an epic hero: The author describes his exceptional deeds, both positive and negative. As a matter of fact, he is a particularly competent magician, since he is introduced as follows: (vv. 1.115–116

---

meaning of the word in 1.16 Bevegni and in 1.389 Bevegni (= 1.290 Ludwich: θεοῦ ζάκορος τάκος ἦλθ' ἱερῆι | ἀγγέλλων, "when he learned these things, the servant of God quickly went to the priest to announce the news"), where the servant who announces the arrival of Cyprian is the deacon (the διάκτορος of v. 1.382 Bevegni = 1.283 Ludwich). In Nonnus the word διάκτορος has the same meaning as διάκονος (*Dion.* 1.1, 21.271, 39.82, 41.291, 43.115) and the one of 'messenger' (*Dion.* 2.591, 30.250, 31.107, 33.57); in the *Par.* (1.216, 2.33, 4.98, 5.22, 6.46, 12.103, 12.107, 13.17, 13.61, 13.90, 18.52, 18.83, 18.105, 18.126) it usually refers to a 'service', except for *Par.* 4.98 and 13.90, where it can mean 'messenger' (see Lampe *s.v.*). The word has the meaning of 'minister of God' also in an epigram from Aphrodisias (155 Roueché = *SGO* 02/09/31) of the 5th–6th century: σῆμα τόδε Στεφάνοιο τὸν ἐν ζωοῖσιν ἀκούεις | εὐσεβίης γεγαῶτα διάκτορον ἤπιον ἄνδρα | ἀκμὴν ἐς βιότοιο τὸν ἥρπασε λοίμιος αἶσα ("this is the memorial of Stephanus, whom you hear about among the living that he had become a minister of piety, a meek man, whom destructive Fate snatched at the peak of his life"). Apart from Nonnus and Eudocia, the word διάκτορος is not widespread among Christian authors; it appears also in Greg. Naz., *carm.* II.2.7.114 *PG* 37.1559: πύματον Χριστοῖο διάκτορος ἠγαθέοισι ("and at last to the holy (oracles) of the messenger of Christ"), where it probably has the meaning of 'messenger'; and in Jo. Gaz. 625 (Lauritzen): ἡ δ' ἑτέρη φαέεσσι διάκτορον ὄμμα τανύσσει ("the other one stretches her ministering eye towards the light"), where it can mean both servant and messenger; see Lauritzen 2015, 43 and 197. For a more detailed analysis of this word see Agosti 2003, 337–346.

18 See Agosti 2003, 339–346. On the Christian interpretation of Hermes see also Kuhn-Treichel in this volume at 100.

Bevegni = 1.16–17 Ludwich) κακοεργέα ... φῶτα, | δυσσεβέος μαγίης ὑποθήμονα, Κυπριανόν γε ("an evil man, Cyprian, advisor of impious magic").[19] After converting to Christianity, Cyprian will become an outstanding Christian too. For example, below we read: (vv. 1.400–404 Bevegni = 1.301–305 Ludwich) ... αὐτὰρ κρατερῶς ἐδάμαξεν | ἀντιθέων γε φάλαγγας ἀναιδήτων, ἀπαλάμνων, | καὶ νούσους στυγερὰς μελέων ἀπόηλαεν ἀνδρῶν· | ἤδη καὶ πολέας Χριστοῦ ἐς πώεον ἦγεν, | εἰδώλων κακόπιστον ἀναινομένους ἀλάωσιν ("with power he tamed the ranks of the godless, the shameless, the lawless ones and healed the horrible diseases of men's limbs. Indeed, he led into the flock of Christ many who rejected the blinding faith of idols").[20] Cyprian, then, not only has extraordinary magic powers but, when he converts to Christianity, he soon becomes bishop of the city, is able to convert other people to Christianity, and even has thaumaturgical powers. His deeds are always astonishing, as a pagan and as a Christian, but after his conversion he is working in order to correct what he was doing before, when he was guided by the devil. Like many epic heroes of antiquity, in the first part of the poem he is antagonistic towards God, just as Achilles is towards Apollo in the *Iliad* and Odysseus towards Poseidon in the *Odyssey*; after his conversion, Satan will be his enemy. The main trait of this character is always his exceptional nature and this, together with the Homeric echoes, turns Cyprian into the epic hero of the poem.[21]

The epic allure of the character is also manipulated at the intradiegetic level: The character often uses Homeric or Homeric-sounding words. As will become clear, it is noteworthy that he uses the epic register especially in the first part of the poem, when he is presented as an enemy of Christianity, suggesting that before his conversion he is closer to pagan culture and, accordingly, uses the language of the classical tradition to a greater extent.

A first example of Cyprian's use of epic language is the next one: (1.129 Bevegni = 1.30 Ludwich) ἔννεπέ μοι τεὰ ἔργα, ὅπως φρεσὶ θάρρος ἔχοιμι ("tell me

---

[19] The word κακοεργής is used only twice in the poem: the first time here and the second time in: *Cypr.* 1.122 Bevegni (= 1.23 Ludwich): κίκλησκεν χαλεπὸν κακοεργέα δαίμονα ῥίμφα; here it refers to the demon. Wizard and demon are depicted similarly (see Bevegni 2006a, 128 n. 42).

[20] Trans. Sowers 2008, 203, slightly modified. The word ἀλάωσιν is a *hapax* and according to Lampe can be translated as 'blinding' (see Lampe s.v.). This is, perhaps, an allusion to Homer: the blinding faith in the pagan gods is related to the blindness of the pagan poet *par excellence*. When Cyprian becomes a Christian, he rejects classical and pagan culture not only from a religious point of view, but also from a literary one: as we will see, epic language is used by Cyprian especially before his conversion. The relationship between the Homeric and pagan blindness is not new: for thorough analysis see Agosti 2011 and Faulkner in this volume at 266.

[21] On the characteristics of the epic hero see Nagy 2005, especially 87–89.

your deeds, so that I may have confidence in my heart"). Here Cyprian has just summoned the first demon and is asking him to outline his accomplishments so that Cyprian might trust him and his power. It is easy here to recognize the Homeric-sounding expression, ἔννεπέ μοι. It is an expression quite typical of epic, usually occurring either with the words placed in this order or in the more Homeric form μοι ἔννεπε. We can consider this form a *variatio* of the more famous μοι ἔννεπε.[22] Nearly all attestations of this expression are an apostrophe to the Muse, but in Eudocia this original meaning is subverted, as Cyprian is speaking to a demon: this is a peculiar case of *Kontrastimitation*, because, although this kind of imitation usually refers something typical of pagan culture or literature to a (superior) Christian context, here the context is demonic, not Christian. Eudocia's aim is not to show the falsity of the pagan model in comparison with Christianity, but to underline the peculiarity of the belief of Cyprian, who – at this point of the story – has a demon as his personal Muse and source of inspiration for his witchcraft.[23]

Furthermore, at 1.197 Bevegni (= 1.98 Ludwich) we find Cyprian enquiring about the whereabouts of the girl: δαίμονα Κυπριανὸς δ' εἰρώτεε· "ποῖ πέλει αὕτη". In this section, Cyprian is speaking with the first demon he summoned, since he should have brought her to the wizard, but he actually ran away after the girl made the sign of the cross. The expression πέλει αὕτη is used in a variation just once before our epic, in *Iliad* 9.324: μάστακ' ἐπεί κε λάβῃσι, κακῶς δ' ἄρα οἱ πέλει αὐτῇ ("wherever she [the mother bird] can find morsels, but as for herself it is suffering").[24] Eudocia's audience probably knew this famous, much-cited Homeric passage.[25] In the Homeric line Achilles is speaking to Odysseus and explaining why he does not want to fight any longer: so, in this case, Cyprian is not only speaking in an epic manner, but he is also using the words of the archetypal

---

22 For the first case we have examples in Opp., *Cyn.* 3.461 (ἔννεπέ μοι ... Μοῦσα) and George Pisides *Carm. vit.* 59 (ἔννεπέ μοι, βασίλεια), and for the second Hom., *Il.* 2.761 (σύ μοι ἔννεπε Μοῦσα), *Od.* 1.1 (ἄνδρα μοι ἔννεπε, Μοῦσα,), *Hymn. Hom. Ven.* 1 (Μοῦσά μοι ἔννεπε), Luc., *Ver. Hist.* 2.24.7 (νῦν δέ μοι ἔννεπε, Μοῦσα) and an inscription from Hama, *IGLS* V 1999 (= *SEG* 17.756: ἄνδρα μοι ἔννεπε, κοῦρε). See also Whitby 2014, 442 on the Byzantine reception.

23 This could reflect back onto the classical model and the controversial role of the Muse for Christian authors, maybe implying that Homer's Muse had some demonic traits (for the problematic role of the Muse in Christian inspiration theory see Shorrock 2011, 13–48). There was also, however, a spiritualized vision of the Muses, who could be analogous to the Evangelists or to the angels; see Agosti 2015, 202–206.

24 Trans. Lattimore.

25 This line is cited by several scholia, see e.g. Ariston., *De sign. Il.* 9.323, and Muson., *Dissert. a Lucio dig. rel.* 15.44, Plut., *Mor.* 494d7, Ath. 9.373b (Olson), John Philoponus, *de aetern. mundi* 323.6, *schol.* in *Il. ad loc.*, and Eustath., *ad Il.* 2.719 (Van der Valk).

epic hero of the *Iliad*, citing part of a verse that should be recognized by the audience.

After a few lines, we read: (vv. 1.205–208 Bevegni = 1.106–109 Ludwich) ὁ δ' αἶψα μάγος κεχαρηὼς | ἔννεπε· "τῇ τόδε, δαῖμον· ὅλον δῶ παρθένου ἀγνῆς | φαρμάκῳ ἐγκατάδευσον. Ἐγὼ δ' ὄπιθεν σέο βαίνω· | πείσειν δ' αἶψ' ὀίω μιν" ("the magician, immediately pleased, said: 'here you are, demon. Sprinkle the potion onto the entire house of the chaste girl. And I will go behind you. I think I will immediately persuade her'"). In these lines, Cyprian is teaching the second demon how to seduce Justa. The expression ἐγὼ δ' ὄπιθεν (v. 207 Bevegni) appears only here and in Homer in the same *sedes*: *Il*. 21.129: ὑμεῖς μὲν φεύγοντες, ἐγὼ δ' ὄπιθεν κεραΐζων ("you in flight, and I making havoc from behind", trans. Murray). In the *Iliad* Achilles, who has just murdered the Trojan warrior Lycaon, is speaking during the carnage along the banks of Scamander. He foresees that the Achaeans are going to take Troy, with the Trojans running away and he himself pursuing and slaughtering them (ἐγὼ δ' ὄπιθεν κεραΐζων). In both texts the one who speaks is explaining his plan: Achilles explains how he is going to avenge Patroclus; Cyprian sets out his final attempt to seduce Justa. Both plans will, in fact, be thwarted: when the Achaeans finally take Troy Achilles will be dead, and Cyprian will never be able to seduce Justa.

In the last two examples cited above, Cyprian uses expressions that can be attributed only to Achilles: they are very famous lines cited by later authors (as in the case at *Iliad* 9.324) or passages in which Achilles' words and actions can be compared to Cyprian's situation (as in *Iliad* 21.129). Moreover, the audience should recognize them easily, supported by their same place in the line. This comparison between Achilles and Cyprian is interesting, as it completely alters the traditional interpretation of Achilles, who was usually represented in a positive way.[26] It is noteworthy that this close relationship between Cyprian and Achilles occurs only before Cyprian's conversion: Homeric language is used to shape the character of this markedly pagan wizard/hero. In the second part of the book (1.301–421 Bevegni, = 1.202–322 Ludwich), the magician understands the power of Christ and the comparison with Achilles does not recur: when Cyprian speaks, he no longer cites Achilles (or other Homeric heroes).

---

[26] See Buffière 1956, especially 24, 128, 327, 331, 334–335, 366–367; and Lamberton 1986.

Conclusions: 'Epic hagiography' between the new Christian culture and the classical literary tradition

This brief overview of Eudocia's *St. Cyprian* may help us to think in more depth about its genre. At this point, it is rather clear that we are talking about a transposition, since Eudocia turned a prose hagiographic model into heroic hexameters. The *St. Cyprian* is both a hagiographic text, because of its content, and an epic poem, because of its language and the way its main character is described: therefore, we can speak of an 'epic hagiography'. This combination of different genres, alongside the synthesis of classical and Christian culture, was quite common in Late Antiquity.[27] It is important to consider why Eudocia chose to re-write the hagiographic text into an epic poem. Several reasons may explain why the *paraphrasis* of Christian prose was so common in early Christianity. First of all, *paraphrasis* was a very common rhetorical exercise in antiquity, and a number of Christian writers (like Juvencus) took it up in the fourth and fifth centuries CE.[28] Moreover, the Scriptures – and Christian texts more widely – did not match the standards required of classical literature.[29] Because of all these reasons, the *paraphrasis* of biblical and hagiographical narratives was straightforward for Christian authors and the outcome was a new kind of text, which had simultaneously an epic and a Christian flavor.

Epic was a natural fit for such paraphrastic enterprises, as it was considered a combination of grand narrative and praise, and since the themes of Christianity always contained these aspects, Christian themes were epic by definition.[30] From this point of view, the choice of Eudocia seems obvious and it appears that a poem like this may fall easily under the traditional rubric of epic without looking too strange or unconventional. Nevertheless, although Eudocia's *St. Cyprian* displays at the same time Homeric and hagiographic features we have seen that Homeric

---

[27] See, e.g., Schottenius Cullhed 2015, 79 on *C. Pr.*
[28] Sandnes 2011, 229. Nevertheless, the connection between biblical epic and the school exercise of paraphrase has been questioned by Herzog, who downplays the importance of the paraphrase and situates biblical epic in a specifically Christian tradition. According to the scholar, biblical epic originates from the practice of the early Christian Fathers, who cited lines from the pagan poets for apologetic and interpretative purposes; see Herzog 1975, lxx–lxxii, 60–68 and 155–211. For a summary and a critique on Herzog's theory see also Roberts 1985, 61–62.
[29] See Sandnes 2011, 24.
[30] Pollmann 2001, 74.

language is used by the author to enrich and strengthen the Christian message of the prose model, but mainly in the first part of the poem, before Cyprian's conversion.

It is noteworthy that Cyprian is not the only 'holy epic hero' of Greek late antique poetry: another one is Eutychius, Patriarch of Constantinople from 552 to 565 and from 577 to 582, celebrated by Paul the Silentiary in *Ekphrasis of S. Sophia* 978–1029.[31] The poet had to praise the patriarch of the city in his *ekphrasis*, even though Eutychius had not accomplished much at that point. The outcome was an encomium with hagiographical content, written in epic hexameters and with a classical touch.[32] Paul the Silentiary's style is different from Eudocia's, but both use classicizing and epic language in order to celebrate the new kind of holy epic hero.[33]

Now, it is mandatory to take the audience into account. Although we do not know what kind of public the *St. Cyprian* addressed, we may still consider that the empress would have been surrounded by a cultured elite, who, like her, were well educated and had thoroughly absorbed classical *paideia*.[34] It is necessary to consider the cultural milieu, and not only its religious preferences, in order to define the kind of audience envisioned here. The loaded Homeric language and allusions in the poem suggest that the addressees of *St. Cyprian* were certainly attached to Greek *paideia* but were not necessarily converts to Christianity.[35] Therefore, the use of the Homeric and classical style for Christian topics may have been useful both to arouse the interest of the cultural elite and also to elevate the

---

31 About this man and Paul's lines see Whitby 1987.
32 Whitby 1987, 299.
33 On the other side, we can find authors such as Sotericus of Oasis, who wrote an enormous number of epics, both historical and mythological, among which is listed one on Apollonius of Tyana, the pagan counterpart of Christ (see Al. Cameron 1965, 475). Of course, the major work on Apollonius is the eponymous *Vita* by Philostratus; see Sowers 2008, 244 with literature.
34 For the importance of *paideia* for the imperial entourage see Cameron 2004, 344–349.
35 Agosti 2001, 100. Hence, we may infer that Eudocia's audience could have been composed of Christians as well as pagans and catechumens who could appreciate epic poetry with a Christian content. As Gregory Nagy wrote in his foreword to Usher 1998, ix-x, whose attribution of the *Homeric Centos* to Eudocia is still debated, the *Centos* were "intended for performance before audiences who were intimately familiar with both Homer and the Bible. To say 'familiar' may well be an understatement. The Homeric Centos presuppose a veritable internalization of both Homer and the Bible for both the composer and the audience." On the *I HC* see also Lefteratou in this volume. Michael Roberts 1985, 223 points out that "for later poets the metrical form given to the biblical message was calculated to appeal to those Christians whose sense of style was sometimes in conflict with their Christian piety."

newly formed Christian literature to the level of its classical counterpart.[36] Readers were meant to recognize the Homeric echoes in Eudocia's text and appreciate how Homer could help in narrating the story of Cyprian and praising the power of God, which are the main objectives of this story. Since the foundational Christian texts were mostly considered rough and uncultured, it is also possible that some cultured pagans could also enjoy this kind of classicizing poetry and appreciate its novelty. In other words, pagans would have been encouraged to appreciate how this poetry forges a relationship between the new, Christian culture and the long-standing, classical literary tradition.

Genre, being not only a theoretical classification of the text but also a literary code that affects the reader's experience of the text, raises specific expectations in the audience about the content and its form.[37] In this case, the meter and style used for Eudocia's *St. Cyprian* would influence both its reception and interpretation: the assumed audience of this work would have been different from that of the hagiographic prose texts. Moreover, presenting Cyprian as a 'holy epic hero' made his story more similar to the kind of highbrow stories that the audience would have been more accustomed to. The epic genre could, thus, pre-shape the audience's expectations in a positive way.[38]

It is clear that a *paraphrasis* of a hagiographical text does not simply subordinate itself to the model, but it should also be considered a work with high literary ambitions, presenting a Christian theme to a different and learned audience.[39] As the genre of the *paraphrasis* and knowledge of Homer were natural consequences of the education system of Late Antiquity, their re-use to convey Christian messages has to be considered a way to submit classical literary culture to the remit of Christianity.[40]

As Karla Pollmann writes in *The baptized Muse*, the versification of a prose model entails changes of perspective, accentuation and effect, apart from adding more details and information, and therefore it cannot be considered a mere paraphrase adding nothing to the hypotext.[41] As shown in this paper, Eudocia actually modifies, strengthens, and enriches the meaning of the prose model, using

---

36 See, e.g., Cameron 2004, 348.
37 Schottenius Cullhed 2015, 11; also pp. 11–13 for a discussion about the genre of the centos.
38 Pollmann 2017, 21.
39 See Fuhrer 2013, 86 and especially 87, who argues that "this in-between status, between heteronomy and autonomy, is in fact programmatic and as a result these works *must* break the boundaries of the old genre system."
40 For a deeper analysis of *paraphrasis* and biblical rewriting in Late Antiquity see Johnson 2006a, 67–112.
41 Pollmann 2017, 130–131.

Homeric language as an instrument. In this work, the sophisticated Homeric echoes are used by Eudocia with the specific aim of shaping the character of Cyprian, clarifying the meaning of the prose text, and raising the linguistic register of the whole poem. In *St. Cyprian* we are looking not only at the hagiographic genre turning into epic, but also at epic poetry turning Christian. Eudocia – like other late antique poets – understood that the themes of Christianity were perfectly suitable for the epic genre and that this could help to strengthen the Christian message. The outcome – as we have seen – was the creation of a new kind of 'Homeric-hagiography' and of a holy epic hero.

Bibliography

Agosti, G. 2001. "L'epica biblica nella tarda antichità greca. Autori e lettori nel IV e V secolo", in F. Stella (ed.), *La scrittura infinita. Bibbia e poesia in età medievale e umanistica*, Firenze, 67–104.

Agosti, G. (ed.) 2003. *Nonno di Panopoli. Parafrasi del Vangelo di S. Giovanni. Canto V*, Firenze.

Agosti, G. 2011. "Le brume di Omero. Sofronio dinanzi la *paideia* classica", in L. Cristante/S. Ravalico (eds.), *Il calamo della memoria. Riuso di testi e mestiere letterario nella tarda antichità. Trieste, 27–28 aprile 2006*, Trieste, 33–50.

Agosti, G. 2015. "Chanter les dieux dans la société chrétienne: les Hymnes de Proclus dans le contexte culturel et religieux de leur temps", in N. Belayche/V. Pirenne-Delforge (eds.), *Fabriquer du divin. Constructions et ajustements de la représentation des dieux dans l'Antiquité*, Liège, 183–211.

Bailey, R. 2009. *The Confession of Cyprian of Antioch: introduction, text, and translation* (diss.), Montréal.

Bevegni, C. 1982. "Eudociae Augustae *Martyrium S. Cypriani* I, 1–99", *Prometheus*, 8, 249–262.

Bevegni, C. 2003. "Per una nuova edizione del *De Sancto Cypriano* dell'imperatrice Eudocia: primi passi", *FuturAntico* 1, 29–46.

Bevegni, C. (ed.) 2006a. *Eudocia Augusta, Storia di San Cipriano*, Milano.

Bevegni, C. 2006b. "Sui modelli del *De Sancto Cypriano* dell'imperatrice Eudocia", in E. Amato (ed.), *Approches de la Troisième Sophistique. Hommages à Jacques Schamp*, Bruxelles, 389–405.

Buffière, F. 1956. *Les mythes d'Homère et la pensée grecque*, Paris.

Burman, J. 1994. "The Athenian empress Eudocia", in P. Castrén (ed.), *Post-Herulian Athens. Aspects of Life and Culture in Athens A.D. 267–529*, Helsinki, 63–87.

Cameron, Alan 1965. *Wandering poets: A literary movement in Byzantine Egypt*, Historia, 14, 470–509 (repr. in: Al. Cameron 2016 *Wandering poets and other essays on late Greek literature and philosophy*, Oxford).

Cameron, Alan 1982. "The empress and the poet", *YCIS*, 27, 217–289 (repr. in: Al. Cameron 2016. *Wandering poets and other essays on late Greek literature and philosophy*, Oxford).

Cameron, Alan 2004. "Poetry and literary culture in Late Antiquity", in S. Swain/M.J. Edwards (eds.), *Approaching Late Antiquity: the transformation from Early to Late Empire*, Oxford, 327–354.
Cox Miller, P. 1994. *Dreams in Late Antiquity. Studies in the imagination of a culture*, Princeton (NJ).
Danesin, C. 2001. "Per un commento al frammento Leidense di Eudocia", *Patavium*, 18, 49–61.
Dickie, M.W. 2003. *Magic and magicians in the Greco-Roman World*, London.
Fuhrer, T. 2013. "Hypertexts and auxiliary texts: new genres in Late Antiquity?", in T.D. Papanghelis/S. Harrison/S. Frangoulis (eds.), *Generic interfaces in Latin Literature*, Berlin, 79–89.
Gow, A.S.F. 1950. *Theocritus. Edited with a translation and commentary*, Cambridge.
Hadjittofi, F. 2019. "Sleeping Europa from Plato Comicus to Moschus and Horace", *CQ*, 69, 264–277.
Herzog, R. 1975. *Die Bibelepik der lateinischen Spätantike. Formgeschichte einer erbaulichen Gattung I*, München.
Holum, K.G. 1982. *Theodosian empresses. Women and imperial dominion in Late Antiquity*, Berkeley (CA).
Johnson, S.F. 2006a. *The life and miracles of Thekla. A literary study*, Cambridge (MA).
Johnson, S.F. 2006b. "Late antique narrative fiction: Apocryphal Acta and the Greek novel in the fifth-century *Life and miracles of Thekla*", in S.F. Johnson (ed.), *Greek literature in Late Antiquity. Dynamism, didacticism, classicism*, Aldershot, 189–207.
Lamberton, R. 1986. *Homer the theologian. Neoplatonist allegorical reading and the growth of the epic tradition*, Berkeley (CA).
Lattimore, R. 1951. *The Iliad of Homer*, Chicago (IL).
Lauritzen, D. (ed.) 2015. *Jean de Gaza. Description du tableau cosmique*, Paris.
Ludwich, A. (ed.) 1897. *Eudociae Augustae Procli Lycii Claudiani Carminum graecorum reliquiae*, Leipzig.
Nagy, G. 2005. "The epic hero", in J.M. Foley (ed.), *A Companion to ancient epic*, Malden (MA), 71–89.
Murray, A.T. 1919. *Homer, Odyssey*, 2 vols., Cambridge (MA).
Pollmann, K. 2001. "The transformation of the epic genre in Late Antiquity," *Stud. Patr.*, 36, 61–75.
Pollmann, K. 2017. *The baptized Muse: early Christian poetry as cultural authority*, Oxford.
Radermacher, L. 1927. *Griechische Quellen zur Faustsage*, *AAWW*, 206, 2.
Roberts, M. 1985. *Biblical epic and rhetorical paraphrase in Late Antiquity*, Liverpool.
Salvaneschi, E. 1981. "Ἐξ ἄλλου ἄλλο. Antico e tardoantico nelle opere di Eudocia Augusta", in G. Fabiano/E. Salvaneschi (eds.), *Δεσμὸς κοινωνίας, scritti di filologia e filosofia*, Genova, 143–180.
Salvaneschi, E. 1982. "Un Faust redento", in C. Angelino/E. Salvaneschi (eds.), *Σύγκρισις α'. Testi e studi di storia e filosofia del linguaggio religioso*, Genova, 1–80.
Sandnes, K.O. 2011. *The Gospel 'according to Homer and Virgil'. Cento and canon*, Leiden.
Schottenius Cullhed, S. 2015. *Proba the Prophet. The Christian Virgilian Cento of Faltonia Betitia Proba*, Leiden.
Shorrock, R. 2011. *The myth of paganism. Nonnus, Dionysus and the world of Late Antiquity*, London.
Sowers, B. 2008. *Eudocia: the making of a Homeric Christian* (diss.), Cincinnati (OH).
Usher, M.D. 1998. *Homeric stitchings: the Homeric Centos of the empress Eudocia*, Lanham (MD).

Van der Valk, M. (ed.) 1971–1987. *Eustathii Archiepiscopi Thessalonicensis commentarii ad Homeri Iliadem pertinentes*, 4 vols., Leiden.

Whitby, Mary 1987. "Eutychius, Patriarch of Constantinople: an epic holy man", in Michael Whitby/P. Hardie/Mary Whitby (eds.), *Homo viator. Classical essays for John Bramble*, Bristol, 297–308.

Whitby, Mary 2014. "A learned Spiritual Ladder? Towards an interpretation of George of Pisidia's hexameter poem *On Human Life*" in K. Spanoudakis (ed.), *Nonnus of Panopolis in Context I. Poetry and cultural milieu in Late Antiquity with a section on Nonnus and the modern world*, Berlin, 435–457.

Domenico Accorinti
Did Nonnus Really Want to Write a 'Gospel Epic'? The Ambiguous Genre of the *Paraphrase of the Gospel According to John*

> Who sayes that fictions onely and false hair
> Become a verse? Is there in truth no beautie?
> Is all good structure in a winding stair?
> May no lines passe, except they do their dutie
> Not to a true, but painted chair?
>
> George Herbert, *Jordan (I)*

Introduction

Francis Barham (1808–1871), in the Preface to *A rhymed harmony of the Gospels* (1870), published in collaboration with Isaac Pitman (1813–1897), the inventor of Pitman's shorthand, justified his choice to write a poetic version of the four Gospels in the following way:

> In order to render the Gospel history more attractive, I have composed this poetic paraphrase of it in that antique ballad verse, which seems most pleasing to the majority of the English. [...] This work may therefore be considered a new experiment in biblical literature. It forms a GOSPEL EPIC, in our old national ballad verse, so prized by the English for its quaint simplicity, pathos, and power. My principal aim is to impress the Divine truths of the Gospel on the minds of the lovers of poetry, and make its leading doctrines and facts familiar as household words, by the aid of rhythm and rhyme. [...] A Harmony of the Gospels is the grandest Epic in the world. What Epic has ever treated of so magnificent a theme as the manifestation of God in the form of man, to redeem mankind? In tracing the history of the Messiah through its successive stages, the Gospel epic exhibits the noblest unity of design, and the noblest variety of wonderful incidents. It is indeed the Epic of epics.[1]

For poetic paraphrases of the Gospels before Barham, we can only look to three hexameter works of the fourth and fifth century: Juvencus' *Evangeliorum libri quattuor* (c. 330, henceforth *ELQ*), Sedulius' *Carmen Paschale* (c. 425–450, hence-

---

1 Barham/Pitman 1870, 4–5.

forth *CP*) – the poet also wrote a prose 'paraphrase' of that poem, the *Opus Paschale*[2] –, and Nonnus' *Paraphrase of the Gospel According to John* (c. 430–450). Not unlike the English religious writer, the Latin poets Juvencus and Sedulius illustrate the aims of writing a Gospel epic in the introductory sections of their poems (*ELQ* 1.19–20 and *CP* 1.23–26), and Juvencus himself adds a programmatic message in the epilogue to the *ELQ* 4.802–805.[3] The Greek poet Nonnus, on the other hand, did not attach either a prologue, as the anonymous author of the *Metaphrasis Psalmorum* did,[4] or an epilogue to his poetic rendering of the Gospel of St John. Scholars are, therefore, still groping for answers about the real intentions of Nonnus in composing such a work. Notwithstanding the absence of an explicit pagan/Christian dichotomy and authorial intrusions in Nonnus' *Paraphrase*,[5] the choice of John's text, the so-called 'Spiritual Gospel',[6] sets Nonnus apart from Juvencus and Sedulius. Juvencus relies mainly on the Gospel of Matthew, but also includes Mark, Luke and John; for his part, Sedulius follows closely the accounts of Matthew and Luke, while drawing on Mark and John in the fifth book.[7] Thus both poets draw principally on Matthew and Luke, two Gospels that begin with infancy narratives about Jesus, which suggests that their intention is to narrate the deeds of a new 'epic' hero (not unlike a classical one) from birth to death/resurrection: the *vitalia gesta* and *miracula* of Christ, the Son of the living God, are, thus, celebrated by Juvencus and Sedulius in a language that aspires to emulate Virgil.[8] On the contrary, Nonnus chooses to rewrite the Fourth Gospel, which opens with the Logos hymn and which is highly Christological, as it focuses on Christ's identity throughout. As a result, Nonnus appears less interested in Christ's 'epic' potential – though comparison with the 'deeds' of Dionysus, the hero of his mythological poem, the *Dionysiaca*, is sometimes unavoidable – than in John's theology. So, if Juvencus, or rather Sedulius, could be labeled the 'Christian Virgil', it is debatable whether Nonnus could be characterized as the 'Christian Homer'.

---

[2] See Mori 2013.
[3] Sedulius does not add an epilogue to his poem, but adopts the conclusion of John's Gospel (21:25): see Springer 2013, 183.
[4] On the paraphrase of the Old Testament Psalms see recently Faulkner 2014, 208–209, who stresses the prologue's authorial intentions.
[5] Faulkner 2014, 207–208 is sceptical about a programmatic reading of the last lines of Nonnus' poem (*Par.* 21.139–143), as suggested by Agosti 2001, 95–96.
[6] Anderson/Just/Thatcher 2007, esp. 75–159; Franchi 2016.
[7] Nevertheless, the question of the sources of Sedulius' Gospel in both his works (the *CP* and the *Opus Paschale*) is a very complex one, as recently demonstrated by Norris 2014 and 2016.
[8] See recently Hutchinson 2016 and McGill 2016a.

Did Nonnus want to write a 'Gospel epic', or – to borrow an expression from Karl Olav Sandnes – a 'Gospel according to Homer'?[9] The Byzantine readers would have probably answered this question in the affirmative. Evidence that biblical paraphrases appealed to Byzantine taste is found in Robert Browning. In his essay "Tradition and originality in literary criticism and scholarship" (1995), he cites the very autograph note that Maximus Planudes inserted in the Venetian MS *Marcianus gr.* 481 (f. 122ᵛ),[10] the codex of the Planudean Anthology (1301), which also contains the *Paraphrase of the Gospel According to John*. Here the Greek monk traces Nonnus' work back to the Homeric tradition and identifies its addressees as the "lovers of learning and literature" – the phrasing almost seems to echo "the lovers of poetry", who are the intended recipients of Barham's *A rhymed harmony of the Gospels*:

> ἰστέον δὲ ὅτι ἀεὶ πρόσεστι τοῖς φιλομαθέσι ποθεινὸν καὶ ἐράσμιον ἡ τῶν Ἑλληνικῶν συγγραμμάτων ἀνάγνωσις, καὶ μάλιστα ἡ τῶν Ὁμηρικῶν, διὰ τὸ εὐφραδὲς καὶ ποικίλον τῶν λέξεων. οὗ ἕνεκεν καὶ ἡ παροῦσα μετάφρασις ἐμμέτρως ἐν ἡρωϊκοῖς ἐγεγράφη στίχοις, πρὸς τέρψιν τοῖς φιλομαθέσι καὶ φιλολόγοις.

> We should note that the reading of Hellenic (i.e. pagan) literature has always been an object of longing and delight for lovers of learning, and particularly the reading of the poems of Homer, because of the grace and variety of the language. That is why the present metrical paraphrase has been written in heroic metre, to give pleasure to lovers of learning and literature.[11] (*Marc. gr.* 481, f. 122ᵛ)

Commenting on the same passage, Edmund Fryde also rightly points out that the scholars of the Palaeologan Renaissance were only concerned with language and style, and that "[t]his blend of Christian content and classical form was a perfect example of Byzantine Christian humanism, though it is notable that Planudes stressed here form, not content."[12] More recently, Konstantinos Spanoudakis has expressed even more strongly the significance of Planudes' assertion in the *Marcianus*, claiming that it was the aesthetic pleasure aroused by Homeric hexameters and not the potential exegetical value that made Nonnus' work palatable to Planudes' circle.[13]

---

9 Sandnes 2011.
10 On this MS see De Stefani 2002, 44–46 and 2016, 677–678; Spanoudakis 2016, 605–607.
11 Trans. Browning 1995, 21.
12 Fryde 2000, 228, followed substantially by Pontani 2015, 414.
13 Spanoudakis 2016, 607.

But a Homer-oriented reading of the *Paraphrase* seems too reductive an approach for a learned poet who in his other *opus magnum*, the *Dionysiaca*, demonstrates his familiarity not only with the epics of his "father Homer" (*Dion.* 25.265),[14] but also with Hellenistic poets (e.g., Callimachus and Apollonius), as well as with imperial poetry and the novel.[15] For Nonnus famously blends genres, subgenres and text types.[16] Moreover, by rewriting the Fourth Gospel Nonnus enters into dialogue with John and the Christian exegetical tradition of the Fourth Gospel, and most importantly with Cyril of Alexandria's exegesis, since the *Paraphrase* seems strictly to follow the patriarch's *Commentary on the Gospel of St John* written between 425 and 428.[17]

To speak of Nonnus' *Paraphrase*, then, would inevitably mean to debate the issue of its literary genre: can one speak of a Gospel paraphrase genre, to echo the title of an article by Norman Petersen?[18] Attempts at defining the genre of Latin poems like those of Juvencus and Sedulius, to whom Nonnus' *Paraphrase* may be compared, have led in the past to different and sometimes diametrically opposed conclusions. Just to mention two Italian scholars, Antonio Vincenzo Nazzaro argued vigorously for the legitimacy of a new literary genre, the "paraphrase (biblical and hagiographic)",[19] whereas Franca Ela Consolino claimed that there is no need to introduce a new literary genre, since works such as Juvencus' *ELQ* and Sedulius' *CP* belong to the epic genre.[20] Most recently, Amélie Alrifaee in her dissertation on the paraphrastic and epic nature of the *ELQ*, states that Juvencus wrote a classical (and not a paraphrastic) epic inspired by the Gospels.[21] Likewise, Scott McGill, in an analysis of Virgil's presence in Juvencus, contends that the Spanish poet himself conceived of his work as an epic.[22] Finally, in an essay originally published in 2012, "Tradition and innovation. The transformation of classical literary genres in Christian Late Antiquity", Karla Pollmann remarks that there is no established classification of late antique genres:

---

[14] Bannert/Kröll 2016.
[15] See Acosta-Hughes 2016; Maciver 2016; Miguélez-Cavero 2016.
[16] See Lasek 2016. On 'text types' and their relation with genres see Görlach 2004, 3–22.
[17] Whitby 2016, 215. The strictness of Nonnus' reliance on Cyril has recently been cast into doubt by Hadjittofi 2018 and Simelides 2018; see also below, n. 28.
[18] Petersen 1994, 157–158 posed the question, "Can one speak of a Gospel Genre?", and reached a negative conclusion; see also Czachesz 2003, 25–27. On the Gospels and their affinity to Graeco-Roman biography see recently Licona 2017, 3–6.
[19] Nazzaro 2008a, 38–54 and 2008b.
[20] Consolino 2005.
[21] Alrifaee 2015, 68. See also Paschalis' contribution in this volume.
[22] McGill 2016a, 52–53. On Juvencus' use of allusion see Kaufmann 2017, 155–157.

Thus, the classification of genres is varied, chaotic, and attempts at establishing a conclusive systematization fail. Currently, literary theory prefers to think rather along the following criteria: the relevance and impact of various historical and cultural factors, 'family resemblance' between various texts; overlapping of literary genres; the diachronic dynamic potential of genre development; and finally, the characterization of a text by more than one genre, that is, a hybrid.[23]

It is precisely this last perspective, "the characterization of a text by more than one genre, that is, a hybrid",[24] that we could apply to read an ambiguous work like Nonnus' *Paraphrase*. The reasons behind this complexity are the following: a) the *Paraphrase* adopts the hexameter, the heroic verse of Homer, but is not an epic, since Nonnus, unlike Juvencus and Sedulius, does not look upon Christ as an epic hero;[25] b) the employment of epic language – namely Homeric quotations, allusions, and formulae – or in other words the Homeric color of Nonnus' *Paraphrase*,[26] does not suffice to read this work only as a Homerizing text, since the author does not write in a continuous intertextual relationship with Homer, but is clearly also familiar with Hellenistic, imperial, and early Christian poetry;[27] c) Nonnus' text is not an autonomous poetic work, nor is it a mere paraphrase of its biblical hypotext, because the tension between dependence on and independence from the Gospel of John is always evident; d) Nonnus' interest in the Gospel of John does not prove that he aimed to offer a complete exegetical paraphrase of the Fourth Gospel, although he does sometimes seem to engage with theological issues.[28]

In order to show the issues at play when dealing with the genre of the *Paraphrase* I will focus on three passages from Book 19, in which Nonnus reworks John's account of the Passion of Christ, because they are particularly representative of this 'ambiguous genre' into which Nonnus composes his work.

---

[23] Pollmann 2017c, 22–23.
[24] Cf. Cullhed 2015, 547.
[25] *Contra*, König 2012, 178: "His *Paraphrase of St John's Gospel* rewrites Christ as an epic hero in Homeric hexameters." Such a statement is misleading. For a general definition of an epic hero see Toohey 1992, 9–11. For Cyprian's ambiguous epic heroism in Eudocia's *Cypr.* see Rigo's contribution in this volume.
[26] See Ypsilanti 2016, esp. 220–222.
[27] See Spanoudakis 2014, 5–16.
[28] For Nonnus' Christology see Grillmeier/Hainthaler 1996, 92–99; Sieber 2016 and 2017; Hadjittofi 2018.

Jesus' silence before Pilate (*Paraphrase* 19.40–48)

I begin with Jesus' silence in front of Pilate in John's Gospel. After entering the praetorium the Roman governor asks Jesus about his origin, but Jesus remains silent. Then Pilate tries again to force him to speak appealing to his own authority over Jesus, because, as the Roman governor, he has the power to release or crucify him:

> καὶ εἰσῆλθεν εἰς τὸ πραιτώριον πάλιν καὶ λέγει τῷ Ἰησοῦ· πόθεν εἶ σύ; ὁ δὲ Ἰησοῦς ἀπόκρισιν οὐκ ἔδωκεν αὐτῷ. λέγει οὖν αὐτῷ ὁ Πιλᾶτος· ἐμοὶ οὐ λαλεῖς; οὐκ οἶδας ὅτι ἐξουσίαν ἔχω ἀπολῦσαί σε καὶ ἐξουσίαν ἔχω σταυρῶσαί σε;
>
> he entered the praetorium again and said to Jesus, "Where are you from?" But Jesus gave no answer. Pilate therefore said to him, "You will not speak to me? Do you not know that I have power to release you, and power to crucify you?"[29] (Jo 19:9–10)

This passage is recast by Nonnus in a vivid narrative that reads as follows:

> σπερχομένοις δὲ πόδεσσιν ἐδύσατο πανδόκον αὐλήν·   40
> Ἰησοῦν δ' ἐρέεινε τὸ δεύτερον ἠθάδι μύθῳ·
> τίς τελέθεις; πόθεν ἐσσί; κατωπιόων δ' ἐπὶ γαίῃ
> κοίρανος ὄμματα πῆξε καὶ οὐ Πιλάτῳ στόμα λύσας
> ἀντίδοτον μύθοισιν ἀμοιβαίην πόρε φωνήν.
> καὶ Πιλᾶτος βαρύμηνιν ἀπερροίβδησεν ἰωήν·   45
> οὔ με τεοῖς ἐπέεσσιν ἀμείβεαι; οὐδέ πω ἔγνως,
> ὅττι κεν εἰς σὲ φέρω δίδυμον κράτος; ἀμφότερον γάρ,
> καὶ σταυρῷ δαμάσαιμι καί, ἢν ἐθέλω, σε μεθήσω.
>
> With hastening feet he entered the all-receiving court. He questioned Jesus a second time with familiar voice, "Who are you? From where are you?" Looking down the Lord fixed his eyes on the ground, and he did not loose his tongue and give an answering voice counteracting his expressions. And Pilate shrieked forth a heavy-wroth voice, "You are not going to answer me with your words? Do you not at all realize that I could bear against you a twin power? For doubly I could both subdue you on a cross and, if I am willing, I could let you go."[30] (*Par.* 19.40–48)

One notes first how Nonnus amplifies his prose model in nine quasi-Homeric lines.[31] While John uses 40 words, none of which are adjectives, Nonnus employs

---

[29] All biblical translations are from *RSV*.
[30] Translations of Nonnus' *Paraphrase* are taken from Sherry 1991, sometimes adapted.
[31] 40a ~ *Il.* 20.189, 21.564, *Od.* 13.261 ταχέεσσι πόδεσσι(ν); 41a ~ *Il.* 6.176 καὶ τότε μιν ἐρέεινε (*), *Od.* 5.85 Ἑρμείαν δ' ἐρέεινε (*), 20.190 αὐτὸς δ' αὖτ' ἐρέεινε (*); 42a ~ Hom., *Il.* 21.150, *Od.* 1.170,

64, seven of which are adjectives, mainly exegetical,[32] two neuter adjectives used adverbially (41: τὸ δεύτερον, 47: ἀμφότερον) and one, σπερχομένοις (40), is an adjectival participle, showing Nonnus' concern with the theatrical potential of the scene. Few words come from John, sometimes with slight adaptation by Nonnus.[33] The first hemistich of v. 42 τίς τελέθεις; πόθεν ἐσσί; combines the formulation of the recognition scene from John 19:9 πόθεν εἶ σύ; ("Who are you? From where are you?")[34] and the formulae used in Homer's *Iliad* and *Odyssey* when questioning a stranger, τίς πόθεν εἰς ἀνδρῶν; ("Who among men are you, and from where?"),[35] and τίς δὲ σύ ἐσσι; ("Who are you?").[36] The result is a hybrid hemistich that conflates two authoritative sources, Nonnus' biblical hypotext and Homer.

Similarly, Eudocia too, in the first recension of the *Homerocentones* (*I HC*), appropriates Telemachus' words to Athena/Mentes (*I HC* 1103 Schembra ~ *Odyssey* 1.170: τίς πόθεν εἰς ἀνδρῶν; πόθι τοι πόλις ἠδὲ τοκῆες;)[37] to phrase the question regarding Jesus' identity, as posed by the Samaritan woman.[38] The second hemistich of v. 42 introduces the silence of Jesus before Pilate,[39] a theme which Nonnus expresses in a paradoxical, unexpected manner:[40] whereas John confines himself to saying that Jesus did not answer Pilate, Nonnus adds a psychological dimension to the Gospel account, focusing on the composure of Jesus, who looks down with his eyes fixed on the ground. This seems to be a reminiscence of the Homeric characterization of Odysseus before a speech at *Iliad* 3.216–

---

etc. τίς πόθεν εἰς ἀνδρῶν + *Il.* 6.123, 15.247, 24.387 τίς δὲ σύ ἐσσι; 42b ~ *Il.* 3.114, 11.161, etc., *Od.* 10.165, 18.92 (δ') ἐπὶ γαίῃ (*); 44a ~ *Il.* 3.171 μύθοισιν ἀμείβετο, 3.437, 23.794, etc. μύθοισιν ἀμειβόμενος; 46a ~ e.g. *Il.* 22.329 ἀμειβόμενος ἐπέεσσιν, 23.492 ἀμείβεσθον ἐπέεσσιν; 47a ~ *Od.* 14.445 ὅττι κεν (*).

32 40 πανδόκον, 41 ἠθάδι, 44 ἀντίδοτον, ἀμοιβαίην, 45 βαρύμηνιν, 46 τεοῖς, 47 δίδυμον.
33 41 Ἰησοῦν, 42 πόθεν ἐσσί, 45 Πιλάτος, 46 οὔ με, 47 ὅττι, σε, 48 καί (2x), σε. At v. 40, probably for metrical reasons, Nonnus avoids the Johannine term πραιτώριον, which he renders with πανδόκος αὐλή (cf. *Dion.* 3.125, 16.304, 31.30; *Par.* 14.6); see Smolak 1984, 9 n. 45; and Agosti 2003, 369–370 on Nonn., *Par.* 5.33.
34 For the recognition scene before Pilate (Jo 18:28–19:16a) see Larsen 2008, 173–180.
35 *Il.* 21.150, *Od.* 1.170, 7.238, 10.325, 14.187, 15.264, 19.105, 24.298.
36 *Il.* 6.123, 15.247, 24.387.
37 Cf. *II HC* 924 Schembra: τίς πόθεν εἰς ἀνδρῶν; τίνα δ' αὖ καλέουσί σε φῶτες; ("Who among men are you? What do people call you?").
38 See Usher 1998, 125–126; Sowers 2010, 27–32.
39 On Jesus' silence in Lk 23:6–12 see Dinkler 2013, 192–202.
40 For the *topos* of eloquent silence see Accorinti 2009, 83–87, esp. 85–87 on Nonn., *Par.* 19.43–44.

224.⁴¹ Like the Homeric hero Odysseus, Jesus in John delivers rhetorical speeches.⁴² Immediately after Jesus' answer (Jo 19:11: "You would have no power over me unless it had been given you from above; therefore he who delivered me to you has the greater sin"), Pilate would even like to release him (Jo 19:12).

But even more striking than this likely Homeric allusion, is a textual echo in Pilate's words (v. 48: καὶ σταυρῷ δαμάσαιμι καί, ἢν *ἐθέλω, σε μεθήσω*) of Hesiod's fable of the hawk and the nightingale in *Works and Days* 202–212. There the hawk says to the nightingale: δεῖπνον δ', αἴ κ' *ἐθέλω*, ποιήσομαι ἠὲ *μεθήσω* (v. 209: "I shall make you my dinner if I wish, or I shall let you go").⁴³ After discussing the various interpretations of Hesiod's fable in *Ainoi, Logoi, Mythoi* (1997, 134), Gert-Jan van Dijk concludes that the "unexpected change of roles" between hawk and nightingale is paralleled in Eunapius (*Hist*. fr. 72.1), who is "virtually the only one to make a literary use of Hesiod's fable" and compares one Ἱέραξ ("Hawk") to Hesiod's nightingale. Here the Dutch scholar clearly ignores the likely allusion to Hesiod's tale in Nonnus' *Paraphrase*.

Furthermore, neither van Dijk nor Francisco Rodríguez Adrados, in *History of the Graeco-Latin Fable*, vol. 3 (2003), mentions Nonnus' passage as a literary reference to the hawk's words in Hesiod's fable. It is not hard to see, however, why Nonnus in the context of Jesus' trial before Pilate would have introduced a moralizing reflection on Roman justice. While the Roman governor thinks he has δίδυμον κράτος (47: "a twin power"), that is, a power of life and death over the prisoner, he really does not have any authority, as Jesus himself says to Pilate, because he is subject to the Power that comes from above: (50–51) οὐδὲ μίαν μεθέπεις αὐτάγρετον εἰς ἐμὲ τιμήν, | εἰ μὴ ἄνωθεν ἔην κεχαρισμένον ("you do not ply any self-appointed rank against me, unless from above it was graciously given").⁴⁴ Thus, the Hesiodic echo cannot be considered a *Usurpation*, nor a *Kontrastimitation*, at least not *stricto sensu*, but rather an act of literary appropriation

---

41 For Antenor's account of Odysseus see Goldhill 1986, 158–159. The passage is imitated by Triphiodorus 114–119: see Miguélez-Cavero 2013, 194–197.
42 For the identification between Odysseus and Christ in the *Homerocentones* see Whitby 2007, 213. On rhetoric in John see Parsenios 2010, esp. 4–9.
43 Trans. Most 2006. On the interpretation of Hesiod's story see Griffiths 1995, 95–96; van Dijk 1997, 127–134; Nelson 1998, 77–81; Adrados 2003, 9–11. For Hesiod in Late Antiquity see Agosti 2016, who does not mention Nonn., *Par*. 19.48.
44 On Jo 19:11 see Carter 2003, esp. 146f.

by a Christian poet.⁴⁵ And this blend of Gospel, Homeric and Hesiodic material provides another example of conflation of sources and hybridization of genres.

The crucifixion (*Paraphrase* 19.91–100)

John's account of the crucifixion of Jesus between two criminals is remarkably restrained. In John 19:18 the description is brief: ὅπου [sc. Γολγοθᾶ] αὐτὸν ἐσταύρωσαν, καὶ μετ' αὐτοῦ ἄλλους δύο ἐντεῦθεν καὶ ἐντεῦθεν, μέσον δὲ τὸν Ἰησοῦν ("there [sc. Golgotha] they crucified him, and with him two others, one on either side, and Jesus between them"), just as those of the synoptic Gospels (Mt 27:38; Mk 15:27; Lk 23:33).⁴⁶ In comparison, Nonnus' retelling of the crucifixion scene is exuberant and astounding:

κεῖθι φονῆες
εἰς δόρυ τετράπλευρον ἐπήορον ὑψόθι γαίης
ὄρθιον ἐξετάνυσσαν, ἐπισφίγξαντες ἀνάγκῃ
πεπταμένας ἑκάτερθε σιδηρείῳ τινὶ δεσμῷ
χεῖρας, ὁμοτρήτῳ δὲ πεπαρμένον ἄζυγι γόμφῳ   95
διπλόον ἦτορ ἔχοντα, μιῇ τετορημένον ὁρμῇ
ποσσὶν ὁμοπλεκέεσσιν, ἀκαμπέα δεσμὸν ὀλέθρου.
κέντροις δ' ἀντιτύποισιν ἐπὶ σταυροῖο δεθέντας
νυκτιλόχους δύο φῶτας ἐνὶ ξύνωσαν ὀλέθρῳ
γείτονας ἀλλήλοισι, μέσον δ' ἔστησαν Ἰησοῦν.   100

95 ὁμοτρήτῳ δὲ γ: ὁμοτρήτοιο V: ὁμοτρήτοισι Scheindler: ὁμότρητον δὲ Golega, at ὁμοτρήτῳ active intellegi potest, sc. 'simul perterebrans' || 96 ἦτορ β iniuria suspectum: ἕλκος Tiedke, alii alia | ἔχοντα β: ἔχοντι Livrea, sc. 'traiectum unico clavo duplicem animum habenti.'

There the murderers stretched him out upright lifted on the four-sided wood above the ground, binding him under compulsion by his outstretched hands on either side with an iron bond, pierced by the co-perforating unyokable nail, but he had a twofold substance, and bored in one motion through his interlaced feet, an unbendable bond of destruction. They made common to one destruction two waylayers of the night, bound on a cross with

---

45 For the German terms *Usurpation* and *Kontrastimitation* see Agosti 2011, esp. 287–295. For further Hesiodean echoes in the *Paraphrase* and their implications for the poem's genre see Hadjittofi in this volume.

46 For the crucifixion in antiquity see Samuelsson 2013. On the Gospel accounts of the crucifixion see Casey 2011, 1359–1360 and, for the "brigandage connotations of crucifixion", Chapman 2008, 226–227.

corresponding pins, neighboring to one another, but they set Jesus in the middle. (*Par.* 19.91–100)

Where John has only 15 words, two of which are adjectives (ἄλλους, μέσον), Nonnus uses 52 (only three come from the original: δύο, μέσον, Ἰησοῦν), 17 of which are adjectives, mainly exegetical,[47] and one, πεπταμένας (94), is an adjectival participle. About thirty years ago, in my thesis on Book 19 of Nonnus' *Paraphrase*, I struggled with this passage, which had been problematic for many scholars.[48] The French Jesuit Nicolas Abram, to cite one name, commented in his edition of Nonnus' *Paraphrase* (1623) as follows: "*quid ista sibi velint ne Oedipus quidem, aut ille Loxias intelligat.*"[49] Here it will be sufficient to stress a point: it is likely that Nonnus wanted to contrast (95: δέ) Jesus' stretched hands on the cross, transfixed by two nails, with his feet, perforated by a single nail.[50] As I suggested, Jesus' interlaced feet, which are transfixed by a single nail, may be a symbol of his double nature, if διπλόον ἦτορ at v. 96 refers to the 'double substance' of Christ as both God and man.[51] This interpretation could be supported by the symbolism of Peter's 'head-downwards' crucifixion in the *Apocryphal Acts of Peter* 38,[52] although there are some textual difficulties in this section which contains an allegorical description of the cross as a mediator between human and divine:

> προσῆκεν γὰρ ἐπιβαίνειν τῷ τοῦ Χριστοῦ σταυρῷ, ὅστις ἐστὶν τεταμένος λόγος, εἷς καὶ μόνος, περὶ οὗ τὸ πνεῦμα λέγει· Τί γάρ ἐστιν Χριστὸς ἀλλ' ὁ λόγος, ἦχος τοῦ θεοῦ; ἵνα λόγος ᾖ τοῦτο τὸ ὀρθὸν ξύλον, ἐφ' ᾧ ἐσταύρωμαι· ἦχος δὲ τὸ πλάγιόν ἐστιν, ἀνθρώπου φύσις·[53] ὁ δὲ ἦλος ὁ συνέχων ἐπὶ τῷ ὀρθῷ ξύλῳ τὸ πλάγιον κατὰ μέσου, ἡ ἐπιστροφὴ καὶ ἡ μετάνοια τοῦ ἀνθρώπου.[54]

---

[47] 92 τετράπλευρον, ἐπήορον, 93 ὄρθιον, 94 σιδηρείῳ, τινί, 95 ὁμοτρήτῳ, ἄζυγι, 96 διπλόον, μιῇ, 97 ὁμοπλεκέεσσιν, ἀκαμπέα, 98 ἀντιτύποισιν, 99 νυκτιλόχους, δύο, ἑνί, 100 γείτονας, μέσον.
[48] Accorinti 1986–1987, 90–102, esp. 94–99 ("Excursus V: La croce cosmica"); Livrea/Accorinti 1988. Justus Lipsius mentions Nonnus' description of the cross in his *De cruce libri tres* (1593): see Pickering 1980, 70–71.
[49] Abram 1623, 76.
[50] On the use of nails in crucifixion see Chapman 2008, 182–183.
[51] Koch 1856, 194, who preferred to conjecture ἔστορ' ("peg"), thought that διπλόον ἦτορ (96) could refer to the double nature of Christ. For the Christological use of the term διπλόος as referring to "Christ as possessing two natures" see Lampe, *s.v.* 'διπλόος', 1.b. On the Homeric ἦτορ, see Sullivan 1996.
[52] Lipsius 1891, 96 = Prieur 2006, 100 (n° 124). On the Gnostic cross of the *AAPetr.* see Bolyki 1998; Voicu 2007, 124–125.
[53] For the Greek tradition of *AAPetr.* 96.7–9 see Baldwin 2005, 286–287 n. 300.
[54] On textual problems of the Greek version of *AAPetr.* 96.10–11 see again Baldwin 2005, 287 n. 302.

For you ought to come to the cross of Christ, who is the extended Word, the one and only, concerning whom the Spirit says, "For what else is Christ than the Word, the sound of God?" The Word is this upright tree on which I am crucified; the sound, however, is the crossbeam, namely the nature of man; and the nail which holds the crossbeam to the upright in the middle is the conversion and repentance of man.[55] (*AAPetr.* 38)

It is also evident that Nonnus' crucifixion draws on the archetypal scene of Odysseus bound to the mast of his ship (*Od.* 12.178–179: οἱ δ' ἐν νηΐ μ' ἔδησαν ὁμοῦ χεῖράς τε πόδας τε | ὀρθὸν ἐν ἱστοπέδῃ, ἐκ δ' αὐτοῦ πείρατ' ἀνῆπτον, "and they bound me in the ship hand and foot, upright in the step of the mast, and made the ropes fast at the ends to the mast itself"),[56] which Christian authors like Clement of Alexandria, Gregory of Nyssa and Hippolytus interpreted as an image of Christ nailed to the cross.[57] Indeed, there are some similarities between the cross of Christ in the *Paraphrase* (19.28, 92–95) and the mast of a ship described in the *Dionysiaca* 40.453–454. But Nonnus could also echo here another famous chained hero, Aeschylus' *Prometheus Bound*,[58] as Prometheus is seen by Christian authors as another prefiguration of Christ.[59]

Let me now take a quick look at other poetic accounts of the crucifixion, two of which are paraphrases, Juvencus' *Evangeliorum Libri Quattuor* and Sedulius' *Carmen Paschale*, and three are centos: the Virgilian cento of Faltonia Betitia Proba (c. 401–460), the *Homerocentones* of Aelia Eudocia Augusta (c. 400–460), and the Euripidean cento *Christus Patiens*, sometimes attributed to Gregory Nazianzen, but usually dated to the eleventh or twelfth century.[60] Passing over the

---

55 Trans. Elliot 1993, 425. On the *Hymn of the Cross* in the *Berlin-Strasbourg Apocryphon* (also known as the *Gospel of the Savior*) and its relation with the *Hymn of the Cross* in the Qasr el-Wizz codex see now Suciu 2017, who dates the composition of the *Berlin-Strasbourg Apocryphon* (preserved only in Coptic by two fragmentary manuscripts, *Papyrus Berolinensis* 22220 and *Strasbourg Copte* 5–7) after the Council of Chalcedon (451 CE).
56 Translations of Homer are those by Murray 1998 and 1999, sometimes adapted.
57 Greg. Nyss., res. = *Gregorii Nysseni opera* 9.302.19–9.303.8; Hipp., antichr. 59 = GCS Hippolytus 1.2.39–40; haer. 7.13.3 = Marcovich, p. 280. See Markschies 2005, esp. 230–239; Zilling 2015, 139–140, 161–164. For the connection between Odysseus' mast and Andrew's cross in the *AAAndr.* (c. 150–200) see MacDonald 1994, 150–155, 257–262; see also Granger Cook 2014, 214–215.
58 Cf. Aesch., *PV* 15, 55–56, 113, 141–142 ~ *Par.* 19.92f.; 76 ~ *Par.* 19.95 and 20.111. Such parallels were suggested to me by the late Vincenzo Di Benedetto. See also Samuelsson 2013, 68.
59 See Smyth 1999, 84–89; González-Rivas Fernández 2018, 304–305. For Prometheus as *figura Christi* in Simone Weil see Accorinti 2014, 464 n. 22.
60 See Friesen 2015, 251–260, esp. 259; Perris 2015, 511; Pollmann 2017b.

brief account of Juvencus (*ELQ* 4.662: *iamque cruci fixum pendebat in arbore corpus*, "now he hung crucified upon the tree"),[61] the cross in Sedulius becomes a *signum salutis* (*CP* 5.186) and a cosmic symbol (*CP* 5.190–195) which "serves as an indication of Christ's rule over the four directional areas of the world."[62] Sedulius' notion finds parallels in Nonnus' description of the cross that is described as stretched to the four (*quadrati*, τετράπλευρον) corners of the universe:

> neve quis ignoret speciem crucis esse colendam,
> quae dominum portavit ovans, ratione potenti
> quattuor inde plagas quadrati colligat orbis: 190 ~ Nonn., *Par.* 19.92 : τετράπλευρον
> splendidus auctoris de vertice fulget Eous;
> occiduo sacrae lambuntur sidere plantae;
> arcton dextra tenet; medium laeva erigit axem.
> cunctaque de membris vivit natura creantis,
> et cruce complexum Christus regit undique mundum.   195

> Lest anyone forget that the form of the cross which carried the Lord
> in triumph is to be cherished, with cogent reasoning let him
> infer from it the four regions of the four-cornered world: 190
> The shining east gleams down from the head of its creator;
> The soles of his holy feet are licked by the western star;
> His right hand holds the north; and his left raises up the southern heaven.
> All nature derives life from the limbs of its creator,
> and Christ rules a world everywhere embraced by the cross.[63]   195 (*CP* 5.188–195)

In the Virgilian cento of Proba, v. 616, Christ is crucified on *ingentem quercum* ("a large oak tree"). Thus, as Schottenius Cullhed emphasizes,[64] the Tree of Knowledge referred to here is associated with the cross, and links "the original sin of Eden with the New Testament sacrifice and redemption", according to the following passage:

tollitur in caelum clamor cunctique repente		*Aen.* 11.745 + *Aen.* 1.594
corripuere sacram effigiem manibusque cruentis	615	*Aen.* 2.167
ingentem quercum, decisis undique ramis,		*Aen.* 11.5
constituunt | spirisque ligant ingentibus ipsum,		*Aen.* 6.217 + *Aen.* 2.217
tendebantque manus | pedibus per mutua nexis,		*Aen.* 6.314 + *Aen.* 7.66
triste ministerium, | sequitur quos cetera pubes,		*Aen.* 6.223 + *Aen.* 5.74
ausi omnes inmane nefas ausoque potiti.	620	*Aen.* 6.624

---

61 Trans. McGill 2016b; on *ELQ* 4.642–649, 662–673 see McGill 2016b, 265–266; McBrine 2017, 51–56. For the epic language of *ELQ* 4.687–713 see Green 2006, 56.
62 Springer 2013, 176.
63 Trans. Springer 2013.
64 Schottenius Cullhed 2015, 153.

They raised their cry to the skies and suddenly everyone | seized the holy figure. With their bloody hands | they put up a large oak tree with cut branches, | tied him with huge twisted bands, | and stretched out his hands and pressed his feet together | – a terrible undertaking – and the other young men followed them. | All dared an atrocious sin and enjoyed what they dared.[65] (*Cento Probae* 614–620 Fassina/Lucarini)

Eudocia's version of the crucifixion is full of descriptive details concerning Christ and the cross, and recalls, like Nonnus' *Paraphrase*, the image of Odysseus tied to the mast of his ship (v. 1886: ἐν ἱστοπέδῃ).[66] Here I quote from the first recension, the longest one,[67] of the *Homerocentones* (*I HC*):

σὺν δὲ πόδας χεῖράς τε δέον κεκοτηότι θυμῷ,	*Od*. 22.189 + 22.477 Melanthius
ἐς μέσσον δ' ἄναγον, τὼ δ' ἄμφω χεῖρας ἀνέσχον 1880	*Od*. 18.89 Odysseus/Irus fight
καρπαλίμως, ἀπὸ δὲ χλαῖναν θέτο φοινικόεσσαν.	*Od*. 14.500 Odysseus
ἦμος δ' ἠέλιος μέσον οὐρανὸν ἀμφιβεβήκει,	*Il*. 8.68 Helios travels in the sky
δεξάμενοι δ' ἄρα τοί γε διαστάντες τανύουσι	*Il*. 17.391 of a bull hide
σταυροῖσιν πυκινοῖσι διαμπερὲς ἔνθα καὶ ἔνθα,	*Il*. 24.453 Achilles' court + *Od*. 14.11 Eumaeus' court
γυμνόν, ἀτάρ τοι εἵματ' ἐνὶ μεγάροισι κέοντο, 1885	*Il*. 22.510 of the dead Hector
ὀρθὸν ἐν ἱστοπέδῃ, ἐκ δ' αὐτοῦ πείρατ' ἀνῆψαν,	*Od*. 12.179 Odysseus on the mast
ὕψι μάλα μεγάλως· ἐπὶ δ' ἴαχε λαὸς ὄπισθεν.	*Il*. 17.723 Patroclus' corpse
ὣς ὁ μὲν αὖθι λέλειπτο, ταθεὶς ὀλοῷ ὑπὸ δεσμῷ,	*Od*. 22.200 Melanthius
μεσσηγὺς γαίης τε καὶ οὐρανοῦ ἀστερόεντος,	*Il*. 5.769 of the horses' flight
ὥρῃ ἐν εἰαρινῇ, ὅτε τ' ἤματα μακρὰ πέλονται, 1890	*Od*. 18.367 the length of a spring day
ὥς κεν δηθὰ ζωὸς ἐὼν χαλέπ' ἄλγεα πάσχῃ.	*Od*. 22.177 Melanthius

And they bound his feet and hands in their furious wrath, and led him into the midst (of the cross) and put up both his hands quickly, and he took off his purple cloak. But when the sun had bestrode mid heaven, and when they have taken him they stand separately and stretch him on a solid cross on either side, a naked corpse, yet in the halls lay his clothes, upright on the wood, and they tied ropes around him, high, very high, and at that the people behind them shouted aloud. So he was left there, stretched in the direful bond, between

---

[65] Trans. Schottenius Cullhed 2015, 153. On the relationship between Proba's crucifixion scene and its Virgilian hypotext see Dijkstra 2008, 46; Sineri 2011, 274–276; Schottenius Cullhed 2015, 151, 153–154, 181–182. For the Virgilian cento of Proba, see also McGill 2007; Curran 2012; Schottenius Cullhed 2016; Kaufmann 2017, 157–159. A useful discussion on the Virgilian centos and the centonist's technique is found in Audano 2012; Elsner 2017, 176–182.
[66] See Sandnes 2011, 210–211 and 2016, 33–34. On Nonnus and Eudocia see Whitby 2007 and more recently Lefteratou 2016. For a good treatment of Nonnus and biblical epic see Whitby 2016; cf. also Miguélez-Cavero/McGill 2018, 264–265; Whitby/Roberts 2018, 230–232.
[67] The first recension of the Homeric centos is commonly attributed to the empress and poet Aelia Eudocia Augusta, Theodosius II's wife: see Whitby 2007, 218–219; Sowers 2010, 23–24. On the different recensions of the Homeric centos see the introduction by Schembra 2007, cxxxiii–clxxxi to his edition of the *HC*; for *I HC* 1879–1891 see Schembra 2006, 506–511.

earth and starry heaven, in the season of spring, when the long days come, that he may keep alive long, and suffer grievous torment. (*I HC* 1879–1891, text Schembra, trans. Accorinti, adapted from Murray 1998 and 1999)

Finally, the Euripidean cento *Christus Patiens* mentions Jesus' hands and feet nailed to the tree, and also displays some similarities with Nonnus' description:

αὐτίχ' ὅμιλος οὐρανοδρόμῳ ξύλῳ	660	*Bacch.* 1064 (cf. *Bacch.* 1067)
ἀνῆγον, ἦγον, ἦγον εἰς ἄκρον τέλος·		*Bacch.* 1065
ὀρθὸς δ' ἐς ὀρθὸν αἰθέρ' ἐστηρίζετο.		*Bacch.* 1073 ~ Nonn., *Par.* 19.92–93
Ἐς κλῶνα δ' ἐγκάρσιον ἄλλον εὐθέως		*Bacch.* 1068 ~ Nonn., *Par.* 19.92
ἔτεινον, ἐξέτεινον, ἥλωσαν χέρας,		~ Nonn., *Par.* 19.93
πόδας δὲ καθήλωσαν ἐν πηκτῷ ξύλῳ. 665		

Straightway the crowd led up him to a wood running along the sky, leading him high, high, up in the sky. And the wood was placed all straight in the air. And immediately they stretched, stretched him out on another transverse branch, nailed his hands, then nailed his feet to the stick wood. (*Chr. Pat.* 660–665, text Tuilier, trans. Accorinti)

Despite some similarities between these accounts and the *Paraphrase*, none of these represents a descriptive *ekphrasis* blended with a symbolic and theological interpretation of Jesus' cross as in Nonnus' case.

The wandering sponge (*Paraphrase* 19.149–157)

I will close with another passage from Book 19 of Nonnus' *Paraphrase* that inserts an ekphrastic digression into the Gospel account. In John 19:29, Jesus is given vinegar: σκεῦος ἔκειτο ὄξους μεστόν· σπόγγον οὖν μεστὸν τοῦ ὄξους ὑσσώπῳ περιθέντες προσήνεγκαν αὐτοῦ τῷ στόματι ("A bowl full of vinegar stood there; so they put a sponge full of the vinegar on hyssop and held it to his mouth"), to fulfil scripture (Jo 19:28; cf. Ps 69:22).[68] Nonnus' rendition has transformed its hypotext so much as to make it almost unrecognizable:

καὶ ἑτοῖμον ἔην παρὰ γείτονι χώρῳ
ὄξεος ἔμπλεον ἄγγος. ἀνὴρ δέ τις ὀξὺς ἀκούσας   150
σπόγγον ὑποβρυχίων ἀδύτων βλάστημα θαλάσσης
πλήσας δριμυτάτοιο ποτοῦ καὶ διψάδος ἅλμης
ἰθυπόρου καλάμου παρὰ νείατον ἄκρον ἐρείσας
ὤρεγεν ὑσσώπῳ κεκερασμένον ὄξος ὀλέθρου,

---

68 See Schiffman 2006, 123.

ἀντίδοτον βασιλῆι μελισταγέος νιφετοῖο 155
ἄρτου θεσπεσίοιο δι' ἠέρος ὑψόσε τείνων
ἄκρον ἀειρομένου καλάμου καὶ σπόγγον ἀλήτην.

> And ready at a neighboring place was a vessel full of vinegar. A certain man keenly heard him and filled a sponge, offshoot of the submarine sanctuaries of the sea, with the most bitter drink and thirsty brine. He balanced it on the uttermost tip of a straight-faring reed and stretched forth the mixed vinegar of death with a hyssop – given to the king in lieu of honey-soaked snow, the divine bread – stretching upward through the air the tip of the rising reed and the wandering sponge. (*Par.* 19.149–157)

Where John uses 15 words, two of which are adjectives (μεστόν, 2x), Nonnus employs 52, of which only three come from the Gospel account: 150, 154 ὄξεος/ὄξος, 151, 157 σπόγγον, 154 ὑσσώπῳ. Moreover, 13 are adjectives, mainly exegetical;[69] one, ἄκρον (153, 157), is a substantival adjective, and one, ὀξύς (150), an adjective used adverbially.[70] Here, however, Nonnus draws on the synoptic Gospels. In fact, both Matthew (Mt 27:48: καὶ εὐθέως δραμὼν εἷς ἐξ αὐτῶν καὶ λαβὼν σπόγγον πλήσας τε ὄξους καὶ περιθεὶς καλάμῳ ἐπότιζεν αὐτόν, "and one of them at once ran and took a sponge, filled it with vinegar, and put it on a reed, and gave it to him to drink") and Mark (Mk 15:36a: δραμὼν δέ τις [καὶ] γεμίσας σπόγγον ὄξους περιθεὶς καλάμῳ ἐπότιζεν αὐτόν, "and one ran and, filling a sponge full of vinegar, put it on a reed and gave it to him to drink") speak of one of the soldiers (~ Nonn., *Par.* 19.150: ἀνὴρ δέ τις) who put a sponge with vinegar on a reed (~ Nonn., *Par.* 19.153: ἰθυπόρου καλάμου) and gave it to Jesus to drink. It is also noteworthy that Nonnus seems to mean that the hyssop was mixed with the vinegar (154).[71]

The strangeness of this *ekphrasis* inserted by Nonnus in his rewriting of Jesus' agony has been highlighted by the Russian scholar Sergej Sergeevič Averincev, who read this passage as a sign of Nonnus' obscure and enigmatic language.[72] Yet, another interpretation remains possible, as I suggested a few years ago.[73] For the poet could recall a text from the imperial period, the ekphrastic poem on the

---

[69] 149 ἑτοῖμον, γείτονι, 150 ἔμπλεον, τις, 151 ὑποβρυχίων, 152 δριμυτάτοιο, διψάδος, 153 ἰθυπόρου, νείατον, 155 ἀντίδοτον, μελισταγέος, 156 θεσπεσίοιο, 157 ἀλήτην.
[70] Moreover, there is a strange numeric coincidence with the previous passage I have dealt with (*Par.* 19.91–100), which has almost the same number of lines as this, because both extend John's original 15 words to 52.
[71] See Mitford 1846, 368; Abbott 1917, 605 argued that "Nonnus [...] read, after τοῦ ὄξους in Jn xix. 29, ὑσσώπῳ παραρτυθέντος '*flavoured with hyssop*' instead of ὑσσώπῳ περιθέντες '*putting round hyssop.*'" For the textual tradition of Jo 19:29, see Nestle/Aland[28] in app.; on the hyssop branch in John see Porter 2015, 222.
[72] Averincev 1988, 203. On the poetry of *ekphrasis* in Nonnus' *Dionysiaca* see Faber 2016.
[73] Accorinti 2009, 94–95.

sponge by Mesomedes of Crete (whose *Hymn to Nemesis*[74] is imitated by Nonnus in *Dionysiaca* 48.378–381), which is transmitted with the title ἔκφρασις σπόγγου. This piece, "a *tour-de-force* lyrical treatment of an unlikely topic [...] is a love-song in which the singer presents the sponge to his mistress and dignifies it with a mythical description of its uses under the sea."[75] The first two lines that may have inspired Nonnus' digression refer to the sponge, and read as follows: (Mesomedes GDRK 9 = Hopkinson 1994, 19) ἄνθος τόδε σοι βυθίων πετρῶν | πολύτρετον ἁλὸς παλάμαις φέρω ("this much-pierced flower of the sea's deep rocks I bring you in my hands");[76] and the Nonnian description (*Par.* 19.151): σπόγγον ὑποβρυχίων ἀδύτων βλάστημα θαλάσσης ("sponge, offshoot of the submarine sanctuaries of the sea").[77]

The last three lines of the Nonnian passage (*Par.* 19.155–157), which begin with the same vowel α (ἀντίδοτον, ἄρτου, ἄκρον), deserve attention for two reasons. First, Nonnus opposes ὄξος ὀλέθρου (154: "the vinegar of death") to Jesus' μελισταγέος νιφετοῖο (155: "honey-soaked snow"),[78] using an antithesis that anticipates the paradox of vinegar and sweet water of Romanos the Melodist in the kontakion *On the Passion of Christ*: (no. 20 Maas-Trypanis 22.1) ὄξος ἐπότισαν τὴν πηγὴν τῶν γλυκερῶν ναμάτων ("they gave the spring of sweet streams vinegar to drink"); here the oxymoron stresses, as Sarah Gador-Whyte points out, "the reversal of all norms in the crucifixion."[79] And second, Nonnus' reference at v. 156 to ἄρτου θεσπεσίοιο ("the divine bread") marks a clear allusion to the bread of life discourse of *Par.* 6.105–163 (~ Jo 6:26–40).[80]

Conclusions

The analysis of the passages discussed above shows that although the language appears *grosso modo* Homeric and Nonnus does appropriate some famous Homeric scenes that were popular among Christian authors, such as the image of Odysseus tied to the mast of the ship, this does not mean that he restricts himself to the Homeric hypotext. Equally important for his poetic and exegetical purpose

---

74 For the melody of this work see Cosgrove 2011, 191–192.
75 Hopkinson 1994, 80–81.
76 On this poem see Hopkinson 1994, 19 (text), 80–82 (commentary); Whitmarsh 2013, 168–171.
77 Cf. Paul. Sil., *AP* 6.66.7 (= 19.7 Viansino).
78 The same clausula occurs in Triph. 119: see Miguélez-Cavero 2013, 196–197.
79 Gador-Whyte 2017, 38.
80 See Franchi 2013, 111–127.

is an exuberant language (e.g. the abundance of adjectives), but also the influence of other models, such as Hesiod's fable of the hawk and the nightingale, whose didactic poem only shares the hexameter verse with Nonnus' *Paraphrase*, and even an imperial ekphrastic poem by Mesomedes of Crete.

On the other hand, the parallels from Sedulius and the centos show that Nonnus was not alone in reworking these images, but, just as the symbol of Odysseus on the mast or the cosmological symbolism of the crucifixion and the references to the four-cornered world, Nonnus' elaboration of John seems to align with contemporary trends in rewriting the Gospel. His poem turns out to be the product of a mixing of literary forms that transcends genre,[81] modulating from verbal intertextuality with multiple texts to exegetical approaches.[82] For Nonnus transforms and distorts both Homeric epic and Gospel prose.[83]

Thus, by combining poetry with exegesis,[84] the *Paraphrase* aims both at departing from the constraints of its hypotext and at becoming a quasi-poetic commentary of John's Gospel, as if Nonnus wanted to smooth the way for some medieval poetic Psalm paraphrases[85] and Erasmus' *Paraphrase upon the New Testament*.[86] There is no doubt that this kind of poetry with its mixture of genres must have been intended "to give pleasure to lovers of learning and literature."[87]

Bibliography

Abbott, E.A. 1917. *The fourfold Gospel. Section V. The founding of the New Kingdom or Life reached through Death*, Cambridge.

Abram, N. (ed.) 1623. *Nonni Panopolitani Paraphrasis Sancti secundum Ioannem Evangelij. Accesserunt notae P.N.A. Societatis Jesu*, Paris.

Accorinti, D. (ed.) 1986–1987. *Nonno di Panopoli. Parafrasi del Vangelo di S. Giovanni. Canto T (= XIX)* (diss.), Firenze.

Accorinti, D. 2009. "Poésie et poétique dans l'oeuvre de Nonnos de Panopolis", in P. Odorico/P.A. Agapitos/M. Hinterberger (eds.), *'Doux remède ...'. Poésie et poétique à Byzance. Actes du IVe colloque international philologique 'EPMHNEIA', Paris, 23–24–25 février 2006*, Paris, 67–98.

---

[81] Cf. Johnson 2006, 84 n. 61 (on the practice of Jewish paraphrase).
[82] Cf. recently Smolak 2016.
[83] See Averincev 1988, 203. On Nonnus' creative reception of Homeric language see Spanoudakis 2014, 6.
[84] For this aspect see the collection of essays edited by Otten/Pollmann 2007.
[85] See Orth 2007.
[86] On Erasmus' theory of paraphrase as 'a kind of commentary' see Cottier 2012.
[87] I would like to thank Fotini Hadjittofi and Anna Lefteratou for their careful editing of my text.

Accorinti, D. 2014. "Simone Weil, reader of the *Dionysiaca*", in K. Spanoudakis (ed.), *Nonnus of Panopolis in context I. Poetry and cultural milieu in Late Antiquity with a section on Nonnus and the modern world*, Berlin, 461–486.

Acosta-Hughes, B. 2016. "Composing the masters: an essay on Nonnus and Hellenistic poetry", in D. Accorinti (ed.), *Brill's Companion to Nonnus of Panopolis*, Leiden, 507–528.

Adrados, F.R. 2003. *History of the Graeco-Latin fable, III: inventory and documentation of the Graeco-Latin fable*, Leiden.

Agosti, G. 2001. "L'epica biblica nella tarda antichità greca. Autori e lettori nel IV e V secolo", in F. Stella (ed.), *La scrittura infinita. Bibbia e poesia in età medievale e umanistica (Atti del Convegno di Firenze, 26–28 giugno 1997)*, Firenze, 67–104.

Agosti, G. (ed.) 2003. *Nonno di Panopoli. Parafrasi del Vangelo di San Giovanni. Canto V*, Firenze.

Agosti, G. 2011. "Usurper, imiter, communiquer: le dialogue interculturel dans la poésie grecque chrétienne de l'antiquité tardive", in N. Belayche/J.-D. Dubois (eds.), *L'oiseau et le poisson. Cohabitations religieuses dans les mondes grec et romain*, Paris, 275–299.

Agosti, G. 2016. "Esiodo nella tarda antichità: prime prospezioni", *SemRom*, 5, 179–194.

Alrifaee, A. 2015. *Le dessein littéraire de Juvencus: étude de la nature paraphrastique et épique des Evangeliorum libri quattuor* (diss.), Ottawa (url: https://ruor.uottawa.ca/handle/10393/33175).

Anderson, P.N./Just, F./Thatcher, T. (eds.) 2007. *John, Jesus, and History, I. Critical appraisals of critical views*, Atlanta (GA).

Audano, S. 2012. "Le molte strade del centone virgiliano cristiano: in margine a tre recenti edizioni", *Sileno*, 38, 225–255.

Averincev, S.S. 1988. *L'anima e lo specchio. L'universo della poetica bizantina*, Bologna (original edn.: *Poetika rannevizantijskoj literatury*, Moscow, 1977).

Baldwin, M.C. 2005. *Whose Acts of Peter? Text and historical context of the Actus Vercellenses*, Tübingen.

Bannert, H./Kröll, N. 2016. "Nonnus and the Homeric Poems", in D. Accorinti (ed.), *Brill's Companion to Nonnus of Panopolis*, Leiden, 481–506.

Barham, F./Pitman, I. 1870. *A rhymed harmony of the Gospels*, London.

Bolyki, J. 1998. "'Head downwards': the cross of Peter in the lights of the Apocryphal Acts, of the New Testament and of the society-transforming claim of Early Christianity", in J.N. Bremmer (ed.), *The Apocryphal Acts of Peter. Magic, miracles and Gnosticism*, Leuven, 111–122.

Browning, R. 1995. "Tradition and originality in literary criticism and scholarship", in A.R. Littlewood (ed.), *Originality in Byzantine literature, art and music. A collection of essays*, Oxford, 17–28.

Carter, W. 2003. *Pontius Pilate. Portraits of a Roman governor*, Collegeville (MN).

Casey, M. 2011. "The role of Aramaic in reconstructing the teaching of Jesus", in T. Holmén/S.E. Porter (eds.), *Handbook for the study of the historical Jesus*, 4 vols., Leiden, II, 1343–1375.

Chapman, D.W. 2008. *Ancient Jewish and Christian perceptions of crucifixion*, Tübingen.

Consolino, F.E. 2005. "Il senso del passato: generi letterari e rapporti con la tradizione nella 'parafrasi biblica' latina", in I. Gualandri/F. Conca/R. Passarella (eds.), *Nuovo e antico nella cultura greco-latina di IV–VI secolo*, Milano, 447–526.

Cosgrove, C.H. 2011. *An ancient Christian hymn with musical notation. Papyrus Oxyrhynchus 1786*, Tübingen.

Cottier, J.-F. 2012. "Erasmus's *Paraphrases*: A 'new kind of commentary'?", in J. Rice Henderson (ed.), with the assistance of P.M. Swan; trans. by K. Mak/N. Senior, *The unfolding of words. Commentary in the age of Erasmus*, Toronto, 27–54.

Cullhed, A. 2015. *The shadow of Creusa. Negotiating fictionality in late antique Latin literature*, trans. by M. Knight, Berlin.

Curran, J. 2012. "Virgilizing Christianity in late antique Rome", in L. Grig/G. Kelly (eds.), *Two Romes. Rome and Constantinople in Late Antiquity*, Oxford, 325–344.

Czachesz, I. 2003. "The Gospels and cognitive science", in A.A. Macdonald/M.W. Twomey/ G.J. Reinink (eds.), *Learned Antiquity. Scholarship and society in the Near-East, the Greco-Roman world, and the Early Medieval West*, Leuven, 25–36.

De Stefani, C. (ed.) 2002. *Nonno di Panopoli. Parafrasi del Vangelo di S. Giovanni. Canto I*, Bologna.

De Stefani, C. 2016. "Brief notes on the manuscript tradition of Nonnus' works", in D. Accorinti (ed.), *Brill's Companion to Nonnus of Panopolis*, Leiden, 671–690.

van Dijk, G.-J. 1997. *ΑΙΝΟΙ, ΛΟΓΟΙ, ΜΥΘΟΙ. Fables in archaic, classical, and Hellenistic Greek literature. With a study of the theory and terminology of the genre*, Leiden.

Dijkstra, R. 2008. *La Passion dans les épopées bibliques de Juvencus, Proba et Nonnos*, Nijmegen.

Dinkler, M.B. 2013. *Silent statements. Narrative representations of speech and silence in the Gospel of Luke*, Berlin.

Elliot, J.K. 1993. *The Apocryphal New Testament. A collection of Apocryphal Christian Literature in an English translation based on M.R. James*, Oxford.

Elsner, J. 2017. "Late Narcissus. Classicism and culture in a late Roman cento", in J. Elsner/ J. Hernández Lobato (eds.), *The poetics of late Latin literature*, Oxford, 176–204.

Faber, R.A. 2016. "Nonnus and the poetry of *Ekphrasis* in the *Dionysiaca*", in D. Accorinti (ed.), *Brill's Companion to Nonnus of Panopolis*, Leiden, 443–459.

Fassina, A./Lucarini, C.M. (eds.) 2015. *Faltonia Betitia Proba. Cento Vergilianus*, Berlin.

Faulkner, A. 2014. "Faith and fidelity in biblical epic. The *Metaphrasis Psalmorum*, Nonnus, and the Theory of Translation", in K. Spanoudakis (ed.), *Nonnus of Panopolis in context. Poetry and cultural milieu in Late Antiquity with a section on Nonnus and the modern world*, Berlin, 195–210.

Franchi, R. (ed.) 2013. *Nonno di Panopoli. Parafrasi del Vangelo di S. Giovanni. Canto VI*, Bologna.

Franchi, R. 2016. "Approaching the 'Spiritual Gospel': Nonnus as interpreter of John", in D. Accorinti (ed.), *Brill's Companion to Nonnus of Panopolis*, Leiden, 240–266.

Friesen, C.J.P. 2015. *Reading Dionysus. Euripides' Bacchae and the cultural contestations of Greeks, Jews, Romans, and Christians*, Tübingen.

Fryde, E. 2000. *The Early Palaeologan Renaissance (1261–c. 1360)*, Leiden.

Gador-Whyte, S. 2017. *Theology and poetry in Early Byzantium. The Kontakia of Romanos the Melodist*, Cambridge.

Goldhill, S. 1986. *Reading Greek tragedy*, Cambridge.

Golega, J. 1966. "Zum Text der Johannesmetabole des Nonnos", *ByzZ*, 59, 9–36.

González-Rivas Fernández, A. 2018. "Aeschylus and *Frankenstein, or The Modern Prometheus*, by Mary Shelley", in R. Futo Kennedy (ed.), *Brill's Companion to the reception of Aeschylus*, Leiden, 292–322.

Görlach, M. 2004. *Text types and the history of English*, Berlin.

Granger Cook, J. 2014. *Crucifixion in the mediterranean world*, Tübingen.

Green, R.P.H. 2006. *Latin epics of the New Testament. Juvencus, Sedulius, Arator*, Oxford.
Griffiths, A. 1995. "Non-aristocratic elements in archaic poetry", in A. Powell (ed.), *The Greek world*, London, 85–103.
Grillmeier, A./Hainthaler, T. 1996. *Christ in Christian tradition*, II: *from the Council of Chalcedon (451) to Gregory the Great (590–604); part four: the Church of Alexandria with Nubia and Ethiopia after 451*, trans. by O.C. Dean, London; original edn.: *Jesus der Christus im Glauben der Kirche*, II/4: *Die Kirche von Alexandrien mit Nubien und Äthiopien*, Freiburg im Breisgau, 1990.
Hadjittofi, F. 2018. "ποικιλόνωτος ἀνήρ: clothing metaphors and Nonnus' ambiguous Christology in the *Paraphrase of the Gospel according to John*", VChr, 72, 165–183.
Hopkinson, N. (ed.) 1994. *Greek poetry of the imperial period. An anthology*, Cambridge.
Hutchinson, E.J. 2016. "The presence of Virgil in the miracles of Sedulius' *Paschale Carmen*", in S. McGill/E.J. Watts (eds.), *A Companion to late antique literature*, Malden (MA), 265–296.
Johnson, S.F. 2006. *The Life and miracles of Thekla. A literary study*, Washington (DC).
Kaufmann, H. 2017. "Intertextuality in late Latin poetry", in J. Elsner/J. Hernández Lobato (eds.), *The poetics of late Latin literature*, Oxford, 149–175.
Koch, H.A. 1856. "*Coniectanea Nonniana*", RhM, 10, 167–194.
König, J. 2012. *Saints and symposiasts. The literature of food and the symposium in Greco-Roman and Early Christian culture*, Cambridge.
Larsen, K.B. 2008. *Recognizing the stranger. Recognition scenes in the Gospel of John*, Leiden.
Lasek, A.M. 2016. "Nonnus and the play of genres", in D. Accorinti (ed.), *Brill's Companion to Nonnus of Panopolis*, Leiden, 402–421.
Lefteratou, A. 2016. "Jesus' late antique epiphanies: healing the blind in the Christian epics of Eudocia and Nonnus", in J.J. Clauss/M. Cuypers/A. Kahane (eds.), *The gods of Greek hexameter poetry. From the Archaic Age to Late Antiquity and beyond*, Stuttgart, 268–287.
Licona, M.R. 2017. *Why are there differences in the Gospels? What we can learn from ancient biography*, New York.
Lipsius, R.A. (ed.) 1891. *Acta Petri. Acta Pauli. Acta Petri et Pauli. Acta Pauli et Theclae. Acta Thaddaei*, in *Acta Apostolorum Apocrypha, post Constantinum Tischendorf denuo ediderunt Ricardus Adelbertus Lipsius et Maximilianus Bonnet*, I, Leipzig (repr. Darmstadt, 1959).
Livrea, E./Accorinti, D. 1988. "Nonno e la Crocifissione", SIFC III s. 6, 262–278 (repr. in: E. Livrea (ed.), 1993. *ΚΡΕCCONA ΒΑΣΚΑΝΙΗC. Quindici studi di poesia ellenistica*, Firenze, 201–224).
Maas, P./Trypanis, C.A. (eds.) 1963. *Sancti Romani Melodi Cantica: cantica genuina*, Oxford.
MacDonald, D.R. 1994. *Christianizing Homer. The Odyssey, Plato, and the Acts of Andrew*, Oxford.
MacIver, C.A. 2016. "Nonnus and imperial Greek poetry", in D. Accorinti (ed.), *Brill's Companion to Nonnus of Panopolis*, Leiden, 529–548.
Marcovich, M. (ed.) 1986. *Hippolytus, Refutatio omnium haeresium*, Berlin.
Markschies, C. 2005. "Odysseus und Orpheus – christlich gelesen", in R. von Haehling (ed.), *Griechische Mythologie und frühes Christentum*, Darmstadt, 226–253 (repr. in: M. Vöhler (ed.), 2005. *Mythenkorrekturen: zu einer paradoxalen Form der Mythenrezeption*, Berlin, 69–92).
McBrine, P. 2017. *Biblical epics in Late Antiquity and Anglo-Saxon England. Divina in Laude Voluntas*, Toronto.
McGill, S. 2007. "Virgil, Christianity, and the *Cento Probae*", in J.H.D. Scourfield (ed.), *Texts and culture in Late Antiquity. Inheritance, authority, and change*, Swansea, 173–193.

McGill, S. 2016a. "Arms and Amen: Virgil in Juvencus' *Evangeliorum libri IV*", in S. McGill/ J. Pucci (eds.), *Classics renewed. Reception and innovation in the Latin poetry of Late Antiquity*, Heidelberg, 47–75.

McGill, S. 2016b. *Juvencus' Four books of the Gospels*, London.

Miguélez-Cavero, L. 2013. *Triphiodorus, The sack of Troy. A general study and a commentary*, Berlin.

Miguélez-Cavero, L. 2016. "Nonnus and the novel", in D. Accorinti (ed.), *Brill's Companion to Nonnus of Panopolis*, Leiden, 549–573.

Miguélez-Cavero, L./McGill, S. 2018. "Christian Poetry", in S. McGill/E.J. Watts (eds.), *A Companion to late antique literature*, Malden (MA), 259–280.

Mitford, J. 1846. "On the hyssop of Scripture", *Gentleman's Magazine*, 25, 367–369.

Mori, R. 2013. *Sedulio: tra prosa e poesia. L'Opus Paschale e il Carmen Paschale*, Padova.

Most, G.W. (ed.) 2006. *Hesiod. Theogony, Works and Days, Testimonia*, Cambridge (MA).

Murray, A.T. 1998. *Homer. Odyssey*, revised by G.E. Dimock (first edition: 1919), 2 vols., Cambridge (MA).

Murray, A.T. 1999. *Homer. Iliad*, revised by W.F. Waytt (first edition: 1924), 2 vols., Cambridge (MA).

Nazzaro, A.V. 2008a. "Motivi e forme della poesia cristiana antica tra Scrittura e tradizione classica", in *Motivi e forme della poesia cristiana antica tra Scrittura e tradizione classica. XXXVI Incontro di studiosi dell'antichità cristiana, Roma, 3–5 maggio 2007*, 2 vols., Roma, I, 9–56.

Nazzaro, A.V. 2008b. "Parafrasi (biblica e agiografica)", in A. Di Berardino (ed.), *Nuovo dizionario patristico e di antichità cristiane*, 3 vols., Genova, III, 3909–3915.

Nelson, S.A. 1998. *God and the land. The metaphysics of farming in Hesiod and Vergil*, New York.

Norris, O. 2014. "The sources for the Temptations episode in the *Paschale Carmen* of Sedulius", in H.A.G. Houghton (ed.), *Early readers, scholars and editors of the New Testament. Papers from the eighth Birmingham colloquium on the textual criticism of the New Testament*, Piscataway (NJ), 67–92.

Norris, O. 2016. *Sedulius's Gospel sources in the Paschale Carmen and the Paschale Opus* (diss.), London (url: https://kclpure.kcl.ac.uk/portal/files/61101200/2016_Norris_Oliver_0715795_ethesis.pdf).

Orth, P. 2007. "Metrische Paraphrase als Kommentar: Zwei unedierte mittelalterliche Versifikationen der Psalmen im Vergleich", *JMLat*, 17, 189–209.

Otten, W.O./Pollmann, K. (eds.) 2007. *Poetry and exegesis in premodern Latin Christianity. The encounter between classical and Christian strategies of interpretation*, Leiden.

Parsenios, G.L. 2010. *Rhetoric and drama in the Johannine lawsuit motif*, Tübingen.

Perris, S. 2015. "Bacchant women", in R. Lauriola/K.N. Demetriou (eds.), *Brill's Companion to the reception of Euripides*, Leiden, 507–548.

Petersen, N.R. 1994. "Can one speak of a Gospel genre?", *Neotestamentica* 28, 3, 137–158.

Pickering, F.P. 1980. "Justus Lipsius' *De Cruce libri tres* (1593), or The historian's dilemma", in F.P. Pickering (ed.), *Essays on Medieval German literature and iconography*, Cambridge, 59–74; originally published in *Festgabe für L.L. Hammerich, aus Anlaß seines siebzigsten Geburtstags*, Copenhagen, 1962, 199–214.

Pollmann, K. 2017a. *The baptized Muse. Early Christian poetry as cultural authority*, Oxford.

Pollmann, K. 2017b. "Jesus Christ and Dionysus. Rewriting Euripides in the Byzantine cento *Christus Patiens*", in K. Pollmann 2017a, 140–157; originally published as "Jesus Christus und Bacchus. Überlegungen zu dem griechischen Cento *Christus patiens*", *JÖByz* 47, 1997, 87–106.

Pollmann, K. 2017c. "Tradition and innovation. The transformation of classical literary genres in Christian Late Antiquity", in K. Pollmann 2017a, 19–36; originally published in J. Ulrich/A.-C. Jacobsen/D. Brakke (eds.), *Invention, rewriting, usurpation. Discursive fights over religious traditions in Antiquity*, Frankfurt a.M., 2012, 103–120.

Pontani, F. 2015. "Scholarship in the Byzantine Empire (529–1453)", in F. Montanari/S. Matthaios/A. Rengakos (eds.), *Brill's Companion to Ancient Greek scholarship*, 2 vols., Leiden, I, 297–455.

Porter, S.E. 2015. *John, his Gospel, and Jesus. In pursuit of the Johannine voice*, Grand Rapids (MI).

Prieur, J.-M. 2006. *La croix dans la littérature chrétienne des premiers siècles*, Bern.

Samuelsson, G. 2013. *Crucifixion in Antiquity. An inquiry into the background and significance of the New Testament terminology of crucifixion*, Tübingen.

Sandnes, K.O. 2011. *The Gospel 'according to Homer and Virgil'. Cento and canon*, Leiden.

Sandnes, K.O. 2016. "A respectable Gospel: the Passion 'according to Homer' in Eudocia's *Homerocentones*", *Svensk Exegetisk Årsbok*, 81, 25–48.

Scheindler, A. (ed.) 1881. *Nonni Panopolitani Paraphrasis S. Evangelii Ioannei*, Leipzig.

Schembra, R. (ed.) 2007. *Homerocentones*, Turnhout.

Schembra, R. 2006. *La prima redazione dei centoni omerici. Traduzione e commento*, Alessandria.

Schiffman, L.H. 2006. "Biblical exegesis in the Passion narratives and the Dead Sea Scrolls", in I. Kalimi/P.J. Haas (eds.), *Biblical interpretation in Judaism and Christianity*, New York, 117–130.

Schottenius Cullhed, S. 2015. *Proba the Prophet. The Christian Virgilian Cento of Faltonia Betitia Proba*, Leiden.

Schottenius Cullhed, S. 2016. "Patterning past and future: Virgil in Proba's biblical cento", in S. McGill/J. Pucci (eds.), *Classics renewed. Reception and innovation in the Latin poetry of Late Antiquity*, Heidelberg, 97–110.

Sherry, L.F. 1991. *The hexameter Paraphrase of St. John attributed to Nonnus of Panopolis. Prolegomenon and translation* (diss.), New York.

Sieber, F. 2016. "Nonnus' Christology", in D. Accorinti (ed.), *Brill's Companion to Nonnus of Panopolis*, Leiden, 308–326.

Sieber, F. 2017. "Words and their meaning. On the chronology of the *Paraphrasis of St John's Gospel*", in H. Bannert/N. Kröll (eds.), *Nonnus of Panopolis in Context II. Poetry, religion, and society*, Leiden, 156–165.

Simelidis, C. 2018. "Παράφραση και ερμηνεία: ο ποιητής Νόννος Πανοπολίτης και το Κατά Ιωάννην" ('Paraphrase and Exegesis: Nonnus of Panopolis and the Gospel of John'), *Δελτίο Βιβλικών Μελετών*, 33B, 65–79.

Sineri, V. (ed.) 2011. *Il centone di Proba*, Acireale.

Smolak, K. 1984. "Beiträge zur Erklärung der *Metabole* des Nonnos", *JÖByz*, 34, 1–14.

Smolak, K. 2016. "'Ἄρτοι αὐτόματοι' – *elementa mundi*. Das exegetische Potential der 'wunderbaren Speisenvermehrung' im Vergleich (Nonnos, *Metabole* 6, 25–55 und Prudentius, *Apotheosis* 706–735)", in R. Merker/G. Danek/E. Klecker (eds.), *Trilogie. Epos – Drama – Epos. Festschrift für Herbert Bannert*, Wien, 371–393.

Smyth, D.B. 1999. *The trauma of the Cross. How the followers of Jesus came to understand the Crucifixion*, New York.

Sowers, B. 2010. "Retelling and misreading Jesus: Eudocia's *Homeric Cento*", in N. Calvert-Koyzis/H. Weir (eds.), *Breaking boundaries. Female biblical interpreters who challenged the status quo*, New York.

Spanoudakis, K. (ed.) 2014. *Nonnus of Panopolis. Paraphrasis of the Gospel of John XI*, Oxford.

Spanoudakis, K. 2016. "Pagan themes in the *Paraphrase*", in D. Accorinti (ed.), *Brill's Companion to Nonnus of Panopolis*, Leiden, 601–624.

Springer, C.P.E. 2013. *Sedulius, The Paschal Song and Hymns*, Atlanta (GA).

Suciu, A. (ed.) 2017. *The Berlin-Strasbourg Apocryphon. A Coptic Apostolic memoir*, Tübingen.

Sullivan, S.D. 1996. "The psychic term ἦτορ: its nature and relation to person in Homer and the *Homeric Hymns*", *Emerita*, 64, 11–29.

Tiedke, H. 1873. *Quaestionum Nonnianarum specimen*, Berlin.

Toohey, P. 1992. *Reading epic. An introduction to the ancient narratives*, London.

Tuilier, A. (ed.) 1969. *Grégoire de Nazianze, La Passion du Christ. Tragédie*, Paris.

Usher, M.D. 1998. *Homeric stitchings. The Homeric Centos of the empress Eudocia*, Lanham (MD).

Viansino, G. (ed.) 1963. *Paolo Silenziario. Epigrammi*, Milano.

Voicu, S.J. 2007. "La croce negli apocrifi", in B. Ulianich/U. Parente (eds.), *La Croce. Iconografia e interpretazione (secoli I-inizio XVI). Atti del convegno internazionale di studi (Napoli, 6–11 dicembre 1999)*, Napoli, 119–126.

Whitby, Mary 2007. "The Bible hellenized: Nonnus' *Paraphrase of St. John's Gospel* and 'Eudocia's' *Homeric Centos*", in J.H.D. Scourfield (ed.), *Texts and culture in Late Antiquity. Inheritance, authority, and change*, Swansea, 195–231.

Whitby, Mary 2016. "Nonnus and biblical epic", in D. Accorinti (ed.), *Brill's Companion to Nonnus of Panopolis*, Leiden, 215–239.

Whitby, Mary/Roberts, M. 2018. "Epic poetry", in S. McGill/E.J. Watts (eds.), *A Companion to late antique literature*, Malden (MA), 221–240.

Whitmarsh, T. 2013. "The Cretan lyre paradox: Mesomedes, Hadrian and the poetics of patronage", in T. Whitmarsh (ed.), *Beyond the Second Sophistic. Adventures in Greek Postclassicism*, Berkeley (CA), 154–175; originally published in B.E. Borg (ed.), *Paideia. The world of the Second Sophistic*, Berlin, 2004, 377–402.

Ypsilanti, M. 2016. "The reception of Homeric vocabulary in Nonnus' *Paraphrase of St. John's Gospel*: examination of themes and formulas in selected passages", in A. Efstathiou/I. Karamanou (eds.), *Homeric receptions across generic and cultural contexts*, Berlin, 215–224.

Zilling, H.M. 2015. "Die Mimesis des Heros: pagane Helden in christlicher Deutung", in H. Leppin (ed.), *Antike Mythologie in christlichen Kontexten der Spätantike*, Berlin, 139–166.

Fotini Hadjittofi
Nonnus' *Paraphrase of the Gospel According to John* as Didactic Epic

Didactic is an ill-defined and much-maligned poetic genre.[1] While modern scholars struggle to stipulate the criteria by which a poem can be termed 'didactic',[2] ancient grammarians generally did not even set such a (sub)genre apart from narrative epic.[3] As well as being difficult to pin down, didactic can also be difficult to appreciate: its aesthetic 'otherness', by our standards, can compel a modern critic to ask, "Why read didactic epic?"[4]

As opposed to modern audiences, the ancients definitely appreciated didactic, but were not entirely sure whether they appreciated it *qua* poetry. In the fourth century BCE, Aristotle was willing to exclude Empedocles' verses from the category of poetry *tout court*, based on their lack of *mimesis*.[5] For Aristotle, at least, what makes 'good poetry' is a good (mythological) plot – and plot is an element that didactic manifestly lacks. According to both Plato and Plutarch, when Socrates felt obliged, by a dream, to turn his hand to poetry, he decided to

---

[1] I am grateful to the audience at the Lisbon workshop, especially Gianfranco Agosti and Anna Lefteratou, for their helpful comments. I would also like to acknowledge the financial support of FCT – Fundação para a Ciência e a Tecnologia – through project PTDC/LLT- LES/30930/2017 (national funds).
[2] See, among others, Dalzell 1996, 9–31; Toohey 1996, 2–19; Gale 2004; Vesperini 2015. Volk's 2002 influential definition of four criteria (explicit didactic intent; a teacher-student constellation; poetic self-consciousness; poetic simultaneity) has also come under criticism – see Sider 2014.
[3] Quintilian, for example, considers Hesiod (*Inst.* 10.52) and Lucretius (10.87) epic poets. The Latin grammarian Diomedes (second half of the 4th century) mentions Empedocles, Lucretius, Aratus, Cicero, and Virgil's *Georgics* as examples of the genre he calls *enarrativum | enuntiativum | exegetikon*, where the poet speaks in his own voice throughout the poem. This category was traditionally reserved for lyric, and indeed Proclus classifies "gnomic" (γνωμολογικά) and "georgic" (γεωργικά) under lyric genres related to circumstance; see Photius 320a. The clearest trace of a didactic genre in ancient criticism is very brief: in the *Tractatus Coislinianus*, possibly by Theophrastus, non-mimetic poetry is subdivided into the historical and "didactic" (παιδευτική), which is further divided into the "expository" (ὑφηγητική) and "theoretical." On this tantalizing text and its authorship see Nesselrath 1990, 102–146.
[4] Toohey 1996, 19.
[5] See *Poet.* 1447b17–1447b20. The question continued to be debated well into the imperial period; see, e.g., Lactant., *Div. inst.* 2.12.

set Aesop's fables into verse, recognizing that he would be an implausible "manufacturer of fictions", which are the essential ingredients of poetry.[6] Plutarch goes on to offer a version of Aristotle's argument: "But the epics of Empedocles and Parmenides, the *Theriaca* of Nicander, and the collections of maxims by Theognis are, rather, speeches which have borrowed meter and sublimity (ὄγκος) as a vehicle from poetry, so that they might escape what is pedestrian [i.e., prose]."[7] Despite the dearth of explicit theorization, then, it is clear that ancient criticism was aware of a didactic tradition that included both archaic and Hellenistic poets, and whose distinguishing feature was the absence of narrative.

Given the cardinal importance of narrativity (or lack thereof) in demarcating didactic from other forms of epic, it might seem strange that this chapter undertakes to examine under the rubric of 'didactic' Nonnus' *Paraphrase of the Gospel According to John*, a poem that does have a narrative structure and whose narrator never addresses a specific audience nor indicates (at least not explicitly) that he aims to teach. In focusing on didactic the objective of this contribution will not be to champion the importance of this subgenre over narrative epic, but rather to highlight the relevance of the long didactic tradition for Nonnus' Christian poem – a relevance that has so far been overlooked. The first part of this chapter will present a more restricted version of the argument, suggesting that the *Paraphrase* 'modulates' didactic specifically in relation to Jesus' speech. The second part will offer a more tentative but broader argument, reading the whole poem as a 'transposition' of John's Gospel into a form which ancient readers might have interpreted as, or associated with, didactic.

---

[6] See Pl., *Phd.* 60c–61b and Plut., *Mor.* 16b-d (= *Quomodo adul.* 2). Plato has Socrates admit he versified Aesop because αὐτὸς οὐκ ἦ μυθολογικός (61b5), while Plutarch says the philosopher would be a bad ψευδῶν δημιουργός (16c6–7). In the 4th century CE, Julian the Emperor (*Or.* 7.3.9–17 = 207b) claims that Archilochus employed myths in his poetry because "he knew well that poetry which lacks myth is mere versification, and is deprived of, one could say, its own essence" (σαφῶς δὲ ἐγνωκὼς ὅτι στερομένη μύθου ποίησις ἐποποιΐα μόνον ἐστίν, ἐστέρηται δέ, ὡς ἂν εἴποι τις, ἑαυτῆς). All translations are my own.

[7] 16c11–16d1: τὰ δ' Ἐμπεδοκλέους ἔπη καὶ Παρμενίδου καὶ θηριακὰ Νικάνδρου καὶ γνωμολογίαι Θεόγνιδος λόγοι εἰσὶ κιχράμενοι παρὰ ποιητικῆς ὥσπερ ὄχημα τὸ μέτρον καὶ τὸν ὄγκον, ἵνα τὸ πεζὸν διαφύγωσιν. For rich commentary on this passage see Hunter/Russell 2011 *ad loc.*

Jesus the teacher: Modulating didactic

The possibility of labeling Latin biblical epic as didactic has been floated and dismissed, in spite of the strong didactic markers some such poems exhibit.[8] Roberts, for example, points out that Arator, in his *De actibus apostolorum*, speaks more as a *predicator* than a *narrator*; and yet the poem, "[d]espite its instructional intent, differs from didactic poetry in its reliance on the order of the biblical narrative rather than a sequence of argument."[9] Nonnus' *Paraphrase* obviously shares this reliance on the structure of biblical narrative, which it replicates without any divergences. Compared, however, to the Latin biblical epics, which are largely episodic and narrate events, the *Paraphrase* is considerably more discursive: just as John's Gospel, it includes extensive passages where the plotline does not advance, as no action takes place apart from Jesus speaking to and instructing single interlocutors, the restricted group of his disciples or larger crowds.[10]

In fact, five whole Books (13–17) are dedicated to a long speech, in which Jesus gives advice to his disciples regarding their behavior and faith after his departure from this world, and tells them how they should confront the difficulties that lie ahead. The speech even includes a kind of 'georgics' in the parable of the true vine (Book 15), where Jesus instructs his disciples how to grow not plants but themselves as offshoots of the eternal and divine plant. Kennedy has characterized the corresponding chapters (13–17) of John's Gospel as an extensive epideictic speech (akin to a *consolatio*),[11] but perhaps 'didactic' would be a better label, at least for the *Paraphrase*, which is composed in dactylic hexameters, given that Jesus is presented repeatedly and obsessively as a teacher throughout this text. While in some cases this emphasis is derived from John and even replicates the phrasing of the Gospel itself, for example by calling Jesus a διδάσκαλος (3:2 = *Par.*

---

8 See, e.g., the explicit didacticism in Claudius Marius Victorius, *Aleth.* 104–105: *dum teneros formare animos et corda paramus | ad verum virtutis iter puerilibus annis* ("as I prepare to shape tender minds and hearts | to the true path of virtue in their youthful years") – in just these two verses we find three out of the four criteria stipulated by Volk 2002 (above, n. 2): explicit didactic intent, a teacher-student constellation, and poetic self-consciousness.
9 Roberts 1985, 179. Cf. Consolino 2005, 515–526.
10 This discursiveness is pointed out by ancient readers (e.g., Greg. Naz., *carm.* I.1.23 = *PG* 37.494: παῦρα δ' Ἰωάννου δήεις ἱερῇ ἐνὶ βίβλῳ | θαύματα δή, πολλοὺς δὲ λόγους Χριστοῖο ἄνακτος. "Now in the sacred book of John you will find few | miracles, but many speeches of Christ the king"), and is precisely what won John the Evangelist the title Θεολόγος.
11 See Kennedy 1984, 73–85.

3.10),[12] very frequently it is the poet who introduces the vocabulary of teaching and learning, without any verbal prompt from the Gospel.[13] Already in Book 1, John the Baptist describes those who have not (yet) received Jesus' divine teaching as an "uninstructed, ignorant crowd" (1.112: ἀδίδακτον ἀπευθέα λαόν), whereas no such notion of teaching and learning is present in the Gospel. In several other cases the verb διδάσκω characterizes Jesus' speeches, where the Gospel uses unmarked verbs such as 'to speak' (λαλῶ or λέγω),[14] 'announce' (ἀγγέλλω),[15] or 'reply' (ἀποκρίνομαι).[16]

In one example, Nonnus turns Johannine Jesus' "the things I speak" (12:50: ἃ οὖν ἐγὼ λαλῶ) into "the things I teach you" (12.199: καὶ ὑμέας ὅσσα διδάσκω), thus not only adding the idea of Jesus' speech as instruction but also bringing the audience to the fore – ὑμέας.[17] The second person (either singular or plural) is central for didactic poetry, whose discourse is always directed at an addressee – the so-called 'didactic "you"', first exemplified in Hesiod's feckless brother, Perses.[18] In the *Paraphrase*, as in John's Gospel, Jesus can (somewhat disconcertingly) move from a singular to a plural 'you' while addressing specific interlocutors: for example, in his long speech to Nicodemus Jesus starts by addressing him personally, in the singular, (3.50: Ἰσραὴλ σὺ μέν ἐσσι διδάσκαλος, οὐ νοέεις δέ;

---

[12] See, further, *Par.* 6.181: διδάσκων (= Jo 6:59); 7.52: ἐδίδαξεν (Jo 7:14 ἐδίδασκεν); 7.59: διδαχή (= Jo 7:16).
[13] Origen, who wrote a commentary on John's Gospel, was one of the first thinkers to conceptualize Jesus primarily as a teacher. For example, in the preface to his *De principiis* he terms believers "those who derive knowledge ... from the very words and teachings of Christ" (*scientiam ... ab ipsis verbis Christi doctrinaque suscipiunt*). For a possible Origenist reading of the *Paraphrase* see Hadjittofi 2018.
[14] See, e.g., *Par.* 3.57: διδάσκομεν (Jo 3:11: λαλοῦμεν); 14.19: ἴαχησε διδάσκων (Jo 14:6: λέγει). For 5.132–133, where διδάσκων | ... μετέρχομαι 'translates' John's λέγω (5:34), Agosti 2003 *ad loc.* notes that the verb διδάσκω frequently appears at the end of the verse, and argues that its use in this case reveals Nonnus' dependence on Cyril's (*Jo.* 2.9 = *PG* 73.397c) διδάσκων δὲ πάλιν.
[15] *Par.* 4.128: διδάξει (Jo 4:25: ἀναγγελεῖ).
[16] In *Par.* 4.61, 8.88, and 9.15 Nonnus uses ἐδίδαξεν where John (4:13, 8:34, and 9:3 respectively) has ἀπεκρίθη. In 14.88 he replaces John's ἀπεκρίθη (14:23) with ἀγόρευεν ... διδάσκων.
[17] The following verse makes it clear that Jesus is an extraordinary kind of teacher, relaying superior knowledge (it is what his Father told him; 12.200: ὥσπερ ἐμοὶ κατέλεξε πατὴρ ἐμός, ὡς ἀγορεύω) to his disciples. We could compare archaic didactic poetry's claim to knowledge through direct contact with the divine, as in Hesiod's encounter with and inspiration by the Muses at the beginning of the *Theogony* or Parmenides' proem, where the narrator describes his journey through the heavens.
[18] For the importance of the addressee in didactic epic see the essays in Schiesaro/Mitsis/Strauss Clay 1994.

"You are a teacher of Israel, but you do not understand"), but as the speech progresses, the focus shifts from Nicodemus to all of humankind, and some ten verses later Jesus is now apostrophizing a plural 'you' (3.61: ὑμείων βαρυπειθέες εἰσὶν ἀκουαί; "your ears are so slow to believe"). Such fluid shifts between singular and plural addressees have a metaleptic effect: it is as if Jesus is speaking to, and teaching, not only the characters inside the text but also the readers themselves.[19]

It is also worth noticing that in the only passage where the narrator of the *Paraphrase* addresses his readers (the external audience), he does so by near-quoting a plural 'you' apostrophe of Jesus to an internal audience (the reluctant Jews). At the end of Book 20, the poet, following the Evangelist (Jo 20:31), offers an aposiopesis of Jesus' miracles, and explains that what is written in the divine book, has been written "so that you may believe" (20.141: ὄφρα κε πίστιν ἔχοιτε), and "those of you who believe" (20.143: ὔμμι δὲ πειθομένοισιν) will be saved. What the poet promises his external audience as a reward for assenting to the truth of his text echoes promises made by Jesus to several audiences earlier in the poem, but the most relevant parallel, perhaps, is Jesus' pledge in Book 8 that truth will save "those of you who believe" (8.81: ὑμῖν πειθομένοισιν). So, even though the *Paraphrase* does not present a stable, straightforward teacher – pupil relationship such as, for example, that of Hesiod and Perses, the poem invites us to discern a thread which binds together, on the one hand, the divine teacher Jesus, the Evangelist, and the poet as conveyors of absolute truth and, on the other, their various audiences, both internal and external, as pupils.[20]

In order to elucidate further the modulation of didactic in Jesus' speech, it would be useful to take a brief look at the vocabulary of Christian *didaxis* in the *Paraphrase* and its possible roots in didactic poetry. A very general point is that Nonnus' Jesus presents an extremely black-and-white view of the world, which goes back to archaic didactic (a genre that is built on the distinction between ἀγαθός and κακός), although, of course, this worldview and the vocabulary that transmits it are mediated and constantly recycled throughout Greek literature.[21]

---

19 For metalepsis in John's Gospel see Eisen 2013, esp. 342 for singular and plural addressees. Jesus' speeches with more than one addressee are usually for either large crowds of (mostly) faithless people or the more restricted group of disciples; they can also be read as a challenge for 'us', the external audience, to consider with which of these internal audiences we are to identify. According to Dalzell 1996, 25–26, it is a hallmark of didactic that the listener is not expected to identify with the speaker/poet, but with the person addressed.
20 On the relationship between Jesus, the Evangelist, and the poet see further Hadjittofi 2020.
21 For a general introduction to Hesiod's afterlife in Late Antiquity see Agosti 2016; for Hesiod and (less so) Theognis in the Christian poems of the Bodmer papyrus (with perceptive comments

Thus, Nonnus' Jesus proclaims that he will save the "deluded sinners" (12.160–161: νοοβλαβέας δὲ σαώσω | ἄνδρας ἀλιτραίνοντας). The word ἀλιτραίνοντας goes back to Hesiod's much cited condemnation of "the man who sins and devises presumptuous deeds" in the *Works and Days* (241: ὅστις ἀλιτραίνῃ καὶ ἀτάσθαλα μηχανάαται). Jesus' words could even be interpreted as a case of *Kontrastimitation*, as he offers to save the same sinners who in Hesiod's world would have been responsible not only for their own fall but also for taking their whole cities down with them.[22]

Another striking example of Hesiodean recasting is Jesus' description of the devil as a fraudster, one who "sends forth a man-beguiling word, wheedling and coaxing" (8.130: αἱμύλα κωτίλλων ἀπατήνορα μῦθον ἰάλλει). This is based on Hesiod's famous warning not to be deceived by the alluring woman who wheedles and coaxes men because she is after their farms (*Op.* 374–375: μηδὲ γυνή σε νόον πυγοστόλος ἐξαπατάτω | αἱμύλα κωτίλλουσα, τεὴν διφῶσα καλιήν). While the hemistich αἱμύλα κωτίλλουσα was renowned as a Hesiodean tag,[23] Nonnus' ἀπατήνορα seems to echo Hesiod's ἐξαπατάτω from the previous verse and thus indicates awareness of the context from which the quotation is derived – a context that the readers are also invited to consider. If they did so, they might infer that by describing the devil in terms of the Hesiodean temptress, Nonnus is implying that it is mainly through sexuality that the devil will attempt to deceive men, although, again, this notion is entirely absent from the Gospel.

Moving now from sinners to believers, and from Hesiod's hexameter to Theognis' elegiac didactic, we could note, for example, that in the long speech to his disciples Jesus tells them they have a "cleansed mind" (13.54: καθαρὸν νόον),[24] an expression which is first found in Theognis' exhortation to Cyrnus either to

---

on how intertextuality intersects with genre) see Agosti 2001, esp. 192–194, 198, 202, 208, 213–215.

22 The Hesiodean context is almost certainly relevant for the only other use of this verb in the *Paraphrase*, when Jesus' disciples ask him if the man born blind was being punished for his own sins or those of his parents (9.12: οὗτος ἀλιτραίνων θεὸν ἤκαχεν ἠὲ τοκῆες); cf. Lefteratou 2016, 287 n. 59.

23 In the 6th century CE the Gazan rhetor Choricius cites the famous hemistich with explicit attribution to "the Ascraian"; see the *Epithalamium for Zacharias*, ed. Foerster/Richtsteig 5.1.14: αἱμύλα κατὰ τὸν Ἀσκραῖον κωτίλλουσαι.

24 The full sentence reads ἄμμορον ἀμπλακίης καθαρὸν νόον ἴστε καὶ αὐτοί, | ἀλλ' οὔπως ἅμα πάντες (*Par.* 13.53–54: "Not having a share in sin, you yourselves experience a cleansed mind, | but not entirely all of you"). Greco 2004 comm. *ad loc.* does not mention Theognis.

love him with "cleansed mind" or to renounce and openly hate him.[25] As Simelidis notes regarding this same expression in Gregory Nazianzen, the conjunction is "common in antiquity, especially in later philosophers and Church Fathers."[26] Gregory, however, echoes, and even names, Theognis elsewhere too,[27] and it is entirely possible that he alludes to the archaic poet in a more conscious way. The same can be true of Nonnus, who could also be evoking, apart from Theognis' repeated stress on inner cleanliness,[28] the 'teacher and pupil against the corrupt world' attitude for which the poet of the *Theognidea* is famous.[29] After all, Jesus' overall objective in this five-Book-length monologue is to exhort his disciples to love him (and each other) and prepare them for the inevitable attack they will suffer from the unjust world. Jesus' vocabulary of steadfastness and of being always the same is also reminiscent of Theognidean instruction. Cyrnus is advised to be a good man, whose mind is "always steadfast" (319: ἔμπεδον αἰεί, at the end of the hexameter); Jesus promises to send the Holy Spirit to the disciples after his departure from the world, and describes him as "an always steadfast guide to certitude" (same *sedes*; 14.63–64: ἔμπεδον αἰεὶ | ἀτρεκίης ὀχετηγόν).[30]

Finally, it can be pointed out that the Nonnian Jesus speaks not only like an archaic didactic poet, but also like a Hellenistic one, and indeed in a context where a genre-specific allusion is supremely appropriate.[31] In his coded prophecy in Book 3, Jesus predicts that

---

25 Thgn. 89–90: ἤ με φίλει καθαρὸν θέμενος νόον, ἤ μ' ἀποειπών | ἔχθαιρ' ἀμφαδίην νεῖκος ἀειράμενος.
26 Simelidis 2009, 134.
27 See Kuhn-Treichel's contribution in this volume. Cf. Gregory's approval of Theognis' views on friendship in *ep.* 13.1 ed. Gallay.
28 See, e.g., Thgn. 447–452, a poem whose basic argument is, "if you want to wash me" (447: εἴ μ' ἐθέλεις πλύνειν), "you will always find me clean" (452: αἰεὶ δ' ἄνθος ἔχει καθαρόν).
29 Cf. Theognis' famous promise of poetic immortality to Cyrnus in 236–254; Jesus also offers his disciples immortality, albeit of a different kind.
30 This word does not appear in the same *sedes* in the *Dionysiaca*. Cf. from the same speech, in the parable of the vine at *Par.* 15.27–28: εἰ δ' ἐν ἐμοὶ μίμνητε, καὶ ἡμετέρης ῥόος αὐδῆς | ὑμέας ἀρδεύων ὑποκάρδιος ἔμπεδος εἴη ("But if you abide in me, and the flow of my voice which irrigates you remains steadfast in your hearts"). In another speech he describes himself as the "steadfast light" (8.6: φάος ἔμπεδον) of life, while he calls the (spiritual) water he offers the Samaritan woman ἔμπεδον ὕδωρ (4.68).
31 In the Beroe episode of the *Dionysiaca* (Book 41) Nonnus alludes, in a layered manner, first to Hesiod and then to Aratus; see Faulkner 2017, with comments on the relevance of the didactic tradition for that episode. For Hellenistic echoes in the *Par.* see also Accorinti in this volume.

οὕτω γυιοβόρων τελέων ἀλκτήρια νούσων
καὶ πάις ἀνθρώποιο βροτοῖς ὑψούμενος ἔσται,   75
λυσιπόνου μίμημα δρακοντείοιο προσώπου,

> thus creating an antidote for limb-devouring diseases,
> the Son of man shall also be raised up for mortals,   75
> in imitation of the pain-loosing serpentine face. (*Par.* 3.74–76)

The conjunction ἀλκτήρια νούσων occurs in exactly the same form and *sedes* in Nicander's *Alexipharmaca* (350), a poem that precisely contains instructions for making antidotes.[32] It is also found in the same poet's *Theriaca*, whose subject, venomous creatures – primarily snakes – is obviously relevant for our passage. In the *Theriaca*, then, we read "Pay attention now; I will set out compound antidotes for diseases. | Take the limb-nourishing root of Sicilian fustic" (528–529: νῦν δ' ἄγε τοι ἐπίμικτα νόσων ἀλκτήρια λέξω. | Θρινακίην μὲν ῥίζαν ἕλευ γυιαλθέα θάψου).[33] Nicander's γυιαλθέα is an *hapax*, just like Nonnus' γυιοβόρων. The stylistic similarity between the poems makes Nonnus' Jesus sound very much like a learned didactic poet and physician, but also underscores the differences between the technical, scientific knowledge (supposedly) imparted by Nicander and the coded, spiritual truth taught by Nonnus' Jesus – a novel kind of physician, as the poem explicitly describes him elsewhere.[34]

Transposing the Gospel into didactic poetry

My discussion of allusions to didactic poetry in the section above has not been interested in Nonnus' paraphrastic *modus operandi* in the technical sense, but has rather aimed to reveal a repertoire of didactic themes, which, together, help to shape Nonnus' Jesus into a *predicator* whose voice is (also) invested with the authority of a venerable succession of didactic poets.[35] This does not mean, of

---

[32] See Massimilla 2016, 266, who also notes Pindar's Apollo as "healer of all manner of diseases" (*Pyth.* 3.7: παντοδαπᾶν ἀλκτῆρα νούσων).

[33] Overduin 2015 *ad loc.* notes that the conjunction νόσων ἀλκτήρια is quasi-formulaic in Nicander, as it also appears (in slightly different versions) in vv. 7, 493, and 837.

[34] See *Par.* 12.162: ἰητὴρ ἀσίδηρος ("a doctor without iron instruments").

[35] On the importance of authority for didactic see Canevaro 2014 and Strauss Clay 2015. The status of Jesus as a "foreigner to this world" (*Par.* 8.53: ξεῖνος ἔφυν κόσμοιο) in a way parallels Hesiod's 'metanastic' persona: on this term see Martin 1992, esp. 28 for how Hesiod's self-positioning as an outsider allows him to inhabit the apparently distinct poetic *personae* of the adviser/critic (*Op.*) and the praiser of gods (*Theog.*).

course, that the weight of the didactic tradition is only felt in Jesus' speeches,[36] although his frequent and longwinded exhortations and warnings are indeed the primary locus of instruction in the poem. The narrator of the *Paraphrase*, whose own authority is based not on his individuality (as he does not identify himself) but on his 'impersonation' of the Evangelist,[37] can also use the language of didactic to guide his readers towards the correct interpretation of the biblical characters' speeches, actions, and mindsets. It has been pointed out, for example, that the narrator of the *Paraphrase* uses the Hesiodean adjective ἁμαρτίνοος, first employed for Epimetheus, who "from the beginning was a bane to men",[38] twice to describe the "mind-erring Pharisees" (1.88 and 7.121: ἁμαρτινόων Φαρισαίων), which is not surprising, and once for the disciples, when they find Jesus' discourse about the bread too harsh, and seem to have second thoughts (6.188: Χριστὸς ἁμαρτινόοισιν ἔπος ξύνωσε μαθηταῖς).[39] This inherent instability in the characterization of the disciples (some things they understand; others escape them; they are mostly faithful but not all of them and not always) makes them ideal didactic addressees,[40] and challenges the readers to consider their own position and understanding, while also highlighting the role of the narrator as a fellow-guide (along with Jesus) on the path towards knowledge.[41]

Indeed, this section will argue that the whole poem can be read as structurally echoing the long, didactic tradition that stretches from the archaic down to the imperial period. A first, and rather obvious, point is that this poem is the

---

36 See Accorinti's contribution in this volume for the identification of a Hesiodean allusion in Pilate's words.
37 I develop this idea in Hadjittofi 2020, where I also argue for the possibility of an allusion to Theognis' famous *sphragis* in the epilogue of the *Paraphrase*.
38 Hes., *Theog.* 511–512: ἁμαρτίνοόν τ' Ἐπιμηθέα· | ὃς κακὸν ἐξ ἀρχῆς γένετ' ἀνδράσιν ἀλφηστῆσι.
39 The allusion is pointed out by De Stefani 2002, n. on 1.88. Cf., recently, Ypsilanti/Franco 2018, 174.
40 Cf. Hesiod's Perses, who is the perfect addressee precisely because of his flaws; see Canevaro 2014, 30 and Aloni 2017, 7.
41 The metaphor of the journey or the path towards knowledge is one of the main "structural metaphors of teaching", according to Fowler 2000, 208–210, and it is omnipresent in both the Gospel and the *Paraphrase*. In fact, the latter occasionally adds this notion without prompt from the Gospel. In 15.92, for example, Nonnus' Jesus says that he has come "to indicate the path of piety to all" (πᾶσι θεουδείης ἐνέπων ὁδόν), where the Johannine Jesus simply says, "I came and spoke" (15:22: ἦλθον καὶ ἐλάλησα). It is telling that Rotondo's 2017 monograph on the *Paraphrase* adopts this metaphor in the second half of its title: *Itinerarium fidei*. Initiation, which is the other major metaphor by which teaching is "emplotted" according to Fowler 2000, 213–214, is also used by the Nonnian Jesus, for example when he speaks of the "true initiates" (4.111: ἀληθέες ... μύσται), where the Gospel has "true worshippers" (4:23: οἱ ἀληθινοὶ προσκυνηταί).

transposition into hexameter verse of a prose model. This is a practice that attaches specifically well to didactic, whose Hellenistic and Roman version relied on the versification of prose treatises,[42] as if didactic poets readily assumed what Plutarch states in the passage quoted in the introduction of this chapter: that their task is to take λόγοι and apply onto them poetry's meter and sublimity so as to 'escape' being prosaic. The late antique trend, especially in the school context, was to paraphrase texts written as elaborate poems, turning them into either more accessible poems or prose: there are such paraphrases of the *Theriaca* and *Alexipharmaka* of Nicander, of the *Halieutica* of Oppian and the *Ixeutica* of Dionysius, as well as various paraphrases of Dionysius Periegetes.[43] Perhaps this considerable traffic between poetry and prose is particularly characteristic of the didactic genre because of its technical nature, which gives authors suitably challenging material to tackle. At any rate, it is conceivable that the mere fact that the *Paraphrase* is the Gospel's close adaptation into verse would have suggested to Nonnus' readers that the poem has a place within the tradition of didactic.

Secondly, we should not ignore the popularity and the very rich production of didactic: this is the genre that is best represented even during the poetic 'Dark Ages' of the first-third centuries CE.[44] Although the didactic poems that have come down to us fit the model of a discursive genre in which the teacher-poet imparts technical knowledge to his addressee(s), there is evidence to suggest that not all didactic poetry stuck so closely to these criteria. The largely lost corpus of Hellenistic metamorphosis poetry (primarily Boios' *Ornithogonia* and Nicander's *Heteroioumena* – both hexameter collections of metamorphosis myths) should be thought of as didactic: these poems would have communicated with prose metamorphosis collections, exhibited an outspoken moralization, and suggested a divinely ordered and rationally governed universe.[45] The narrativity of the myths (arranged as collected fragments) would have been subordinated to the didactic framework of the poems.

---

42 See Dalzell 1996, 9 and Fowler 2000, 205. Gutzwiller 2007, 99 suggests that in the Hellenistic period, perhaps as a reaction to Plato's critique of poetry's claim to wisdom, the didactic poet "no longer represented himself as the source of knowledge about the subject at hand, but his role was more limited to providing poetic expertise, that is, the ability to express the material well in verse."
43 See Livrea 1989, 37–38.
44 See Cameron 2004, 327–328.
45 See Fletcher 2012, esp. 90–91, who highlights the importance of collection as a marker of didactic.

Another Hellenistic subgenre that is now hopelessly fragmentary is that of philosophical didactic. Here, we find a poem whose structure and tenor are somewhat reminiscent of Nonnus' *Paraphrase*. Timon of Phlius (third century BCE) wrote the elegiac *Indalmoi*,[46] a dialogue with his teacher, Pyrrho, in which the poet-disciple celebrates his master and presents him as a superior being, invested with divine attributes.[47] Pyrrho, in his turn, proclaims to Timon that his words "hold the straight canon of truth," and affirms that "the nature of the good and the divine is eternal, and from that derives for man the most equable life."[48] A reader familiar with such a tradition of philosophical didactic would have probably seen the *Paraphrase* as belonging in, or having strong affinities with, this tradition: after all, this is also a dactylic poem whose narrator takes up the persona of a disciple glorifying his master, the literally divine Jesus, who, like Pyrrho, left no writings, is an austere teacher, and even speaks in similarly self-assertive terms, declaring, for example, that "I am the life, the truth, and the straight road."[49]

The desire to elevate the didactic master to the stars might be particularly striking in Timon, but several other didactic poems evince a clear hymnic 'modulation', especially close to the beginning of the composition. The extended hymn to the Logos, which we find at the head of the *Paraphrase* and which greatly amplifies the Gospel, can be compared with the 'hymns to Zeus' that open Hesiod's *Works and Days* and Aratus' *Phaenomena*.[50] In the second century CE, Dionysius Periegetes begins his *Description of the inhabited world* with a quasi-hymn

---

46 On this author see Long 1978. For his poetry as didactic see Harder 2011, 180.
47 See *SH* F841 = F67 Diels, where Timon addresses a question to Pyrrho and compares him to the Sun god, who guides men by turning around the earth (5–6: μοῦνος δ' ἀνθρώποισι θεοῦ τρόπον ἡγεμονεύεις, | ὃς περὶ πᾶσαν ἑλῶν γαῖαν ἀναστρέφεται). Cf. Jesus as the "light of life" (Book 6) and also as the only mortal to have ever "stepped onto the untrodden rim of the heavenly circles" (*Par.* 3.65–66: οὔποτε δὲ βροτὸς ἄλλος ... | οὐρανίων ἐπάτησεν ἀνέμβατον ἄντυγα κύκλων).
48 See *SH* F842 = F68 Diels: ἦ γὰρ ἐγὼν ἐρέω, ὥς μοι καταφαίνεται εἶναι, | μῦθον, ἀληθείης ὀρθὸν ἔχων κανόνα, | ὡς ἡ τοῦ θείου τε φύσις καὶ τἀγαθοῦ αἰεί, | ἐξ ὧν ἰσότατος γίνεται ἀνδρὶ βίος.
49 *Par.* 14.20: ζωὴ ἀληθείη τε καὶ ὀρθιός εἰμι πορείη.
50 Cf. Kneebone 2017, 220–221, who also points out that the 'technical' material in both poems is itself presented as evidence of Zeus' ordering of the universe. Another scholar – Sider 2014, 27 – suggests that a more appropriate title for the *Works and Days* would have been the *Zeusiad*, given that the entire poem is about Zeus and how he observes and judges human actions. In the imperial period, the *Cynegetica* opens with an encomiastic dedication to Caracalla, where the emperor is praised as "sweet scion of Ausonian Zeus" (1.3: Αὐσονίου Ζηνὸς γλυκερὸν θάλος).

of Oceanus – both a god and part of the poet's vast subject matter.[51] The poem ends with a farewell to all lands and to the waters of Oceanus, a proud proclamation of the difficult mission the poet has accomplished (1184–1185: "I have already traversed the swell of the whole sea and the crooked paths of the land"), and a request that the gods reward the poet for his "hymns" (ὕμνων)."[52] Nonnus' *Paraphrase* can, arguably, be read as a Christian version of this didactic tradition which presents itself as a hymn to the gods and their providential ordering of the world.[53]

Another, related hallmark of didactic, at least from the Hellenistic period onwards, is the creative tension between a vast subject matter, which is difficult if not impossible for mortals to master, and the necessity to select, order, and present this material in a poem.[54] Aratus' endeavor to chart the sky and the myriads of stars comes up against the poet's confessed "lack of courage" to speak about "the circles and heavenly signs of the planets";[55] Dionysius Periegetes admits that some tribes live so far away that "no mortal could speak about them with clarity; only the gods can do everything easily;"[56] Oppian's attempt to set out the innumerable multitudes of fishes has to contend with the boundlessness of the sea, where many things have to remain "hidden, and no mortal can speak about these obscure things; the mind and strength of humans is slight."[57] In this context, Nonnus' rendition of two passages where the Gospel indicates humans' inability fully to capture and contemplate the divine, can be interpreted as both belonging in and upstaging this didactic tradition. In 14.64–67 Jesus announces that he will send to his disciples the Holy Spirit,[58]

---

[51] The poet praises the renowned "power of indefatigable Ocean, who, while being one, has come to be called by many names" (Dionys. Per. 27–28: πάντη δ' ἀκαμάτου φέρεται σθένος Ὠκεανοῖο, | εἷς μὲν ἐών, πολλῇσι δ' ἐπωνυμίῃσιν ἀρηρώς); for polyonymy as a hallmark of the hymnic genre see Bremer 1981, 194–195.
[52] Dionys. Per. 1181–1186: ... χαίρετε νῆσοι ... ἤδη γὰρ πάσης μὲν ἐπέδραμον οἶδμα θαλάσσης, | ἤδη δ' ἠπείρων σκολιὸν πόρον· ἀλλά μοι ὕμνων | αὐτῶν ἐκ μακάρων ἀντάξιος εἴη ἀμοιβή.
[53] Cf. Toohey's 1996, 208–211 comments on Prudentius as a Christian didactic poet.
[54] See Kneebone 2017 *passim*.
[55] Aratus, *Phaen.* 460–461: οὐδ' ἔτι θαρσαλέος κείνων ἐγὼ ἄρκιος εἴην | ἁπλανέων τά τε κύκλα τά τ' αἰθέρι σήματ' ἐνισπεῖν.
[56] Dionys. Per. 1168–1169: οὓς οὐκ ἄν τις ἀριφραδέως ἀγορεύσαι | θνητὸς ἐών· μοῦνοι δὲ θεοὶ ῥέα πάντα δύνανται.
[57] Opp., *Halieut.* 1.86–87: κέκρυπται, τά κεν οὔ τις ἀείδελα μυθήσαιτο | θνητὸς ἐών· ὀλίγος δὲ νόος μερόπεσσι καὶ ἀλκή.
[58] This renders Jo 14:17: ὃ ὁ κόσμος οὐ δύναται λαβεῖν, ὅτι οὐ θεωρεῖ αὐτό.

> ... ὅπερ πολύμορφος ἀείρειν
> οὐ δύναταί ποτε κόσμος, ὅτι βροτὸς οὔποτε λεύσσει
> τηλίκον ἀνδρομέοισιν ἐν ὄμμασιν ἀρχέγονον φῶς,
> πνεῦμα θεοῦ γενετῆρος.
>
> whom the manifold-shaped world
> is never able to hold, because a mortal never gazes   65
> with his human eyes upon such primordial light,
> upon the spirit of God the begetter. (*Par.* 14.64–67)

In the very last lines of the poem, John's admission that many miracles have been omitted from his account, because not even the world could contain so many books,[59] is rendered thus:

> ὅσσα καθ' ἓν στοιχηδὸν ἀνὴρ βροτὸς αἴκε χαράξῃ,
> βίβλους τοσσατίας νεοτευχέας οὐδὲ καὶ αὐτὸν
> ἔλπομαι ἀγλαόμορφον ἀτέρμονα κόσμον ἀεῖραι.
>
> [miracles] so numerous that if a mortal inscribed them one by one, line by line,
> so many newly wrought books I think
> not even the beautiful, boundless world itself could hold. (*Par.* 21.141–143)

Nonnus (and John) share with the didactic tradition an acute awareness of the limitations of human understanding: just as parts of the world are inaccessible for the eyes of the didactic poets mentioned above, human eyes cannot contemplate the Holy Spirit. As is frequent with Nonnus, however, his addition of adjectives to the plain account of the Gospel is not merely decorative.[60] The world, which can hold neither the Holy Spirit nor the unwritten books containing Jesus' miracles, is "manifold-shaped" (14.64: πολύμορφος) and "boundless" (21.143: ἀτέρμονα). In a didactic poem aiming to describe the world (or significant parts thereof), its multiple shapes and boundlessness would have been themselves the obstacles to scientific enquiry. The difficulty here, on the contrary, is not caused by the immensity of the world, but something (the divine, the numerous miracles) that lies even beyond this world and its capacities. The scope of Nonnus' poem, therefore, surpasses the already vast subjects of earlier didactic poems, as it provides mortals with a glimpse of the divine and of transcendental truth.

---

59 Jo 21:25: ἅτινα ἐὰν γράφηται καθ' ἕν, οὐδ' αὐτὸν οἶμαι τὸν κόσμον χωρῆσαι τὰ γραφόμενα βιβλία.
60 Cf. Accorinti in this volume.

Conclusions

Nonnus chose to versify a Gospel whose genre is already "bent".[61] John's account is very far from being a straightforward telling of Jesus' life and deeds: it is structured as a series of didactic encounters either with single interlocutors (Nicodemus, the Samaritan, the paralytic, Mary and Martha, Pilate, Thomas, and, finally, Peter) or with larger groups (the disciples, the Jewish 'multitudes', the Pharisees), resulting in a sense that these scenes are put together as if they were fragments belonging in a *sylloge* rather than an integrated narrative plot. Aloni's recent reading of Hesiod's fully extant works in terms of collection poetry, which can easily be broken down into 'fragments' for re-composition, can, to a certain degree, also be applied to John's Gospel and, by extension, Nonnus' *Paraphrase*.[62]

What binds together these didactic encounters is, of course, the presence of Jesus, who imparts knowledge and guides his interlocutors towards the truth. The first section above has suggested that Nonnus presents Jesus as a didactic master throughout, and invests his speech with the authority of earlier didactic poetry by alluding to both archaic and Hellenistic models. The second section has drawn attention to poorly preserved didactic subgenres that might lie at the periphery of what we nowadays consider 'didactic poetry', but which provide a richer picture of the tradition in which the *Paraphrase* inserts itself or in which (some) readers might have perceived it to belong. Finally, it has been suggested that two important features of didactic poetry, its 'modulation' of hymn and its emphasis on the limitations of human knowledge, have parallels in the *Paraphrase*, which might signal to a late antique reader that this poem has considerable affinities with the didactic tradition. As a whole, Nonnus' Christian poem may ultimately be forging its own place on the generic grid; my contention has been that this new place should have didactic as one of its main coordinates.[63]

---

61 See Attridge 2002.
62 See Aloni 2017, with comments on the importance of oral performance for this process. For the absence of an independent narratorial voice in the *Paraphrase* and how it might encourage oral performance and re-performance see Hadjittofi 2020.
63 This conclusion is strengthened by Faulkner's identification (in this volume) of didactic markers in the only contemporary large-scale paraphrase that is extant in Greek, the *Metaphrasis Psalmorum*.

Bibliography

Agosti, G. 2001. "Considerazioni preliminari sui generi letterari dei poemi del Codice Bodmer", *Aegyptus*, 2, 185–217.
Agosti, G. (ed.) 2003. *Nonno di Panopoli, Parafrasi del Vangelo di S. Giovanni. Canto V.* Firenze.
Agosti, G. 2016. "Esiodo nella tarda antichità: prime prospezioni", *SemRom*, 5, 179–194.
Aloni, A. 2017. "Hesiod between performance and written record", in C. Tsagalis (ed.), *Poetry in fragments: studies on the Hesiod Corpus and its afterlife*, Berlin, 3–28.
Attridge, H.W. 2002. "Genre bending in the Fourth Gospel", *JBL*, 121, 3–21.
Bremer, J.M. 1981. "Greek hymns", in H.S. Versnel (ed.), *Faith, hope and worship: aspects of religious mentality in the ancient world*, Leiden, 193–215.
Cameron, Alan 2004. "Poetry and literary culture in Late Antiquity", in S. Swain/M.J. Edwards (eds.), *Approaching Late Antiquity: the transformation from Early to Late Empire*, Oxford, 327–354.
Canevaro, L.G. 2014. "Genre and authority in Hesiod's *Works and Days*", in C. Werner (ed.), *Gêneros poéticos na Grécia Antiga: confluências e fronteiras,* São Paulo, 23–48.
Consolino, F.E. 2005. "Il senso del passato: generi letterari e rapporti con la tradizione nella 'parafrasi biblica' latina", in I. Gualandri/F. Conca/R. Passarella (eds.), *Nuovo e antico nella cultura greco-latina di IV–VI secolo*, Milano, 447–526.
Dalzell, A. 1996. *The criticism of didactic poetry: essays on Lucretius, Virgil, and Ovid*, Toronto.
De Stefani, C. (ed.) 2002. *Nonno di Panopoli. Parafrasi del Vangelo di S. Giovanni. Canto I.* Bologna.
Diels, H. (ed.) 1901. *Poetarum Philosophorum Fragmenta*, Berlin.
Eisen, U. 2013. "Metalepsis in the Gospel of John – narration situation and 'Beloved Disciple' in new perspective", in U. Eisen/P. von Möllendorff (eds.), *Über die Grenze. Metalepse in Text- und Bildmedien des Altertums*, Berlin, 318–345.
Faulkner, A. 2017. "Nonnus' 'younger legend': the birth of Beroë and the didactic tradition", *G&R*, 64, 103–114.
Fletcher, K. 2012. "Divine agency and morality in Hellenistic metamorphosis poetry", in A. Harder/R.F. Regtuit/G.C. Wakker (eds.), *Gods and religion in Hellenistic poetry*, Leuven, 81–102.
Foerster, R./Richtsteig, E. (eds.) 1929. *Choricii Gazaei opera*, Leipzig (repr. Stuttgart, 1972).
Fowler, D. 2000. "The didactic plot", in M. Depew/D. Obbink (eds.), *Matrices of genre: authors, canons, and society*, Cambridge (MA), 205–219.
Gale, M. 2004. "Introduction: genre, tradition and individuality", in M. Gale (ed.), *Latin epic and didactic poetry*, Swansea, xi–xxiii.
Gallay, P. (ed.) 1964–1967. *Saint Grégoire de Nazianze. Lettres.* 2 vols., Paris.
Greco, C. (ed.) 2004. *Nonno di Panopoli. Parafrasi del Vangelo di S. Giovanni. Canto XIII.* Alessandria.
Gutzwiller, K. 2007. *A guide to Hellenistic literature*, Malden (MA).
Hadjittofi, F. 2018. "ποικιλόνωτος ἀνήρ: clothing metaphors and Nonnus' ambiguous Christology in the *Paraphrase of the Gospel according to John*", *VChr*, 72, 165–173.
Hadjittofi, F. 2020. "The poet and the evangelist in Nonnus' *Paraphrase of the Gospel according to John*", *CCJ*, 66, in press.

Harder, A. 2011. "More facts from fragments?", in D. Obbink/R. Rutherford (eds.), *Culture in pieces. Essays on ancient texts in honour of Peter Parsons*, Oxford, 174–187.
Hunter, R./Russell, D. (eds.) 2011. *Plutarch. How to study poetry (De audiendis poetis)*, Cambridge.
Kennedy, G.A. 1984. *New Testament interpretation through rhetorical criticism*, Chapel Hill.
Kneebone, E. 2017. "The limits of enquiry in imperial Greek didactic poetry", in J. König/G. Woolf (eds.), *Authority and expertise in ancient scientific culture*, Cambridge, 203–230.
Lefteratou, A. 2016. "Jesus' late antique epiphanies: healing the Blind in the Christian epics of Eudocia and Nonnus", in J. Claus/M. Cuypers/A. Kahane (eds.), *The gods of Greek hexameter poetry: from the Archaic Age to Late Antiquity and beyond*, Stuttgart, 268–287.
Livrea, E. (ed.) 1989. *Nonno di Panopoli. Parafrasi del Vangelo di S. Giovanni. Canto XVIII*, Napoli.
Long, A.A. 1978. "Timon of Phlius: pyrrhonist and satirist", *PCPhS*, 204, 68–90.
Martin, R.P. 1992. "Hesiod's metanastic poetics", *Ramus*, 21, 11–33.
Massimilla, G. 2016. "Nel laboratorio del parafraste: i richiami alla poesia ellenistica nella *Parafrase del Vangelo di San Giovanni* di Nonno di Panopoli", *Prometheus*, 42, 249–279.
Nesselrath, H.-G. 1990. *Die attische mittlere Komödie: Ihre Stellung in der antiken Literaturkritik und Literaturgeschichte*, Berlin.
Overduin, F. 2015. *Nicander of Colophon's Theriaca. A literary commentary*, Leiden.
Roberts, M. 1985. *Biblical epic and rhetorical paraphrase in Late Antiquity*, Liverpool.
Rotondo, A. 2017. *Ascoltare, vedere, credere. Itinerarium fidei nella Parafrasi di Nonno di Panopoli*, Calabria.
Schiesaro, A./Mitsis, P./Strauss Clay, J. (eds.) 1994. *Mega nepios. Il destinatario nell'epos didascalico. The addressee in didactic epic, MD* 31, Pisa.
Sider, D. 2014. "Didactic poetry: the Hellenistic invention of a pre-existing genre", in R. Hunter/A. Rengakos/E. Sistakou (eds.), *Hellenistic studies at a crossroads: exploring texts, contexts and metatexts*, Berlin, 13–30.
Simelidis, C. (ed.) 2009. *Selected poems of Gregory of Nazianzus: I.2.17; II.1.10, 19, 32*, Göttingen.
Strauss Clay, J. 2015. "Commencing cosmogony and the rhetoric of poetic authority", in P. Derron (ed.), *Cosmologies et cosmogonies dans la littérature antique: huit exposés suivis de discussion et d'un épilogue. Entretiens sur l'Antiquité classique 61*, Vandœuvres, 105–147.
Toohey, P. 1996. *Epic lessons: an introduction to ancient didactic poetry*, London.
Ypsilanti, M./Franco, L. 2018. "Characterization of persons and groups of persons in the *Metabole*", in H. Bannert/N. Kröll (eds.), *Nonnus of Panopolis in context II. Poetry, religion, and society*, Leiden, 166–183.
Vesperini, P. 2015. "La poésie didactique dans l'Antiquité: une invention des modernes", *Anabases*, 21, 25–38.
Volk, K. 2002. *The poetics of Latin didactic*, Oxford.

Andrew Faulkner
Davidic Didactic Hexameters: The Generic Stance of the *Metaphrasis Psalmorum*

The *Metaphrasis Psalmorum*, a paraphrase of the Septuagint Psalms in hexameter verse,[1] is a prominent example of the flourishing genre of biblical poetic paraphrase in the Greek and Latin literature of Late Antiquity.[2] Already in the first half of the fourth century CE, Juvencus recast the Gospels in Latin hexameters in his *Evangeliorum Libri Quattuor*.[3] Among other examples in Latin over the next two centuries are Paulinus of Nola's (353/4–431 CE) paraphrases of select Psalms (*carm.* 6–9),[4] a poetic *Heptateuch* of uncertain authorship (fifth century),[5] Sedulius' *Carmen Paschale* (fifth century), freely based upon the Gospels, and Victorinus' *Alethia* (fifth century), which retells Genesis with much exegetical intervention.[6] In Greek, the poems of the Bodmer papyri uncovered in Egypt provide fourth-century examples of biblical paraphrase on a smaller scale,[7] while in the fifth century the empress Eudocia paraphrased the Octateuch, Zacharias, and Daniel (now lost), and Nonnus retold St John's Gospel in hexameter verse, a poem

---

1 The exact date and authorship of the *Metaphrasis Psalmorum* (henceforth, *Met. Pss.*) are uncertain. Following the designation of some manuscripts, it has been attributed to the 4th-century bishop Apollinaris of Laodicea; see Dräseke 1892, 63–80; Ludwich 1912, v–xi; Raven 1923, 154–155. But more recent opinion has strongly favored a 5th-century date under the reign of the patriarch Gennadius (458–471 CE); see Golega 1939 and 1960, 5–24; Agosti 2001a, 87; De Stefani 2008. In Faulkner 2020 I re-evaluate this debate and argue that the attribution to Apollinaris is plausible.
2 For recent overviews see Agosti 2012, 371–372, who labels biblical paraphrases "the most characteristic Christian genre", Whitby 2016, 218–220, and Miguélez-Cavero 2018. On ancient views of fidelity to the source text see Green 2006, 44–46; Faulkner 2014.
3 Jerome dates the poem to 329 CE. See Green 2006, 3–7.
4 See Roberts 1985, 92–96; Trout 1999, 85–86; Green 2006, 146–148.
5 See Green 2006, 151–152.
6 See Roberts 1985, 96–99.
7 Hurst/Rudhardt 1999 is the standard edition; the precise date of the poems is disputed, but they belong to the 4th century. One 30-line poem retells the Binding of Isaac from Gen 22:1–19, a 19-line poem on Cain and Abel expands upon Gen 4:13–15, while a 69-line poem, again on the theme of Cain and Abel, paraphrases elements of Psalm 101. See further, among others, Agosti/Gonnelli 1995, 301–308; Agosti 2001a, 71–74, 2001b, 2002; Miguélez-Cavero 2008, 61–63.

https://doi.org/10.1515/9783110696219-015

which shows marked influence by Cyril of Alexandria's commentary on the Gospel and other early Christian exegesis.[8]

Alone of the surviving Greek paraphrases of the period, the *Metaphrasis Psalmorum* is transmitted together with an extended programmatic prologue (110 lines), which lays out the poet's spiritual and apostolic mission. This begins with an address to a certain Marcianus, whose wisdom and advice have inspired the poetic labor (1–9); Marcianus' counsel is then depicted in direct speech, calling upon the poet to restore the grace (χάρις) of the meter lost in the Septuagint translation of the Hebrew,[9] so that the Psalms will be attractive even to non-Christians (10–43);[10] further praise of Marcianus' dedication to the Psalms, said to be his companion in old age (51: γήραος εὐφήμοιο συνέμπορον), leads to a lengthy excursus on the power of the Holy Spirit to communicate universally through the Apostles, whose teaching of Christ will convert all nations (44–104); a final section links Marcianus' call to recast the Psalms in hexameter verse to this apostolic mission and claims the living Christ as the helper of the poet's song (105–110).

Alongside its expression of the poet's faith, the prologue lays down markers of poetic aesthetic, influence and genre. In its opening lines, the poet likens himself to Homer, on the surface aligning his paraphrase with the epic hexameter tradition:

ἔλπομαι ἀθανάτοιο θεοῦ κεκορυθμένος οἴμῃ
σοὶ χάριν ἀντὶ πόνων φορέειν καὶ κέρδος ἐπ' ἔργῳ
καὶ τυφλὸς γεγαὼς δοκέειν φάος ἄλλο κομίζειν,
Μαρκιανὲ κλυτόμητι· τί γάρ νύ τοι ἔπρεπεν ἄλλο
ἢ τό μοι εὑρέμεναι σέθεν ἄξιον; οὐ γὰρ ἐφετμῆς
σεῖο, πάτερ, λαθόμην· ἐθέλω δέ τοι ἤπιος εἶναι
εἰς ἀγαθὸν σπεύδοντι. τί δ' ἥδιον ἠὲ μερίμναις
σῇσιν ἐπ' ἀτρύτοισι νόον φιλόμολπον ἐγείρειν,
μεμνῆσθαι δ' ἐπέων, ὧν φθέγξαο τοῖα πιφαύσκων·

---

8 Eudocia's lost works are attested by Photius *Bibl.* Codex 183–184. Cf. Accorinti 2016, 17–19. On Nonnus' poem see, *inter alia*, Livrea 1989; Agosti 2003; Whitby 2016; Simelidis 2016, all with further bibliography.

9 For ancient ideas concerning the shared origins of Greek and Hebrew verse see Agosti/Gonnelli 1995, 359.

10 See in particular *praef.* 18–19: ἀτὰρ μετ' Ἀχαιίδα γῆρυν | αὖτις ἀμειβομένων κατὰ μὲν χάρις ἔφθιτο μέτρων ("But during translation into the Greek language, the grace of the meter was in turn lost, although the words in this way remain true"); 32–34: ἵνα γνώωσι καὶ ἄλλοι | γλῶσσ' ὅτι παντοίη Χριστὸν βασιλῆα βοήσει | καί μιν πανσυδίῃ γουνάσσεται ἔθνεα γαίης ("In order that others (i.e. pagans) as well should know that every tongue will shout Christ the king and all nations of the earth will with all speed supplicate him").

> I hope, armed with the song of immortal God,
> to bring to you joy in return for pains and reward for work,
> and, although being blind, to be able to convey another light,
> Marcianus, famed for skill. For what else is indeed now more fitting,
> than for me to find something worthy of you? For your command
> I have not forgotten, father, and I want to be pleasing to you,
> who strive after good. What then is sweeter than to
> rouse the song-loving mind upon your limitless thoughts,
> and to recall the words, which you uttered speaking thus. (*Met. Pss. proem*, 1–9)

The poet's claim to be blind, an expression of spiritual rather than literal blindness,[11] clearly evokes the figure of Homer, without naming him. Moreover, for an educated audience intimately familiar with the Hellenic literary tradition, the particular language used to describe Marcianus' literary vision recalls an earlier poetic expression of Homer's influence on his successors.[12] The phrase μερίμναις | σῇσιν ἐπ' ἀτρύτοισι brings to mind the only other surviving occurrence of the combination μέριμναι ἄτρυτοι in a fragment of Hellenistic anapaestic poetry:

> τήν τ' ἀπὸ Μουσῶν ἄφθιτον αὐδὴν
> ἣν σὺ μερίμναις ταῖσιν ἀτρύτοις
> καθυφηνάμενος πόντος τις ὅπως ἔπτυσας ἄλ[λο]ις.
>
> the deathless voice of the Muses,
> which, weaving in your limitless thoughts,
> you spit out for others like the ocean. (*Lyrica Adespota, CA* 10)

In his vast intellect, Homer weaves the inspirational voice of the Muses into poetry, which in turn provides inspiration to others.[13] Marcianus too provides poetic inspiration, although in the new Christian context he does so in the role of a spiritual father inspired by Christ, just as the poet himself is armed by God (1: ἀθανάτοιο θεοῦ κεκορυθμένος) and helped by Christ (110: Χριστὸν ἀεὶ ζώοντα ... ἐπαρωγὸν ἀοιδῆς). The authority of the Muses and Homer are thus usurped by

---

11 See Gitschel 1936; Golega 1960, 26; Agosti 2001a, 88. The adjective τυφλός is used elsewhere in early Christian literature of an inability to understand. On the meaning of blindness see also Agosti 2011b.
12 Cf. Faulkner 2014, 202–204.
13 Compare a report by Aelian of a painting on a third-century Hellenistic temple, in which poets were shown collecting what Homer spit out (*VH* 13.22: Γαλάτων δὲ ὁ ζωγράφος ἔγραψε τὸν μὲν Ὅμηρον αὐτὸν ἐμοῦντα, τοὺς δὲ ἄλλους ποιητὰς τὰ ἐμημεσμένα ἀρυτομένους). On the motif of Homer as the sea and the *tabula Galatonis* see e.g. Traill 1998, with bibliography.

Christ and the poet's Christian spiritual father Marcianus,[14] even as Homer's traditional epic language is marked as the aesthetic vehicle of the Christian message. A similar, if more complex, strategy is found in Juvencus' hexameter preface to his *Evangeliorum Libri Quattuor* (a rare example of a hexameter preface in the Latin poetry of Late Antiquity), where the poet cites Homer and Virgil as exemplary epic poets (9–10: *hos celsi cantus, Smyrnae de fonte fluentes | illos Minciadae celebrat dulcedo Maronis*, "The high-flown verse that flows from Smyrna's spring lifts some, the charm of Mincian Virgil others"), at the same time invoking the inspiration of the Holy Spirit to speak things worthy of Christ, in language that seems to allude pointedly to a Virgilian passage concerning Apollo (27: *ut Christo digna loquamur* ~ *Aen*. 6.662: *Phoebo digna locuti* [*vates*]); whereas the *vates* of the *Aeneid* who speak fitting things for Apollo are in Elysium, Juvencus implies that his hopes for eternal salvation as a poet are based on speaking fitting things for Christ.[15]

The *Metaphrasis Psalmorum* is steeped in far more than the language of Homeric epic, drawing upon a broad range of classical sources at the level of expression,[16] and interweaving classical idioms and motifs with biblical and early Christian language. Ultimately, the evocation of the figure of Homer in the opening lines of the prologue is not indicative of deep generic affiliation with the epic tradition, but is a more superficial marker of the poet's use of hexameter verse and Homeric language. This is the case at least in comparison to the preface of Juvencus, who by calling to mind Homer and Virgil not only signals his use of epic hexameter language, but reflects deliberately upon the traditional epic themes of *fama* and *gloria* from his new Christian perspective.[17]

In its structure and thematic focus, the prologue of the *Metaphrasis Psalmorum* is more properly aligned with the didactic hexameter tradition, a natural fit for biblical paraphrase, given the frequency with which didactic poetry

---

[14] On the typical strategies of *Usurpation* and *Kontrastimitation* in early Christian poets see Agosti 2011a, esp. 287–289, with earlier bibliography. The invocation of Christ or the Holy Spirit in place of the Muses is a common strategy of early Christian poets; cf. in Latin, Juvenc., *ELQ* 1.25–27, Sedul., *CP* 1.85, Arator 2.577–578, and in Greek, Greg. Naz., *arc*. 1.22 = *PG* 37.400a. See further Green 2006, 21–22 and 300–302; Shorrock 2011, 22–33.

[15] See Van der Nat 1973; Green 2006, 15–23, also 50–71 on the influence of epic on Juvencus. On Juvencus' preface see also Paschalis' contribution in this volume.

[16] A good sense of this breadth is given by the linguistic parallels collected by Golega 1960, even if these are not in every case significant. A similar case for the (not exclusively epic) generic affiliation of Nonnus' *Paraphrase* is made by Accorinti in this volume.

[17] See Green 2006, 17: "The main thrust of the Preface is a meditation (and perhaps also a manifesto) on fame, not a new topic by any means but one that he wishes to reconfigure."

after the second century BCE is closely linked to prose treatises.[18] The presence of the addressee at the outset of the poem, a common feature of Greek and Latin didactic literature, is a prominent generic marker.[19] In this instance, a limited number of details paint a picture of Marcianus as an educated teacher and patron of the poet. Apart from the advice and inspiration he gives for the poet's literary activity, his reported speech portrays him as welcoming and supporting the poet when he came to Constantinople (42–43: πὰρ γὰρ ἐμοὶ πρώτῳ προμολὼν χθόνα Κωνσταντίνου | ἤθεα καὶ λαόν τ' ἐδάης καὶ ἐπάσσαο σίτου; "For through me above all, having come to Constantinople, you became familiar with its customs and people and partook of food"). The precise identity of Marcianus has long been debated, in conversation with the question of the poem's date and authorship. In support of a fourth-century date and Apollinarian authorship, Dräseke identified him as the Syrian recluse Marcianus, who, Theodoret says, was from a noble family and lived in the desert of Chalcis (died c. 380–390 CE).[20] Alternatively, in line with his now commonly accepted fifth-century date for the poem, Golega names the addressee as the Marcianus who served as priest and *oikonomos* of St. Sophia under the patriarch Gennadios,[21] an educated member of the elite who played a role in several church building projects.[22] Others have identified him less plausibly with the very emperor Marcianus (450–457 CE); but one would not expect an emperor to be addressed as "father" (v. 6) and not lauded more explicitly.[23]

Whatever the actual identity of Marcianus, the addressee of the paraphrase is to some extent at least a literary construct, as is the poet's persona. A well-read Christian audience may have detected in the addressee an echo of Irenaeus'

---

18 See Hutchinson 2009 on the permeable border between didactic prose and poetry. See also Hadjittofi in this volume for Nonnus' *Paraphrase* and its relationship with the didactic tradition.
19 For the addressee in Greek and Latin didactic poetry see the collection of essays in Schiesaro/Mitsis/Strauss Clay 1994. Dr F. Hadjittofi suggests to me that the Psalms might also be viewed as collection of poetry, which is another marker of the didactic genre; cf. Aloni 2017 on Hesiod.
20 See Dräseke 1892, 72. Thdt., *h.rel.* 3. Theodoret, however, also indicates that this Marcianus condemned the folly (φρενοβλάβεια) of Apollinaris. Cf. Golega 1960, 23. Lebon 1946, 192 argued that this ascetic was the Marcianus who authored fragments in the *Florilegium Edessenum*, and who may have joined a delegation of Apollinaris to the Council of Alexandria in 362, but the identification is unlikely. See Brock 1969 and van Roey 1975.
21 Golega 1939, 18–20; 1960, 23–24. See also Agosti 2001a, 87; De Stefani 2008, 3–4.
22 The epithet κλυτόμητις (4), used of the god Hephaestus and in Late Antiquity as an honorific epithet of governors and bishops, is appropriate to an official involved in building projects. See further Agosti 2015, 26–27.
23 This was proposed by Bandini (*Catal. Codd. Graec. Bibl. Med. Laur.*, I. 66), followed most recently by Gonnelli 1989, 51–52. *Contra* Dräseke 1892, 72; Golega 1960, 23 n. 1.

Demonstration of the Apostolic Preaching (Ἐπίδειξις τοῦ Ἀποστολικοῦ Κηρύγματος), a didactic treatise addressed to a certain Marcianus, a baptized Christian of unknown identity, with the aim of deepening his faith.[24] Be that as it may, Agosti has shown how the description of Marcianus' hospitality in the *Metaphrasis Psalmorum* can be read figuratively as shepherding the poet into the Christian faith:[25] πὰρ γὰρ ἐμοὶ πρώτῳ προμολών (42) is reminiscent of οἱ πρώτως προσιόντες of converts (*Const. App.* 15), after which ἐπάσσαο σίτου (43) could stand either for eucharistic communion or more general spiritual nutrition provided by Marcianus. The ἤθεα learned by the poet may refer broadly to Christian character or ethics, but in this context might imply more specifically the ethics learned by Scripture,[26] recalling the use of the word a few lines above regarding the moral teachings of the glorious David's Psalter (15: Δαυίδου μὲν ἀγακλέος ἤθεα). The effect of this parallelism, within the unusual direct speech of the addressee, is to layer the didactic voices of David, Marcianus, and ultimately the poet himself, who with his paraphrase brings the moral teachings of David to an even wider audience.

The language of conversion here also connects the figure of the poet and his audience, in that Marcianus' stated aim in advising the paraphrase of the Psalms is to educate "others" (32: ἄλλοι, i.e. non-Christians or heretics)[27] and presumably convert them to the Christian faith. This does not exclude as well an educated Christian audience, who could equally have appreciated the hexameter paraphrase of the Psalms. The figurative language of Marcianus' hospitality and teaching might be taken more simply to suggest the deepening of the poet's Christian faith rather than absolute conversion. Two of the reasons given by Gregory Nazianzen for writing his classicizing Christian verse (*carm.* II.1.39 = *PG* 37.1312–13) are to surpass pagans and heretics (49: τοὺς ξένους) in literature and to provide a pleasing and persuasive medicine to sweeten the bitterness of Christian education for the young (37–42: τοῖς νέοις ... | ὥσπερ τι τερπνὸν τοῦτο δοῦναι φάρμακον | πειθοῦς ... | τέχνῃ γλυκάζων τὸ πικρὸν τῶν ἐντολῶν).[28] The image of

---

24 On this text, which now survives only in an Armenian translation, see Rousseau 1995; Behr 1997; Graham 2001.
25 Agosti 2001a, 90 on vv. 42–43, cited above.
26 Cf. Or., *princ.* 3.1.11–12 (Lampe s.v.). Agosti 2001a, 90 proposes that it refers to the sacraments of the church, as does ἔθος at Greg. Nyss., *Eun.* 3.9.58 (cf. Lampe s.v.).
27 vv. 32–34, quoted in full above in n. 10.
28 See Simelidis 2009, 24–30; Whitby 2008. Cf. *carm.* II.1.11.6–8: παίζει δὲ μέτρον τῆς ἀνίας φάρμακον | παίδευμα καὶ γλύκασμα τοῖς νέοις ἅμα, | τερπνὸν παρηγόρημα ("Poetry is a medicine against sorrow, both sweet and educational for the young, a pleasing means of instruction").

poetry as sweet and pleasing medicine has roots in the didactic tradition[29] and is used prominently by Clement of Alexandria (c. 150–215 CE) near the beginning of his *Protrepticus*, an appeal to pagans to turn towards Christianity: in contrast, he says, to the pagan poetry of Eunomus or Terpander, his new Levitical song of God is mixed with a true and sweet medicine of persuasion (1.2: γλυκύ τι καὶ ἀληθινὸν φάρμακον πειθοῦς ἐγκέκραται τῷ ᾄσματι), a message he delivers amidst quotation of Homer and the usurpation of Hesiodic motifs.[30]

The prologue to the *Metaphrasis Psalmorum* does not present the re-versification of the Psalter as educational medicine (φάρμακον), but it is bound to the imagery of sweetness used by Clement and Gregory in its aim to reawaken the honey-sweet song of David's Psalms (30–31: εἰς δὲ μελιχρὴν | Δαυίδου βασιλῆος ἐγείρομεν αὖτις ἀοιδήν). Elsewhere, Basil speaks of the Psalms themselves, in their Septuagint version, as an ideal educational vehicle for the young, because the sweetness of their song is mixed with good doctrine, just as the best doctors coat the rim of the cup with honey when giving the most difficult medicines (*hom. in Ps.* 1.1–2: τὸ ἐκ τῆς μελῳδίας τερπνὸν τοῖς δόγμασιν ἐγκατέμιξεν ... κατὰ τοὺς σοφοὺς τῶν ἰατρῶν, οἳ τῶν φαρμάκων τὰ αὐστηρότερα πίνειν διδόντες τοῖς κακοσίτοις, μέλιτι πολλάκις τὴν κύλικα περιχρίουσι).[31] In this respect the Psalms are inherently linked to the aesthetic and educational aims of early Christian classicizing poetry. Gregory Nazianzen himself likens his poetry to the Psalms (*carm.* II.1.39.82–89),[32] while others connect their work to David as poet.[33] Perhaps most famously, Jerome, in a letter to Paulinus (53.8), compared David to pagan poets

---

29 See Cameron 2016, 168–169, who notes Lucr. 1.935–950 = 4.10–25. For poetry as φάρμακον, cf. Theoc., *Id.* 11.1–3, Callim., *Epigr.* 46.4. See also the Introduction to this volume.
30 Earlier in the same passage Clement calls upon pagans to turn away from Mt Helicon and toward Mt Sion. See Scully 2015, 155: "Adapting and cannibalizing the *Theogony*'s vision, he uses it to argue that the old tradition is benighted and as a vehicle to carry his audience to a true understanding of the light that shines from Mt. Sion."
31 On the sweetness of the Psalms as an educational tool cf. Jer., *ep.* 107.4 (of the education of the soul): *adhuc tenera lingua psalmis dulcibus inbuatur* ("its tender tongue must be imbued with the sweetness of the Psalms"); Greg. Nyss., *Pss. titt.* 8: ὁ μέγας Δαυὶδ τῇ περὶ τῶν ἀρετῶν φιλοσοφίᾳ τὴν μελῳδίαν κατέμιξεν, οἷόν τινα μέλιτος ἡδονὴν τῶν ὑψηλῶν καταχέας δογμάτων ("Great David mixed melody with the philosophy of virtue, thus pouring the sweetness of honey over elevated teachings").
32 Cf. Greg. Naz., *ep.* 101.73; see Simelidis 2009, 28.
33 Cf. Paulinus, *Laus Sancti Iohannis* (*carm.* 6) 1–26; Prudentius, *Cath.* 9.2 (David as pagan priest); Sedul., *CP* 1.23–25.

such as Simonides, Pindar, Alcaeus, and Horace.³⁴ Indeed, a hexameter paraphrase of the Psalms would have had a natural educational function for early Christians. Not only was the practice of paraphrase linked to the school curriculum,³⁵ but the Psalms were one of the most widely known texts in Late Antiquity. The remains of school exercises in Egypt show that the Psalms were at times taught together with classical poetry such as Homer and Menander.³⁶

While the evocation of the figure of Homer at the beginning of the prologue of the *Metaphrasis Psalmorum* is underscored by an allusion to classical verse, which depicts the broad influence of Homer, the language of the opening lines also brings to mind Hesiod's didactic voice. The poet states in v. 2 his intention to bring to Marcianus joy in return for pains and reward for work (2: σοὶ χάριν ἀντὶ πόνων φορέειν καὶ κέρδος ἐπ' ἔργῳ). The second half of the line recalls and combines Hesiod's advice to Perses on farming and sailing in *Works and Days* 381–382: σοὶ δ' εἰ πλούτου θυμὸς ἐέλδεται ἐν φρεσὶν ᾗσιν, | ὧδ' ἔρδειν, καὶ ἔργον ἐπ' ἔργῳ ἐργάζεσθαι ("If you desire wealth in your heart, act thus and undertake work upon work") and 644 μείζων μὲν φόρτος, μεῖζον δ' *ἐπὶ κέρδει κέρδος* ("The greater the cargo, the greater the profit piled upon profit"). The phrasing ἔργον ἐπ' ἔργῳ does appear once more in Theocritus (*Id.* 15.20, at line end as here) and Aeschylus echoes ἐπὶ κέρδει κέρδος (*Sept.* 437: καὶ τῶιδε κέρδει κέρδος ἄλλο τίκτεται);³⁷ also similar is Dolon's aphorism in Euripides *Rhes.* 162–163: παντὶ γὰρ προσκείμενον | κέρδος πρὸς ἔργῳ τὴν χάριν τίκτει διπλῆν ("For a reward placed upon any work bears a double favor"). But the combination κέρδος ἐπ' ἔργῳ in the context of the prologue's didactic address to Marcianus naturally summons up Hesiod. The allusion is another instance of *Konstrastimitation*: Whereas the Hesiodic advice concerns the accumulation of material and worldly profit, the Christian poet hopes to bring spiritual profit in return for ascetic labor. Through the prologue's structure and allusive language, the poet of the *Metaphrasis Psalmorum* becomes a new Davidic Hesiod,³⁸ who, to echo Clement, inhabits Mt Sion rather than Mt Helicon, a prophet instructing pagans and Christians alike.

---

34 See Green 2006, 146–148, who suggests that Jerome's letter may have inspired Paulinus' paraphrase of Psalms 1, 2, and 137 (*carm.* 7–9).
35 See *inter alia* Roberts 1985, 37–60; Miguélez-Cavero 2008, 309–316.
36 See Cribiore 1996, nos. 388 and 396; cf. nos. 295, 297, 397 and 403.
37 For similar repetitive phrasing cf. Hes., fr. 204.105: ἄλγος ἐπ' ἄλγει, *Od.* 7.120: μῆλον δ' ἐπὶ μήλῳ. For the first half of the line cf. Thuc. 4.86: οὐκ ἂν ἀντὶ πόνων χάρις καθίσταιτο ("there would be no thanks in return for our labor"); Agathias, *AP* 6.80.5: αἰτεῖ δ' ἀντὶ πόνων. In Pind., *Isthm.* 5.24–25: μὴ φθόνει κόμπον τὸν ἐοικότ' ἀοιδᾷ | κιρνάμεν ἀντὶ πόνων ("Do not resent mixing in song a fitting boast in return for labors"), song is a reward for athletic efforts.
38 On the wider influence of Hesiod in Late Antiquity see Agosti 2016.

Bibliography

Accorinti, D. 2016. "The poet from Panopolis: an obscure biography and a controversial figure", in D. Accorinti (ed.), *Brill's Companion to Nonnus of Panopolis*, Berlin, 11–53.
Agosti, G. 2001a. "L'epica biblica nella tarda antichità greca. Autori e lettori nel IV e V secolo", in F. Stella (ed.), *La scrittura infinita. Bibbia e poesia in età medievale e umanistica (Atti del Convegno di Firenze, 26–28 giugno 1997)*, 67–104.
Agosti, G. 2001b. "Considerazioni preliminari sui generi letterari dei poemi del *Codice Bodmer*", *Aegyptus* 81, 185–217.
Agosti, G. 2002. "I poemetti del *Codice Bodmer* e il loro ruolo nella storia della poesia tardoantica", in A. Hurst/J. Rudhardt (eds.), *Le Codex des Visions*, Genève, 73–114.
Agosti, G. 2003. *Nonno di Panopoli: Parafrasi del Vangelo di S. Giovanni. Canto V*. Firenze.
Agosti, G. 2011a. "Usurper, imiter, communiquer: le dialogue interculturel dans la poésie grecque Chrétienne de l'antiquité tardive", in N. Belayche/J.-D. Dubois (eds.), *L'oiseau et le poisson. Cohabitations religieuses dans les mondes grec et romain*, Paris, 275–299.
Agosti, G. 2011b. "Le brume di Omero. Sofronio di fronte alla paideia classica", in L. Cristante/ S. Ravalico (eds.), *Il calamo della memoria. Riuso di testi e mestiere letterario nella tarda antichità. Trieste, 27–28 aprile 2006*, Trieste, 33–50.
Agosti, G. 2012. "Greek poetry", in S.F. Johnson (ed.), *The Oxford Handbook of Late Antiquity*, Oxford, 361–404.
Agosti, G. 2015. "Per una fenomenologia del rapporto fra epigrafia e letteratura nella tarda antichità", in L. Cristante/T. Mazzoli (eds.), *Il calamo della memoria. Riuso di testi e mestiere letterario nella tarda antichità, VI*, Trieste, 13–34.
Agosti, G. 2016. "Esiodo nella tarda antichità: prime prospezioni", *SemRom*, 5, 179–194.
Agosti, G./Gonnelli, F. 1995. "Materiali per la storia dell'esametro nei poeti cristiani greci", in M. Fantuzzi/R. Pretagostini (eds.), *Struttura e storia dell'esametro greco*, Roma, 289–434.
Aloni, A. 2017. "Hesiod between performance and written record", in C. Tsagalis (ed.), *Poetry in fragments: studies on the Hesiod Corpus and its afterlife*, Berlin, 3–28.
Behr, J. 1997. *St. Irenaeus of Lyons: On the Apostolic Preaching*, New York.
Brock, S. 1969. "Review of Lebon (1968)", *JThS* 20, 646–649.
Cameron, Alan 2016. *Wandering poets and other essays on late Greek literature and philosophy*, Oxford.
Cribiore, R. 1996. *Writing, teachers, and students in Graeco-Roman Egypt*, Atlanta.
De Stefani, C. 2008. "La *Parafrasi di Giovanni* di Nonno e la *Metafrasi dei Salmi* dello Pseudo-Apollinare: un problema di cronologia", in S. Audano (ed.), *Nonno e i suoi lettori*, Alessandria, 1–16.
Dräseke, J. 1892. *Apollinarios von Laodicea. Sein Leben und seine Schriften*, Leipzig.
Faulkner, A. 2014. "Faith and fidelity in biblical epic: the *Metaphrasis Psalmorum*, Nonnus, and the theory of translation", in K. Spanoudakis (ed.), *Nonnus of Panopolis in context I. Poetry and cultural milieu in Late Antiquity with a section on Nonnus and the modern world*, Berlin, 195–210.
Faulkner, A. 2020. *Apollinaris of Laodicea: Metaphrasis Psalmorum*, Oxford.
Gitschel, P.J. 1936. "War der Verfasser der dem Apolinarius zugeschriebenen Psalmenmetaphrase wirklich körperlich blind?", in *Munera philologica L. Ćwikliński oblata*, Posnan, 104–110.
Golega, J. 1939. "Verfasser und Zeit der *Psalterparaphrase* des Apolinarios", *BZ*, 39, 1–22.

Golega, J. 1960. *Der Homerische Psalter*, Ettal.
Gonnelli, F. 1989. "Il Salterio esametrico. I. Edizione e traduzione del *ps.* 21", *Koinonia*, 13, 51–59.
Graham, S.L. 2001. "Structure and purpose of Irenaeus *Epideixis*", *Stud. Patr.*, 36, 210–221.
Green, R.P.H. 2006. *Latin epics of the New Testament. Juvencus, Sedulius, Arator*, Oxford.
Hurst, A./Rudhardt, J. (eds.) 1999. *Papyri Bodmer XXX-XXXVII, 'Codex des Visions': poèmes divers*, München.
Hutchinson, G.O. 2009. "Read the instructions: didactic poetry and didactic prose", *CQ*, 59, 196–211.
Lebon, J. 1946. *Le moine saint Marcien (Miscellanea historia in honorem Alberti De Meyer)*, Leuven.
Livrea, E. (ed.) 1989. *Nonno di Panopoli. Parafrasi del Vangelo di S. Giovanni. Canto XVIII*, Napoli.
Ludwich, A. (ed.) 1912. *Apolinarii Metaphrasis Psalmorum*, Leipzig.
Miguélez-Cavero, L. 2008. *Poems in context: Greek poetry in the Egyptian Thebaid 200–600 AD*, Berlin.
Miguélez-Cavero, L. 2018. "Christian poetry", in S. McGill/E. J. Watts (eds.), *A Companion to late antique literature*, New Jersey, 259–280.
Raven, C.E. 1923. *Apollinarianism: an essay on the Christology of the Early Church*, Cambridge.
Roberts, M. 1985. *Biblical epic and rhetorical paraphrase in Late Antiquity*, Liverpool.
Rousseau, A. 1995. *Irénée de Lyon: Démonstration de la prédication apostolique*, Paris.
Schiesaro, A./Mitsis, P./Strauss Clay, J. (eds.) 1994. *Mega nepios. Il destinatario nell'epos didascalico. The addressee in didactic epic*, MD 31, Pisa.
Scully, S. 2015. *Hesiod's Theogony: from Near Eastern creation myths to Paradise Lost*, Oxford.
Shorrock, R. 2011. *The myth of paganism: Nonnus, Dionysus and the world of Late Antiquity*, London.
Simelidis, C. (ed.) 2009. *Selected poems of Gregory of Nazianzus: I.2.17; II. 1.10, 19, 32*, Göttingen.
Simelidis, C. 2016. "Nonnus and Christian literature", in D. Accorinti (ed.), *Brill's Companion to Nonnus of Panopolis*, Berlin, 289–307.
Traill, D.A. 1998. "Callimachus' singing sea (*Hymn* 2. 106)", *CP*, 93, 215–222.
Trout, D. 1999. *Paulinus of Nola: life, letters, and poems*, Berkeley (CA).
Van der Nat, P.G. 1973. "Die *Praefatio* der Evangelienparaphrase des Iuvencus", in W. den Boer/J.H. Waszink (eds.), *Romanitas et Christianitas*, Amsterdam, 249–257.
van Roey, A. 1975. "Remarques sur le moine Marcien", *Stud. Patr.* 12, 160–177.
Whitby, Mary 2008. "'Sugaring the pill': Gregory of Nazianzus' advice to Olympias (*carm.* 2. 2. 6)", *Ramus*, 37, 79–98.
Whitby, Mary 2016. "Nonnus and biblical epic", in D. Accorinti (ed.), *Brill's Companion to Nonnus of Panopolis*, Berlin, 215–239.

Anna Lefteratou
The Lament of the Virgin in the *I Homeric Centos*: An Early *Threnos*

"Il existe une chanson religieuse d'une grande beauté ... la Déploration de la Vierge" – it is with these words that Bertrand Bouvier opens his book *Le Mirologue de la Vierge*. Bouvier's study is a collection of Byzantine and Medieval Greek folksongs which were gradually included within the liturgy of Good Friday and are performed to this day.[1] The text of what is nowadays called Ἐγκώμια, namely an eulogy, goes back to the fourteenth century, but its forerunners can be traced to a much earlier date: the first prose text suggesting a lament of the Virgin is the fourth-century *Apocryphal Acts of Pilate* B,[2] as nowhere in the canonical texts is the Virgin depicted mourning. A weeping mother would have shattered the theological underpinning of the Cruxifiction and subverted Mary's initial humble willingness to participate in the plan of Redemption: Mary, above all, ought not to disbelieve in Jesus' promised resurrection.[3] In the canonical sources, only John 19:25 presents Mary at the feet of the Cross together with Mary the Magdalene and the Beloved Disciple. But in the fifth century the time for a more touching representation of Mary was ripe. The Church Fathers increasingly crafted her *ethopoeia* and dwelled on her maternal suffering:[4] Cyril of Alexandria, for example, interprets Jesus' address to

---

1 Bouvier 1976.
2 For a 4th-century date for the so-called Gospel of Nicodemus, or the Cycle of Pilate, see Gounelle 2013, 251–253. Tischendorf 1987 (1876), lxvii for a 5th-century date for the Greek text. On the influence of these apocrypha on Byzantine literature see Cameron 1991, 90 and 93–106.
3 Cf. Origen's commentary (*Jo.*, *PG* 14.4.32), where Mary is expected to see in the beloved disciple John the risen Christ.
4 Cf. already a mention of Mary's suffering in John Chrysostom, *Hom. in Jo.*, *PG* 59.462; Jesus' saying is a manifestation of filial love to his mother. The most characteristic of Mary's suffering was the reworking of Lk 2:35: σοῦ αὐτῆς τὴν ψυχὴν διελεύσεται ῥομφαία ("a sword will pierce your own soul too", trans. *NRSV)* interpreted as foreshadowing Mary's grief at the cross, which begins with Origen, *PG* 13.1845. For more sources see Constas 2003, 331: e.g., Athanasius (*PG* 28.996) restages the dialogue between Mary and Simeon and prompts Mary to show philosophical temperance. Cf. Cyr. Alex., *Jo.*, *PG* 74.663 (= 3.91, Pusey): ῥομφαίαν γὰρ ἔλεγε τὴν ὀξεῖαν τοῦ πάθους προσβολὴν πρὸς λογισμοὺς ἐκτόπους κατατέμνουσαν τοῦ γυναίου τὸν νοῦν. δοκιμάζουσι γάρ οἱ πειρασμοὶ τὰς τῶν πασχόντων καρδίας, καὶ τοὺς ἐνόντας αὐταῖς ἀπογυμνοῦσι λογισμούς ("for by sword he meant the sharp infliction by sorrow that tears the woman's sanity [urging her] towards unfitting thougths. For the temptations are testing the hearts of the suffering and they strip them [the hearts] naked of the thoughts they contain"). See also Kalavrezou 1990; Constas, forthcoming, on the Byzantine reception of these patristic interpretations; and Chapter 6 in Reynolds 2012 for an overview.

https://doi.org/10.1515/9783110696219-016

his mother and John as a way of assuaging her grief.[5] Nonnus' *Paraphrase*, probably written some twenty years after the first edition of the *Homeric Centos* (henceforth *I HC*), is influenced by Cyril but does not significantly alter the Fourth Gospel: Nonnus has only Mary the Magdalen weeping at the feet of the cross, an innovation when compared with his *Vorlage*.[6]

Researchers cite among the earliest poetic versions of Marian lamentations in Greek the works of two Syrians: Ephrem's (d. 373) homily and Romanos' (d. 566) Kontakion on the Crucifixion.[7] Both of these texts are embedded in the liturgical context of Eastern Orthodoxy and despite their emphasis on Mary's *ethopoeia*, they are not theatrical sketches, as opposed to some of the later medieval and Byzantine reworkings.[8] A theatrical revision of Mary's lament is the Euripidean Cento *Christus Patiens*, which will not be discussed here, because its date and authorship are heavily contested.[9] Importantly, however, an unnoticed poetic reworking of Mary's lament from the mid-fifth century is found in the *I HC*.[10] The *Homeric Centos*, Christian poems composed with verses lifted verbatim from Homer and reassembled into new poems, are transmitted in several editions. From these, the first and longest one (*I HC*) is dated in the mid-fourth century, consists of 2,354 lines, and narrates briefly the *Genesis* and the major events of the canonical Gospels, both the Synoptics and John. The poem is probably to be

---

[5] Jo 19:25–27. Cyr. Alex. interprets it as a sign of filial love but also as a way of restraining Mary's maternal reaction, *Jo.*, PG 74.663–665.

[6] Nonnus avoids the spectacle of Maria lamenting but instead focuses on Mary Magdalene: in Nonn., *Par.* 19.136 on Jo 19:25: Μαγδαληνὴ φιλοδάκρυος; echoing Cyr. Alex., *Jo.*, PG 74.661: φιλόδακρυ γάρ πως ἀεί τὸ θηλειῶν ἐστι γένος ("women are always fond of tears").

[7] The bibliography is immense; see, e.g., Emereau 1918; Tomadakis 1993; Sticca 1984; Tulier 1997; Tsironis 1998; Shoemaker 2011. For Christians and theater see Easterling/Miles 1999 and Barnes 2008; see also Cameron 1991, 83; for performances and Christian responses see, e.g., Leyerle 2001; Webb 2008; Elm 2012, 348–350. Between Ephrem's and Romanos' laments of the Virgin appear a Coptic fragmental apocryphon, the *Gospel of Gamaliel* (Elliott 1993, 159–160) and the Syriac *Homily on Good Friday* by Jacob of Serugh (Tsironis 1998, 110–111).

[8] This is the main focus of Sticca's 1984 work on medieval religious theater. For secular pantomime in Late Antiquity see Wasyl in this volume.

[9] For *Chr. Pat.* as an early Byzanatine drama see Sticca 1974; for the attribution to Gregory Nazianzen see Tulier 1997; for a 10th /11th-century date see Pollmann 2017, ch. 6.

[10] But this is not included in all subsequent abbreviated editions besides the brief HCy 331–340.

attributed, though its authorship is still debated, to the wife of Theodosius II, Eudocia Athenais, the daughter of a sophist,[11] but also empress and sister-in-law of Pulcheria, who allegedly popularized the Marian cult in Constantinople.[12]

Classicists and Byzantinists alike largely ignore the lament in the *I HC*,[13] although its study might help to bridge the gap between the fourth-century *Acts of Pilate* B and the sixth-century *Kontakion* of Romanos, and also add to the classical pedigree of such ritual lamentations, as already argued in the magisterial work of Alexiou (2002). This is not the place to discuss the influence of Ephrem on the Marian Lament found in the *I HC*; that of the *Acts of Pilate* B, however, is more than certain.[14] The focus of this paper is twofold: On the one hand, I will illustrate the continuity and the subversion of classical versions of *goos* and rhetorical lamentations in this Christian lament for the Son of Man and explore the significance of this generic modulation for the reception of classicizing genres in Late Antiquity. Secondly, I will address the question of authorship and religious context of the *I HC* within the setting of events following the Council of Ephesus in 431 CE, which declared the Virgin the 'Theotokos', given that, surprisingly enough, this early Marian lament does not resurge in the second edition of the *Homeric Centos*.

Laments in Late Antiquity and in the Homeric interpretation

The earliest epic *gooi* are found in the *Iliad*, with the laments of Briseis for Patroclus, and of Andromache, Hecuba, and Helen for Hector being the most typical of the kind. These share a formulaic structure and similar themes, such as the tri-

---

11 Schembra 2007, cxxxiii–cxlii.
12 For the context see Holum 1982. For Eudocia's life and work see Van Deun 1993. For the literary production under Theodosius II see now Whitby 2013.
13 The edition of Usher 1999 was based on a narrow selection of manuscripts; see now Schembra 2007 and 2006. Mary's lament in the *I HC* is not included, to my knowledge, in any discussion of Marian laments such as Alexiou 2002, Sticca 1984, or even the more recent discussion of Ephrem's homily in Bakker/Philippides 2000 or in the otherwise exhaustive treatment of Mary by Brubaker/Cunningham 2011.
14 For Ephrem and his influence in the 4th-century homilies see Emereau 1918, 98–100; Brock 2001, 13; Bakker/Philippides 2000. For apocryphal literature in the *Homeric Centos* see Rey 1996 and esp. Schembra 2006 *ad loc.*, esp. on the crucifixion and the entombment.

partite division, past-present oscillation, ring composition, and antiphonal elements.[15] While these stereotypical *gooi* were influential for the late antique *Homeric centos*, as they would have provided the relevant lines to be reused in the Christian poem, it is equal important to contextualize Mary's lament within the contemporary rhetorical tradition.[16] By the fifth century Homeric *gooi* were the models of rhetorical declamation: in the third century Menander Rhetor describes *goos* thus:

> Ὅμηρος ὁ θεῖος ποιητὴς τά τε ἄλλα ἡμᾶς ἐπαίδευσε καὶ τὸ τῆς μονῳδίας εἶδος οὐ παραλέλοιπε· καὶ γὰρ Ἀνδρομάχῃ καὶ Πριάμῳ καὶ τῇ Ἑκάβῃ λόγους μονῳδικοὺς περιτέθεικεν οἰκείους ἑκάστῳ προσώπῳ, ὥσπερ ἐκδιδάξαι βουλόμενος ἡμᾶς μηδὲ τούτων ἀπείρως ἔχειν. [...] διαιρήσεις δὲ τὴν μονῳδίαν εἰς χρόνους τρεῖς, τὸν παρόντα εὐθὺς καὶ πρῶτον· μᾶλλον γὰρ ὁ λόγος κινητικώτερος εἰ ἀπὸ τῶν ἐπ' ὄψιν καὶ τῶν νῦν συμβάντων οἰκτίζοι τις, εἰ τὴν ἡλικίαν ἢ τὸν τρόπον τοῦ θανάτου λέγοι τις, εἰ μακρᾷ νόσῳ περιπεπτωκὼς εἴη, εἰ ὀξὺς ὁ θάνατος· <ἢ> ἀπὸ τῆς συνόδου τῶν παρόντων, ὅτι συνεληλύθασιν οὐκ εἰς θέατρον εὔδαιμον, οὐκ εἰς θέαν εὐκταίαν. εἶτα ἀπὸ τοῦ παρεληλυθότος χρόνου, οἷος ἦν ἐν νέοις ὅτε ἦν νέος, οἷος ἐν ἀνδράσιν ἀνὴρ τυγχάνων, ὅπως ὁμιλητικός, ὅπως ἤπιος, ὅπως ἐπὶ λόγοις διαπρέπων, ὅπως ἐν νεανίσκοις καὶ ἡλικιώταις γαῦρος, οἷος ἐν κυνηγεσίοις, οἷος ἐν γυμνασίοις· ἀπὸ δὲ τοῦ μέλλοντος, οἵας εἶχεν ἐλπίδας ἐπ' αὐτῷ τὸ γένος.

> Homer the divine poet, has instructed us in so many things without even omitting the genre of monody (καὶ τὸ τῆς μονῳδίας εἶδος); for he attributed to Andromache, Priam and Hecuba monodic speeches, fitting for each character, as if he wished to teach us in detail, so that there is nothing that we are not aware of in these matters. [...] The monody should be divided into three periods: (i) the present, since the speech is more effective if pity is induced by reference to visible events and present happenings – e.g. if reference is made to his age or manner of death – whether he endured a long illness or died suddenly – or to the present gathering, people who have come not to a happy theatre or sight they hoped to see; (ii) the past: e.g. what he was like when he was young among the young, what he was like among men when he became a man (if so), how accessible, how gentle, how distinguished in speaking, how proud among the lads and his contemporaries, how he was at hunting, at athletics; (iii) the future: what hopes the family placed in him. (Men. Rhet. 434–435 trans. Russell/Wilson)

Menander's discussion of *gooi* is intriguing, because it provides a rhetorical frame for monodies and adds an extra touch of theatricality that enhances the inherent performativity of the Homeric lament.[17] Already in classical times, *Iliad* 18, the lament of Briseis, and the cluster of lamentations for Hector in Book 24 inspired

---

15 Tsagalis 2004, 32–51; Alexiou 2002, 1976, 131–133. For a psychoanalytical interpretation of classical mourning mothers see also Loraux 1998.
16 Pernot 1993; Cribiore 2001, 239; Hose 2004.
17 On laments and performance see, e.g., Alexiou 2002, 12; Tsagalis 2004, 6.

tragic revisions.[18] Hellenistic and later epics did not hesitate to infuse their narratives not only with tragic allusions but also with a deeper tragic mode.[19] It comes, therefore, as no surprise, that Menander describes the attendees at a funeral as the audience of an unhappy drama. Lucian's *De luctu* (13) satirically illustrates this attitude: in funerals, he argues, the parents of the deceased tend to exaggerate their act in order "to intensify the staged (funerary) drama" (ἵνα καὶ ἀκμαιότερον τὸ ἐπ' αὐτῷ δρᾶμα) by throwing themselves on the corpse with "unintelligible and vain shrieks (φωνὰς ἀλλοκότους καὶ ματαίας), lamenting as if the dead could respond." The cynical pepping aside, Lucian highlights the quasi-theatrical flair of imperial-age lamentations, which are presented as tragic monologues including movement and wailing. Chaniotis (2013, 173) rightly observes that theatrically staged emotions were a way to control excessive reactions since Roman culture advocated moderation.[20] Indeed, from Plato[21] to the Christian Fathers,[22] there was an emphasis on emotional restraint,[23] although this did not always reflect reality. Equally difficult was the dissociation of lament from the theater. Whereas Gregory, for example, in his funerary speech for his sister Gorgonia advises restraint, he still cannot resist the theatrical cliché and thus describes her family and friends assisting her in the last hours like a chorus.[24] It appears, therefore, that lamentations were inherently performative, and from the imperial times onwards they were conceptualized in relation to theater and theatrical metaphors.

But it was not only rhetorical lamentations that became increasingly theatrical. More illuminating for the transformation of *goos* in the *I HC* is probably the observation of a Homeric scholiast a propos of Briseis' lament that shows the

---

18 Cf. Aeschylus' anecdotal claim that tragedies were the leftovers of the Homeric banquet recorded in Athen. 8.347e; see also Pl., *Resp.* 607a; Arist., *Poet.* 1462a15. Cf. Kaufmann 1968, 136–163. See also the modern takes on what makes a plot tragic, e.g., Most 2000; Liebert 2017. For the theatricality of the imperial and later public life see Chaniotis 1997 and Cameron 1991, 83; see also Leyerle 2001; Webb 2008; and Elm 2012, 348–350.
19 E.g., Sistakou 2016 on Apollonius.
20 Roman elite was advised to show restrained emotions; see Fögen 2009. Cf. Mustakallio 2014 for the mourners in the iconography of sarcophagi, which suggests that there was a need to at least have theatrical mourning on display. Zanker/Ewald 2012, 67–69 note that the embedded elite mourners were depicted as more restrained whereas the expression of grief was delegated to professional mourners and slaves.
21 Pernot 1993, 531.
22 Greg. Naz., *PG* 35.813. Cf. Basil of Caesarea's condemnation of mourners who wail excessively, tear their clothes, and pour dust over themselves (*PG* 31.229c). See also Hughes 2004, 75–76.
23 E.g., Plut., *Mor.* 309a-b (= *Cons. ad. ux.* 3–4).
24 Greg. Naz., *PG* 35.813.

trans-generic reception of the passage. The commentator here reads the Homeric text through the lens of Athenian drama, and 'sees' a chorus of captive women:

> Βρισηῒς δ' ἄρ' ἔπειτ'<—κήδε' ἑκάστη>: ... ἐπεὶ γὰρ ἐπ' ἀλλοδαπῆς τέθνηκε Πάτροκλος, ἔνθα μὴ πάρεισι συγγενεῖς γυναῖκες, αἳ λίαν χεῖν δάκρυα φιλοῦσι, χορὸν αἰχμαλωτίδων πεποίηκε θρηνοῦντα, ἐξάρχοντος ἐνδόξου προσώπου. ὁ δὲ τόπος μέσου χαρακτῆρος ὑπάρχων τῷ μὲν διηγηματικῷ σεμνῶς πέφρασται καὶ λίαν ἐστὶ γραφικός, τῷ δὲ μιμητικῷ συμπαθὴς καὶ γοερός.

> Because Patroclus died abroad, where there were no women relatives that like to shed streams of tears, (Homer) created a chorus of captive women, with an outstanding character (i.e. the Aphrodite-like Briseis) as the chorus leader. The passage being of the middle character is told in the narrative mode with dignity and is very lively described; whereas in the mimetic mode it (i.e. direct speech) is emotional and mournful. (*schol. in Il.* 19.282–302)

In reusing the respective verses from the Iliadic *gooi*, therefore, the *I HC* was dealing with a passage that already had a prominent epic and dramatic coloring,[25] since Briseis in the *scholia* balances between epic and drama.[26] Equally important is another *scholion* on an earlier episode from Book 18: there the scholiast observes that in describing Patroclus' death Homer depicts everything neatly in two verses without the long emotive digressions found in drama.[27] This suggests that the commentator was 'reading' the *Iliad* through its later tragic revisions, pointing out the aesthetic differences. There was something manifestly theatrical about lamentations and there was something typically tragic in emotional monologues. In other words, by the fifth century CE, *goos* was a 'minor' epideictic sub-genre, which, depending on its treatment, could be used to 'transpose' a 'major' narrative, such as Homeric epic, onto a tragic register.

---

25 On tragedy and the Homeric scholiasts cf. Nünlist 2009, 268 and 358.
26 This is significantly different from the case of Hosidius Geta's Virgilian Cento *Medea* that, albeit composed of Virgilian hexameters, was highly dialogical, an element that increased theatricality. The reason is that the centos used in *Medea* come from passages such as *Aen.* 4 which were already heavily indebted to tragedy. The same is true for the theatrical lament of Mary in the *Chr. Pat.*, which presents Mary as the leader of a chorus. Since tragedy did not exist in Homer's time, the situation with the Homeric centos is slightly different. For the *Medea* see McGill 2002; for *Chr. Pat.* see Alexiou 2002, 65. See also the introduction to this volume.
27 *schol. in Il.* 18.20–21, b (BCE3E4) T.

Mary's lament in the *I Homeric Centos*

μήτηρ δ', ἥ μιν ἔτικτε καὶ ἔτρεφε τυτθὸν ἐόντα, 2050 [28]	*Od.* 23.325, Anticlea
ἀμφ' αὐτῷ χυμένη λίγ' ἐκώκυε, χερσὶ δ' ἄμυσσε	*Il.* 19.284, Briseis
στήθεά τ' ἠδ' ἁπαλὴν δειρὴν ἰδὲ καλὰ πρόσωπα.	*Il.* 19.285, ibid.
ἐκπάγλως γὰρ παιδὸς ὀδύρετο οἰχομένοιο,	*Od.* 15.355, Laertes
ὀξὺ δὲ κωκύσασα κάρη λάβε παιδὸς ἑοῖο,	*Il.* 18.71, Thetis
ἀμβρόσιαι δ' ἄρα χαῖται ἐπερρώσαντο ἄνακτος. 2055	*Il.* 1.529, Zeus and Thetis
τὴν δὲ κατ' ὀφθαλμῶν ἐρεβεννὴ νὺξ ἐκάλυψεν,	*Il.* 22.466, Andromache
ἀλλ' ὅτε δή ῥ' ἄμπνυτο καὶ ἐς φρένα θυμὸς ἀγέρθη,	*Od.* 5.458, Odysseus
καί ῥ' ὀλοφυρομένη ἔπεα πτερόεντα προσηύδα·	*Il.* 5.871 or 18.72, Thetis
"τέκνον ἐμόν, πῶς ἦλθες ὑπὸ ζόφον ἠερόεντα	*Od.* 11.155, Anticlea in Hades
ζωὸς ἐών; χαλεπὸν δὲ τόδε ζωοῖσιν ὁρᾶσθαι. 2060	*Od.* 11.156, ibid.
οἴμοι, τέκνον ἐμόν, περὶ πάντων κάμμορε φωτῶν,	*Od.* 11.216, ibid.
πῶς ἂν ἔπειτ' ἀπὸ σεῖο, φίλον τέκος, αὖθι λιποίμην;	*Il.* 9.473, Phoenix to Achilles
πῆ γὰρ ἐγώ, φίλε τέκνον, ἴω; τεῦ δώμαθ' ἵκωμαι;	*Od.* 15.509, Theoclymenos
πῶς ἔτλης Ἄϊδόσδε κατελθέμεν, ἔνθα τε νεκροί;".	*Od.* 11.475, Anticlea
ἀμφὶ δὲ παιδὶ φίλῳ βάλε πήχεε δάκρυ χέουσα, 2065	*Od.* 17.38, Penelope with Telemachus
κύσσε δέ μιν κεφαλήν τε καὶ ἄμφω φάεα καλὰ	*Od.* 16.15, Eumaeus & Telemachus
χεῖράς τ' ἀμφοτέρας, θαλερὸν δέ οἱ ἔκπεσε δάκρυ·	*Od.* 17.39, Penelope /16.16, Eumaeus
τέκνον, ⌐ἐμοί γε μάλιστα λελείψεται ἄλγεα λυγρά.	*Il.* 1.362+24.742, Andromache
οὐ γάρ μοι θνῄσκων λεχέων ἐκ χεῖρας ὄρεξας,	*Il.* 24.743, ibid.
οὐδέ τί μοι εἶπες πυκινὸν ἔπος, οὗ τέ κεν αἰεὶ 2070	*Il.* 24.744, ibid.
μεμνῄμην νύκτας τε καὶ ἤματα δάκρυ χέουσα.	*Il.* 24.745, ibid.
ἀλλά με σός τε πόθος σά τε μήδεα, φαίδιμε υἱέ,	*Od.* 11.202, Anticlea
σή τ' ἀγανοφροσύνη μελιηδέα θυμὸν ἀπηύρα·	*Od.* 11.203, ibid.
τῶ σ' ἄμοτον κλαίω τεθνηότα, μείλιχον αἰεί.	*Il.* 19.300, Briseis
νῦν δὲ σὺ μέν ῥ' Ἄϊδαο δόμους ὑπὸ κεύθεσι γαίης 2075	*Il.* 22.482, Andromache
ἔρχεαι, αὐτὰρ ἐμὲ στυγερῷ ἐνὶ πένθεϊ λείπεις".	*Il.* 22.483, ibid.
ὣς ἔφατο κλαίουσ', ἐπὶ δ' ἔστενε δῆμος ἀπείρων,	*Il.* 24.776, Helen
οὐδὲ γὰρ ⌐οὐδέ τις⌐ ⌐αὐτόθ' ἐνὶ πτόλεϊ λίπετ'⌐ ἀνὴρ	*Od.* 8.32+*Il.* 24.707, for Hector
οὐδὲ γυνή· πάντας γὰρ ἀάσχετον ἵκετο πένθος,	*Il.* 24.708, ibid.
αἶψα τοῖσι δὲ πᾶσιν ὑφ' ἵμερον ὦρσε γόοιο. 2080	*Il.* 23.108, Achilles for Patroclus
καί νύ κ' ὀδυρομένοισιν ἔδυ φάος ἠελίοιο·	*Od.* 16.220/23.154

> But his mother who gave him birth and milk when he was a baby   2050
> fell on him, lamented with shrieks, and tore with her hands
> her breast, her soft skin, and her beautiful face.
> And she lamented violently her dying son
> with a shriek she hugged her child's head
> and then the holy locks flowed waving from his head.   2055

---

[28] The passage covers broadly the events in Jo 19:38; Mt 27:57; Mk 15:42–46; Lk 23:50–53.

> Then a dark night covered her eyes,
> but when she breathed and regained her senses
> lamenting she uttered these volatile words:
> "My child, how did you descend in the dark mist,
> you a living one? It is unbearable for mortals to see this spectacle! 2060
> Oh! You my child, are the most wretched human.
> How, my dear child, can I stay here after your death?
> Where, my dear child, to whose house shall I return?
> How did you bear to descent to Hades, where the dead dwell?"
> With both hands she hugged her son shedding big tears, 2065
> she kissed his head and both his pretty eyes,
> and his two hands, and big tears fell from her eyes.
> "My child, I have been left in dreadful misery
> for you did not die stretching out your hands to me from the bed.
> You did not leave me any advice, nothing at all 2070
> so that I may recall it and lament over days and nights.
> But my longing for you, and your counsel, my brave son
> your gentleness, that took away sweet life from me.
> Thus I lament you endlessly now that you are dead, who were always kind.
> Now you are heading to Hades' palaces, the underworld, 2075
> and you have left me behind in dreadful sorrow."
> Thus she lamented, and with her wept also the crowds,
> for not one man was left there in the city (without crying)
> not even one woman; everybody was grieving heavily,
> and immediately she urged everyone to weep. 2080
> And thus as they lamented the light of the sun set. (*I HC* 2050–2081)

The first line of the passage introduces Mary with a line that originally referred to Anticlea, Odysseus' mother. It is precisely this line that is used throughout *I HC* as a *Leitmotiv* for the Virgin and which will introduce her formulaically in the subsequent editions too.[29] The *I HC* highlights Mary's role in the Redemption in the aftermath of the Ephesus Council (431 CE), where she was named the 'Theotokos.'[30] By giving birth and milk to the Word the Virgin participated in the miracle of Incarnation,[31] what might have appeared as recalling the alleged claim of Nestorius that one should not imagine God as a baby breastfeeding.[32] Yet, whereas in the Homeric epics lamenting characters are announced with a formulaic opening,

---

29 E.g., *I HC* 296, 304, 360, 2179, 2338; *II HC* 158, 234, 895, 1822; *HCa* 122, 155, 200, *passim*.
30 E.g., Holum 1982, 142.
31 Schembra 2006, 560–561 and 637. The passage also alludes to the *Acta Pilati B* (*cod.* C) 10.2: τὸ θυλλαγγάλακτον τῶν μασθῶν μου ("the one who drank the milk from the pouches of my breasts"); Cf. *Chr. Pat.* 908–909 and 1335.
32 Coll. Vat. 53. *ACO* I.1. See Bevan 2016, 60 with literature.

often of a couple of lines,[33] Mary's suffering is described in 8 lines and in two snap-shots.[34] These include: the account of lamenting gestures (2051–2052), the sound effect of her lamentation (2053–2054), a description of her hugging the head of Jesus, his hair flowing down her hands (2054–2055), her fainting (2056–2057), and another round of lamentation starting at v. 2058. Whereas there is nothing unusual about Mary's gestures, given that they were excerpted from their Iliadic model,[35] the descriptive character of the first lines and the two snapshots are indicative of the tragic tonality of the passage. This is not just a case of *amplificatio*, I believe, but this tone serves the *I HC* both at the level of characterization and also at the level of generic transposition of the epic *goos* onto a tragic register.

On the level of characterization, each of the foils offered for Mary contribute to an all-encompassing portrayal and flesh out her multi-layered relationship to her Son as a virgin bride, virgin mother, and a Second Eve.[36] These foils are used either by assimilating (*Usurpation*) their respective intertext to the needs of narrating the Christian poem without signaling so, or by subverting and contrasting the Christian content/character to the Iliadic narrative/character (*Kontrastimitation*).[37]

a) *Usurpation*. The foils of the two young women, Briseis and Andromache, and that of the immortal nymph Thetis, represent lamentations for the deceased beloved: for example Briseis' non-sexual relationship to Patroclus (2041, 2044, 2051–2052) mirrors Mary's immaculate relationship to Jesus: just as Briseis is a young girl and a slave, so Mary is a virgin and also an obedient handmaiden of God;[38] like Briseis who loses Patroclus, Mary will lose Jesus. Contrarily, the Andromache analogue (2056 and esp. 2068–2071) evokes the wedding imagery surrounding Mary's relation to her Son and God,[39] who, like Hector, dies young.

b) *Kontrastimitation*. Three foils of women, one negative and two positive, address the theme of tragic motherhood through contrast: the immortal Thetis

---

[33] Tsagalis 2004, 55 and 58 notes that the introductory lines can be up to three.
[34] This contrasts also with the introduction of other laments in the subsequent editions of the *HC*, e.g., the Widow of Nain at *II HC* 881–885 is presented with one line (*Od.* 11.155, Anticlea to Odysseus) but closes with her hopes for a speedy resurrection.
[35] E.g., Andromache at *Il.* 24.726; cf. Usher 1998, 140 on Mary's "moving elegy" and Sandnes 2011, 240, briefly.
[36] E.g., Constas 2003, 274–294.
[37] For the terms see Thraede 1962.
[38] Schembra 2006, 562 on Lk 1:38: ἡ δούλη κυρίου. See also Usher 1999, 140 on the Homeric models.
[39] See Lefteratou, forthcoming, for the nuptial imagery at the Cana wedding in the *I HC*.

(2054, 2058) illustrates the tragic mother who loses her only semi-mortal son, though Mary loses hers temporarily. Thetis famously prays to Zeus to grant her otherwise soon-to-die son *kleos*.[40] Verse 2054, on the flowing locks, conjures Zeus' confirmation by headshake, understood as a majestic move;[41] it thus links Jesus to Zeus *qua* Pantocrator and reminds the audience that Jesus is the immortal God. Penelope (2065–2067), on the other hand, laments her son whom she falsely believes to be dead at the suitors' hands. Penelope is thus a positive foil that, through *Kontrastimitation*,[42] signals Jesus' nearing Resurrection: like Telemachus, Mary's son too will come back alive as, unlike Telemachus, her son is immortal. Yet, more interesting is the Anticlea analogue so prominent in the formula used to describe Mary throughout, especially given that the queen of Ithaca in the *Odyssey* is dead and already in the Underworld. It is there where she meets Odysseus during his descent: like Odysseus, who makes it to Hades and back again, Jesus dies as a Man but is resurrected; Mary's mortality associates her to Anticlea, but, since she is alive, it likens her even more so to Eve, of whom she is the positive type;[43] and since Mary redeems the deeds of Eve, the Anticlea foil foreshadows Mary's/Eve's redemption and resurrection.[44] Yet for redemption to take place, both birth and death were prerequisites, as was the mortal body of the Virgin; this is why Mary's role in the plan of Salvation is exalted by emphasizing her role as a womb and a nursing mother (ἔτικτε, ἔτρεφεν).[45]

---

40 Hom., *Il.* 1.505.
41 Cf. Dio Chrys., *Or.* 12.26. The line from *Il.* 1.528–529 was much cited: see, e.g., Strab. 8.3.30 and Dio Chrys., *Encom. comae* 49, or criticized by Christians, such as Clem. Al., *Prot.* 2.33.1.
42 On the not always 'contradictory' nature of *Kontrastimitation* see in this volume Paschalis esp. 203–205.
43 Constas 1995, 131.
44 The *I HC* is aware of the theme of the Harrowing of Hell that appears in the *Gospel of Nicodemus*, an apocryphal narrative dated around the 5th century CE, though some versions might have appeared earlier. Cf. Schembra 2006, 526–550, and further the lamentation of Mary in this article. In the *Gospel of Nicodemus* 22–24 Jesus meets Adam in Hades and draws him to Paradise "holding him by the right hand." The resurrection of Adam appears also in the apocryphal *Life of Adam and Eve* 28.4 and 41.3; see also De Jong/Tromp 2005. The first instances of Eve being drawn upwards appear later; the *I HC* might be one of the earliest allusions to Eve being in Hades, together with the Latin *recension B* of the apocryphon of *Nicodemus*; see Flood 2011, 55–58 with further literature.
45 Constas 2003, 330–331, esp. n. 35. On the importance of Mary's body in the creation of Jesus in Nonn., *Par.* see now Hadjittofi 2018, esp. 175–176.

On the other hand, the extant *ekphrasis* of Mary's suffering has a particular theatrical touch, both at the level of the descriptive body language that introduces the lament and at that of the rhetorical reworking of the actual *goos*. We observed above that, contrary to the Iliadic *gooi*, the *I HC* states Mary's grief in an extensive introduction. The detailed references to Mary's body, suggest, I believe, a kind of ekphrastic *didaskalia* that enables the audience both to 'hear' and to 'see' Mary lamenting.[46] This language can be read as a kind of visual paratext adding to the ekphrastic spectacle: at 2051 she throws herself over Jesus' body, tearing her face; she hugs his head at 2054, his locks flowing down in waves; at 2057 she faints and regains her senses. In fact, the actual lament is split into two sequels and the next digression zooms further in on Mary's gestures: at 2065 she hugs and kisses his head, eyes, and hands. Additionally, there is an attempt to recreate a tragic impression and give the *ekphrasis* an acoustic dimension not present in Homer[47] by suffusing lament-related centos.[48]

The dramatic aspirations of Mary's *goos* also need to be seen through the rhetorical lens. It is not a coincidence that the cento follows Menander's tripartite separation of present, past, and future: vv. 2059 and 2060 are prompted by the current situation; the violent death of Jesus is also mentioned at 2069, since, like Hector, he did not die bed-ridden surrounded by family. The flashback consists of praise of his kindness (ἀγανοφροσύνη), good counsel (μήδεα), bravery (φαίδιμος), and sweetness (μείλιχος).[49] As for the future, this is foreshadowed as one of total loss. The second lamentation speech begins at 2068 and Mary's woes are repeated at 2077-2078, as in a kind of *Ringkomposition*. But whereas structure remains, the *topoi* of lamentation undergo rehabilitation and resemantization.

The oscillation between life and death brings forth the antithetical mourning imagery of light (life) and darkness (death); companionship and solitude; hope and despair.[50] But the Christian revisions of these *topoi* suggest an innovative treatment:[51] for example, the reuse of the cento originally belonging to the de-

---

46 For the theatrical dimension of *ekphrasis* see Webb 2009, 54–55.
47 Tsagalis 2004, 55–66.
48 E.g., *I HC* 2051: λίγ' ἐκώκυε; 2053: ἐκπάγλως ὀδύρετο; 2054: ὀξὺ κωκύσασα; 2058: ὀλοφυρομένη. Cf. *Chr. Pat.* esp. 865–866: ἒ ἒ ἒ ἒ ... αἲ αἴ. For the acoustic dimension in an *ekphrasis* cf. Laird 1993 on Catullus 64.
49 Menander's terms are (435): ὁμιλητικός, ἤπιος, λόγοις διαπρέπων.
50 For the reuse of the funerary *topoi* in Christian epitaphs see Gullo in this volume, e.g. 61–65.
51 Cf. the similar findings a propos of the *epithalamion* as a genre in Paulinus of Nola in Basson 1996.

scription of Zeus' divine locks at 2055, assimilates Jesus to Zeus – and in a Christian context that would evoke the *pantokrator* of the *Creed*[52] – despite his current mortal suffering. The alliteration of *z* (2059–2060: ζόφον - ζωός - ζωοῖσιν) not only contrasts darkness (ζόφος) with life, but mainly opposes the death of the living God (ζωός) to the short-living mortals (ζωοῖσι).[53] Furthermore, the description of mortals as φῶτες accentuates, through a paretymological play, the oxymoron of man's mortality versus the eternal life and light (φῶς) embodied by Jesus.[54] The theme of *mors immatura*, or violent death, exemplified in the assimilation of Jesus to Achilles, Patroclus or Hector, is equally subverted, since at the core of Jesus' suffering is his willingness to take up this task, which is vividly narrated at the beginning of *I HC*.[55] Accordingly, Mary's impasse as to where to go as a widow and a bereaved mother is not just an indication of her despair, but also alludes to John 19:26–27: there Jesus arranges, before dying, for John to take care of his mother. Given that the *Centos*' Jesus does not do this, Mary in the poem appears even more tragic in her despair.[56] The semantic reworking implies that the lament of the Virgin was meant to cast her as existing in a different league from that of mythical mortal women. Ultimately, the pathetic fallacy that follows the death of Jesus (2081: ἔδυ φάος ἠελίοιο) is not only a reprise of similar motifs, but also has a further allegorical and exegetical twist: in Christian belief Jesus *is* the light (Jo 8:12).

Conclusions

Despite the Church Fathers' polemics against the theater and dramatic performances, there were other ways to revisit the dramatic genre, brilliantly illustrated in Mary's lament in the *I HC*. Our poem is probably the first classicizing text in Greek that links the apocryphal tradition and Ephrem with the sixth-century Kontakion of Romanos, leading into the long tradition of Marian Laments in both East

---

[52] *Creed* 1: πατέρα παντοκράτορα.
[53] Cf. Cyr. Alex., *Jo.*, *PG* 74.662 (= Pusey 3.90): ἐγώ εἰμι λέγων ἡ ζωή· πῶς ἐσταυρώθη; ("the one who said 'I am the life', how was he crucified?") Later see Jesus' reply to Mary in Romanos, *Hymn* 35 (Grosdidier de Matons), str. δ, 6: μὴ τάφον οἰκήσω; πῶς ἑλκύσω πρὸς ζωὴν τοὺς ἐν τῷ ᾅδη; ("Shall I not dwell in a tomb? But how will I pull those who are in Hades towards life?").
[54] Cf. Jo 8:12; see also Nonn., *Par.* 5.22: οὐ γὰρ ἔχω τινὰ φῶτα διάκτορον ("for I do not have one to minister to me", trans. Hadjittofi, forthcoming); see also Agosti 2003, 345.
[55] E.g., *I HC* 99–205.
[56] I am indebted to Fotini Hadjittofi for pointing out this discrepancy to me.

and West. In concluding this article, and like Gianfranco Agosti in this volume and Ramsay MacMullen and E.A. Judge before him,[57] we need to ask again, "What difference did Christianity make?" The answer, I believe, is not easy, as it suggests a variety of more or less definitive observations:

On the one hand, conclusions should address the adaptation of 'minor' genres into 'major' ones. In Archaic and Classical Antiquity, the *goos* was initially intended to be a ritual lamentation performed antiphonically between a (non-/professional) mourner and a crowd/chorus of co-mourners. This 'minor' genre was often embedded in 'major' host genres such as epic and tragedy. Yet, after the tragedians, in Hellenistic and imperial rhetorical manuals *goos* is no longer a ritual song but a sub-genre of epideictic rhetoric, with a well-defined structure and peppered with theatricality. Even Homeric reception, illustrated in the Iliadic *scholion* on Briseis' lament quoted above, bears the marks of the on-going theatralization of lament. The lament of Mary in the *I HC* revisits not only the Homeric but also the rhetorical *gooi* adding a theatrical paratext that focuses on her body language (a quasi-*didaskalia*) and highlights the acoustic performative dimension. This passage thus becomes an eloquent ekphrastic representation of late antique rhetorical epidictic. This generic entanglement might have encouraged the oral performance of Mary's lament in even more theatrical terms.

Secondly, the passage needs to be evaluated within the milieu of the first half of the fifth century in the aftermath of the Council of Ephesus. It is surprising that this lament appears only in the *I HC* and not in most later, shorter *Centos*. Apocryphal sources and Cyril's interpretation of Mary's weakness at the Cross[58] suggest that a lamentation scene might not have been implausible by orthodox criteria, since a more emotional representation of Mary was already available. The classicizing reworking of Mary's lament, however, is extremely eloquent for the time of the poem's composition, the ascent of Marian worship and the related issues regarding Jesus' incarnation from a mortal woman. Whoever the poet of the *Homeric Centos* was, s/he seems to have been aware of the patristic interpretations of Mary's motherhood found both in Cyril and in Proclus of Constantinople. Mary as a sorrowful mother and the role of Mary's flesh – in our poem exemplified in the imagery of breastfeeding – in the mystery of the Incarnation, which culminates in the crucifixion, were important parameters in the interpretation of Jesus' human nature. The fact that the lament appears in the *I HC* might be a reflection of the development of the Marian Cult in Constantinople after the Council of

---

[57] Agosti in this volume esp. 39–42 on MacMullen 1986.
[58] Cyr. Alex., *Jo.*, *PG* 74.661.

Ephesus and the Theotokos Controversy at the aftermath of Nestorius' condemntation, which was connected to the environement of Eudocia's sister-in-law Pulcheria. On the other hand, the absence of the lament from most subsequent editions might be indicative of the *I HC*'s gendered poetics. Research has repeatedly described lamentation as a female 'narrative' par excellence,[59] and as Karanika (2014) shows, the *I HC* often focuses and voices the plot through female characters. *I HC* differs from other editions in that the description of Mary underscores, despite the centonic mode, maternal suffering. Although more research is required before reaching a definite conclusion about a female poetess for the *I HC*, it is tempting to attribute this pathetic dramatic lament of Mary in Homeric hexameters to a woman, herself a bereaved mother,[60] and a learned poetess: the empress Eudocia.

Ultimately, the religious context is important for evaluating the subversion of the epic genre in the *I HC*. The passage analyzed above paints a perennial portrait of the tragic mother by describing Mary alongside famous Homeric and tragic models. Yet, whereas classical literature and the *progymnasmata* trained the young to provide *ethopoeiae* for 'Hecuba lamenting' her mortal sons in the ashes of Troy,[61] the Christian poet set off to represent an oxymoron: the mourning of a virginal mortal mother for a suffering, albeit immortal son. The differentiations suggest that Christianity gave an ideological twist to the content and redefined the aesthetics and concretization of tragic pleasure: no longer was it human misfortunes on stage but the suffering in the flesh[62] of the immortal God and the emotional outburst of his virginal mother. Subsequently, the notions of fear and pity were displaced well beyond the human condition. Namely, lamentation was no longer seen as depicting the limitations of mortal nature but as an exercise in

---

[59] E.g., Murnaghan 1999, Dué 2002 for female lamenting voices in the epic; Foley 2001 for the revolutionary female lamenting voices in tragedy. For female authorship and voice in the cento see also Karanika 2014. For female authors see also Wasyl in this volume, e.g. 171 and 175 and Schottenius Cullhed 2016 on Proba.
[60] Eudocia had three children with Theodosius II: Licinia Eudoxia, Flaccilla who died in 431, and Arcadius who died in infancy; *PLRE* 2: 410–412 Licinia Eudoxia; 130 Arcadius; 473 Flaccilla 2. An extra pathetic motherly touch is also found in *I HC* 787–798 in the description of the resurrection of Jairus' daughter where the mourning mother is described in twelve lines whereas at *II HC* 562–565 in four lines. On other themes such as weaving, which is typical of the female voice, and the gender of the *I HC* author see Lefteratou 2017, 1013.
[61] Hermog., *Prog.* 9 (Andromache); Aphthon., *Prog.* 11 (Hecuba); Miguélez-Cavero 2008, 316–320 on *ethopoeia* in both classicizing and Christian epic poems.
[62] For martyrdom as spectacle see Leyerle 2001, focusing on bodily suffering. On Christian perceptions of the body see Averincev 1988, esp. ch. 2. For perceptions of the body in Late Antiquity see Brown 1988 and Bynum 1995.

maternal *pathos* and as a drama of emotional turmoil.[63] Ultimately, the *I HC* shows Mary gradually developing from a tragic mother into the later *mater dolorosa*.[64]

Bibliography

Agosti, G. (ed.) 2003. *Nonno di Panopoli. Parafrasi del Vangelo di S. Giovanni. Canto V*, Firenze.
Alexiou, M. 2002. *Ritual lament in Greek tradition* (revised by D. Yatromanolakis and P. Roilos), (first printed: 1974) London.
Averincev, S.S. 1988. *L'anima e lo specchio. L'universo della poetica bizantina*, Bologna.
Bakker, W.F./Philippides, D. 2000. "The lament of the Virgin by Ephrem the Syrian", in S.E. Kaklamanes (ed.), *Enthymesis Nikolaou M. Panagiotake*, Herakleion.
Barnes, T. 2008. "Christians and the theater", in I. Gildenhard/M. Revermann (eds.), *Beyond the fifth century. Interactions with Greek tragedy from the fourth century BCE to the Middle Ages*, Berlin, 315–334.
Basson, A. 1996. "A transformation of genres in late Latin literature. Classical literary tradition and ascetic ideals in Paulinus of Nola", in R.W. Mathisen/H.S. Sivan (eds.), *Shifting frontiers in Late Antiquity*, Aldershot, 267–276.
Bevan, G. 2016. *The New Judas: The case of Nestorius in ecclesiastical politics, 428–451 CE*, Leuven.
Bouvier, B. 1976. *Le mirologue de la Vierge*, Roma.
Brock, S.P. 2001. "Greek into Syriac, Syriac into Greek", in S.P. Brock (ed.), *Syriac perspectives on Late Antiquity*, (first printed: 1984) Hampshire, 1–17.
Brown, P. 1988. *The body and society: men, women, and sexual renunciation in early Christianity*, New York.
Brubaker, L./Cunningham, M.B. (eds.) 2011. *The cult of the Mother of God in Byzantium: texts and images*, London.
Bynum, C.W. 1995. *The resurrection of the body in Western Christianity, 200–1336 AD*, New York.
Cameron, Averil 1991. *Christianity and the rhetoric of Empire: the development of Christian discourse*, Berkeley (CA).
Chaniotis, A. 1997. "Theatricality beyond the theater: staging public life in the Hellenistic world", in B. Le Guen (ed.), *De la scène aux gradins: théâtre et représentations dramatiques après Alexandre le Grand*, Toulouse, 219–259.

---

[63] In the later *Chr. Pat.* the drama of the Theotokos consists mainly in the *metabole* of her previous bliss, e.g., 106: ἡ πάλαι μακαρία; 148: ἡ τὸ πρὶν πανόλβια; on pathos and emotional turmoil as suffering see *ibid*. A9: μητροπρεπῶς θρηνοῦσαν.
[64] I would like to thank DFG and Heidelberg University for funding and hosting respectively my project on Late Antique Christian poetry.

Chaniotis, A. 2013. "Staging and feeling the presence of God: emotion and theatricality in religious celebrations in the Roman East", in L. Bricault/C. Bonnet (eds.), *Panthée. Religious transformations in the Roman Empire*, Leiden, 169–189.
Constas, N. 1995. "Weaving the body of God: Proclus of Constatninople, the Theotokos and the loom of the flesh", *JECS*, 3, 169–194.
Constas, N. 2003. *Proclus of Constantinople and the cult of the Virgin in Late Antiquity*, Leiden.
Constas, N. Forthcoming. "'I wish I could always weep like that'. Abba Poemen and Mary at the Cross. On the origins of Byzantine devotion to the Mother of God", in N. Tsironis/Th. Kampianaki (eds.), *Lament as performance in Byzantium*, London.
Cribiore, R. 2001. *Gymnastics of the mind: Greek education in Hellenistic and Roman Egypt*, Princeton (NJ).
De Jong, M./Tromp, J. (2005). *The Life of Adam and Eve in Greek (Pseudepigrapha veteris testamentis graeca 6)*, Leiden.
Dué, C.L. 2002. *Homeric variations on a lament by Briseis*, Lanham (MD).
Easterling, P./Miles, R. 1999. "Dramatic identities: tragedy in Late Antiquity", in R. Miles (ed.), *Constructing identities in Late Antiquity*, London, 95–111.
Elliott, J.K. 1993. *The apocryphal New Testament*, Oxford.
Elm, S.K. 2012. *Sons of Hellenism, Fathers of the Church: Emperor Julian, Gregory of Nazianzus, and the vision of Rome*, Berkeley (CA).
Emereau, C. 1918. *Études critiques de littérature et de philologie byzantines: Saint Ephrem le Syrien; son oeuvre littéraire grecque*, Paris.
Flood, J. 2011. *Representations of Eve in Antiquity and the English Middle Ages*, New York.
Fögen, T. (ed.) 2009. *Tears in the Graeco-Roman world*, Berlin.
Foley, H.P. 2001. *Female acts in Greek tragedy*, Princeton (NJ).
Grosdidier de Matons, J. (ed.) 1967. *Romanos le Mélode, Hymnes. Tome IV (Nouveau Testament, XXXII-XLV, SC 128)*, Paris.
Gounelle, R. 2013. "Christian apocryphal literature: an overview", in E. Rose (ed.), *The Apocryphal Acts of the Apostles in Latin Christianity*, Leiden, 7–30.
Hadjittofi, F. 2018. "ποικιλόνωτος ἀνήρ: clothing metaphors and Nonnus' ambiguous Christology in the *Paraphrase of the Gospel according to John*", *VChr*, 72, 165–173.
Hadjittofi, F. Forthcoming. "Nonnus of Panopolis: *Paraphrase of the Gospel According to John*", in E. Kneebone/P. Avlamis (eds.), *Collected imperial Greek epics, vol. 3*, Berkeley (CA).
Holum, K.G. 1982. *Theodosian empresses: women and imperial dominion in Late Antiquity*, Berkeley (CA).
Hose, M. 2004. *Poesie aus der Schule. Überlegungen zur spätgriechischen Dichtung*, München.
Hughes, R. 2004. *Lament, death and destiny*, New York.
Kalavrezou, I. 1990. "Images of the Mother: when the Virgin became *Meter Theou*", *DOP*, 44, 165–172.
Karanika, A. 2014. "Female voice, authorship, and authority in Eudocia's *Homeric Centos*", in F.J. Martínez García (ed.), *Fakes and forgers of classical literature*, Leiden, 95–108.
Kaufmann, W.A. 1968. *Tragedy and philosophy*, Princeton (NJ).
Laird, A. 1993. "Sounding out *ekphrasis*: art and text in Catullus 64", *JRS*, 83, 18–30.
Lefteratou, A. 2017. "From Haimorrhooussa to Veronica? The weaving imagery in the *Homeric Centos*", *GRBS*, 57, 1085–1119.
Lefteratou, A. Forthcoming. "The Cana wedding in Eudocia and Nonnos: poetics, rhetoric, and exegesis", in G. Agosti/A. Rotondo (eds.), *Studies in the Paraphrasis of Nonnus*, Berlin.

Leyerle, B. 2001. *Theatrical shows and ascetic lives: John Chrysostom's attack on spiritual marriage*, Berkeley (CA).
Liebert, R.S. 2017. *Tragic pleasure from Homer to Plato*, Cambridge.
Loraux, N. 1998. *Mothers in mourning*, Ithaca (NY).
MacMullen, R. 1986. "What difference did Christianity make?", *Historia*, 35, 322–343.
McGill, C.S. 2002. "Rewriting Vergil as tragedy in the cento *Medea*", *CW*, 95, 143–161.
Miguélez-Cavero, L. 2008. *Poems in context: Greek poetry in the Egyptian Thebaid 200–600 AD*, Berlin.
Most, G.W. 2000. "Generating genres: the idea of the tragic", in M. Depew/D. Obbink (eds.), *Matrices of genre. Authors, canons and society*, Cambridge (MA), 15–35.
Murnaghan, S. 1999. "The poetics of loss in Greek epic", in J. Tylus/S. Wofford (eds.), *Epic traditions and the contemporary world*, Berkeley (CA), 203–220.
Mustakallio, K. 2013. "Grief and mourning in Roman context", in A. Chaniotis/P. Ducrey (eds.), *Unveiling Emotions II*, Leipzig, 237–250.
Nünlist, R. 2009. *The ancient critic at work: terms and concepts of literary criticism in Greek Scholia*, Cambridge.
Pernot, L. 1993. *La rhétorique de l'éloge dans le monde gréco-romain*, Paris.
Pollmann, K. 2017. "Jesus Christ and Dionysus: rewriting Euripides in the Byzantine Cento *Christus Patiens* (repr. from: *JÖByz*, 47, 1977, 87–106).", in K. Pollmann, *The baptized Muse*, Oxford, 140–160.
Pusey, P.E. 1872. *Sancti patris nostri Cyrilli archiepiscopi Alexandrini in D. Joannis evangelium*, 3 vols., Oxford.
Rey, A.-L. 1996. "*Homerocentra* et littérature apocryphe chrétienne: quels rapports?", *Apocrypha*, 7, 123–134.
Reynolds, B.K. 2012. *Gateway to Heaven. Marian doctrine and devotion, image and typology in the Patristic and Medieval Periods*, New York.
Russel, D./Wilson, N.G. (eds.) 1981. *Menander Rhetor. A commentary*, Oxford.
Sandnes, K.O. 2011. *The Gospel 'according Homer and Virgil': Cento and Canon*, Leiden.
Schembra, R. 2006. *La prima redazione dei centoni omerici: traduzione e commento*, Alessandria.
Schembra, R. (ed.) 2007. *Homerocentones* (CCSG 62), Turnhout.
Schottenius Cullhed, S. 2016. *Proba the prophet. The Christian Virgilian Cento of Faltonia Betitia Proba*, Leiden.
Shoemaker, S.J. 2011. "A mother's passion: Mary at the Crucifixion and Resurrection in the earliest *Life of the Virgin* and its influence on George of Nikomedeia's *Passion Homilies*", in L. Brubaker/M.B. Cunningham (eds.), *The cult of the Mother of God in Byzantium: texts and images*, London, 53–67.
Sistakou, E. 2016. *Tragic failures: Alexandrian responses to tragedy and the tragic*, Berlin.
Sticca, S. 1974. "The *Christos Paschon* and the Byzantine theatre", *Comparative Drama*, 8, 13–44.
Sticca, S. 1984. *Il Planctus Mariae nella tradizione dramatica del Medio Evo*, Sulmona.
Thraede, K. 1962. "Epos", *RAC*, 5, 983–1042.
Tischendorf, C. (ed.) 1987. *Evangelia Apokrypha adhibitis plurimis codicibus Graecis et Latinis. Editio Altera*, Hildesheim.
Tomadakis, B.N. 1993. *Ἡ Βυζαντινὴ ὑμνογραφία καὶ ποίησις. Εἰσαγωγὴ εἰς τὴν Βυζαντινὴν φιλολογίαν Β'*, (first published: 1965) Athens.
Tsagalis, C.K. 2004. *Epic grief: personal lament in Homer's Iliad*, Berlin.

Tsironis, N.J. 1998. *The lament of the Virgin Mary from Romanos the Melode to George of Nicomedia* (diss.), London.

Tuiler, A. 1997. "Grégoire de Nazianze et le *Christus Patiens*", *REG*, 110, 632–647.

Usher, M.D. 1998. *Homeric stitchings: the Homeric Centos of the empress Eudocia*, Lanham (MD).

Usher, M.D. (ed.) 1999. *Homerocentones Eudociae Augustae*, Leipzig.

Van Deun, P. 1993. "The poetical writings of the Empress Eudocia: an evaluation" in J. den Boeft/A. Hilhorst (eds.), *Early Christian poetry: a collection of essays*, Leiden, 273–282.

Webb, R. 2006. "Logiques du mime dans l'antiquité tardive", *Pallas*, 71, 127–136.

Webb, R. 2008. *Demons and dancers: performance in Late Antiquity*, Cambridge (MA).

Webb, R. 2009. *Ekphrasis, imagination and persuasion in ancient rhetorical theory and practice*, Farnham.

Whitby, Mary 2013. "Writing in Greek: classicism and compilation, interaction and transformation", in C.K. Kelly (ed.), *Theodosius II: rethinking the Roman Empire in Late Antiquity*, Cambridge (MA), 195–218.

Zanker, P./Ewald, B.C. 2012. *Living with myths. The imagery of Roman sarcophagi*, Oxford. Trans. J. Slater.

Hartmut Leppin
George Pisides' *Expeditio Persica* and Discourses on Warfare in Late Antiquity

In contrast to philologists, historians are allowed to deal with literary texts in a way that might seem barbarous, as I will do in the following in order to show how poetry of the early seventh century can yield insights into the perception of politics amongst the educated elites of the Eastern Roman Empire at this time.[1] While not dwelling on aesthetic issues for their own sake, I will discuss narrative strategies as a means of source criticism. To put it more precisely: I would like to discuss the question of how the transformation of warfare during the sixth and seventh centuries was reflected in a poem, i.e. George Pisides' *Expeditio Persica*.

Let me start with some notes on the historical background. My main focus is on emperor Heraclius, who ruled between 610–641 CE. He is perhaps best known among classicists for being the emperor who made Greek the primary language of the empire of the *Rhomaioi*. In terms of warfare, his reign was shaped by extreme defeats and losses in war on the one hand, but then by astounding victories on the other.

The emperor grabbed the throne as a usurper in 610 amidst a time of war in which the Persians had made significant military advances. During the following years they overran the eastern provinces, advancing as far as Egypt. The loss of Jerusalem and the True Cross in 614 left a deep impression on contemporaries. The Romans faced more conflicts in the Balkans, where Avars and Slavs were formidable enemies. In a few years, Heraclius managed to reorganize the army and extract new economic resources from his subjects by, for example, devaluing the currency and melting down church treasures. In doing so, he relied on Sergius, the patriarch of Constantinople, a most influential figure at this time. In 622, Heraclius started to fight back effectively. Nevertheless, Constantinople was besieged in 626 and nearly captured by the Avars and the Persians. Finally, the Romans managed to fend off the Avars and to turn the tables on the Persians. In 627, Heraclius triumphantly won a battle near Nineveh in the Persian heartland, where he annihilated their army. The Persians overthrew their king, and his successor accepted a peace treaty that restored the eastern territories to the Roman Empire in their entirety. Heraclius was at the height of his power. None of his predecessors had achieved similar success. A few years later, however, Arabic

---

[1] I am grateful to Charlotte Hamway, Christian Scheidler, Sebastian Weinert, and the editors of this volume for their comments.

https://doi.org/10.1515/9783110696219-017

troops united under the banner of Islam would inflict disastrous losses on the exhausted empire. The Romans suffered a decisive defeat at the river Yarmouk in 636. When Heraclius died five years later, he left behind a weakened empire.[2]

Two changes in warfare occurred during his time, the first being a major involvement of the emperor in actual fighting. From the time of Arcadius (395–408) onwards most of the eastern Roman emperors spent their whole lives in Constantinople and did not take to the field even in times of war. The emperor was bound to the city. This has been called *urbanes Kaisertum* in German scholarship, a term that does not translate easily into English; 'urban imperial rule' might give an idea of its meaning.[3] Heraclius, however, abandoned the city in order to lead the struggle against the Persians himself, thus fundamentally changing the role of the emperor. This also meant that he put both his own person and the empire at considerable risk. The emperor's involvement in warfare relied on certain immaterial resources, which are highlighted by some literary texts. This led to a second major development in the ideology of warfare: wars acquired a sacred and even religious dimension.

Contemporary poetry such as the *Expeditio Persica* composed by George of Pisidia echoes and in part even debates these developments. The *Expeditio* describes Heraclius' first successful campaign: After some futile attempts, Heraclius launched a new attack against the Persians probably in April 622.

His panegyrist George Pisides was a well-educated cleric who served in various functions in the patriarchal administration.[4] In addition to his so-called panegyrical poems, he also composed religious poetry displaying his theological education. In the Byzantine tradition, his epigrams were regarded as exemplary. The *Hexaemeron* on the creation was most famous in Byzantium, much more so than the epics discussed here.[5]

George claims to know emperor Heraclius personally (3.343–346) and gives the impression of having joined him on the campaign.[6] Indeed, this seems to be

---

[2] For Heraclius' reign Haldon 1997; Reinink/Stolte 2002; Kaegi 2003; Booth 2014. Speck 1988 is a strange mixture of acute observations and arbitrary judgements.
[3] Pfeilschifter 2013.
[4] For George Pisides see Whitby 1998, 250 n. 21 (only tenuous evidence that George accompanied Heraclius); Whitby 2002, underlining differences between the various poems; 162–167 for the *Expeditio Persica*; Whitby 2003; Howard-Johnston 2010, 16–35; Meier 2015, especially 170–174, with bibliography. His panegyrics have been edited, translated and commented by Agostino Pertusi 1959, with a useful introduction (*Introduzione*) 9–67.
[5] On the respective manuscripts see Lauxtermann 2003, 57f.; 334–337 for the epigrams. For the *Hexaemeron* see Gonnelli 1998; for its political significance Ludwig 1991, 104–128.
[6] 2.122–126; 3.131–136.

a rare relationship between ruler and poet. The *Expeditio* is only one in a series of epic poems on the achievements of emperor Heraclius and his advisers. But given the limited length of this contribution, I will only be able to focus on this one. Although it is an epic poem, the meter is not dactylic hexameter, but iambic trimeter, which is already on the road to the Byzantine dodecasyllable.[7]

How does George perceive the campaign, which went well but was by no means decisive?[8] From the very beginning of the poem, George stages the expedition as a holy war. With the first lines of his poem he invokes the Trinity instead of the Muses.[9] He asks the Trinity, which aligns the immaterial (ἄυλος) armies of heaven (1.1f.), to teach him to move the sword, the tongue, to describe the miracles (θαύματα) of the Trinity's power (1.13–16). Following the orders of the Trinity, the emperor wages war against the barbarians who worship things created (κτίσματα) instead of the creator (1.19f.: κτίσας) – this is a traditional Christian polemic against polytheistic religions.[10] The enemies believe that right is wrong and vice versa (1.21f.). Thus, George does not define the war as a conflict of political interests, of territorial claims or of honor. Rather, he describes it as a combat between right and wrong, between true and false religion and, at the same time, as a war against lawless barbarians.[11] The Battle of the Frigidus (394) was interpreted, perhaps even staged as a clash of religions; Theodosius' campaign against the Persians in 421/2 was interpreted in terms of religion. Yet, Heraclius' propaganda of a religious war seems to go much further.[12] Thus, George seems to invoke the so-called Mosaic Distinction between true and false religion, a distinction that has been regarded as crucial for a tendency towards religious violence characteristic of monotheistic religions.[13] Fittingly, George Pisides goes so far as to praise a Christian emperor who is stained with the blood of the enemy (3.121f.;

---

7 Agosti 2012, 361–404, 386 n. 6; compare Rhoby 2011.
8 Theophanes the Confessor, *Chronogr.* AM 6113 (302.32–306.8), describes the war as a prose historian who was influenced by imperial representation. But he also mentions the economic resources (302.34–303.3) and the emperor's aides Sergius and Bonus (303.3–6). Regarding the *acheiropoietos*, he has some allusions to George's text (303.17–214), but he confounds the two passages in George. More allusions are noted in de Boor's edition. The difficulties of using Theophanes are notorious; see for example Howard-Johnston 2010, 268–312, especially 275; 277; 283 on Theophanes' use of George's *Expeditio Persica* compare Speck 1988.
9 For the avoidance or not of the invocation to the Muses see Shorrock 2011, 32f.
10 Arist., *apol.* 3.2; Or., *Cels.* 7.65; cf. Rom 1:25.
11 For parallels see 2.240; 3.305, 410.
12 For the battle of the Frigidus see Eck 2008; for 421/2 Holum 1977.
13 For the complex debate, however, see Assmann 2003; Thonhauser 2008.

cf. 405).¹⁴ This is a very unusual depiction in late antique Christian texts. Earlier Christian accounts of war had generally praised military successes while advocating bloodless victories in war.¹⁵

In the poem's opening lines, George unabashedly admits the Persians' successes thus far. Dark night covers the whole world, as he says (1.104–111). After some debate, the emperor decides to lead a military expedition in person with the campaign starting immediately after Easter (1.132–157); it is thus embedded in the liturgical calendar of the year. Heraclius takes with him the most famous holy image, the *Acheiropoietos*, the icon of Christ not painted by human hands.¹⁶ George explains the theology behind it at length: Since the image represents the all-informing λόγος, it is impossible for a human to have painted it. The emperor relies on this holy object, as the war is defined here as a religious act, and therefore connected to the idea of Easter in a very broad sense.

In the poet's narration it is the emperor himself who carries the image and, although the story unfolds during a Christian holiday, there is no mention of priests or bishops. The poem focuses on the emperor and the λόγος. In addition, the poet completely disregards patriarch Sergius' financial support of the campaign, which is well known from other sources.¹⁷

George mentions the icon again in the second book of the poem. The poet sets the scene of troops having successfully crossed the sea and assembling in order to praise the emperor's power, which is strengthened by God (78).¹⁸ The soldiers bow their necks to the ground, hailing the emperor "benefactor" (εὐεργέτης) and "powerful ruler" (2.84f.: κρατῶν δεσπότης) in a classical mode. The emperor again reaches for the God-made image and explains that he sees his soldiers as brothers, an evidently Christian concept. Thus, the poet evokes the idea of the army as a Christian community. In the following lines, Heraclius proceeds along the same lines. His power is not based on fear, but on love, he claims. Consequently, he contrasts the law of love to the tyrant's law of violence.¹⁹ Not fear, but

---

14 George apparently does not see any contradiction in the ascription of mildness, which the emperor shows towards enemies and future allies from small tribes, who are comparable with wild beasts in the poet's view (2.213–234). For blood connected with piety see also *Heracl.* 1.195–198.
15 Leppin 2012 and 2015.
16 Probably the Kamuliana according to Pertusi 1959, 142f.; Whitby 1998, 253 n. 33; compare *Heracl.* 1.218. Kaegi 2003, 113 erroneously identifies it as a depiction of Mary.
17 Theoph. Conf., AM 6113 (p. 302f.).
18 I do not think that George sees this as part of the hymn, since the following episode would become pointless if this were the case.
19 According to Pertusi 1959, 151 this refers to Phocas.

love, with its benevolent violence (φιλάνθρωπος βία), should shape the relationship between the emperor and his soldiers.[20]

Yet, what is the point of these remarks? The soldiers behave as if they were subjects of the Persian rulers, performing an act of reverence strongly reminiscent of Persian adoration, the *proskynesis* so offensive to the Greeks of Classical Antiquity. But Heraclius wants to leave no doubt about his role as emperor. He is not a Persian ruler who expects submissiveness, but rather the well-meaning, loving emperor of his Christian brethren.[21]

In the second part of the speech he spurs his soldiers to march against the infidels who have defiled Christian altars and churches in an attempt to eliminate the true faith. This speech ends (115) with a brutal quote from Psalm 137:9: "Blessed shall he be who takes your little ones and dashes them against the rock!"[22] For George and Heraclius, this psalm represents the work of another important ruler, King David: the psalmist directed this blessing against the Babylonians. George, however, turns it against the Persians (2.88–115). The poem again evokes the religious dimension of war, and is indicative of how this concept of war might have contributed to brutalizing warfare in Late Antiquity.

The *acheiropoietos* is characterized by the word φρικτός (86), which means something causing a shudder, a holy thrill.[23] This is not the first time Romans used Christian sacred objects in war; Philippicus, a commander under Mauricius (582–602), had asked for relics and had taken the *acheiropoietos* on campaign previously.[24] However, the holy icon did not so much serve as an instrument of military victory as an aid for restoring the troops to proper behavior and to remind them of their religious obligations. In terms of power, George does not seem to doubt that Heraclius is entitled to use the icon freely. The emperor does not allow any religious institution to interfere with the military exploits of the Roman army. The whole idea of victory is centered on Heraclius despite its religious impact.

The emperor's piety, although rarely mentioned explicitly (but see 1.164), is crucial for his success. This is illustrated repeatedly by his behavior: perhaps the most salient feature is his prayer at night (1.110f.). Sleeplessness had become an important trait in imperial representation in Late Antiquity. Justinian – obviously wanting to impress his subjects – boasted about his sleeplessness and how he

---

[20] 2.86–106. Cf., for his mildness, 1.82–99.
[21] For George's depiction of the Persians see Huber 2008.
[22] For a psalter epigram by Georgios Pisides see Lauxtermann 2003, 202–204. For the late antique metrical recasting of David's Psalms in the *Met. Pss.* see Faulkner in this volume.
[23] Lampe *s.v.* The word appears again in 2.125 when he describes military training.
[24] Evagr. 1.13 (p. 23); Thphyl. 2.3.4–6; 3.1.11f.

was filling his time musing on laws and theological issues.²⁵ Procopius, however, paints a damning picture of the emperor in his *Anekdota* by insinuating how sleeplessness was an expression of the emperor's demonic character. Evidently, this practice could also be made to stand for habits going beyond normal human behavior. From his depiction of Heraclius, it becomes clear that George understood this behavior to be a point of strength. The emperor's sleeplessness represents his concern for the empire. At the same time, the poet understands piety to be intimately connected with the imperial office when the emperor fulfils his religious obligations at night. Another example of George's strong Christian faith is the fact that he cannot bear the pagan-sounding toponym of Heraea (1.156–161).

As the totalizing Christian discourse of Late Antiquity²⁶ becomes apparent in George's writing, it does not come as a surprise that Heraclius' deeds are equated to miracles. A telling episode at the end of Book 1 is George's description of the passage to Bithynia. This episode seems to be all the more important since it is attested only by George. The noise of a ship's crew interrupts the emperor's prayers. The ship had run aground on a high rock, and the sailors are almost dead when they catch sight of the light emanating from the emperor – a light more glorious than sunlight as it does not burn. For the sailors this is a spark of hope. The emperor draws closer to the stranded ship and unassumingly lends his own hand to help (αὐτουργία). Instantly, everyone present – even the eunuchs – join in helping, and they manage to salvage the ship (1.177–220). In the following verses George describes Heraclius' excellent abilities as a helmsman not only on this occasion, but in general (221–239).

Two elements of imperial representation concur in this episode. Just like Alexander the Great or Caesar, Heraclius is a good comrade to the soldiers under his command and does not hesitate to participate in physical work. In addition to this, however, he is also – and this is all the more important for my argument – a figure invested with a certain degree of holiness. The light emanating from Heraclius reminds Christian readers of the transfiguration of Jesus as described in the synoptic gospels.²⁷ But the emanation of light was also connected with ascetic practices. The emperor is likened to Jesus Christ as well as to holy men.²⁸

---

25 Leppin 2011, 287.
26 For this concept see Cameron 1991, esp. 220–222.
27 Mt 17:1–9; Mk 9:2–8; Lk 9:28–36; Geo. Pis., *Pers.* 1.191–193 seems to evoke Mt 17:2; in general, Wallraff 2010, 100–137, especially 121f. (imperial representation); 129 (holy men and Christ); see also Lauxtermann 2003, 181f.
28 For the association between Heraclius and Jesus see Meier 2015, 186–189. For the imperial associations of Jesus' 'calming of the sea' miracle in Juvencus see Paschalis in this volume.

Yet envy, as the poet says (1.239), cannot bear the salvific power of the emperor. In one scene, envy takes the form of a stone and strikes the emperor's toe. The blood bathes the ground as a witness of his suffering and a sign of his piety. George describes this scene in religious semantics: βάπτειν, μάρτυς, στίγματα are words used in this context. Again, the emperor is assimilated to Jesus and to holy men,[29] but the same episode leaves no doubt as to his human character – given the intense Christological debates of the time, the audience must have been extremely sensitive in this regard.[30]

The poet is adept in handling theological issues: He does not depict the emperor as a priest, as had been done with some of his predecessors.[31] And although there is holiness in Heraclius, he definitely remains a human being. George performs a balancing act. He extols the emperor's spiritual qualities and his religious impact without investing him with a religious role that could be regarded as the expression of heretical belief.

While the emperor spends his nights praying, he uses the daytime to organize the empire and especially the army, as George repeatedly demonstrates. Early on in Book 1, turning to the figure of the emperor himself, he calls him the general of wise counsel. The poet does not feel that he is strong enough to describe the emperor's πόνοι (hard work), his γνῶμαι (ways of thinking), διαιρέσεις (his analytical capacities) and εὐτολμία (courage, 1.46f.). He is an extremely circumspect general who looks after everything and is respected for his military competence (2.19–24). He attends to all strategic questions and even to the supply of the troops with food (esp. 2.39–49).[32] Moreover, he introduces new forms of military training that, in their intensity, remind the poet of real battles (2.120–149). The emperor had found the army in bad shape but is able to reform it completely (2.44–48). Filled with the Holy Spirit, the emperor is capable of moving his soldiers with his speech (2.162–177).

Repeatedly, the poet highlights that the emperor acts alone (esp. 2.163) while never neglecting anything (2.206). The Roman army does not depend on any other military leaders. In short, the emperor holds every virtue a general needs. Although George keeps underlining that the emperor puts his trust in God, he

---

29 1.239–247; Trilling 1978, 259 ("a token martyrdom"); Meier 2015, 186 n. 145.
30 For the Christological debates see Lange 2012, 531–622; and Booth 2014.
31 George comes close to this when he calls the emperor a "herdsman in chief" (3.322: ἀρχιποίμην).
32 Pertusi 1959 *ad loc.* interprets the τράπεζα mentioned in 40 as an altar, which is possible. The context, however, seems to invite a more pragmatic meaning.

leaves no doubt about how the emperor's personal virtue and his intellectual capacities are decisive for the victory of the Roman troops. With all his spiritual glory the emperor is able to meet the practical needs of a ruler. The Persians, however, eschew battle (2.239–256). Their plan to make use of the night as an element of surprise is foiled by the moon, their own god, as George underlines quite gloatingly (2.368–3.6).

In consequence, Heraclius leads his troops through several brilliant tactical manoeuvres. His measures put the Roman troops in an excellent position before battle (2.257–375). The third Book of the *Expeditio Persica* is an extensive description of the victory achieved by Heraclius against the fraudulent Persians. The emperor fights in person. He shows even more boldness than Alexander (3.48f.)[33] and is covered in dust and sweat – this depiction of the imperial persona is in clear contrast to the conventional late ancient image of an emperor sitting aloof in his palace, surrounded by splendor.[34] In addition, Jesus also sweat while praying in Gethsemane according to Luke (22:44), which again suggests closeness between the emperor and Christ. In contrast to other passages, George does not mention any miracle or the icon, but praises the emperor's νοῦς and φύσις. His strategy is the real miracle (3.255: θαῦμα again). Fittingly, the troops glorify at the same time the emperor and God (3.279–281) for the victory that was unexpected and thus all the more miraculous (3.296f.).

Everything seems to be set for the continuation of this campaign, but now the city needs the emperor and the soldiers entreat him in tears to return to Constantinople (3.314–321). In fact, the empire is under pressure by the Avars in the West. Having praised the emperor so extensively, the poet changes gears in the end: In a prayer he calls God the highest general of all (385: στρατηγός), whereas Heraclius is the ὑποστρατηγός (401). The poet asks God to make Heraclius fearsome to his enemies. The sweat he sheds shall serve as a purification of former errors, and he shall conquer both passions and barbarians (3.405–410).[35] This passage seems to hint at his contested marriage to Martina, his own niece whom he had chosen as his second wife against the advice of clerics who reprimanded him for incest. Christ is asked to protect the empire and to help the emperor against envy, especially against that of his descendants (3.456–461). This is an astonishingly

---

[33] In other passages the emperor is compared to Moses in his fight against the Pharaoh, who is still outstripped by the Persian king when it comes to impiety (135–139; cf. 3.415–425). For a comparison with Elijah cf. 3.412–414.
[34] But see also *Heracl.* 1.195–206 and *hex.* 1853 with Ludwig 1991, 117f. The Dioscuri are sometimes portrayed as soaked in sweat: Plut., *Aem.* 25.1 (the horses); Val. Max. 1.8.1 (they themselves and the horses).
[35] Howard-Johnston 2010, 33f.

blunt allusion to the patchwork family of the emperor, who had sons from two (successive) wives.

With these verses the poem comes to an end. It is a splendid praise of the first Roman victory after a long series of defeats against the Persians and a dire warning against domestic infighting, which had unsettled the Roman Empire all too often. It is a document of an early stage of Heraclius' imperial representation: George does not express the desire to win back the True Cross abducted by the Persians, which was to become crucial for imperial representation later, when George took the opportunity to compose a poem *In restitutionem Sanctae Crucis*.[36] The quotation of a psalm ascribed to David (2.113–115) is not necessarily a hint at the emperor's depiction as a new David, which was central to his image later on.[37] Nevertheless, although the *epos* mirrors Heraclius' representation in his early years in many aspects, it is not merely part of his propaganda, as will be shown in the following paragraphs.

What is the context of this poetic description of war? One major theme is the importance of the emperor himself as a warrior. Another is the belief in the considerable relevance of immaterial resources for success in war. The emperor is the best fighter as well as the most holy man. Should we expect anything else from a panegyrical poem about the emperor? It is obvious that the *Expeditio Persica* could not but extol the virtues of the emperor, but Greco-Roman tradition offered various options for doing so. An emperor could be praised for choosing his advisers wisely, for his trust in priests or philosophers, or for his splendor, but Heraclius is, to put it casually, a do-it-yourself emperor.

George certainly did not avoid mentioning patriarch Sergius in order to belittle his achievements.[38] Rather, he praises him in other poems, for example in the *Bellum Avaricum*. As a member of the patriarchal administration, George must already have been close to Sergius during the composition of the *Expeditio Persica*. Perhaps he heaped lavish praise on Heraclius in order to be able also to allude to the criticism raised by the patriarch, especially concerning the marriage with Martina. Focusing on Heraclius was a feature of poetic stylization: George makes it very clear that God grants military success, but the emperor alone is enough to guarantee divine help; he does not need the intervention of religious authorities, be they monks or bishops.

George also comments on a conflict prevailing in Constantinople at the time of war, which is unusual for poems of this kind. Apparently, a debate had been

---

36 Drijvers 2002, 182f.
37 Trilling 1978; Ludwig 1991, 93–104; Meier 2015.
38 Rather, he seems to have been close to him; see, for example, Pertusi 1959, 13.

raging about whether the emperor should actually take to the field or stay in the city or whether something in between was possible (1.111–123).[39] The poet underlines that the conflicting parties had the best intentions. The debate was not a power struggle or argument between the emperor's friends or foes: it was about finding the best solution to an existential challenge. Here, George clearly defends those who were critical of Heraclius. Nevertheless, the transformation of the concept of imperial rule becomes evident. Was the emperor expected to stay in the city quietly or should he venture outside in order to quell all the dangers the empire faced?

The debate resurfaces under another guise in the third Book, where George describes the great victory. Two soldiers discuss the role of the emperor during wartime. They are shocked but also impressed by the fact that the emperor takes on the physical efforts of war. In the end, they see a hero in him. The poet himself declares that he is oscillating between joy and tears at this image (3.93–136). It is obvious that George does not consider the personal involvement of the emperor in combat as normal, but that he still accepts it as necessary under extreme circumstances such as those in which his intervention proved successful.

The *Expeditio Persica* is an assertion of imperial power and virtue. Heraclius proves to be an excellent military leader who acts on his own initiative. Like Justinian, the emperor mediates divine help through his piety and does not depend on clerics or monks. But Heraclius goes far beyond Justinian's model by being a competent military leader himself and also by employing a wide range of traditional and religious resources. George rarely takes economic issues such as food supply into account (but see 2.40), although Heraclius did spend a lot of energy on these problems. Thus, the importance of the emperor's character for the well-being of the empire itself takes center stage. Everything depends on his personality and his piety.

Let us try to contemplate the bigger picture. The Christianization of warfare was a major and powerful feature in the transformation of war that took place in Late Antiquity. It was not, however, a linear process but rather a complex development which allowed a broad range of interpretations; Christians lacked a uniform concept of war. Many emperors interpreted the role of the Christian emperor in war quite differently from Heraclius. As mentioned earlier, Eastern rulers such as Theodosius II or Justinian, in fact almost every ruler after Theodosius I, stayed in Constantinople during times of war, offering prayers for victory, which, if it

---

39 See also 3.93–125. Pertusi 1959 thinks it possible to connect those concepts with various circus parties. There had been an aborted attempt of Heraclius to join the siege of Caesarea and Antioch.

came to pass, would then be ascribed to the praying emperor. The idea that emperors do not fight in war was one feature of the *urbanes Kaisertum*. The city of Constantinople was the emperor's permanent base. No emperor had left the capital for a long time, and thus Heraclius represents something new.

This change did not mean the end of the *urbanes Kaisertum*, but it showcased an alternative. Relying on the protection of mobile religious resources, the emperor could be present everywhere and was not confined within the walls of one city. Despite the risks involved in his personal participation and his absence from the center of power, Heraclius' engagement in warfare seemed successful for some years until things changed dramatically with the Arab expansion – except for the fact that immaterial resources again proved to be a major factor during these wars.

Another important element in the discourse of war in the *Expeditio Persica* is the question of the necessary resources for warfare, the most important of which are there thought to be immaterial, as has been shown. Again, this is not so unusual: late antique literary sources usually tend to focus on individuals and questions of virtue and piety and are not intended to be systematic treatises about strategies of war. Despite this tendency towards one-sidedness, various ideas about resources in war can be identified.

In classicizing historiography, military leadership is the most important resource. Belisarius for example, Justinian's famous general, is a core figure in Procopius' *Wars*. His ruses and his influence over the troops contribute heavily to military victories. Nevertheless, the historian leaves no doubt that a dearth of troops and food can severely restrict the general's options. He even insinuates that the emperor is responsible for human and material resources, thus possibly inserting a critical note.

Religious resources, in the guise of divine support, are also decisive on several occasions. They can be considered the main issue of debate on successful warfare during the sixth and seventh centuries. According to Procopius and other historiographers, divine intervention is decisive for the outcome of many battles and no military success is imaginable without divine support. But there are many innovations in the depictions of Heraclius. Justinian, for example, who never actively took part in a military expedition, makes very clear that he does not rely on weapons, soldiers, generals or his own capacities when it comes to war, but only on God.[40] Although the emperor does show a certain degree of humility in that

---

40 *Constitutio Deo auctore, praef.*: *ita nostros animos ad dei omnipotentis erigimus adiutorium, ut neque armis confidamus neque nostris militibus neque bellorum ducibus vel nostro ingenio, sed omnem spem ad solam referamus summae providentiam trinitatis: unde et mundi totius elementa*

sense, he makes it unambiguously clear that he is the crucial figure on earth: He claims to be the mediator of divine help, thus relating all his successes to his possession of God's favor, and he presents himself accordingly. When Belisarius defeated the Vandals he was allowed to celebrate a triumph, but he had to walk on foot and to prostrate himself in front of the emperor. Although this kind of triumph was new, the fundamental idea goes back to the beginnings of the Principate, when every victory was ascribed to the auspices of the emperor.[41]

Another strand of discourse on military victory had gained popularity in the periphery during the 540s; it is visible in the work of Procopius and still more in that of Evagrius Scholasticus. During those years the Persians forcefully attacked Syria, while Justinian barely lent any military support. Several provincial cities that managed to fend off the Persians ascribed their success to holy icons or relics. As is well known, even pagan Romans used to carry holy objects with them during war, but these had never acquired the central position of being seen as the explanation for military success. Whenever cities had to rely on holy objects, this highlighted the failures of the political and military elites of the late antique Roman Empire, which did not supply enough troops. Interestingly, holy objects that had been proved to be successful in the periphery were highly contested and were often appropriated by the center. The icon of the Virgin Mary, another *acheiropoietos*, was regarded as decisive when Sergius and Bonus fended off the siege of Constantinople in 626. The emperor was not present during this siege, one of the dangerous results of his method of warfare. George gratefully praises Mary in the so-called *Bellum Avaricum*, which celebrates the failure of this siege (especially 1–9). He also sings to the glory of the general Bonus and the patriarch Sergius, which might have been regarded as risky politically, even though the poem also acclaims the absent emperor who gives his support by writing a letter and sending troops (246–307).

Finally, there was also a non-religious discourse on warfare. A text written during the sixth century, the *Strategikon* of Pseudo-Mauricius, illustrates just how important knowledge about warfare was. It highlights the significance of military and especially strategic knowledge on how best to fight the enemies of Rome.[42] This text does not mention any religious resources. It is difficult to say

---

processerunt et eorum dispositio in orbem terrarum producta est ("Thus we lift up our minds towards the assistance of all-powerful God, so that we trust not in military campaigns, soldiers, generals or our own abilities, but so that all our hope may be placed solely in the providence of the highest Trinity: it is from there that the elements of the entire world proceeded and their arrangement on the earth was produced").

41 Goldbeck/Wienand 2016.
42 See Koehn 2018, 121–133.

whether this should be considered a counter discourse, but it is nevertheless possible to deduce that the question of necessary resources for war was highly contested and that our knowledge about these debates is restricted. The non-religious discourse on war must have been much more important in everyday life, especially among functional elites, than the religious discourses that dominate the literary texts.

The *Expeditio Persica* is one of the foremost sources for the discourses on warfare in Late Antiquity. The new military concept of personal imperial participation in war meant that the restriction of imperial presence to Constantinople was abandoned. If the emperor ventured outside his capital, it was in an extreme situation, justified by the need to protect the empire and the true faith, and he was expected to return to the city, to his proper place, as soon as possible. George is aware of the ambivalences of the emperor's personal engagement in war and does not shy away from mentioning them.

The *Expeditio* assembles various ideas about the resources needed for war: The emperor as both an impressive warrior and a competent leader is the most important human resource. Religious resources, especially the icon, are also crucial for success. Weapons and economic resources are almost completely excluded from the picture. In effecting such an exclusion, the poet emphasizes that nobody can replace the emperor or even come close to him.

This observation is within our expectations for a poem of this kind. But George goes a step further: He also reveals that there were debates on the role of the emperor and that he himself saw risks in the emperor's absence from his capital – his poem on Bonus, probably written shortly before the Perso-Avarian siege of Constantinople, is for the most part an open appeal for the emperor to return to his capital (esp. 111–113).[43] Moreover, the poet stresses that the emperor performs seemingly miraculous deeds and is favored by God, that he is a valiant warrior and a provident general, that he is even close to Jesus in some respects, but still remains a vulnerable human being.

In doing so, the poet, writing at a time when the Roman-Sassanian war was by no means decided, imbues his praise of the emperor's military achievements with a notable dose of scepticism which must have been widespread among the elites in Constantinople. This panegyrical poem is not the work of a mere adulator, but the product of a prudent advisor. George's *epos* is not simply a mouth-

---

[43] See Howard-Johnston 2010, 21.

piece of imperial propaganda (and it is not a version of the official history of Heraclius' campaign)⁴⁴ but a contribution to the ongoing debate about warfare during his reign.

It is therefore not pure coincidence that the poet seems to have received no imperial commission during the following years (and it is by no means clear that the *Expeditio* was an imperial commission). It would be wrong to call him a court poet, as has often been done; he is but one voice in the debates on the emperor's role in war.⁴⁵ No doubt, a poem featuring the emperor during this time had to include some praise and glorification. It has become clear, however, that George's praise of the emperor is highly nuanced. George assimilates Heraclius to Christ but at the same time underlines the emperor's human persona. He duly praises the emperor's military achievements but does not ignore the risks involved.

Six years after the campaign described in the *Expeditio Persica*, Sassanian king Chosroes II (590–628) was dead (having been overthrown and killed) after lengthy, daring, but in the end impressively successful military operations led by the emperor himself. George commemorates these events in his *Heraclias*, which arguably was comprised of three Books, two of which have been preserved in their entirety. This poem is characterized by unabated joy and relief and is, in that sense, a kind of tacit palinody of the *Expeditio*. George compares Chosroes II to the brutal oriental kings from both the classical and Hebrew traditions, whereas Heraclius is obviously another, stronger Heracles and also represents the tradition of great Greek and Roman generals. George admonishes no lesser a figure than Plutarch to keep quiet, claiming that it does not make sense to write parallel lives of Greek and Roman generals, as a biography of Heraclius would include and surpass all of them (1.110). The lengthy absence of the emperor earns him respect because he does not listen to the entreaties of his family, instead displaying a body of bronze and a heart of iron which are praiseworthy (1.173; compare 2.144–166). The section on the absence of the emperor ends with an allusion to

---

44 For diverging standpoints see Howard-Johnston 1994. He thinks that George wrote a history that incorporated verses as the official history. On 71f. he suggests that there was an estrangement between emperor and poet after the composition of the *Expeditio Persica* (but see his footnote 31); Ludwig 1991, 128 calls him a "Hofpoet"; Huber 2008 defines George as "eine Art Hofpropagandist" (163) although she is aware that his position is much more nuanced (175).
45 According to Howard-Johnston 2010, 32f. he even lost imperial favor, which is an educated guess. In contrast, Lauxtermann 2003, 38f. believes that George served Heraclius faithfully throughout his career; he calls Pisides a "court poet" (42), even "a poet laureate at the court of Herakleios" (58); compare Speck 1988, 360 ("Hofdichter").

the icon from heaven, which is the real foundation of victory (1.218).[46] The fundamental change to warfare is beyond doubt by now. But George also writes that Heraclius is willing to dedicate some of his time to learning the theory of warfare (2.118–121; 135–142):[47] As in the *Expeditio*, the emperor possesses every virtue a general needs. The criticism George had taken seriously in the *Expeditio* is now no more than idle talk (2.122–126). The concept of war is the same as it was in the *Expeditio*, but now the emperor's method of warfare seems to have been vindicated.

The relief of the eastern elites after this success pervades this poem. The personal participation of the emperor and the support of God, materialized in the icon of Christ, seem to establish the Roman Empire as the effective ruler of the world. Eight years later, a new enemy would humiliate the Roman army. We would love to know how George would have commented on this change. Perhaps he was lucky enough not to see it. The generations to come were forced to experience the gruesome consequences of the idea that war could be about true religion.

Bibliography

Agosti, G. 2012. "Greek Poetry", in S.F. Johnson (ed.), *The Oxford Handbook of Late Antiquity*, Oxford, 361–404.
Assmann, J. 2003. *Die Mosaische Unterscheidung oder der Preis des Monotheismus*, München.
Booth, P. 2014. *Crisis of Empire. Doctrine and dissent at the end of Late Antiquity*, Berkeley (CA).
Cameron, Averil 1991. *Christianity and the rhetoric of Empire. The development of Christian discourse*, Berkeley (CA).
de Boor, C. (ed.) 1883–1885. *Theophanis Chronographia*, 2 vols., Leipzig.
Drijvers, J.W. 2002. "Heraclius and the *Restitutio Crucis*. Notes on symbolism and ideology", in G.J. Reinink/B.H. Stolte (eds.), *The reign of Heraclius (610–641). Crisis and confrontation*, Leuven, 175–190.
Eck, W. 2008. "Vom See *Regillus* bis zum *flumen Frigidus*. Constantins Sieg an der Milvischen Brücke als Modell für den Heiligen Krieg?", in K. Schreiber (ed.), *Heilige Kriege. Religiöse Begründungen militärischer Gewaltanwendung: Judentum, Christentum und Islam im Vergleich*, München, 71–91.
Gonnelli, F. (ed.) 1998. *Giorgio di Pisidia, Hexaemeron*, Pisa.

---

[46] Interestingly, George now even mentions that the icon of the Virgin Mary, again characterized as φρικτός (2.14), was crucial for Heraclius' success against Phocas, which is not mentioned in his poem on the return of Heraclius to Constantinople.
[47] His ascetic behavior at this time is compared to that of Elijah: 2.133f.

Goldbeck, F./Wienand, J. (eds.) 2016. *Der römische Triumph in Prinzipat und Spätantike*, Berlin.
Haldon, J. 1997. *Byzantium in the seventh century: the transformation of a culture*, Cambridge.
Holum, K.G. 1977. "Pulcheria's Crusade A.D. 421–22 and the ideology of imperial victory", *GRBS*, 18, 153–172.
Howard-Johnston, J.D. 1994. "The official history of Heraclius' Persian campaign", in E. Dąbrowa (ed.), *The Roman and Byzantine army in the East. Proceedings of a colloquium held at the Jagiellonian University, Kraków in September 1992*, Kraków, 57–87. (repr. in: J.D. Howard-Johnston (ed.) 2006. *East Rome, Sasanian Persia and the end of Antiquity. Historiographical and historical studies*, Aldershot, ch. IV, 57–87).
Howard-Johnston, J.D. 2010. *Witnesses to a world crisis. Historians and histories of the Middle East in the seventh century*, Oxford.
Huber, I. 2008. "Ansichten eines Zivilisierten über die unzivilisierte Welt: das Sāsāniden-Bild des Georgios Pisides und sein historischer Wert für den spätantiken Iran", *Klio*, 90, 162–192.
Kaegi, W.E. 2003. *Heraclius. Emperor of Byzantium*, Cambridge.
Koehn, C. 2018. *Justinian und die Armee des frühen Byzanz*, Berlin.
Lange, C. 2012. *Mia energeia. Untersuchungen zur Einigungspolitik des Kaisers Heraclius und des Patriarchen Sergius von Constantinopel*, Tübingen.
Lauxtermann, M.D. 2003. *Byzantine poetry from Pisides to Geometres: texts and contexts*, WBS 24, Wien.
Leppin, H. 2011. *Justinian. Das christliche Experiment*, Stuttgart.
Leppin, H. 2012. "Der Loyalismus der Kirchengeschichtsschreibung. Bemerkungen zu Magnentius bei Sokrates und Sozomenos und zur Selbstdarstellung Constantius' II.", in M. Cassia (ed.), *Pignora amicitiae: Scritti di storia antica e storiografica offerti a Mario Mazza I*, Roma, 325–335.
Leppin, H. 2015. "Coping with the tyrant's faction: civil war amnesties and Christian discourses in the fourth century AD", in J. Wienand (ed.), *Contested monarchy. Integrating the Roman Empire in the 4th century AD*, Oxford, 198–215.
Ludwig, C. 1991. "Kaiser Herakleios, Georgios Pisides und die Perserkriege", W. Brandes/S. Kotzabassi/C.L.P. Speck (eds.), *Poikila Byzantina 11*, Bonn, 73–128.
Meier, M. 2015. "Herakles – Herakleios – Christus. Georgios Pisides und der *kosmorhýstes*", in H. Leppin (ed.), *Antike Mythologie in christlichen Kontexten der Spätantike*, Berlin, 167–192.
Pertusi, A. (ed.) 1959. *Giorgio di Pisidia, Poemi I. Panegirici epici*, Ettal.
Pfeilschifter, E. 2013. *Der Kaiser und Konstantinopel. Kommunikation und Konfliktaustrag in einer spätantiken Metropole*, Berlin.
Reinink, G.J./Stolte, B.H. (eds.) 2002. *The reign of Heraclius (610–641). Crisis and confrontation*, Leuven.
Rhoby, A. 2011. "Vom jambischen Trimeter zum byzantinischen Zwölfsilber. Beobachtung zur Metrik des spätantiken und byzantinischen Epigramms", *WS*, 124, 117–142.
Shorrock, R. 2011. *The myth of paganism. Nonnus, Dionysus, and the world of Late Antiquity*, London.
Speck, P. 1988. *Das geteilte Dossier. Beobachtungen zu den Nachrichten über die Regierung des Kaisers Herakleios und die seiner Söhne bei Theophanes und Nikephoros*, Bonn.

Thonhauser, J. 2008. *Das Unbehagen am Monotheismus. Der Glaube an den einen Gott als Ursprung religiöser Gewalt? Eine aktuelle Debatte um Jan Assmanns Thesen zur 'Mosaischen Unterscheidung'*, Marburg.

Trilling, J. 1978. "Myth and metaphor at the Byzantine court. A literary approach to the David Plates", *Byzantion*, 48, 249–263.

Wallraff, M. 2010. "Licht", *RAC*, 23, 100–137.

Whitby, Mary 1998. "Defender of the Cross: George of Pisidia on the Emperor Heraclius and his deputies", in Mary Whitby (ed.), *The propaganda of power: the role of panegyric in Late Antiquity*, Leiden, 247–276.

Whitby, Mary 2002. "George of Pisidia's presentation of the Emperor Heraclius and his campaigns: variety and development", in G.J. Reinink/B.H. Stolte (eds.), *The reign of Heraclius (610–641). Crisis and confrontation*, Leuven, 157–173.

Whitby, Mary 2003. "George of Pisidia and the persuasive word: words, words, words...", in E. Jeffreys (ed.), *Rhetoric in Byzantium. Papers form the thirty-fifth spring Symposium of Byzantine Studies, Exeter College, University of Oxford, March 2001*, London, 173–186.

Contributors

Accorinti, Domenico, Ph.D. from Scuola Normale Superiore di Pisa, is an Independent Researcher and teaches Classics at the Gymnasium Galilei, Pisa, Italy.

Agosti, Gianfranco is Professor of Classical and Late Antique Philology at Sapienza University of Rome, Dipartimento di Scienze dell'Antichità, Italy.

Falcone, Maria Jennifer is Senior Assistant Professor (RTD-B) at Università di Pavia – Dipartimento di Musicologia e Beni Culturali, Cremona, Italy.

Faulkner, Andrew is Professor of Classical Studies at the University of Waterloo, Canada.

Fischer, Susanna is Privatdozentin at der Fakultät für Sprach- und Literaturwissenschaften der LMU München, Germany.

Gullo, Arianna is Fellow in Byzantine Studies at Dumbarton Oaks Research Library and Collection, Washington DC, and Leverhulme Early Career Fellowship at the University of Newcastle, UK.

Hadjittofi, Fotini is FCT Research Fellow at Centro de Estudos Clássicos, Universidade de Lisboa, Portugal.

Kuhn-Treichel, Thomas is DFG Research Fellow at Heidelberg University, Germany.

Lefteratou, Anna is DFG Research Fellow at Heidelberg University, Germany.

Leppin, Hartmut is Professor of Ancient History at the Historisches Seminar Fachbereich Philosophie und Geschichtswissenschaften at Johann Wolfgang-Goethe-Universität, Frankfurt a. M., Germany.

McDonald, James is an AHRC-funded PhD candidate in Classics at University of Glasgow, UK.

Onorato, Marco is Senior Assistant Professor (RTD-B) of Latin language and literature at the Dipartimento di Civiltà Antiche e Moderne (Di.C.A.M.), Univerisity of Messina, Italy.

Paschalis, Michael is Emeritus Professor of Classics at the University of Crete, Department of Philology, Rethymnon, Greece.

Rigo, Maria-Sole is PhD holder from Università degli Studi 'La Sapienza' Roma, Dipartimento di Scienze dell'Antichità Department, Italy.

Wasyl, Anna Maria is Associate Professor at Instytut Filologii Klasycznej at Uniwersytet Jagielloński, Krakow, Poland.

Wolff, Étienne is Professor of Latin at Université Paris Nanterre, France.

Index Auctorum Locorumque

Aelian
Varia Historia
13.22   267 n.13

Aeschylus
Prometheus Bound
15   235 n.58
55–56   235 n.58
76   235 n.58
113   235 n.58
141–142   235 n.58
941   213 n.17
Seven Against Thebes
437   272

Anonymi
Constitutio Apostolica
15   270
Constitutio Deo Auctore
Praef.   303 n.40
Corpus Hermeticum
1.31   100 n.27
13.17–20   100 n.27
F29   100 n.28
Lyrica Adespota
CA 10   267
Oracula Sibyllina
13.65   49 n.32
Orphic Hymns
2.11   52 n.39
59.20   52 n.39
Rhetorica ad Herennium
4.11.16   79 n.23
4.13.18   79 n.23
4.23.32   79 n.23
Theosophia Tubingensis
13   49 n.32

Anthologiae
Anthologia Latina (Riese)
7–18   169 n.3
15.2   174
15.3   181
15.45   174
15.79–83   175
15.105–113   176
111   140 n.6
310   140 n.6
376   132 n.29
389   132 n.29
664   154 n.15
Anthologia Palatina
1.34–36 (Agath.)   62 n.16
4.3b.115 (Agath.)   61
4.3b.122–123 (Agath.)   61
6.66.7 (Paul. Sil.)   240 n.77
6.80.5 (Agath.)   272 n.37
6.274.4 = *HE* III 2870 (Pers.) 70 n.59
7.12.5–6 = *FGE* XXXIX 1226–1227   69 n.52
7.13.2–3 = *HE* XCVIII 2564–2565
(Mel. or Leon.)   70 n.55
7.17.1–2 = *GPh* 3909–3910
(Tull. Laur.)   68 n.48
7.45.1–2 = *FGE* I 1052–1053   69 n.51
7.290.3 = *GPh* 3809 (Stat. Fl.)   50
7.310 (Anon.)   65 n.32
7.356–360 (Anon.)   65 n.32
7.368 = *GPh* VI 2232–2235 (Eryc.) 67 n.41
7.451 (Call.)   68 n.48
7.529.1 = *HE* X 3544 (Theodorid.) 66 n.36
7.580–581 (Jul. Aegypt.)   65–66
7.587 (Jul. Aegypt.)   66–67
7.590 (Jul. Aegypt.)   67–68
7.594 (Jul. Aegypt.)   68–69
7.599 (Jul. Aegypt.)   71
7.600 (Jul. Aegypt.)   71
7.603 (Jul. Aegypt.)   69–70
7.604 (Paul. Silent.)   70
7.605 (Jul. Aegypt.)   70–71
7.671 = *GPh* V 1667
(Anon. or Bianor)   70 n.56
7.695 (Anon.)   71 n.62
9.808.2 (Cyrus?)   52 n.39
11.133 (Lucill.)   70 n.56
16.98.1 (Stat. Fl.)   50
For the epigrams of Greg. Naz. see *s.v.*
'Gregory Nazianzen'

Aphthonius
Progymnasmata
11   288 n.61

[Ps.-]Apollinaris
Metaphrasis Psalmorum

Proem, 1–9	266–267
Proem, 2	272
Proem, 10–110	266
Proem, 15	270
Proem, 18–19	266 n.10
Proem, 30–31	271
Proem, 32–34	266 n.10, 270
Proem, 42–43	269, 270
Proem, 110	52 n.39
36.14	52 n.39
36.50	52 n.39
88.22	52 n.39
96.8	52 n.39
103.18	52 n.39

Apollonius of Rhodes
Argonautica

3.132–150	157 n.31
4.54–65	158 n.33

Arator
De actibus apostolorum 251

2.577–578	268 n.14

Aratus
Phaenomena

1–18	259
460–461	260

Aristides
Apologia

3.2	295 n.10

Aristonicus
De signis Iliadis

9.323	216 n.25

Aristotle
Poetics

1447b17–1447b20	249 n.5
1447b20–22	109 n.2
1459b37–1460a2	109 n.2
1462a15	279 n.18

Athanasius of Alexandria
Homilia de descriptione deiparae (PG)

28.996	275 n.4

Athenaeus
Deipnosophistae

8.347e	279 n.18
9.373b	216 n.25

Augustine of Hippo
Confessions

3.6.2	162

Contra secundam Juliani responsionem imperfectum opus

4.55	80 n.27

De doctrina Christiana

2.97	178 n.34

Sermons

293.2	133 n.31

Tractatus in evangelium Iohannis

20.1	80 n.27
124.7	80 n.27

Aulus Gellius
Noctes Atticae

5.14	133

Ausonius
Precationes variae

2	132 n.29

Avitus of Vienne
De spiritalis historiae gestis

Prologue 1	4 n.5
3.336f.	94 n.7

Barham, Francis
A rhymed harmony of the Gospels

4–5	225

Basil of Caesarea
De gratiarum actione (PG)

31.229c	279 n.22

Homilies on the Psalms
1.1–2   271

Bede the Venerable
De arte metrica
7.259   15

Bible
New Testament
Apocalypse (Vulgate)
21:12–16   77 n.12
21:19–20   77
John
1:1   10
1:12–14   49 n.32
3:2   251–252
3:11   252 n.14
4:13   252 n.16
4:23   257 n.41
4:25   252 n.15
5:34   252 n.14
6:26–40   240
6:59   252 n.12
7:14   252 n.12
7:16   252 n.12
8:12   286
8:34   252 n.16
9:3   252 n.16
12:50   252
13–17   251
14:6   252 n.14
14:17   259 n.58
14:23   252 n.16
15:22   257 n.41
18:28–19:16a   231 n.34
19:9–10   230
19:11–12   232
19:18   233
19:25   275, 276 n.5, 286
19:28–29   238
19:38   281 n.28
20:31   253
21:25   226 n.3, 261 n.59
Luke
1:38   283 n.38
2:35   275 n.4
8:22–25   197

9:28–36   298 n.27
9:32   50
22:44   300
23:6–12   231 n.39
23:33   233
23:50–53   281 n.28
Mark
4:35–41   197
9:2–8   298 n.27
15:27   233
15:36a   239
15:42–46   281 n.28
Matthew
5:6   68 n.49
6:12   129
8:23–27   197–198
17:1–9   298 n.27
18:21–22   129
22:21   204
27:38   233
27:48   239
27:57   281 n.28
Epistles
Col 1:15–20   10 n.29
Col 15:3–4   10 n.29
Col 19:1–8   10 n.29
1 Cor 3:16   78 n.16
1 Cor 15:35–58   49
Phil 2:5–11   10 n.29
Rom 1:25   295 n.10
1 Tim 3:16   10 n.29
New Testament Apocrypha
Apocrypha Acta Petri
38   234–235
Apocrypha Acta Pilati B (cod. C)
10.2   282 n.31
Apocrypha Acta Thomae
108–113 (Hymn of the Pearl)   10
Gospel of Nicodemus
22–24   284 n.44
Life of Adam and Eve
28.4   284 n.44
41.3   284 n.44
Old Testament
Genesis
4:13–15   265 n.7
22:1–19   265 n.7

2 Kgs
1:12	116 n.22
2:1	143

Psalms
1–2	272 n.34
18:3	80 n.27
44:2	80 n.27
69:22	238
101	265 n.7
118:171	80 n.27
137	272 n.34, 297
145:7	80 n.27

Callimachus
Epigrammata (Anthologia Palatina)
7.451.2	68 n.48
46.4	271 n.29

Hymns
1.60	101 n.30, 193 n.10
2.58	52 n.39

Catullus
64	285 n.48
64.1–15	85

Choricius of Gaza
Epithalamium for Zacharias
5.1.14	254 n.23

Cicero
De oratore
1.50	79 n.23
1.218	79 n.23
2.36	79 n.23
3.96	79 n.23
3.201	79 n.23

Orator ad M. Brutum
134	79 n.23

Partitiones oratoriae
72	79 n.23

Claudian
Carmina minora
22–23	129 n.20
22.28–32	133

Clement of Alexandria
Paedagogus
3.12.101.4 (Hymn to the Savior)	11

Protrepticus
1.2	271
2.33.1	284 n.41

Stromata
6.4.35.3	100 n.28
6.5.35	101 n.32
6.5.43	101 n.32

Commodian
Carmen Apologeticum
9–10	11

Instructiones
2.35	11

Corippus
Iohannis
7.25	133 n.38

Cyprianus Gallus
Heptateuchos
Exodus 213	200 n.33

Cyril of Alexandria
Commentary on John's Gospel (PG)
73.397c	252 n.14
74.661	276 n.6, 287 n.58
74.662	286 n.53
74.663	275 n.4, 276 n.5

Dio Chrysostom
Encomium comae
49	284 n.41

Orationes
12.26	284 n.41

Diogenes Laertius
2.78	102 n.35

Dionysius of Halicarnassus
Ars rhetorica
2.5	85 n.41

Dionysius Periegetes
Description of the inhabited world
27–28	259–260
1168–1169	260
1181–1186	260

Dracontius
De laudibus Dei
1.52–91	146
1.363–370	144
1.653–655	146
2.1	131 n.28
2.15–27	146
2.440–463	146
2.588–593	142
3.217–221	142

Orestis Tragoedia
13–15	139
44–107	140
153–203	141
258–262	141
719–728	141
732	141
763–774	143
792–794	141
963–966	162 n.54
973	143, 162

Romulea
1.14	146
2	139, 157 n.31
5	145, 146
5.1	140
8.3	142
8.11–30	139–140
8.55–56	143
8.57–60	142–143
8.80	143
8.131	142–143
8.185–187	143
8.191	142–143
8.198	142–143
8.286–290	144
8.304–308	144
8.535–539	143
8.571–585	144
8.638–651	144
8.655	142
10.1	153
10.16–18	154
10.16–30	139
10.17	182
10.20–21	154
10.26–28	154–155, 182
10.30–31	155
10.41	147 n.24
10.49–85	157
10.102–109	146
10.127–134	157 n.31
10.136–140	156 n.22
10.146–155	157
10.188–194	160 n.47
10.199–200	147 n.24
10.200–208	160 n.47
10.254	158
10.291–300	158–159
10.297	158 n.37
10.321–327	159
10.326–327	157–158
10.328–329	147 n.24
10.366	160
10.374–80	160
10.396–518	160–161
10.545	158 n.37, 160 n.44
10.556–569	143, 156 n.23, 160–161
10.570–601	143, 162
10.587–601	156
10.591–93	162–163
10.600–601	161–162, 163

Satisfactio
1–18	131–132
19–26	127
26	135
27–48	132–133
41–44	127
42	135
49–52	130
53–54	127
53–92	126, 133–134
81–86	132
93–94	127–128
95–100	128
101–114	130–131

101–116	132	*Hippolytus*	
105–107	128	1328f.	159 n.41
107–108	129	*Phoenissae*	
117–120	130	40	103 n.37
121–136	135	1380	103 n.37
137–148	133	*Rhesus*	
149–151	131	162–163	272
152–190	133		
192–192	131 n.23	**Eusebius**	
215–264	126, 133–134	*Praeparatio evangelica*	
284	135	9.21.1	9 n.27
297–302	133	*Vita Constantini*	
305–309	128–129	2.40	48
311–312	130		
312	135	**Evagrius Scholasticus**	

Eudocia
Homerocentones s.v. 'Homer'
Life of Saint Cyprian (Bevegni)

		Historia ecclesiastica	
		1.13	297 n.24
1.16	213–214		
1.115–116	214–215	**Fulgentius**	
1.122	215 n.19	*Mythologiae*	
1.129	215–216	1.22	170, 174
1.152–155	211–213		
1.197	216–217	**George of Pisidia**	
1.205–208	217	*Bellum Avaricum*	
1.301–421	217	1–9	304
1.379	213 n.17	246–307	304
1.382	213 n.17	*Carmen de vita humana*	
1.389	214 n.17	59	216 n.22
1.397	213 n.17	*Expeditio Persica*	
1.400	213 n.17	1.1–21	295
1.400–404	215	1.46f.	299
2.374	52 n.39	1.82–99	297 n.20
		1.104–111	296, 297–298
Eunapius		1.111–123	301–302
Fragmenta historica		1.132–157	296
72.1	232	1.156–161	298
		1.164	297
Euripides		1.177–239	298
Bacchae		1.191–193	298 n.27
317f.	102	1.239–247	299
836	102	2.19–24	299
1064–1073	238	2.39–49	299, 302
Fragments		2.78–84	296
895 K.	103 n.37	2.86–106	297 n.20
		2.88–115	297, 301
		2.120–149	299
		2.122–126	294 n.6

2.162–177	299	I.1.17.7	116
2.206	299	I.1.18	115, 117 n.28, 118, 119
2.213–234	296 n.14		
2.239–256	300	I.1.19	118, 119 n.34
2.257–375	300	I.1.20.7	117–118
2.368–3.6	300	I.1.23	251 n.10
2.240	295 n.11	I.1.25.6	117
3.48f.	300	I.1.27.15	117
3.93–136	294 n.6, 302	I.2.10.277–279	101 n.29, 103 n.37
3.121f.	295–296		
3.255	300	I.2.10.585–588	103 n.37
3.279–281	300	I.2.15.84	96 n.10
3.296f.	300	I.2.25	117
3.305	295 n.11	I.2.31.31–47	110 n.6
3.314–321	300	II.1.10	101–104
3.322	299 n.31	II.1.11.7	111
3.343–346	294	II.1.11.6–8	270 n.28
3.385–410	300	II.1.11.249–264	112
3.405	295–296	II.1.11.1804f.	103 n.37
3.410	295 n.11	II.1.12.134f.	103 n.37
3.412–425	300 n.33	II.1.34A	95–98, 105 n.44
3.456–461	300–301	II.1.39	4–5, 111, 121, 270–271
Heraclias			
1.110	306	II.2.6	118
1.218	306–307	II.2.7	98–101, 214 n.17
1.173	306	*Epigrammata (Anthologia Palatina)*	
1.195–198	296 n.14	8.8.3	66 n.35
1.195–206	300 n.34	8.12	65 n.31, 66 n.38
1.218	296 n.16	8.15.3a	98 n.22
2.14	307 n.46	8.33.1	66 nn.35 and 38
2.118–126	307	8.35.5	66 n.35
2.133f.	307 n.47	8.53.2	66 n.35
2.135–142	307	8.59.1	66 n.35
2.144–166	306	8.60.1	65 n.31
Hexaemeron		8.61.1	66 n.35
1853	300 n.34	8.69.1	66 n.35
In Bonum patricium		8.71.1	65 n.31
111–113	305	8.72.1	66 n.38
		8.81.1	65 n.31
Gregory Nazianzen		8.82	49 n.32, 66 n.35
Carmina		8.85b.3	70 n.58
I.1.1.22	268 n.14	8.97.6	65 n.31
I.1.12–27	109–122	8.104.6	65 n.31
I.1.12	109, 113–116	8.107.6	65 n.31
I.1.13	119 n.34	8.126.1	65 n.31
I.1.14.12	116–117	8.152.1	70 n.58
I.1.16.10	116	8.170–172	65 n.31

8.171	65 n.30	*Theogony*	
8.176–254	65 n.31	27	193
8.192.4	65 n.31	30–34	252 n.17
8.218.1	65 n.31	511–512	257 n.38
8.226	65 n.31	*Works and Days*	
8.246–248	65 n.31	1–10	259
Epistulae		202–212	232–233
13.1	255 n.27	241	254
101.73	96 n.15, 271 n.32	313	104
114.4	99 n.23	374–375	254
198–201	98 n.21	381–382	272
In laudem sororis suae Gorgoniae (PG)		644	272
35.813	279 nn. 22 and 24	**Hippolytus of Rome**	
Orationes		*Demonstratio de Christo et antichristo*	
27.9	99 n.23	59 = *GCS* 1.2.39–40	235 n.57
44.10	99 n.23	*Refutatio omnium heresium*	
		7.13.3	235 n.57
[Ps.–]Gregory Nazianzen			
Christus Patiens		**Homer**	
A9	289 n.63	*Iliad*	
106	289 n.63	1.129	47
148	289 n.63	1.362	281
660–665	238	1.505	284 n.40
908–909	282 n.31	1.528–529	284 n.41
865–866	285 n.48	1.529	281
1335	282 n.31	2.103	213 n.16
		2.231 = 5.9	45 n.25
Gregory of Nyssa		2.761	216 n.22
Contra Eunomium		3.114	231 n.31
3.9.58	270 n.26	3.171	231 n.31
In Christi resurrectionem		3.216–224	231–232
9.302.19–9.303.8	235 n.57	3.437	231 n.31
Psalmorum tituli		5.769	237
8	271 n.31	5.871 = 18.72	281
		6.123	231 n.31, 231 n.36
Heliodorus			
Aethiopica		6.176	230 n.31
4.7	211 n.8	8.68	237
		9.324	216–217
Hermogenes		9.413	97 n.18
Progymnasmata		9.473	281
9	288 n.61	9.528–599	96 n.10
		11.161	231 n.31
Hesiod		11.844	49 n.32
Fragments		14.433	45 n.25
204.105	272 n.37	15.207	45 n.25

Index Auctorum Locorumque — **321**

15.247	231 n.31, 231 n.36	8.32	281
17.391	237	8.335	213 n.16
17.723	237	8.338	213 n.16
18.71	281	8.345	45
19.284–285	281	10.165	231 n.31
19.300	281	10.325	231 n.35
20.189	230 n.31	11.64–65	66 n.37
21.129	217	11.155–156	281, 283 n.34
21.150	230 n.31, 231 n.35	11.202–203	281
		11.216	281
		11.218–222	66 n.37
21.497	213 n.16	11.475	281
21.564	230 n.31	11.601–604	66 n.37
22.329	231 n.31	12.178–179	235, 237
22.466	281	12.390	213 n.16
22.482–483	281	13.261	230 n.31
22.510	237	14.11	237
23.108	281	14.187	231 n.35
23.492	231 n.31	14.445	231 n.31
23.794	231 n.31	14.500	237
24.339	213 n.16	15.264	231 n.35
24.378	213 n.16	15.319	213 n.16
24.387	231 n.31, 231 n.36	15.355	281
		15.509	281
24.389	213 n.16	16.15–16	281
24.410	213 n.16	16.220	281
24.432	213 n.16	17.38–39	281
24.445	213 n.16	18.89	237
24.453	237	18.92	231 n.31
24.707–708	281	18.367	237
24.726	283 n.35	19.105	231 n.35
24.742–745	281	19.541	212
24.776	281	19.581	212, 213
Odyssey		20.190	230 n.31
1.1	48, 216 n.22	21.79	212, 213
1.84	213 n.16	22.177	237
1.170	230 n.31, 231 n.35	22.189	237
		22.200	237
5.43	213 n.16	23.154	281
5.75	213 n.16	23.325	281
5.85	230 n.31	22.477	237
5.94	213 n.16	24.99	213 n.16
5.145	213 n.16	24.298	231 n.35
5.291–453	197		
5.458	281	**Homeric Hymns**	
7.120	272 n.37	5.1	216 n.22
7.238	231 n.35	30.12	104 n.41

Homeric Scholia
in Il. 9.324	216 n.25
in Il. 9.338	213 n.17
in Il. 18.20–21	280 n.27
in Il. 19.282–302	280
in Od. 2.103	213 n.17

Homerocentones (Schembra)
apologia (Vat. suppl. gr. 388) 30 n.90, 94 n.7

I HC 99–205	286 n.55
I HC 296	282 n.29
I HC 304	282 n.29
I HC 360	282 n.29
I HC 787–798	288 n.60
I HC 1879–1891	237–238
I HC 2050–2081	281–286
I HC 2179	282 n.29
I HC 2338	282 n.29
II HC 158	282 n.29
II HC 234	282 n.29
II HC 562–565	288 n.60
II HC 881–885	283 n.34
II HC 895	282 n.29
II HC 924	231 n.37
II HC 1822	282 n.29

Horace
Epistulae
3.119–123	159

Carmina
3.30	193
4.2.33	8

Isidore of Seville
Etymologies
8.7.11	15

Jerome
Adversus Jovinianum
1.45	170

De viris illustribus
103	42

Epistulae
53.8	271–272
65.5	80 n.27
69.2	80 n.27
70.5	196
107.4	271 n.31

Explanatio in Danielem
1.4.1	133 n.31

John Chrysostom
Homiliae in Joannem
59.462	275 n.4

John of Gaza
Ekphrasis
1.159	52 n.39
625	214 n.17

John Philoponus
De aeternitate mundi
323.6	216 n.25

Julian the Emperor
Orationes
7.3.9–17 = 207b	250 n.6

Juvencus
ELQ
Praef. 6–14	191–192
Praef. 9–10	94 n. 7, 268
Praef. 15–24	192–193
Praef. 25–28	194
Praef. 27	268
1.19–20	226
1.25–27	196 n.22, 268 n.14
2.25–38	197–198
2.38	201, 203
2.243–245	201
2.828	80 n.27
3.42	193 n.11
4.628	193 n.11
4.642–649	236 n.61
4.662	236
4.662–673	236 n.61
4.687–713	236 n.61
4.802–805	226
4.806–812	199–201

Lactantius
Divinae Institutiones
2.12   249 n.5

Lucan
Pharsalia
1.67   153
5.560–677   197

Lucian
De luctu
13   279
Verae Historiae
2.24.7   216 n.22

Lucretius
De Rerum Natura
1.62–101   143
1.935–950 = 4.10–25   4 n.7, 271 n.29

Macrobius
Saturnalia
1.17.2–3   132 n.29

Martial
4.64   88–89, 89 n.64
5.11.3–4   79 n.23
6.42   89 n.60

Martianus Capella
De nuptiis Philologiae et Mercurii
2.185ff.   132 n.29

Maximus of Tyre
Dialexeis
4.6   4 n.7

Melito of Sardis
Homily on the Passion
731–733   10

Menander Rhetor
On Epideictic Speeches
400.15–22   85 n.41
409.5   85 n.41
434–435   278–279, 285 n.49

Mesomedes of Crete
Ekphrasis of a sponge / ἔκφρασις σπόγγου
9 *GDRK* = 19 Hopkinson   240

Methodius of Olympus
Symposium
12.3–128 (Hymn to the Nymphios) 11

Metrical Inscriptions
IC II 24, 13 = 80 Bandy   49–50
IG IX 1, 720–721 = 569 Felle   46–47
IG X 2, 1, 876 = 23 Vérilhac   68 n.48
SEG 17.756 = *IGLS* V 1999   216 n.22
SEG 24.1243   51
SEG 34.1003 = 493 Samama   50
SEG 59.1723 = *IGLS* XXI 323   50
SGO 02/06/15 = *LSA* 657   47–48
SGO 02/09/31 = 155 Roueché   214 n.17
SGO 16/43/06   47 n.28
SGO 20/03/03 = 111 Preger = *IGLS* 832   43–44
SGO 20/05/06   51–52
SGO 20/06/01 = *LSA* 878   48
SGO 21/22/01   47 n.28
SGO 21/23/03–04   53
SGO 22/35/02   44–46

Michael the Syrian
Chronicle
9.29   70 n.60

Musonius Rufus
Dissertationum a Lucio digestarum reliquiae
15.44   216 n.22

Nicander of Colophon
Theriaca
528–529   256
Alexipharmaca
350   256

Nonnus of Panopolis
Dionysiaca
1.1   214 n.17
1.399   52 n.39

2.591	214 n.17	5.144	80 n.27
3.125	231 n.33	6	259 n.47
5.50	52 n.39	6.46	214 n.17
5.104	154 n.15	6.51 = 21.34	49 n.32
16.304	231 n.33	6.105–163	240
17.135	52 n.39	6.188	257
21.271	214 n.17	7.121	257
25.265	94 n.7, 228	8.6	255 n.30
30.250	214 n.17	8.53	256 n.35
31.30	231 n.33	8.81	253
31.107	214 n.17	8.88	252 n.16
32.54	52 n.39	8.130	254
33.57	214 n.17	9.12	254 n.22
39.82	214 n.17	9.15	252 n.16
40.453–454	235	9.29	52 n.39
41	255 n.31	10.125	212 n.15
41.291	214 n.17	12.9	212 n.15
43.3	52 n.39	12.103	214 n.17
43.115	214 n.17	12.107	214 n.17
48.378–381	239–240	12.160–161	254
Paraphrasis		12.162	256 n.34
1.1–13	259–260	12.199	252
1.34	52 n.39	12.200	252 n.17
1.40–41	49 n.32	13–17	251
1.88	257	13.17	214 n.17
1.112	252	13.54	254–255
1.134	52 n.39	13.61	214 n.17
1.201	52 n.39	13.90	214 n.17
1.216	214 n.17	14.6	231 n.33
2.33	214 n.17	14.19	252 n.14
3.10	251–252	14.20	259 n.47
3.50–61	252–253	14.64–67	260–261
3.57	252 n.14	14.88	252 n.16
3.65–66	259 n.47	15.27–28	255 n.30
3.74–76	255–256	15.92	257 n.41
4.61	252 n.16	15.105	52 n.39
4.68	255 n.30	16.74	52 n.39
4.98	214 n.17	17.11	52 n.39
4.111	257 n.41	17.14	52 n.39
4.128	252 n.15	18.48	52 n.39
5.22	214 n.17, 286 n.54	18.52–53	214 n.17
		18.105	214 n.17
5.33	231 n.33	18.126	214 n.17
5.41	69	19.40–48	230–233
5.70	52 n.39	19.43–44	231 n.40
5.80–82	69 n.54	19.91–100	233–238
5.132–133	252 n.14	19.136	276 n.6

19.149–157	238–240	**Papyri**	
19.151	240	*PBodmer*	
19.155–157	240	29–37 (*Codex Visionum*)	11, 12, 15 n.54, 19, 40, 50, 93 n.4, 253 n.21, 265
20.141–143	253		
21.139–143	226 n.5		
21.141–143	261		

P.Monts. Roca inv. 158–161
(Alcestis Barcinonensis)

Oppian
Halieutica

		32–33	183
1.86–87	260	35–40	172
		48–50	183
[Ps.–]Oppian		54	173
Cynegetica		57–63	172, 173 n.22
1.3	259 n.50	69–70	173 n.22
3.461	216 n.22	77–78	173
		90–92	172
Origen		93–95	173
Commentary on John's Gospel		100–101	172
14.4.32 (*PG*)	275 n.3	101–102	183
Contra Celsum		109–114	173
7.65	295 n.10	122	173
De principiis		*POxy*	
I prol. 1	252 n.13	1786	10
3.1.11–12	270 n.26		
Homiliae in Lucam		**Parmenides**	
13.1845 (*PG*)	275 n.4	B1 (DK)	252 n.17

Ovid
Amores

Paulinus of Nola
Carmina

1.2.37	157	6–9	265
Heroides		6.1–26	271 n.33
6.151	153 n.8	7–9	272 n.34
12	152	10	4 n.5, 5, 132 n.29
Metamorphoses		27	5–9, 18, 80 n.27
1	146, 153	*Epistulae*	
1.3	181	15.4	80 n.27
1.454–465	157	19.1	80 n.27
7.1–424	152–153		
11.474–572	197	**Paul the Silentiary**	
15.871–879	193	*Descriptio Sanctae Sophiae*	
Tristia		195	62 n.16
1.1.84	130 n.22	221	62 n.16
2	125, 131	273	62 n.16
3.3	173 n.21	978–1029	219
3.5.33–36	133		

Photius
Bibliotheca
183–184	266 n.8
320a	249 n.3

Pindar
Isthmian Odes
5.24–25	272 n.37

Nemean Odes
4.76	49 n.32

Pythian Odes
3.7	256 n.32

Plato
Laws
659e–660a	4 n.7

Phaedo
60c–61b	250 n.6

Republic
394b	13 n.43
607a	279 n.18

Pliny
Naturalis historia
8.48	133

Plutarch
Moralia
16b–d (= *Quomodo adul.* 2)	250
309a–b (= *Cons. ad. ux.* 3–4)	279 n.23
494d7	216 n.25

Vitae
Aemilius Paulus 25.1	300 n.34

Proba
Cento Vergilianus / Cento Probae
praef. 3	94 n.7
13–17	4 n.5
614–620	236–237

Procopius
De bello Vandalico
2.6.7	154 n.15

Propertius
Elegiae
4.11	173 n.21

Prudentius
Apotheosis
93	80 n.27
386–392	7 n.21

Cathemerinon
9.2	271 n.33

Peristephanon
12.49–54	87 n.51
12.54	78 n.19

Psychomachia
804–822	76
823–887	76
851–865	76–80

Quintilian
Institutio oratoria
10.52–87	249 n.3

Res gestae divi Augusti
34.2	200 n.34

Romanos the Melodist
Kontakia
20.22.1	240

Hymni
35 str. δ, 6	286 n.53

Sedulius
Carmen Paschale
1.17–22	94 n.7
1.23–26	226, 271 n.33
1.85	268 n.14
3.62–69	202–203
5.186–195	236

Seneca
Ad Marciam de consolatione
10.5	173 n.22

Epistulae
95	143

Medea
1ff.	158
910	153
1026–1027	151

Phaedra
186–189	157

Sextus Empiricus
Πυρρώνειοι ὑποτυπώσεις
3.204 102 n.35

Sidonius Apollinaris
Carmina
9 75, 85 n.42
10 85
11.1–16 82–86
11.17–33 80–82
22 88
23 88
Epistulae
2.10 86–89

Silius Italicus
Punica
17.236–291 197

Socrates of Constantinople
Historia Ecclesiastica
3.15–16 15

Sozomen
Historia Ecclesiastica
5.18.3–4 15–16

Sophocles
Oedipus Tyrannus
629 103 n.37

Statius
Silvae
1.2 84
1.3 88, 89 n.60
1.5 84, 88, 89 n.60
2.2 84
3.1 88
Thebaid
2.65 160
5.335–421 197
6.238–549 88

Tacitus
Dialogus de oratoribus
22.4 79 n.23

Tertullian
Paenitentia
8.9 127 n.13
9.2 127 n.13

Theocritus
Idyllia
11.1–3 271 n.29
12 96 n.13
15.20 272
20.5 212 n.15

Theodoret
Epistulae S
146 96 n.14
Historia religiosa
3 269

Theognis
89–90 255 n.25
175f. 104 n.40
236–254 255 n.29
319 255
447–452 255 n.28
1253 96 n.13
1335 96 n.13
1375 96 n.13

Theophanes the Confessor
Chronographia (AM 6113)
302.32–306.8 295 n.8, 296 n.17

Theophylactus Simocatta
Historiae
2.3.4–6 297 n.24
3.1.11f. 297 n.24

Thucydides
4.86 272 n.37

Timon of Phlius
Indalmoi
SH F841–842 = F67–68 Diels 259

Triphiodorus
114–119 232 n.41
119 240 n.78

Valerius Flaccus
Argonautica
1.574–699	197
4.54–65	158 n.33

Valerius Maximus
1.8.1	300 n.34

Verecundus of Junca
Carmen de satisfactione paenitentiae
22–23	127
40–41	127
64–65	128 n.16
68	129 n.18
117	129 n.18

Virgil
Aeneid
1.10	200
1.11	143
1.50–156	198
1.85–86	203 n.41
1.102	203 n.41
1.103–105	199
1.107	198 n.29
1.115	198 n.29
1.130	201
1.151	199, 200
1.594	236
2.167	236
2.217	236
2.692–698	201
4	178
4.553–570	198
4.554–555	198 n.29, 203–204
4.571–573	204
5.74	236
5.114–267	88
6	178
6.15	6 n.16
6.217	236
6.223	236
6.314	236
6.624	236
6.662	196 n.22, 268
7.66	236
8.369–453	84–85
11.5	236
11.745	236

Eclogues
4	146

Georgics
4.559–562	200 n.35

Epitaph
F2 (Courtney)	67 n.41

Victorius, Claudius Marius
Alethia
104–105	251 n.8

Thematic Index

Christian Appropriation cf. *s.v.* 'Late Antiquity'
Allegorical exegesis 25, 76–77, 78, 83, 147, 170, 172, 196, 202, 234, 241, 286, 295
– Symbolic appropriations 54, 77, 80, 161, 173–178, 216, 236, 241, 267, 286
chrêsis 6, 27, 213
Christian content and classical form (dissonance) 3, 4, 8, 40, 43, 49, 51, 64, 226, 295
Christian interpretation 161, 194, 213, 284
Christian polemical approaches 5, 22, 96, 99, 105, 121, 147, 151, 161–163, 295
– laity *vs.* clergy and apologetics 4–6, 25, 74; cf. *s.v.* 'Ascetism/Christian notions'
Classicizing *vs.* non-classicizing poetry/prose 10, 26, 40, 61, 118, 240, 276
Continuity as adaptation/appropriation of form and context 3, 15, 21–24, 41–43, 60–62 ('Christian interferences'), 64 (nugatory), 81–88 (nugatory), 101, 128, 135, 140, 148, 153, 193–194, 231, 240, 258, 271, 287
– 'Democratization of culture' (Agosti, G.) 42
– Hellenistic *vs.* late antique appropriation 18, 23, 59, 64, 110, 139 (miniaturization), 193, 195, 228, 238–240, 250–255, 279
– 'Levels of literariness' (Agosti, A.) 3, 48
Continuity *vs.* discontinuity 3, 5, 18, 19, 25, 28, 31, 40–52, 75, 94, 121, 146, 152, 193, 226, 285, 302
Embellishing the Bible 41, 193–195, 213, 218, 225, 266–268; cf. *s.v.* 'Jeweled style' and *'poikilia'*
Kontrastimitation and *Usurpation* 6, 21–30, 45–47, 97, 232, 254, 268, 283
– *Kontrastimitation* 6, 98, 196, 203, 205, 213, 232, 254, 268, 284

– *Kontrastimitation* as restrictive term 191–208; 216–217 (*Kontrastimitation* between pagan and demonic context)
– *Usurpation* 6, 20, 27, 45–47, 89, 271, 283
Moralizing agenda/ Didacticism 4, 6, 30, 71, 79–90 102–103, 152–159, 142–144, 170–176, 213, 232, 251 (biblical epic as didactic), 258, 268–269, 276
– Collections of moralizing quotations 103
– Poetry as (didactic) medicine 4–6, 111, 270–271
– Schoolroom poetry 9, 94, 111–112, 155, 171, 193, 205, 218, 258, 272
Philosophical echoes 3, 6, 103 (Aristippus), 128, 172, 255, 259, 275
– Plato (and Mimesis) 3, 4, 14, 40, 102, 250, 258, 279
– Stoicism/Seneca 129, 143, 147, 151, 176
Spoliation aesthetics 47, 53

Christian notions cf. *s.v.* 'Pagan notions'
Afterlife/Underworld 59, 64, 71, 161, 170, 173, 284
Angels 216, 268, 295
Apologetic agendas 5, 101, 126, 128, 139, 218, 260
Asceticism 4, 5, 25 (ascetics as poets), 107, 194, 269, 272, 298, 307
Christology 6, 67, (Incarnation), 234 (double substance), 277–288 (Incarnation), 299 (humanity in Christ); cf. *s.v.* 'Logos/Christian notions'
Church 5 (St. Felix), 6, 11, 39, 46 (Hagia Sophia), 47, 53, 78 (Hagia Sophia), 86–87 (Lyonnais Church), 219 (Hagia Sophia), 269, 294
Cross 209, 216, 234, 236 (as Wood of Paradise), 233–238 (Crucifixion), 236 (as mast), 276 (Foot of the Cross), 301 (True Cross)
Demons 99, 161, 209, 211, 216, 298
Eucharist 240

Exegesis 30, 191, 205, 227, 228, 234, 239, 241, 265, 286
Forgiveness/mercy 48, 126–132, esp. 128
Holy Spirit 7, 9, 44, 45, 114, 194, 255, 261, 268, 295 (or trinity), 299; cf. also s.v. 'Muses/Pagan notions/gods'
Humility 47, 275, 303
Icons/*acheiropoietos* 295, 296, 304
Liturgy 10, 11, 276, 296
Logos 3, 10, 226, 259, 296
Mary/Theotokos 25, 277, 282, 283, 288–289 (Mater Dolorosa), 304
Miracles 7, 143, 145, 191–205, 226, 261, 298, 300–305
Monotheism 100, 161, 295, 304
Pentecost 7–9
Proskenysis 129, 297, 304
Salvation /immortality 3, 65–70, 87, 173, 268, 283
–and poetic immortality 69, 193–194, 255
–resurrection 71, 170, 226, 275, 284
Satan/Devil 23, 211, 215, 254
Trinity 45, 51, 52, 97, 295
Typology 51, 236, 283
Virginity 153 (Medea), 209 (Justa), 213, 275 (the Virgin; cf. s.v. 'Mary/Christian notions')
Virtue *vs.* vice/sin 3, 5, 76–79, 101, 126–130, 141–145, 170, 172, 175, 191, 254, 271, 299

Christian Literary Production
Christian Poetry
–Hymns 6, 9–12, 26, 93, 95, 100, 126, 131, 136, 226, 259, 262, 296 (cf. s.v. 'Hymns/Ancient categories')
–*kontakion* 10, 26 (Akathist Hymn), 240, 276
–Psalms 226, 241, 265, 266, 272, 297, 301
Christian Prose 20, 29, 49
–Apocalypses 77, 78, 82
–Apocryphal works 10, 234, 275–277, 284

–Bible 10 (Septuagint, Vulgate), 14, 15, 100, 110, 114, 115, 170 (Jerome's Bible), 192, 194 (Old Latin Bible), 196, 219, 264
–*confessio* 126, 162, 209
–Gospels (Canonical) 3, 8, 10, 15, 50, 115, 191, 196, 204, 214, 226 ('Spiritual Gospel'), 262 (John's Gospel as *sylloge*)
–Hagiographies 210
–Homilies 3, 10, 276
–*paenitentia* 126, 127, 128
–Theological commentaries 14, 110 (poetry as auxiliary literature) 121, 228, 241, 252, 266, 270

Genre (Ancient categories of genre)
Ancient readers and classical *paideia* / readerly approaches 13, 27, 53, 60, 62, 64, 85, 105, 125, 132, 148, 179, 196–198, 219–220, 250, 262, 279, 288, 293; cf. s.v. 'Audiences/Genre/Modern Categories'
–Aristotle 249
–Apollinarii (Apollinaris the Elder and Apollinaris the Younger) 9, 15–16
–Bede, Venerable 15
–*didaxis* 253
–Diomedes Grammaticus 15, 179–182, 183–184, 249 n.32
–*genera* (ancient) 15, 98, 179, 182, 249, 280
–Isidore of Seville 15
–*gnomae* 68, 103, 249
–*species heroica* 183
–*species lyrica* 179
–*progymnasmata* 13, 18, 28, 272, 278
–Scholiasts/*scholia* 216, 279, 282
–Socrates of Constantinople 15
–Sozomen 16
–Theodorus 68
–*Tractatus Coislinianus* 249
–Quintilian 171, 249
Drama/theater 15, 24, 28, 101, 106, 116, 151–155, 164–169, 177–183 (performance), 177 (costume), 182 (recitation), 276 (performance), 279 (theatricality), 286 (Christians and theater), 285 (*didaskali*a)

Thematic Index — **331**

- Comedy/comic 69, 115, 116 69, 158
- Pantomime 21, 154 (Polymnia), 158, 164, 177 (*tragoedia saltata/fabula saltica*), 178, 179 182, 285
- Tragedy/tragic 9, 12, 15, 29, 85, 94, 103, 115, 139, 140, 151 (Seneca), 152 (Euripides), 154, 174 (Euripides), 141, 154, 182 (Melpomene)

Elegy 22, 28, 94, 95, 98, 125, 127, 157, 164, 173, 254, 259

Epic / hexameter poetry
- Archaic *vs.* Hellenistic didactic epic 240, 250, 255–260
- Didactic elegy 254, 259
- Didactic epic 4, 12, 23, 94, 241, 249, 272, 250–262, 266–274
- Didactic markers 251 (teacher), 256 (*predicator*), 252–269 (addressees/disciples), 258, 262, 269 (*sylloge*); 95, 115 (lists/catalogues); 11, 23, 226, 258, 269, 271 (prose into poetry); 259 (hymnic preambles); 268 (didactic preambles)
- Heroic epic 20, 24, 129–131, 192, 200 (Jesus/Emperor/epic hero), 215, 218 (epic/Homeric hagiography) 255 (Gospel epic), 218 ('holy epic hero'), 226, 272, 286; 76 (Allegorical epic); 139, 153, 182 (Calliope); 192, 209, 226 (*vitalia gesta*), 301 (epic hero)
- Hesiod 12, 24, 94, 100, 110, 118, 232, 249, 252, 253, 254 (Ascra), 257, 262, 271, 272 (Hesiod *vs.* Homer), 272 ('Davidic Hesiod')
- Homer 12, 13, 26, 44, 48, 62, 66, 94, 95, 100–101 (Christian bard as Sibyl), 104, 110, 118, 120, 139, 180, 192, 210, 213, 215 (blindness), 216–220, 226–228 (Christian Homer?), 229 (Homeric *Kunstsprache*), 233, 240, 266 (blindness), 267–268 (*Homeric Kunstsprache*), 272, 278, 280
- Jewish Hellenistic Epic 9 n. 27 (Ezekiel, Theodotus, Philon), 9–10, 102 (*Sib. Or.*)
- Lucan 153, 160
- Ovid 83, 125, 130, 132, 139, 146, 153, 157, 170 (*Ovide moralisé*), 178, 181

- Statius 84, 156, 160, 197
- Virgil 6–9 (Christian Virgil), 14, 27, 62, 67, 84, 88, 112, 139, 143, 169, 174, 180, 181, 191–195, 226 (Christian Virgil), 251, 268 (Christian bard as *vates*)

Epigrams/Metrical inscriptions 42, 59, 62, 76, 88, 96

Hymns (classical) 20, 52, 94, 100 (*Corpus Hermeticum*), 131, 240 (Mesomedes), 259, 260 (hymns in didactic poetry); cf. *s.v.* 'hymns/Christian Works'

Lyric 11, 14, 88, 96, 179, 249, 267, 272 (David as lyric poet); cf. *s.v.* 'lyric meters/Genre/Ancient categories'

Meter and genre 5, 13, 16, 28, 64, 75, 88, 180, 209
- Anapests 11, 115, 116
- *ametria* 121
- Choriambs 116
- Classical meters 3, 5, 12, 210
- Dactylic meter / elegiac couplets 4, 21, 28, 93–96 (pederastic elegiacs), 114, 127
- Dactylic meter / hexameter 22, 40, 88, 95, 100, 106, 109, 118, 137, 251, 259, 295
- Dochmiac 116
- Dodecasyllabe (Byzantine) 64, 116, 295
- Iambic trimeter 22, 24, 94, 101, 103, 107, 115, 139, 154, 295
- Lyric meters 11, 12, 93–96, 115, 249, 267
- 'Modern style' 51, 60, 120
- Phalaecian hendecasyllable 86, 87, 88
- *polymetria* 75, 105, 109–123
- Quantitative meter *vs.* prosodic meter 10, 26, 30, 42 (problematic prosody), 116–122, 295

Rhetorical concepts and terms; rhetorical techniques as genre 18, 20, 135, 199, 209, 266
- *aemulatio* 82
- *cento* 8, 9, 14, 18, 140, 169, 171, 174, 181, 219, 235, 276
- *consolatio* 172, 173, 251
- *controversia* 27, 140, 152, 173
- *deprecatio* 125–136

−*ekphrasis* 5, 13, 45, 76, 80, 83, 87, 88, 219, 238, 239, 285
−*encomium* 13, 23, 29, 88, 219, 259
−*epideictic* 13, 24, 287
−*epithalamium* 18, 21, 75, 84–90, 125, 140–144, 152, 170, 254, 285
−*ethopoeia* 14, 173, 214–218, 275, 288
−*exempla* 22, 126, 132
−*excursus* 133, 266
−Lament 275, 278
−memorization of classical texts 110, 115, 176, 194
−*metaphrasis* 120
−Panegyric 88, 294, 295–301 (panegyric as propaganda)
−*paraphrasis* 16, 18, 27, 111, 120, 191, 204–205 (and exegesis), 209–210, 220–225, 228, 238–241 (and exegesis), 258, 265 (as sub-genre of biblical poetry), 261 (and exegesis), 268
−*pathos* 29, 140, 172, 289
−*poikilia/varietas* 7, 75–79, 84–86, 93, 140, 177; cf. *s.v.* 'Jeweled Style/Genre/Modern Categories'
−*progymnasmata* 13,15, 27, 278, 288
−*prosopopoeia* 13, 20, 82
−Ring-composition 124, 278
−*suasoria* 22, 125
−*topoi* 11, 22, 59–63, 71, 79, 81, 88, 132–136, 285–287
Performance 12–14, 28–30, 182–183, 219, 262, 287; cf. *s.v.* 'Drama/Genre/Ancient Categories'

Genre (Modern Categories of appropriation and genre)
Audiences/Contexts 9, 12, 17, 20–26, 65, 71, 105–110, 129, 145, 170, 178, 181–183, 194, 196, 199, 211, 219, 241, 253, 272
−Christian audiences *vs.* non-Christian audiences 64, 105, 146, 219, 298
−Female audiences/authors Eudocia 42, 209, 237, 265, 277; Proba 9, 14, 26, 171, 199, 236; Siria 171, 174; Feminist readings/themes 170–175
−Greek-speaking East and Latin-speaking West 11, 14, 25, 26, 42, 104, 151

−*Horizon of Expectations* (Jauss, R.) 17, 19, 126, 178, 220
Epyllion 20, 22, 29, 85, 125, 140; *vs Kleinepos* 155; *vs* 'Miniature Epic' 180, 184
Exile Literature 135
'Gospel Epic' (Barham, F.) 225, 226
Ideology and Genre 3, 4, 16, 20, 21, 24, 29, 39–47, 51, 61, 184, 202, 295; *Sitz im Leben* 10, 17, 20, 24, 30, 145–146, 172, 294; cf. *s.v.* 'Christianization/Christian vs. Pagan Conflict'
−emperor/imperial ideals 129–131, 200–204, 300
−'enlightened' Christian bard 101
−'epigraphy of the Christians' 44
−*deprecatio* 125–136
−*fama* 193–195
−familial love 162, 170, 275, 301
−female chastity 170, 175, 213, 284
−heroism 68 (ἄφθιτον κλέος), 194 (*sublimia facta/virtutis honos*), 300 (spiritual glory)
−hexameter as the embodiment of pagan poetry/ideology 41, 96, 99, 100, 215, 217, 271
−Holy War 295, 296
−Profit/toil 272
−'Transvaluation' (Genette, G.) 196
−Tragic suffering 288
−'Triumphalism' 39, 52, 53, 54, 131, 201, 204, 295, 304
Intergenericity 17 ('Generic Enrichment', Harrison, S.), 76, 88, 141, 182; 287; cf. *s.v.* 'Modulations/Genre/Musical Metaphor'
Intertextuality 5, 13, 17, 27, 41, 71, 76, 153, 155, 158, 163, 181, 194–202, 229; cf. *s.v.* 'Meter/Genre/Ancient Categories'
−Explicit *vs.* implicit references 5, 94–105, 111, 126–132, 151, 164, 193, 214, 250–256
−Intertext *vs.* allusion (Hinds, S.) 195
−Intertextuality and genre 82, 94, 109, 125, 132, 157, 139, 181

—Intertextuality and meter 75, 103, 115, 116, 125
—Narratological terms: 14, 120–121, 185, 287 (paratext); 45, 81–84, 174, 220, 229, 237, 241 (hypotext); 115, 226, 253, 257 (metalepsis); 18, 25, 61, 79, 94–98, 160, 200, 222, 226, 266 (metatext/metaliterary)
—'Non–referential allusions' (McGill, S.) 7, 195
'Jeweled Style' (Roberts, M.) 8, 75, 79; cf. s.v. 'poikilia/Rhetorical Concepts/Genre/Ancient Categories'
Innovation vs Tradition (Pollmann, K.) 9, 11–13, 41, 75, 110, 121, 152, 228, 285, 303; cf. also s.v topoi/Rhetorical Concepts/Genre/Ancient Categories
—Experimentation 27, 109, 141, 225
—'Implosion of genre' (Kaufmann, H.) 40
Kreuzung der Gattungen (Kroll, W.) 16, 17, 125
Mixture of genres 18–19, 98, 109, 140, 121–126 (of meters), 164, 170, 182, 218, 241, 268, 287
—Hybrid (Fuhrer, T.) 17, 18, 85, 106, 110, 125, 141, 220, 229, 231, 233 (hybridization of genres)
—'Mélange des genres' (Fontaine, J.) 19
—Mixture and ambiguity 18, 126, 131, 220 (blurry), 229 (ambiguous), 64 (nugatory), 81–88 (nugatory)
Prison Literature (and Drac., Satisf.) 135

Genre (Musical metaphor)
Fugue (as metaphor) 20, 21
Major tonalities and/vs. minor/major forms/themes/registers
—Christian epic between tragedy and epidictic *goos* (in *I HC*) 280–283
—Christian epic vs. Homer and Hesiod (in Met. Pss. and Nonn., Par.) 251–262, 265–271
—Christian epic and Archaic/Hellenistic didactic (in Nonn., Par.) 238–240, 249–255, 251–262, 265–271
—Christian epic and heroic epic (in Juv., ELQ) 193–202

—Christian hagiographic epic and Homeric epic (in Eudoc., Cypr.) 210–218
—Iambic Christian panegyric epic (in Georg. Pisid., Exped. Pers.) 294–300
Minor tonalities and/vs. major/minor forms/themes/registers
—Metrical inscriptions and Homeric epic (in Christian epigrams) 47–50
—Funerary Epigram and Hellenistic epigram (in Julian the Egyptian) 66
—*Epyllion* and *Epithalamium* vs Christian allegorical epic (in Sid. Apoll.) 85, 90
—Elegiac poetry and epic modes (in Greg. Naz.) 95, 121
—Penitential genre/*deprecatio*, enriched with minor tonalities (in Drac., Satisf.) 136
—*Kleinepos*/Miniature *epos* between grand epic, tragedy, and pantomime (in Drac., Romul. and Orest. Trag.) 141, 152, 155, 169
Modulations/Alternate registers (between major and minor keys) 8–12, 21–28, 71, 75, 85, 122, 131, 152, 155, 241, 250–253, 277
—high/low characterization 47, 220
—high/low theme 6, 7, 60, 76, 178, 192, 268, 55 (contra highbrow vs. lowbrow poetry division)
—large/small scale/form 8, 75, 76, 90, 154
—Modulation as oscillation between minor and major genres (in Greg. Naz.) 121
—Modulation of the hymnic mode within didactic (in Nonn., Par.) 259–260
—Modulation of Christian epic within minor genres (in Sid. Apoll.) 80–90
—Modulations across minor genres (in Drac., Satisf.) 131
—Modulations across tragic tonalities (in Greg. Naz.; Alcesta, Alc. Barc.; Drac., Medea; the *I HC*) 103, 104, 277
Polyphony 7 (Pentecost and musical polyphony), 20 (Bakhtin), 26, 31, 136
Transpositions/Transfer 8, 15–16, 22–30, 45, 71, 75, 88, 120, 151, 164, 250, 256, 280–283

– Transposition of Christian grand epic onto epigram (in Sedulius, *ep.* 2.10.4) 88
– Transfer of hexametric revelatory poetry onto Christian hexameter (in Greg. Naz., *carm.* II.2.7) 100
– Transposition of prose hagiography onto epic (in Eudoc., *Cypr.*) 209
– Transposition/transfer of the Scripture onto biblical poetry (in Greg. Naz., Biblical Poems) 120
– Transposition as secularization of tragic myth (in Drac., *Romul.* and the *Orest. Trag.*) 144
– Transposition from grand epic to tragic mode (in Drac., *Medea*; in the *I HC*) 164, 283
– Transposition of drama onto *Kleinepos* (in Drac., *Medea*) 164
– Transposition of the Gospel onto heroic hexameters (in Juvenc., *ELQ*; Nonn., *Par.*) 193, 225
– Transposition of the Gospel onto the didactic mode (in *Met. Pss.*; in Nonn., *Par.*) 156, 268

Historical figures and events
Alexander III of Macedon, Alexander the Great (356–323, BCE) 298
Apollonius of Tyana (and Christ) 219
Augustus, Gaius Octavius, Roman Emperor (63BCE–14CE) 131
Barbarians / Barbarian migrations 127, 131, 145, 146, 155, 181, 184, 295, 304
Caesar, Gaius Julius, Roman general and dictator (100 BCE – 44 BCE) 200
Chosroes II (Khosrow II), Sassanian king (d. 628 CE) 306
Constantine the Great, Roman Emperor (272–337 CE) 200, 201
Council of Ephesus – The Theotokos Controversy (431 CE) 277
Council of Nicaea (325 CE) 205
Cyprian of Antioch, pagan sorcerer and Christian convert (and Faust) 209

Erasmus of Rotterdam (1467?–1536) 30–31, 241
Eudocia Aelia, Augusta (400?–460 CE) 42, 277
Fall of Rome (476 CE) 145
Genseric, Vandal king (389–477 CE) 133
Heraclius, Roman Emperor (575–641 CE) 293
Honorius, Flavius, Western Roman Emperor (384–423 CE) 18
Jerome, Eusebius Sophronius, Latin priest and theologian (347–420 CE) 170, 194, 265
Jesus (as holy man) 251
Julian, Flavius Claudius, Roman Emperor, the Apostate (330–363 CE) 9, 15
Julian's School Edict (362–364 CE) 9, 25, 93, 112
Justinian I, the Great, Eastern Roman Emperor (d. 565 CE) 60, 71, 297, 302
Pax Augusta and *Pax Constantiniana* 200
Ruricius, Gallo–Roman aristocrat, bishop of Limoges (d. 510 CE) 80
Siege of Constantinople (626 CE) 304
Theodosius I, Roman Emperor (347–395 CE) 302
Theodosius II, Eastern Roman Emperor (401–450 CE) 209, 265
Valentinian III, Western Roman Emperor (419–455 CE) 145

Late Antiquity
'Anxiety of influence' (Bloom, H.) 98
Christian truth *vs.* pagan falsehood 3, 9, 23, 101–103, 105, 193, 295 (the Mosaic Distinction)
Christianization (process of) 9, 14, 39–55, 40, 59 , 63, 79, 111, 194, 295; cf. *s.v.* 'Ideology and Genre/Genre and Modern Categories'
Classical forerunners of Christian criticism 3, 143, 193
Conflict and anxiety 25, 40, 219, 295,
Intercultural dialogue' (Agosti, G.) 27, 40, 170, 176, 218
Periodization 10, 30, 39

Scholarly bias 39–43, 61–62, 94, 109–112
'The Postmodern Vision' (Athanassiadi, P.) 40

Pagan notions
Hospitality 89, 270
Hybris 201, 215
Magic 210–214
Mythenkritik 3, 4, 22, 141 (secularization/romanesque), 143–144, 151–159, 152–159, 170 (*Ovide moralisé*), 174 (Fulgentius), 193, 250
Mythological characters
–Achilles 215, 217
–Aeneas 23, 84, 175, 181, 194, 198, 200, 201, 203
–Alcestis 23, 169–179
–Andromache 277, 281, 283
–Anticlea 281
–Briseis 277, 281, 283
–Clytemnestra 141
–Dido 14, 175, 181, 198,
–Hector 278, 283, 285
–Helen 139
–Icarus 6
–Medea 152, 153
–Odysseus 213, 231–237, 284
–Penelope 213, 284
–Thetis 85, 281, 283, 285
–Turnus 175
Pagan gods
–Apollo 157, 170, 174, 215, 256, 268
–Charon 70, 71
–Cupid 143
–Diana/Artemis 142, 144, 155, 157
–Dionysus/ Bacchus 159
–Hades 62, 67 (Christianization), 70, 284
–Hermes 100, 101, 213, 214
–Muses and the *fons Musarum* 69, 104, 155, 182, 194, 216, 268, 295 cf. *s.v.* 'Holy Spirit/ Christian notions'
–Neptune / Poseidon 45, 198, 215
–Prometheus 235
–Venus /Aphrodite 80, 84, 143, 157
–Vulcan/Hephaestus 45, 80, 82, 85, 163, 269 n.22
–Zeus / Jupiter 84, 143, 160, 259, 284, 286
Polytheism/idols 53, 127, 128, 142, 215, 294; cf. *s.v.* 'Christian notions'
–body and soul 66
–*religio* 159–163
–Ritual 287
–Statues / civic space 47–48, 53
–Temples 39, 76, 80, 158
(Roman) Statesmen 199–205; *contra*, Christian Emperor 295–297

www.ingramcontent.com/pod-product-compliance
Lightning Source LLC
Chambersburg PA
CBHW030520230426
43665CB00010B/700